Edited by two leading analysts of postcommunist politics, this book brings together distinguished specialists on Albania, Bosnia Herzegovina, Bulgaria, Croatia, Macedonia, Romania, Serbia/Montenegro, and Slovenia. The authors analyze the challenge of building democracy in the conflict-riven lands of the former Yugoslavia and in neighboring states. They focus on oppositional activity, political cultures that often favor strong presidentialism, the role of nationalism, and basic socioeconomic trends. Karen Dawisha and Bruce Parrott contribute theoretical and comparative chapters on postcommunist political development. This book will provide students and scholars with detailed analysis by leading authorities, plus the latest research data on recent political trends in each country.

Democratization and Authoritarianism in
Postcommunist Societies: 2

Politics, power, and the struggle for democracy in South-East Europe

Editors

Karen Dawisha
University of Maryland at College Park

Bruce Parrott
The Paul H. Nitze School of Advanced International Studies
The Johns Hopkins University

These four volumes, edited by two leading analysts of postcommunist politics, bring together distinguished specialists to
provide specially commissioned, up-to-date essays on the
postcommunist countries of Eastern Europe and the former Soviet
Union. Each contributor analyzes both progress made toward
democratization, and the underlying social, economic, and cultural
factors shaping political change. All chapters contain information on
the emergence of political parties, elections, institutional reform, and
socioeconomic trends. Each volume also contains chapters by the
editors juxtaposing the overall trends in these countries with
comparable transitions and democratization processes elsewhere.

1. *The consolidation of democracy in East–Central Europe*

2. *Politics, power, and the struggle for democracy in
   South-East Europe*

3. *Democratic changes and authoritarian reactions in Russia,
   Ukraine, Belarus, and Moldova*

4. *Conflict, cleavage, and change in Central Asia and
   the Caucasus*

Politics, power, and the struggle for democracy in South-East Europe

edited by

Karen Dawisha

University of Maryland at College Park

and

Bruce Parrott

The Paul H. Nitze School of Advanced International Studies
The Johns Hopkins University

 CAMBRIDGE
UNIVERSITY PRESS

135571

PUBLISHED BY THE PRESS SYNDICATE OF THE UNIVERSITY OF CAMBRIDGE
The Pitt Building, Trumpington Street, Cambridge CB2 1RP, United Kingdom

CAMBRIDGE UNIVERSITY PRESS
The Edinburgh Building, Cambridge, CB2 2RU, United Kingdom
40 West 20th Street, New York, NY 10011-4211, USA
10 Stamford Road, Oakleigh, Melbourne 3166, Australia

First published 1997

Printed in the United Kingdom by Bell & Bain Ltd, Glasgow

Typeset in 10/12 pt CG Times

A catalogue record for this book is available from the British Library

Library of Congress Cataloguing in Publication data applied for

ISBN 0 521 59244 5 hardback
ISBN 0 521 59733 1 paperback

To Adeed, Nadia and Emile,
with love

K.D.

To Sindy,
partner in all seasons,
with love

B.P.

Contents

Albania, Bulgaria, and Romania

Tables

Figures

Contributors

JOHN D. BELL is Professor of History at the University of Maryland, Baltimore County. He is the author of numerous publications on the nineteenth- and twentieth-century Balkans, including *Peasants in Power* (1977) and *The Bulgarian Communist Party: From Blagoev to Zhivkov* (1986). He is currently editing a volume on developments in Bulgaria since 1989. He received his Ph.D. in history from Princeton University.

STEVEN L. BURG is Professor of Politics at Brandeis University. He is the author of *Conflict and Cohesion in Socialist Yugoslavia* (1983), *Introduction to Comparative Politics: Regimes and Regime Change* (1991, with Roy C. Macridis), and *War or Peace? Nationalism, Democracy, and American Foreign Policy in Post-Communist Europe* (1996). With Paul Shoup, he is presently completing a study of the domestic and international dimensions of the war in Bosnia Herzegovina to be published by M.E. Sharpe. He received his Ph.D. in political science from the University of Chicago.

LENARD J. COHEN is Professor of Political Science at Simon Fraser University in British Columbia. His books include include *Broken Bonds: Yugoslavia's Disintegration and Balkan Politics in Transition* (2d ed., 1995); *The Socialist Pyramid: Elites and Power in Yugoslavia* (1989); and *Political Cohesion in a Fragile Mosiac: The Yugoslav Experience* (1983) (co-author). He is currently completing a book entitled, *"'Serpent in the Bosom': Slobodan Milosevic and Serbian Nationalism."* He received his Ph.D. from Columbia University.

KAREN DAWISHA is Professor of Government and Director of the Center for the Study of Postcommunist Societies at the University of Maryland at College Park. She graduated with degrees in Russian and politics from the University of Lancaster in England and received her Ph.D. from the London School of Economics. She has served as an advisor to the British House of

Commons Foreign Affairs Committee and was a member of the policy planning staff of the US State Department. Her publications include *Russia and the New States of Eurasia: The Politics of Upheaval* (co-authored with Bruce Parrott, 1994), *Eastern Europe, Gorbachev and Reform: The Great Challenge* (1989, 2d ed., 1990), *The Kremlin and the Prague Spring* (1984), *The Soviet Union in the Middle East: Politics and Perspectives* (1982), *Soviet–East European Dilemmas: Coercion, Competition, and Consent* (1981), and *Soviet Foreign Policy toward Egypt* (1979).

NICHOLAS J. MILLER is Assistant Professor of History at Boise State University in Idaho. The focus of his research is Serbian history in the nineteenth and twentieth centuries. His book, *Between Nation and State: Serbian Politics in Croatia, 1903-1914*, is forthcoming from the University of Pittsburgh Press. He received an IREX advanced research grant for research in Croatia and Serbia in 1995-96; his current project examines the role of Serbian intellectuals in political change in Serbia and Yugoslavia after 1958. He received his Ph.D. in history from Indiana University.

NICHOLAS C. PANO is Professor of History and Associate Dean of the College of Arts and Sciences at Western Illinois University. His research has focused on Albanian history and politics. He is author of *The People's Republic of Albania* (1968) and a contributing author to *East Central Europe: Yesterday, Today and Tomorrow* (1982), *Communism in Eastern Europe* (1984), and the *Columbia History of Eastern Europe in the Twentieth Century* (1992). His articles and reviews have appeared in such publications as *Problems of Communism*, *Far Eastern Economic Review*, *Slavic Review*, *Canadian Slavonic Papers*, and the *Baltimore Sun*. He is also president of the Society for Albanian Studies.

BRUCE PARROTT is Professor and Director of Russian Area and East European Studies at the Paul H. Nitze School of Advanced International Studies of The Johns Hopkins University. He is author of *Russia and the New States of Eurasia: The Politics of Upheaval* (with Karen Dawisha, 1994), *The Soviet Union and Ballistic Missile Defense* (1987), and *Politics and Technology in the Soviet Union* (1983). He is editor of *The End of Empire? The Transformation of the USSR in Comparative Perspective* (with Karen Dawisha, 1996), *State-Building and Military Power in Russia and the New States of Eurasia* (1995), *The Dynamics of Soviet Defense Policy* (1990), and *Trade, Technology, and Soviet–American Relations* (1985). He received his Ph.D. in political science from Columbia University.

DUNCAN M. PERRY is Dean for Graduate Studies and Research and Professor of History at Central Washington University. He served as founding executive director of the Open Media Research Institute in Prague from 1994 to 1996. He is the author of *Stefan Stambolov and the Emergence of Modern Bulgaria* (1993), and *The Politics of Terror: The Macedonian Liberation*

Movements, 1893-1903 (1988). He has also written a variety of scholarly and topical articles about Eastern Europe. He received his Ph.D. from the University of Michigan.

SABRINA P. RAMET is Professor of International Studies at the University of Washington. She is the author of seven books, including *Balkan Babel: The Disintegration of Yugoslavia from the Death of Tito to Ethnic War* (2d ed., 1996), *Whose Democracy? Nationalism, Religion, and the Doctrine of Collective Rights in Post–1989 Eastern Europe* (forthcoming, 1997), and *Nihil Obstat: Religion, State, and Social Change in East-Central Europe and Russia* (forthcoming, 1998), and editor of eight others. Born in London, England, she has also lived for extended periods in Germany, Austria, Yugoslavia, and Japan. Her work has appeared in *Foreign Affairs*, *World Politics, Political Science Quarterly, Orbis,* and other journals. She received her Ph.D. from the University of California at Los Angeles.

VLADIMIR TISMANEANU is Professor in the Department of Government and Politics and Associate Director of the Center for the Study of Postcommunist Societies at the University of Maryland at College Park. His most recent publications include *Reinventing Politics: Eastern Europe from Stalin to Havel* (1992; expanded and updated paperback, 1993) and *Political Culture and Civil Society in Russia and the New States of Eurasia* (1995). He is currently completing two books: "Fantasies of Salvation: Post-Communist Political Mythologies," and "Stalinism for All Seasons: A Political History of Romanian Communism." He received his Ph.D. from the University of Bucharest.

Preface

This study of democratization in South-East Europe is one of four books produced by the produced by the Project on Democratization and Political Participation in Postcommunist Societies. The project has been sponsored jointly by the Paul H. Nitze School of Advanced International Studies of The Johns Hopkins University and the University of Maryland at College Park. It draws on the talents of scholars from a wide array of other universities and research institutions.

As codirectors of the project, we are grateful for material support furnished by two organizations. Principal funding for the project has been provided by the United States Department of State as part of its external research program. In addition, the intellectual planning of the project was aided at a crucial juncture by a grant from the Joint Committee on Eastern Europe of the American Council of Learned Societies. However, none of the views or conclusions contained in the book should be interpreted as representing the official opinion or policy of the Department of State or of the Joint Committee.

The three other volumes in the series deal with the countries of East-Central Europe, with the countries of Central Asia and the Caucusus, and with Russia, Ukraine, Belarus, and Moldova. Any student of contemporary international affairs knows that the delineation of "Europe" and its constituent regions frequently generates intellectual controversy about which countries belong to Europe or to "the West." We adopted our quadripartite grouping of countries to facilitate the management of a large research project, and to produce books that match the curricular structure of many college and university courses devoted to the countries of the postcommunist world. Neither the grouping nor the names were chosen with any intention of suggesting that some countries are necessarily more "advanced" or "backward" politically than others. Most of the regional groups exhibit considerable internal political diversity among the member countries, and the comparative judgments presented in the volumes are based on the findings of the individual country-studies, not on preconceptions about one or another region.

In the course of this project we have received assistance from many individuals and incurred many personal obligations. We wish to thank John Parker and Susan Nelson of the Department of State for proposing the general idea of the project to us, for making helpful suggestions about how it could be carried out, and for encouraging the project participants to draw whatever conclusions the evidence supports. We are grateful to Jason Parker of the ACLS Joint Committee on Eastern Europe for his assistance. We also wish to thank several scholars for their valuable help in sorting out the basic issues at an initial planning workshop: Nancy Bermeo, Valerie Bunce, Ted Robert Gurr, Joan Nelson, and Robert Putnam. Herbert Kitschelt was likewise very helpful in this regard.

We are deeply indebted to the country-study writers for the high level of effort that they invested in writing their chapters, for their active participation in the project workshops, and for undertaking more extensive revisions than are customary in collective enterprises of this kind. We also are grateful to the four authors who served as coordinators of the workshops: Sharon Wolchik, Vladimir Tismaneanu, Ilya Prizel, and Muriel Atkin. We benefited from their advice during the organizational stage of the project, and we profited from the written comments that they made on the draft chapters presented at the workshops.

We express our special thanks to Griffin Hathaway, the Executive Director of the project, who performed a nearly endless series of administrative and intellectual tasks with exemplary efficiency; to Florence Rotz, staff person of the SAIS Russian Area and East European Studies program, who managed the production and revision of several versions of the chapters with admirable calmness and consummate skill; and to Steve Guenther, who helped with the logistics of the workshops. Not least, we are grateful to Murray Feshbach for generously providing demographic data for a number of the country-studies.

Finally, we express our thanks to Michael Holdsworth of Cambridge University Press for his willingness to take on this large publishing project and see it through to the end. Bruce Parrott also thanks Gordon Livingston, without whose help he could not have completed his portion of the project.

K. D.
B. P.

1 Perspectives on postcommunist democratization

Bruce Parrott

Of all the elements of the international wave of democratization that began some two decades ago, the transformation of communist political systems, once thought impervious to liberalization, is the most dramatic.[1] Since 1989, more than two dozen countries within the former Soviet bloc have officially disavowed Marxist–Leninist ideology and have dismantled, in varying degrees, the apparatus of communist dictatorship and socialist economic planning. In many cases this transformation has led to a reinvention of politics, in the sense of genuine public debate about the purposes of society and the state, and has produced significant progress toward the establishment of a liberal–democratic order.[2]

This extraordinary turn of events has evoked a surge of scholarly research and writing from specialists on the former communist countries and other social scientists. Analysts have probed the causes of the demise of communism in Eastern Europe and the former Soviet Union.[3] They have examined the communist legacies inherited by the East European and Soviet successor states and have constructed parallel narratives of early postcommunist developments in regional groupings of these states.[4] They also have produced detailed studies of recent trends in individual countries.[5] Extensive analysis and debate have likewise been devoted to the political and institutional aspects of market reform.[6]

To date, however, scholars have devoted relatively little effort to systematic cross-country comparisons of political change in the postcommunist states. With some notable exceptions, Western thinking about attempts to democratize these polities has generally been based on the experience of the countries of North America, Western and Southern Europe, and Latin America.[7] Among scholars and laypersons alike, there has been an unconscious tendency to view postcommunist political developments through interpretive lenses derived from the experiences of countries that have not undergone the historical transformations and traumas associated with communism. Yet the relevance of the paradigms of democratization (and failed democratization) derived from these countries is far from self-evident. Just as some economists have challenged the applicability of models drawn from noncommunist societies to the dilemmas of economic reform in postcommunist states, some political scientists have questioned whether paradigms of democratization drawn from noncommunist countries are relevant to the study of postcommunist political change.[8] This is an issue of central importance both for social theory and for the day-to-day policies of Western governments and nongovernmental organizations.

An adequate understanding of this exceptionally complex theoretical issue, however, requires a better understanding of the nature of the political changes occurring inside the postcommunist countries themselves. Because the communist era saddled these countries with many similar political and socioeconomic dilemmas, it is logical to examine them for similar processes of political change. A strong case can be made that communist countries passed through a distinctive set of profound political and socioeconomic alterations that makes comparisons among postcommunist patterns of political development especially fruitful. On the other hand, these societies also have been shaped by dissimilar processes - witness the contrast between the Czech Republic and Turkmenistan, which today have little in common besides the fact that they were once called communist - and analysts cannot assume that they are destined to follow identical political trajectories. Controlled comparisons among postcommunist countries can help us identify the causes of the varying national outcomes that have begun to crystallize roughly a half-decade after the demise of communism.

Some valuable comparative work on postcommunist political development has already been done.[9] But the immense forces that have been unleashed and the profound questions that they raise demand much fuller exploration. Only a sustained research effort by the broad community of scholars can provide a surer baseline for evaluating recent trends and the prospects for democracy in particular postcommunist states. This long-term effort must address many aspects of each country's political life – its constitutional arrangements, the objectives of its leaders, public attitudes toward politics, ethnonational sentiments, the interplay of politics and economics, and the effects of international influences, to name only a few – and juxtapose them with comparable phenomena in other postcommunist states.

Although the project that produced this book touches on a number of these themes, the central goal has been to trace changes and continuities in elite and mass political participation in each of the postcommunist countries of Eastern Europe and the former Soviet Union.[10] By examining the major political actors and the means through which they exercise power, the project has sought to assess the extent of democratization in each country and the strength of countervailing authoritarian tendencies. In particular, we have examined the degree to which postcommunist political arrangements have fostered or inhibited an expansion of popular political participation through the introduction of competitive elections and the formation of competitive political parties. Where feasible, we also have offered preliminary assessments of the strength and orientation of the network of groups and institutions sometimes known as "civil society" – or, more generally, as political society.[11] The writers of the country-studies have necessarily approached these topics from various angles, depending on the particulars of the country being analyzed. In each instance, however, the writer has sought to clarify whether formative influences and political choices have propelled the country's postcommunist politics in a democratic or an authoritarian direction, and how durable the new constellation of power appears to be.

This approach has both intellectual advantages and limitations. The contributors to the project have harbored no illusions that we could treat all the relevant issues in the necessary depth. Separate volumes could easily have been written on particular facets of the overall comparisons we have undertaken. The value of our enterprise is that it presents a comprehensive set of carefully researched case-studies based on a common research agenda and on close interaction among the country-study writers and editors. The project provides a useful picture of each country's political development up to the mid–1990s, along with a sense of the national trends that may prevail during the next few years. In addition, it lays the groundwork for delineating and explaining alternative paths of democratic and nondemocratic change in postcommunist societies. Today, less than a decade since communist regimes began to fall, the challenge of charting these paths remains daunting. In the words of one scholar, "it is a peculiarity of political scientists that we spend much of our time explaining events that have not finished happening."[12] Identifying and explaining patterns of postcommunist political development will become easier as additional events and a longer historical perspective make those patterns more distinct; but it is not too early to begin the task.

The remainder of this chapter situates the country-studies in a general intellectual framework and highlights some of the principal themes they address. First it examines the meaning of key concepts, such as democracy and democratic transition, and sketches the types of regimes that may emerge from the wreckage of communism. Next the chapter explores the impact of the international environment and of national historical legacies on the evolution of postcommunist regimes. It then turns to a discussion of elections, party systems, and their role in the success or failure of democratization. Finally, the chapter surveys the potential effects of political culture and the intermediate groups that constitute a country's political society. In treating each theme, I draw on the chapters included in this book and the companion volumes.[13]

Democracy and the alternatives

Because the general notion of democracy has been interpreted in many different ways, it is essential to begin by discussing some of these variations and their implications for the study of postcommunist countries. After all, during their heyday Marxist–Leninist regimes claimed to be quintessentially democratic and ridiculed the "bourgeois" democracies found in other parts of the world. More to the point, proponents of liberal democracy have long disagreed among themselves about which institutional arrangements constitute the essence of a democratic system. Equally significant, some admirers of the advanced industrial democracies prefer to call such systems "polyarchies" and to treat democracy as a set of normative standards against which all political systems must be measured, in order not to gloss over the serious defects of contemporary liberal polities.[14]

For the purposes of this project, we have adopted a less stringent criterion for classifying a country as democratic. According to this standard, democracy is a political system in which the formal and actual leaders of the government are chosen within regular intervals through elections based on a comprehensive adult franchise with equally weighted voting, multiple candidacies, secret balloting, and other procedures, such as freedom of the press and assembly, that ensure real opportunities for electoral competition. Among the various attributes of democracy, competitive elections are the feature that is most easily identifiable and most widely recognized around the world. Competitive elections are arguably a precondition for the other political benefits that a democratic system may confer on its citizens, and they are a valuable yardstick for analyzing and distinguishing among postcommunist countries. One fundamental question is why some countries, such as Poland, have introduced fully competitive elections, while others, such as Uzbekistan, have not. Another question is why some postcommunist countries have continued to choose their governmental leaders through free elections, whereas other countries that initially introduced such elections, such as Armenia and Albania, have recently fallen victim to large-scale electoral fraud.

Although useful, our minimalist definition of democracy also involves potential pitfalls. Because it does not stipulate all the individual liberties that most Western observers consider an essential element of genuine democracy, it groups together the majoritarian and constitutionalist/libertarian traditions of democratic governance.[15] Under certain conditions, a competitively elected government is capable of behaving in a despotic fashion toward large numbers of its citizens or inhabitants, especially when those persons belong to a distinct ethnic or religious minority.[16] The behavior of the Croatian government toward many ethnic Serbian inhabitants of Croatia is a graphic example. Other postcommunist governments, such as those of Estonia and Latvia, have faced major dilemmas posed by the presence of sizable minorities, but they have dealt with these issues in a more humane though sometimes controversial manner. Confronted with ethnic mixes that pose less obvious risks to the state, still other governments have accorded full rights to citizens of minority extraction; Bulgaria is a case in point. In a fully functioning constitutional democracy, the rights of citizens and inhabitants are legally specified and protected by the government, no matter how sweeping a mandate it has received at the polls.

Another caveat concerns the application of the criterion of competitive elections. The project's case-studies show that in several countries postcommunist elections have been considerably more competitive than the typical stage-managed charades of the communist era, yet have not been entirely free by strict democratic standards. In the long run, however, this movement from communist-style to semidemocratic elections may constitute an important step in the process of liberalization and may lead, despite powerful resistance, to voting procedures that are fully democratic. One strand of the scholarly literature emphasizes that democracy is sometimes the unintended consequence of political struggles among antagonists who did not initially seek to create it. The political import of semi-competitive elections thus depends on whether they mark a national step forward from completely rigged elections or a regression from elections that were genuinely democratic. Semi-competitive elections in Turkmenistan would be a sign of dramatic democratic progress, whereas similar elections in the Czech Republic would not.

Care is also required in applying the notion of democratic transitions. Due to the astonishing cascade of events that brought about the collapse of communism and a Western victory in the Cold War, virtually all postcommunist leaders proclaimed their commitment to democratization – sometimes sincerely, sometimes not – and a considerable number of outside observers assumed that democracy would be the natural result of communism's demise. However, when thinking about the evolution of the postcommunist states it is important to maintain the distinction between transitions from communism and transitions to democracy. It may be true that liberal democracy has become the prevailing model of modern politics in much of the world.[17] But both historical experience and a priori reasoning suggest that a spectrum of possible postcommunist outcomes still exists. This spectrum includes variants of democracy, variants of authoritarianism, and some hybrids in between.

The consolidation of democracy is another important idea that warrants careful handling. To say that democracy has been consolidated in a country suggests, at a minimum, that the introduction of fully competitive elections has been completed and that the new political system has become stable. In this discussion, consolidation denotes the condition of a political system in which all major political actors and social groups expect that government leaders will be chosen through competitive elections and regard representative institutions and procedures as their main channel for pressing claims on the state.[18] A few scholarly critics have challenged the idea of consolidation, arguing that some democracies have demonstrated considerable staying-power without ever satisfying certain commonly accepted criteria of consolidation.[19] Nevertheless, the concept remains useful for differentiating democratic systems that have achieved internal stability from systems that have not, and for making probabilistic assessments of a particular democracy's political prospects. It calls attention to internal factors, such as fundamental divisions over national identity, constitutional structure, and criteria of citizenship, that can destroy a democratic polity. Because all systems are subject to political decay, consolidation does not guarantee that a democracy will survive, but does improve its chances. Although democratic consolidation typically required a long time in earlier eras, the contemporary ascendancy of liberal-democratic norms in many parts of the globe may accelerate the process. Since the 1970s the consolidation of new democratic systems has occurred quite quickly in some noncommunist countries, though not in others.[20]

Whether any of the postcommunist states have achieved democratic consolidation is a complex issue. A case can be made that the Czech Republic, Poland, and Lithuania have reached this political watershed, even though controversy persists over the shape of the Polish constitution. But most postcommunist states have not reached it. Some, such as Latvia and Estonia, have established representative institutions and political structures that work quite smoothly, but have not yet admitted large ethnic minorities to citizenship. Others, such as Russia, have made impressive progress in introducing competitive elections, but contain particular political parties and social groups whose loyalty to democratic principles remains highly questionable. Still others, such as Uzbekistan and Belarus, are plainly developing along authoritarian lines.

The spectrum of possible postcommunist outcomes includes such variants of democracy as parliamentary rule and presidential government. Each of these forms of government has been adopted by some postcommunist countries, and each has champions who argue that it is the least susceptible to political breakdown.[21] In addition, the spectrum of potential outcomes includes hybrid systems similar to the "delegative democracy" identified by students of comparative politics.[22] In a delegative democracy, the president is chosen through competitive elections. Once in office, however, he rules in the name of the whole nation, usually on the pretence that he transcends the petty concerns of particular parties and interest groups. Unconstrained by the legislature or the courts, the president governs without significant checks on his power, save for the constitutional requirement that regular presidential elections be held and the de facto power held by other officials, and he often seeks to change the constitution so as to prolong his time in power.[23] Several postcommunist countries, particularly some former Soviet republics, have concentrated governmental power in an executive president with the authority to issue decrees having the force of law. Depending on the future course of events, this hybrid arrangement has the potential to become either a constitutional democracy or a clear-cut form of authoritarianism.

The main potential forms of postcommunist authoritarianism are personal dictatorships, one-party states, and military regimes. The socioeconomic turmoil following the collapse of communism may make it hard to build stable versions of any of these types of authoritarianism, but oscillations among them may still preclude successful democratization. In countries where a substantial part of the population has already undergone sociopolitical mobilization, the lack of a well developed party structure makes a personal dictatorship vulnerable to sharp shifts in the public mood and to unbridled power-struggles when the dictator is incapacitated or dies.[24] Nonetheless, a few postcommunist countries are likely to come under the sway of such dictatorships. Contemporary Belarus fits this model, and Turkmenistan bears a significant resemblance to it.

Generally speaking, authoritarian states built around a single ruling party are more stable than personal dictatorships. A ramified party organization helps harness mass political participation to the leaders' objectives, reduces elite conflict, and smooths the process of succession. For postcommunist leaders set on following this path, the challenge is to create a party mechanism that can actually control mass participation and the behavior of any quasi-democratic governmental institutions that already have been set up. This stratagem is often more difficult to apply than it might seem. Once the old communist mechanisms of control have been weakened, building a stable new ruling party is a problematic undertaking, as developments in Kazakstan indicate. Success depends both on the top leader's willingness to assign high priority to building such a party and on the party's capacity to contain new socioeconomic forces within its structure. Absent these two conditions, leaders with a dictatorial bent may move toward a system of personal rule, eliminating quasi-democratic institutions and processes, such as elections, that they cannot effectively control.

As of the mid–1990s, direct military rule seemed the least likely postcommunist authoritarian outcome. Historically, one-party states have proven less susceptible to military coups than have other forms of authoritarianism.[25] Ruling communist parties exercised especially close civilian control over their military professionals, and this heritage of subordination appears to have shaped military behavior in most postcommunist countries. The rare episodes in which the armed forces have intervened collectively to affect the selection of national leaders have usually been precipitated by "demand pull" from feuding politicians eager to defeat their rivals rather than by any military desire to rule.[26] That said, it should be noted that irregular military forces and militias have played a sizable role in the politics of some postcommunist countries, especially those parts of the former Soviet Union and the former Yugoslavia that have become embroiled in warfare. In a number of countries the parlous economic and social condition of the regular military has facilitated transfers of weapons and personnel to irregular military forces. Although irregular forces have caused a change of government leadership in only a few cases, such as Georgia and Azerbaijan, they frequently have had a strong effect on the political balance inside their "host" states, whether those states are nominally democratic or authoritarian in character.[27]

The international environment and national historical legacies

The dynamics of postcommunist political change have been shaped by several major variables. One of the most important is the international environment, which includes geopolitical, institutional-normative, and cultural elements. Historically, the overall effect of the international environment on attempts to promote democratization has ranged from highly beneficial to extremely harmful.[28] By historical standards, the contemporary international setting has been relatively favorable to the creation and consolidation of new democracies, although there have been important regional variations in this respect. The generally propitious international environment has been shaped by a number of factors: the heightened Western commitment to human rights as a major aspect of interstate relations; the gradual absorption of liberal ideas into once-autarkic societies made increasingly permeable by competitive pressures from an open global economy; the decision of the Soviet leadership not to shore up communist regimes in Eastern Europe with military threats or intervention; the "gravitational pull" exerted by highly prosperous Western democracies and by multilateral institutions prepared to assist postcommunist liberalization; and the intensifying bandwagon effects exerted by leading exemplars of reform, such as Poland, on other former communist countries that initially dragged their feet.[29]

International conditions have not favored all postcommunist efforts at democratization in equal measure. The effects of the international setting have varied sharply by region and by the form of outside influence in question. For the most part, the Western powers have refused to intervene with decisive military force to suppress the savage ethnic violence that has undermined the chances for democratization in parts of the former Yugoslavia and the Transcaucasus.[30] In contrast to the situation after World War II, when the geostrategic interests of the Western Allies required the imposition of democratic institutions on the defeated Axis powers, the West has had no compelling strategic reason to impose liberal-democratic arrangements on such countries as Serbia.[31] Perhaps as significant, the West's political and economic impact on most European postcommunist states has exceeded its influence on the postcommunist states of the Transcaucasus and Central Asia. The scale of such influence is not determined solely by the receiving state's location or culture; witness the isolation of Belarus from the countries to its west. But the large cluster of established European democracies and the prospect of close political and economic ties with them have had a much stronger effect in Eastern Europe than in other postcommunist regions. In Eastern Europe, a desire to be admitted to NATO and the European Union has tempered the political conduct even of lagging states such as Romania.

Several factors account for this variation in Western influence: the greater physical and cultural distance between the West and most of the non-European postcommunist states; the lower level of Western strategic interest in these countries, coupled with a tendency to manifest less concern about their internal liberalization than about their potential as sources of energy and raw materials; the countries' greater vulnerability to pressures from a Russia preoccupied with ensuring the stability of its southern flank; and the substantial limits on the West's diplomatic leverage in Asia, where booming economies have emboldened some authoritarian regimes, such as China, to defy Western human-rights standards.[32]

In addition to being influenced by the international environment, the direction of postcommunist political development has been shaped by whether struggles over political change have taken place within the arena of a firmly established nation-state. In a handful of postcommunist countries, politics has unfolded within the boundaries and administrative framework of the old communist state. In most cases, however, the struggle over democratization has coincided with efforts to create the political scaffolding of a new state on a portion of the territory of the old communist regime. Due to the breakup of Czechoslovakia, Yugoslavia, and the Soviet Union, twenty-two of the twenty-seven postcommunist states are new sovereign entities. This is one of the main features that distinguishes postcommunist efforts to build democracy from comparable processes in Latin America and Southern Europe.[33]

The break-up of states severely complicates efforts to achieve democratization. The process frequently triggers incendiary controversies over the national identity of the new states, contested borders, and rival groups' competing claims to be the only indigenous inhabitants of their new country. In cases as diverse as Croatia, Azerbaijan, Georgia, Moldova, and

Russia, national declarations of independence from a larger communist regime have coincided with simultaneous attempts by local minorities to declare their own independence from the newly established states. Such centrifugal processes, which cannot be resolved by appealing to the principle of national self-determination, increase the probability of violent communal conflict and the emergence of ultranationalist sentiments harmful to democratization.[34] The conflicts between Serbia and Croatia and between Armenia and Azerbaijan provide examples. The collapse of an established state also accelerates the disintegration of the government bureaucracies that must function smoothly to ensure the administrative effectiveness of democratic institutions. This, in turn, may undermine the popular appeal of democracy as a political system.[35]

The creation of new states from old does not always preclude democratic development, however. The Czech Republic and Slovakia, Russia and the Baltic states, and the former Yugoslav republic of Slovenia are cases in point. Democratization is liable to fail when efforts to dismantle the old state interact with the mobilization of large internal ethnic "diasporas" and the emergence of ultranationalism in internal ethnic "homelands" to ignite large-scale violence. Democratization stands a greater chance of success when internal ethnic diasporas are small or are willing to be incorporated into successor states outside their "homeland," and when nationalist movements in the ethnic homelands are moderate rather than extremist.[36] In new, ethnically divided states, the political impact of ethnic differences depends on the actions both of the dominant group and of ethnic minorities and outside parties, as the contrasting internal political dynamics of Croatia and Estonia demonstrate.

Whether linked to the collapse of an established state or not, manifestations of nationalism and efforts to democratize can affect each other in very different ways. Careful observers have distinguished between two types of nationalism: inclusionary "civic" nationalism, which is compatible with the observance of individual rights, and exclusionary ethnic nationalism, which tends to subordinate such rights to the collectivist claims of the nation.[37] Rarely if ever do these two types of nationalism exist in pure form, but the weighting of the two tendencies in citizens' attitudes varies enormously from one country to another.[38] For example, Ukraine might be placed close to the "civic" end of the spectrum, Latvia nearer the middle, and Serbia near the "ethnic" end.[39] Before the final third of the nineteenth century, when nationhood in Europe became closely linked to ethnicity, nationalism was commonly understood to be a concomitant of democracy, and in postcommunist cases such as Poland, this connection can still be seen.[40] A modicum of nationalism is indispensable for the creation and cohesion of a modern state; without it many citizens will lack an incentive to participate actively in democratic politics, as the case of Belarus demonstrates. On the other hand, exclusionary nationalism can lead to the effective disenfranchisement of substantial segments of the population – witness the behavior of the Serbian and Croatian governments toward minorities within their borders – and undergird dictatorial practices.

In addition to examining the historical roots of national identity in each country, analysts of postcommunist political change must examine other effects of the country's precommunist political legacy. Studies of democratization in states lacking a communist past have shown that countries which have had a prior experience of democracy, even if the experience has been unsuccessful, have a better chance of democratizing successfully on their second attempt.[41] Prior democratic experience may promote current democratization in several ways. If fairly recent, it may provide "human capital" – that is, persons with a first-hand understanding of democratic institutions and practices who can help launch and maintain the new political arrangements. Even if historically remote, previous experience may provide instructive lessons in the design of democratic institutions matched to the particular features of the country in question. Finally, previous experience may help legitimize new democratic institutions by protecting them against the xenophobic charge that they are an alien cultural import.

By comparison with many democratizing countries that were never communist, the postcommunist countries have little prior democratic experience on which to draw, as Valerie Bunce has forcefully argued. This disadvantage is clearest with respect to human capital. Measured against Latin America and Southern Europe, where authoritarian and democratic rule frequently alternated with one another in the past, "Eastern Europe has no such democratic tradition. The so-called democratic experiments of the interwar period lasted less than a decade and are best understood, in any case, as authoritarian politics in democratic guise." Lacking "the 'feel' for democracy that Latin America and Southern Europe enjoyed," postcommunist states face special political obstacles.[42]

These obstacles are not insurmountable, however. Even if short-lived, a nation's previous attempts to build democracy can give reformers not only potential models for contemporary governmental arrangements but also lessons about constitutional flaws that have contributed to past democratic failures. Political learning of this kind has occurred, for example, in Estonia and Latvia. More broadly, national memories or even myths of a democratic past may facilitate popular acceptance of democratic political structures.[43] This sort of process has occurred in both the Czech Republic and Poland. Citizens of Slovakia, by contrast, tend to regard interwar Czechoslovakian history as a period of alien domination by the Czechs rather than as an integral part of their own national past, and countries such as Ukraine effectively lack any modern experience of independent statehood. But even in nations such as these, a strong popular aversion to decades of communist oppression may compensate for the absence of a "usable" democratic past. Due to the exceptional severity of most communist regimes, this kind of negative learning may be considerably stronger in postcommunist countries than in noncommunist countries that aspire to democratize.

Like the effects of the precommunist legacy, the effects of communist rule on the prospects for democratic political participation warrant careful scrutiny in each country. Exactly what constitutes political participation, it should be said, is a matter of some disagreement among Western scholars. Defining the concept narrowly, specialists on the "classic" democracies have tended to concentrate on citizen involvement in such activities as voting and contacting government officials, and have frequently excluded citizen involvement in such "unconventional" activities as peaceful protests and demonstrations.[44] This narrower definition may stem from an understandable concern, sharpened by the history of Fascism and Communism, that authoritarian elites bearing the standard of "direct democracy" can manipulate mass movements to destroy the institutions of representative democracy.[45] By contrast, scholars interested in comparative political development have tended to define participation more broadly and have sometimes classified nearly all politically motivated activities, including political violence, under this rubric.[46] Analysts also have differed over the importance of the distinction between voluntary and compulsory participation. Specialists on established democracies have generally treated the contrast between these two forms of political involvement as a key difference between democratic and non-democratic systems, whereas some students of political development have minimized its significance.[47]

Voluntary participation and compulsory participation can each be found in both authoritarian and democratic polities. However, the relative proportions of these types of participation differ dramatically in authoritarian and democratic systems and help explain the qualitative differences between the two.[48] Main-line communist regimes systematically excluded most kinds of voluntary participation – particularly competitive elections for high government office and the freedom to form independent associations – and introduced novel forms of compulsory mass participation directed from above. Mandatory participation reached its zenith in the stage of full-fledged totalitarianism. Communist totalitarianism rested on the discovery that under certain conditions the expansion of mass education and the creation of new social organizations could be joined with mass coercion to multiply rather than diminish the power of the state.[49]

The totalitarian approach to political participation was linked with a radical stance toward society. In the Stalin era, Marxist–Leninist regimes sought to create a political system that not only compelled every citizen to endorse a common sociopolitical program but excluded the very notion of a pluralist society with autonomous interests distinct from those of the ruling elite.[50] In essence, these regimes sought to obliterate the dividing-line between state and society. Although they never completely succeeded, some of them came quite close. For most of the twentieth century, communist systems remained the most stable form of dictatorship – a form so stable that their transformation into liberal polities was said by some observers to be impossible.[51]

The erosion of communism did, of course, pave the way for the expansion of autonomous political participation by citizens and groups acting outside the control of the political elite. To begin with, not all national societies went through so shattering a totalitarian experience as did the nations of the USSR, and this lent them greater political resilience. Poland, where the Catholic Church retained a substantial measure of autonomy and agriculture was never fully collectivized, is probably the best example. Moreover, although communist regimes went to unprecedented lengths to instill the official ideology, their simultaneous drive to transform the economy and raise educational levels gradually expanded the social groups whose members later found those ideological claims implausible or absurd. For example, during the early stages of Stalin's industrialization drive, citizen support for the Soviet regime was directly correlated with an individual's youth and level of education – no doubt partly because education served as an important vehicle of upward social mobility. During the next four or five decades, the stratum of persons with higher education grew dramatically, but at some point support for the regime became inversely correlated with youth and level of education.[52] In many communist countries a small group of citizens became the nucleus of a nascent civil society – that is, in the broadest sense, a society whose members insisted on a separation between state and society and on the moral primacy of societal interests – which ultimately contributed to the downfall of the political regime.[53]

Although communist regimes have generally pursued similar social and economic policies, the effects of communist rule have varied among countries and have contributed to different national patterns of postcommunist political change. At each stage in the transition from communism, the course of events has been shaped by the strength of the ruling elite vis-à-vis the political opposition, as well as by the relative strength within each camp of hard-line groups hostile to compromise and groups favoring compromise for the sake of peaceful change.[54] The overall disposition of the ruling communist elite for or against reform has thus had an important effect on the political development of individual countries. The dynamics of change have also been affected by the presence or absence of a vigorous dissent movement, which has sometimes exerted an indirect but powerful long-term influence on both elite and mass attitudes toward democratization. The influence of a generation of liberal Soviet dissenters on the policies of Mikhail Gorbachev contrasts strikingly with the absence of reformist currents among the intellectuals and communist party leaders of Belarus during the same period. In addition, disparate levels of social development and varying mass political cultures have affected the political evolution of individual countries. A case can be made, for instance, that Central Asia's comparatively low levels of urbanization and education have impeded efforts to democratize the states of the region. In such countries as Kyrgyzstan, these low levels have made it difficult to subordinate particularistic loyalties and local ties to a countrywide sense of political engagement and civic responsibility.

Ruling elites and opposition leaders have typically crafted their stances toward democratization with an eye to the shifting national constellation of political forces, and each group's successes and failures have been strongly influenced by its capacity to generate political power. In struggles over the postcommunist order, new forms of democratic participation, ranging from peaceful mass demonstrations to competitive elections, have frequently been pitted against antidemocratic forms of political action, ranging from attacks by hired thugs to mob violence or all-out civil war, as in Tajikistan and Georgia. Intermediate types of political action, such as organized boycotts of elections and general strikes, have been resorted to by both advocates and opponents of democracy. In cases where hostile camps of similar strength have confronted one other, the outcome has depended not only on elite objectives and tactics, but on the content of mass attitudes and the level of mass mobilization in behalf of democratic reforms.[55]

The impact of violence on struggles over the postcommunist order is complex. The prevalence of nonviolent and noncoercive forms of politics improves the chances for a democratic outcome but does not guarantee it. Under certain conditions, dictators and authoritarian parties may be voted into office and then roll back a political system's democratic features, as the example of Belarus shows. In authoritarian systems, many forms of voluntary participation regarded as normal in democratic systems are illegal, and "unconventional" forms of participation such as mass demonstrations and strikes may be indispensable for launching and sustaining the process of democratization. In these circumstances, eyeball-to-eyeball confrontations and the implicit threat of violent escalation may be a spur to reform.[56] Nor does limited violence necessarily eliminate the possibility of further democratic change; instead it may sharpen leaders' and citizens' awareness of the high risks of further violence, as it arguably did in the clash between Russian president Boris Yeltsin and his parliamentary opponents in the fall of 1993. The example of Georgia suggests that even civil war may not completely block a state's subsequent movement in a democratic direction.[57]

Nevertheless, the threshold between nonviolent and violent political action remains extremely important. Violence makes the political stakes a matter of life or death. It deepens grievances among the losers, intensifies fears of liberalization among the winners, and reduces the chances for political compromise. Often it creates armed camps that are prepared to resort to force and have a vested interest in the continued use of force to decide political conflicts, as in the countries of the Transcaucasus. Even if it sweeps away old communist structures, it may make noncommunist dictatorship more likely. Paradoxically, it also may extend the political life of established elites that are tied to the military or the security police but manage to shift the blame for past misdeeds onto the shoulders of a few fellow culprits – as the first phase of Romania's postcommunist development illustrates. The absence of violence does not guarantee a democratic outcome, but it improves the chances for substantial progress in this direction; witness the contrast between Georgia's first violence-laden years of postcommunist politics and Bulgaria's relatively peaceful transition to democracy.

Elections, parties, and political development

The introduction of competitive elections as a means of selecting a country's governmental leaders is a watershed in the transition to democracy. Because electoral rules can decisively affect the prospects for the survival of particular parties – and sometimes for the survival of an entire country – they generally become an object of intense struggle.[58] In transitions from communism, this struggle has been shaped both by the attitudes of established communist elites and by the power at the disposal of the proponents of full-fledged democratization. In a large number of cases, a combination of ideological erosion within the elite and vigorous public pressure for reform have led the elite to accept electoral procedures that are genuinely democratic by Western standards. In some instances the elite has accepted a major expansion of democratic participation partly because of doubts about the strength or reliability of the instruments of coercion needed to block it. Some major turning-points in the history of the "classic" democracies of North America and Western Europe were shaped by a similar calculus of power.[59] In contrast to most of the classic cases, however, the introduction of competitive elections at the close of the communist era generally entailed an extremely rapid expansion of voluntary political participation.[60]

Numerous postcommunist countries, of course, have experienced only a partial liberalization of electoral rules and conditions; a handful have experienced none at all. In Uzbekistan and Kazakstan, for example, where popular pressure for democratization was relatively weak, established elites managed to exert a large measure of influence over the quasi-competitive elections introduced near the close of the communist era, and thereby kept enough control over national politics to avoid comprehensive democratic reforms.[61] In lands such as Belarus, the postcommunist manipulation of electoral rules was initially more oblique, but led within a few years to flagrant violations of democratic electoral practices. Another graphic illustration of this trend is the refusal of the Serbian and Croatian regimes to recognize the victories of opposition parties in national rounds of urban elections conducted in 1995 and 1996.

In those transitions from communism in which the balance of political forces has favored the introduction of genuinely democratic elections, the choice of possible electoral systems has been wider than in most noncommunist countries. By comparison with cases of democratization in Latin America, far fewer preauthoritarian political parties have survived in the former communist states; this has reduced pressures to return to preauthoritarian electoral rules and has increased the scope for political maneuver in framing new rules.[62] Communist successor parties and nascent noncommunist parties have often altered their stance on the specifics of electoral reform according to apparent shifts in their chances under one or another electoral dispensation. However, by the mid–1990s it became clear that many of the postcommunist regimes that have introduced genuinely competitive elections have adopted rules for legislative elections that show certain broad similarities. These rules, which commonly distribute some or all legislative seats on the basis of proportional representation, have been tacitly designed to reduce the risk of extra-constitutional clashes by ensuring that all major groups will be represented in the legislature.[63]

Competitive elections have given rise to a host of postcommunist parties.[64] But just how these parties have affected the development of democracy remains an open question. Western observers have long debated the positive and negative consequences of parties for democracy and democratic values.[65] Political parties often fail to perform some functions deemed essential by democratic theorists, and in many established democracies the political salience of parties has diminished in recent decades.[66] Nonetheless, every contemporary political system that satisfies either the minimalist or a more rigorous definition of democracy has political parties. This fact indicates that the political mechanisms which enable citizens to replace governmental leaders through competitive elections cannot function effectively in the absence of parties. In this sense, parties are indispensable for the survival of democratic systems.

Party-formation in postcommunist countries has been subject to some influences that are distinctive and others that are common to postcommunist and noncommunist countries alike. As noted above, the industrial and social policies of communist regimes created many of the socioeconomic conditions – especially vastly expanded education and urbanization – that facilitate the emergence of voluntary associations and political parties. On the other hand, after seizing power communist regimes typically destroyed all noncommunist parties – with the occasional exception of one or two small "satellite" parties. Moreover, the high level of mandatory participation in communist party activities reportedly imbued the public in many countries with a distrust of parties of any kind. Also, the turbulence of postcommunist socioeconomic upheavals has hampered the efforts of voters to assess their short- and long-term interests and to pick a party that will represent those interests.[67]

Postcommunist party-formation thus appears to face an unusual array of structural obstacles. Unlike many post-authoritarian transitions in Latin America and other parts of the Third World, there are virtually no shadow-parties, independent trade unions, or other societal organizations that have roots in the pre-authoritarian period and that can quickly be reactivated to fight new elections.[68] This suggests that the rate at which postcommunist parties crystallize into reasonably stable institutions might be closer to the rates of party-formation during the nineteenth century than to the rates in other new democracies near the end of the twentieth.[69] Preliminary results of studies currently under way suggest that in several cases, postcommunist levels of electoral volatility – that is, the aggregate shift of voters among parties from one national election to the next – are unusually high by comparison with democratizing countries that lack a communist past.[70]

Other considerations, however, point in the opposite direction. Techniques of party-formation may be learned from abroad by ambitious political leaders and activists who have a large stake in party development. In addition, the proportional-representation features of the electoral systems hammered out in many postcommunist countries facilitate the formation of new parties. The sudden expansion of the scope of participation in meaningful elections also must be taken into account. In the nineteenth century, the step-by-step expansion of the franchise in most countries provided an incentive to create programmatic parties that appealed to the interests of each newly enfranchised segment of the population. By contrast, the simultaneous admission of all social strata and economic groups into postcommunist electoral systems has created an incentive to establish catch-all parties that appeal to many different constituencies.[71] Hence the low level of programmatic coherence in many postcommunist parties should not necessarily be equated with institutional weakness. Finally, the postcommunist states show major differences in the rate at which reasonably stable parties and competitive party systems are taking shape. For instance, parties in the Czech Republic and Poland appear to be fairly well institutionalized and to have established partisan attachments with a significant proportion of the citizenry. In Russia and Ukraine, by contrast, the level of party identification remains very low.[72]

In evaluating the relationship between party systems and democratization, it is important to remember that parties and party systems are overlapping but distinct concepts.[73] As used here, party system denotes all a country's politically significant parties – that is, those parties, small as well as large, whose behavior has a major impact on national politics – and the dominant characteristics of those parties taken as a constellation of political actors. Although the classification of party systems is a notoriously tricky matter, some of the relevant criteria are the number of significant parties, the strength of parties' linkages to particular social groups, the ideological range separating major parties on any given issue, and whether the strongest parties are situated near the extremes of the political spectrum or clustered near the center. Among polities lacking meaningful party competition, Giovanni Sartori has distinguished strictly one-party systems from systems dominated by a hegemonic party that permits but may not be challenged by "satellite" parties. Among polities with meaningful party competition, he has differentiated polarized multiparty systems, moderate multiparty systems, two-party systems, and systems characterized by one dominant party that is open to real electoral challenge. Sartori also has emphasized the importance of whether a particular party system promotes centripetal or centrifugal forms of competition among the parties.[74]

Scholars disagree about the effects of different types of party systems and electoral arrangements on democracy. In particular, these disagreements center on the effects of multiparty systems versus two-party systems and of proportional-representation versus winner-take-all electoral arrangements.[75] However, scholars generally agree that systems having a large number of significant parties with weak ties to a volatile electorate are harmful to democracy. They also agree that democracies with relatively strong extremist parties are vulnerable to authoritarian takeovers. Such anti-system parties may function under democratic conditions for an extended period without giving up their authoritarian orientation. This point is illustrated by the communist parties of Western Europe after World War II: most retained an anti-system orientation for many years, whereas socialist parties tended to undergo a gradual change of political ethos.[76] The largest anti-system parties, in France and Italy, appear to have been sustained by the political orientations of party activists and intellectuals, national levels of personal dissatisfaction among ordinary citizens that were unusually high by international standards, and the polarizing effects of the Cold War.[77]

Writing in 1990, Samuel Huntington observed that the international wave of democratization that began in the mid–1970s was characterized by a "virtual absence of major antidemocratic movements" that posed "an explicit authoritarian alternative" to new democratic regimes.[78] It is important to ascertain whether the same can be said of the postcommunist parties and political movements that have arisen since Huntington wrote these words. In a number of countries, such as Hungary and Lithuania, communist successor-parties have shed their hostility toward liberal democracy and accepted alternations in control of the government as the normal state of affairs. In cases such as Russia and Belarus, however, the main successor-party has not clearly disavowed its past authoritarian ethos.

As a rule, the postcommunist evolution of a party's goals and strategy depends on both elite and mass attitudes. Some observers have suggested that substantial rates of continuity between communist-era and postcommunist elites give members of the old guard a personal stake in the emerging democratic and economic system and reduce the incentive to try to restore authoritarianism. According to this analysis, extremely low or extremely high rates of elite continuity invite an antidemocratic backlash or a smothering of democratic reforms.[79] By themselves, quantitative measures of elite turnover cannot explain democratization's victories and defeats. But they may explain a great deal when combined with an analysis of elite values and the institutional structures through which elite members strive to advance their interests.[80] Taken together, these factors can help identify the point at which personal attitudes and the national political context "tip" old elites into acceptance of democratic political arrangements and practices.

Broadly speaking, the likely causes of moderating change among communist successor parties include the erosion of authoritarian ideas through the discrediting of Marxism–Leninism and generational turnover among top party leaders; a sense of "democratic inevitability" produced by shifts in the balance of organized political forces inside the country and by the seeming international triumph of liberal democracy; and widespread opportunities for personal enrichment through privatization and insider dealing.[81] In Hungary, for example, the path of political reform has been smoothed by elite opportunities for personal gain. Conversely, the factors that have facilitated the persistence of anti-democratic orientations in some successor parties include low leadership turnover; an exodus of moderate and liberal members who joined the party purely to advance their professional careers; the weakness of popular pressures for political liberalization; and a centripetal pattern of inter-party competition caused in part by deepening socioeconomic cleavages.

New anti-system parties based on ethnicity can also disrupt the process of democratization. The apparent explosion in the worldwide incidence of ethnic conflicts in the 1990s is largely a product of the increased public salience accorded such conflicts due to the end of the Cold War.[82] Still, extremist parties do pose a special danger to societies in which deep ethnic cleavages override or coincide with other socioeconomic divisions. Under these conditions, as Donald Horowitz has shown, the ethnicization of political parties and party competition for immobile blocs of ethnic supporters can lead to polarizing elections that preclude democratic alternations of government and pave the way for violence and an authoritarian seizure of power.[83] Whether postcommunist ethnic cleavages are as deep and unmitigated as the Third-World cleavages analyzed by Horowitz is a matter for careful consideration. In such countries or regions as Bosnia Herzegovina and the Transcaucasus, they often are. But in other countries, such as Kazakstan and the Baltic states, they appear to be more susceptible to political management and more compatible with democratization. Occasionally, ethnic cleavages are deeper among national elites than among ordinary citizens, and the competition to mobilize voters for electoral campaigns actually serves to reduce ethnic polarization, as in Moldova.

Anti-system parties that promote antidemocratic goals through nonviolent means should be differentiated from parties that are closely linked with paramilitary forces and are prepared to initiate large-scale violence. Although parties of both types constitute threats to democratization, the latter are probably a greater threat than the former. Nonviolent anti-system parties may gradually be coopted into the status of semi-loyal or even loyal supporters of a democratic system.[84] By contrast, parties predisposed to violence may trigger cycles of political conflict that spiral out of control. They also may precipitate military intervention in politics, either by design or as a result of the violent civil clashes that they set in motion, as some radical parties did in Latin America during the 1970s. To date, most postcommunist antidemocratic parties appear to fall in the nonviolent category. But there have been exceptions, as in Tajikistan, and under the stresses of prolonged social and economic turmoil, this broad pattern might change.[85]

A country's party system, it should be emphasized, can undercut democracy even in the absence of significant antidemocratic parties. One threat to the survival of democratic government is a widespread public perception that it is incapable of dealing with the numerous political and socioeconomic problems bequeathed by the collapse of communism. Such a perception may be fostered by feuding parliaments and inertial cabinets that seem unable to solve critical problems, or by frequent changes in governing coalitions that give the appearance of failing even to address the problems. Some types of multiparty systems are especially conducive to frequent changes of government; to the degree that they contribute to the formation of ineffectual coalition governments, they may erode the legitimacy of the whole democratic enterprise.

Such debilitating party systems may be less common than one might suppose, however. Certain types of coalition governments may last nearly as long as single-party ones, and turnover in the partisan make-up of governing coalitions does not always result in sharp changes of policy.[86] Much depends on the political longevity of individual cabinet ministers – which may considerably exceed the duration of a particular government coalition – and on the degree of public consensus or division over policy questions. Some postcommunist countries, such as Poland, Lithuania, and Hungary, have experienced several changes in the governing coalition but still have sustained quite consistent macroeconomic and social policies for several years. Moreover, a democratic government may experience several failures of performance in the economic and social realms without necessarily undermining the popular legitimacy of democratic institutions, as we shall see below.

Some postcommunist countries, of course, have remained in the grip of a single monopolistic party, or a hegemonic one. Sartori has distinguished totalitarian and authoritarian one-party systems from "one-party pragmatic systems" that have low levels of ideological intensity and are based primarily on political expediency.[87] This characterization bears a close resemblance to Turkmenistan and might become applicable to a few other postcommunist countries. The question is whether such parties have become effective instruments of authoritarian rule or have encountered serious challenges from other political forces. In addition, it is important to determine whether the satellite parties tolerated by hegemonic rulers have acquired real political influence or have become even more marginal since the cresting of pro-democratic symbolism and gestures immediately after the fall of communism. The experience of Kazakstan suggests that the role of these parties depends in part on whether elite factions seek to develop them as a means of defending their interests against attacks from other elite groups.

The effects of political culture and political society

As already noted, the political development of any postcommunist country is strongly influenced by the attitudes and strategies of elites and the character of the parties and other institutions through which they vie for power. Equally important to long-term postcommunist outcomes are the initial condition and subsequent evolution of the country's political culture and political society. Broadly speaking, a country's political culture reflects the inhabitants' basic attitudes toward such matters as the trustworthiness of their fellow citizens, the legitimacy of others citizens' rights and interests, the fashion in which conflicting interests ought to be reconciled, the ability of citizens to influence government policies, and the legitimacy of existing political institutions. A civic political culture embodies high levels of interpersonal trust, a readiness to deal with political conflict through compromise rather than coercion or violence, and acceptance of the legitimacy of democratic institutions.[88] It stands to reason that political culture affects whether citizens choose to support moderate or extreme political movements and parties, and whether they choose to engage in democratic or anti-democratic forms of political participation.[89]

Empirical evidence suggests that a country's political culture is neither fixed once and for all, nor completely malleable. It changes in response to new historical events and personal experiences, but with a considerable lag, and primarily through the generational turnover of citizens.[90] This makes political culture an important determinant of the way that political institutions evolve and operate. Over time political institutions and major sociopolitical events exert a reciprocal influence on the content of the country's political culture. But in any given period, the content of the political culture shapes the perceptions and actions of the political elite and the mass public.

A country's political culture and its political society are closely intertwined. The notion of political society is often defined broadly to include political parties, but here it is used to denote those nonparty, nongovernmental groups and associations that participate, directly or indirectly, in shaping a country's political life. The nature of these groups and associations varies widely according to the type of political society in question.[91] Civic associations, commercial enterprises, extended clans, and criminal organizations are examples of such groups. As some of these examples suggest, a political society may include a sizable number of organizational components but still not embody the values of a civic culture. In a statistical sense, social structure and the content of political culture are related; witness the widely accepted proposition that the rise of the middle class is a source of liberal democracy, and the more controversial notion that the working class is the main social basis of authoritarianism.[92] Analytically, however, social structure and political culture are distinct, and the relationship between them may vary from one country to the next. Taken in the aggregate, a country's political society generally reflects its prevailing political culture and significantly affects the operation of its governmental institutions.[93]

Civil society is a form of political society based on a dense network of nongovernmental associations and groups established for the autonomous pursuit of diverse socioeconomic interests and prepared to rebuff state efforts to seize control of these activities.[94] The components of a civil society may include such elements as independent media, religious confessions, charitable organizations, business lobbies, professional associations, labor unions, universities, and non-institutionalized movements for various social causes. The existence of a civil society depends not only on the presence of large numbers of associations and organized groups but on the spirit in which they act. The divergent fashions in which political thinkers have depicted civil society reflect the reality that relations among societal groups inevitably entail conflict as well as cooperation.[95] A society is civil only if its constituent groups demonstrate a substantial measure of self-restraint rooted in a recognition of the legitimacy of the interests of other groups – a recognition often reinforced by the existence of overlapping group memberships – and a commitment to forgo violence as means of deciding social conflicts. Because in the aggregate the structures of a civil society embody a civic culture, such a society is conducive to the consolidation of democratic governmental institutions. Under a democratic dispensation, the relationship of civil society to the state involves a large measure of cooperation as well as conflict.[96]

The application of the concepts of political culture and civil society to countries during their communist phase entails several difficulties. Until the late communist era, systematic survey data on citizens' political attitudes were generally unavailable for most communist countries; this created a risk that analysts would erroneously attempt to infer the characteristics of mass political culture from the history and structure of the regime rather than from the empirically measured values of the population.[97] Confusion also has arisen from the attribution of several disparate meanings to the concept of civil society: these range from the notion of small oppositional movements under communist regimes to the notion of the macrostructure of entire societies in noncommunist or postcommunist states.[98] Certainly the *idea* of a civil society with values and interests superior to those of the party–state apparatus was ardently embraced by many dissidents and played an important role in delegitimizing the quasi-totalitarian pretensions of a number of communist regimes. But how widely this idea was held by ordinary citizens in most countries is difficult to establish. During the communist era the notion of civil society was plainly not embodied in a ramified network of independent social organizations and associations, although elements of such a network began to crystallize during the late communist era in Poland.[99]

In addition, it is important to inquire whether all the activists who tenaciously championed the concept of civil society as a source of resistance to communism have been capable of making a postcommunist transition to tolerance and cooperation with groups whose central values and concerns differ from their own. Put differently, not all dissidents and anticommunist groups were liberals. Adamant opposition to communist rule was not necessarily equivalent to support for democracy or for compromise among conflicting societal groups, as the examples of Georgia's Zviad Gamsakhurdia and Croatia's Franjo Tudjman show. Nor do all autonomous social institutions find the transition from communism to liberal democracy easy; witness the controversies in Poland over the efforts of the Roman Catholic hierarchy to influence legislation on abortion and the curriculum of public schools.

Applying the concepts of political culture and civil society to postcommunist countries has proved easier but still entails some complexities. In many countries a wealth of survey data on popular attitudes and behavior has now become available. However, scholars have tended to disagree about the implications of political culture for postcommunist democratization.[100] Those who believe that it constitutes a serious obstacle have generally argued that the political culture which existed before the end of communism has considerable staying-power. The sources of this inertia may include enduring precommunist traditions of dictatorship and ultranationalism, as well as authoritarian attitudes absorbed by citizens from Marxist–Leninist propaganda and frequent contact with the party–state apparatus. According to this view, the content of mass political culture increases the possibility of a reversion to some form of authoritarian rule – or to its preservation in countries where the political hold of the old elite has never been broken.

Other scholars have taken a different approach that stresses the compatibility of postcommunist political culture with democratization in many countries. Research along these lines has revealed that major West European democracies and some East European countries show broad if incomplete similarities in political culture – and that some East European citizens exhibit greater acceptance of the rights of ethnic minorities than do most West Europeans.[101] Analysts of this school have often stressed the depth of the ideological erosion that occurred during the final decades of communist rule. Arguing that postcommunist political culture is more prodemocratic than Marxist–Leninist propaganda would lead one to expect, they have suggested that memories of the violence and repression experienced under communism have strengthened citizens' attachment to attitudes of tolerance and non-violence conducive to democratization.[102] Adherents of this school of thought also maintain that intergenerational turnover strongly favors democratization because younger citizens are more enthusiastic about a transition to democratic politics and market economies, partly because they can adapt more easily and have longer time-horizons in which to enjoy the personal benefits of reform.

Closely related to such issues is the question whether a particular country's postcommunist political society bears any resemblance to a civil society in the social-structural sense. Mapping the organizational density and value orientations of a whole society is an enormous intellectual task that scholars have only begun to attempt. Nonetheless, several things seem clear. Without key components of civil society, governmental structures that are formally democratic cannot be expected to operate in a fashion that is substantively democratic. This is particularly true of independent media, which serve not only as direct advocates for societal interests but as important channels through which the members of societal groups communicate with one another and voice demands on the government. In Poland, for instance, independent print and broadcast media have played a major part in the democratic process. In Serbia, by contrast, government manipulation of the media has been so extensive that opportunities for fair electoral competition at the national level have virtually been eliminated.

The character of political society varies sharply among postcommunist countries. Networks of nongovernmental organizations and voluntary associations are growing far more rapidly in states such as Poland and the Czech Republic than in states such as Belarus and Uzbekistan. But even in countries where this growth has been relatively rapid, the infrastructure of civil society has not yet approached the density and durability of such social networks in long-established democracies; in many countries the heavy dependence of the non-profit sector on funding from the state or foreign sources makes it particularly vulnerable.[103] Moreover, processes occurring after the collapse of communism may profoundly alter a country's political society and political culture – and not necessarily in a direction favorable to democracy. Of particular consequence are economic stabilization and liberalization, the privatization of state property, and changes in the levels of legality and public order.

Economic stabilization and liberalization hold out the promise of a long-term improvement in living standards, but at the cost of bruising economic hardships in the short run. When communism first collapsed, outside observers tended to adopt the pessimistic view that democratization and market reform were basically incompatible.[104] This outlook appears to have been shaped by a tendency to analyze the political behavior of economic groups schematically and to view the issue through the lens of a few dramatic but unrepresentative cases such as Chile.[105] With time it has become clear that the relationship between postcommunist democratization and economic reform varies from one phase to another and from one country to another. Economic elites and members of the working class are not monolithic blocs and do not pursue static goals. Moreover, the goals of more narrowly defined economic groups, including labor unions, encompass interests that are broadly political as well as strictly economic.[106] The citizens of many postcommunist countries do regard economic prosperity as a central feature of liberal democracy, but they seem prepared to endure material hardships so long as they believe that economic circumstances will ultimately improve.[107] On the other hand, the severe hardships inflicted on many persons by economic reform may ultimately sharpen disillusionment with democracy – especially if these hardships are accompanied by rapidly increasing disparities of income and extensive corruption.[108]

The effects of privatization on the prospects for democratization also are likely to vary. A wide distribution of private property has long been regarded by many political theorists as an essential check on the authoritarian tendencies that may arise even in popularly elected governments. In addition to this putative benefit, the privatization of state property may facilitate democratization by offering members of the old elite a means of personal aggrandizement more lucrative and far less risky than attempting to reinstate an authoritarian order. However, the insider dealings that help neutralize the former elite as a source of collective opposition also may give rise to mass sentiments that equate democracy with social injustice and rampant corruption. This is especially likely to occur if elite corruption and an equivocal elite attitude toward economic reform produce a protracted depression of popular living standards. Although national understandings of corruption and conflict of interest vary substantially from country to country, the process of economic transformation has made postcommunist countries susceptible to corruption on an unusually large scale.[109] Under these conditions, threats to democracy may come not so much from political and economic elites as from newly enfranchised citizens embittered by the emergence of a plutocracy. In Russia and several East Europe states, public disapproval of the privatization of state economic enterprises has grown substantially since 1991.[110] For most voters, political patience has thus far outweighed economic dissatisfaction, but a long-term economic downturn and an appearance of unchecked social injustice might alter their outlook.

This is one reason that changes in the level of legality and public order are significant. Economic liberalization may lead toward a civil society sustained by the growth of socioeconomic groups with a vested interest in further democratic change, predictable commercial laws, and vigorous civic associations. But the legacy of the totalitarian state may favor elements of an "uncivil" society rather than a civil one. Unless augmented by the growth of smaller civic associations, quasi-corporatist labor and industrial organizations like those in Slovakia and the Czech Republic may become the sort of large, impersonal entities that some Western political theorists view as endangering rather than embodying a civil society.[111] Similarly, deregulation of economic life in the absence of an adequate legal structure and a trustworthy state bureaucracy may lead to the domination of economic activity by predatory business and criminal groups indifferent or hostile to democracy, especially a democracy which blocks some highly profitable activities through effective laws and institutions.[112] At its worst, deregulation of this sort could generate not only citizen disillusionment with the elected leaders who set the process in motion, but also a widespread reaction against basic democratic values.

Perhaps the most fundamental question is whether most citizens in each country believe that democratization and economic reform are essential or that realistic alternatives exist. Comparing the initial phases of dual transitions – that is, the simultaneous liberalization of national political and economic systems – in selected countries of Latin America and Eastern Europe sheds light on this question. One striking difference between the two sets of countries is that elites and citizens were much more strongly convinced of the necessity for fundamental economic change in Eastern Europe than in Latin America.[113] This conviction, in turn, apparently has given greater impetus to the postcommunist drive for liberalization and has reduced the potential for a powerful political backlash against economic reforms. Evidence from some cases, such as Russia, shows that despite economic turmoil and dissatisfaction, public support for democratic political practices has grown substantially since 1991.[114]

In other words, the "deep beliefs" of the citizens of postcommunist countries – their most strongly held attitudes and values, as opposed to transient opinions about day-to-day politics – may be of decisive importance. In Western countries, disillusionment and cynicism about particular leaders and governmental institutions coexist with a continuing commitment to democratic principles.[115] The project's case studies suggest that similar split-level outlooks exist among the citizens of a number of postcommunist countries. The fact that significant proportions of citizens believe that their new governments are unresponsive or corrupt may be taken as a loss of faith in democracy. But it also may be interpreted quite differently – as an accurate assessment of current political realities, and as the social foundation for further efforts to achieve a full-fledged democratic order.

NOTES

I am grateful to Joan Nelson, Valerie Bunce, and Karen Dawisha for helpful comments on an earlier version of this chapter.

1 For a penetrating analysis of the global process of democratization, see Samuel Huntington, *The Third Wave: Democratization in the Late Twentieth Century* (Norman, OK: University of Oklahoma Press, 1991). For shifting Western views of communist systems, including the assertion that they could never be liberalized, see Abbott Gleason, *Totalitarianism: The Inner History of the Cold War* (New York: Oxford University Press, 1995), pp. 198–209.

2 The notion of the reinvention of politics is borrowed from Vladimir Tismaneanu, *Reinventing Politics: Eastern Europe from Stalin to Havel* (New York: Free Press, 1992).

3 See, among many possible examples, J. F. Brown, *Surge to Freedom: The End of Communist Rule in Eastern Europe* (Durham, NC: Duke University Press, 1991); Gale Stokes, *The Walls Came Tumbling Down: The Collapse of Communism in Eastern Europe* (New York: Oxford University Press, 1993); Sabrina Petra Ramet, *Social Currents in Eastern Europe: The Sources and Consequences of the Great Transformation*, 2d ed. (Durham, NC: Duke University Press, 1995); Tismaneanu, *Reinventing Politics*; Brendan Kiernan, *The End of Soviet Politics: Elections, Legislatures, and the Demise of the Communist Party* (Boulder, CO: Westview Press, 1993); Archie Brown, *The Gorbachev Factor* (Oxford: Oxford University Press, 1996); John Dunlop, *The Rise of Russia and*

the Fall of the Soviet Empire (Princeton: Princeton University Press, 1993); and M. Stephen Fish, *Democracy from Scratch: Opposition and Regime in the New Russian Revolution* (Princeton: Princeton University Press, 1995).

4 For example, *The Social Legacy of Communism*, ed. James R. Millar and Sharon L. Wolchik (Washington, DC and Cambridge: Woodrow Wilson Center Press and Cambridge University Press, 1994); *The Legacies of Communism in Eastern Europe*, ed. Zoltan Barany and Ivan Volgyes (Baltimore: Johns Hopkins University Press, 1995); J. F. Brown, *Hopes and Shadows: Eastern Europe after Communism* (Durham, NC: Duke University Press, 1994); Karen Dawisha and Bruce Parrott, *Russia and the New States of Eurasia: The Politics of Upheaval* (New York: Cambridge University Press, 1994); *New States, New Politics: Building the Post-Soviet Nations*, ed. Ian Bremmer and Ray Taras, 2d ed. (New York: Cambridge University Press, 1996); Anatol Lieven, *The Baltic Revolution: Estonia, Latvia, Lithuania and the Path to Independence*, 2d ed. (New Haven: Yale University Press, 1994); and *Central Asia and the Caucasus after the Soviet Union: Domestic and International Dynamics*, ed. Mohiaddin Mesbahi (Gainesville: University Press of Florida, 1994).

5 See, for instance, *Transition to Democracy in Poland*, ed. Richard F. Starr (New York: St. Martin's, 1993); Raymond Taras, *Consolidating Democracy in Poland* (Boulder, CO: Westview Press, 1995); Rudolf Tőkés, *Negotiated Revolution: Economic Reforms, Social Change, and Political Succession in Hungary, 1957–1990* (Cambridge: Cambridge University Press, 1996); Lenard J. Cohen, *Broken Bonds: Yugoslavia's Disintegration and Balkan Politics in Transition*, 2d ed. (Boulder, CO: Westview, 1995); Sabrina Petra Ramet, *Balkan Babel*, 2d ed. (Boulder, CO: Westview, 1996); Susan Woodward, *Balkan Tragedy: Chaos and Dissolution after the Cold War* (Washington, DC: Brookings Institution, 1995); Richard Sakwa, *Russian Politics and Society* (New York: Routledge, 1993); *Elections and Political Order in Russia*, ed. Peter Lentini (New York and Budapest: Central European University Press, 1995); *The New Russia: Troubled Transformation*, ed. Gail W. Lapidus (Boulder, CO: Westview Press, 1995); Stephen White, Richard Rose, and Ian McAllister, *How Russia Votes* (Chatham, NJ: Chatham House Publishers, 1997); *Independent Ukraine in the Contemporary World*, ed. Sharon Wolchik (Prague: Central European University Press, forthcoming); and Alexander Motyl, *Dilemmas of Independence: Ukraine after Totalitarianism* (New York: Council on Foreign Relations, 1993).

6 For example, Anders Åslund, *Post-Communist Economic Revolutions: How Big a Bang?* (Washington, DC: Center for Strategic and International Studies, 1992); Adam Przeworski, *Democracy and the Market: Political and Economic Reforms in Eastern Europe and Latin America* (Cambridge: Cambridge University Press, 1991); *A Precarious Balance: Democracy and Economic Reforms in Eastern Europe*, ed. Joan Nelson (Washington, DC: Overseas Development Council, 1994); Joan Nelson et al., *Intricate Links: Democratization and Market Reforms in Latin America and Eastern Europe* (Washington, DC: Overseas Development Council, 1994); *The Privatization Process in Central Europe*, ed. Roman Frydman et al. (Budapest and New York: Central European University Press, 1993); *The Privatization Process in Russia, Ukraine, and the Baltic States*, ed. Roman Frydman et al. (Budapest and New York: Central European University Press, 1993); Roman Frydman et al., *Corporate Governance in Central Europe*

and Russia, 2 vols. (Budapest and New York: Central European University Press, 1996); *Banking Reform in Central Europe and the Former Soviet Union*, ed. Jacek Rostowski (Budapest and New York: Central European University Press, 1995); Max Ernst et al., *Transforming the Core: Restructuring Industrial Enterprises in Russia and Central Europe* (Boulder, CO: Westview, 1996); and Anders Åslund, *How Russia Became a Market Economy* (Washington, DC: Brookings Institution, 1995).

7　Although the fullest coverage of democratization in the Third World has been devoted to Latin America, in the past few years more attention has been paid to democratization in other Third-World countries. See, for instance, *Politics in Developing Countries; Comparing Experiences with Democracy*, ed. Larry Diamond, Juan J. Linz, and Seymour Martin Lipset (Boulder, CO: Lynne Rienner, 1990).

8　For differing views on this question, see Kenneth Jowitt, *The New World Disorder: The Leninist Extinction* (Berkeley: University of California Press, 1992), pp. 284–305; Sarah Meiklejohn Terry, "Thinking about Post-Communist Transitions: How Different Are They?" *Slavic Review* 52, no. 2 (Summer 1993), 333–37; Philippe C. Schmitter and Terry Lynn Karl, "The Conceptual Travels of Transitologists and Consolidologists: How Far to the East Should They Attempt to Go?" *Slavic Review* 53, no. 1 (Spring 1994), 173–85; Valerie Bunce, "Should Transitologists Be Grounded?" *Slavic Review* 54, no. 1 (Spring 1995), 111–117; idem., "Comparing East and South," *Journal of Democracy* 6, no. 3 (July 1995), 87–100. See also Beverly Crawford and Arend Lijphart, "Explaining Political and Economic Change in Post-Communist Eastern Europe: Old Legacies, New Institutions, Hegemonic Norms, and International Pressures," *Comparative Political Studies* 28, no. 2 (July 1995), 171–99. The most comprehensive empirical examination of this issue is Juan J. Linz and Alfred Stepan, *Problems of Democratic Transition and Consolidation: Southern Europe, South America, and Post-Communist Europe* (Baltimore: Johns Hopkins University Press, 1996), which appeared just as this book was going to press.

9　*Developments in East European Politics*, ed. Stephen White, Judy Batt and Paul G. Lewis (Durham, NC: Duke University Press, 1993); *Developments in Russian and Post-Soviet Politics*, ed. Stephen White, Alex Pravda, and Zvi Gitelman (Durham, NC: Duke University Press, 1994); *The New Democracies in Eastern Europe: Party Systems and Political Cleavages*, 2d ed., ed. Sten Berglund and Jan Ake Dellenbrant (Brookfield, VT: Edward Elgar, 1994); *Party Formation in East-Central Europe*, ed. Gordon Wightman (Aldershot: Edward Elgar, 1995); *Public Opinion and Regime Change: The New Politics of Post-Soviet Societies*, ed. Arthur H. Miller et al. (Boulder, CO: Westview Press, 1993); *Political Culture and Civil Society in Russia and the New States of Eurasia*, ed. Vladimir Tismaneanu (Armonk, NY: M. E. Sharpe, 1995); Richard Rose, *What Is Europe?* (New York: HarperCollins, 1996); *Social Justice and Political Change: Public Opinion in Capitalist and Post-Communist States*, ed. James R. Kluegel, David S. Mason, and Bernd Wegener (New York: Aldine de Gruyter, 1995); *Stabilising Fragile Democracies: Comparing New Party Systems in Southern and Eastern Europe*, ed. G. Pridham and P. G. Lewis (London: Routledge, 1996).

10 As noted in the Preface, the term "Eastern Europe" is employed for the sake of conciseness; in this book it does not presuppose political or cultural uniformity among the countries that it encompasses.

11 The distinction between civil society and other forms of political society is discussed below.

12 Barbara Geddes, "Challenging the Conventional Wisdom," *Journal of Democracy* 5, no. 4 (October 1994), 117.

13 *The Consolidation of Democracy in East-Central Europe*, ed. Karen Dawisha and Bruce Parrott (New York: Cambridge University Press, 1997); *Democratic Changes and Authoritarian Reactions in Russia, Ukraine, Belarus, and Moldova*, ed. idem (New York: Cambridge University Press, 1997); and *Conflict, Cleavage, and Change in Central Asia and the Caucasus*, ed. idem (New York: Cambridge University Press, 1997).

14 See especially Robert Dahl, *Polyarchy: Participation and Opposition* (New Haven: Yale University Press, 1971), and Dahl, *Democracy and Its Critics* (New Haven: Yale University Press, 1989).

15 I am obliged to Sabrina Ramet for bringing this important point to my attention.

16 It is worth noting that such cases have not been confined to postcommunist democracies but have occurred in other democracies as well. India and Turkey, for example, have harshly suppressed some ethnic minorities among their citizens. (Samuel Huntington, "Democracy for the Long Haul," *Journal of Democracy* 7, no. 2 [April 1996], 10.)

17 Ghia Nodia, "How Different Are Postcommunist Transitions?" *Journal of Democracy* 7, no. 4 (October 1996), 15–17, 22–24.

18 This definition is derived from Joan Nelson, "How Market Reforms and Democratic Consolidation Affect Each Other," in Nelson et al., *Intricate Links*, pp. 5–6. For a similar but stricter definition designed to take direct account of military threats to democracy, see Juan J. Linz, "Transitions to Democracy," *Washington Quarterly*, 13 (1990), 156. For a more complex definition that deals also with the social and economic realms, see Juan J. Linz and Alfred Stepan, "Toward Consolidated Democracies," *Journal of Democracy* 7, no. 2 (April 1996), 34–51.

19 Guillermo O'Donnell, "Illusions about Consolidation," *Journal of Democracy* 7, no. 2 (April 1996), 38 and passim. Cf. Richard Guenther et al., "O'Donnell's 'Illusions': A Rejoinder," ibid. 7, no. 4 (October 1996), 151–59.

20 For example, a team of scholars has argued that consolidation was achieved within five years of the first democratic elections in Spain and within seven years of such elections in Greece. About a decade after the elections, elite and public acceptance of the superiority of democracy over all other forms of government in these two countries matched the average level in the countries of the European Union. By contrast, in Brazil, where the process of electoral democratization began at about the same time as in Spain, the level of elite and public acceptance of democracy remained far lower. Guenther et al., "O'Donnell's 'Illusions,'" 155-56.

21 For a sample of the Western debates over which form of democracy is more stable, see the chapters in Part II of *The Global Resurgence of Democracy*, ed. Larry Diamond and Marc F. Plattner (Baltimore: Johns Hopkins University Press, 1993).

22 Eugene Huskey discusses the applicability of this concept to Kyrgyzstan in his chapter in *Conflict, Cleavage, and Change*.
23 Guillermo O'Donnell, "Delegative Democracy," *Journal of Democracy* 5, no. 1 (1994), 59–60, 67.
24 Cf. Huntington, *Political Order in Changing Societies*, p. 177 f.
25 Huntington, *The Third Wave*, pp. 231–32.
26 On the other hand, the breakdown of communism has frequently been accompanied by a blurring of the line between civilian and military affairs and by the participation of some military men, as individuals, in civilian politics. See *State Building and Military Power in Russia and the New States of Eurasia*, ed. Bruce Parrott (Armonk, NY: M. E. Sharpe, 1995), esp. chs. 2, 8, and 13. Cf. Cohen, *Broken Bonds*, pp. 85–88, 183–88, 227–33, and Woodward, *Balkan Tragedy*, pp. 166–69, 255–62.
27 Charles Fairbanks, Jr., "The Postcommunist Wars," *Journal of Democracy* 6, no. 4 (October 1995), 18–34.
28 Assessing the character of the international environment leaves considerable room for disagreement among observers, especially where ideological and cultural currents are concerned. For example, Samuel Huntington has asserted that Marxist–Leninist regimes, Nazi Germany, and the advanced capitalist democracies shared some ultimate political values because they were all parts of the same Western civilization. In my view these three Western traditions were divided at least as fundamentally as are liberal democratic thought and the authoritarian strands of non-Western cultural traditions. See Huntington, "The Clash of Civilizations?" *Foreign Affairs* 72, no. 3 (Summer 1993), 23, 44, plus the reply from Fouad Ajami in ibid., 72, no. 4 (September-October 1993), 2–9.
29 Huntington, *The Third Wave*, pp. 86–100; see also the chapters by Geoffrey Pridham, Laurence Whitehead, John Pinder, and Margot Light in *Building Democracy? The International Dimension of Democratisation in Eastern Europe*, ed. Geoffrey Pridham et al. (New York: St. Martin's Press, 1994), pp. 7–59, 119–68; and Nodia, "How Different are Postcommunist Transitions?" 15–16, 20–23.
30 Richard Ullman, "The Wars in Yugoslavia and the International System after the Cold War," and Richard Sobel, "U.S. and European Attitudes toward Intervention in the Former Yugoslavia: *Mourir pour la Bosnie?*" in *The World and Yugoslavia's Wars*, ed. Richard H. Ullman (New York: Council on Foreign Relations, 1996), pp. 9–41, 145–81.
31 During the critical early phases of the Yugoslav civil war, NATO's member-states were preoccupied with managing the consequences of the unification of Germany, other major European-security problems thrown up by the collapse of the Soviet bloc, and the Persian Gulf War. See Ullman, "The Wars in Yugoslavia and the International System after the Cold War," Stanley Hoffman, "Yugoslavia: Implications for Europe and for European Institutions," and David C. Gombert, "The United States and Yugoslavia's Wars," in *The World and Yugoslavia's Wars*, pp. 14–15, 24–31, 36, 102–18, 122–30, 136–37.
32 Samuel Huntington, *The Clash of Civilizations and the Remaking of World Order* (New York: Simon and Schuster, 1996), pp. 192–98.
33 Bunce, "Comparing East and South," 91.

34   In such instances, democratic theory provides no reliable means of determining which proposed outcome is preferable. This, in turn, often spurs the advocates of each proposed outcome to argue their case in still more vehement and uncompromising terms. See Dahl, *Democracy and Its Critics*, pp. 32–33.

35   Linz and Stepan, "Toward Consolidated Democracies," 20–21; Jacek Kochanowicz, "Reforming Weak States and Deficient Bureaucracies," in *Intricate Links*, pp. 195–96.

36   For a fuller treatment of this question, see my "Analyzing the Transformation of the Soviet Union in Comparative Perspective," in *The End of Empire? The Transformation of the USSR in Comparative Perspective*, ed. Karen Dawisha and Bruce Parrott (Armonk, NY: M. E. Sharpe, 1996), pp. 13–14, 16–20.

37   Liah Greenfeld, *Nationalism: Five Roads to Modernity* (Cambridge: Harvard University Press, 1992), pp. 8–12. Cf. John Breuilly, *Nationalism and the State*, 2d ed. (Chicago: University of Chicago Press, 1993), pp. 404–24.

38   For a penetrating discussion of this issue, see Rogers Brubaker, *Citizenship and Nationhood in France and Germany* (Cambridge: Harvard University Press, 1992).

39   One set of opinion surveys suggests considerable variation in the levels of acceptance or hostility expressed by members of several East European nations toward other ethnic groups. The levels of hostility expressed by Serbs in 1992 appear to be unusually high, although this contrast may be due partly to the fact that Serbia was at war when the survey was conducted. Mary E. McIntosh and Martha Abele MacIver, *Transition to What? Publics Confront Change in Eastern Europe*, Occasional Paper No. 38, Woodrow Wilson International Center for Scholars, Washington, DC, 1993, pp. 15–17.

40   On these linkages in the nineteenth century, see E. J. Hobsbawm, *Nations and Nationalism since 1780: Programme, Myth, Reality*, paperback ed. (New York: Cambridge University Press, 1990), ch. 1.

41   Huntington, *The Third Wave*, p. 44.

42   Bunce, "Comparing East and South," 89. Bunce grants that interwar Czechoslovakia constitutes a partial exception to this generalization.

43   Note, too, that democratic experience is a matter not simply of kind but of degree; hence scholars may apply different chronological and substantive standards to assess whether a country has had prior national experience with democracy.

44   See, for example, Sidney Verba, Norman H. Nie, and Jae-on Kim, *Participation and Political Equality: A Seven-Nation Comparison* (Chicago: The University of Chicago Press, 1978).

45   For an analogous trend in historians' treatment of American populism, see Peter Novick, *That Noble Dream: The "Objectivity Question" and the American Historical Profession* (New York: Cambridge University Press, 1988), pp. 337–41.

46   See, for example, Samuel Huntington, *Political Order in Changing Societies* (New Haven: Yale University Press, 1968), chs. 1, 3; and Samuel Huntington and Joan Nelson, *No Easy Choice: Political Participation in Developing Countries* (Cambridge: Harvard University Press, 1976), p. 13.

47 In his classic study of political development, Huntington adopts a definition that conflates voluntary and compulsory forms of political participation and attaches little explanatory significance to the differences between the two. (*Political Order in Changing Societies*, chs. 1, 3; cf. Theodore H. Friedgut, *Political Participation in the USSR* [Princeton: Princeton University Press, 1979], ch. 5.) In a later book he and Joan Nelson do emphasize the distinction by differentiating "autonomous" from "mobilized" participation. (Huntington and Nelson, *No Easy Choice*, pp. 7–15.) In *The Third Wave*, Huntington sometimes employs the narrower definition favored by students of liberal democracy. For example, he states that one-party systems, among which he includes communist regimes, have "suppressed both competition and participation" (p. 111).

48 Huntington and Nelson, *No Easy Choice*, pp. 7–15.

49 In Russia, for example, the tsarist regime long feared the expansion of mass education as a threat to its legitimacy. The Soviet regime quickly recognized that the expansion of mass education would allow it to indoctrinate individuals during a stage of social and personal development when their capacities for abstract thought were weakly developed, making them highly susceptible to manipulation from above.

50 Gregory Grossman, "The USSR – A Solidary Society: A Philosophical Issue in Communist Economic Reform," in *Essays in Socialism and Planning in Honor of Carl Landauer*, ed. Gregory Grossman (Englewood Cliffs, NJ: Prentice Hall, 1970); Robert F. Miller, "Civil Society in Communist Systems: An Introduction," in *The Developments of Civil Society in Communist Systems*, ed. Robert F. Miller (New York: Allen and Unwin, 1992), p. 5.

51 Huntington, *Political Order in Changing Societies*, emphasizes the stability of communist dictatorships. See also Gleason, *Totalitarianism*, pp. 198–209.

52 Brian D. Silver, "Political Beliefs and the Soviet Citizen," and Donna Bahry, "Politics, Generations, and Change in the USSR," in *Politics, Work, and Daily Life in the USSR: A Survey of Former Soviet Citizens*, ed. James Millar (New York: Cambridge University Press, 1987), pp. 116–121; Donna Bahry, "Society Transformed? Rethinking the Social Roots of Perestroika," *Slavic Review* 52, no. 3 (Fall 1993), 514–17.

53 Miller, "Civil Society in Communist Systems: An Introduction," pp. 6–11; Moshe Lewin, *The Gorbachev Phenomenon* (Berkeley, CA: University of California Press, 1988). The concept of civil society as a separate sphere of social life superior to the state first emerged in the late eighteenth and early nineteenth centuries. See John Keane, "Introduction," and idem., "Despotism and Democracy," in *Civil Society and the State*, ed. John Keane (New York: Verso, 1988), pp. 22–25, 35–71.

54 For a general discussion of these factors, see Huntington, *The Third Wave*, ch. 3, and Guillermo O'Donnell and Philippe C. Schmitter, *Transitions from Authoritarian Rule: Tentative Conclusions about Uncertain Democracies*, paperback ed. (Baltimore: Johns Hopkins University Press, 1986), pp. 61–64.

55 For an illuminating analysis of this general issue based on noncommunist cases, see Sidney Tarrow, "Mass Mobilization and Regime Change: Pacts, Reform, and Popular Power in Italy (1918–1922) and Spain (1975–1978)," in *The Politics of Democratic Consolidation: Southern Europe in Comparative Perspective*, ed.

Richard Gunther et al. (Baltimore, MD: Johns Hopkins University Press, 1996), pp. 204–30.

56 For example, in the spring of 1991 the radical reform forces led by Boris Yeltsin staged a peaceful mass demonstration in Moscow, and Soviet miners launched a damaging strike that included demands for political reform and the resignation of President Mikhail Gorbachev. The sequence of events suggests that these public demonstrations of support for Yeltsin helped persuade Gorbachev to abandon his temporary reliance on conservative political forces and grant large concessions to the advocates of further reform. Brown, *The Gorbachev Factor*, pp. 283–88; Jonathan Aves, "The Russian Labour Movement, 1989–91: The Mirage of a Russian Solidarność," in Jeffrey Hosking et al., *The Road to Post-Communism: Independent Political Movements in the Soviet Union, 1985–1991*, paperback ed. (New York: St. Martin's Press, 1992), pp. 151–52.

57 In addition to the chapter by Darrell Slider in *Conflict, Cleavage, and Change*, see Jonathan Aves, *Georgia: From Chaos to Stability?* (London: Royal Institute of International Affairs, 1996).

58 In conditions of acute political tension, certain electoral rules can heighten the probability of civil war; and different electoral rules can lead to a legitimate victory of right–wing, centrist, or left–wing parties under the same distribution of popular votes. See Rein Taagepera and Matthew S. Shugart, *Seats & Votes: The Effects & Determinants of Electoral Systems* (New Haven: Yale University Press, 1989), ch. 1.

59 For example, the weakness of the US government's coercive capacities played a major role in the Federalists' reluctant decision to accept the creation of the Democratic–Republican party in the 1790s, when parties were still generally regarded as illegitimate factions harmful to democratic government. (Martin Shefter, *Political Parties and the State: The American Historical Experience*, paperback ed. [Princeton: Princeton University Press, 1994], pp. 9–10; James R. Sharp, *American Politics in the Early Republic: The New Nation in Crisis* [New Haven: Yale University Press, 1993], pp. 208–25).

60 One noteworthy historical exception is revolutionary France. For a concise historical description of the complex struggles over the scope and forms of electoral participation in several European countries, see Stein Rokkan, "Elections: Electoral Systems," *International Encyclopedia of the Social Sciences*, vol. 5 (London: Macmillan and the Free Press, 1968), pp. 7–13.

61 White et al., *How Russia Votes*, pp. 29–34; Dawisha and Parrott, *Russia and the New States of Eurasia*, pp. 148–53.

62 Barbara Geddes, "A Comparative Perspective on the Leninist Legacy in Eastern Europe," *Comparative Political Studies* 28, no. 2 (July 1995), 261–65.

63 Krzysztof Jasiewicz, "Sources of Representation," in *Developments in East European Politics*, pp. 137–46. Most of these new electoral systems also have established a minimum-vote threshold for party representation, meant to avoid a paralyzing proliferation of splinter parties in the legislature.

64 In this discussion a political party is defined as an organization that (a) is identified by an official label (b) seeks to place its representatives in government office or to change the governmental system and (c) employs methods that include mobilizing citizens and participating in free elections if the state allows such elections. This definition encompasses both political organizations that

pursue or exercise power solely through democratic methods and organizations that pursue or exercise power largely through non-democratic means. On the other hand, it excludes single-issue interest groups whose avowed purpose is not to place their representatives in government office. It also excludes organizations that pursue power solely through violent means.

65 For a brief historical account of American distrust of the impact of parties on democracy, see Alan Ware, *Citizens, Parties, and the State: A Reappraisal* (Princeton: Princeton University Press, 1987), ch. 1.

66 A list of important democratic functions includes (a) mobilizing a large proportion of the citizenry to participate in politics (b) ensuring the representation of all social groups (c) allowing citizens to select individual governmental leaders directly (d) promoting the optimal aggregation of social interests (e) ensuring that government officials fulfill their electoral promises and (f) punishing the originators of failed governmental policies. Note that not all these functions can be fulfilled simultaneously. For example, (b) and (c) are at odds, as are (b) and (d). (Ware, *Citizens, Parties, and the State*, pp. 23–29, 150–241; G. Bingham Powell, Jr., *Contemporary Democracies: Participation, Stability, and Violence*, paperback ed. [Cambridge: Harvard University Press, 1982], pp. 73–78.) The causes of party decline include such factors as media-based political campaigns, the "surrogate" effects of public opinion surveys, the displacement of some party activities by narrowly-focused interest groups, and a tendency for some citizens to regard themselves as political independents unwilling to vote automatically for any party's slate of candidates. (Robert D. Putnam, "Troubled Democracies: Trends in Citizenship in the Trilateral World," paper prepared for the planning workshop of the Project on Democratization and Political Participation in Postcommunist Societies, Washington, DC, April 1995; and Thomas Poguntke, "Explorations into a Minefield: Anti-Party Sentiment," *European Journal of Political Research* 29, no. 3 (April 1996), 319–44.)

67 Valerie Bunce, "Uncertainty in the Transition: Post-Communism in Hungary," *East European Politics and Societies* 7, no. 2 (Spring 1993), 240–75.

68 Nelson, "Introduction," in *A Precarious Balance*, pp. 4–5; Robert H. Dix, "Democratization and the Institutionalization of Latin American Political Parties," *Comparative Political Studies* 24, no. 4 (January 1992), 488–511.

69 In nineteenth-century democracies, most political parties crystallized and expanded gradually, as the suffrage was widened and as socioeconomic changes made more citizens susceptible to political mobilization. In England, for example, Liberal and Conservative elites took at least 20 years to build party structures capable of exploiting the widening of the suffrage that occurred in mid-century. Ware, *Citizens, Parties, and the State*, pp. 22–23.

70 Conference on Political Parties and Democracy, sponsored by the International Forum for Democratic Studies, National Endowment for Democracy, November 18–19, 1996, Washington, DC.

71 Geddes, "A Comparative Perspective," 253–57.

72 See the chapters by Andrew Michta and David Olson in *The Consolidation of Democracy in East–Central Europe*; the chapters by Michael Urban and Ilya Prizel in *Democratic Changes and Authoritarian Reactions in Russia*; Dawisha and Parrott, *Russia and the New States of Eurasia*, p. 131; and White et al., *How Russia Votes*, p. 135.

73 The pioneering scholarly writings on parties focused solely on individual parties rather than on party systems, and a tendency to blur the distinction has persisted in some more recent scholarly analyses. (Harry Eckstein, "Parties, Political: Party Systems," *International Encyclopedia of the Social Sciences*, vol. 11, pp. 436–53.) One weakness of Huntington's seminal treatise on political development is that it assigns great weight to parties but tends to conflate parties with party systems. See Huntington, *Political Order in Changing Societies*, ch. 7.

74 Giovanni Sartori, *Parties and Party Systems: A Framework for Analysis* (New York: Cambridge University Press, 1976); Powell, *Contemporary Democracies*, pp. 74–80. For a discussion of the problems of classifying party systems, particularly by numerical criteria alone, see Eckstein, "Party Systems."

75 See especially Powell, *Contemporary Democracies*, pp. 74–80.

76 Sartori, *Parties and Party Systems*, pp. 132–42.

77 For the correlation between levels of personal dissatisfaction and the strength of extreme parties of the Left or Right in these two countries, see Ronald Inglehart, *Culture Shift in Advanced Industrial Society*, paperback ed. (Princeton: Princeton University Press), pp. 36–40.

78 Huntington, *The Third Wave*, p. 263.

79 John Higley et al., "The Persistence of Postcommunist Elites," *Journal of Democracy* 7, no. 2 (April 1996), 133–47; Michael Burton and John Higley, "Elite Settlements," *American Sociological Review* 52 (June 1987), 295–307.

80 For a critique of past elite studies and comparative survey data showing unusually deep attitudinal cleavages within the Soviet/Russian political elite during both the Gorbachev and Yeltsin eras, see David Lane, "Transition under Eltsin: The Nomenklatura and Political Elite Circulation," forthcoming in *Political Studies*.

81 For data showing that the political attitudes of former communist party members and individuals who never belonged to the communist party are quite similar in Bulgaria, Romania, and several countries of East–Central Europe, see the table in Rose, *What Is Europe?* p. 142. (The table pools the national data sets, so that no conclusions for individual countries can be drawn from it.)

82 According to a careful study, in the past decade the number of ethnic conflicts has grown at approximately the same rate as in the 1960s and 1970s. See Ted Robert Gurr and Barbara Harff, *Ethnic Conflict in World Politics* (Boulder, CO: Westview, 1994), pp. 11, 13.

83 Horowitz, *Ethnic Groups in Conflict*, Part Three.

84 Juan Linz, *The Breakdown of Democratic Regimes: Crisis, Breakdown, & Reequilibration* (Baltimore: Johns Hopkins University Press, 1978), ch. 2.

85 For a general discussion of the connection between political parties and terrorism, see Leonard Weinberg, "Turning to Terror: The Conditions under Which Political Parties Turn to Terrorist Activities," *Comparative Politics* 23, no. 4 (July 1991), 423–38.

86 Arend Lijphart, *Democracies: Patterns of Majoritarian and Consensus Government in Twenty-One Countries*, paperback ed. (New Haven: Yale University Press, 1984), ch. 7; Powell, *Contemporary Democracies*, ch. 7.

87 Sartori, *Parties and Party Systems*, pp. 221–25.

88 My interpretation of these concepts, which have sparked vigorous scholarly debate, is derived from such works as Gabriel Almond and Sidney Verba, *The Civic Culture: Political Attitudes and Democracy in Five Nations*, paperback ed.

(Boston: Little, Brown and Co., 1965), and Inglehart, *Culture Shift in Advanced Industrial Societies*. Most of the controversial issues are well covered in *The Civic Culture Revisited*, ed. Gabriel Almond and Sidney Verba (Newbury Park, CA: Sage Publications, 1980). For reasons of space, my discussion omits several important distinctions, such as the existence of national political subcultures and differences between elite and mass political cultures.

89 However, scholars have disagreed about the particular cultural dispositions that actually support democracy. See especially Edward Muller and Mitchell Seligson, "Civic Culture and Democracy: The Question of Causal Relationships," *American Political Science Review* 88, no. 3 (September 1994), 635–52. Naturally, an important role is also played by non-cultural factors, such as the behavior of the state and major changes in citizens' socioeconomic circumstances.

90 Inglehart, *Culture Shift*, chs. 1–3. For evidence of dramatic increase in the democratic elements of German political culture and a decline in the civic elements of British and US political culture during the three decades following World War II, see the chapters by David Conradt, Dennis Kavanagh, and Alan Abramowitz in *The Civic Culture Revisited*.

91 For a discussion that relates civil society to other forms of political society, see Ernest Gellner, *Conditions of Liberty: Civil Society and Its Rivals* (New York: Allen Lane/The Penguin Press, 1994).

92 Seymour Martin Lipset, *Political Man: The Social Bases of Politics* (New York: Anchor Books, 1963), ch. 4.

93 Robert Putnam, *Making Democracy Work: Civic Traditions in Modern Italy* (Princeton: Princeton University Press, 1993). Cf. Sidney Tarrow, "Making Social Science Work Across Space and Time: A Critical Reflection on Robert Putnam's *Making Democracy Work*," *American Political Science Review* 90, no. 2 (June 1996), 389–98.

94 This paragraph is based on Dawisha and Parrott, *Russia and the New States of Eurasia*, pp. 123–25. For a nuanced discussion of the historical evolution of the concept of civil society, see Keane, "Despotism and Democracy," pp. 35–72.

95 For an exposition of these theoretical differences, which have centered especially on whether commercial organizations based on private property belong to civil society or undermine it, see Keane, "Introduction," pp. 13–14, and "Despotism and Democracy," esp. pp. 62–66. On the connection between civil society and relations within the family, see Carol Pateman, "The Fraternal Social Contract," pp. 101–28 in the same volume.

96 Larry Diamond, "Rethinking Civil Society: Toward Democratic Consolidation," *Journal of Democracy* 5, no. 3 (July 1994), 4–17.

97 For a discussion of this and other problems of analyzing political culture in the USSR and Russia, see Frederick J. Fleron, Jr., "Post-Soviet Political Culture in Russia: An Assessment of Recent Empirical Investigations," *Europe–Asia Studies* 48, no. 2 (March 1996), 225–60.

98 In keeping with prevailing usage before about 1800, the concept of civil society has sometimes been construed even more broadly to include both democratic governmental institutions and social structures conducive to democracy. However, this definition prevents analysis of the interactions between government and society that may fundamentally change the political system.

99   "Under whatever name – 'parallel *polis*,' 'independent culture,' or 'independent society' – the idea of civil society remained largely restricted to narrow circles of independent intellectuals in every East and Central European country save one. The exception . . . was Poland." Aleksander Smolar, "From Opposition to Atomization," *Journal of Democracy* 7, no. 1 (January 1996), 26.

100 Of necessity, this short excursus oversimplifies the analytical issues and omits discussion of the empirical variations among countries. For a general discussion of scholarly tendencies to explain postcommunist political development in terms of either "communist legacies" or "liberal institutional" determinants, see Crawford and Lijphart, "Explaining Political and Economic Change in Post-Communist Eastern Europe."

101 McIntosh and MacIver, *Transition to What? Publics Confront Change in Eastern Europe*, esp. pp. 6, 14.

102 For an insightful juxtaposition of survey data gathered from displaced Soviet citizens after World War II and data collected from Soviet emigrants during the late Brezhnev period, see Bahry, "Society Transformed? Rethinking the Social Roots of Perestroika." The data suggest that in the late Stalin years up to 50 percent of Soviet citizens may have favored a relaxation of intellectual controls, and that by the late Brezhnev period this percentage may have increased substantially (ibid., p. 539). On the role of authoritarian violence in strengthening the appeal of democracy, see Giuseppe di Palma, *To Craft Democracies: An Essay on Democratic Transitions*, paperback ed. (Berkeley: University of California Press, 1990), pp. 19–23, 150–51.

103 For a survey of the voluntary sector in advanced industrial democracies, see *Between States and Markets: The Voluntary Sector in Comparative Perspective*, ed. Robert Wuthnow (Princeton: Princeton University Press, 1991).

104 Geddes, "Challenging the Conventional Wisdom," 104; Jose Maria Maravali, "The Myth of the Authoritarian Advantage," *Journal of Democracy* 5, no. 4 (October 1994), 17–31; Joan Nelson, "Labor and Business Roles in Dual Transitions: Building Blocks or Stumbling Blocks?" in *Intricate Links*, p. 147. This issue was, of course, the subject of vigorous public debate in the West.

105 Geddes, "Challenging the Conventional Wisdom," 109–111.

106 In Eastern Europe, for example, labor unions have played a role in dislodging some government coalitions from power and have pressed governments to adopt their policy preferences. However, anti-democratic union violence and general strikes have been unusual and have tended to occur in countries, such as Romania, whose party systems have been least capable of representing workers' interests. Nelson, "Labor and Business Roles in Dual Transitions," pp. 154–63.

107 Linz and Stepan, "Toward Consolidated Democracies." For example, in Russia's 1996 presidential run-off, Boris Yeltsin won the votes of more than two-thirds of the persons who believed the government would solve the economy's problems in 10 years or less. By contrast, Genadii Zyuganov, the communist party candidate, won the support of 70 percent of those who thought the government would never be able to solve these problems. (*New Russia Barometer VI: After the Presidential Election*, Centre for the Study of Public Policy, University of Strathclyde, Glasgow, 1996, p. 13.) Considerable evidence also suggests that many categories of workers, though hard-hit by economic reform, have devised unofficial sources of income that are not reflected in

gloomy official estimates of declining output. See Daniel Kaufman and Aleksander Kaliberda, "Integrating the Unofficial Economy into the Dynamics of Post-Socialist Economies: A Framework of Analysis and Evidence," in *Economic Transition in Russia and the New States of Eurasia*, ed. Bartlomiej Kaminski (Armonk, NY: M. E. Sharpe, 1996), pp. 81–120.

108 In Russia and several democracies of Eastern Europe, public opinion has shifted since 1991 toward more support for government involvement in the economy, although acceptance of economic inequalities has simultaneously grown in most of the same countries. A recent survey of several postcommunist countries found that the only one in which public attitudes have moved toward greater support for egalitarianism is Russia. (James Kluegel and David S. Mason, "Social Justice in Transition? Attitudinal Change in Russia and East-Central Europe," paper presented at the annual convention of the American Association for the Advancement of Slavic Studies, Boston, November 1996.) In the early 1990s, measurable economic inequalities in postcommunist countries generally remained smaller or no larger than than those in Western democracies. (Branko Milanovic, "Poverty and Inequality in Transition Economies: What Has Actually Happened," in *Economic Transition in Russia and the New States of Eurasia*, pp. 180–81.)

109 For a discussion of national variations in the understanding of corruption, see Michael Johnston, "Historical Conflict and the Rise of Standards," in *The Global Resurgence of Democracy*, pp. 193–205.

110 Kluegel and Mason, "Justice Perceptions in Russia and Eastern Europe, 1991–1995"; Richard Dobson, "Is Russia Turning the Corner? Changing Russian Public Opinion, 1991–1996," *Research Report*, Office of Research and Media Reaction, US Information Agency, September 1996, pp. 11–13.

111 Miller, "Civil Society in Communist Systems," p. 9; Keane, "Despotism and Democracy," pp. 64–66.

112 Richard Rose, "Toward a Civil Economy," *Journal of Democracy* 3, no. 2 (1992), 13–25, and Kochanowicz, "Reforming Weak States and Deficient Bureaucracies," pp. 195–204, 214–22. The fullest account of the criminalization of economic activities in Russia is Stephen Handelman, *Comrade Criminal* (New Haven: Yale University Press, 1995).

113 Nelson, "How Market Reforms and Democratic Consolidation Affect Each Other," pp. 11–13.

114 Dobson, "Is Russia Turning the Corner?" pp. 8–9.

115 For example, surveys of citizens in the European Community's member-countries show that the average percentage of respondents saying they were "very satisfied" or "fairly satisfied" with the way democracy works ranged between 66 and 41 percent in 1985–1993. Leonardo Morlino and Jose R. Montero, "Legitimacy and Democracy in Southern Europe," in *The Politics of Democratic Consolidation: Southern Europe in Comparative Perspective*, p. 239.

2 Democratization and political participation: research concepts and methodologies

Karen Dawisha

The primary objectives of the Project on Democratization and Political Participation have been to gauge the prospects for democratization in Eastern Europe and the former Soviet Union by systematically examining and comparing trends in the organized political activities of society in each country and to contribute to the theoretical discussion about the determinants of these trends. This chapter has several objectives. It begins with an discussion of how the concepts of democracy, democratization, and democratic consolidation are defined and operationalized in this project. Three sections then follow in which the research questions which have guided the project are discussed (the questions themselves are presented in the Appendix), along with propositions and hypotheses derived from the existing literature on democratization. The sections substantively address three disparate parts of the democratization process: two sections on inputs to the process, namely factors influencing the formation of political groups and parties, and the political evolution of society, and one section on outcomes, namely the factors affecting the possible emergence of party systems in postcommunist states.

Conceptualizing democracy and democratization

What is meant by democracy, and how is the process of democratization understood in this project? In line with recent research,[1] a procedural or minimalist conception of democracy was employed. Democracy is defined as a political system in which the formal and actual leaders of the government are chosen through regular elections based on multiple candidacies and secret balloting, with the right of all adult citizens to vote. It is assumed that leaders chosen via free and fair elections, using universal adult suffrage, will be induced to modify their behavior to be more responsive to popular wishes and demands than leaders in authoritarian states.

There remains, however, the crucial task of making the transition from the conceptual level to the empirical-observational level. Even if the features of the conception can be elaborated, how does one determine their presence or their absence over time, within individual countries or across the postcommunist world? Simply put, how does one know when the level of democracy is high, or when it is low or non-existent? Over the past thirty years or so, there have been numerous attempts at objectively measuring democracies.[2] Some of the more recent efforts such as those of Kenneth Bollen have, arguably, resulted in more finely calibrated instruments.[3] These measures are most useful as indicators of the extent to which democracy exists in a country at a specific time. In and of themselves, they are not useful for explaining democratic change. As noted recently, "with these scores, one can only estimate the extent to which democracy has advanced or regressed in that given country over a very long period of time or compare the country with others similarly scored."[4] Indeed most analysts who draw up such indicators would be the first to recognize that their contribution has been in measuring democracy, not explaining its underlying dynamics.

Civil liberties and political rights can be viewed as two distinct conceptual dimensions of democracy. The dimension of political rights can be, more or less, directly observed. The degree to which adult suffrage is universal, elections are fairly conducted, and all persons are eligible for public office can be directly observed through objective analysis of electoral laws and practices. The degree to which leaders freely compete for votes can be ascertained in a similar manner. An analysis of political rights allows one to draw conclusions about the level of democracy, since it can reasonably be hypothesized that the higher the number of rights universally enjoyed by the population, the greater will be the level of democratization.

Democracy is also dependent upon the provision of civil liberties, specifically: (1) freedom to form and join organizations; (2) freedom of expression; and (3) access to multiple and competing sources of information. Empirical data can be garnered to support a judgment about the extent to which the three components of civil liberties exist. It is assumed that the more the number and level of civil liberties enjoyed by a country's population, the greater will be the level of democratization. Thus, political rights and civil liberties serve as indicators of democracy and both must be present in order for a country to be classified as democratic. Through the assignment of numerical values to the empirical properties representing political rights and civil liberties, according to consistent rules, one could draw up a representation of the level of democracy existing within a country at any given time.

*

Such a measure, however, would not necessarily allow one to conclude that any given democracy was likely to be both stable and durable. Indeed, the free and unfettered exercise of political rights and liberties has been seen on occasions as negatively affecting the durability of democracies, sometimes obliging leaders and populations to accept various trade-offs which would limit the degree of representation of societal groups in return for sustaining democratic institutions over time. A good example is the tendency of democracies to introduce measures which effectively limit the number of parties that can be represented in the legislature to those which gain above a certain percentage threshold of the popular vote, so as to lessen the impact of minority opinion and of groups at the left and right of the political spectrum and magnify the influence of majoritarian views and centrist groups. Such measures, while in fact denying some voters the right to have their votes have an equal impact upon outcomes, are justified by reference to the universal interests of all voters in ensuring the long-term durability of democratic institutions.

Equally, democracies vary in their protection of civil liberties such as freedom of speech and assembly. Many established democracies curtail the rights of groups which have in the past shown their intent to overthrow the democratically elected order. These actions, too, are justified by reference to the right of the state to limit the liberties of some in the short term in order to ensure the liberty of all in the long-term.

Finally, one must distinguish between democracy and democratization. To a certain extent, all states, even those that call themselves, and are recognized by others as, democratic are still evolving, either towards or away from more democracy. The perennial debates in even the most stable democracies about justice, liberty, equity, rights, and governability reflect this continuing concern. But more problematic is drawing the line between an authoritarian polity which is breaking down and a democratic entity which is emerging. When can one say that the process of democratization actually begins? For the purposes of this project, democratization is said to begin when the first set of free and fair elections for national-level office takes place. This first set of elections must be accompanied in short order by the granting of civil liberties and political rights and the establishment of both state institutions that operate according to the rule of law and intermediate organizations that mediate between the citizen and the state. If these events do not take place, then it is likely that the process of democratization will not be fully consolidated.

Measuring democratic consolidation

Unlike the numerous efforts to measure democracy systematically, relatively few attempts have been made to measure democratic consolidation. Central to this notion is acceptance that not all states that start out on the road to democracy will complete the transition. Some will fall back into authoritarianism, others might regress into civil war, others will maintain a low equilibrium democracy for decades, verging constantly on the brink of collapse.[5] And all transitions will differ, combining as they do on the one hand individual historical legacies, leaders, socioeconomic foundations and international interactions and on the other hand the policies pursued by elites and their varied impact on individual societies at any given time.

A consolidated democracy is one in which most major social groups expect that government leaders will be chosen through competitive elections and regard representative institutions and procedures as their main channel for processing claims on the state. One way of measuring consolidation is to apply a "two-turnover test," in which a democracy "may be viewed as consolidated if the party or group that takes power in the initial election at the time of the transition loses a subsequent election and turns over power to those election winners, and if those election winners then peacefully turn over power to winners of a later election.[6] Thus, for example, when communism fell, a first round of elections was held. Typically two to four years later, a second round was held: if the group in power since the fall of communism was displaced, this would count as the first turnover. Only after this group or party was displaced by a second round of elections could one then speak of a country having passed the 'two turn-over test.' Of the postcommunist states, only postcommunist Lithuania had by the end of 1996 passed such a test: the Lithuanian Democratic Labor Party, the renamed Communist Party, took power from the conservative Sajudis led by Vytautas Landsbergis in 1992, and then surrendered it back to Landsbergis' party (the renamed Homeland Union) when they lost parliamentary elections in November 1996. However, such a test has been criticized on the grounds that it would fail to classify either interwar Eastern Europe or postwar Italy or Japan as democracies. Moreover, if used alone, it does not provide levels of calibration and gradation adequate for the comparative scope of the project. Also while a determination could be made if a democracy were consolidated or not using a two-turnover test, it would not be possible to answer the questions "why?" or "why not?" using the test.

In measuring democratic consolidation over time within a given country or across nations, it may prove more theoretically informative to treat it as a continuum, rather than a two-step process. There are at least four distinct conceptual aspects of democratic consolidation, each of which could be observed by various measures: the two-turnover test, low public support for anti-system parties or groups, high public commitment to the fundamental values and procedural norms of democratic politics, and elite consensus about the desirability of institutionizing and legitimizing democratic norms and values.[7]

An index could be constructed by combining the latter three indicators if the criteria for the two-turnover test are not met. This would serve at least three purposes. First, several variables relating to democratic consolidation could be represented by a single score, thereby reducing the complexity of the data and facilitating comparison. Second, such an index could provide a quantitative measure of democratic consolidation amenable to statistical manipulation. Finally, because it measures several properties, the index is inherently more reliable than a measure based on a single factor.

Clearly, democratic consolidation is still a goal in almost all of the postcommunist countries, yet significant strides have been made. Autonomous societal action has largely replaced communist dictatorship in most countries; and the notions of choice, competition, and tolerance are increasingly salient. As emphasized in the working definition of democracy, elections should be based on multiple candidacies that ensure real opportunities for electoral competition. Informal alliances rapidly evolved into political parties in the wake of the communist collapse: these parties are gradually becoming rooted and stable. The following section examines some of the factors influencing the formation of political groups and parties across the countries under investigation. In each of the following sections, the research questions (as presented in the Appendix) which were given to the authors are used as the basis for deriving hypotheses and propositions, and a consideration is made of the range of results which might be expected from the various hypotheses. This section is followed by sections on the political evolution of society and on the emergence of political parties and party systems.

Factors influencing the formation of parties

Authors were presented with a number of questions, listed in the Appendix, which addressed the factors influential in forming the political groups and parties, considered as a cornerstone in any country's move toward democracy. The comparative literature is deeply divided over the relative influence of historical, ethnic, social, cultural, institutional, and economic factors in determining the success of a country's move toward democracy. This section was intended to elicit the panel's responses to these various issues.

In the literature on transitions, it is generally assumed that those countries which have to establish a national identity before going on to build the institutions of the state and inculcate civic virtues in the populace will face the greatest challenge.[8] In doing so they will have to replace other national identities which may command popular support if the new state was carved out of old ones and strive to surpass and mobilize the other nested identities of family, clan, region, and ethnicity in the service of a new civic minded-ness.

Authors were asked to elaborate the key elements of the precommunist historical legacy of each country. They were additionally asked to focus on any precommunist experience of democracy, and whether elements of the postcommunist polity, such as particular government structures, intermediary associations, and political parties have been modeled on precommunist patterns.

The literature would appear to support three interrelated hypotheses: polities with a strong, unified national identity based on a precommunist legacy of independence will be able to make the most rapid and peaceful transition to sovereign independence; those polities with a precommunist tradition of exclusivist nationalism will have more difficulty in making the transition to democracy; and those polities with a precommunist tradition of competitive multiparty systems are most likely to be successful in establishing stable multiparty democracies.

It could reasonably be assumed that those countries which are being "reborn" after a period of communist suppression would have an enormous advantage over states being established for the first time. One would expect a shorter time in putting basic institutions in place, in passing a constitution and other basic laws, and in regularizing state-society relations on the basis of a national accord. States coming into existence for the first time are not able to operate on the basis of historical trust or on a shared remembrance of the role the state played in the past in forging a partnership between state and society to nourish and sustain the nation. On the contrary, given the role of the state in the communist period in suppressing both nation and society (although to be sure the nation was often harnessed to the needs of the state during times of crisis in all the communist states and was symbiotically allied to the state in Yugoslavia, Hungary, and Romania in particular), any state without a precommunist legacy of trust might reasonably be expected to falter in the project of legitimization.

There are, however, two related dilemmas: first, countries that are resurrecting states which, in the precommunist era, had an authoritarian character may have more difficulty overcoming the burden of this legacy than countries that are creating state institutions anew. Secondly, while a regeneration of a previous national identity is expected to facilitate the process of state-building, if the national identity was exclusivist, then its renaissance might promote state-building but impede democratization. This tendency is underscored by Beverly Crawford and Arendt Lijphart, who address the problem that unlike in France or England, where nationalism had its origins in the Enlightenment, in Eastern Europe and the former Soviet Union, it had its roots "in the Russian and German tradition of *Volk*, blood, *narod*, and race as the basis for membership in the nation."[9] To be sure, the distinctions between the historical origins of the national identities of the Germans and Russians on the one hand and the British and the French on the other are clear. Yet this view does not account sufficiently for the fact that even in England, the process of transforming narrow English identity centered in the Home Counties into a greater United Kingdom entailed the forcible suppression of independent national aspirations in Wales and Scotland, as we;; asa lengthy and continuing struggle with Northern Ireland. And despite this, democratization proceeded apace in Great Britain, suggesting that the connections between a state's formative national identity and the identity which underpins its institutions is not fixed for all time.

It is also posited in the transitions literature that those states with precommunist traditions of multiparty elections and capitalist development are more likely to be able to reestablish these institutions. There are two reasons: one is that to the extent that a state had already adopted a multiparty system and/or capitalism in the past, protracted and often divisive national debates on paths of development could be avoided. Additionally many of the actual laws governing political and economic life can be resuscitated with only minor amendments. Of course, given the number of ultra-nationalist parties that inhabited the landscape of interwar Eastern Europe, the resuscitation of these parties has not necessarily promoted simultaneous liberalization.

Postcommunist states have had to sift through, resurrect, and overcome elements not only of their precommunist heritage, but also of their communist past. Authors were asked to identify key elements of the legacy of the communist era. In addition, they were asked to speculate on how the political and social evolution of each country in the late communist era (e.g., the emergence or nonemergence of a significant dissent movement) affected the postcommunist formation of societal interest groups and parties.

Prevalent in the field are two core assumptions that require some systematic elaboration: first, the assumption that the more and the longer a country was subjected to the antidemocratic and totalitarian features of Stalinism, the less likely will be the chances of democracy succeeding, and secondly, if there is a prior history of democracy and civil society, and a communist legacy of reform and openness, then the chances of a successful transition to democracy will be greater and the speed of transition will be quicker.

The literature on the legacy of the communist era is vast, growing, and divided. Most would agree that communism left a "poisonous residue"[10] on virtually all aspects of society, but whether that residue can easily be washed away is open to controversy. Those who subscribe to the view that the legacy of communism will be significant and abiding look at its effect in several areas.[11] Politically, the fact that there essentially were no public politics in the communist era is presumed to have left a deep legacy: there were no self-governing institutions, no interest groups or rival parties operating independent of the state, and no competing sources of information. At the same time, Soviet systems were characterized by a single elite which, while capable of being split into factions, did not regularly or routinely circulate into and out of power. These elites, it was assumed by some, would resist the construction of new institutions which would limit the reach of their authority.[12] Some would see these features as a significant barrier to the emergence of democracy and civil society.[13] Other authors also assume that the Soviet-era largely succeeded in one of its aims, namely to destroy the pre-Leninist past, thus robbing these societies of their ability to resurrect precommunist identities, parties, and institutions.[14]

Soviet-style systems, in addition, were command economies controlled from the center, without private ownership of the means of production or market relations. As the sector ideologically most suited to the Stalinist world view and economically most capable of thriving under command conditions, the military-industrial complex grew to become not only the dominant sector of the economy but also the only sector which functioned more or less according to plan. The performance of this sector in most communist countries (most notably the USSR, Yugoslavia, and the Slovak sector of Czechoslovakia) not only gave central planning whatever credibility it enjoyed but also was designed to form the protective outer shell for the entire system, leading analysts inside and outside the country to attribute far more capability to the economy and the system as a whole than ultimately it possessed.[15] This sector bequeathed to the successor states industries which could produce high quality goods but which required both continued subsidies and a Cold War-style mission concomitant with its size and orientation. Additionally, it is believed by some that sectors of the military-industrial complex in Russia, in support of like-minded groups within the Ministry of Interior, the revamped KGB, and the Ministry of Defense, have been a major buttress of a strong but not necessarily democratic or non-imperial state.[16]

Underneath this strong outer shell resided the light industrial and consumer sectors of the economy which were denied funds, resources, initiative, and personnel – virtually everything except planning targets; and after de-Stalinization ended the use of terror to force compliance, these could be met only by bribery, corruption, distortion, and the formation of informal and illegal production networks. The fact that such a high percentage of total state economic interactions took place outside the plan meant that whatever performance the economy achieved was bought at the expense of the integrity of the planning mechanism of the state and the trust, loyalty, and ultimately the compliance of the population. These socioeconomic and political failures weakened central control, but also left a legacy of cynicism and disrespect for the state, to say nothing of the vast array of informal economic networks which fell out of the state and beyond the law when the regimes collapsed.[17] In *New World Disorder*, Ken Jowitt predicted that the combined legacy of bureaucracy, corruption, and interpersonal distrust would hinder the implementation of democratic reforms, although it is unclear from his analysis whether and why this legacy might vary across countries and whether and why it might be relatively transient.[18]

The great difficulty of establishing political and economic institutions from the bottom up cannot be overstated: Samuel Huntington found that twenty-three of the twenty-nine countries that democratized during the so-called "third wave" (between 1974 and 1990) had previous democratic experience. Equally, those that had not democratized by 1990 had no democratic past. So while states are not condemned necessarily to relive their past, clearly the results of Huntington's study would support the thesis that all other factors being equal, previous democratic experience greatly facilitates the transition to democracy.[19]

The hypotheses generated in the remainder of the section are designed to address not the legacy of the precommunist or communist era, but the nature of the transition and the actual social situation inherited by the first postcommunist leaders. In particular, questions focus on the possibility of overcoming the Leninist legacy through what Crawford and Lijphart call "the imperatives of liberalization." As they state, this approach "suggests that new institutions can be crafted and new international pressures can be brought to bear that shut out the negative influences of the past."[20] Even those authors like Samuel Huntington who favor a strong political cultural argument are supportive of the view that the success of one country or region in introducing democratic reforms can have a snowballing effect in encouraging democratization elsewhere. The economic, political, and cultural policies pursued by actors in the external environment also are seen as extremely consequential for stimulating and supporting movement toward liberalization, particularly in an era when communication is global and international norms favor human rights and democracy.[21]

From this discussion and the literature on transition, it is possible to generate a number of propositions and hypotheses: the following are among the most salient. In those countries whose transition was non-violent and pacted between the elites and the opposition, a party system is most likely to be quickly established.[22] In those countries whose transition was non-violent and pacted between different groups of elites, the ruling party or group will be most able to maintain their elite status, if not their monopoly.[23] In those countries where the new elites moved most quickly to impose rapid liberalization, privatization, and democratization, extremist opposition parties will be less likely to gain a foothold amongst the populace.[24] In those transitions marked by violence, the elites are most likely to attempt to preempt the emergence of independent associations and parties.[25]

Another crucial aspect of transition is the assertion of civilian control over violent coercion in society. Many theorists, most notably Robert Dahl, have underlined the civilian control of the military as a crucial requirement for successful democratization,[26] leading one to suppose that it should be possible to demonstrate the validity of the following propositions: the greater the popular support for democracy as opposed to other political systems or of democratic values as opposed to other political ends (for example, stability, social justice, and so forth), the lower the levels of military intervention in domestic politics;[27] the greater the participation of the citizenry in electoral politics, the lower the levels of military intervention in politics;[28] and the greater the tradition of civilian control of the military within a country, the less will be the tendency of the military to intervene in politics.[29]

Also of concern is the need to analyze the impact on democratization of the political balances among the transitional groups, since much has been made by Adam Przeworski, Mancur Olson, and others of the likelihood that transitional elites would attempt to shape new institutions to maximize their interests. Thus it could be hypothesized that the more that the transition is coopted by hard-liners on the ruling side and radical factions amongst the opponents, the greater will be the prospect for failure of talks to produce a workable and democratic electoral system.[30] And conversely, the more evenly balanced the power amongst diverse elite groups at the time of transition, the more will be the tendency to design electoral legislation which does not favor any particular electoral constituency.[31]

Social and ethnic cleavages suppressed under communism are likely to emerge in the transition and are often intensified by economic changes and political and personal uncertainty. The challenge facing authors is both to identify these cleavages and to analyze the extent to which they have shaped the formation of parties and other political groups. The literature suggests the following relationships exist between social and ethnic cleavages and the prospects for democratization: the more that societies are characterized by spatial distances between mutually reinforcing and exclusivist ethnic, social, economic, and religious groups, the greater will be the tendency for parties to be formed reflecting these divisions;[32] the larger the size of ethnic minorities as a proportion of the total population, the greater is the probability that democratization using majoritarian formulas will fail to contain communal violence if it breaks out;[33] as long as no group has a monopoly over control of resources, then social divisions and unequal access to those resources can be mitigated within a democratic regime;[34] and to the extent that parties and associations promote and facilitate social mobility and civic awareness, then their aggregative function will assist democratization.

The pattern and pace of postcommunist economic change is another independent variable seen as having an impact on democratic outcomes, affecting the emergence of political parties, and increasing the stakes of winning and losing in the political arena. On the whole, it is accepted that the pattern and pace of economic change is a function of the political will of the ruling elites, but that both elites and social groups interact to maximize their access to resources. Thus, political elites will structure economic reforms to maximize their political and economic interests, while setting the pace of change in order to minimize the chances of systematic and widespread social unrest.[35]

Among the greatest challenges to successful democratization is the existence of violent conflict either inside the country or with other states. Indeed, it would appear that the greater the level of violent conflict within a society, the more democratic institutions will be undermined.[36] But its actual impact, upon observation, is diverse, depending on the level and direction of conflict, elite reaction, state capacity to terminate, suppress, resolve, or withstand the violence, and the impact of the violence on the attitude of core social groups toward the process of democratization. Violence may weaken existing institutions in an emerging democracy, but it can also increase pressure toward the adoption of changed institutional arrangements which maintain democracy, ranging from the introduction of nonmajoritarian consociational arrangements to widen the representation of marginalized and alienated minorities[37] to the adoption of corporatist forms of democracy in which large interest-based groups mediate between the state and the citizenry, to a certain degree suppressing citizens' direct involvement in policy making and aggregating overlapping and pluralistic intermediate groups into larger and more monopolistic associations.[38]

The political evolution of society

Central to the questions in this section is the assumption that citizens' attitudes matter. Gabriel Almond and Sidney Verba's theory of civic culture[39] postulates that the viability of democratic institutions is significantly affected by attitudes such as belief in one's ability to influence political decisions, feelings of positive affect for the political system, and the belief that fellow citizens are trustworthy. Challenges to political culture theory have taken place primarily on two levels and have emerged from two intellectual camps.

One challenge emerged in the 1960s and lasted throughout the 1970s as radical scholars polemicized against political culture theory. These scholars, many of them Marxist or neo-Marxist, argued that the dominant political culture in any society was a necessary reflection of the relationships between the ruling and subordinate classes. As Almond later wrote, political culture theory, in particular, "was challenged on the grounds that political and social attitudes were reflections of class and/or ethnic status or else were the 'false consciousness' implanted by such institutions as schools, universities and media."[40]

Also in the 1960s another challenge to political culture theory emerged with the ascension of rational choice models, which asserted that all individuals and institutions in a political system – whether ordinary members of society or politicians or parties, coalitions, intermediate organizations, and governmental institutions comprised of or representing those individuals – would act efficiently to maximize interests, often defined in economic terms.[41] By the late 1960s models based on rational choice and game theoretic approaches had become a dominant mode of social analysis. This emergence of "rational choice," "public choice," and "positive political theory" challenged the very premise of political culture theory. From within this perspective, examining political culture amounted to little more than a superfluous exercise. It was widely held that sufficient explanatory power could be generated by assuming self-interested, short-run rationality. Contributing to the ascension of this mode of analysis, especially within comparative political science, were the availability of economic data and the lack of sufficient cross-national data on political attitudes.

This paucity of aggregate data or large-N studies that would allow researchers to go beyond individual country or region case-studies and draw broader conclusions about factors outside the economic realm hampered efforts by those interested in political culture to reach generalizable conclusions. However, by 1988, Ronald Inglehart[42] had compiled data on attitudes of the general public for a sample of countries large enough to permit multivariate statistical analysis of the relative influence of mass political attitudes as compared with macro-socioeconomic variables on democratization. The accumulation of cross-national data on attitudes of the general public combined with the collapse of Marxism as an alternative explanatory system and the reorientation of some public choice theorists toward a "new institutionalism" has led to a resurgence of interest in political culture as an explanatory variable.

It is now more generally accepted that democracy requires a supportive culture, even if it is agreed that this culture can be strongly shaped both by transient and short-term factors including economic performance and by more underlying variables, including the institutional setting in which this culture is set. Democratic institutions both promote and are promoted by a democratic political culture. In a democracy, popular support for the creation of an independent civil society embodying intermediate groups and associations which feed into the political process and aggregate different societal interests is also required. Because freedom of speech, media, religion, assembly and the right to form independent groups and opposition parties were all suppressed in the communist era, the norms associated with a civic culture cannot be expected to emerge overnight. The legacy of mistrust must first be overcome in order for a previously atomized society to establish the basic level of tolerance and civic responsibility required to sustain even the most basic levels of freedom.[43] Even then, clearly, underlying cultural factors independent of the communist legacy could accelerate or impede the emergence of the kind of civil society associated with liberal democracy.[44]

When examining the emergence of political associations in early transitional societies, authors were asked to collect data on the types of political associations or actors that have become most prominent in each country's political life, that is, political parties, state sector managerial lobbies, trade unions, business organizations, professional associations, religious organizations, clans, paramilitary units, criminal groups, and so forth. In addition, data was collected on how the public perception of political parties and what they claim to represent has affected citizens' attitudes to the political system. Authors were asked to comment on the relative importance of parties as vehicles for new elites intent on accumulating political power and wealth, as opposed to alternative vehicles, such as associations, informal groupings, and the like.

The assumptions in the comparative politics literature that underlie the section on the emergence of political parties are several, including: the higher the level of citizen distrust of political institutions, the greater will be the difficulty of establishing a viable party system; parties will gain preeminence as intermediary institutions only if elections are regular, free, and fair; and the holding of regular, and free and fair elections will increase civic trust over time.[45]

Also central to an understanding of the evolution of societies in transition is the extent to which attempted marketization and privatization have affected the political strength and behavior of various economic groups in society. Operating at the level of abstraction, one could envision distinct responses from economic groups along a continuum ranging from strategies of intransigent resistance to reforms which directly (and in the short-term, negatively) impact their respective economic interests to strategies of ready accommodation with the reforms based on the assumption that these individuals are, or could easily become, aware of the long-term benefits of marketization and privatization which are readily observable throughout the West. With this continuum in mind, authors were asked to analyze the extent to which attempted marketization and privatization have affected the political strength and behavior of business and managerial groups, agricultural groups, and organized industrial labor. Authors were asked to gather information on whether these groups had formed or formally affiliated themselves with political parties and what role they had assumed in the financing of elections and the control of the media.

Monitoring of the emergence of new economic strata in transitional polities is important because of the assumptions about the relationship between marketization and democratization which underpin the literature. The transition to democracy has previously been thought to occur as a result of a long period of capitalist development in which previously subordinate classes – the middle class, most notably, but also the urban working class and small and medium-sized farming interests – evolved an economic interest in the promotion of democracy as a way of balancing class power. Thus, a strong middle class allied with commercial and industrial elites in the private sector is generally seen as a necessary but not sufficient condition for successful democratization.[46] Economic winners are thought to support democracy to the extent they feel it legitimizes and sustains their dominant economic position, whereas economic losers are seen as supporting democracy to the extent they feel the existence of democratic state autonomous of dominant economic classes erodes economic inequality.[47]

This obviously raises the question of whether an economy which liberalizes before the rule of law is in place can prevent the rise of organized criminal activity which in turn can disrupt, impede, and even capture the process of democratization itself. Authors were asked to analyze the political impact of organized criminal groups in the respective countries under review and to discuss the extent to which associations or political parties have become linked with organized crime. In general, it can be assumed that the emergence of organized crime will not be welcomed by the population, and authors were asked to gather data on how the public perception of the role of organized crime has affected citizens' attitudes toward the political system. But studies done in economic theory suggest that to the extent that organized crime provides stability and economic security and benefits, the population will be more likely to acquiesce in its existence.[48] And further, it is postulated that the existence of widespread random criminality will predispose the population to allow organized crime to establish rules and norms over geographic regions.[49] The public's predisposition to prefer organized criminal activity to large-scale inchoate activity does not necessarily translate into greater support for democracy, however, and indeed one could suppose that the existence of connections between elected officials and organized crime would erode public confidence in democracy and increase public support for a "strong hand" to end corruption, even if democracy is put on hold for a time.[50]

The redistribution of wealth, the emergence of political parties tied to diverse societal interests, the struggle to control marketization – all have an impact on citizen attitudes toward the democratic process. The collapse of communism has allowed researchers to conduct public opinion surveys and collect data on the changes over time in the level of public support for democratization. Many of these countries have had declines in economic performance which have matched or even exceeded rates seen in the West during the Great Depression, a depression in which democracy endured the test in most of Western Europe and North America, but was wiped out in Germany, Austria, and Italy by the rise of fascism. Based on past trends, it can obviously be expected that the impact of poor economic performance can and will erode support for government leaders, but it is not clear that such performance will necessarily also diminish popular support for democracy as a whole; and authors were asked to collect data on this where it exists.[51]

Surveys also exist which measure a number of factors – such as attitudes toward specific institutions, levels of tolerance in the society, the likelihood of participation in elections, and membership in political parties and intermediary associations – as among different sectors of the society: specifically, authors were asked to gather data which surveyed attitudes by various groups. As with other democratic countries, one would expect attitudes toward democratization to vary across generations, ethnic identification, region, class, and gender.[52]

Popular attitudes are in constant interaction with a free media, which both reflects those attitudes and helps to shape them. What is at stake in postcommunist countries is the establishment of a media which is a channel for the expression of a range of societal interests independent of the preferences of the government. And while the media in all countries are subject to some regulation, what is vital to examine is whether control of the media has affected the conduct of elections and other forms of political participation. It can generally be assumed that the greater the independence and pluralism of the media from the outset of the democratization process, the greater will be the level of civic trust and civic involvement.

Political parties and the party system

With the political evolution of society and increases both in levels of tolerance and in civic involvement, it is assumed in a democracy that a system which promotes parties' sustained competition and pluralism over time will enhance the possibility that political parties will develop and become rooted. Clearly, the comparative literature supports the proposition that a strong civil society is a necessary but not sufficient condition for a strong party system, and it is difficult to find examples where party systems have been established in states with weak civic cultures.[53] Authors were presented with a number of questions addressing the actual emergence of party systems in postcommunist states. They were asked to assess the strength and durability of political parties and the impact of electoral laws, electoral competition, and the type of government on the development of a party system. Particular attention was paid to the renamed communist parties and extremist anti-democratic parties and social movements. Finally, the effect of the party system on the strength of government itself was studied.

Literature in the field traditionally has been divided over the prerequisites for the creation of a strong party system between those who assess the strength of political parties by reference to their intrinsic qualities (internal structure, leadership, platform) and those who emphasize their strength in terms of their ability to perform effectively as a channel for, and reinforcement of, citizens' interests. The former view minimizes the relationship between civil society and political parties; the latter sees that relationship as intrinsic to, and the *raison d'etre* for, a party system. Thus, the former would see a strong party system existing without civic engagement as unproblematic for democracy: the latter would see such a situation as inimicable to the very aims of democracy.

Authors were also asked to comment on the type of electoral system introduced in the postcommunist states and the results. Electoral laws provide the method for the conversion of votes into the selection of leaders for electoral office. There are two major types of electoral systems – majoritarian and proportional representation (or PR). Plurality and majority systems reflect a majoritarian philosophy – the candidate who garners the largest number of votes wins. These formulas can be used to elect both individual leaders, as with presidential elections, and multimember bodies, as with parliaments and legislatures. The PR model, which can be used only for multimember bodies, provides proportional allocation of seats according to the percentage of votes parties received. These differences in electoral systems have an impact on party evolution, with parties in majoritarian systems tending to move toward the center of the political spectrum (median voter theorem), and parties in PR systems likely to be more diverse and more extreme in their approach.[54] The desire to favor majoritarian rule while not disenfranchising minorities has also produced a large number of mixed systems, including in the postcommunist states. Mixed systems typically utilize a version of PR to elect the legislature, and one of several majoritarian formulas to select the chief executive, thereby balancing the benefit of governability produced by majoritarian results with the value of representativeness exhibited by PR formulas.[55]

The strength and structure of the party system is also affected by the structure of government, especially whether the system is parliamentary or presidential. Studying the failures of presidential regimes in Latin America, Juan Linz has concluded that parliamentarism imparts greater flexibility to the political process, promotes consensus-building, and reconciles the interests of multiple political parties. Presidentialism, by focusing on the election of a single individual to an all-powerful post, diminishes the influence of the party system. Political parties tend to be less cohesive in presidential than in parliamentary systems. Presidential systems foster the creation of a two-party or two-bloc system.[56] It has also been shown that presidentialism favors the emergence of two large parties and reduces their distinctiveness and internal cohesion. Party discipline is stronger in parliamentary systems where the prime minister or chancellor belongs to the legislative branch and depends on disciplined and cohesive parties for the survival of government. It is possible for presidential systems to maintain a strong party system and better represent minorities by encouraging federalism and separation of powers, but one cannot ignore findings which point to the tendency of presidentialism to overrepresent the majority, thereby increasing the chance that an alienated and mobilized minority might drop out of party life and pursue political objectives by other, often violent, means.[57]

The attitudes and activities of extremist and communist parties and movements are central to an analysis of the future stability and cohesiveness of party systems in postcommunist countries. The impact of all these parties will depend on their leadership, the institutional and legal setting, constituency, and organization. But postcommunist regimes are challenged to build consensus at the center at the same time they are trying to overcome the institutional and bureaucratic inheritance of a one-party system which still has many well-organized adherents at the political extreme. Trying to construct an electoral and legal system which favors a shift to the center while these groups remain powerful is, therefore, a significant and indeed unprecedented challenge.

Turning to parties of the left and the right, authors were asked to examine the extent to which the renamed communist parties have actually changed (a) their attitudes toward liberal democracy (b) their political leadership, and (c) the interests that they represent as a result of their experience in the emerging democracies. On the other side of the political spectrum, anti-democratic parties and social movements based on clericalism, fascistic traditions, or radical nationalism have arisen in some countries, and authors were asked to determine, among other things, the number and importance of such parties, their willingness to endorse political violence, and their links with paramilitary forces. The literature is split between those who maintain that when electoral systems provide the possibility of coming to power by legal means, the tendency of communist and extremist parties to support the overthrow of the current elected government will subside and those who assert that extremist parties become most destructive to the democratic process when they win elections. These two views are reconciled by the notion that extremist groups will become less extreme through participation in the democratic process, that they will lose their authoritarian and anti-democratic impulse and cease to be a threat to the democratic order. This assumption works best when there is a strong and stable center, fairly good economic conditions, and low levels of social mobilization. However, as the example of Weimar Germany demonstrated, both the Nazis and the Communists won seats in the legislature; and the violent fighting between them paralysed the body in the face of Hitler's rise to power. Concern about the possibility of a repeat of the Weimar example has been widespread in postcommunist countries, most notably Russia, with many analysts concerned about the growth of extremist groups. It is assumed that such groups have the best chance of coming to power without a significant moderation of their political platform when poverty is on the rise, when elected officials are perceived as unable or unwilling to take steps to ameliorate the situation, and when the electoral system is so structured in favor of a pure PR formula as to give parties little incentive to moderate their stand.[58]

Authors were asked to assess the strength of the countries' political parties and party system, including whether emerging party systems are characterized only by the creation of ephemeral parties, or by more stable parties, as indicated by patterns of leadership, electoral results, and survey data. Studies have shown that the more a party exhibits a stable constituency, a consistent party platform, and internal consensus, the greater its durability over time.[59] In looking at parties, authors were also asked to speculate on how the structure and durability of political parties has been affected by any laws on campaign finance and by the timing of elections – including regional versus countrywide elections. Additionally, the literature suggests many propositions which deserve analysis in light of results from postcommunist elections: that the number of coalitions amongst parties will be lower in countries with a proportional representation system than in a majoritarian electoral system; that parties representing women and minorities will fare better in proportional representation systems than in majoritarian systems; that voter turnout will be less among women and minorities in majoritarian systems; that majoritarian systems produce moderate parties, weak in ideological and social class definition, whereas proportional representation systems encourage parties defined along class, ethnic, and regional lines, including extreme right-wing and left-wing parties. All of these propositions can be tested in the new environment provided by postcommunist transitions. Elsewhere, it has been shown that even in a mixed presidential/parliamentary system with proportional representation used for the legislative elections, the large parties which are favored in a winner-take-all presidential election continue to be favored in elections to the legislature, particularly if they are held at the same time, thereby reducing the bias of proportional representation toward greater inclusion of minorities, regional elites, and women.[60]

The party system as it has emerged in postcommunist countries has sometimes facilitated and sometimes obstructed the creation of governments able to formulate and carry through reasonably coherent policies. And conversely the capacity of postcommunist regimes to formulate and implement policies has affected citizen support of democratization and marketization processes. This interaction and essential circularity makes the identification and isolation of variables responsible for shaping the process of democratization difficult. Yet the reasons for undertaking the attempt go beyond the normal intellectual curiosity of academe: never before have so many countries which cover such a large percentage of the world's surface started at the same time along the path of transition from one single kind of regime to another; never before have populations embarking upon a democratic path been so educated, urban, and mobile; and never before has the international system been so clear and unequivocal (if not unanimous) in its support for democracy and marketization as the dominant paradigm. This unique opportunity essentially to control for so many variables makes it all the more likely that observers will be able to judge whether differential strategies for democratic development will also have predictable outcomes. Democracy may be the "only game in town" but as with any game there can be winners and losers, and the winners will be those countries where social, economic, and institutional engineering has received the most attention by elites, parties, and citizens alike.

Notes

For their generous and insightful comments on an earlier draft of the chapter, the author wishes to thank Valerie Bunce, Joan Nelson, Bruce Parrott, Darya Pushkina, Melissa Rosser, and DelGreco Wilson.

1 *Politics in Developing Countries: Comparing Experiences with Democracy*, ed. Larry Diamond, Juan Linz, and Seymour M. Lipset (Boulder, CO: Lynne Rienner, 1990); *Elites and Democratic Consolidation in Latin America and Southern Europe*, ed. John Higley and Richard Gunther (Cambridge: Cambridge University Press, 1992); Samuel Huntington, *The Third Wave: Democratization in the Late Twentieth Century* (Norman, OK: University of Oklahoma Press, 1992); Stephanie Lawson, "Conceptual Issues in the Comparative Study of Regime

Change and Democratization," *Comparative Politics* 25 (January 1993), 88–92; Scott Mainwaring, "Transition to Democracy and Democratic Consolidation: Theoretical and Comparative Issues," in *Issues in Democratic Consolidation*, ed. Scott Mainwaring, Guillermo O'Donnell, and J. Samuel Valenzuela (Notre Dame, IN: University of Notre Dame Press, 1992).

2 Among the more pioneering works are Daniel Lerner, *The Passing of Traditional Society* (Glencoe, NY: Free Press, 1958); Seymour M. Lipset, "The Social Requisites of Democracy," *American Political Science Review* 53 (1959), 69–105; James P. Coleman, "Conclusion: The Political Systems of the Developing Areas," in *The Politics of Developing Areas*, ed. Gabriel A. Almond and J. S. Coleman (Princeton: Princeton University Press, 1960); Phillips Cutright, "National Political Development: Its Measures and Analysis," *American Sociological Review* 28 (1963), 253–64; *On Measuring Democracy*, ed. Alex Inkeles (New Brunswick, NJ: Transaction Publisher, 1991); and Arthur S. Banks and R. B. Textor, *A Cross Polity Survey* (Cambridge, MA: MIT Press, 1963).

3 For example, see Kenneth Bollen, "Issues in the Comparative Measurement of Political Democracy," *American Sociological Review* 45 (1980), 370–90; Kenneth Bollen, "Political Democracy: Validity and Method Factors in Cross-National Measures," *American Journal of Political Science* 37 (November 1993), 1207–30; Raymond D. Gastil and Freedom House, *Freedom in the World* (New York: Freedom House, annual); and Ted Robert Gurr, et al., Polity I, II and III data sets, Inter-University Consortium for Political and Social Research.

4 Doh Chull Shin, "On the Third Wave of Democratization," *World Politics* 47 (October 1994), 148.

5 See Valerie Bunce, "It's the Economy, Stupid . . . Or Is It?" Paper presented for the Workshop on Economic Transformation, Institutional Change and Social Sector Reform, National Academy of Sciences/National Research Council, Task Force on Economies in Transition, Washington, DC, September 19-20, 1996.

6 Huntington, *The Third Wave*, 266–67.

7 Peter McDonough, Samuel Barnes, and Antonio Lopez Pina, "The Growth of Democratic Legitimacy in Spain," *American Political Science Review* 80, no. 3 (September 1986), 735–60. While focusing on the prerequisites and indicators of democratic legitimacy they nevertheless are concerned with consolidation more broadly. Also see *Transitions from Authoritarian Rule: Prospects for Democracy*, ed. Guillermo O'Donnell, Philippe C. Schmitter, and Laurence Whitehead (Baltimore, MD: Johns Hopkins University Press, 1986).

8 For a classic statement of this view and the corollary that factors other than a country's level of economic development were crucial to the explanation of why some countries embarked upon democratization and others did not, see Dankwart Rustow, "Transitions to Democracy," *Comparative Politics* 2 (April 1970), 337–63.

9 Beverly Crawford and Arend Lijphart, "Explaining Political and Economic Change in Post-Communist Eastern Europe: Old Legacies, New Institutions, Hegemonic Norms, and International Pressures," *Comparative Political Studies* 28, no. 2 (1995), 187.

10 Tina Rosenberg, "Overcoming the Legacies of Dictatorship," *Foreign Affairs* 74, no. 3 (May–June 1995), 134.

11 There are many articles and books in the literature, but one which approaches the subject thematically is *The Legacies of Communism in Eastern Europe*, ed. Ivan Volgyes (Baltimore, MD: Johns Hopkins University Press, 1995).

12 The best case is made by Ken Jowitt, *New World Disorder: The Leninist Extinction* (Berkeley, CA: University of California Press, 1992).

13 See Jacques Rupnik, *The Other Europe: The Rise and Fall of Communism in East Central Europe* (London: Pantheon, 1989); Roy Medvedev, *Let History Judge: The Origins and Consequences of Stalinism* (Oxford: Oxford University Press, 1989); Jeffrey Goldfarb, *After the Fall: The Pursuit of Democracy in Central Europe* (New York: Basic Books, 1992); Timothy Garton Ash, *The Uses of Adversity: Essays on the Fate of Central Europe* (New York: Vintage Books, 1989); Milovan Djilas, *The New Class: An Analysis of the Communist System* (New York: Praeger, 1957); and Vladimir Tismaneanu, *Reinventing Politics: Eastern Europe from Stalin to Havel* (New York: The Free Press, 1992).

14 Richard Rose in doing cross-national surveys found support for the hypothesis that "if the common historical experience of Sovietization has had a decisive influence, generational differences in attitudes should be similar from one former Communist country to another." "Generational Effects on Attitudes to Communist Regimes: A Comparative Analysis," *Post-Soviet Affairs* 11, no. 1 (January–March 1995), 37. Also see Ellen Comisso, "Legacies of the Past or New Institutions?" *Comparative Political Studies* 28, no. 2 (July 1995), 200–38; and Barbara Geddes, "A Comparative Perspective on the Leninist Legacy in Eastern Europe," ibid., 239–74. Both maintain that the Soviet era destroyed popular support for pre-Leninist parties and traditions in most countries.

15 See, for example, Anders Åslund, *Gorbachev's Struggle for Economic Reform* (Ithaca, NY: Cornell University Press, 1989); and Ed A. Hewett, *Reforming the Soviet Economy* (Washington, DC: Brookings Institution Press, 1988).

16 The varied political views and splits within the military/security services are discussed in Karen Dawisha and Bruce Parrott, *Russia and the New States of Eurasia* (Cambridge: Cambridge University Press, 1993), ch. 6. Although she is dealing only with the security service, the role and political attitudes of this service are discussed by Amy Knight, *Spies without Cloaks* (Princeton, NJ: Princeton University Press, 1996).

17 Janos Kornai, *The Socialist System: The Political Economy of Communism* (Princeton, NJ: Princeton University Press, 1992). See also Peter Wiles, *The Political Economy of Communism* (Cambridge, MA: Harvard University Press, 1962).

18 Jowitt, *New World Disorder*. Also see Sten Berglund and Jan Dellenbrant, "Prospects for the New Democracies in Eastern Europe," in *The New Democracies in Eastern Europe*, ed. Sten Berglund and Jan Dellenbrant (Brookfield, VT: Edward Elgar Publishing Company, 1991).

19 Huntington, *The Third Wave*, pp. 40–6; also see Valerie Bunce and Maria Csanadi, "Uncertainty in the Transition: Post-Communism in Hungary," *East European Politics and Societies* 7 (Spring 1993), 240–75.

20 Crawford and Lijphart, "Explaining Political and Economic Change," p. 172.

21 Huntington, *The Third Wave*, pp. 85–108.

22 For a consideration of the impact of previous regime type on transition success
and of transition type on prospects for consolidation, see Juan J. Linz and Alfred
Stepan, *Problems of Democratic Transition and Consolidation: Southern Europe,
South America, and Post-Communist Europe* (Baltimore, MD: Johns Hopkins
University Press, 1996), ch. 4.

23 For a discussion of pacted transitions, see Arend Lijphart, *Democracy in Plural
Societies: A Comparative Perspective* (New Haven: Yale University Press, 1977);
and in the Arab world, see *Democracy without Democrats? The Renewal of
Politics in the Muslim World*, ed. Ghassan Salame (New York: I. B. Taurus,
1994).

24 This hypothesis is drawn from Joan Nelson, "How Market Reforms and
Democratic Consolidation Affect Each Other," in *Intricate Links*, ed. Joan Nelson
(New Brunswick, NJ: Transaction Publishers, 1994).

25 See Alfred Stepan, "Paths toward Redemocratization: Theoretical and Comparative Considerations," in *Transitions from Authoritarian Rule*, ed. O'Donnell,
Schmitter, and Whitehead, pp. 79–81.

26 Robert A. Dahl, *Democracy and Its Critics* (New Haven: Yale University Press,
1989).

27 The idea that a state's movement toward democracy is conditioned by its ability
to exercise civilian control of violent coercion is most fully developed by Dahl in
Democracy and Its Critics.

28 See, for example, Jendayi Frazer, "Conceptualizing Civil–Military Relations
during Democratic Transition," in *Africa Today*, Quarters 1 & 2 (1995), 39–48;
Philippe Schmitter, "Dangers and Dilemmas of Democracy," *Journal of
Democracy* 5, no. 2 (April 1994); and *Civil–Military Relations in the Soviet and
Yugoslav Successor States*, ed. Constantine Danopoulos and Daniel Zirker
(Boulder, CO: Westview, 1996).

29 S. E. Finer, *The Man on Horseback: The Role of the Military in Politics*, 2d ed.
(Boulder, CO: Westview Press, 1988); and Morris Janowitz, *The Military in the
Political Development of New Nations* (Chicago: University of Chicago Press,
1964).

30 This proposition is derived from Adam Przeworski, *Democracy and the Market:
Political and Economic Reforms in Eastern Europe and Latin America* (Cam-
bridge: Cambridge University Press, 1991). It largely coalesces with the view
promoted by rational choice theorists such as Douglass C. North, *Institutions,
Institutional Change, and Economic Performance* (Cambridge: Cambridge
University Press, 1990); Anthony Downs, *An Economic Theory of Democracy*
(New York: Harper and Row, 1957); and Mancur Olson, "Dictatorship,
Democracy, and Development," *American Political Science Review* 87 (September
1993), 567–76.

31 G. Bingham Powell, Jr., *Contemporary Democracies: Participation, Stability and
Violence* (Cambridge, MA: Harvard University Press, 1982); Larry Diamond and
Marc F. Plattner, *The Global Resurgence of Democracy* (Baltimore, MD: Johns
Hopkins University Press, 1993).

32 See, for example, Phillippe C. Schmitter, "The Consolidation of Democracy and
Representation of Social Groups," *American Behavioral Scientist* 35 (March–June
1992), 422–49.

33 See Ted Robert Gurr, *Minorities at Risk: A Global View of Ethnopolitical Conflict* (Washington, DC: US Institute of Peace, 1993). Also Linz and Stepan, *Problems of Democratic Transition and Consolidation: Southern Europe, South America and Post-Communist Europe*.

34 This problematic relationship between capitalism and democracy is most fully explored in Przeworski, *Democracy and the Market*.

35 The debate over whether shock therapy or gradualism is the best policy is extensive and is well analyzed in *The Postcommunist Economic Transformation: Essays in Honor of Gregory Grossman*, ed. Robert W. Campbell (Boulder, CO: Westview Press, 1994); and in articles by Anders Åslund and Bela Kadar in *Overcoming the Transformation Crisis: Lessons for the Successor States of the Soviet Union* (Tubingen, 1993). Public choice literature has contributed most to a discussion of rational calculations in polities which are already established, not in those being formed, so its contribution has been more limited, but is discussed in Dennis Mueller, "Public Choice: A Survey," in *The Public Choice Approach to Politics*, ed. Dennis Mueller (Brookfield, VT: Edward Elgar, 1993), pp. 447–89.

36 Donald L. Horowitz, *Ethnic Groups in Conflict* (Berkeley, CA: University of California Press, 1985); Juan Linz, *The Breakdown of Democratic Regimes: Crisis, Breakdown, and Reequilibration* (Baltimore, MD: Johns Hopkins University Press, 1978).

37 See especially Arendt Lijphart, "Consociational Democracy," *World Politics* 21 (January 1969), 207–25.

38 Charles Tilly, *Coercion, Capital, and European States*, rev. ed. (Oxford: Blackwell, 1992); Harry Eckstein, ed., *Internal War: Problems and Approaches* (Glencoe, IL: Free Press, 1963); and *Organizing Interests in Western Europe: Pluralism, Corporatism, and the Transformation of Politics*, ed. Suzanne Berger (Cambridge University Press, 1981).

39 Gabriel Almond and Sidney Verba, *The Civic Culture: Political Attitudes and Democracy in Five Nations* (Princeton: Princeton University Press, 1963).

40 Gabriel Almond, "Foreword: The Return to Political Culture," in *Political Culture and Democracy in Developing Countries*, ed. Larry Diamond, ix–xii. Among the more important critiques lodged against mainstream comparative politics during this era were the following: Mark Kesselman, "Order or Movement? The Literature of Political Development as Ideology," *World Politics* 26, no. 1 (1973); Fernando H. Cardoso and Enzo Faleto, *Dependency and Development in Latin America* (Berkeley: University of California Press, 1979); and André Gunder Frank, *Latin America: Underdevelopment or Revolution* (New York: Monthly Review Press, 1969).

41 Among the seminal works are Downs, *Economic Theory of Democracy*, and William Riker, *The Theory of Political Coalitions* (New Haven: Yale University Press, 1962).

42 Ronald Inglehart, "The Renaissance of Political Culture," *American Political Science Review* 82, no. 4 (December 1988), 1203–30; and idem., *Culture Shift in Advanced Industrial Society* (Princeton: Princeton University Press, 1990).

43 This requirement is explored most fully by Ernest Gellner, *Conditions of Liberty: Civil Society and Its Rivals* (New York: Allen Lane, The Penguin Press, 1994).

44 The debate about this possibility was begun by the publication of Samuel P. Huntington, "The Clash of Civilizations," *Foreign Affairs* 72 (Summer 1993), 22–49.

45 See Seymour M. Lipset, "The Social Requisites of Democracy Revisited," *American Sociological Review* 59 (February 1994), 1–22; Inglehart, "The Renaissance of Political Culture"; and Inglehart, *Culture Shift in Advanced Industrial Society*; Almond and Verba, *The Civic Culture*. The dilemma of how to build trust in societies where the state had systematically gone about its destruction is deftly argued in Richard Rose, "Postcommunism and the Problem of Trust," in Diamond and Plattner, *The Global Resurgence of Democracy*, 2d ed., pp. 251–63.

46 Barrington Moore, *Social Origins of Dictatorship and Democracy* (Boston: Beacon Press, 1966); and Charles Lindblom, *Politics and Markets: The World's Political-Economic Systems* (New York: Basic Books, 1977). They were among the first to assert the connection between a strong bourgeoisie and democracy. This view has been challenged only rarely, including by Dietrich Reuschemeyer, Evelyne Huber Stephens, and John D. Stephens in *Capitalist Development and Democracy* (Chicago, IL: University of Chicago Press, 1993) who argued that it was the working class that had proved over time to have been the greatest supporter of democracy.

47 Mancur Olson, "Dictatorship, Democracy, and Development," *American Political Science Review* 87, no. 3 (September 1993), 567–76; Rueschemeyer, Stephens, and Stephens, *Capitalist Development and Democracy*; and Edward N. Muller, "Democracy, Economic Development and Income Inequality," *American Sociological Review* 53 (1988), 50–68.

48 Louise Shelley, "The Internalization of Crime: The Changing Relationship Between Crime and Development," in *Essays on Crime and Development*, ed. Ugljesa Zvekic (Rome: UN Interregional Crime and Justice Research Institute, 1990); J. S. Nye, "Corruption and Political Development: A Cost-benefit Analysis," *American Political Science Review* 61, no. 2 (1967), 417–27.

49 This is a central tenet of Olson, "Dictatorship, Democracy and Development."

50 James Walston, *The Mafia and Clientism* (London: Routledge, 1988); Rensselaer W. Lee III, *The White Labyrinth* (New Brunswick, NJ: Transaction Publishers, 1989).

51 Studies done in six Central European countries suggest that respondents continue to have a very positive perception of the political benefits of democracy even as they hold a very negative perception of the economic benefits of marketization. See Richard Rose and Christian Haerpfer, "New Democracies Barometer III: Learning from What is Happening," *Studies in Public Policy* 230 (1994), questions 26,35,36,39,40,42, as presented in Linz and Stepan, *Problems in Democratic Transition and Consolidation*, 443.

52 The first attempt to see democracy as strongly affected by culture was Almond and Verba, *The Civic Culture*. Page and Shapiro have argued that irrespective of cleavages within public opinion, overall the public in aggregate is able to make rational and informed judgments (Benjamin Page and Robert Shapiro, *The Rational Public: Fifty Years of Trends in Americans' Policy Preferences* [Chicago: University of Chicago Press, 1992]). One of the first attempts to gauge public opinion and attitudinal shifts in the Soviet Union was Ada W. Finitfer and Ellen

Mickiewicz, "Redefining the Political System of the USSR: Mass Support for Political Change," *American Political Science Review* 86 (1992), 857–74. More recently, a wide array of authors have examined changes in public opinion and political culture in postcommunist states: see, for example, James L. Gibson, "The Resilience of Mass Support for Democratic Institutions and Processes in the Nascent Russian and Ukrainian Democracies," and Jeffrey W. Hahn, "Changes in Contemporary Political Culture," in *Political Culture and Civil Society in Russia and the New States of Eurasia*, ed. Vladimir Tismaneanu (Armonk, NY: M. E. Sharpe, 1995).

53 In *Making Democracy Work: Civic Traditions in Modern Italy* (Princeton, NJ: Princeton University Press, 1993), Robert Putnam argues that a strong party system can operate within a weak civic culture; also see Robert Putnam, "Troubled Democracies," paper prepared for the University of Maryland/Johns Hopkins University Workshop on Democratization and Political Participation in Postcommunist Societies, US Department of State, May 1995; and Robert Putnam, "Bowling Alone: America's Declining Social Capital," in Diamond and Plattner, *The Global Resurgence of Democracy*, 2d ed., pp. 290–307.

54 Connections between electoral laws and political parties are the subject of many works, of which some of the best are Arend Lijphart, *Democracies* (New Haven, CN: Yale University Press, 1984); Arend Lijphart, *Electoral Systems and Party Systems: A Study of Twenty-seven Democracies, 1945–1990* (Oxford: Oxford University Press, 1994); Richard S. Katz, *A Theory of Parties and Electoral Systems* (Baltimore, MD: Johns Hopkins University Press, 1980); and *Electoral Laws and Their Political Consequences*, ed. Bernard Grofman and Arend Lijphart (New York: Agathon Press, Inc., 1986). Also see Part II of Dennis Mueller, *The Public Choice Approach to Politics* (Brookfield, VT: Edward Elgar, 1993).

55 On the effects of different varieties of electoral systems, see Douglas W. Rae, *The Political Consequences of Electoral Laws*, 2d ed. (New Haven: Yale University Press, 1971); and Rein Taagapera and Matthew Soberg Shugart, *Seats and Votes: The Effects and Determinants of Electoral Systems* (New Haven: Yale University Press, 1989).

56 See Juan Linz and Arturo Valenzuela, *The Failure of Presidential Democracy* (Baltimore, MD: Johns Hopkins University Press, 1994), for an argument in support of this hypothesis. By contrast, see Donald Horowitz, *A Democratic South Africa? Constitutional Engineering in a Divided Society* (Berkeley: University of California Press, 1991), who finds no necessary link, and W. H. Riker, who theorizes that all party systems converge to two coalitions of equal size (*The Theory of Political Coalitions* [New Haven, CN: Yale University Press, 1962]).

57 Juan Linz, "Presidential or Parliamentary Democracy: Does it Make a Difference?" in Linz and Valenzuela, *The Failure of Presidential Democracy: Comparative Perspectives*, 3–91; and Arend Lijphart, "Democracy in Plural Societies: A Comparative Exploration," in *The Failure of Presidential Democracy*, 91–105. Also see Vladimir Tismaneanu, *Fantasies of Salvation: Post-Communist Political Mythologies* (Princeton, NJ: Princeton University Press, forthcoming).

58 Quentin L. Quade examines the impact of an unmodified proportional representation system on the potential for takeover by extremist groups in "PR and Democratic Statecraft," in Diamond and Plattner, *The Global Resurgence of*

Democracy, 2d ed., pp. 181–7. The case for the likely rise in extremist politics was first and most forcefully made in Jowitt, *The New World Disorder*.

59 Giovanni Sartori, *Parties and Party Systems* (Cambridge: Cambridge University Press, 1976), 6; and Lijphart, *Democracies;* in opposition to Robert Michels (*Political Parties* [Glencoe, IL: The Free Press, 1958]) who dismissed the need for constituency support, focusing instead on the centrality of elites and their ability to instill beliefs in the masses. On the need for a party to show internal consensus, see Katz, *A Theory of Parties and Electoral Systems*.

60 The seminal work on the relationship between party and electoral systems is Maurice Duverger, *Political Parties: Their Organization and Activity in the Modern State* (New York: Wiley, 1954); see also Douglas J. Amy, *Real Choices/New Voices: The Case for Proportional Representation in the United States* (New York: Columbia University Press, 1993); and Michel L. Balinski and H. Peyton Young, *Fair Representation: Meeting the Ideal of One Man, One Vote* (New Haven, CN: Yale University Press, 1982).

The former Yugoslavia

3   Embattled democracy: postcommunist Croatia in transition

Lenard J. Cohen

We have democracy and in our war conditions we even have too much of it. We are even allowing some anarchy but of course we will have full freedom and total democracy when we liberate every inch of land.

Franjo Tudjman, president of Croatia, August 1993

There is no state in Europe that is more centralized than Croatia. All funds and decision-making concerning people have been concentrated in the presidential palace. In that way the incumbent party is exercising unlimited power.

Mika Tripalo, Head of "Action of Croatia's Social
Democrats" and former communist leader,
December 1994

Croatia's first five years of postcommunist rule (1990–95) were marked by trends that may be viewed as both promising and inauspicious. Thus, for many Croatian citizens and leaders it was an exhilarating period filled with achievements: jettisoning a one-party communist regime, holding competitive elections, obtaining statehood and international recognition, embarking on a transformation of the economy. For many others, however, the same years were characterized by dashed hopes, societal deterioration, and repressive regime policies as Croatia experienced a tumultuous secession from the former Yugoslav socialist federation (including warfare, severe economic disruption, interethnic polarization, and territorial fragmentation).

On balance, postcommunist Croatia has exhibited important aspects of both incipient democratization and residual authoritarianism. Croatia represents a classic example of how self-determination and state formation by an ethnic group seeking freedom may generate new communal violence, socioeconomic dislocation, and illiberal tendencies that can seriously jeopardize the democratic prospects of the newly "liberated" state. Indeed, as the second half of the 1990s began, it remained an open question whether Croatia would move forward in the process of democratic consolidation, or remain stalled as a mixed case, exhibiting significant features of authoritarian control.

This study will explore the problems and contradictory developments in postcommunist Croatia with special attention to those factors which have served to facilitate or impede the establishment of democratic rule. Because the nature of postcommunist political development is profoundly affected by political history, and particularly by the circumstances associated with the demise of the former one-party regime, this analysis will begin with a brief examination of the salient experiences and expectations which marked the last stages of communist rule in Croatia: Tito's crack-down on the reformist and nationalist strivings in Croatia which flourished during the late 1960s, the de-legitimation of the Croatian communist leadership in the 1970s and 1980s, and the emergence of pluralist pressures prior to the important "founding election" of 1990. The discussion will then turn to the initial stage of Croatian postcommunism, including the serious challenges facing the new self-styled democratic regime, the drift toward an "imperial presidency" and anti-pluralist practices, and also the intractable schism between the regime and segments of the Serbian minority that finally ended in a violent alteration of the country's demographic make-up. The last section of the study will focus on the outcome of the October 1995 election, and the subsequent political conflict between the regime and the opposition in Zagreb.

Authoritarian breakdown and democratic transition: the "Silent Republic" finds its voice

In late 1971, the Titoist regime launched a brutal campaign to suppress reformist and national currents in Croatia, thereby ushering in a seventeen-year period of rigid one-party control in the republic. Tito's ire was aimed at Croatian leaders and their sympathizers within and outside the Croatian League of Communists (SKH) – participants in the so-called "Croatian Spring" or MASPOK (mass movement) – who, between 1966 and 1971, had attempted to blend advocacy of political reform and enhanced autonomy for their republic with an assertion of pride in Croatian national traditions. Top officials in Belgrade regarded the surgical political strike to remove Croatia's communist and non-communist reformers and nationalists as essential to the maintenance of Yugoslavia's one-party state, and the territorial cohesion of the country.

The post-1971 Croatian communist elite – a conservative coalition between Croat and Serb elements in the leadership of the SKH (in which Serbs were markedly over-represented compared with their roughly 12 percent proportion of the republic's total population) – dutifully stifled all stirrings of Croatian nationalism, and at least superficially upheld the tenets of the Titoist "self-managing," socialist model. Indeed, from 1971 to the late 1980s, that is, well beyond Tito's death in May 1980, the Croatian communist leadership proved to be one of the most conformist and docile branches of the regionally segmented communist apparatus in Yugoslavia. Throughout this period, most communist and non-communist political activists who had been associated with the MASPOK were either barred from political activity or chose to live outside the country. Meanwhile, Croatian political dissidents who remained in the republic and continued to work on behalf of reformist or nationalist goals, were subjected to sporadic political imprisonment or police harassment.

Transition triggers and the prelude to pluralism

In retrospect, one might say that after the suppression of the MASPOK, Croatian political life became more or less frozen. During the late 1980s, however, the influence of new political developments simply caused a rapid meltdown of the old regime, thereby allowing the re-activation of many well-known political forces and perspectives that had unsuccessfully attempted to gain momentum some twenty years earlier. Most notably, the ruling SKH leadership was required once again to come to terms with the question of fundamental political reform and Croatian nationalism. Indeed, most of the non-communist political actors who emerged as leaders of new parties in Croatia during 1989 had been significant figures during the 1971–72 period or dissidents in the politically authoritarian years that followed. By 1988–89, four additional and interrelated factors can be considered as important stimulants for the transition to postcommunism: (1) the rapidly advancing de-legitimation of the SKH as a result of the economic and political crises which overwhelmed the country and the ruling party during the post-Tito period; (2) the negative Croatian reaction, in both elite and non-communist circles, to the advent of Slobodan Milošević's strident Serbian nationalist-communism; (3) the demonstration effect of reformist communism and pluralist development in neighboring Slovenia, and; (4) the rapid demise of orthodox communist rule elsewhere in Eastern Europe during the second half of 1989.

As political and economic difficulties mounted for the Yugoslav communist regime during the post-Tito period (interregional squabbling, a resurgence of ethnonationalism, increasing indebtedness, inflation, unemployment, strikes, and so forth) the Croatian communist leadership was placed in a particularly precarious position. Forced to endorse a conservative and anti-nationalist platform since the purge of 1971–72, linked and subordinated to the bankrupt policies of the federal communist party leadership in Belgrade, and under the strong influence of officials from Croatia's Serbian minority (who regarded any political expression of autonomous Croatian national feeling as potentially subversive and threatening to ethnic relations in the republic), the SKH elite had very little scope to recast its negative image. Moreover, those reform-minded communist leaders who perceived the danger of maintaining the status quo, and urged changes that might enable the SKH to develop new sources of legitimacy, constituted a politically weak minority.

Croatian officials were also faced with a potentially serious challenge from the brash leader of the communist apparatus in Serbia. Having come to appreciate the deep malaise and latent nationalist sentiments in his own republic – following a legendary 1987 meeting with Serbs protesting Albanian nationalism in the province of Kosovo – Slobodan Milošević had abandoned traditional Titoist-communist methodology regarding the national question. Seeking to enhance and re-legitimate his own position and control of his party organization, Milošević elaborated a crafty admixture of warmed-over socialist ideas and an appeal to Serbian patriotism that would completely and quickly alter the character of Yugoslav political discourse. Thus by 1988, Milošević had launched a populist brand of nationalist mobilization in Serbia, and signaled that only a fundamental alteration of the country's existing constitutional arrangements could provide Serbia with the fair treatment and political influence it deserved. He had also decided, albeit not overtly, to embrace elements of the controversial 1986 Memorandum of the Serbian Academy of Science and Arts which claimed, among other things, that the Serbian minority in Croatia was politically oppressed and threatened.

Milošević's exploitation of Serbian nationalism, and particularly his attack on Croatia's treatment of its Serbian minority – views that were echoed by many Serbian intellectuals and political figures in Croatia – were a major impetus to the re-emergence of Croatian nationalism. The general deterioration of Serbian-Croatian relations in Yugoslavia and Croatia created an extremely awkward situation for the anti-nationalist coalition of Croatian and Serbian communist conservatives who were governing Croatia. A great many Croatian citizens already regarded the SKH leadership as an oligarchy of opportunistic ethnic Croatians and members of Croatia's Serbian minority who were devoted solely to their own power and the suppression of legitimate Croatian nationalist interests. Thus during 1987 and 1988, as Milošević began his political ascendancy, the Croatian communist elite enjoyed little political leverage or legitimacy to effectively resist the new Serbian leader. It was primarily the reformist communists in Slovenia who led the attack against Milošević, and first suggested the dangers for Yugoslav cohesion that might flow from unchecked populist nationalism. Unlike their Croatian comrades, the Slovene communists had, for several years, associated themselves with the advancement of their republic's regional interests, and also encouraged the pluralization of their republic's communist regime.

Table 3.1 *Social and demographic trends in Croatia since 1948*

	1948	1971	1991
Total population	3,779,858	4,426,221	4,784,265
Agricultural population (%)	62.4	32.3	9.1
Non-agricultural population (%)	37.6	67.7	90.9
Level of education[a] (%)	(1953)	(1971)	(1991)
0–3 years	30.5	18.0	10.1
4–8 years	60.8	59.8	44.6
Secondary	7.3	18.5	36.0
Technical/Higher	0.7	3.2	9.3
Age distribution (%)	(1953)	(1971)	(1991)
0–14 years	27.1	22.7	19.4
15–49 years	52.7	52.9	48.8
50+ years	20.2	24.4	31.8

Note: [a]Population aged 10 and over for 1953 and 1971, and aged 15 and over for 1991.
Sources: Federal Institute for Statistics (Belgrade, Yugoslavia) and Republic of Croatia, Central Bureau of Statistics (Zagreb, Croatia).

Many leading Croatian communists quickly came to the realization that a strong stand against Milošević and Serbian nationalism might provide an opportunity for recasting and re-legitimizing the SKH. For example, in the fall of 1988, Stipe Šuvar, a Croatian communist ideologue whose dogmatic views were widely unpopular in Croatian intellectual circles, became president of the Yugoslav League of Communists' federal organization (SKJ). When Šuvar, after coming under attack by the Serbian party apparatus, began to sharply attack Milošević, the Croatian leader's popularity temporarily soared in his native republic. For liberal and reformist Croatian communists, who were even more repelled than Šuvar by Milošević's program and tactics, the building confrontation with the Serbian leadership demonstrated the urgency of transforming the SKH into an organization committed to the advancement of Croatian interests. Initially, however, there was little support for fundamental political reform and the adoption of a genuinely Croatian perspective at the apex of Zagreb's petrified communist power structure. Thus, many members of Croatia's small socialist intelligentsia were either closely tied to the communist regime, and often were under the spell of the idea that Yugoslavia's self-management model represented the most "progressive" model of socialist development. Moreover, having already witnessed Belgrade's harsh reaction to ethno-regional strivings for autonomy and economic reform, few Croatian communist moderates were inclined to independently initiate fundamental political and economic changes.

The views of Croatia's unpopular and weak communist leadership contrasted sharply with the beliefs and predominant aspirations of the Croatian public. Thus, throughout the 1970s and 1980s, devotion to traditional Croatian values and nationalist sentiments remained a powerful latent force in both the general population of the republic, and in intellectual circles (not to mention among the hundreds of thousands of Croats living abroad). An interesting indicator of such traditional beliefs was the increasing religiosity of the population as indicated in numerous public opinion surveys, church attendance figures, and the circulation of religious publications. The relationship between the Roman Catholic church and communist authorities remained rocky, but throughout the 1980s Catholic sentiments and bonds were gradually reemerging as an important facet of Croatia's civil society. When such religiosity – traditionally a phenomenon closely linked to national consciousness in Croatian society[1] – is considered together with the reservoir of accumulated anti-regime sentiments arising from several decades of communist control, and particularly popular resentment at the suppression of the 1971 Croatian Spring, the potential for mass political mobilization by aspiring traditionalist and nationalist political forces becomes apparent. Overall, the social composition of the Croatian population had changed considerably during the four decades between the establishment of the communist state in the mid-1940s and the last period of the Tito regime in the late 1980s. Thus, the population had become overwhelmingly non-agricultural, was far more educated, and had aged considerably (table 3.1). At the same time, the ideological bankruptcy of Titoist "self-managed" socialism had created both a revitalization of old values (including religion) and a yearning for new political options.

Emergent pluralism and the 'founding election'

By late 1988, with the League of Communist's federal organization severely weakened by quarrelling among the regional communist oligarchies, and with Croatia's republican leadership sharply divided over how to deal with the delicate and long-suppressed issues of political reform and Croatian nationalism, the dynamics of political debate and political action in the republic underwent a rapid change. Sensing that the communists were in a quandary, and that a political vacuum existed, Croatia's non-communist and anti-communist political dissidents (the most well-known of whom had been involved in the Croatian Spring), and also a widening circle of politicized intellectuals, were finally emboldened to become more politically active.

Although multiparty pluralism was still technically illegal and officially condemned, a number of intellectuals decided to take political advantage of the ruling party's apparent confusion and lack of self-confidence.

The first political group formed was the Association for a Yugoslav Democratic Initiative (UJDI) launched in early February 1989 by the Zagreb economist Branko Horvat and a few other well-known intellectuals. UJDI activists did not aspire to organize a political party, but rather a movement advocating "a legally guaranteed pluralism of political actors." In late May 1989, Dražen Budiša, a former youth activist during the Croatian Spring, who had served several years in prison for his activities, joined with several intellectuals to form Croatia's first non-official party organization, the Croatian Social Liberal Party (HSLS). Although UJDI and HSLS were sharply criticized by the regime and denied legal registration as organizations, their members remained free and were allowed to continue their activity. Thus, party pluralism had essentially been decriminalized through a tacit understanding by the main actors on the Croatian political landscape that old methods of rule could simply not be revived.

The next party-like organization to make its formal appearance on the political scene was the Croatian Democratic Union (HDZ). The HDZ – initially deemed a "movement" and not a "party" owing to legal restrictions – was the brainchild of the Croatian historian and political dissident, Dr. Franjo Tudjman, and would soon emerge as the most powerful force in the republic. Although the new organization was officially launched at a meeting in mid-June 1989, the formation of the HDZ actually had been underway since late 1988, and its draft program was publicly discussed at an important February 1989 meeting of key members from its "Initiating Circle."[2] Tudjman had fought in the communist-led Partisan forces, and until 1961 served as a high-ranking officer in the Yugoslav People's Army (JNA). However, during the 1960s, embittered by the belief that his parents had died at the hands of local Croatian communists, that the role of Croatia in the anti-fascist victory had been denigrated by Serbian officials, and that his native republic's interests were being side-tracked by the Belgrade-centered communist regime, Tudjman had become increasingly committed to Croatian nationalist views.[3] For example, in 1967, when Serbo-Croatian (or Croato-Serbian) was Yugoslavia's official language, he signed a controversial petition insisting that Croatian was a separate language. Actively sympathetic to the goals of the Croatian Spring in 1971, and subsequently engaged full-time in dissident work during the 1970s and 1980s, he was periodically imprisoned, and barred from disseminating his views during the 1970s and 1980s. Tudjman also travelled extensively abroad, where he established a network of contacts and sources of financial support within the large Croatian diasporic community (over three million people) that was later to prove vital to the success of the HDZ.

Briefly, Tudjman's platform for political change in Croatia consisted of two related planks: eliminating the communist regime, and establishing Croatia as an independent state. His organizational formula for accomplishing these ambitious tasks, which also differentiated him from other aspiring political actors in Croatia, derived from the concept of "national reconciliation." Essentially Tudjman argued that the termination of communist control and the creation of a Croatian state would only be feasible if a bond was established between those who had formerly participated in the anti-fascist struggle – the Partisans (such as Tudjman himself) – and those who had actively served, or sympathized with, the Ustaša political organization and other agencies that had been part of the World War II Independent State of Croatia.[4] Such reconciliation entailed not only an end to open quarrelling between the Partisans and the Ustaša elements, but also close cooperation between first-generation émigrés, their children, and those who were still living in Croatia, not to mention unity among all classes of the Croatian social structure. Tudjman also was confident that he could personally bridge the gap that divided the democratically oriented political subculture in Croatian society – expressed during the interwar years by Stjepan Radić's Croatian Peasant Party – from the more violent, and anti-democratic ("dinaric") political subculture that had found radical expression in Croatia's wartime fascist state. Tudjman did not specify precisely how – besides reliance on his own judgment – a future Croatian state would protect itself against the illiberal or intolerant proclivities deriving from either the extremist Ustaša tradition (including the dinaric/heroic political subculture), or the Partisan mono-party mentality. It was an important omission that would seriously trouble the development of postcommunist Croatia.

Significantly, "national reconciliation" was a concept conceived by Tudjman to enhance pan-Croatian solidarity, and explicitly not a means of bridging historical antagonism or distrust between Croats and Serbs, or between Croatia and Serbia. Thus for Tudjman, Serbs and Croats constituted two fundamentally incompatible "civilizations." Moreover, Tudjman was deeply concerned, as he pointed out (quoting himself at his own trial in 1981) that "every time the Croatian national problem and interests are mentioned and brought to light . . . this move is immediately generalized and branded as nationalism, separatism and Ustaša extremism."[5] In much the same way as Slobodan Milošević would reassure Serbs that they need not feel guilty about expressions of patriotism or prior episodes of Serbian political domination in Yugoslavia, Tudjman reassured Croats that they should need not feel uncomfortable about Croatia's World War II pro-fascist affiliations, or exhibiting nationalist sentiments. In Tudjman's analysis of Croatian political history, the communal violence and atrocities during World War II, and particularly the magnitude of Serbian losses due to terror by Croatian extremists, had been greatly exaggerated. Such revisionism infuriated Croatia's Serbs, but for Tudjman, the "correction" of the historical record was politically useful as a means to bridging the gulf between anti-fascist and pro-fascist veterans of the war.

Already regarded by many Croats as a skillful and articulate patriot, Tudjman quickly overshadowed other non-communist political figures actively organizing party organizations throughout 1989 and early 1990. Tudjman also cleverly cultivated contacts with the small group of reform communists (almost all of whom were ethnic Croats), and other members of the SKH who were prepared to accept a working relationship with the HDZ leadership – and indeed even the possibility of a free election and possible HDZ rule in the republic – in order to better resist Milošević's Serbian national revival, and also end the domination of communist conservatives in Croatia.[6] Because a sizeable portion of the SKH membership consisted of nominal communists, who had joined the ruling party simply out of careerist motives or the absence of other alternatives, Tudjman believed that his policy of reconciliation would encourage a wholesale migration of individuals from the SKH directly into the HDZ. Thus, when Yugoslavia's federal party organization collapsed in January 1990 at the 14th SKJ Congress – after a walkout by the Slovene reform communist leadership who had crossed swords with Milošević, followed by the refusal of Croatia's delegation to proceed without the Slovenes (as Milošević urged) – Tudjman shrewdly sent a message of congratulations to the Slovene communists praising their initiative. Through such gestures, Tudjman signaled communists in Croatia that, if they behaved appropriately, they might find a place for themselves under his umbrella of reconciliation.

In late 1989, just prior to the break-up of the SKJ, the Croatian communist leadership – bowing to internal pressures, the example of Slovenia, and news of the collapse of communist regimes elsewhere in Eastern Europe – finally endorsed the legalization of multiparty pluralism, and scheduled Croatia's first post-World War II competitive election for April–May 1990. Efforts by the communist apparatus to rapidly reconfigure and reorient their organization – through cosmetic measures such as a name change to League of Communists of Croatia-Party of Democratic Change (SKH-SDP) – did little to improve the organization's electoral prospects or forestall a hemorrhage of party members. By the eve of the election, HDZ membership had soared, while the SKH was in a stage of sharp decline. Tudjman's intuition about the potential realignment of activists and voters in Croatia proved to be highly accurate. For example, it is estimated that in a very short time before the elections, approximately 27,000 party members left the SKH and joined the recently formed HDZ.[7]

As the election campaign proceeded, over three dozen parties registered to compete. The most important new party besides Tudjman's HDZ and Budiša's HSLS, was the Croatian Democratic Party (HDS), headed by Savka Dabčević-Kučar and Mika Tripalo, the two leaders who had been ousted by Tito in late 1971 for permitting the MASPOK. The HDS would soon join with the HSLP and other smaller parties of the center–left to form the Coalition for National Accord (KNS). Thus by the time of the election, the KNS, the SKH-SDP (leading a "left-bloc"), and the HDZ (leading a "Croatian democratic bloc") were the three major contenders. Most of the smaller parties appealed to narrow segments of the electorate, and linked themselves to the loose "blocs" dominated by the leaders of the three principal parties.

All of the major contending parties espoused the principle of establishing a democratic country. But, in contrast to its major competitors, Tudjman's HDZ was distinguished by its pledge to establish a democratic and capitalist country on the basis of Croatian national and religious values, its promise to eliminate the strong influence of Croatia's Serb minority in political life, and its explicit appeal to those who had earlier been involved at either the left or right ends of the political spectrum. Tudjman and other HDZ leaders also made it clear that the creation of Croatian state sovereignty, and the retention of the existing Yugoslav federation, were mutually exclusive. "Let us decide ourselves, the destiny of our own Croatia," was the electoral slogan of the HDZ. As for Croatia's neighbors, Tudjman maintained that at most he would try to negotiate a loose confederation – an "alliance of independent states" – with Serbia and the other republics. Unlike the other two major parties – which attempted to balance their promise to advance Croat interests with a commitment to uphold Serbian and minority rights and to negotiate a restructuring of Yugoslav federalism on a less centralized basis – Tudjman and the HDZ presented an essentially Croato-centric program which left no doubt that if elected to power, the Serbs of Croatia would be treated as just one of several minorities, albeit with appropriate constitutional protections.

A public opinion survey conducted on the eve of the first competitive election revealed that in comparison to findings from five years earlier, a radical change had taken place in attitudes regarding the value of a multiparty system (table 3.2). For example, although party competition had only been formally legalized for a few months by the election campaign of 1990, more than one-half of manual workers, two-thirds of clerical workers, over four-fifths of professional people, and 95 percent of managers surveyed, embraced the notion that a multiparty system was the best guarantee for group expression. Interestingly, members of the League of Communists and

Table 3.2 *Attitudes in Croatia concerning the value of a multiparty system, 1985 and 1990 (%)*

Groups	1985			1990 (eve of the election)		
	Positive	Negative	No opinion	Positive	Negative	No opinion
Manual workers	40.5	40.9	18.7	54.5	23.1	22.4
Office workers	31.8	53.0	15.2	64.7	18.1	17.3
Professionals	37.5	50.1	12.3	83.7	8.9	7.4
Managers	18.8	72.3	8.4	94.9	2.6	2.6
Croats	39.3	42.8	17.9	65.7	16.4	17.9
Serbs	30.5	56.7	12.8	48.0	29.7	22.3
Yugoslavs	38.3	40.7	21.0	57.7	26.3	16.0
Others	33.6	55.6	10.9	56.6	21.0	22.4
Members of SKH	27.9	63.4	8.6	65.3	22.0	12.5
Ex-members of SKH	47.6	42.8	9.5	64.2	21.2	14.5
Never a member of SKH	40.2	39.8	20.0	61.3	18.4	20.4

Question: "Do you feel that a multiparty system guarantees the expression of the interests of all groups?"

Notes: The 1985 sample surveyed 2,119 persons; the 1990 sample was of 1,599 persons. Respondents were classified as Croats, Serbs, or Yugoslavs on the basis of self-identification.
Source: *Croatian Society on the Eve of Transition*, ed. Katarina Prpić (Zagreb: Institute for Social Research 1993), pp. 43-55.

managers who had indicated the most skepticism about multiparty competition in 1985, were now the most ardent supporters of the same idea. Overnight, what was politically correct and regime-endorsed had changed – from self-management non-party pluralism to multiparty pluralism – and those who had run the communist regime, and now hoped to manage or survive postcommunism, had dramatically shifted their opinion. Majority support for multipluralism was expressed by all occupational groups, irrespective of age, gener, or former party affiliation. Only among Croatia's Serbian minority, who had been rather well integrated into the operation of communist Croatia, was there less than an absolute majority supporting the virtue of party competition. Thus in 1990, about 30 percent of the Serbs interviewed had a negative opinion on this question, and 22 percent cautiously expressed no opinion at all.

Deeply troubled by the HDZ nationalist agenda, and the threat of radical political changes in the republic, most of Croatia's Serbs opted to give their electoral support to either the familiar League of Communists, or the newly formed (February 1990) Serbian Democratic Party (SDS), a non-communist Serb organization led by the psychiatrist Jovan Rašković. Rašković's main support was among rural Serbs who were concentrated in a chain of thirteen communes in the Croatian regions of northern Dalmatia, eastern Lika, the Kordun, the Banija, and western Slavonia – parts of the so-called "krajina" or "borderland" area of Croatia.[8] Although the Serbs of the Krajina constituted only about one-quarter of all Serbs residing in Croatia, their regional concentration and intense ethnic consciousness made them a very significant factor in the political life of Croatia and Yugoslavia.

The election held in late April and early May 1990 was a rout for the communists. Tudjman's HDZ won a total of 205 out of 356 seats in Croatia's legislature, including a majority in each of that body's three chambers. The communists ranked second with 75 seats, and their smaller "left bloc" allies picked up 26 more seats.[9] The performance of the centrist Coalition for National Accord was much weaker than anticipated, despite the personal popularity of some of its top leaders. As predicted, most Serbs in Croatia voted heavily against the HDZ, choosing to support either the communists or the increasingly vocal and more nationalistic SDS. Interestingly, survey research conducted in April 1990, on the eve of the election, revealed that a large majority of Serbian citizens in Croatia were strongly opposed to plans by Croatian nationalists, such as Tudjman, to work for either the restructuring of the Yugoslav federation on a confederal basis, or Croatia's outright secession from Yugoslavia. Even more disturbing for future political development, the same data also demonstrated that close to half of the Serbian minority population believed that it was discriminated against by the republic's majority Croats, a viewpoint most strongly felt in the heavily Serbian-populated Krajina.[10] For example, other findings from a survey conducted near the end of 1989 – that is, just prior to the onset of legal multiparty competition – revealed a relatively low level of tension among nationalities in Croatia.[11] An obvious explanation for the contrasting results in the two surveys is that the character of the election campaign, and particularly the utilization of ethnonationalist appeals by various party leaders and the media, had significantly polarized interethnic relations within the republic.

Initial postcommunism: the pitfalls of sovereignty and the "ethnic state"

Although the pattern of Serbian voting, especially in the Krajina, was an ominous portent of problems ahead, the HDZ had won an impressive victory in the election. On May 30, 1990, one month following Croatia's first competitive election, deputies at the inaugural session of Croatia's first multiparty parliament elected Tudjman as the republic's president, by a margin of 281 out of 331 votes cast. Significantly, Tudjman and the HDZ leadership viewed their electoral victory not only as a change in the governing party, but also as a mandate to prepare for Croatia's departure from the already enfeebled Yugoslav federation. Thus, having won legitimate authority in a free election, the HDZ leaders quickly turned (1990–91) to the crucial tasks of state-formation: removing the personnel and artifacts of the old regime, installing new symbols of statehood (a flag, insignia, etc.), adopting a new constitution, and holding a referendum on independence. For the Serbs of Croatia's Krajina region – already reeling from the rapid collapse of communist control and the loss of their pre-election influence, angst-ridden because of their community's earlier persecution and suffering during World War II, and believing that the preservation of Yugoslavia was crucial to their survival – Tudjman's strategy and tactics amounted to state formation by means of shock therapy.[12]

Serbian-Croatian tensions took a sharp turn for the worse not long after the first competitive elections when Tudjman's new government proposed draft amendments to the Croatian constitution which made specific reference to the republic as the "national state of the Croatian nation." The same sentence went on to note that Croatia was also "a state of members of other nations and minorities who are its citizens." The Serbs were mentioned as an example of a minority, but only along with seven other groups. The amendments also provided for the adoption of traditional Croatian ethnic symbols (a new coat of arms, flag, and national anthem) as the official insignia of the republic. Ethnic Serbs saw the new symbols as a throw-back to a time when their ethnic community was in an inferior or persecuted position. The Latin script used by ethnic Croats was explicitly identified as the republic's official alphabet, although it was specified that legislation could be adopted providing for the use of the Cyrillic alphabet by the Serbs (and also the alphabets of other minorities). The Krajina Serbs were outraged by the draft constitutional provisions, and the republic's use of symbols. Their deeper fear, however, was that Tudjman was determined to sever Croatia from the Yugoslav state – either through creation of a loose confederation or outright secession – thereby leaving the Serbian minority at the political mercy of the Croatian majority, and the nationalist HDZ government now firmly ensconced in Zagreb.

From the Serbian vantage point, the first steps taken by the new regime were not encouraging. Thus, while many former communist officials retained their posts in the republican administrative organs, the new regime rapidly initiated a purge of Serbs in the police, judiciary, media, and educational system. More importantly, power at the summit of the political hierarchy shifted dramatically. Serbian representation in the political elite was reduced largely to those Serbs belonging to the "opposition" communist caucus in the republic's legislature, and another five Serbian deputies belonging to

Rašković's SDS. Tudjman offered Rašković a position in the new government, but the Serbian leader refused a job which was likely to be purely symbolic.

During the summer of 1990, the Krajina Serbs – encouraged by the Milošević regime in Serbia – announced plans to hold a referendum among the republic's Serbs on the question of their autonomy, and adopted a "Declaration on the Sovereignty and Autonomy of the Serbian People." Croatian leaders claimed, with some justification, that they were witnessing the creation of a "state within a state." Intending to prohibit the Serbian referendum on autonomy scheduled for August, Tudjman proceeded to form special new police detachments that would be entirely Croatian in their ethnic composition. But the regime's measures only served as a pretext for greater resistance by the Krajina Serbs. Plans for the reorganization of the police and justice system were particularly offensive to many Serbian officials, who not only feared for their jobs but also resented having to display the regime's national Croatian insignia. As the planned referendum approached, Serbian vigilante groups began to form in the Knin area and to erect barricades on the roads leading to the predominantly Serbian communes. The protests marked the onset of an armed uprising – the so-called "log revolution" – and the prelude to Serbian-Croatian clashes in Croatia that would become far more serious. By late summer 1990, Croatia had begun to disintegrate into two jurisdictions: one under the control of the Zagreb authorities, and another under the control of rebellious Serbs. It was the beginning of a bifurcated arrangement that over the next five years would severely complicate the process of Croatian state formation and democratic development.[13]

Whether the sharp Serbian-Croatian divisions that emerged within Croatia during the first period of postcommunist government could have been avoided remains an important question. Some observers have suggested that Tudjman's hurried timetable for securing Croatian independence, and particularly his "revolution of symbols,"[14] provoked the Krajina Serbs into anti-regime resistance and armed rebellion. Thus, the use of symbols and insignia that had been associated with Croatia's precommunist history reminded Serbs of a period when they had been subjected to political discrimination or outright violence. Croatia's Serbian leaders place special blame on constitutional changes formally promulgated in December 1990 in the so-called "Christmas Constitution," which technically relegated Serbs to the status of a minority (rather than their previous position as one of the republic's constituent nations). Such assertions are strongly rejected by Croatian leaders, who argue that the constitution guaranteed equality to all citizens of Croatia, regardless of religion or nationality. The deeper and real issue, it seems fair to say, is not the constitutional provisions themselves but the matter of timing, sensitivity to perceptions, and political judgment. Thus, although Serbian anxiety about the new regime may have been deliberately exacerbated by the SDS leaders, and also shamelessly fanned by Belgrade's nationalist media, blame for the breakdown in ethnic relations must also be assigned to Tudjman's Croato-centerism, his high tempo transition schedule, and the ethno-exclusivist nature of his "reconciliation policy." Indeed, Tudjman's key lieutenant during the drafting of the constitution – Vladimir Šeks, a member of the HDZ right-wing – later admitted that the constitutional changes were designed to create an "ethnic state," and not the "pure civil state" urged by the Serbian SDS and various left-wing intellectuals (including the members of UJDI). The constitution, Šeks claims, "does not negate the civil state, [but] it is not in conflict with the original foundation of Croatia as an ethnic state. After all one does not eliminate the other."[15]

As Tudjman pushed ahead with his plans for Croatia's secession from the Yugoslav federation during the first part of 1991, it became increasingly clear that Croatia would be confronted with outside support for the "autonomy" of the Krajina Serbs. Thus in March 1991, after armed clashes between Croatian policemen and Krajina Serbs seeking to join with other municipalities belonging to the "Serbian Autonomous District of Krajina," the Yugoslav federal army intervened to prevent further conflict. These actions marked the beginning of a new pattern: predominantly Serbian JNA units acting with Serbian paramilitary forces in Croatia to obstruct moves by Croatian police and security troops. In May, Tudjman held a referendum on the issue of Croatian independence and received overwhelming support (93 percent of those voting) for his plans to create a "sovereign and independent" country. The Krajina Serbs boycotted the referendum, and held a separate poll in which an alleged 99.8 percent of those voting endorsed the idea of the region's union with Serbia. Less than a month later, Tudjman unilaterally declared Croatia's independence from Yugoslavia (following a similar decision by Slovenia). After brief but intense fighting in Slovenia, the EEC negotiated a cease-fire, and both secessionist republics agreed to temporarily postpone plans for independence. Retreating from Slovenia into Croatia, the JNA joined together with Serbian paramilitary forces to resist Zagreb's assertion of sovereignty over the Krajina. In the ensuing military struggle between July and December 1991, Croatia lost control over roughly one-third of its territory. The bitter war resulted in extensive Croatian casualties (officially 11,702 dead and missing, and 26,448 wounded),[16] savage atrocities, the dislocation of hundreds of thousands of people, and the widespread destruction of property and historical monuments.

The savage bombardment and capture of the eastern Slavonian city of Vukovar by Serbian forces in the fall of 1991 created a particularly deep scar on Croatia's political psyche regarding future treatment of and co-existence with the state's Serbian minority. For ethnic Croats, especially the thousands who had lived in the break-away Krajina and were driven from their homes, revenge against the militant Serb minority became a visceral emotion. In December 1991, just as it became clear that Croatia would be formally recognized by Germany and other European states (the Croatian parliament had again declared independence on October 8), the Krajina Serbs adopted their own constitution and proclaimed the independent Republika Srpska Krajina (RSK). Full-scale hostilities ended with the signing of a peace agreement in January 1992, and deployment of United Nations Protection Force (UNPROFOR) troops in the spring.[17] Over the next four years, the Krajina would function as a politically autonomous para-state entity, although Croatia would re-take some territory in two short offensives (January 1993 and September 1993), and regain a sizeable portion of western Slavonia in a large military thrust during May 1995.

The politics of survival and reintegration: semi-presidential rule and the drift toward party hegemony

The territorial fragmentation and economic disruption of Croatia resulting from the Serbian rebellion of 1990–91, and the so-called "homeland war" during the second half of 1991, would shape the tenor of the country's postcommunist political development during the next five years. Thus, the new regime's initial insecurity, together with the imperatives of military defense, and a natural obsession to reclaim parts of the country that had fallen under the control of rebel Serbs, encouraged the formation of a defensive elite mindset and a siege mentality in Croatia (including a tendency to mythologize and romanticize the recent war and ongoing conflict with the Serbs).[18] The fact that HDZ-led Croatia was in some respects a garrison state, motivated and provided justification for the regime's adoption of many illiberal practices. In many instances, such initiatives also tended to reflect a strong disposition for paternalistic government and semi-authoritarian modes of governance that were already prevalent in Croatian political tradition, as well as in a segment of the HDZ leadership and its political base.[19]

One of the most pronounced features of the regime that soon became apparent after the 1990 election was a concentration of power in the hands of President Tudjman and the executive branch of the HDZ government. Tudjman's proclivity to maintain tight control over the operation of Croatian political life is not surprising considering his key role in the formation and electoral victory of the HDZ, his strong personality, and his early political socialization in the military bureaucracy of the communist state. Tudjman resembled many self-proclaimed "democrats," who have demonstrated records of struggle against oppressive one-party regimes, but who, once in power, are not necessarily ideologically or temperamentally inclined to foster pluralistic political development. Thus, although a former political dissident who had been subjected to over twenty years of official ostracism and periodic imprisonment by the previous communist leadership, Tudjman was ill-prepared to compromise with domestic critics – whether within or outside the HDZ – regarding his agenda for change in Croatia. Indeed, even before the HDZ-designed 1990 constitution had elaborated a "semi-presidential" form of government, Tudjman and his inner sanctum had established an executive-centered political system in Croatia.[20] Once Croatia became an independent state, such tendencies accelerated. For many Croatian journalists, various new features of the presidential office – such as the creation of an elaborately uniformed presidential guard, a large personal staff, bodyguards, expensive cars, and the purchase of a presidential jet – although perhaps justified by the dignity and tasks of the new state, represented ominous expressions of Tudjman's taste for power and the underlying realities of excessive executive control.

While the executive branch quickly came to dominate the postcommunist Croatian governmental system, the organizational prerequisites for democratic pluralism and a division of power had also been established. As a result of the Sabor's multiparty composition, for example, parliamentary life was more lively than under the previous system. However, internally divided, lacking a coordinated strategy, suffering from an acute shortage of material resources, and still unsure about the best manner to control a large and popularly legitimated hegemonic party such as the HDZ, the opposition parties were essentially forced to monitor events, and express dismay at the obvious drift toward strong presidential rule. Indeed, in the wake of the founding election, the political base of the largest opposition parties – the former communist SDP and the liberal HSLS – rapidly eroded, while the membership of the ruling HDZ continued to increase.[21] Moreover, although the major Croatian parties of the center–left expressed strong reservations about Tudjman's hurried timetable for declaring statehood – referring to extend negotiations for an accommodation with the other republics in some sort of confederal system to replace the disintegrated Yugoslavia – once open hostilities broke out with the JNA and the Krajina Serbs, strong pressure developed for Croatians of all political stripes to support the regime. Thus in August 1991, not long after the onset of major fighting with the JNA, the leading opposition parties agreed to join the HDZ in a "Government of Democratic Unity," a coalition arrangement which lasted until the cessation of hostilities and the arrival of UN troops in the spring of 1992. It was significant that, just at the crucial initial point in postcommunist Croatia's evolution, when societal and regional stability might have assisted the renaissance of democratic elements in Croatia's political culture, the war and pressing security concerns necessitated an emphasis on contrived consensus, or tended to reinforce non-democratic tendencies that were also a part of the country's political traditions.[22] A less turbulent period following the acquisition of statehood may not necessarily have guaranteed democratic consolidation in Croatia, but it certainly would have helped such a process.

Three significant aspects of the new regime's operation reflected and accentuated the emerging asymmetry of power between the president and the opposition: (1) the proliferation of intelligence services under the close personal control of the president; (2) executive controls limiting the independence of the judiciary and the "rule-of-law" and; (3) the regime's manipulation of the media. In regard to all three areas, Tudjman and the HDZ leadership used the imperatives of the ongoing Krajina rebellion to justify their course of action.

The key figure in the elaboration of Croatia's intelligence network was Tudjman's trusted associate, Josip Manolić. Manolić had served for many years as a communist police official, and had only become a dissident after having supported the failed 1971 Croatian Spring. Along with Tudjman, he was a co-founder and high official of the HDZ. Appointed in 1991 to head the Bureau for the Defense of the Constitutional Order (after serving for a time as prime minister), Manolić coordinated several agencies designed to protect the country and the regime: (1) the Service for the Protection of the Constitutional System (SZUP, later the Office for National Security, UNS); (2) the Security Information Service (OBS) of the Ministry for Foreign Affairs; (3) the Security and Information Service (SIS), which served as the counter-intelligence service for the Ministry of Defense, and; (4) the Intelligence Service of the Croatian Army (OSHV). Purging the old security service of personnel, especially Serbs appointed under the previous regime, Manolić created, as one observer put it, a security-intelligence network "that Serbs in the republic were more afraid of than the Croats" (unlike in communist Croatia when many Serbs served as high police officials).[23]

Opposition party members and journalists frequently complained that Croatia's intelligence gathering and security services were far larger than the new state required. In view of continuing internal subversion, and also the active role of Belgrade-based intelligence operatives against Croatia, it was not difficult, however, for the Tudjman regime to justify strong counter-measures. Thus, the most important question for political development was who would control the intelligence community, and how the services would be used? In 1993, Manolić, who opposed Tudjman's anti-Muslim policies in Bosnia, and had differences with the president on other matters, was removed from his posts. The move was highly popular in the right-wing of the HDZ, whose leading figure, Minister of Defense Gojko Šušak, now enhanced his own control of the intelligence branches in the military. Šušak had been one of Tudjman's key links to the diasporic Croats, had reportedly played a crucial role in arranging finance for the HDZ's electoral victory, and also was responsible for the Croatian military's first purchases of armaments abroad. Šušak, whose roots were in the highly Croatian nationalist area of Herzegovina, strongly supported Tudjman's policy in Bosnia. Tudjman left no doubt, however, as to who was in overall control. In the spring of 1993, worried about increasing disaffection and factionalism in the HDZ leadership, he appointed his older son, Miroslav Tudjman, to oversee the network of Croatian intelligence agencies (initially as head of a branch called the "Croatian Information Service," HIS).[24] The appointment suggested that the president was less concerned with the appearance of liberal and unbiased democratic rule, than with absolute loyalty and the maintenance of personal control over the levers of power.[25]

Changes in the Croatian judiciary during the first period of the Tudjman regime also initiated some worrisome trends with respect to problems of democratic transition. The initial decision of the Tudjman government to purge judicial officials from the old regime was designed to achieve both ethnic and political goals. Thus, the disproportionately high representation of ethnic Serbs in Croatia's justice system during the communist period made the judiciary an attractive target for nationalist forces in the new Zagreb government. The fact that a large number of the newly elected Croatian political elite were disillusioned communists and former political dissidents, who had been persecuted and imprisoned by the previous regime, also made changes in the judicial sector a particularly high priority for the postcommunist government. Less than six months after taking power in Croatia, for example, the government had already replaced 280 judicial officials.[26]

In October 1990, the Croatian legislature also adopted a controversial new law which gave Tudjman's Minister of Justice wide latitude over the appointment and removal of personnel in the judicial sector. Judges and public prosecutors no longer needed to demonstrate their political suitability in terms of ideological perspectives, but under the new laws the top officials of the regime would now be able to decide whether judicial officials had the proper "human, working, civil and moral qualities" to fulfill their responsibilities. Some members of the legal community in Croatia objected to the broad discretionary power given to the Minister of Justice, and cautioned that the vagueness of the new legislation threatened the independence of the Croatian judiciary to the same degree as the communists' former use of ideological criteria in judicial appointments and dismissal. For example, one observer noted that the postcommunist legislation would result in the creation of a "state judiciary" in which judicial appointments were based on "newly devised" and "flexible criteria."[27] Thus, another provision which made it illegal for judicial personnel to be card-carrying members of political parties clearly was aimed at the removal of former communist judges and prosecutors, and their replacement by new judges supportive of the Tudjman government (although not necessarily members of the HDZ). Reservations were also expressed concerning the lack of parliamentary debate prior to the adoption of the new legislation, as well as about the centralization of future judicial recruitment and the inability of Croatian judges to appeal personnel decisions made by the Minister of Justice.[28] One former reform communist leader even suggested that empowering President Tudjman to appoint judges to the republican Constitutional Court, and also to a judicial council which would select (together with the Minister of Justice) judges and prosecutors, had the potential of creating a new one-party state.[29]

The utilization of state-run television and radio to enhance the views of the government and ruling party, as well as a willingness to periodically take punitive measures against critical voices in the media, also emerged as hallmarks of the postcommunist Croatian state. The politicization and manipulation of the state media was rather rapidly accomplished through the appointment of a HDZ vice-president to head Croatian Radio and Television (HRT), and the intervention of the government and parliament in choosing directors and department heads throughout the public broadcasting network. Although criticism of government policies was not entirely absent in the state media, such views have generally been quite muted. Dealing with the large number of critical voices in the media has been a more difficult challenge for the regime. Seeking to maintain a democratic image and avoid overt censorship, Tudjman and the HDZ elite primarily used economic measures – and particularly the April 1991 privatization law – to suppress aggressive anti-government criticism. This legislation allowed the state-run Croatian privatization fund to select new managing bodies for enterprises undergoing transformation from social to private ownership. Control and pressure by means of privatization were used, for example, with considerable success against the Zagreb weekly *Danas* and the Split-based daily *Slobodna Dalmacija*, both renowned for their outspoken opposition to government policies.[30]

Harassment, and on occasions even criminal prosecution, were also used against individual journalists who consistently and vocally attacked the government and the ruling party. Thus, independent journalists viewed as overly critical of the authorities, or who were deemed to be unpatriotic and "Yugoslav-oriented" sometimes found themselves directly attacked in the state media. Despite the documentation of such regime practices, President Tudjman dismissed charges that independent expression by the Croatian media had been stifled or subjected to manipulation. Croatia had become "a modern democracy," Tudjman claimed in early 1993, that is "underpinned by a free media." After all, he added, "Croatia has ten private newspapers whose editors write about the government openly and freely. Everyone is free to establish or purchase a newspaper."[31] Ironically, the best confirmation that Tudjman's claim had at least partial credence, was the existence of several independent publications – most notably the *Feral Tribune* and *Novi List* – and audacious journalists who routinely subject the regime to ridicule and withering criticism. For example, Jelena Lovric, writing in the *Feral Tribune*, expressed views that have given her special notoriety in the ranks of the media opposition. "Tudjman has already demonstrated his leanings towards ostentatious courtly spectacles. That was in fact the first thing that he demonstrated . . . by his guard, his sash, the flag and coat of arms, protocol, airplanes, residences, boats . . . But this is no longer a matter of love for kitschy and pretentious protocol. There is a system behind this affinity for ostentation . . . Tudjman is in fact turning into a hybrid of president and king, whereby royal manners are increasingly prevalent."[32]

Economic problems, privatization, and the formation of a new power elite

Although the Tudjman regime firmly established a hold on power during its difficult initial stage, economic conditions in the ravaged and truncated state were hardly conducive to a smooth postcommunist transition. For example, Tudjman estimated the cost of direct material damage from the 1991 war at between $US20–22 billion. Industry, tourism and communication all seriously deteriorated, GDP declined steeply compared to 1990,[33] while the unemployment rate was at an all time high (17.8 percent in 1992). The regime's plans to develop a free market economy were also disrupted, thereby severing the potentially positive link between economic progress and political pluralization that can prove crucial to political stability. Moreover, the cost of caring for thousands of refugees who had been displaced in the fighting or had fled Serbian-controlled areas of the country, together with an influx of Croatian and Muslim refugees fleeing the outbreak of war in neighboring Bosnia, put a tremendous burden on the Zagreb government.[34] The combined expenditures associated with the "homeland war" of 1991, ongoing military preparedness aimed at defense and the potential armed reintegration of the Krajina, and the costs of maintaining Croatian troops in Bosnia (both regular Croatian army and Bosnian Croat formations), also constituted an enormous financial drain on the new state.

The nature and consequences of Croatia's privatization program in the years following the war for independence would prove to be one of the most important factors affecting the overall process of transition. At the onset of the postcommunist regime in 1990, those employed outside the public sector constituted about 3.7 percent of the workforce, or only a slight increase from the 2.5 percent in that sector in 1980. Employment in Croatia's small private sector more than doubled during the first year of Tudjman's rule, and by 1992 that figure had risen to 10.8 percent. However, although legislation authorizing a rapid process of privatization was already in place by the spring of 1991, the results achieved during the first year were rather disappointing.[35] For example, by the end of June 1992, the agency managing the process had received about 1,000 requests for privatization, but only 119 requests had been approved (about 3 percent of the 3,619 socially owned enterprises scheduled for transformation), and only 60 enterprises had completed the process. For the time being, this meant that the Croatian Fund for Development became the principal owner of all so-called "socially owned" or non-private enterprises in the country. Thus, rather ironically, the centralized political control of the state over the economy was actually expanding in comparison with the decentralized social ownership pattern during the communist period. Economically, Croatia was undergoing a process of "quiet etatisation" and the recentralization of economic activities.[36]

The process of privatization – that is, the sale of shares to employees in socially owned firms – accelerated markedly in 1993 and 1994,[37] although with some contradictory consequences for Croatia's overall transition. For example, during 1993, about 550,000 small shareholders, mainly employees who wished to keep their jobs, had become the new owners of privatized socially owned property. The sharp erosion of living standards as a result of war-related difficulties, however, meant that many of the small shareholders could not cope with the repayment schedules and were forced to return their shares to the Croatian Privatization Fund. In order to reverse this trend, and preserve popular support for privatization, the government passed special legislative amendments to boost the number of small shareholders. During 1993, there was also a one-time free distribution of shares to war invalids and to the families of dead war veterans.

Despite such measures, however, the impact of privatization on the overall division of political and economic power in Croatia served to reinforce tendencies toward elite control by those associated with the new ruling party. Thus, while there are no in-depth studies providing econometric measurement of privatization's impact on income and welfare, descriptive analyses indicate that privatization has created a very small "private elite" or "new rich" consisting of those individuals who possessed sufficient capital to buy the most profitable socially owned assets (for example, in food processing, textiles, electronics, etc.). Most of this new class of wealthy entrepreneurs are rich expatriates from the Croatian diaspora who helped finance Tudjman's 1990 victory, as well as local entrepreneurs who are either members of, or closely connected with, the ruling HDZ. Some Croatian critics have charged that these émigré entrepreneurs have provided a major political base for right-wing and illiberal tendencies in the country's political life.[38] In the absence of systematic data, it is difficult to generalize about the views and influence of the diasporic Croats on Croatia's political development. However, it seems fair to observe that many of the returning emigres have more interest in personal economic benefit than in the encouragement of democracy (although the two are not necessarily mutually exclusive). Right below the new elite of wealth and connections are members of the techno-managerial stratum who previously directed the socially owned enterprises, and were subsequently able to obtain substantial asset holdings in the privatized sector through management buyout loan schemes.

Although over half a million small shareholders also benefited from privatization,[39] this latter group is constituted of individuals with far less cohesiveness and influence than the top elite and managers. Moreover, it is also important to consider that the roughly half a million Croatians who lost their jobs at different points throughout the 1990s, and also the bulk of the 4.8 million Croatian population who have suffered a sharp decline in their standard of living, have derived almost no direct benefit from the privatization process (by 1995, more than 250,000 people were unemployed, and there were approximately 800,000 pensioners). The uneven results of the privatization process, general economic deterioration, and growing income inequality, also resulted in a contraction and relative economic decline of the former "socialist middle class" (skilled industrial workers, public employees, intellectuals, and so forth), who helped build and operate most of Croatia's existing infrastructure before 1990. The weakening of the former middle class (which also lost members due to substantial economically motivated emigration), along with the initial failure of the economic transformation to create a strong new class of small shareholders, significantly slowed the evolution of a vital and autonomous civil society in Croatia.

In August 1993, President Tudjman admitted that "the passage from the socialist system to a normal society with a free market is not an easy job," and that it is necessary to fight against "the plundering of the people's property." However, Tudjman vehemently rejected criticism that members of the relatively wealthy Croatian diaspora had improperly enriched themselves by using the privatization process to invest money in the new state. Indeed, he has referred to cases where returned Croatian immigrants have faced obstacles to investing their money, and occasions when he has personally intervened to facilitate matters. As for charges that the process of economic transformation has been affected by rampant corruption, Tudjman's reply is that even advanced industrial countries have their mafias and criminal activities.[40] In a frequently used formulation, the president insists that there will only be "a rich Croatia if we have rich Croatians." "There are among us those who are apt, more capable of making money, of finding their way around, or accumulating larger properties, launching new companies and opening factories . . . from biblical times to now there have always been the rich and poor . . . there has always been justice and injustice. This is something that cannot be avoided."[41]

New elections and new political divisions

In mid-1992, notwithstanding the country's serious economic difficulties, Tudjman and the HDZ surprised the opposition parties by abandoning the continuation of the coalition "unity" government, and announcing presidential and legislative elections. The twenty-nine parties contesting the August election included many of the same organizations and political personalities that had competed in 1990. However, the issues in the election had changed, causing most of the Croatian political spectrum to shift markedly to the right. Thus, the "homeland war" had made vigorous support for Croatian nationalism a very respectable and popular sentiment. At the same time, pronounced advocacy of cooperation with Yugoslavia (Serbia-Montenegro), or reform of the communist system had disappeared as viable political options. As a result, left-wing and moderate parties now included defense of the country, reversal of Serbian gains, and other patriotic perspectives in their appeal to the public.

Meanwhile, Tudjman's HDZ had moved from the right to the center. No longer simply a broad nationalist movement focusing upon an end to communism and state-formation, the HDZ now portrayed itself as the ruling centrist party guiding the destiny of an established Croatian national state. Indeed, the HDZ had become a more structured organization which was gradually evolving into a center–right Christian democratic party modelled along Western European lines. To the immediate left of the HDZ was Croatia's second most popular party, the HSLS, whose polls showed to have a narrow if constant segment of about 15–20 percent of the electorate behind it. The HSLS – whose leader, Dražen Budiša, had resigned from the coalition government in 1992 because of Tudjman's failure to consult with his cabinet on the United Nations peace plan – was now running separately from its former partner in the 1990 election, the rather weakened Croatian National Party led by Savka Dabčević-Kučar. Among the parties to the right of the HDZ were two organizations that had appeared to gain in strength since 1990, the Croatian Peasant Party (HSS) which had a strong base in Croatia's rural sector, and the Croatian Party of [Historic] Rights, led by the radical nationalist, Dobroslav Paraga.

Unlike 1990, the electoral debate now focused on the policies and behavior of the new regime's leaders, and not the radical transformation of the existing state. Opposition parties charged that the ruling party was autocratic and corrupt, and that Tudjman himself – who was allegedly preoccupied with the pomp and luxury of high office – was responsible for tolerating the UN-patrolled division and "occupation" of the country. Tudjman was also criticized for encouraging Croatia's intervention in the war in Bosnia, and particularly his willingness to support the planned cantonization or partition of Bosnia, a view favored by Serbia's Milošević and the Bosnian Serbs. Despite such criticism, Tudjman easily won a first-round victory over his competitors for the post of president, receiving 57 percent of the vote to Budiša's 22 percent. None of the other six candidates for president received more than 6 percent of the vote.[42] In the new Sabor, the HDZ controlled eighty-five seats, or 58.7 percent of the total number (compared to the remarkably similar 57.6 percent they controlled in 1990). Only fourteen seats were won by the HSLS, the second most successful party. The ex-communist SDP which had received a vote of about 28 percent in 1990, managed to garner only 5.4 percent in 1992. A feared surge from the extreme right owing to disenchantment with the recent war and occupation did not materialize. The radical ultranationalist, Dobroslav Paraga, received 5.4 percent of the vote for president, and his HSP 6.9 percent of the vote in the proportional races for the Sabor.[43]

The democratic character of the 1992 election was somewhat undermined by the regime's ability to dictate the timing of the election, its special access to the state media, and also the symbolic nature of minority representation.[44] However, the opposition parties were permitted to campaign freely, and the balloting occurred without any regime interference. Voter turnout in the presidential race was 79.4 percent, and 75.6 percent in the legislative election (down from 84.5 percent in 1990). If the election failed to demonstrate significant qualitative progress in Croatia's democratic development, blame could be placed on the extraordinary circumstances which the country had experienced over the proceeding two years. Indeed, Tudjman's ability to replicate his 1990 victory, despite the consequences of the war and so much economic suffering, was undoubtedly due to strong citizen support for his role as the state's founder and as a spokesman for Croatia's national interests. The electoral success was also a real testament to Tudjman's ability at firmly grasping the levers of political control, and convincing Croatian voters that no other party or leader yet deserved responsibility for guiding the new state's destiny.

However, even a record of successful state-formation and patriotism does not provide immunity from the will of a free electorate. Thus, the existence of important islands of popular dissatisfaction with the regime emerged

Table 3.3 *Members of local government assemblies in Croatia by party affiliation and ethnicity, 1993 election*

	County assemblies		Town councils		District councils		Total local assemblies	
	N	%	N	%	N	%	N	%
Party affiliation								
HDZ (ruling party)	453	54.4	826	47.7	3,551	58.2	4,830	55.7
SDPH	19	2.3	68	3.9	77	1.3	164	1.9
Others	361	43.3	836	48.3	2,473	40.5	3,670	42.4
Total	833	100.0	1,730	100.0	6,101	100.0	8,664	100.0
Ethnicity								
Croatian	795	95.4	1,636	94.6	5,830	95.6	8,261	95.3
Serb[a]	8	1.0	18	1.0	29	0.5	55	0.6
Other[b]	27	3.2	74	4.3	216	3.5	317	3.6
Unknown	3	0.4	2	0.1	26	0.4	31	0.5
Total	833	100.0	1,730	100.0	6,101	100.0	8,664	100.0

Notes: Acronyms: HDZ–Croatian Democratic Union (ruling party); SDPH–Party of Democratic Changes (former League of Communists); Others – other opposition parties (and individual candidacies). [a]Serb-majority districts in the rebellious Krajina did not participate in the 1993 elections for local assembles. From 1991 to 1993, it is estimated that Serbs dropped from 12.2 percent of Croatia's population to roughly 8 percent. [b]126 or 1.5 percent of all local assembly members classified themselves as "Istrians" or "Istrian Croats." However, members of the Istrian Democratic Assembly constitute 7.1 percent of all members.
Source: Republic of Croatia, Central Bureau of Statistics.

somewhat more clearly in February 1993, when elections were held for the upper chamber of the Sabor, and for local governments. Twenty-eight of the fifty-eight registered parties ran candidates in the 1993 election. As a result of demands by the opposition parties, a system of proportional representation was utilized. The HDZ again emerged victorious in these elections, but this time a number of opposition parties scored impressive successes. In the competition for the upper chamber, for example, the HDZ obtained thirty-seven of the sixty-eight seats, but the HSLS and the HSS won sixteen and five seats respectively. Even more important, and perhaps a portent of the future, the ruling party lost its monopoly in a large number of local government bodies. Thus, the HDZ failed to win an absolute majority in seven out of twenty-one countries including Zagreb, in two-thirds of the sixty-eight towns, and in roughly half of the 324 municipalities.[45]

As a result of the election, members of the opposition parties now constituted a significant part of Croatia's local political elite (table 3.3), a group that was overwhelmingly composed of ethnic Croats owing to the non-participation of the rebellious Serb regions, and also the nationalist or patriotic orientation of most political parties. The main opposition winners on the local level were Budiša's moderate HSLS and the Croatian Peasant Party. In many areas, the results forced the HDZ to negotiate coalition arrangements with the opposition and to share power. The success of the opposition in the local elections was all the more remarkable because, only two weeks before the voting, the regime had scored its first military success against the Krajina Serbs, a modest offensive in Dalmatia that was conveniently timed in connection with the election.

The setback for the HDZ in the local elections was particularly striking in the western Croatian region of Istria, where regional nationalists organized in the Istrian Democratic Assembly (IDS) made notable headway. The Istrians, who together with the Dalmatian Action (DA) and Rijeka Democratic Alliance (RDS), had already made some modest gains in the August 1992 election, began to agitate for greater regional decentralization or the federalization of the country. Similar views on regionalization had also been advanced as a solution for the Krajina problem by the Serbian People's Party (SNS), an organization of Croatia's urban Serbs which in 1992 had been awarded three seats in the Sabor. With roughly one-third of the country already under Serbian control, Tudjman regarded all suggestions for regional autonomy, and especially for federalization, as bordering on treason.[46] For the moment, Croatia remained a highly centralized unitary state, with a constitutionally strong president, but the election of 1993 revealed new societal divisions and a new grassroots political stirring in the electorate that might potentially challenge the control of the ruling party.

The election of 1993 heartened the opposition parties, but the reality of political life in Croatia was that Tudjman's HDZ had won three elections in a three year period, and was still firmly in power. During the second part of 1993, criticism of the regime intensified, however, primarily as a result of Tudjman's inability to reestablish control over the Krajina, and also the outbreak of Croatian-Muslim hostilities in Bosnia. In September 1993, for example, six prominent Croatian intellectuals published an open letter in which they accused President Tudjman of bringing his country "to the brink of national tragedy and catastrophe," and called upon him to resign. Tudjman's persistent efforts to join with Milošević in a Serbo-Croat partition of Bosnia, the letter alleged, had fostered the rift between Muslims and Croats, and also jeopardized Zagreb's ability to reintegrate the rebellious Krajina Serbs. The root of the problem, the letter bluntly informed President

Tudjman, was his intolerance toward free expression. This attitude had, they maintained,

reversed the course of Croatian democracy in its fledgling state, crippled the competencies of parliament and the government, limited the freedom of the press, and degraded the institution of opposition and the multiparty system . . . In the name of national reconciliation you [President Tudjman] have allowed an invasion of Ustashe symbols, songs, renaming [of streets and institutions], the rewriting of history, chauvinistic statements and methods which change the constitutionally designed democratic identity of the country, and your occasional anti-fascist statements seem like an unconvincing screen and hence do not lessen the detrimental doubts about the possible future fascist development of the Croatian state.[47]

By early 1994, the intensity of political debate in Croatia had markedly escalated particularly with respect to three controversial issues: (1) Zagreb's policy toward the war in Bosnia; (2) how to deal with the Krajina Serbs, and; (3) how to carry forward the privatization of the economy. These issues, along with Tudjman's paternalistic management style, had also led to a deep divisions in the ruling HDZ itself. Thus, as the HDZ underwent a transition from a movement into a ruling party it became increasingly difficult for Tudjman – even with his considerable talents at political juggling and maneuvering – to retain harmony among the party's different political currents and strong personalities. Constituting what almost amounted to a parallel party system, several different factions of the HDZ co-existed under the large tent of reconciliation constructed by the president for the transition to postcommunism. Three major factions were most significant: (1) a group of right-wing nationalists, sometimes referred to as the "Herzegovinian lobby," led by Defense Minister Šušak and the vocal Vladimir Šeks; (2) the centrists, epitomized by those devoted to President Tudjman's policy preferences, and which included the bulk of the "techno-managerial stratum" running most of Croatia's economy and public administration, and; (3) the "soft," "moderate," or "left" faction, led by Josip Manolić and Stjepan Mesić, and which included many of the former communists who had bolted to the HDZ in 1989–90. Generally speaking, the rightists were "hawks" on the question of advancing Croatia's interests in Bosnia-Herzegovina (even at the expense of the Muslims), favored the use of force in order to reintegrate the Krajina (although in this case and on Bosnia they were not adverse to reaching a deal with Milošević in order to achieve their aims), and were supportive of a state-managed slow privatization process which allowed time for expatriate Croats to invest money in the country. In contrast, most moderates supported a non-compromising posture toward Milošević on Bosnian matters, constitutional adjustments with the Serbian minority to solve the Krajina issue, restoration of the Croatian-Muslim alliance against the Bosnian Serbs, and an emphasis on a rapid privatization process providing for a more populist distribution of property. Moreover, while the right-wing of the HDZ was relatively untroubled over the questions of executive domination and occasional rights violations, the moderates feared for the future of democracy and the preservation of the rule-of-law. Meanwhile, avoiding extreme positions, the centrist managerial forces followed a more interest-based and pragmatic mode of behavior, supporting "efficient government," and the current Tudjman-led flow of policy.

During the initial years of postcommunism, Tudjman tried to bridge the sharp differences in the HDZ, although his natural tilt was generally to the right of center. For example, at a HDZ convention in October 1993, Tudjman intervened to prevent a right-wing takeover of the ruling party. During the same year, however, the left faction's leaders, Manolić and Mesić, were also subjected to a humiliating erosion of their power and given sinecure posts as heads of the Sabor's two chambers. The two politicians finally broke with Tudjman and the HDZ in the spring of 1994 and formed their own political party, the Croatian Independent Democrats (HND). Although by this time Tudjman had renewed the Croat-Muslim alliance in Bosnia, he still retained prominent members of the Herzegovinian lobby in his government, including Minister of Defense Šušak, and periodically negotiated with Milošević over the future of the Krajina Serbs. Only about a dozen members of the ruling party defected together with Mesić and Manolić, but the walkout presented the first major threat to the cohesion of the broad HDZ coalition established by Tudjman during the late 1980s.

Mesić and Manolić had collaborated with Tudjman in the creation of the postcommunist Croatian state, held high positions in the ruling party and political system, and were closely acquainted with the inner workings and secrets of the Croatian regime. Tudjman accused his two comrades of failing to transcend their earlier communist affiliations, and an unwillingness to cooperate with those HDZ leaders having a non-communist and more nationalist background. Tudjman's own political background was quite similar to the two defectors, but he saw himself as a centrist linchpin who could bridge the extreme poles – right and left, fascist and anti-fascist – of Croatia's political spectrum and historical legacy. For Tudjman, the HDZ policy of reconciliation required party leaders to regard both the communist Partisans and the wartime fascist-leaning Independent State of Croatia (NDH) as legitimate parts of the Croatian "nation-building tradition." For example, Tudjman was untroubled about changing the name of Croatia's currency from the dinar to the kuna (marten), although the new name had been used by earlier regimes in Croatian history, including the infamous wartime NDH. Moreover, if such a name offended the minority Serbs or others in Croatia, Tudjman was not particularly concerned. The "Serbs in Croatia," Tudjman observed in late May 1994, "must understand one thing, they are a minority

Figure 3.1   *The Croatian Party System 1994-95*

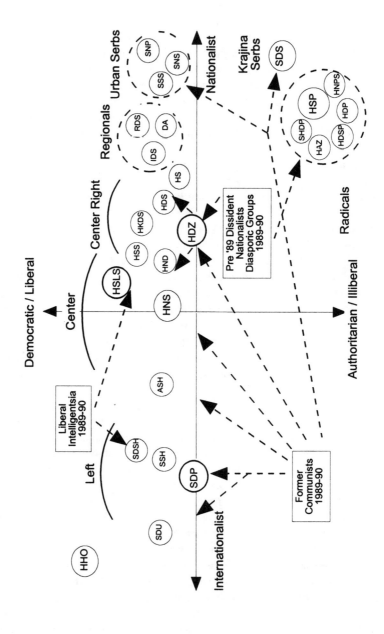

here, and they must recognize Croatia as their homeland. They can take an equal part in it . . . but they cannot, as they did in the past, impose solutions on state policies, and least of all, on the name of the Croatian national currency."[48]

Manolić and Mesić had demonstrated their credentials as ardent Croat patriots, but they claimed to offer an approach to the Serbian question, and even more urgently to the Bosnian Muslim issue, that was far more prudent than the methods employed by Tudjman, not to mention polices advanced by the right-wing of the HDZ. The defectors had similar reservations about Tudjman's habit of making gratuitous negative remarks concerning Serbs, Muslims, and Jews. According to Tudjman, the emergence of "turncoats," such as Mesić and Manolić was not surprising in view of the fact that the HDZ was transforming itself from a broad "movement" into a "party" based on the principles of "Christian civilization."[49] The alleged "turncoats," whose break with the HDZ created a temporary public sensation, saw matters rather differently. Mesić, for example, claimed that Tudjman catered to certain "totalitarian" strivings in the HDZ that sometimes resulted in the use of "Bolshevik" methods. Moreover, the HDZ had increasingly hewed, Mesić suggested, to the model of a one-party system, with President Tudjman's office functioning like a "power center" manipulating both parliament, and the choice of judges. The ruling party leadership had shut itself up behind a "Balkan wall," Mesić maintained, and Tudjman's closest advisers simply told him what he wanted to hear. In earlier years, according to Mesić, the HDZ had responded positively to its two major historic challenges, that is, shedding the communist system, and creating a Croatian state. But the party now faced a new challenge, namely, "what kind of state that should be."[50]

Although the ruling HDZ was internally divided, and also weakened by the Manolić–Mesić defections during 1994, it still remained the dominant force in Croatian political life. The opposition parties were also weak and divided, both internally, and from one another. The Croatian party system remained in its very early phase of development. The ideological pattern of the party system can be seen in figure 3.1, which locates the most important parties in the 1994–95 period on a grid in relation to two factors: (1) the extent of nationalist sentiment manifest by the parties, and; (2) their degree of support for democratic norms. Utilizing this admittedly very general and approximate scheme for differentiating among party organizations, it is possible to identify five distinct political constellations: (1) left-wing parties having an essentially non-nationalist orientation; (2) the ruling HDZ and other center–right parties; (3) regional nationalist parties advocating the federalization of Croatia; (4) Serbian parties, either in the Krajina, or working within the system for Serbian interests, and; (5) radical right-wing Croatian nationalist groups clustered around the Croatian Party of Rights

(HSP). Programmatically, all of the parties espoused democracy, and supported respect for human rights and a free economy. But there was considerable variance among the parties regarding how to implement those goals.

Trends and prospects in Croatia's democratic consolidation (1994–95)

Viewed in comparative terms, Croatia enjoyed an unusually smooth transfer of power from communism to postcommunism. Thus, serious difficulties in the transition process did not begin until after the Croatian communist organization had opened the door for pluralism, and had been defeated in the first multiparty election in over half a century. Many of the political and economic problems which surfaced during the initial years of postcommunist rule in Croatia can undoubtedly be attributed to the circumstances of the Serbian rebellion, and to Belgrade-directed military and political aggression against the country. However, obstacles to postcommunist democratization can also be traced to illiberal proclivities emanating from various sources, including Croatian political culture, segments of the HDZ's ruling elite, and President Tudjman himself. Indeed, some Croatian critics not only blamed such illiberal trends on the circumstances in which the country found itself, but also on the political "immaturity" of both the new elite and the majority of the electorate.[51]

As the regime celebrated its fifth anniversary in mid-1995, the crucial question was whether the anti-democratic or ademocratic overtones apparent in postcommunist Croatia's initial development would gradually abate, or would become magnified during the next phase of the transition process. There was some evidence that, after a difficult beginning, matters were improving and that the prospects for economic health and democratic growth were quite bright. For example, a June 1994 survey conducted by a Croatian polling firm on behalf of the United States Information Agency revealed that Croatians exhibited very high levels of support for a market economy, privatization, and foreign investment. Ethnic Croats also exhibited broad general approval for the principles of a multinational state, interethnic relations based on tolerance, and for the rights and institutions characteristic of a free and democratic society.[52]

However, a close examination of other results from the same survey – which were excluded from the partial report of the findings enthusiastically circulated to the media by Croatian governmental agencies[53] – reveal a far more ambiguous and troubling side of Croatian political development. For example, attitudes on the economy are far from uniformly positive or hopeful. While most Croats expressed support for a market economy and market reforms, only a third felt that privatization was being carried out in the correct manner, and seven in ten felt that it was not being properly implemented. As a rule, those Croats who were most economically satisfied and were profiting from the course of privatization were most likely to have a favorable attitude to President Tudjman. A majority of the respondents (57 percent) also said that the state, rather than the individual, should assume responsibility for providing for the individual.

Moreover, although Croats in the survey expressed strong confidence in the leader of the Catholic church (Cardinal Kuharić), the army, and President Tudjman – all associated with essentially hierarchically ordered institutional sectors – less than a majority of the respondents expressed confidence in the parliament, and one-third indicate a lack of confidence in the judiciary (tables 3.4 and 3.5).

The findings also revealed that those who preferred that the government ensure *order* over political *rights* had the most favorable attitude toward President Tudjman, as did those who expressed agreement with various specifically authoritarian ideas. The strong support expressed for the religious and military establishment are not surprising in view of Croatia's recent turmoil and societal disruption. The fact that substantial numbers of Croatians lacked confidence in all three major media sectors was, however, somewhat troubling. For example, 57 percent of those surveyed had no, or not very much, confidence in television, while the equivalent figures for the press were 47 percent, and for radio, 42 percent. According to the survey, those who felt that television and radio were doing a good job in informing people, were more likely to favor President Tudjman, while support for prominent opposition leaders was higher among those who felt that the newspapers performed best. A potentially bright spot was that although public confidence for the parliament and media was rather weak, the survey data and recent elections revealed substantial and cohesive support in the republic for the major opposition parliamentary parties.[54]

The potentially most worrisome aspect of the survey findings lay in the area of ethnic relations. Thus, despite a clear rejection of ethnic exclusivity in principle, the ethnic Croats surveyed in June 1994 exhibited extremely strong negative feelings toward Serbs. Anti-Serb feeling, not surprisingly, ran highest toward members of that nationality who were living in the rebellious Krajina region. However, Croatian respondents also exhibited strong negative feelings toward Serbs who live in Serbia.[55] Public opinion toward Croatia's urban Serbs was split, with 52 percent of the Croats surveyed expressing an unfavorable view (about the same percentage held a negative view of Bosnian Muslims who are currently allied with Croatia under a confederal structure designed by the United States). Interestingly, a survey conducted by the same researchers during March 1995 indicated that while the opinion of ethnic

Table 3.4   *Levels of public confidence in Croatia's principal institutions/personalities, 1994*

Institutions/personalities	Confidence %	No confidence %
Cardinal Kuharić	95	5
President Tudjman	87	13
Army	93	7
National government	74	26
Judiciary	67	31
Parliament	48	52
Media	43	57

Note: The survey is based on a sample of 1,000 Croatian respondents.
Source: *Public Opinion in Croatia: A Special Report* (Washington, DC: Office of Research and Media Reaction, USIA, November 1994).

Table 3.5   *Croatian attitudes toward other nationalities in the state and region, 1994*

Nationality	% favorable	% unfavorable
Serb minority in Croatia:		
Krajina Serbs (occupied Croatia)	6	94
Urban Serbs (in Zagreb & other cities)	48	52
Serbs in Serbia	21	78
Montenegrins	29	68
Bosnian Moslems	45	54
Albanians	64	34
Macedonians	73	25
Slovenians	60	39
Hungarians	92	6

Note: The survey is based on a sample of 1,000 Croatian respondents.
Source: *Public Opinion in Croatia: A Special Report* (Washington, DC: Office of Research and Media Reaction, USIA, November 1994).

Croats toward the Krajina Serbs remained substantially unchanged, the Croat view of urban Serbs had become far more unfavorable (rising from 52 percent to 68 percent). Such feelings may have contributed to President Tudjman's decision to finally attempt a military push into the Krajina only a few months later.[56]

Overall, Croatian support for minority rights in the June 1994 survey was very uneven. Thus, respondents were willing (86 percent) to give non-Croatian minorities the right to have their own representatives in parliament, and to have their own political parties (81 percent), but two-thirds of those surveyed did not believe minorities should have radio and television facilities in their own language or the right to a separate "autonomous (independent) region still under Croatian sovereignty." An index of ethnic tolerance developed from a number of related questions in the survey, revealed that 37 percent of the Croatian respondents could be described as "tolerant," 10 percent as "intolerant," and 54 percent as "inconsistent."[57] Interestingly, no differences emerged among these three groups in their positive assessment of President Tudjman, a fact which seemed to suggest his rather secure and critical role in the immediate future of the Croatian state.

Reintegration of the Krajina: the Serbian exodus and its consequences

In early August 1995, just a few months after celebrating its fifth anniversary in power, the Tudjman regime launched a major military offensive (operation "Storm") against the Krajina parastate. In only a few days Zagreb had regained control over the rebel capital of Knin, as well as almost all of the Croatian territory which had fallen into Serbian hands during 1990–91 (the exception was the resource-rich area of eastern Slavonia adjacent to Serbia). After having followed a two-track policy with regard to the Krajina for several years – that is, diplomatic negotiation and limited military action against the rebel Serbs – Tudjman had finally chosen the military road to Croatian reintegration. Only six months earlier, Tudjman had reluctantly agreed to the so-called Z-4 plan formulated by diplomats in Zagreb which offered the Krajina substantial self-government rights. But the plan had been cavalierly rejected by the Serb side.

By the early summer of 1995, roughly one-fifth of Croatia was still outside Zagreb's control, but the overall situation had changed significantly. Most importantly perhaps, Tudjman was now confident, unlike in 1990–91, of having tacit agreement from Serbia's Milošević that the Third Yugoslavia would not militarily intervene to assist the Krajina Serbs. A number of additional factors also appeared to influence Tudjman's decision to abandon the frustrating and unsuccessful diplomatic option: Croatian military forces had been significantly strengthened, and in May 1995 had successfully demonstrated (operation "Flash") their new prowess by retaking western Slavonia; Bosnian Serbs were under considerable pressure from the predominantly Muslim forces of the Bosnian government and were unlikely to come to the assistance of the Krajina Serbs; Zagreb expected little opposition to its military plans from the international community, and was particularly reassured by the sympathetic and cooperative posture of the United States and Germany. Although at the eleventh hour the US Ambassador to Croatia, Peter Galbraith – well aware of Zagreb's preparation for an armed strike against the Krajina – finally prevailed on the Krajina Serb leaders to accept a politically modified version of the Z-4 plan, Tudjman was set upon the military option, and believed he had at least "an amber light" to push ahead militarily (just before the military action, Vice-President Gore made an unsuccessful personal call to the Croatian president urging restraint).

One dramatic outcome of the swift Croatian victory in the Krajina was the exodus of almost the entire Serbian population inhabiting the area. By the end of August 1995, it was estimated that between 150,000 and 200,000 Krajina Serbs – descendants of families that had first settled in Croatia over 400 years earlier – had fled the region. Having previously announced that the Krajina Serbs were welcome to remain in their localities, and would be offered the full protection of Croatian democracy, officials of the Tudjman regime vehemently rejected the notion put forward by some observers that Zagreb had ethnically "cleansed" the Krajina. High-ranking American officials maintained that the Serbs had "involuntarily" departed the region, but were careful to distinguish such a mode of departure from ethnic cleansing. Such a characterization really amounted, however, to a distinction without much of a difference. Thus, the bombardment of the Serb civilian population during the military campaign against Knin and other Krajina towns, as well as the subsequent strafing of fleeing refugees by the Croatian air force, and the harassment of Serb civilians by Croatian military personnel and gleeful civilians, undoubtedly motivated or hardened the determination of most Krajina Serbs – already angst-ridden as a result of historically conditioned feelings of victimization, earlier experiences, and the ultranationalist message from their own leaders – to seek safety outside Croatia.

Publicly Croatian officials claimed that the Serbian exodus was totally unintended and unnecessary, but a more typical sentiment suggested by Croatian officials and citizens was that the country's "Serbian question" had been favorably resolved. After all, many Croatians recalled, only five years earlier over 10,000 Croats had died in a war with Serbian paramilitary forces and their Yugoslav army compatriots following Croatia's declaration of independence. Indeed, in that period Serbian militia in the Krajina had ruthlessly burnt down Croatian villages, blown-up churches, not to mention forcing thousands of Croats from the Krajina to flee to other areas of Croatia. Such memories of the 1991 war, and the natural desire of the displaced Croats to return to their homes had been important factors fueling the revanchist syndrome and militaristic mind-set prevalent in Croatia during the first half of the 1990s. It was therefore not surprising that reporters visiting the Knin area directly after its capture by Croatia witnessed the systematic arson and razing of Serb homes, and heard versions of the representative view expressed by one Croat that the few hundred Serbian old people who remained should "celebrate mass to President Tudjman" for having spared their lives.[58] Significantly, the head of Croatia's Roman Catholic church, Cardinal Kuharić, condemned reports of killing, looting, and house-burning by members of the Croatian army. In any case, by the fall of 1995 the Serbian population of Croatia, which before World War II had constituted over one-fifth of the region's total population, had dwindled to under 5 percent. Tudjman's state-building strategy of "reconciliation" developed during the late 1980s had conveniently excluded the Serb minority community. Now the direct and indirect impact of that strategy, and their own anxious, militant, and often self-destructive behavior, had forced the Serbs to leave Croatia. Visiting Knin after its recapture by the Croatian army, an emotional Tudjman used the same kind of divisive nationalist phraseology that had helped to frighten the Serbian minority during the first years of HDZ rule: "This was not only a battle between Serbia and Croatia, but rather a battle between two worlds."[59] For Tudjman and many of his ethnic brethren, Croatia belongs squarely in the *European* world; the August 1995 military victory simply hastened the return of Croatia's Serbs to *Balkan* "civilization."

Zagreb's military reintegration of the Krajina – that had been executed with at least the tacit cooperation of the United States – had a profound impact on both Croatian political development and the balance of power in the Balkans. In the course of a few days, the long festering "Serbian problem," which had historically colored so much of Croatian political life, had essentially disappeared. The country was now far more homogeneous in both an ethnic and religious sense (nearly 90 percent Croat and Catholic), and the ruling party had strengthened its claim that it was governing a "national state." A small Serbian minority still existed, principally living in urban areas, and Zagreb's attitude toward minorities remained an important litmus test of the country's democratic development. But the Serbs in Croatia had been effectively marginalized as a political force.

Equally significant, the victory of Croatian military forces, and the rout of the Krajina Serbs, began a chain-reaction of events – orchestrated by the Clinton administration and its chief envoy for Balkan affairs, Richard Holbrooke – which ultimately led to the signing of a peace agreement among the warring sides in Bosnia and Herzegovina. A more pro-active and anti-Serb American policy in Bosnia had begun in mid-1995, prompted by both the imminent 1996 presidential election in the United States, and also the brutal Bosnian Serb seizure of Srebrenica and other Muslim enclaves in eastern Bosnia. However, once Croatian forces had demonstrated their prowess on the battlefield, the White House and Holbrooke were in a much better position to push their new Bosnian strategy to a successful conclusion. In effect, Croatian forces opened the road to the Dayton peace conference, though it was only after further successful Croatian-Muslim military offensives in Bosnia, NATO bombing of the Bosnian Serbs at the end of August and in early September, and the assistance of Serbia's wily Slobodan Milošević, that all the pieces were in place for ending hostilities.[60]

But Bosnia aside, the US decision to assist Croatia's military build-up for the reintegration of the Krajina, and to temporarily enlist Croatia as a junior ally of the United States, greatly enhanced both the political strength of President Tudjman and the military-security facets of his regime. In shaping its policy toward Croatia in 1995, the Clinton administration's paramount consideration clearly was not the democratization of the Croatian state. Although Washington's policy proved to be highly successful in achieving a temporary end to the savage war in Bosnia – undoubtedly a formidable achievement – to a large extent it actually may have slowed the process of democratic development in Croatia. Indeed, as Tudjman basked in the immediate afterglow of Croatian battlefield successes, it appeared that the Croatian president's tendency to aggrandize and wield power in a rather "ademocratic" if not "anti-democratic" manner, was likely to intensify.[61] The most pessimistic evaluation of trends was advanced by the idiosyncratic and strident opposition figure, Ivan Čičak: "We are entering a dark tunnel in Croatian political life. If you are a Sparta, you don't need a parliament, you just need soldiers."[62]

The election of October 1995

Evidence of Tudjman's illiberal orientation, and also the narrow parameters of Croatia's emergent democracy, became increasingly evident after the Krajina victory. Only six weeks after ending the rebellion of Croatia's Serbs, and a year before he was technically required to do so, Tudjman called for new legislative elections. The Croatian president obviously felt he could exploit the mood of triumphalism and pride that had enveloped Croatia, and also (on the eve of the Dayton meeting) benefit from Croatia's significant military and political role in the unfolding Bosnian story. Such a move was undoubtedly a rational calculation by a politician wishing to maintain power, but it also exposed Tudjman to the dangers faced by all political leaders who hope to derive long-term political capital and legitimacy from a military triumph. Tudjman expected a substantial victory at the polls, but his earlier reservations about democracy's fickle and disorderly character were soon confirmed.

In the October 29, 1995 election, 1,403 candidates ran for seats in the Sabor's 127-person lower "House of Representatives." Turnout was 68.8 percent, or roughly 2.5 million of the over 3.6 million Croatian citizens eligible to vote. Competition for 115 of the 127 seats took place in Croatia: 80 proportionally distributed from state rosters, 28 in single-member constituencies, and 7 in special districts for minority representation. Determination of an additional 12 seats (or 8 percent of the House) was made by Croats living outside the country. For the election, this latter diasporic constituency consisted of approximately 365,000 émigré Croats and their descendants, and was comprised largely (over 83 percent) of Croats living on territory under the control of Croatian military forces in Bosnia-Herzegovina.

Tudjman's HDZ won 45.3 percent of the popular votes cast for the state rosters, and 45.8 percent of the vote in the single-member constituencies (winning 21 of those 28 constituencies). All 12 of the seats allocated to Croats "living abroad" went to the HDZ, since no opposition party managed to win the 5 percent of the diasporic vote necessary to obtain seats. Overall, the HDZ won 75 seats (59 percent) in the House, while the opposition received 45 seats (35 percent), and 7 seats (5.5 percent) went to the national minorities. The regime had abrogated pre-election provisions giving the Serbs a proportion of seats that reflected their demographic strength in 1991, thereby downgrading Serb representation in the House from 13 members to 3 (2.9 percent).

The timing of the election, which caught the opposition by surprise, together with the circumstances surrounding the election, the HDZ's grip over the diasporic Croat constituency, and also the suspension of earlier provisions for minority representation, put the ruling party at a considerable advantage. The state media network, Croatian radio and television (HRT), also were able to manipulate media access to favor the ruling party.[63] But despite these factors – which gave the election a decisively less than democratic coloring – Tudjman's HDZ was far less successful than expected. Beyond the failure of the HDZ to win a landslide, or even an absolute majority of the popular votes, several of its officials failed in their election bids. As a result, the HDZ found itself lacking the two-thirds majority in the Sabor necessary to single-handedly amend the constitution. Coalitions of opposition parties succeeded in capturing a majority of votes in the politically restless region of Istria, as well as in several large cities, including Rijeka, Split, and for the first time, Zagreb. Geographically, HDZ support was highest in the more rural and less economically developed areas of the country, and in areas that had been adversely affected by the war. Socially, the ruling party did best among older and less educated voters.

In percentage terms, the number of votes won by the HDZ was slightly better than its showing in the 1990 and 1992 elections for the popularly

Table 3.6 *Party composition of the Croatian Sabor's major chamber (the Socio-political Chamber in 1990, the House of Representatives in 1992 and 1995)*

Political party	1990		1992		1995	
	N	%	N	%	N	%
Croatian Democratic Union (HDZ)	54	67.5	85[a]	61.5	75[a]	59.1
Social-Democratic Party (SDP)[b]	20	25.0	11	7.9	10	7.9
Croatian Social-Liberal Party (HSLS)			14	10.1	12	9.4
Croatian Party of Rights (HSP)			5	3.6	4	3.1
Croatian People's Party (HNS)			6	4.3	2	1.6
Istrian Democratic Assembly (IDS) & smaller regional parties[c]			6	4.3	4	3.1
Croatian Peasant Party (HSS)			3	2.2	10[d]	7.9
Deputies of parties representing the Serbian minority[e]			3	2.2	3	2.4
Others	6	7.5	5	3.6	7	5.5
Total	80	100	138	100	127	100

Notes: [a]Fluctuation in the party identification of 24 deputies changed the Sabor's party composition between 1992 and 1995. For example, in 1994 the defection of 10 HDZ deputies to the newly formed Croatian Independent Democrats (HND) reduced the ruling party to 75 deputies or 54.3 percent of the chamber. The break-away HND captured 1 seat in the 1995 election. Thus, in 1995 the HDZ caucus retained the same number of seats (75) it held just prior to the election, but within a chamber having 9 fewer members. [b]And smaller allied parties on the left. In 1990, the SDP was part of the SKH-SDP (League of Communists of Croatia – Party of Democratic Change). [c]Dalmatian Action and the Rijeka Democratic Alliance. [d]As part of a five-party joint alliance. [e]Does not reflect several ethnic Serb candidates of other parties who were elected to the Sabor.

elected legislative chamber (though changes in the electoral system make it difficult to compare successive races). But despite the events in the Krajina, and Croatia's changed ethnic composition, the HDZ failed to expand its appeal to the ethnic Croat majority. Having designed the electoral rules in its own interest, the HDZ was able to obtain a substantial "manufactured majority,"[64] in terms of seats won (table 3.6). That majority position dropped only slightly compared with the elections of 1990 and 1992. However, segments of the regionalist, centrist, and left-oriented opposition forces significantly improved their relative strength, especially in urban areas. For example, in 1995, the Istrian Democratic Assembly (IDS) consolidated a stronger hold in Istria, while the moderate Croatian Peasant Party (HSS) made significant progress in many areas. The HSS, in coalition with other center–right parties, even replaced the Croatian Social-Liberal Party (HSLS) as the strongest opposition force. The Social Democratic Party (SDP), which grew out of the former League of Communists, also made some modest gains.

Had the HDZ not manipulated the electoral system in order to inflate the party's strength, it is likely that the regime's grip on control would have been seriously weakened. Indeed, despite the special electoral measures taken by the authorities, and the notable political and military achievements of the Tudjman regime, more than half of the Croatian electorate appeared to be searching for alternatives to the ruling HDZ. Many Croats undoubtedly felt that with the struggle for the territorial reintegration of Croatia nearly complete, and the war in Bosnia reaching a conclusion, the time had come to find a new approach that would remedy the economic difficulties of the early 1990s (table 3.7). Although by the end of 1995 over 50 percent of national income was being generated from the private sector, the war and the process of establishing a market economy had created serious economic disruption. The fact that the hierarchy of the Roman Catholic church had begun to take a more arms-length posture toward the regime may also have proved useful to opposition parties.

The overall electoral results were clearly a disappointment to Tudjman. But in Zagreb the outcome of voting for local assemblies provoked a real crisis. Briefly, Tudjman was faced with the fact that a coalition of seven opposition parties had won thirty-one seats in the fifty-person Zagreb City Assembly; only seventeen seats were captured by the HDZ, and two went to the right-wing Croatian Party of Rights (HSP). This situation technically gave the opposition an opportunity to gain control of both the City Assembly, and also the eighty-person Zagreb County Assembly (which includes the members of the City Assembly). Should Tudjman cede control of Zagreb – a former HDZ stronghold – to the opposition, the ruling party's organizational apparatus and record would undoubtedly be subjected to unfriendly scrutiny. At a minimum, property and operations previously controlled by the HDZ would be at the disposal of his adversaries. In order to forestall such a possibility, Tudjman decided to invoke a legal provision permitting him to block the selection of top Zagreb officials. Returning home during the deliberations in Dayton, Tudjman explained his planned obstruction: "It is important that our public understands that the situation in which Croatia finds itself regarding the problems of the liberation of the remaining occupied territories and the crisis in Bosnia-Herzegovina is such that we cannot allow that sort of opposition which would rock Croatia's stability to take root in the city of Zagreb, capital of Croatia, where a quarter of the population of Croatia lives."[65] When, despite Tudjman's plans, opposition deputies met at the Assembly and chose a mayor and speaker of the City Assembly from

Table 3.7 *Indicators of economic trends in Croatia since 1990*

	1990	1991	1992	1993	1994	1995[a]
GDP	-8.6	-14.4	-9.0	-3.2	0.8	2.0
Industrial output	-11.3	-28.5	-15.0	-6.0	-3.0	0.3
Rate of inflation	136	149	937	1,150	-3.0	3.7
% Unemployment	9.3	15.5	17.8	17.5	17.2[c]	12.5
% Workforce in private activity[b]	n.a.	21.8	26.9	37.5	46.6	n.a.
% GDP from private sector[b]	18.8	25.2	34.9	41.2	44.9	n.a.

Notes: GDP – % change over previous year; Industrial output – % change over previous year; Rate of inflation – % change in end-year retail/consumer prices; Unemployment – as of end of year. [a]Estimate. [b]Data prior to 1993 for private firms only; data for 1993–94 include mixed firms with over half private ownership. [c]November 1994.
Sources: European Bank for Reconstruction and Development, *Transition Report 1995: Economic Transition in Eastern Europe and the Former Soviet Union* (London: EBRD, 1995); European Bank for Reconstruction and Development, *Transition Report Update, April 1996: Assessing Progress in Economies in Transition* (London: EBRD, 1996); Republic of Croatia, Central Bureau of Statistics (Zagreb, Croatia).

among their own ranks, HDZ members boycotted the session, and Tudjman refused to confirm the newly selected officials. The opposition appealed to the Constitutional Court, but without success. Public opinion polls indicated that Tudjman's action was widely resented in Zagreb, and also that another election would actually improve the position of the opposition. In early March 1996 – after turning down an opposition mayoral candidate for a second time – Tudjman completely circumvented the electoral results and named his own Commissioner to manage Zagreb's affairs. Opposition leaders asserted that the City Assembly would not confirm Tudjman's appointment, and that eventually the Zagreb crisis would determine whether the existing level of democracy in Croatia would "stay or vanish."

The president's adamant refusal to bow to the electoral outcome in Zagreb appeared to confirm accusations by his critics that he was fundamentally uncommitted to a democratic system, that he professed a devotion to democracy largely in order to secure Western recognition and financial support, and also that Croatian pluralist development was unlikely to flourish so long as he remained in power. Whether the October 1995 election would prove to be the beginning of the end for the HDZ's control of Croatia, as some observed, and indeed whether Tudjman was in the process of committing "political suicide," remained to be seen. But after five years of postcommunist rule, the Zagreb stalemate indicated that democratic transition in Croatia was still very tenuous and incomplete. Tudjman still enjoyed widespread respect and support, but the long-term prospects for his regime and Croatian democratic development were very much in doubt. Deep divisions also existed within the HDZ leadership between moderates and hard-liners about how to deal with such serious problems as the City Assembly crisis, the American-engineered alliance with the Muslims in Bosnia, requests by the Hague tribunal for the extradition of indicted Croatian war criminals, and urgent matters of economic reconstruction and development.

At the HDZ party convention in February 1996, Tudjman still appeared feisty and in charge. But he also was increasingly defensive and emotional in responding to the attacks of his critics. Brushing aside the results of the recent election, Tudjman pointed to polls that revealed his personal popularity. His paramount theme, however, was the continued threat to Croatia from forces that were allegedly attempting to sabotage the country's independence, that wished to return to some kind of Yugoslavia or "Euroslavia," and who hoped to eventually topple the HDZ from power.[66] Commenting on the festering crisis in Zagreb, Tudjman stressed that his party had garnered twice as many votes as the second place party in the capital (which led the seven-party opposition coalition). He denounced the motives of striking railway workers, left and right political parties, and various intellectuals who were endeavoring to present an alleged "democratic alternative" to the HDZ. But Tudjman assured his party colleagues that he could effectively deal with those elements who desired to subvert the regime and to alter the course of development that had been launched by the HDZ in 1990. It appeared that the struggle between the impulses of "Franjoism," and the imperatives of democratic pluralism, would continue to animate Croatia's postcommunist political evolution.

Afterword: soft dictatorship or quasi-democracy?

Throughout 1996, the Tudjman regime continued to exhibit the same executive-centered and anti-pluralist impulses that had been characteristic of Croatian political life during the first half of the 1990s. For example, in spring 1996 the regime obtained parliamentary approval for a new libel law that made it a crime for journalists to "offend" leading officials. Several top political posts were identified in the new law prohibiting the defamation of state leaders, including the president of the Republic, the prime minister, the president of the Parliament, and the presidents of the Supreme Court and Constitutional Court. The legislation did not, however, define precisely what constituted criminal defamation. Two editors of the satirical weekly, *Feral*

Tribune, who had allegedly defamed President Tudjman were soon charged under the new law. Tougher legislation was also adopted against the dissemination of state secrets.

President Tudjman also remained steadfast in his refusal to acknowledge the 1995 electoral success of the opposition parties in Zagreb. In April 1996, after having vetoed four successive opposition candidates to serve as mayor of Zagreb, Tudjman instructed the government to dissolve the Zagreb Assembly and to appoint a commissioner to run Zagreb. In a remarkable flourish of judicial independence, the Constitutional Court of Croatia (by a 6-4 decision) annulled the government's dissolution order and also the appointment of a commissioner. The court's move prompted the Council of Europe to delay Croatia's application for full membership temporarily, but Tudjman adamantly rejected the idea of allowing the opposition to control Zagreb. An effort by the president to resolve the Zagreb crisis in June through a non-binding referendum turned into a fiasco when less than 19 percent of the capital's eligible electorate turned out to vote.

Although the stand-off between the regime and the opposition continued, it seemed that the president's tenacity was paying off. Thus, in early November, the Council of Europe finally extended membership to Croatia after the regime promised to cooperate with the International Tribunal on War Crimes at the Hague (several Croats had already been indicted) and also to respect human and minority rights. But though "Europe"now seemed to have accepted the Croatian regime on its own terms, tensions arising from the politically schizophrenic character of the country had not abated. Infuriated with those he referred to as "brainless" opposition elements who encouraged foreign criticism of Croatia, Tudjman remained determined to place limits on media pluralism and democratic expression. In November, not long after the editors of the *Feral Tribune* were acquitted – thanks mainly to international pressure and a growing independent spirit in the judiciary – Tudjman proceeded to ban the popular independent news source, Radio 101. However, the regime was forced to back down and extend the radio station's license as a result of a demonstration in Zagreb by a crowd estimated at over 100,000 citizens. But by the end of the month, regime harassment of individual opposition journalists was renewed. Returning to the country after a trip to the United States for medical treatment, Tudjman angrily promised to clamp down on "false prophets of pseudo-democratic illusionism, who are today preaching great ideas about human rights and media freedom."[67] In November the regime-controlled State Judicial Council also removed the head of the Supreme Court for alleged sexual offenses, although he contended that the dismissal was political retribution for his failure to ensure the judiciary's subservience to the regime.

The massive scale of public protest in Zagreb, along with spreading strikes for higher wages by public sector employees and also demonstrations by Croatia's large population of pensioners, revealed the growing disenchantment with the Tudjman regime at the end of 1996. The regime's admission of widespread corruption in the ruling party (in November thirty-three HDZ officials were suspended, including the Zagreb mayor appointed by Tudjman) also fueled public cynicism. Evidence of growing anti-regime sentiment, together with the country's serious economic situation (one survey indicated that two-thirds of Croats felt that they were poorer than before independence in 1991), and also indications that the seventy-four-year-old president was suffering from serious health problems, suggested that Croatia's turbulent postcommunist transition was approaching a crossroads. Important elements of democratic development had clearly become more established in Croatia, as shown by the tenacity of the opposition forces, the increasing independence demonstrated by some members of the judiciary, and the routine reliance on peaceful public demonstrations as a mode of protest. But the attitude of President Tudjman (whose candidacy in the 1997 presidential election was uncertain) and his more hard-line supporters regarding the illegitimacy of certain kinds of democratic expression also indicated that important facets of authoritarianism continued to survive in the country.

Acronyms of Croatian political parties and organizations

ASH	Action of Social Democrats of Croatia (Akcija socijaldemokrata Hrvatske)
DA	Dalmatian Action (Dalmatinska Akcija)
HDP	Croatian State-Building Movement (Hrvatski Državnotvorni Pokret)
HDS	Croatian Democratic Party (Hrvatska Demokratska Stranka)
HDSP	Croatian Democratic Rights Party (Hrvatska Demokratska Stranka Prava)
HDZ	Croatian Democratic Union (Hrvatska Demokratska Zajednica)
HHO	Croatian Helsinki Committee (Hrvatski Helsinki Odbor za Ljudska Prava)
HKDS	Croatian Christian Democratic Party (Hrvatska Krščanka Demokratska Stranka)
HND	Croatian Independent Democrats (Hrvatski Nezavisni Demokrati)
HNPS	Croatian National Movement/Freedom of Croatia (Hrvatski Narodnia Pokret)
HNS	Croatian People's Party (Hrvatska Narodna Stranka)
HRT	Croatian Radio and Television
HRZ	Croatian Republican Community (Hrvatska Republikanska Zajednica)
HS	Croatian Party (Hrvatska Stranka)
HSLS	Croatian Social-Liberal Party (Hrvatska Socijalno-Liberalna Stranka)

HSP	Croatian Party of Rights (Hrvatska Stranka Prava)
HSS	Croatian Peasant Party (Hrvatska Seljačka Stranka)
IDS	Istrian Democratic Assembly (Istarski Demokratski Sabor)
JNA	Yugoslav People's Army (Jugoslovenska Narodna Armija)
KNS	Coalition for National Accord (Koalicija Narodnog Sporazuma)
MASPOK	Mass Movement (Masovni Pokret)
OBS	Security Information Service, Ministry for Foreign Affairs
OSHV	Intelligence Service of the Croatian Army
RDS	Rijeka Democratic Alliance (Riječki Demokratski Savez)
RSK	Republika Srpska Krajina
SDSH	Social Democratic Party of Croatia (Socijaldemokratska Stranka Hrvatske)
SDP	Social Democratic Party/Party of Democratic Change (Socijaldemokratska Stranka Hrvatske)
SDS	Serbian Democratic Party (Srpska Demokratske Stranke)
SDU	Social Democratic Union of Croatia (Socijaldemokratska Unija Hrvatske)
SHDP	Party of Croatian State's Rights (Stranka Hrvatska Državna Prava)
SIS	Security and Information Service, Ministry of Defense,
SKH	Croatian League of Communists (Savez Komunista Hrvatske)
SKH-SDP	League of Communists of Croatia-Party of Democratic Change (Savez Komunista Hrvatske-Stranka Demokratskih Promjena)
SKJ	Yugoslav League of Communists (Savez Komunista Jugoslavije)
SNP	Serbian National Party (Srpska Narodna Partija)
SNS	Serbian People's Party (Srpska Narodna Stranka)
SSH	Socialist Party of Croatia (Socijaldemokratska Stranka Hrvatske)
SSS	Independent Party of Serbs (Samostalna Stranka Srba)
SZUP	Service for the Protection of the Constitutional System
UJDI	Association for a Yugoslav Democratic Initiative (Udruženje za Jugoslovensku Demokratsku Inicijativu)
UNPROFOR	United Nations Protection Force
UNS	Office for National Security

NOTES

1 Nikola Dugandžija, *Kriza i religija* (Zagreb: Institut za društvena istraživanja Sveučilišta u Zagrebu, 1987), and Dragomir Pantić, *Klasična i svetovna religioznost* (Belgrade: Institut društvenih nauka, 1988).

2 *Bilten za članstvo* (Zagreb: Hrvatska demokratsa zajednica, June 1989), and Mate Piškor, "Stranka hrvatske sudbine," *Obzor*, no. 7 (29 May 1995), 11–12.

3 Tudjman claims that soon after the war, when he was working at the headquarters of the Yugoslav People's Army, he was visited by his father, and that the elder Tudjman warned that Croatia had fallen under communist and Serbian domination. The younger Tudjman claims that he only became suspicious about his parents' death years later when he had become an historian, and that only in 1986 was it confirmed that two Croatian hardline communists had carried out the killing on orders from the chief of the secret police in Croatia, a Serb. S. Coll, "Franjo Tudjman, at War with History," *Washington Post*, 1 March 1993, p. B1.

As director of an institute for party history in Zagreb (1961–67), and a professor of history at Zagreb University, Tudjman devoted himself to publicizing research demonstrating that the communist regime had unfairly portrayed recent Croatian history. In particular, he alleged that estimates of the number of Serbs who had died at the hands of the fascist-oriented Independent State of Croatia (NDH) during World War II had been deliberately inflated. Although he occupied a number of senior political functions in Croatia's communist regime, Tudjman soon found himself at odds with both the communist leadership (in 1967 he was expelled from the SKH) and its intellectual establishment.

4 Tudjman told the first general assembly of the HDZ in February 1990 that the Independent State of Croatia (NDH) "wasn't just an ordinary 'Quisling' creation and a 'fascist crime,' but an expression of the historic striving of the Croatian people for an independent state." *Reuters*, 27 February 1990. Writing during World War II, the Croatian sociologist Dinko Tomasić provided a good historical treatment of Dr. Ante Pavelić's Ustasa movement, which established and controlled the World War II NDH, and which influenced a fragment of the Croatian diasporic community that left Croatia after 1944: "This movement became definitely anti-Yugoslav, anti-pan-Slav, anti-Bolshevik, and anti-liberal. Its followers believed in the use of force and violence as a means of fighting the terror employed by Belgrade regimes . . . an anti-Semitic note was added, but it never became very strong because the anti-Serb attitude inherited from the past dominated the movement." "Croatia in European Politics," *Journal of Central European Affairs* (April 1942), 77. Tudjman has emphasized that not all Ustashi in the NDH were fascists, "not all committed crimes, just as . . . not all Chetniks were fascists and perpetrators of crimes . . . both sides had their positive ideas." *Vreme News Digest Agency*, no. 82 (19 April 1993), 12.

5 *Croatia on Trial: The Case of the Croatian Historian Dr. F. Tudjman* (London: United Publishers, 1981), p. 30.

6 Zdravko Tomac, *Iza zatvorenih vrata: tako se stvarala Hrvatska država* (Zagreb: "Organizator," 1992), pp. 35–55.

7 It is estimated that from the end of 1989 to June 1990, membership in the SKH–SDP fell from 298,000 to 46,000, and during 1990 roughly 70,000 members of the SKH–SDP joined the HDZ. Vladimir Goati, *Jugoslaviji na prekretnici: od monizma do gradjanskog rata* (Belgrade: Jugoslovenski institut za novinarstvo, 1991), p. 39.

8 In 1991, the Serbs of the Krajina constituted an absolute majority in eleven of those communes, and a relative majority in two of them.

9 In the most important branch of the legislature, the eighty-seat Socio-Political Chamber, the HDZ won a majority of more than two-thirds (fifty-four seats), compared with nineteen seats for the communists and left bloc, and only seven seats for the other parties. The nature of the electoral system – an absolute majority single-member district, with a double-ballot model similar to the one employed in France – was a contributing factor to the Croatian communists' electoral debacle. Because the system favors strong popular parties on the first ballot and coalitions among like-minded parties on the second ballot, the organizational strength and popularity of the HDZ, and the desire of most opposition parties to defeat the old regime at any cost, helped to ensure a major communist defeat.

10 Ivan Grdešić et al., *Hrvatska u izborima '90* (Zagreb: Naprijed, 1991), pp. 150–61, 171.

11 Nikola Dugandžija, "The Level of National Absorption," in *Croatian Society on the Eve of Transition*, ed. Katarina Prpić et al. (Zagreb: Institute for Social Research, 1993), pp. 136–41.

12 Deprecatory comments made by Tudjman and his party comrades about the Serbs during the electoral campaign only contributed to Serbian anxiety about Croatia's plan for statehood. Equally important as a factor in interethnic polarization were steps taken by the Serbian regime in Belgrade and the top echelons of the Yugoslav People's Army (JNA) to excite the fears and concerns of the Krajina Serbs regarding their future in a postcommunist Croatian state decoupled from Yugoslavia.

13 According to Serbian leaders, their August referendum attracted a "100 percent turnout" of those eligible to vote and resulted in a near-unanimous outpouring of support for the notion of political autonomy. Fearing that direct police action to stop the vote would invite federal military intervention on the Serbian side, Tudjman did not interfere with the referendum. But he described the voting as an event that "had no legal basis whatsoever" and "will mean nothing for the Croatian republic." Foreign Broadcast Information Service, *Daily Report: Eastern Europe* (hereafter *FBIS-EEU*), 22 August 1990, p. 28.

14 Vesna Pusić, "A Country By Any Other Name: Transition and Stability in Croatia and Yugoslavia," *East European Politics and Societies* 6, no. 3 (Fall 1992), 242–59.

15 *FBIS-EEU*, 31 December 1992, p. 35. Kosta Čavoški has argued that in the early 1990s, the framers of both the Serbian and Croatian constitutions produced documents that had a "civil form externally," but their "fundamental aim is *national* or *ethnic*." Čavoški sees the lack of any provision for minority territorial autonomy in the 1990 Croatian constitution, and a "lack of clarity" about cultural autonomy, as factors generating fear of assimilation among the Serbs of Croatia. "Nationalism and Constitutionality: The National and the Universal in the Constitutions of Serbia and Croatia" (unpublished paper prepared for the Centre for Slavonic and East European Studies, Macquarie University).

16 Franjo Tudjman, Croatian Radio, 22 December 1994.

17 In April, Croatia was recognized by the United States, and it became a full member of the UN in May.

18 Ivan Rogić, "Vukovar '91. i Hrvatski nacionalni identitet," *Društvena Istraživanja* 2, nos. 4–5 (March-June 1993), 501–20, and *Croatian War Writing 1991/1992* (Zagreb: Zavod za Znanosti i Književnost, 1995).

19 Josip Županov, "Dominantne vrijednosti Hrvatskog društva," *Erasmus*, no. 2 (June 1993), 2–6.

20 Formally, the Croatian governmental structure includes a separation of powers into three branches. The executive branch is headed by the president, elected for a term of five years, who shares authority with an appointed government, composed of the prime minister, deputy prime ministers, and ministers. The legislative branch, the Croatian Sabor, consists of two houses, the House of Representatives and the House of Counties, members of which are elected for a term of four years. The judicial branch consists of courts of general jurisdiction and specialized courts. There is a Supreme Court, which ensures the "uniform

application of laws and equality of citizens," and a Constitutional Court, deciding matters pertaining to the conformity of laws and other regulations with the constitution, and also rules on jurisdictional disputes among the different branches of the government. Although consisting of distinct branches, the Constitution of 1990 was explicitly conceived not as a "classical parliamentary system," but as a "semi-presidential model," which would reduce the "instability of parliamentary government, create political security, and ensure the harmony of the political process." Davor Gjenero, *Hrvatska u demokraciji* (Zagreb: Azur, 1992), p. 15.

21 A political socialization study of young people in Croatia (grades 4–6) conducted shortly after the 1990 election revealed very high support for the HDZ, and almost none for the former communists or other parties. The author of the study viewed the results as an indication of an emerging pattern of party identification tending to magnify the relative strength of the HDZ in relation to preferences expressed in the actual election. Vladimir Vujčić, *Politička kultura i politička socijalizacija* (Zagreb: "Alinea," 1993), pp. 120–1.

22 Not long after the 1990 election, Savka Dabčević-Kučar, the leader of the opposition HNS, emphasized that the chief problem of the opposition is that "Croatia doesn't have a legacy of democratic practice. We must take account of the fact that democracy in Croatia is extraordinarily young and fragile . . . The opposition is underdeveloped because some parties are internally conflicted, while others are still in rudimentary form." She also mentioned that early on in the postcommunist period some parties deliberately refrained from attacking the new government for fear of hurting Croatia's new sovereignty. "In the marketplace of political ideas the final contours of individual parties are still not stabilized." *Hrvatska gibanja*, ed. Davor Butković (Zagreb: Azur, 1990), p. 117.

23 *FBIS-EEU*, 19 April 1993, p. 38. See also, Marko Milivojevic, "Croatia's Intelligence Services," *Jane's Intelligence Review* 6, no. 9 (September 1994), 404–9.

24 In 1990, Miroslav Tudjman had disagreed with his father on political questions, and had been a member of the Social Democratic Party.

25 The charges of nepotism often levelled against the president by his critics usually include allegations that his younger son, daughter, and grandson are all managing firms that have been given special access to government contracts, or a niche in lucrative sectors of the economy.

26 This included fourteen presidents of District Courts, eighty-seven presidents of Communal Courts, the presidents of the Economic Court and the Administrative Court of Croatia, seven presidents of District Economic Courts, thirteen district prosecutors, and fifty-eight communal public prosecutors.

27 Z. Nikolić, "Vlada i sudstvo: nezavisnost bez zaštite," *Danas*, no. 453 (23 October 1990), 26.

28 D. Gregović, "Što je sucima zabranjeno," *Vjesnik*, no. 643 (3 October 1990), 8, and A. Crnjaković, "Zakon o sudovima pred sudom," *Vjesnik*, 16 December 1990, 8.

29 M. Tripalo, "Kakav Hrvatski ustav," *Danas*, no. 450 (2 October 1990), 15. In March 1995, the Croatian Minister of Justice, Ivica Crnić, resigned after all of his candidates for the Supreme Court were rejected by the State Council on the Judiciary – a body of magistrates created to appoint and discharge the members of the judiciary. Crnić's candidates were rejected in favor of nominees proposed

by the President of the Supreme Court, a former legal adviser to President Tudjman. In his letter of resignation, Crnić denounced a trend toward "non-democratic and totalitarian processes" and said that the earlier election of the State Council on the Judiciary was "rigged." When he was appointed, Crnić was the only person in the cabinet who was not a member of the ruling HDZ. *Agence France Presse*, 3 March 1995.

30 Ken Kasriel, "Croatia," *Index on Censorship*, no. 2 (1993), 18–19.

31 *Facts About the Media in Croatia* (Zagreb: Department of Information, Ministry of Foreign Affairs, May 1993), p. 16.

32 *FBIS-EEU*, 3 March 1995, p. 40. The diverse response of Croatia's journalists to regime manipulation of the media is detailed in Darko Hudelist, *Novinari pod sljemom* (Zagreb: Globus, 1992).

33 The last year with a positive GDP growth rate was 1989. Subsequent increasing negative growth rates reflected the transitional crisis and war. Ante Cicin-Sain, "Croatia," in *Political and Economic Transformation in East Central Europe*, ed. H. Neuhold et al. (Boulder: Westview Press, 1995), p. 161. See also table 3.7 in this chapter.

34 In September 1992, there were 626,796 refugees and displaced persons in Croatia. Croatian Radio, 22 December 1994.

35 By the eve of the 1990 election, support for privatization had markedly increased, according to public opinion surveys. Branimir Kristofić, "Privatization, Work, Surveillance," in *Croatian Society on the Eve of Transition*, ed. Katarina Prpić et al. (Zagreb: Institute for Social Research, 1993), pp. 48–58.

36 See Nevenka Čučković, "Privatization in Croatia: What Went Wrong?" *History of European Ideas* 17, no. 6 (1993), 725–33, and by the same author, "Privatization Process and its Consequences for Distribution of Welfare: The Case of Croatia," *EACES Conference on Privatization and Distribution* (Trento, 3–4 March 1995). See also Ivo Bićanić, "Privatization in Croatia," *East European Politics and Societies* 7, no. 3 (Fall 1993), 422–39.

37 By November 1994, about 2,900 socially owned enterprises had submitted applications for privatization, and 2,578 had been given approval. By December, 1,138 firms had been fully privatized, and 892 were more than 50 percent privatized. *Reuters European Business Report*, 23 December 1994.

38 Davor Glavaš, "The Roots of Croatian Extremism," *The Mediterranean Quarterly* 5, no. 2 (Spring 1994), 42. Other observers, of course, claim that the émigrés who have returned from democratic states in the West provide excellent leadership in the process of democratization.

39 In December 1994, President Tudjman claimed that 540,000 Croatians, or approximately 12 percent of the country's population, had become shareholders. Croatian Radio, 22 December 1994.

40 One of Tudjman's former advisors, Slaven Letica, claims that "the main mechanism of illegal enrichment has been through privatization funds. [State-controlled] banks issue suspicious credits and offer loans to people close to the government who then buy valuable pieces of state property for one-tenth of the real value." *Reuters International Business Reports*, 2 April 1995.

41 British Broadcasting Company, Summary of World Broadcasts (hereafter cited as BBCSWB), 17 August 1993, EE/1769/C1.

42 Bowing to pressure from the opposition, a complicated electoral system for the lower house of the legislature provided that half of the seats would be chosen in proportion to the votes for party lists. Under this system, the HDZ took thirty-one of the sixty seats allocated by the proportional method, and fifty of the sixty seats based on the majority system.

43 The HDZ-led regime kept up a campaign of hounding and political pressure against Paraga and parliamentary members of his party. This was clearly a punitive measure by Tudjman intended to weaken a political rival's competition for the ultra-nationalist portion of the electorate. Of course, the extremist behavior of the Paraga forces provided justification for Tudjman's move against them. After having been cleared of various legal charges by a civilian court in 1992, Paraga and a few of his comrades again faced criminal charges in mid-1993, this time in relation to terrorism and anti-constitutional activities, but they were subsequently acquitted by a military court. By the summer of 1994, the Tudjman regime had effectively crippled the HSP, but police units continued to monitor the right-wing organization. See Jill Irvine, "Nationalism and the Extreme Right in the Former Yugoslavia," forthcoming in *Neo-fascism in Europe* (Longman).

44 Because voting could not be held in the rebellious Krajina, the electoral law set aside thirteen seats for Croatia's Serbian minority. These seats were filled by individuals of Serbian nationality who were on the party lists of the competing parties that shared in the proportional distribution of seats. Five other seats were provided for smaller minorities, four of which were elected in majority-based races, while one set aside for the Jewish community, was filled by a member of the HSLS. See *Parliamentary and Presidential Elections in an Independent Croatia* (Washington, DC: CSCE, August 1992).

45 Ivo Bićanić and Iva Dominis, "The Multiparty Elections in Croatia: Round 2," *Radio Free Europe/Radio Liberty Research Report*, 7 May 1993, 17–21.

46 Tudjman blames the "roots" of the idea of Istrian autonomy on "Belgrade, Moscow and some Western services which want to destabilize Croatia" and "those who want a bunch of Italian irredentists or fascists to enslave Istria." BBCSWB, 1 May 1995, p. EE/2291/C. In February 1995, Croatia's constitutional court annulled parts of Istria's regional (county) constitution that gave local authorities taxing powers and provided for dual Croatian/Italian linguistic rights.

47 The letter was signed on September 20, 1993 and later published in the journal, *Erasmus*. One of the co-signers of the letter, Ivo Banac, also presented a polemical indictment of the Tudjman regime in "Croatianism: Franjo Tudjman's Brutal Opportunism," *New Republic* 209, no. 17 (25 October 1993), 20–2. For a similar view, see Ines Sabalic, "Authoritarianism in Croatia and Prospects for Change," *New Politics* 5, no. 1 (Summer 1994), 77–82.

48 *FBIS-EEU*, 1 June 1994, p. 42.

49 *FBIS-EEU*, 3 June 1994, p. 26.

50 *FBIS-EEU*, 9 June 1994, p. 46.

51 Davor Glavaš, "The Roots of Croatian Extremism," *The Mediterranean Quarterly* 5, no. 2 (Spring 1994), 37–50, and Vesna Pusić, "Constitutional Politics in Croatia," *Praxis* 13, no. 4 (1993), 389–404.

52 *Public Opinion in Croatia: A Special Report* (Washington, DC: Office of Research and Media Reaction, USIA, November 1994).

53 "Public Opinion in Croatia," *Croatia Today, Newsletter of the Embassy of the Republic of Croatia*, no. 4 (March 1995), 3.

54 Ivan Grdešić has argued that because Croatia has "one predominant party" no other party can win elections alone, and parliamentary parties are "pushed to the margins of political life," and "treated as politically irrelevant and dilettante." "This may indicate," he claims, "that the struggle for civil society in Croatia is not over," and it depends on the creation of a "state with self-imposed limits." "Croatia 1971–1992: The Politics of Non-representation," paper presented at a conference in Albuquerque, New Mexico, May 19–22, 1994.

55 A US State Department report maintained that in 1994 "Serbs continued to suffer from ever-present, subtle, and sometimes open discrimination in such areas as the administration of justice, employment, housing, and the free exercise of their cultural rights. In fewer numbers than in previous years, Serbs were also victims of anonymous threats, vandalism, and – more rarely – physical attacks." *Croatia Human Rights Practices, 1994* (Washington, DC: US State Department, March 1995).

56 "Public Opinion in Croatia," *Briefing Paper*, United States Information Agency (15 August 1995).

57 The ethnically "tolerant" consist of about one in three of the respondents who voice a favorable view of urban Serbs, believe that Croatia is not only for the majority group, and think people of different nationalities can live together peacefully. In contrast, about one in ten disagree with those views and are termed "intolerant." The "inconsistent" respondents fall between the extremes. Demographically, the members of the tolerant group are more likely to be male, slightly better off financially, well educated, less religious, and older. *Public Opinion in Croatia: A Special Report* (Washington, DC: Office of Research and Media Reaction, USIA, November 1994), pp. 5–6.

58 Michael Kelly, "Damage Control," *New Yorker*, 21 and 28 August 1995, p. 64. After the reintegration of the Krajina, the United Nations reported serious human rights abuses against Serb civilians, including wanton killing and the destruction of property by members of the Croatian security forces and Croatian civilians. However, such activity declined substantially at the end of 1995 and early 1996. *Report on Human Rights in Croatia, UN Security Council Report, S/1996/109* (New York: UN Security Council, 14 February 1996). For other facets of the Tudjman regime's flawed record on human rights, see *Civil and Political Rights in Croatia* (New York: Human Rights Watch, October 1995).

59 *Times* (London), 8 August 1995.

60 Lenard J. Cohen, "Bosnia and Herzegovina: Fragile Peace in a Segmented State," *Current History* 95, no. 599 (March 1996), 103–12.

61 Julian Borger, "Victorious Croatia Closes Doors to Ethnic Minorities," *Guardian*, 21 August 1995, p. 7.

62 Ibid. Vesna Pusić claims that various post-1989 features of Croatia have led to a trend toward "democratically sanctioned dictatorship" in which certain limitations placed on pluralism and minority rights – owing to the existence of internal rebellion and external threats, and also the idea that the domination of the majority ethnic group constitutes democracy – becomes an essentially anti-democratic ideology of transition. "Dictatorships with Democratic

Legitimacy: Democracy Versus Nation," *East European Politics and Societies* 8, no. 3 (Fall 1994), 383–401.

63 *Report of the National Democratic Initiative for International Affairs, Pre-Election Assessment Delegation, Croatia*, 16 October 1995 (Washington, DC), p. 4.

64 Mirjana Kasapović, "Analiza rezultata upravo završenih parlamentarih izbora u Hrvatskoj," *Globus*, 10 November 1995, p. 4, and by the same author, "Izborni rezultati – analiza," *Erasmus*, no. 14 (December 1995), 13–23.

65 BBCSWB, Part 2, Central Europe, The Balkans, EE/D2453/A.

66 BBCSWB, Part 2, Central Europe, The Balkans, EE/D2545/A.

67 Reuters, 29 November 1996.

4 Bosnia Herzegovina: a case of failed democratization

Steven L. Burg

Bosnia Herzegovina is an example of failed democratization. The Bosnian republic was an ethnically divided society. Muslims, Serbs, and Croats constituted three distinct ethnocultural communities whose relations over the centuries were characterized by both intergroup conflict and accommodation. Conflict had, at times, taken the form of warfare between the groups including, during World War II, genocidal war. Accommodation had taken the form of power-sharing among the respective ethnic leaderships, largely as the result of sponsorship by more powerful outside actors. It also took the form of an emerging, multiethnic, or "civil" identity, expressed in the 1970s and 1980s as "Yugoslavism." The failure of democratization between 1990 and the outbreak of war in 1992 represented the triumph of one tradition over the other.

In an effort to maintain legitimacy, the Yugoslav communist regime had permitted a substantial degree of liberalization to take place. But the local communist leadership of Bosnia Herzegovina did not permit this process to proceed as far in its own republic as in some others. In neither Yugoslavia as a whole nor any of its regions did actual democratization take place under the old regime. With the breakdown of communist authoritarianism, liberalization accelerated in Bosnia Herzegovina, the political rules of the game were altered, and a significant pluralization of politics took place. More than forty new political groups of varying size and character came into existence in the republic in 1990.

The process of democratization can be said to have begun with the onset of electoral competition. But, elections bestowed power upon those who mobilized the conflicting nationalisms of the republic's three major ethnic groups. Those who appealed to liberal democratic principles were excluded from power. The establishment of a coalition government among three nationalist parties might still have produced further democratization had internal social conditions, the organization and procedure of political institutions, the behavior of ethnic leaders, and external circumstances all favored success. All four factors, however, weighed heavily *against* the possibility that democracy might be established. The declaration of sovereignty adopted by the Bosnian parliament in October 1991, less than one year after the election, marked the collapse of the fragile tripartite government and the failure of democratization.

Social conditions

Social conditions in Bosnia Herzegovina varied greatly among the republic's geo-historical regions, and especially between urban and rural areas. Overall, the republic was among the socio-economically less-developed of the Yugoslav republics, although even in this respect the statistical evidence is mixed. Only 34.2 percent of the population was classified urban in 1981. But this was up from 19.5 percent in 1971, suggesting that modernization and the social changes that accompany it were indeed progressing. However, 23.3 percent of the female population and 5.5 percent of males remained illiterate. In 1953 only 0.3 percent of the population over age ten had completed post-secondary education and about 6.4 percent had completed secondary education.[1] Almost 22 percent of the population aged fifteen and over had acquired at least some secondary education, and 4.3 percent had acquired some post-secondary education by 1981.[2] Only 0.4 percent of the workforce in the socialized sector of the economy was employed in scientific-technical work, as compared to 0.7 percent in Croatia and 0.9 percent in Slovenia, former Yugoslavia's most developed republics.[3] For purposes of comparison with other chapters, table 4.1 gives an overview of demographic trends in the area prior to 1991.

Bosnia Herzegovina was in most respects also an economically "peripheral" zone with respect to the rest of Yugoslavia. GNP per capita was 35 percent below the Yugoslav average. Average wages were 16.3 percent below the Yugoslav average and 32 percent below the average wage in Slovenia.[4] The relatively lower level of socioeconomic development of the republic contributed to substantial net out-migration, a strong indication of the overall peripheral status of the republic within the Yugoslav context. But net out-migration consisted very largely of the movement of ethnic Serbs and Croats to their eponymous republics. About 17 percent of Serb out-migration was directed toward neighboring Croatia. Migration into and out of the republic by Muslims was nearly in balance.[5] These patterns reflect the fact that while Croats and Serbs viewed their eponymous republics as the core of their respective homelands, for Muslims Bosnia Herzegovina represented the core of their perceived homeland, rather than its periphery.

Table 4.1 *Demographic trends in Bosnia Herzegovina since the 1950s*

	1950s	1970s	1980s
Percentage of population	(1953)	(1971)	(1981)
Rural	85.0	72.0	65.8
Urban	15.0	28.0	34.2
Average annual rates	(1953–61)	(1971–81)	(1981–91)
of population growth (%)	1.7	0.9	0.5
Age distribution (%)	(1953)	(1971)	(1990)
15–24	23.9	19.5	16.4
25–49	27.0	32.2	37.1
50–59	6.5	5.8	10.8
over 60	5.2	7.7	9.6
Levels of education[a] (%)	(1953)	(1971)	(1981)
Primary	26.1	64.0	51.4
Secondary	6.4	10.8	21.7
Post-secondary[b]	0.3	1.8	4.3

Notes: [a]Indicates attainment of completed or partial education at each level among persons over fifteen years of age. [b]Data are for persons over ten years of age.
Sources: US Department of Commerce, *Statistical Abstracts of the United States*; Paul S. Shoup, *The East European and Soviet Data Handbook*; UNESCO, *Statistical Yearbooks*; United Nations, *Demographic Yearbooks*; Eduard Bos et al., *World Population Projections 1994–95 Edition*; *Yugoslav Survey* #3 (1991); Savezni Zavod za Statistiku (Federal Institute for Statistics), *Popis stanovništva domaćinstava i stanova u 1981. godini* (Census of the population, households and apartments in 1981), table 001 (population according to sex and age), p. 2 and table 004 (population 15 and older according to sex and education), p. 2 (Belgrade: Federal Institute for Statistics, 1984); idem, *Materijalni i drustveni razvoj SFR Jugoslavije 1947-1972* [Material and social development of SFR Yugoslavia, 1947-1972] (Belgrade: Federal Institute for Statistics, 1973), p. 81.

Data on social relations between the major ethnic groups also yield a mixed picture. Survey research on social distance among ethnic groups conducted in 1991, for example, revealed that less than 12 percent of respondents considered nationality an important factor in determining whether someone could be a good friend. But, for some groups, nationality was far more important in determining the suitability of a potential marriage partner. Among Muslims, almost 43 percent of respondents ranked nationality as an important or very important factor, as did more than 39 percent of Croats and more than 25 percent of Serbs. Among self-declared "Yugoslavs," however, only 8.2 percent of respondents took this view.[6]

From the late 1960s on, the number of mixed marriages increased. Mixed marriages accounted for 15.3 percent of the total number of marriages in the republic in 1981. However, 95.3 percent of Muslim women, and 92.9

percent of Muslim men entered into homogeneous marriages. Intermarriage rates were higher among Serbs, and still higher among Croats. Most of the intermarriage in the republic was thus taking place among non-Muslims.[7]

Differences in outlook between "Yugoslavs" and others in Bosnia Herzegovina reflected the difference between "Yugoslav" and other forms of self-identification. The declaration of Yugoslav identity was, by the 1980s, an expression of civic consciousness, or a "transnational" sense of "belonging to the society, the community."[8] There is strong behavioral evidence, in the form of rates of Yugoslav identification in the regional, federal, and military party organizations during the 1970s and early 1980s,[9] that such identification was associated with active support for multinational political institutions. The more open attitudes of "Yugoslavs" toward interethnic marriage, cited above, suggest openness toward multiethnic social relations, as well. While there are significant differences in emphasis among analytical explanations of the sources and meaning of such identification,[10] it is clear that interethnic contact in the modernized, urban sector of society was producing a shared "Yugoslav" identity across Yugoslavia as a whole. This was occurring despite the strong institutional and political disincentives to declare such identity inherent in the official personnel policy of the regime, which apportioned elite positions according to a strict ethnic "key" that favored the eponymous group of each republic and thus disadvantaged "Yugoslavs" in the competition for public employment.

The proportion of "Yugoslavs" varied from region to region. In Bosnia Herzegovina, almost 8 percent of the republic population – as opposed to 5.4 percent of the total population of Yugoslavia – declared "Yugoslav" identity in the 1981 census, and over 75 percent of these individuals were resident in urban areas. In the larger cities, "Yugoslavs" constituted from one-fifth to one-quarter of the population.[11] Thus, it can be said that, at least in the major urban areas of the republic, a multiethnic civic culture was emerging. However, the emergence of that culture depended on the continued existence of the broader multinational state of which the republic was then a part. The collapse of that state would eliminate the very foundation for the emergence of a multiethnic civic culture in Bosnia.

Ethnic exclusiveness and feelings of insecurity remained strong among the major groups in the republic. The study of social distance cited above, for example, also produced data on attitudes toward living in ethnically mixed environments. Among Croats, 38 percent of respondents agreed that a person feels more secure living where his own nation constituted a majority of the population, while 37 percent disagreed. Among Serb respondents, almost 36 percent agreed while more than 41 percent disagreed. Among Muslims, almost 31 percent agreed while almost 40 percent disagreed.[12] These data do not necessarily contradict the view that integrative processes leading to the growth of a shared civic culture were underway in Bosnia Herzegovina in the 1980s. However, they underscore the fact that there was still a great deal of "social distance" between ethnic groups in the republic. The sharp socioeconomic and cultural differences between urban and rural areas in the republic suggest the likelihood that these were associated with differing beliefs, especially with respect to interethnic relations.[13]

Such differences might have been bridged by a conscious effort on the part of the political leadership to socialize the population to a shared, civic culture. One potentially powerful means through which such an effort might have been carried out was the mass media. During the 1980s, television became the dominant medium of mass communication. Partly as the result of the increasing economic hardship of the population, newspaper circulation in the republic dropped precipitously. This also reflected the relatively small size of the urban, modernized sector of society. The four major dailies originating in the republic had an average daily circulation of only 165,000 in 1990; a reflection, perhaps, of the declining appeal of a press tightly controlled by a conservative political elite that still hewed to a rapidly obsolescing ideology. By 1989 more than a quarter of the total daily press circulating in the republic originated in Serbia, and almost 10 percent originated in Croatia. More than half the circulation of weekly publications originated outside the republic.[14] Part of the attraction of the external press was surely its greater openness. The most prominent weekly in Croatia, *Danas*, remained a lively, open, and critical publication. The communist party newspaper *Borba*, which originated in Belgrade but was distributed nationally and took a national – that is, all-Yugoslav – perspective, also provided a stimulating alternative to the regional press. But other Serbian and Croatian publications appealed to Bosnian Serbs and Croats on the basis of their more nationalistic content. Much of the Serbian press had become the active exponent of the increasingly nationalist orientation of the Serbian leadership under Milošević, and served as a forum for the expression of concern for the fate of Serbs outside Serbia including, of course, Bosnia Herzegovina. The press in Croatia actively polemicized with the Belgrade press from an increasingly nationalist perspective of its own. The spread of these views among the Serbs and Croats of Bosnia Herzegovina contributed to the difficulties of forging a civic culture among Serbs, Croats, and Muslims.

In contrast to the declining importance of Bosnian newspapers as a means of influencing mass beliefs, television had penetrated over 88 percent of all households, and over 93 percent of all non-agricultural households in the republic. However, large proportions of television programming also originated in other republics. Over 28 percent of programming originated in Belgrade, and over 27 percent originated in Zagreb. Only about 30 percent

of programming on TV Sarajevo was locally produced.[15] With the establishment of the coalition government in late 1990, Sarajevo television became the
state television of Bosnia Herzegovina, and coverage came under increased
political control by the three nationalist leaderships. Thus, television
contributed little to forging a common Bosnian political culture in the period
before the elections. It devoted greater attention to representing the competing
views of the three nationalist government coalition parties than to fostering
a shared identity in the period following the elections. An attempt in late
1990 by the federal government to establish an independent
Yugoslav-oriented television production enterprise, Yutel, to counteract the
nationalist messages of the regional television stations was attacked from all
sides and failed.[16]

Social conditions in Bosnia Herzegovina thus presented a mixed picture
when democratization was initiated. There were elements of a shared identity
and, perhaps, a civic culture among a significant proportion of the population
in the major cities. But there was also substantial social distance, as well as
feelings of insecurity between the three major ethnic groups. These feelings
were reinforced by the growing conflicts surrounding the collapse of
Yugoslavia.[17]

Political institutions

Following the collapse of the Yugoslav Communist Party at its extraordinary
Congress in January 1990, the Bosnian party leadership accepted the
establishment of opposition parties, but on the condition that they not be
based on ethnicity – a position explicitly justified by reference to the damage
to interethnic relations that would result from the establishment of such
parties. Such fears were shared in the general population. In a survey of
public opinion in the republic conducted by the Zagreb-based news weekly
Danas in spring 1990, 74 percent of the 1,039 respondents supported this
limitation.[18] This restriction on parties was ended in 1990, however, when
the Constitutional Court of the republic declared it unconstitutional. Thus, the
onset of democratization in the republic also opened the door to ethnic
mobilization.

More than forty parties and party-like organizations were established in
the republic in the course of 1990. Most of these were exceedingly small, and
either formed coalitions under the sponsorship of a more prominent party,
such as the Alliance of Reform Forces (see below), or were of no consequence in the politics of the republic. Only thirteen parties put candidates
forward in the November 1990 elections.

Three explicitly ethnic parties dominated the campaign and secured the
largest number of seats in parliament. The Party of Democratic Action

(PDA–Stranka Democratske Akcije, created in May 1990, was organized by Muslim elites who defined it as "the party of Muslim cultural-historic circle"[19] and led by Alija Izetbegović. Izetbegović had been an active proponent of the idea of an Islamic state, a view reflected in his Islamic Declaration of 1970, although that document did not call explicitly for such a state in Bosnia. It was for Islamic activities that he had twice been imprisoned under the communists. Within the PDA, he was associated with those elites inclined toward an identity defined largely in terms of Islam, and insistent on securing a dominant role for the Muslims in Bosnia Herzegovina. While the party formally affirmed support for the continuation of a Yugoslav state, it defined that state as "a community of sovereign nations and republics, within current federal borders." Thus, the PDA appeared more sympathetic to the emerging Slovenian-Croatian tendency toward confederalization of Yugoslavia, if not outright secession, than to preserving Bosnia's association with Serbia. Indeed, Izetbegović made it clear during the campaign that if these republics did secede, then he would not keep Bosnia Herzegovina "in a mangled Yugoslavia, in other words, in a greater Serbia."[20]

The overtly Islamic and Muslim nationalist orientation of the PDA leadership around Izetbegović, and its confrontational stance toward the Serbs and Yugoslavia, led to a split within the party between it and the more secular Muslims led by Adil Zulfikarpašić.[21] Zulfikarpašić was a proponent of *Bošnjaštvo*, or Bosnianism rather than Muslim nationalism. *Bošnjaštvo* was a concept developed under Austrian rule to denote the existence of a distinctive Bosnian identity shared by all who lived in the region, regardless of religion. It was developed specifically as a counterweight to the politicization of religious identities.[22] Because this sentiment was historically stronger among secular Muslims than among others, the party founded under Zulfikarpašić's leadership in October 1990 was called the Muslim Bosniak Organization (MBO–Muslimanska Bošnjačka Organizacija). Although it attempted to appeal to the "national-historic integration of people living in Bosnia-Hercegovina and their lives"[23] rather than to the interests of Muslims alone, it held little appeal outside of liberal Muslim circles.

The PDA secured 41 out of the 130 seats in the Chamber of Citizens, and 45 out of the 110 seats in the Chamber of Municipalities. The Muslim Bosniak Organization secured 2 seats in the Chamber of Citizens, and none in the Chamber of Municipalities.[24]

The Serb Democratic Party (SDP–Srpska Demokratska Stranka), established in July 1990, was at first an extension of the party of the same name established by the Serbs in Croatian Krajina. The Bosnian organization formally stood for the "national, cultural, spiritual, and every other unification of Serbs in Bosnia-Hercegovina"[25] as well as the preservation of

Yugoslavia as a "modern federal state." Radovan Karadžić, leader of the SDP, made it clear that the party actually functioned as the nationalist leadership of the Serbs in Bosnia, opposed to any form of Bosnian independence from Serbia, or to any changes in Bosnia itself that might subject the Serb minority to rule by a hostile majority.[26] Another Serb party, the Serb Movement of Renewal (SMR–Srpski Pokret Obnove), also played a minor role in the campaign. The SDP secured 34 of 130 seats in the Chamber of Citizens, and 38 of 110 seats in the Chamber of Municipalities. The SMR secured only 1 seat in the latter chamber.

The Croatian Democratic Union (CDU–Hrvatska Demokratska Zajednica) was established in August 1990 under the leadership of Stjepan Kljuivć as a branch of the ruling party in Croatia, and "the only party which protects the rights of Croats in Bosnia-Hercegovina."[27] The positions of the party reflected precisely those of the leadership in Croatia, calling for the independence of the republic and ignoring the existence of Yugoslavia. It secured twenty seats in the Chamber of Citizens, and twenty-four in the Chamber of Municipalities.

While the three nationalist party leaderships mobilized and further politicized ethnic identities, two other major parties adopted non-nationalist positions and attempted to appeal across ethnic boundaries on the basis of liberal ideals. Both linked their appeals to support for the preservation of the Yugoslav federation, a preference supported by over 69 percent of the respondents in a survey conducted in the republic in June 1990.[28]

Following the models established by the Slovenian and Croatian party organizations, the League of Communists of Bosnia Herzegovina transformed itself into a party supporting pluralistic political democracy and a market-based economy. The political orientation of the reformed communists could be explained in terms of the multi-ethnic character of its membership. Although Serbs constituted the largest single group in the party (42.8 percent in 1982), Muslims and Croats together outnumbered them (35.0 and 11.9 percent, respectively). And, in a reflection of both demographic and political realities, the Muslim share of the party had been increasing over time. Yugoslavs, at least in 1982, also represented an important party constituency, comprising 8.4 percent of the membership.[29] Neither the Muslim, Croat, nor Yugoslav constituencies in the party would accept a Serb nationalist orientation. Moreover, the communist elite was itself nominally triethnic and, as later events would show, genuinely opposed to nationalism.

The reformed communists supported continuation of the Yugoslav federation, but called for maximum autonomy for the constituent republics. It tried to appeal to voters in non-ethnic terms, affirming the full equality of all citizens. It adopted the name League of Communists-Social Democratic Party (LC-SDP–Savez Komunista-Socijalistička Demokratska Partija), and was led by Nijaz Djuraković, an ethnic Muslim. It worked in alliance with the political successor to the communist party's popular front organization, which adopted the name Democratic Socialist Alliance of Bosnia Herzegovina (DSA–Demokratski Socijalistički Savez), in a relationship that essentially continued the communist-era relationship between the two organizations. The LC-SDP secured eighteen seats (five in coalition with the DSA) in the Chamber of Citizens. The DSA won one seat on its own, and one seat in coalition with a minor environmental party. The Socialist Youth Organization, another splinter group of the old communist popular front organization, also won one seat in coalition with the environmentalists. The LC-SDP won only one seat in the Chamber of Municipalities.

Despite polls that suggested it would secure more support than any other party in the republic,[30] the party of the reformed communists of Bosnia Herzegovina turned out to be the politically weakest of all the regional party organizations. It secured the smallest proportion of the popular vote and the smallest parliamentary representation of any of the former ruling parties in the republics.[31] This reflected, in part, the fact that the nationalist parties appear to have worked together to encourage their respective constituencies to reject reformers, socialists, and communists in favor of their own more clearly anti-communist candidates. This appears especially to have been the case with respect to the vote for candidates for the presidency.[32] The three ethnic parties thus seem to have captured the anti-communist vote as well as the nationalist vote in Bosnia Herzegovina.

The Alliance of Reform Forces of Yugoslavia (ARFY–Savez Reformskih Snaga Jugoslavije) was a party formed in August 1990 to support federal Prime Minister Ante Marković in his efforts to preserve a reformed, democratized Yugoslav federation, and to continue the program of economic reforms initiated with great success by his government. The branch of ARFY for Bosnia Herzegovina was headed by Nenad Kecmanović. Kecmanović was rector of Sarajevo University, a prominent exponent of liberal political views on both Bosnian and Yugoslav politics, and an ethnic Serb. The ARFY functioned as an umbrella organization for many smaller, local groups with liberal-democratic and reformist views,[33] and thereby appealed across the boundaries of ethnic identity. The ARFY secured twelve seats in the Chamber of Citizens (one in coalition with the Democratic Party of Mostar), and one in the Chamber of Municipalities.

Elections to the Chamber of Citizens were conducted on the basis of seven large, multi-member districts, within which seats were distributed proportionally. The number of seats varied with the population of the district. There were a total of 130 seats in the chamber. The Chamber of Municipalities (*opštine*) consisted of 110 single-member districts. These were based on

Table 4.2 *Distribution of votes for major parties in elections to the Bosnia Herzegovina Chamber of Citizens, 1990 (first results - in percent of valid votes)*

Regions	Major parties							Invalid votes[a]
	PDA	SDP	CDU	LC-SDP	ARFY	DSA	MBO	
Banja Luka	21.83	40.85	11.24	10.50	7.32	3.14	–	23.4
Doboj	19.41	23.11	23.05	12.57	12.21	1.30	2.38	27.5
Mostar	7.04	14.35	71.59	2.27	1.95	0.31	0.18	11.8
Sarajevo	32.63	22.97	7.97	13.38	11.27	1.48	1.85	24.9
Zenica	41.17	8.81	26.29	13.66	3.52	1.76	–	21.0
Tuzla	36.04	27.15	8.38	13.78	6.14	–	1.54	27.5
Bihac	63.20	21.56	0.44	5.97	3.29	6.50	0.91	25.4

Note: [a]Percent of all votes cast declared invalid.
Source: *Oslobodenje*, November 20, 1990, p. 3.

the existing opštine, most often translated in official and Western materials as "municipalities" but properly understood as the equivalent of counties. These units ranged in character from sparsely populated rural areas to densely populated urban centers. Elections in these districts were based on a majoritarian principle. If no candidate achieved a majority in the first round of voting, the two candidates who achieved the highest number of votes competed in a second round, or run-off, election.

Although the three nationalist parties dominated the voting, almost one-quarter of the seats in the Chamber of Citizens, distributed proportionally in large multi-member districts, were won by non-nationalist parties – most of them by the LC-SDP and ARFY. As can be seen from the data presented in table 4.2, these two non-nationalist parties together showed substantial electoral strength; in some instances outpolling one or two of the three nationalist parties. The data in table 4.2 also reveal a troubling, but uninterpretable fact: the large proportion of ballots that were declared invalid. No additional information is available to explain the large number of votes that were negated.

The resulting distribution of seats, shown in table 4.3, reflects the relative strengths of the parties in each region, and underscores the extent to which the population of Bosnia Herzegovina supported the non-nationalist alternative in 1990. But they also reveal that there were no potential coalition partners to whom these parties might turn to form a government.

The majoritarian-based elections to the Chamber of Municipalities effectively negated the votes gained by the non-nationalist parties in the first round of elections, and excluded them from power. Data for the individual

Table 4.3 *Distribution of seats among parties in the Bosnia Herzegovina Chamber of Citizens, 1990 (first election results)*

Regions	Total	PDA	SDP	CDU	LC-SDP	ARFY	DSA	MBO	SYO-DP
Banja Luka	25	5	12	2	3	2	1	–	–
Doboj	14	3	4	3	2	2	–	–	–
Mostar	15	3	2	8	1	1	–	–	–
Sarajevo	24	9	6	1	3	3	–	1	1
Zenica	15	6	2	4	2	1	–	–	–
Tuzla	28	10	6	2	5	3	1	1	–
Bihac	9	5	2	2	–	–	–	–	–
Total	130								

Source: *Oslobodjenje*, November 24, 1990, p. 3.

opštine (counties) are incomplete and consist largely of preliminary data published in the daily press at the time of the election.[34] Based on these data, the LC-SDP and ARFY appear to have showed far greater electoral strength in the counties than is indicated by the small number of seats they were able to secure. The former communists won 20–24 percent of the vote in nineteen additional districts, and twenty-five or more percent in an additional seven districts. The ARFY secured 20–24 percent of the vote in seven additional districts, and 25 or more percent in one additional district. The combined vote for these parties exceeded 30 percent in over twenty districts in addition to those won by one or the other of them. These included districts in such major cities as Jajce, Sarajevo (four districts), Travnik, and even Zenica, a city now seen as a bastion of extreme Islamic nationalism. These results are consistent with the view that a civic, or multiethnic, political culture was developing in the cities of Bosnia by 1990.

In most of these districts, however, these results failed to produce even a run-off. Fifty-four seats in the Chamber of Municipalities remained undecided after the first round of voting. The non-nationalist parties lost a dozen contests to the PDA in the second round. Turnout for second-round elections was in almost every instance substantially below the 80 percent recorded in the first round, further favoring the most highly mobilized or nationalist electorates. The final distribution of seats, which differs from the distributions based on preliminary results as shown in tables 4.2 and 4.3, is presented in table 4.4.

Table 4.4 *Final distributions of seats among parties in the Bosnia Herzegovina parliament, 1990*

Party	Chamber of Citizens		Chamber of Municipalities	
	Seats	Percent	Seats	Percent
PDA	43	33.08	43	39.09
SDP	34	26.15	37	33.64
CDU	21	16.15	24	21.82
LC-SDP[a]	15	11.54	4	3.64
ARFY[a]	12	9.23	1	0.91
DSA	1	0.77	–	–
MBO	2	1.54	–	–
ECO	1	0.77	–	–
SYO/DP/ECO	1	0.77	–	–
SMR	–	–	1	0.91
Total	130	100	110	100

Note: [a]Includes seats won in coalitions.
Source: *Oslobodjenje*, December 5, 1990, p. 3.

The elections to the collective State Presidency, held coterminously with those to parliament, required the voter to choose seven members, two from each of the three major ethnic communities, and one from among a slate of candidates who declared another ethnic identity.[35] The results of the balloting are shown in table 4.5. The outcome was a clear victory for the nationalist parties. Fikret Abdić, an immensely popular Muslim businessman who ran under the banner of the PDA but represented the tendency among some sectors of the Muslim elite toward secularism and interethnic cooperation, won the greatest number of votes, entitling him to claim the post of president of the collective presidency. However, Abdić turned down the post in favor of the leader of the PDA, and second-largest vote-getter, Alija Izetbegović. Thus, a popular Muslim politician with a long track record of working successfully with both Croats and Serbs was supplanted by a leader with a more narrow basis of appeal, and no experience in interethnic accommodation. Nijaz Djuraković, the Muslim head of the LC-SDP, secured 23.8 percent of the vote and therefore failed to qualify for either of the two seats reserved for Muslims. Similarly, Nenad Kecmanović, leader of the ARFY, won 21 percent of the vote, but was out-polled for the two Serb seats by the candidates of the SDP – Biljana Plavšić, a nationalist extremist, and Nikola Koljević. Thus, the Muslim and the Serb non-nationalist candidates were defeated. Stjepan Kljuivć and Franjo Boras, candidates of the CDU, qualified for the two seats reserved for Croats with fewer votes than were secured by Kecmanović. The third-largest number of votes went to one of the candidates

Table 4.5 *Distribution of votes in Bosnia Herzegovina presidential elections, 1990 (percent of votes cast, top three only)*

	Number of votes	Percent of votes
Muslim candidates		
Fikret Abdić[a]	867,702	44.29
Alija Izetbegović[a]	726,567	37.08
Nijaz Djuraković	466,887	23.83
Serb candidates		
Biljana Plavšić[a]	482,914	24.65
Nikola Koljević[a]	470,595	24.02
Nenad Kecmanović	421,012	21.49
Croat candidates		
Stjepan Kljuić[a]	413,432	21.1
Franjo Boras[a]	365,532	18.65
Ivo Komšić	298,176	15.22
Other nations and nationalities		
Ejup Ganić[a]	584,090	29.81
Ivan Cerešnjes	307,649	15.70
Josip Pejaković	266,225	13.58

Note: [a]Denotes elected candidates.
Source: *Oslobodjenje*, November 22, 1990, p. 3.

for the position reserved for "others." But this result was not a reflection of the strength of the non-ethnic, multiethnic, or pro-Yugoslavia sentiment in the republic. The vote was secured by Ejup Ganić, a candidate of the PDA and a member of the hardline nationalist faction of the Muslim leadership, who had declared "Yugoslav" identity. His support reflected the voting power and degree of mobilization of the Muslim constituency. Thus, the non-nationalist population was denied representation on the collective presidency.

The elections delivered substantial political power to the Muslims, but not enough for them to rule without support from another party or parties. In the flush of victory, the nationalist parties pledged to cooperate with one another. But no consideration was given to extending cooperation to the non-nationalist parties in an effort to establish a "grand coalition." Instead, an uneasy "partnership" was established among the nationalists. It was reported in the press that the parties had adopted a consensus rule,[36] and a division of the three most prominent positions in the state leadership was achieved after what seem to have been somewhat difficult negotiations.[37] Izetbegović assumed the most visible office, president of the state presidency as representative of the PDA; Jure Pelivan, a Croat and representative of the CDU, was chosen as prime minister, and Momčilo Krajišnik, a Serb of the SDP, was made president of the National Assembly. Thus, the government appeared to adopt some of the characteristics of a consociational, or power-sharing regime. But conditions critical for the success of such a system were absent. The most obvious of these was elite cooperation.

Behavior of elites

Political science literature on deeply divided societies is characterized by widespread support for the view that political elites can bridge ethnic divisions and stabilize the political system through cooperative behavior. In Bosnia Herzegovina, we appear to have an example of precisely the reverse behavior. Both in their behavior during the electoral campaign, and in their actions upon assuming political power, the leaderships of the three nationalist parties contributed to intensifying the salience of ethnicity for politics, and refused to engage in compromise. Only their shared anti-communism appears to have united them.

With the establishment of the coalition government, each of the three nationalist parties began to establish its control over sectors of the state. Under the old regime, personnel in state and government institutions had been appointed according to an ethnic "key" or quota. Following the 1990 election, ethnic identity alone was no longer enough to qualify for positions controlled by the nationalist parties. Appointments were subjected to both ethnic and partisan political criteria. The result was the division of state institutions into Muslim-, Croat-, and Serb-nationalist controlled institutions. Institutions also were divided internally. In the Ministry of Internal Affairs penetration by the three nationalist parties and the conflicting perspectives and priorities of their representatives led, in the words of the minister, to "a type of Lebanonization of Bosnia's police."[38]

The lack of goodwill and the argumentativeness of the three nationalist parties produced a dispute over appointments on the very first day of parliamentary work. Members from the SDP objected to nomination of an PDA candidate for general secretary of the parliament. Significantly, they claimed that the PDA had failed to consult with the other parties over this position, a charge that was not denied by the PDA. Debate over the proposed text for the ceremonial oath of office produced a further change for the worse in the political atmosphere in parliament. Disputes broke out over the definition of "Yugoslavia" allegedly implied by the text. One Serb SDP member demanded that the oath be printed in the Cyrillic as well as the Latin alphabet. Croat members demanded that it be "translated" into Croatian (the only issue in this case, it appears, was one letter: the perceived difference between "demokratija" and "demokracija"). The latter demand was opposed by an SDP member who suggested sarcastically that the oath might also then be translated into "Muslim" (*na muslimanskom*).[39] The deterioration in relations among the self-proclaimed partners in government was reflected during the debate over appointment of the general secretary when the vice-president of the PDA, Muhamed Cengić, referred in his remarks to the SDP as the opposition, and disputed its right to participate in negotiations over the division of government positions.[40]

The situation was no better at the local level. Each of the nationalist parties proceeded to establish its control over those counties (opštine) in which its constituency represented the majority. The parties contested bitterly the division of government power in several mixed areas. In Bijelina, for example, the PDA refused to participate in local parliamentary sessions in which the SDP, using its parliamentary majority, monopolized leading government positions instead of splitting them with the PDA. Similar disputes were unfolding in Banja Luka, Goražde, and other communities.[41] Whole swaths of republic territory (for example, western Bosnia under SDP control, centered in Banja Luka, and western Herzegovina under CDU control) ceased to recognize the authority of Sarajevo. As one journalist for the newspaper *Oslobodjenje* has suggested in a recent paper, "instead of power sharing, power grabbing abounded."[42]

For most of the period in which democratization of Bosnia Herzegovina remained possible, that is, from early 1990 until the declaration of sovereignty in October 1991, the leaders of the three ethnically defined parties remained significantly more nationalist than their constituencies. Their behaviors can only be interpreted as having contributed to intensifying conflict in the republic. The declaration of sovereignty adopted by the Bosnian parliament in October 1991, over the objections of the SDP, marked the final collapse of the attempt to govern the republic through tripartite agreement. Since the beginning of the year the SDP had opposed proposals by its government partners that the republic declare its sovereignty. Adoption of the declaration was inconsistent with an agreement among the three nationalist parties that no legislation affecting the status of any of their constituencies could be submitted unless it was supported by all three parties.[43] After almost a year in office, the three leaderships proved unable to reach a negotiated compromise on an issue that had divided them from the very beginning. Thus the rudimentary "power sharing" arrangement established in the wake of the 1990 elections failed.

Power sharing failed in Bosnia Herzegovina because of the absence of cooperative efforts on the part of participating leaderships. Indeed, their behaviors were more aggressive than conciliatory. But it also failed because of the growing conflicts and increasing prospect of violence between the major ethnic groups at the grass roots, beyond the control of the leaderships.

The domestic conditions necessary for successful operation of a system based on power sharing were simply absent in Bosnia Herzegovina. It also failed because external circumstances impelled the nationalist parties and their constituencies toward confrontation rather than cooperation.

External circumstances

The timing of elections in Bosnia Herzegovina contributed to increasing the dominance of ethnic identities in defining the pattern of voting, and to pushing the three nationalist parties toward conflict. The elections were held in November 1990, months after elections in Slovenia and Croatia had installed independence-minded governments in those two republics. They also came months after the conflict between the nationalist government in Zagreb and the Serb minority in Croatian Krajina, mobilized by Serb nationalists with ties to Belgrade, intensified the politicization of the Serb and Croat communities in Bosnia Herzegovina. Past animosities among Serbs, Croats, and Muslims in Bosnia Herzegovina were agitated further by the exhumations of mass graves of the victims of genocide in World War II, and the extensive coverage given to these events.[44]

The rise of extreme Serb nationalism in Serbia, and especially the example of repression of the Albanian minority in Kosovo, made the prospect of remaining part of a Yugoslav state that did not contain Slovenia and Croatia, and thereby constituted little more than a greater Serbia, simply intolerable for the Muslim nationalist leadership. Moreover, the example of Serb efforts to dismember the Croatian republic hardened non-Serb leaders in Bosnia Herzegovina against compromise. On the eve of the elections, the Slovenian and Croatian leaderships proposed their program for confederalization of the Yugoslav state, increasing the likelihood that the federation would not survive. Thus, the elections in Bosnia Herzegovina unfolded in a context that called into question the republic's continued survival.

The pluralization of politics in Bosnia Herzegovina also was accompanied by its increasing militarization. The larger context of increasing interethnic violence in Yugoslavia in 1990 and the outbreak of war in 1991 was reflected in the spread of weapons and rise of paramilitary organizations in Bosnia Herzegovina, most of them Serb and Croat. The influx of Croat and Serb refugees from Croatia in 1991 also contributed to the militarization of politics. The Yugoslav army, or at least elements thereof, contributed greatly to this process by arming the local Serb population.

By October 1991, Slovenia and Croatia had already declared their independence and war had already broken out in those two republics. The prospect of armed conflict in Bosnia Herzegovina was rising. And the international community, in the form of the European Community's

Conference on Yugoslavia, was already proceeding on the assumption that Yugoslavia was disintegrating and that the relationships between the former federal republics would be redefined in bilateral and multilateral negotiations among the republics themselves. Adoption of the declaration of sovereignty thus represented an attempt by the Muslim leadership of the PDA, supported by the CDU and the other non-nationalist parties represented in parliament, to claim for the republic the same status in international negotiations over the future of Yugoslavia – and the same attention and support from the major western powers – as Slovenia and Croatia, and thereby prevent it from being considered a constituent part of what remained of the Yugoslav state.

The failure of democratization

The failure of democratization in Bosnia Herzegovina offers few opportunities to enhance our understanding of the more general process. The literatures on democracy and democratization are characterized by debate over the relationship between culture and institutions. While some analysts argue that the successful operation of democratic institutions depends on the prior existence of a civic culture,[45] others have argued that the civic culture itself may be the product of the operation of such institutions.[46] The weakness of the civic or democratic element in the political culture of Bosnia Herzegovina might have represented a test of the effectiveness of democratic institutions as instruments for the transformation of culture. However, democratic institutions were never established, or had little opportunity to function before becoming overwhelmed by rising conflict. The dominant, nationalist political parties performed no aggregative, integrative functions. There was little agreement on the rules of parliamentary procedure and governmental decisionmaking when the tripartite coalition took power. Indeed, the very shape of those institutions remained in dispute, as the SDP continued to demand the establishment of a parliamentary chamber of nations in which each nation might exercise a unilateral veto.

For institutions to affect political culture, they must operate effectively over a significant period of time. According to David Easton's widely cited theory of political support,[47] long-term successful operation creates the possibility that instrumental support for governmental incumbents, arising out of governmental performance that produces improved material conditions for the population, will be transformed into more generalized, or diffuse, support for the political system itself. The example of democratization in the Federal Republic of Germany offers strong empirical support for this view.[48] In Bosnia Herzegovina, in contrast, there was effectively no opportunity for parliament, government, and other institutions to produce material results that might increase support for the system among the population.

Consociational, or power-sharing approaches to the stabilization of deeply divided societies, depend entirely on cooperative behavior among the leaderships of communal groups. No such cooperation was present in Bosnia Herzegovina. Moreover, the crucial institutional component of a power-sharing approach was missing in Bosnia Herzegovina: the mutual veto. Although the tripartite coalition appears to have been formed on the basis of an agreement to rule by consensus, the most controversial parliamentary and governmental decisions were taken over the objections of one of the ostensibly ruling parties. Moreover, there is no evidence to suggest that, had such a veto been established, the nationalist leaders would not have used it to paralyze and destroy the new state in much the same way that regional leaders used such a veto to paralyze Yugoslavia.

Thus, the breakdown of the authoritarian regime in Bosnia Herzegovina did not lead to democratization. It led instead to ethnic stalemate, and civil war. Because almost *all* of the factors associated with successful management of ethnic conflict through democratic means were absent – that is to say, the variables all had strongly negative values – it is difficult to use this case to test the relevance of any one of them for understanding democratization processes more generally.

The Dayton agreement and beyond

With the imposition of a cease-fire and deployment of a heavily armed international force to oversee it, an uncertain peace has come to Bosnia as this is being written. The war appears to have destroyed most, but not all, of the bases of political accommodation between the major ethnic groups. The nationalist leadership of each group has consolidated its power, although individual leaders may yet be subjected to prosecution for war crimes. The constitutional provisions for the much-weakened Bosnian state and its constituent units – the Bosnian (Muslim-Croat) Federation and the so-called Republika Srpska – adopted as part of the Dayton agreement locate most of the power in the constituent units and the hands of the local, nationalist leaders.[49]

The constitution for the Republic of Bosnia-Herzegovina establishes a bicameral parliament consisting of a House of Peoples and a House of Representatives. The House of Peoples institutionalizes the ethnic division of the country. It is to be composed of fifteen delegates, including five Muslims (referred to as "Bosniacs" in the Dayton documentation) and five Croats from the Muslim-Croat federation [formally known as the Federation of Bosnia-Herzegovina], and five Serbs from the Republika Srpska, each to be selected by their respective regional parliament. This formulation appears to exclude ethnic minorities from representation in this chamber. The House of

Representatives is to consist of forty-two members, twenty-eight from the (Muslim-Croat) Federation and fourteen from the Serb entity, selected by direct elections. While this does not necessarily exclude other groups from representation, it will be difficult for candidates not supported by the dominant parties to succeed.

The general rules for decisionmaking sketched out in the Dayton document attempt to balance majoritarian principles that support the integrity of the overall state and principles of ethnic-based decisionmaking that grant each group the power to protect its perceived interests. Parliamentary rules are to be adopted by a majority vote. All legislation is to be approved by both houses, with decisions to be taken by a majority vote of those present and voting. The parliamentary leadership is required to attempt to ensure that at least one-third of the delegates from each territorial entity are present. Legislation can be vetoed by a vote of two-thirds of the delegates from either entity. One provision of the Dayton agreement appears to grant each ethnic delegation in parliament a veto over all decisionmaking: a majority of either the Bosniac, Croat, or Serb delegates may declare a decision destructive of the vital interests of their group. But the precise consequence of such a declaration is unclear. Moreover, such a declaration must be confirmed by a majority vote of each of the three ethnic delegations, substantially weakening the apparent veto power granted by this provision. Until the actual composition of the parliament is determined by election, it is difficult to foretell how these provisions will operate.

The presidency of the Republic is to consist of three members; one Bosniac and one Croat elected from the Federation, and one Serb elected from the Republika Srpska. Because voters are apparently to be given one vote, this provision implies either that voters will have to ask for an ethnic ballot, or that Croats and Muslims in the Federation will have to decide between candidates of their own group and those of the other, while only ethnically Serb candidates will be allowed to stand for election in the Serbian entity. It also means, of course, that other groups are excluded from membership in presidency.

The presidency is to attempt to make decisions by consensus. Each member of the presidency may declare a decision destructive of the vital interests of his entity. Such a declaration by the Serb member will be referred to the parliament of the Republika Srpska. However, a Bosniac objection will be referred to the Bosniac delegation to the House of Peoples and a Croat objection will be referred to the Croat delegation, rather than to the parliament of the (Muslim-Croat) Federation. These provisions reflect the priority of the ethnic cleavage in post-Dayton Bosnia Herzegovina even within the Muslim-Croat, or Bosnian Federation.

The salience of the ethnic cleavage is also reflected in the agreement between the Croats and the Muslims over the division of authority between the Republic of Bosnia-Herzegovina and the Federation.[50] The authority of the Republic reflects the narrow domain assigned to it under the Dayton agreement: foreign affairs, customs, monetary policy, immigration and citizenship, civilian "coordination" of the military, and international criminal law enforcement. The latter ensures that the Muslims, who expected to control Republic institutions, will be responsible for pursuing the prosecution of war criminals. The Republic is also to be responsible for common telecommunications and air traffic control. The (Muslim-Croat) Federation is responsible for all other governmental functions, including defense, internal affairs, justice, finance, commerce, agriculture, education and culture, and public health. The agreement calls for the Federation to assume "exclusive governmental authority on the Federation, cantonal, and municipal levels in the entire Federation territory within the areas of its responsibilities." This effectively excludes the Republic from any internal affairs of state and society. It specifically calls for both Croatian and Bosnian military and civilian authorities to turn control of their respective territories over to federation institutions. Yet, each side has been reluctant to relinquish control over territory to the other. This reluctance reflects the absence of any underlying intergroup consensus that supports the Dayton agreement.

Thus, the Dayton agreement appears to have advanced the political institutionalization of the ethnic partition of Bosnia Herzegovina that was established by war rather than its re-integration. Yet, remnants of the multiethnic, civic constituency of the pre-war system remain, and appear to be organizing in anticipation of new elections scheduled for September 1996. Former Bosnian Prime Minister Haris Silajdzić, for example, perhaps the most prominent advocate of reconstructing a multiethnic rather than a nationalist state, has established a new "Party for Bosnia Herzegovina" dedicated to this goal, and has become the leading potential candidate for the presidency. But any effort to represent and mobilize popular support for a multiethnic, democratic government must compete against the determined efforts of the nationalist leaderships to hold onto power.[51]

Whether the elections of 1996 will repeat the experience of 1990 cannot yet be foretold. The electoral rules under which they will be conducted, and even the parties that will eventually run candidates are unclear. But the conditions under which they will take place seem even less favorable to successful democratization than those present in 1990.

Acronyms for post-1990 parliamentary political parties

ARFY	Alliance of Reform Forces of Yugoslavia (Savez Reform-skih Snaga Jugoslavije)
CDU	Croatian Democratic Union (Hrvatska Demokratska Zajednica)
DP	Democratic Party (Demokratska Stranka)
DSA	Democratic Socialist Alliance (Demokratski Socijalisticki Savez)
ECO	Ecological Movement (Ekologiski Pokret)
LC-SDP	League of Communists-Social Democratic Party (Savez Komunista-Socijalisticka Demokratska Partija)
MBO	Muslim Bosniak Organization (Muslimanska Bosnjacka Organizacija)
PDA	Party of Democratic Action (Stranka Democratske Akcije)
SDP	Serb Democratic Party (Srpska Demokratska Stranka)
SMR	Serb Movement of Renewal (Srpski Pokret Obnove)
SYO	Socialist Youth Organization (Socijalisticki Savez Omladina)

NOTES

1 Srdjan Bogosavljević, "Bosna i Hercegovina u ogladalu statistike" [Bosnia Herzegovina in the mirror of statistics], in *Bosna i Hercegovina izmedu mira i rata*, ed. Srdjan Bogosavljević et al. (Belgrade-Sarajevo: 1992), pp. 24–39.
2 Savezni Zavod za Statistiku (Federal Institute for Statistics), *Popis stanovništva, domaćinstava i stanova u 1981. godini* [Census of the population, households and apartments in 1981], table 002 (population according to sex and age), p. 2 and table 004 (population 15 and older according to sex and education), p. 2 (Belgrade: Federal Institute for Statistics, 1984). Note that the categories and definitions in these sources differ from those used in the source cited in note 1.
3 *Statističvki Godišnjak Jugoslavije 1990* [Statistical Yearbook of Yugoslavia, 1990], p. 596.
4 Bogosavljević, "Bosna i Hercegovina u ogladalu statistike," p. 31.
5 Ibid., p. 28.
6 Dušan Janjić, "Bosna i Hercegovina: Otvorena pitanja državno-političkog identiteta multietnicke i multikonfesionalne zajednice," in Bogosavljević et al., eds., *Bosna i Hercegovina izmedu mira i rata*, p. 15.
7 Composition of marriages is calculated from data presented in Savezni Zavod za Statistiku (SZS), *Demografska statistika 1981* (Belgrade: SZS, 1986), pp. 228–9.
8 Jovan Mirić, *Sistem i kriza* [System and crisis] (Zagreb: Čekade, 1984), p. 109. For additional discussion of this issue, see Steven L. Burg and Michael L.

Berbaum, "Community, Integration, and Stability in Multinational Yugoslavia," *American Political Science Review* 83, no. 2 (June 1989), 535–54.

9 Cited in Burg and Berbaum, "Community, Integration, and Stability," 539–40.

10 Compare, for example, Burg and Berbaum, "Community, Integration, and Stability" and Duško Sekulić et al., "Who were the Yugoslavs? Failed Sources of a Common Identity in the Former Yugoslavia," *American Sociological Review* 59 (February 1994), 83–97.

11 Calculations based on data in Savezni Zavod za Statistiku, *Nacionalni sastav stanovništva SFR Jugoslavije po naseljima i opštinama* [National composition of the population of SFR Yugoslavia], vol. 1 (Belgrade: Savremena Administracija, 1991), pp. 16ff.

12 Janjić, "*Bosna i Hercegovina: Otvorena pitanja*," p. 15.

13 Janjić summarizes these differences in "*Bosna i Hercegovina: Otvorena pitanja*,", pp. 18–21.

14 Slavujević Dj. Zoran, "Medijski sistem Bosne i Hercegovine" [The media of Bosnia Herzegovina], in Bogosavljević et al., eds., *Bosna i Hercegovina izmedu mira i rata*, pp. 54–6.

15 Zoran, "Medijski sistem," pp. 55–6.

16 Ibid., pp. 57–8.

17 For a poignant account of the breakdown of ethnic relations in Sarajevo, see Ljiljana Smajlović, "From the Heart of the Heart of the Former Yugoslavia," *Wilson Quarterly* (Summer 1995), 100–113.

18 *Danas*, 22 May 1990, as cited in Vladimir Goati, "Politički život Bosne i Hercegovine, 1989–1992" [Political life in Bosnia Herzegovina, 1989–1992], in Bogosavljević et al., eds., *Bosna i Hercegovina izmedu mira i rata*, p. 45.

19 *Borba*, 10–11 November 1990, p. 3 as trans. in *FBIS-EEU*, 19 November 1990, p. 77.

20 Milan Andrejevich, "Bosnia-Herzegovina: Yugoslavia's Linchpin," *Report on Eastern Europe* 1, no. 49 (7 December 1990), 24.

21 *Borba*, 23 October 1990, p. 3 as trans. in *FBIS-EEU*, 30 October 1990, p. 57.

22 Steven L. Burg, *The Political Integration of Yugoslavia's Muslims: Determinants of Success and Failure*, Carl Beck Papers no. 203 (Russian and East European Studies Program, University of Pittsburgh, 1983), pp. 6–12.

23 *Borba*, 10–11 November 1990, p. 3 as trans. in *FBIS-EEU*, 19 November 1990, p. 78.

24 These and the further results reported below are compiled from *Oslobodjenje*, 24 November 1990, p. 1 as trans. in *FBIS-EEU*, 27 November 1990, p. 66 and *Tanjug*, 12 December 1990, as trans. in *FBIS-EEU*, 15 December 1990, pp. 47–8.

25 *Borba*, 10–11 November 1990, p. 3 as trans. in *FBIS-EEU*, 19 November 1990, p. 77.

26 See, e.g., the interview in *Borba*, 12 November 1990, p. 4 as trans. in FBIS, EEU, 19 November 1990, p. 78–80.

27 *Borba*, 10–11 November 1990, p. 3 as trans. in *FBIS-EEU*, 19 November 1990, p. 77.

28 Goati, "Politički život Bosne i Hercegovine," pp. 46–7.

29 Steven L. Burg, "New Data on the League of Communists of Yugoslavia," *Slavic Review* 46, no. 3-4 (Fall/Winter 1987), table 4, p. 556.
30 Andrejevich, "Yugoslavia's Linchpin," p. 25 and *Start*, 27 October 1990, pp. 35-8 as trans. in *FBIS-EEU*, 7 November 1990, pp. 54-6.
31 Goati, "Politički život Bosne i Herzegovina," pp. 47-8.
32 *Borba*, 14 November 1990, p. 3 as trans. in *FBIS-EEU*, 19 November 1990, p. 80.
33 For a partial list, see *Tanjug*, domestic service, 8 October 1990, as trans. in *FBIS-EEU*, October 10, 1990, p. 59.
34 All calculations are based on data published in the Sarajevo daily, *Oslobodjenje*. The most detailed, district-by-district preliminary returns are to be found in the issues for 20-24 November and 2, 4, and 5 December 1990.
35 *Oslobodjenje*, 6 December 1990.
36 Ibid., 6 December 1990.
37 For intimations of difficulties, see *Oslobodjenje*, 13 December and 14 December 1990.
38 Milan Andrejevich, "The Future of Bosnia and Herzegovina: A Sovereign Republic or Cantonization?" *Report on Eastern Europe* 2, no. 27 (5 July 1991), 32.
39 *Oslobodjenje*, 21 December 1990, pp. 1, 3.
40 Ibid., 22 December 1990, p. 3.
41 Ibid., 22 December 1990, p. 4, 26 December 1990, p. 4 and 27 December 1990, p. 4.
42 Ljiljana Smajlović, "Origins of the Bosnian War" (seminar paper, East Europe Program, Woodrow Wilson International Center, Washington, DC, 21 June 1995), p. 12.
43 Milan Andrejevich, "The Future of Bosnia and Herzegovina," pp. 29-30, and by the same author, "Bosnia and Herzegovina Move toward Independence," *Report on Eastern Europe* 2, no. 43 (25 October 1991), 22-5.
44 See, e.g., *Oslobodjenje*, 25 December 1990.
45 See, for example, Robert D. Putnam, *Making Democracy Work* (Princeton: Princeton University Press, 1993).
46 See, for example, Terry Lynn Karl, "Dilemmas of Democratization in Latin America," in *Comparative Political Dynamics*, ed. Dankwart A. Rustow and Kenneth Paul Erickson (New York: HarperCollins, 1991), p. 168; and Edward N. Muller and Mitchell A. Seligson, "Civic Culture and Democracy: The Question of Causal Relationships," *American Political Science Review* 88, no. 3 (September 1994), 635-52.
47 David Easton, "A Re-assessment of the Concept of Political Support," *British Journal of Political Science* 5 (1975), 437, 444-5.
48 See, e.g., Sidney Verba, "Germany: The Remaking of Political Culture," in *Political Culture and Political Development*, ed. Lucien W. Pye and Sidney Verba (Princeton: Princeton University Press, 1965), pp. 130-70 and David P. Conradt, "Changing German Political Culture," in *The Civic Culture Revisited*, ed. Gabriel A. Almond and Sidney Verba (Boston: Little, Brown and Co., 1980), pp. 212-72.

49 The following summary is based on the text contained in the document "Proximity Peace Talks," Wright-Patterson Air Force Base, Dayton, Ohio, November 1–21, 1995, Annex 4 ("Constitution of Bosnia Herzegovina").
50 "Dayton Agreement on Implementing the Federation of Bosnia and Herzegovina of 9 November 1995" (text).
51 Marshall Freeman Harris, "Three Months After Dayton: The View from the Ground," *Balkan Monitor*, no. 9 (5 April 1996), electronic mail edition.

5   A failed transition: the case of Serbia

Nicholas J. Miller

Five years after the first free elections in postwar Serbia, the stated aim of most of its political actors there is still a true transition to democracy. The reason for this is simple. Although Serbia has the structures and institutions necessary for democratic government, there is no democratic culture. Instead, Slobodan Milošević has governed in an authoritarian manner in the name of the Serbian nation. The Serbian opposition offers little but the rhetorical promise of bringing liberal democracy to the state, and any politician wishing to succeed must offer a vision for the defense of Serbs from a variety of threats, real and unreal. Serbia's minorities, which constitute about a third of its population, have been excluded from politics by this political culture of intolerance. Today, the only positive sign for the future is the fact that the wars in Croatia and Bosnia are (at least temporarily) over, which might enable Serbian political leaders to attempt to broaden their appeal to non-Serbs.

There are numerous reasons for the failed transition in Serbia. Firstly, it is a product of historical conditions and rivalries in the former Yugoslavia. The ethnic nationalism that links all of the most popular and most powerful parties in Serbia today has roots in the Second World War, during which Serbs were the target of attempted genocide by the Croatian Ustaša. Secondly, it is a result of conditions related directly to the wars accompanying Yugoslavia's collapse. The fact that Serbs have been embroiled in a number of wars that threaten the existence of their communities outside of Serbia has enabled the current socialist leadership to claim to be the protector of Serbs at home and abroad. Thirdly, the failure of the transition represents the failure of Serbia's intelligentsia to embrace a civic culture rooted in respect for the individual as opposed to the nation. Finally, the inability of the Serbian people to produce a coherent, anti-authoritarian, anti-nationalist opposition to the Milošević regime reflects a collectivist political culture and the aftermath of forty-five years of communism.

146

Until 1991, Serbia was one of six republics in Yugoslavia. It included two autonomous provinces, Kosovo and Vojvodina. From June 1991, the Yugoslav state disintegrated as Slovenia, Croatia, Bosnia, and Macedonia all declared their independence. Serbia and Montenegro remained, and on April 27, 1992, created the Federal Republic of Yugoslavia. They are the two constituent republics in the new Yugoslav state. Kosovo and Vojvodina are now provinces of Serbia. The republics and provinces are now governed by a three-tiered system: the federal government is centered in Belgrade; the governments of each republic, Serbia and Montenegro, are based in Belgrade and Podgorica, respectively; and Kosovo and Vojvodina each have regional administrations, although the 1992 Yugoslav constitution greatly circumscribes their authority. Serbia and Montenegro each have unicameral parliamentary systems, while Yugoslavia has a bicameral parliament. In Serbia and Montenegro, the national assemblies and the republican presidents are elected by universal suffrage. At the federal level, the Yugoslav Chamber of Citizens is also elected by universal suffrage.

The electoral laws for each level of government in today's Federal Republic of Yugoslavia establish single-member constituencies, which reward the party that receives the most votes in a given district with representation in the various assemblies rather than allowing for proportional representation. There were elections in Serbia in 1990, 1992, and 1993; Montenegro held elections in 1990 and 1992; at the federal level, there were elections in 1992 and 1996. The system has worked to the advantage of the party in power in each of the elections. Furthermore, power in the Serbian constitution is weighted towards the president. Such a system thus assures that the governing party and its leader enjoy overwhelming authority in the state. The judiciary in Serbia provides no balance to the power of the president. It is a continuation of the judiciary which existed in Yugoslavia before 1991, and today it is subservient to Milošević and his Socialist Party of Serbia.

Serbia is a multiethnic society. Only about 66 percent of its population is Serb. The remainder is Albanian, Hungarian, Muslim, and others. Most of the non-Serbs live in Kosovo and Vojvodina. Kosovo is about 90 percent Albanian, whereas Vojvodina is a patchwork of ethnic groups, including Serbs, Hungarians, Romanians, Slovaks, and Croats. Although the Serbian constitution describes Serbia as "the democratic state of all citizens living within it," the political culture is restrictive.[1] Non-Serbs today are alienated and marginalized by the climate of intolerance that has accompanied the collapse of Yugoslavia and the aggressive nationalism of Serbian politics and society.

This chapter will consider the origins of the democratization process in Serbia, the roots of the ethnic nationalism that plagues that process, the elections of 1990, 1992, and 1993, the sources of power of the Milošević regime, and the challenges that the non-Serbian peoples of the state pose to a successful democratic transition.

Background to the elections of 1990

Josip Broz "Tito" and his communist partisans emerged victorious from the civil war that occurred in Yugoslavia between 1941 and 1945. In that war, fought between the communists, the Ustaša of the Independent State of Croatia, and Serbian nationalist Četniks, over 500,000 Serbs were killed, more than any other ethnic group. Many of the dead were victims of the Ustaša, who attempted to cleanse their puppet state of its Orthodox Christians. In spite of the victimization of Serbs during the war, the postwar verdict on Serbia was mixed, because the communists and many others believed that Serbia's domination of the interwar Yugoslav state had led to its violent collapse in 1941. In Tito's Yugoslavia, Serbs were blamed for the interethnic war as much as they were mourned for their suffering. The tension regarding the role of Serbs in the state would result in more blame, anger, and mourning after Tito's death in 1980.

Titoism was the Yugoslav variation on the Leninist-Stalinist model after 1948. The system developed as a result of specific conditions in Yugoslavia and of the Tito–Stalin split in 1948, which compelled the Yugoslav leadership to seek its own source of Marxist legitimacy. Its three most important components were self-management, non-alignment, and a solution to competitive nationalisms in Yugoslavia. The first two answered Tito's need for ideological and political legitimacy in a bipolar world; self-management would also contribute, in the Titoist lexicon, to the solution of the national problem in the state. But Titoism's most basic assault on national identity involved territory, redefining the state, to the detriment of a unified Serbia. Serbian communities were scattered among all of the republics and provinces of Yugoslavia but Slovenia after 1945. By 1981, of 8.1 million Serbs in Yugoslavia, only about 58 percent lived in Serbia proper (Serbia minus Kosovo and Vojvodina).[2]

Yugoslavia was technically a federation after 1945, but the six republics had little authority within their borders until the 1960s. One reason for the centralization was to stifle the competitive nationalisms that had destroyed interwar Yugoslavia. To the same end, one of the stated purposes of self-management was to nurture the growth of a new identity among the peoples of Yugoslavia, but there is little evidence that it succeeded, or that any supranational identity became popular for any reason. Rather, the system of self-management encouraged stable employment and residence, which did little to break down local identities in favor of either a working-class identity or supranational Yugoslavism.[3] The few who did claim to be Yugoslavs rather than Serbs, Croats, or others appear to have done so as an ideological commitment or because other census alternatives did not fit their circumstances (for instance, the products of mixed marriages and, until 1971, Muslim South Slavs).

In the early 1960s, reforms altered the path that Yugoslav federalism had taken. Federalism became more substantive with the reforms. The central purpose of the reforms was economic: Tito and Edvard Kardelj wished to encourage economic growth by allowing republics to have more authority over economic decisions. They did not recognize the danger that decentralized decisionmaking posed for the unified Yugoslav market. The Slovenian and Croatian leaderships, which urged the reforms, viewed decentralization as a step toward confederation and an affirmation of statehood. The goal of a supranational identity no longer made sense; instead, the system envisioned a balance of nationalisms in Yugoslavia, with only Serbian and Croatian nationalism retaining their negative connotations. Republics and provinces would become homes to the major nations and nationalities of Yugoslavia. The revised approach to the administration of the state and the national question implied rapid changes, all of which could be interpreted as detrimental to Serbs.

For instance, in the one major bureaucratic purge initiating the reforms, Aleksandar Ranković was removed from his posts in 1966. Ranković was a Serb who controlled UDBa (Yugoslavia's security service) and was vice-president of Yugoslavia. The fall of Ranković would eventually provide one of the critical pieces in the puzzle of Serbian political mythology after the death of Tito: Ranković, Tito's jailer, would enter revised history books as the symbol of Titoism's subjugation of Serbia. Major administrative changes followed Ranković's fall: Tito overhauled Kosovo's administration and created, in effect, an Albanian state within Yugoslavia. Furthermore, Muslim South Slavs attained the status of a constituent nation in Yugoslavia by 1971. For the Serbs and Croats of Bosnia, recognition of a Muslim nation represented a huge setback to national mythology. These events could be (and eventually were) interpreted by Serbs as hostile acts directed at them. Nothing made this situation clearer in the opinion of most Serbs than the 1974 constitution.[4] That constitution gave the republican governments more authority than ever and prompted the further bureaucratization of the leaderships on a local level. Kosovo and Vojvodina now had powers almost identical to those of the republics with the exception of the right to secede.

The 1974 Constitution ended an era of constitutional reform designed to spread political leadership and economic decisionmaking among the republics. Unfortunately, at just about that moment, Yugoslavia began to suffer from economic problems that demanded more rather than less centralization of decisionmaking. The global debt crisis of the 1980s led to the imposition of

Table 5.1 *Indicators of socioeconomic trends in Serbia since 1956*

	1956–64	1965–72	1973–79	1980–84	1985–90
GDP	7.7	5.0	5.1	-0.3	n.a.
Personal income, Yugoslavia	6.3	6.1	2.7	-2.0	n.a.
Agricultural population	(1953)	(1961)	(1971)	(1981)	(1990)
Serbia, Kosovo, Vojvodina	66.7	56.1	44.0	25.4	n.a.
Unemployment	(1953)	(1961)	(1971)	(1981)	(1990)
Serbia	n.a.	6.9	8.7	17.7	16.4
Kosovo	n.a.	19.3	23.9	39.1	38.4
Vojvodina	n.a.	4.3	6.7	14.6	16.6

Notes: GDP – annual % growth per capita; personal income – annual % growth in real personal income.
Sources: Lenard Cohen, *Broken Bonds: Yugoslavia's Disintegration and Balkan Politics in Transition*, 2d ed. (Boulder, CO: Westview Press, 1995), p. 31, and Susan Woodward, *Socialist Unemployment: The Political Economy of Yugoslavia, 1945–1990* (Princeton: Princeton University Press, 1995), pp. 383–5.

austerity measures which cut domestic consumption but did little to cut the debt. Remittances from workers abroad fell as recession hit Western Europe, and unemployment rose precipitously as workers returned home. The Yugoslav "experiment" was foundering by the mid-1980s. Every indicator showed that the country verged on economic collapse. Between 1953 and 1981, Serbia's agricultural population (including Kosovo and Vojvodina) declined from 67 percent to 25 percent. The rural exodus in the 1970s and 1980s, especially of youth, combined with the decline of the Yugoslav economy to create a surge in unemployment. In Serbia proper, the rate of unemployment shot from 9.9 percent to 18.9 percent between 1970 and 1980; in 1990 it remained at 16.4 percent. For Kosovo, the numbers were more staggering: from 32.3 percent in 1970, the rate of unemployment was 38 percent in 1990. The rate among youth was over 30 percent in Serbia in 1985; in Kosovo, it exceeded 70 percent.[5] Gross domestic product (GDP) per capita rose an average of 5.1 percent a year from 1974 to 1979; from 1980 to 1984, it fell an average of 0.3 percent. Real incomes for Yugoslavia as a whole declined 2 percent between 1980 and 1984, after constant growth in the previous three decades.[6] International agencies (the International Monetary Fund) and many Yugoslavs (Serbs above all) believed that the cause of Yugoslavia's problems was the dispersion of decisionmaking. The 1974 constitution had to be revised.[7]

When Tito died in May 1980, his achievement was already being questioned. The reforms of the late 1960s and 1970s had resulted in inefficient of investments, an immobile labor supply, and a system unable to respond to the demands of international creditors. For the Serbian party leadership of the early 1980s, the answer to these economic ills was clear: economic and political leadership had to become the domain once again of the federal government, not local republican administrations. As in the 1960s, the debate over the economic future of Yugoslavia led inescapably to debate over its political organization. Slovenia supported looser federal ties, Serbia supported recentralization. The failure of the various actors in this drama (republican leaders, federal government, army) to reach a consensus on a strategy to address Yugoslavia's failing economy created tensions between republics that opened the door to the emergence of nationalism as the language of debate in the state. By 1985, Slovenes and Serbs in particular had concluded that no consensus would be reached and began to interpret their failure to communicate in nationalist terms.

Serbs evaluate Tito's legacy

The Serbian reassessment of Titoism began immediately after the president's death in May 1980. Although there were a variety of sources of opposition to Titoism in Serbia, the single most powerful one was nationalist and focused on the critical perception that Titoism's crime was its characterization of Serbs as hegemonic, authoritarian, and thus incapable of coexistence with the other nations of Yugoslavia. The issue that enabled the crystallization of the anti-Titoist movement in Serbia was Kosovo. Kosovo is simultaneously the mythic heartland of Serbia and an overwhelmingly Albanian region (over 90 percent of the population today). It is the home of the many important Serbian Orthodox monasteries, and until the fourteenth century it was the center of the medieval Serbian kingdom. The battle of Kosovo (1389), which signalled the end of that state, was fought there. In spite of the cultural importance of the region to Serbs, the fact that it had an Albanian majority led Tito to grant it autonomy within Serbia. Its history made it impossible for Serbs to accept its separation from Serbia proper. In 1968, 1981, and 1988–89, large-scale demonstrations illustrated the desire of the Albanians of the region for republican status. Those demonstrations also provoked the emigration of about 30,000 Serbs and Montenegrins from Kosovo,[8] which prompted cries that the Albanians of Kosovo were purposefully clearing the land of non-Albanians. Serbian intellectuals first labeled this process "genocide" in the early 1980s amid a flurry of petitions and meetings in Belgrade in support of the emigrant Serbs.[9] The Serbian reevaluation of Titoism proceeded on two tracks: one institutional, the other intellectual. The two avenues of opposition merged after 1987, when Slobodan Milošević came to power in Serbia.

Initially, some opposition to Titoism came from within the League of Serbian Communists (LCS – Savez komunista Srbije) and began long before Slobodan Milošević appeared. The LCS had been purged of its most capable leaders in 1972. The LCS had continued to resist changes to the constitutional status of Serbia after the purges, but they had robbed the party of much of its intellectual capital.[10] By the middle 1980s, the Serbian party was viewed by Serbian intellectuals and many within the party leadership itself as a failure for its inability to successfully articulate Serbian grievances, which were mainly economic and constitutional at that point. Intraparty opposition did not mirror the strength or answer the demands of the non-party intellectual opposition, which grew exponentially after the Albanian rebellion of 1981. The Serbian party, although supportive of a revision of the federal constitution, was still Titoist in its insistence that only the party could solve the national question, by modernizing Serbian society. It proposed revisions of the constitution, which would reintegrate the Yugoslav market and remove economic power from the corrupt Kosovo (Albanian) party. But as the 1980s progressed, the party's failure to make its case regarding the economy at the federal level, combined with its alleged unwillingness to act aggressively against the Albanian "genocide" of Serbs in Kosovo, left it hopelessly unpopular.

The intellectual opposition to Titoism in Serbia focused ever more on rehabilitating Serbian nationalism after decades of perceived denigration by the official ideology of the state.[11] Dobrica Ćosić, a novelist and member of the central committee of the LCS, heralded the beginning of this movement in May 1968 at a meeting of that committee, when he spoke on the failure of the revolution and of a growing bureaucracy to democratize Yugoslav society. His speech had a pronounced anti-Albanian character, but focused on Yugoslav communism's failure to modernize the state and thus eliminate nationalism. Ćosić added martyrdom to his presentation with a 1977 speech popularly titled "Literature and History Today." In it, he railed against Titoism and its bureaucracy, but also blazed a trail that would be well-traveled after Tito's death when he claimed for Serbia a special place as one of Europe's most heroic yet underappreciated nations.[12] Ćosić had little influence in Serbia until Tito died and Kosovo's Albanian population revolted in 1981. From that point, with the death of the charismatic leader and waves of Serbian and Montenegrin emigration from Kosovo, other Serbian intellectuals picked up Ćosić's themes. Ćosić's self-indulgent, self-pitying reflections in the name of Serbia would be welcome to a society deeply convinced of its own victimhood. Ćosić was instrumental in formulating the Memorandum of the Serbian Academy of Arts and Sciences (SANU), composed in 1986 (but never completed or formally issued), which can be considered the public declaration of both the party opposition and the intellectual anti-Titoist orientation, although the randomness of its grievances attested to the unsorted nature of the Serbian belief that Serbia had suffered at the hands of Tito and Kardelj.[13] It proposed that there were two separate categories of Serbian suffering in Yugoslavia. The first was institutional: the economic evolution of the Yugoslav state since the reforms of the 1960s had systematically ignored Serbian needs. The second was political and cultural: Serbs outside of Serbia proper suffered from the persecution of others. This complaint was directed mainly at Kosovo's Albanians, but ominously noted the growth of anti-Serbian sentiment in Croatia as well.

In Serbia in the 1980s, free-ranging political and social dialogue existed.[14] But instead of prompting the pluralization of society, alternative voices fell victim to a new ethnic nationalist orthodoxy. Since 1980, the seductiveness of the Serbian national idea, of the fear of dispersion, and of the myth of historical subjugation have outweighed civic options for intellectuals in Serbia. In other words, the hegemony of the ethnic idea replaced that of the communist idea. The nationalist articulation of Serbian grievances did not emerge from below, among the general population of Serbs; nor was it the result of the manipulations of Slobodan Milošević. Nationalism grew because Serbian intellectuals encouraged it. When Milošević began to use nationalism, he did so because it had become the dominant alternative to Titoist discourse in Serbia.

Slobodan Milošević bridges the opposition

Slobodan Milošević became president of Serbia by eliminating the discrepancy between intellectual dissenters and the party in Serbia. In essence, he used the powerful issue of Kosovo. Milošević promised and delivered what he called an "anti-bureaucratic revolution." In reality nothing more than a party purge, such a revolution could appeal to a variety of participants with mutually contradictory goals: it was a general panacea for a people with wildly varying hopes for the future. Bureaucracy was the bane of ongoing socialist revolution, as Yugoslavia's own Milovan Djilas had so famously pointed out. It had also been blamed by Ćosić and others for institutionalizing human rights abuses against Serbs in Kosovo. Generally, bureaucracy is an easy mark for those wishing to assess blame for an unresponsive political system. Thus an anti-bureaucratic revolution could satisfy socialists who feared their revolution was bogging down, nationalists who blamed bureaucracy for genocide in Kosovo, and any others who believed that change was necessary (just about everyone in Serbia).

Milošević's career was not extraordinary until 1986, when, with the help of his patron, Ivan Stambolić, Milošević became chair of the Serbian League of Communists. From that point, his ambition became apparent. Milošević's first aggressive move was to push out the leadership of the Serbian party, which he accomplished by the Eighth Session of the Central Committee of the Serbian League of Communists, which was held in September 1987 and saw the removal of the president of the Belgrade city committee of the Serbian LC, Dragiša Pavlović. In December, Stambolić, the president of Serbia, was removed from his position, ostensibly due to his support for Pavlović.[15] The turnover was merely a purge. Kosovo, the issue that would enable Milošević to build support throughout Serbia thereafter, was an important part of the backdrop to the purge. Thus Milošević initiated the anti-bureaucratic revolution in classic bureaucratic style.

After the purge of the party, the anti-bureaucratic revolution became populist. Milošević and his supporters mobilized thousands of Serbs who moved around Serbia, Vojvodina, Kosovo, and Montenegro in 1988 and 1989 and demanded the removal of the party leaderships of the latter three entities. Although these demonstrations purported to be spontaneous bursts of rage against an aging and unresponsive party, in fact they were the work of Milošević and his allies, who paid the demonstrators and exaggerated their numbers in the press. The Serbian Resistance Movement of Kosta Bulatović and the organization Božur (Peony), headed by Bogdan Kecman, both representing Kosovo Serbs, aided Milošević. As a result, the party leaderships of Vojvodina (October 1988) and Montenegro (January 1989) were overthrown and replaced by loyalists of Milošević. Milošević and his allies concocted an aura of democracy around the movement, claiming that it represented the will of the Serbian people and that it returned power from an immobilized party to Serbs themselves.

By March 1989, Milošević, riding his populist defense of Serbian rights in Kosovo, immensely popular, and in complete control of his party, produced constitutional revisions that reincorporated the two autonomous provinces in Serbia. In May of 1989, the Serbian skupština (national assembly) elected him president of Serbia, and in a December referendum, 86 percent of Serbs expressed confidence in his presidency. But whereas Milošević had promised much more than the defense of Serbs, ultimately he could only answer the most visceral demands of his constituency. He could not deliver on his other promises, which included privatization, efficient government, or federal centralization, because these questions had to be addressed on a Yugoslav level. At that point, Milošević's hold on Serbia began to wane, and the impulse for institutional (as opposed to populist) democratization grew. That impulse also grew out of concurrent events in the rest of Eastern Europe, where 1989 saw the overthrow of the communist regimes. Not only did the revolutions in the Soviet bloc alert Serbs (and other Yugoslavs) to the availability of new models for political behavior, they alerted Serbia's communists of the likelihood of threats to their monopoly on power.

1990: creating Serbia's tenuous democracy

The formation of political parties

The movement toward Serbia's first multiparty elections began in summer 1990. On June 13, a large meeting of opposition leaders was held in Belgrade.[16] The legal basis for Serbia's first free elections was laid rapidly thereafter. It must be remembered that elsewhere in Yugoslavia, elections had either been announced or already held. Obviously against its will, the Serbian government recognized that it had to announce elections too. No longer could it repeat its claim that it reflected democracy from below. Still, as he would demonstrate repeatedly, as the leader in power with the resources of the LCS, Milošević was able to create a democratic process that he could manipulate. Opposition parties were legalized in Serbia in August 1990, and the basic outlines of today's party system in Serbia emerged by the end of that year. By the date of the first free elections in postwar Serbia (December 9, 1990), dozens of parties had announced themselves, several of which merit more than cursory examination: the Socialist Party of Serbia, the Serbian Renewal Movement, the Democratic party, and the Alliance of Reform Forces of Yugoslavia.

On July 16, 1990, the League of Communists of Serbia was reborn as Socialist Party of Serbia (SPS, Socialistička partija Srbije).[17] Technically the party represented a merger of the LCS and the Socialist Alliance of the Working People of Serbia, the LC's front organization. Many observers therefore assumed it was merely a renamed communist party, a crude attempt by Milošević to reinvent himself. However, it included elements that had found no home in the old LCS. Mihailo Marković, the Praxis philosopher and long time socialist critic of Titoism, became the vice-president of the SPS. Antonije Isaković, a novelist who helped formulate the Memorandum of SANU, also joined the new party, as did several other noncommunist intellectuals. Between 1989 and 1991, absolute membership in the LCS/SPS declined by half, but one-third of the 430,000 members in late 1990 were new, indicating a real transition. There is no clear evidence on the nature of the exodus: it certainly included sincere, reform-minded members who now gravitated to the opposition, and the party undoubtedly picked up portions of the nationalist electorate. Thus, a substantially new party emerged during its transition.[18] The SPS enjoyed the highest membership of all of the new parties, which should be no surprise. In spite of its new name and significant new membership, it enjoyed many inherited advantages: Milošević's relationship with the most important print and electronic media in Serbia (described below), the funds of the Socialist Alliance (which may have been Milošević's main reason for merging it into the new party), and the manipulative political skills that followed forty-five years of experience. Finally, the SPS was the party of the anti-bureaucratic revolution and Milošević's takeover of the nationalist issue. It had the combined advantages of its long past and recent transition.

The Serbian Renewal Movement (SRM, Srpski pokret obnove), which formed in spring 1990,[19] was the first and most critical opposition party to face the LCS and then the SPS. In late 1990, it had between 15,000 and 25,000 members throughout Serbia. The movement and its leader, Vuk Drašković, capitalized on the exhaustion of Milošević's rhetoric, which had long concentrated on the need for economic reform and a solution of some sort to the distress of Kosovo's outnumbered Serbs. The SRM was a conservative, traditionalist party. Its appeal was threefold: opposition to Milošević, opposition to communism, and Serbian tradition. Regarding the first, Drašković's attacks were relentless and clear through the summer and fall of 1990: the people who supported Milošević two years earlier now "feel deceived and duped, and . . . are bitter because none of the promises that were made two years ago have been fulfilled." Milošević, in other words, had failed to satisfy popular demands for the reintegration of Kosovo in Serbia. Regarding communism, the leader of the SRM was quite as clear: it was "darkness, half a century of darkness and chaos . . ."[20] The central appeal of Drašković and the SRM was not simply anti-communist, however: it was a return to Serbian tradition, the precommunist past. With long black hair, beard, and moustache reminiscent of the most exaggerated images of the wartime Četnik movement, with his thumb and first two fingers extended in a salute to Serbian solidarity, Drašković proclaimed that if Yugoslavia were to fall apart, the internal borders of the state could not stand as new international borders. He declared that territories with a Serbian majority "before the Ustaša genocide," or which were part of Serbia before 1918 "are the inalienable, historical, and ethnic property of the Serbian people."[21] Full of the rhetoric of the ethnic nationalist, Drašković asserted that Bosnian Muslims were really Serbs, that Macedonia was a Serbian land, and that if war were necessary to defend those proposals, he would support war unconditionally.

The Democratic Party (DP, Demokratska stranka),[22] emerged in February 1990 as the locus of Serbia's intellectual, democratically oriented opposition. It drew together the majority of the members of the Praxis group who had not joined the SPS, including Dragoljub Mićunović and Ljuba Tadić, and others in Belgrade's intellectual opposition community, including Kosta Čavoški, Vojislav Koštunica, and the novelist Borislav Pekić. In late 1990,

Table 5.2 *Voter characteristics and inclinations in Serbia, 1990 (by party identification)*

	SPS		SRM		DP	
Religion						
Atheist[a]	54.1	(28.5)	33.3	(16.4)	61.4	(35.3)
Believer[a]	45.9	(71.5)	66.6	(83.6)	38.6	(64.7)
Education						
Less than primary	18		6		2	
Primary	25		17		8	
Secondary (worker)	26		32		18	
Secondary (other)	20		31		33	
Post-secondary	11		14		39	
Nationalism						
"Hard"	66		92		70	
"Mixed"	30		7		14	
"Soft"	4		1		16	
Authoritarianism						
Authoritarian	60		42		20	
"Mixed"	20		21		18	
Antiauthoritarian	20		37		62	
Property						
Prefer private	38		69		75	
"Mixed"	26		16		16	
Prefer socialized	36		15		9	

Note: [a]Figures for 1991 in parenthesis.
Sources: Miroslav Pečujlić, "U začaranom krugu politike: Političke institucije u Jugoslaviji (Srbiji) juče i danas," in Pečujlić et al., *Radjanje javnog mnjenja i političkih stranaka: Analiza empiriskih istraživanja u Srbiji 1990–1991* (Belgrade: Institut za političke studije, Centar za javno mnjenje i marketing "Medium," Pravni fakultet, 1992), pp. 77–8; Srbobran Branković, "Determinante političkog javnog mnjenja u Srbiji," in Pečujlić et al, *Radjanje javnog mnjenja*, pp. 212, 216–17.

it had between 10,000 and 15,000 members.[23] The Democratic party was the least likely of the new parties to pander to the nationalism of the masses, but that, in part, can be attributed to its elitist rejection of Milošević's and Drašković's populism. The Democrats' major enemy was the Democrats themselves – the party was plagued by disagreements about tactics, which eventually fragmented the leadership and split the party. The party's potential was limited anyway, as it appealed most to the educated urbanites of Belgrade.

The Democrats and their offspring have prided themselves on their advocacy of all of the standard liberal solutions to autocracy: the usual freedoms of the press, assembly, speech; and, before the dissolution of

Yugoslavia, bicameralism, by which Yugoslavs would have elected one house proportionally by republic, whereas in the other each republic would have been represented equally.[24] Most difficult was the balancing act that the party had to accomplish between its own distaste for the national issue and the absolute necessity that it be addressed, lest the party be completely marginalized. Thus, although assuring its constituents (and one suspects outsiders) of its commitment to constitutionalism rooted in the rights of citizens as individuals, it also made clear its commitment to defending the Serbian nation. In the words of Dragoljub Mićunović, "we are a national party and are equally Serbian and as patriotic as any other party, but we are also a modern democratic party which does not take the view that people can be treated as labels."[25] The party floundered in spite of its intellectual capital and support for liberal democratic institutions. By the late fall, with elections planned, the party divided into two factions, one "nationalist," the other not. The nationalist faction coincided with that group which was willing to cooperate with other opposition parties (most importantly, the SRM) in the elections; the others were unwilling to work with Drašković.[26]

Until the middle of 1990, Ante Marković, the prime minister of Yugoslavia, was the most popular politician in Yugoslavia and in Serbia itself. His popularity was due to his early success with economic reform. In June 1990, Marković founded the Alliance of Reform Forces of Yugoslavia (ARFY – Savez reformskih snaga Jugoslavije),[27] which would be one of only two parties that would enter elections in Serbia as a federal, Yugoslav party with no republican or ethnic commitment (the Association for a Yugoslav Democratic Initiative [AYDI – Udruženje za jugoslovensku demokratsku inicijativu] was the other). A pragmatic reform party, by all accounts the ARFY struck fear in the hearts of the nationalist leaders, because Marković had been so popular to that point.[28] The nationalist parties were able to portray the League as the party of the nationalities – Albanians, Hungarians, Romanians, Muslim South Slavs – who would inevitably flock to it as coalition partners in event of electoral victory.

The legal basis for the elections

The most contentious issue of the summer of 1990 was whether the elections would be held before or after the passage of a new constitution. The Serbian *skupština* (parliament) decided on June 26 that this important question would be answered by a referendum on July 1 and 2, which gave the opposition less than one week to convince voters that a constitution should rightly be formulated by representatives that had been freely elected. The polling proceeded fairly, but the short window of opportunity for the opposition gave it little chance to counteract the influence of the initiative's regime supporters. Voters chose to adopt a constitution before free elections, allegedly by a vote of 97 percent in favor. The inability of the opposition to make its case, combined with regime control of the media, probably assured the affirmative vote in the referendum. On the other hand, it is possible that Serbian voters wished immediately for a strong constitution incorporating Kosovo (and less critically Vojvodina) into Serbia.[29]

The Serbian skupština began discussions of the constitutional draft in August. The opposition had no voice in its formulation. It created a presidential system of government in which the executive would have extensive powers with undefined limitations by the assembly.[30] The constitution did state that new elections for the assembly had to be held within four years, whereas a presidential term would last five years. A president could only serve two terms in office. The constitution promised strong presidential government in the future, which frightened the opposition. The existing skupština, obviously dominated by members of the SPS and other descendants of the LCS, promulgated the Serbian constitution of 1990 on September 28. As Robert Hayden has noted, "the primary purpose of the Serbian constitution of 1990 was to provide the basis for the one-man rule of Slobodan Milošević."[31] It placed sovereignty in the hands of all citizens of Serbia, which included all who lived there, making it a superficially liberal document. Of course, the constitution also answered a venerable demand of opponents of Titoism in Serbia to reunite the two autonomous provinces with the Serbian core.

Other laws accompanied the passage of the constitution. The skupština had already passed its "law on political organizations" on August 27, 1990.[32] According to that law, any organization with 100 members and a clearly stated political purpose could be registered as a political party. The skupština discussed the electoral law at the same time, and without dialogue with the opposition parties. The law as passed in September called for single-member constituencies. It established 250 constituencies: 160 in Serbia proper, 56 in Vojvodina, and 34 in Kosovo.[33] The law also called for two rounds of voting. Any candidate who won 50 percent of the vote in the first round was elected; in cases in which no candidate received half the vote, the top two candidates would enter a second-round runoff. The law did not unequivocally state that the elections be organized with the input of opposition parties, it did not promise any particular length of time to prepare for the elections, and it did nothing to assure that the print media would provide balanced coverage – although it did promise 90 minutes of television and radio exposure to each registered party. Finally, party finances have been obscured by the illegality that pervades Serbian society today. A law on financing political parties was not passed by the Serbian assembly until 1992, but by then the general trends were clear. The SPS was the best funded party, because it inherited the

LCS's resources. The law, when passed, allowed for 3 percent of a party's donations to be anonymous. Parties were not to receive funds from governments of foreign states or government agencies. Although there were no limits placed on donations from foreign individuals (which could include anyone from George Soros to Serbian émigré organizations), there is a stigma attached to such funds that has led all of the parties to deny that they receive them. Recent scandals have revealed the extent of contributions to the SPS by sanction-breakers and criminals.[34]

Elections were announced in late November 1990, to be held on December 9 and 23. In response to the short-notice announcement, the opposition parties demanded revisions to the law, including allowing workers temporarily abroad to vote. They also requested that the time frame for the elections be extended, because according to the law, the opposition would hardly have time to organize for the polling. But the electoral law was not changed.[35] The elections of December 9 and 23, 1990 demonstrated that the fears of the opposition were well-founded, but they also demonstrated the immaturity of the opposition in the face of a well-prepared government used to heavy-handed political behavior. The SPS swept through the elections with a victory that assured its control of Serbia. Milošević, who won the presidential election with 63 percent of the vote to Drašković's 16 percent, would not need to rely on his extensive executive powers, thanks to the single-member system by which his party won 46 percent of the votes cast in the first round but emerged with 78 percent (194 of 250) of the seats in the skupština.[36] The SRM came out with nineteen seats, the DP gained seven, and the ARFY picked up six.

Of registered voters, 71 percent voted in both the presidential and skupština elections in Serbia.[37] As opposed to the Croatian elections, in the Serbian voting only residents of Serbia could take part, which drastically limited the influence of the anti-communist Serbian émigré community.[38] Dennison Rusinow reported at the time that there were few violations at the polls, although it was impossible to measure.[39] There were important regional variations in voter turnout: in Vojvodina, the turnout was somewhat higher at 80 percent, and in Kosovo it was extremely low at 18.6 percent, as the Albanian population boycotted the vote. Several non-Serbian parties did relatively well at the polls (in comparison with the Serbian opposition). The Democratic Community of Vojvodina Hungarians (DCVH – Demokratska zajednica vojvodjanskih madjara) won eight seats, the Party of Democratic Action (PDA – Stranka demokratske akcije), a Muslim South Slav party in the Sandžak, won three seats, the Democratic Union of Croats in the Vojvodina (DUCV – Demokratski savez Hrvata u Vojvodini) won one seat, and the non-national Alliance of Reform Forces (ARFY) won two seats.[40] One group that gained no representation was the Kosovo Albanians, due to their boycott.

Table 5.3 *Parliamentary elections in Serbia, 1990*

Party	Votes	%	Seats	%
SPS	2,320,507	46.08	194	77.6
SRM	794,786	15.78	19	7.6
Group of Citizens (Independents)	456,318	9.06	8	3.2
DP	374,887	7.44	7	2.8
DCVH	132,726	2.63	9	3.6
PDA	84,156	1.67	3	1.2
ARFY	74,748	1.48	6	2.4
PPP	68,045	1.35	4	1.6
ND–MS	67,356	1.33	-	-
PRP	63,041	1.29	-	-
PLPS	52,663	1.04	-	-
SNR	40,359	.80	-	-
Total			250	

Notes: Voter turnout: 71.48 percent; total votes and percentages of votes are from the first round; total seats and percentages of seats include both rounds.
Source: Srećko Mihailović et al., *Od izbornih rituala do slobodnih izbora: Sondaža javnog mnjenja uoči prvih višestranačkih izbora u Srbiji* (Belgrade: Univerzitet u Beogradu, Institut društvenih nauka, Centar za politikološka istraživanja i javno mnjenje, 1991), pp. 281–2.

Interpreting the 1990 elections

The 1990 elections were the first held in a time of peace in postwar Serbia. The war in Croatia began in June 1991, and in essence the system established in Serbia in 1990 has remained static. Why did Slobodan Milošević win in 1990? And why did no non-nationalist party succeed at the polls? The answers need to be sought in the character of the Serbian electorate and the conditions under which it voted. The elections illustrated that Serbs felt comfortable with the existing regime, in spite of the tangible opposition to it that had arisen since early 1990. Two explanations exist for that fact: first, opinion polling before and after the elections (and since 1990) has shown that Serbs were generally anticommunist but inclined to strong presidential (or even authoritarian) rule; second, the regime's takeover of the nationalist issue in the mid-1980s served it well. Some have claimed that Milošević benefited from the existence of a disenfranchised underclass in Serbia in the late 1980s, but polling data indicate that all of the major parties gained support among the youthful unemployed, which constitutes much of that group.[41] There are several points to be made about the nature of the electoral campaigning and its effect on the outcome.

Table 5.4 *Presidential elections in Serbia, 1990*

Candidate	Votes	%
Slobodan Milošević (SPS)	3,285,799	63.34
Vuk Drašković (SRM)	824,674	16.40
Ivan Djurić (Independent)	277,398	5.52
Sulejman Ugljanin (PDA)	109,459	2.18
Vojislav Šešelj (Independent)	96,277	1.91
Blažo Petrović (YU Bloc)	57,420	1.14
Others	n.a.	9.5

Note: Voter turnout: 71.50 percent.

Source: Srećko Mihailović et al., *Od izbornih rituala do slobodnih izbora: Sondaža javnog mnjenja uoči prvih višestranačkih izbora u Srbiji* (Belgrade: Univerzitet u Beogradu, Institut društvenih nauka, Centar za politikološka istraživanja i javno mnjenje, 1991), pp. 278-9.

Miroslav Pečujlić of the Institute for Political Studies in Belgrade noted in 1992 that "the central contradiction in political life [in Serbia] is the fundamental disharmony between democratic forms of political institutions and an undeveloped democratic political culture."[42] Pečujlić and other analysts have concluded that an "authoritarian spirit" settled over Serbia during decades of communist rule. These commentators note that the regime itself is authoritarian, the opposition behaves in an authoritarian fashion (uncompromising rather than as a "loyal opposition"), parties appear which are only distinguishable by the personalities of their leaders, and Serbs themselves are inclined to authoritarian governance.[43] One way that the disharmony noted above has been manifested is in the contradictory voting/belief patterns professed by Serbs who demand democracy yet vote for its antithesis.

A crude measure of inclinations of Serbs suggests that they embraced strong presidential rule. In polling done in 1990, 60 percent of followers (not members) of the SPS claimed to have an "authoritarian orientation"; 42 percent (a plurality) of SRM followers felt the same way. Of followers of the DP, only 62 percent professed to be anti-authoritarians.[44] The category itself is imprecise: what exactly is an "authoritarian orientation"? Given that the Milošević government was the referent, however, we can draw the conclusion that it indicates an inclination to government by a strong, single, authoritative ruler. Another poll elicited less convincing evidence for an authoritarian inclination among Serbs: 27 percent in November 1990 agreed that "there must be a single master obeyed by all," whereas 49 percent favored a system in which officials "serve according to the people's will."[45] The elections since 1990 illustrate, however, that the people's will can be to elect a strong authoritarian figure. Further evidence for that generalization includes the lengthy list of minuscule parties whose strongest appeal for voters was their leaders, as well as the inability of even the larger opposition parties to form electoral or parliamentary coalitions due to interpersonal rivalries.

Whereas polling indicated that Serbs retained respect for strong, centralized governance, it also depicted an electorate that was tired of communism. Thus attitudes towards communism and socialism were generally negative by 1990. Instead, what now drew Serbs to the SPS was that party's ability to use an issue vital to the majority of Serbs: the fate of the Serbian people in a divisive, virtually confederated Yugoslavia. Milošević's nationalist turn, in other words, had satisfied all but the most demanding opponents of the regime. In November 1990, 40 percent of Serbia's population had a favorable view of socialism; 39 percent called themselves non- or anti-communists.[46] On the other hand, all of the parties had recognized the necessity of embracing the nationalist movement surging through Serbia. The vast majority of the supporters (not members) of the three leading parties claimed to have a "hard nationalist" position (66 percent of the SPS, 70 percent of the DP, and 92 percent of the SRM). Attesting to the importance of the national question is the fact that, in spite of his leadership on the issue, it was Milošević's failure to adequately solve the problem of Kosovo and the fate of Serbs outside Serbia's borders that most influenced the growth of opposition.[47] The relatively low percentage of "hard" nationalists in the SPS was partially a result of its Marxist inheritance, according to which many Serbs rejected the notion that they were nationalists at all – rather, they were opponents of other nationalisms (Albanian most of all).

The SPS's dominance of the media clearly influenced the outcome of the elections of 1990.[48] In fact, the issue of the media was the single most divisive question between the legalization of parties and the beginning of the war in Croatia and Slovenia in June 1991. Whereas in earlier decades Serbian print and broadcast media had benefitted from the freedom allowed them by the party, Milošević demanded that they conspire in the government's manipulation of the situation in Kosovo and in the president's consolidation of power. In 1987, Milošević had gained the loyalty of the directors of the Politika publishing house and Radio-Television Belgrade; they conspired in the anti-bureaucratic revolution, playing up the lurid imagery of a Kosovo under siege by Albanians. Serbs, accustomed to believe in what they read and saw in the media, fell victim to this newly radicalized press. As the reputation of Milošević began to fall in 1990, so did the reputation of his media. Nonetheless, his control of it served to confuse an unsophisticated electorate unused to multiparty elections. The publications of the *Politika* house, under the leadership of Milošević minion Živorad Minović, and the programming of Radio-Television Belgrade (RTB), under the guidance of general director Dušan Mitević, proved critical to Milošević. By 1990, several independent media sources had arisen in Serbia. *Vreme*, an independent weekly newsmagazine, began publication; Studio B, an independent television station in Belgrade, started broadcasting; B-92 (a student radio station) could be heard after 1989. The sophisticated nature of their message, the weakness of their signals (in the case of the radio and television stations), and their inability to improve their equipment and supplies limited their influence to Belgrade and its environs.[49] The Milošević government has allowed supportive illegal stations to flourish while clamping down on opposition ones.[50]

One of the characteristics of Serbian democracy in action has been the fact that a plethora of parties appears at the sign of elections, only to disappear after having garnered no support. In 1990, for example, fifty-three parties were registered, of which few gained seats in the skupština. Some observers suspect that many of the small parties are encouraged by the SPS, to confuse the public but also for a more practical reason: the media coverage that each party can demand as its legal right clouds the message of more viable parties. In the lead-up to the elections of 1990, every registered party was guaranteed 90 minutes of airtime on radio and television, and each presidential candidate got 60 minutes (and the registration process was welcoming: any organization with over 100 members and a stated political goal could register as a party).[51] Given that many of the parties were either not serious or not competitive, much airtime was wasted or had the effect of confusing rather than informing the electorate. Opponents of Milošević thus rightly suspect that the "democratic" rules of access to the media were designed to flood the electorate with useless information, diluting the effect of serious participants.

There is mixed evidence regarding the effectiveness of the media with the Serbian public. Before the outbreak of war in June 1991, Serbs claimed not to trust their media. A *Borba* poll in December 1990 showed that 40 percent of Serbs polled did not trust television, but 15 percent trusted it completely; only 4 percent trusted *Politika* completely, whereas 30 percent believed little or nothing of what they read.[52] Other research showed that in 1990, 30 percent of adults in Serbia never read the newspaper, whereas 44 percent read it daily, 26 percent occasionally. *Politika*, *Politika ekspres*, and *Večernje novosti* (all loyal to the government) were read by 40 percent of those polled, but *Srpska reč* (SRM) and *Demokratija* (DP) were read by 9 percent and 5 percent respectively.[53] So the government press had the faith of a plurality of Serbs. Although 92 percent of those polled watched the televised electoral campaign, many were skeptical of the fairness of the conditions under which the opposition parties were allowed access to the media. The SPS and the SRM both left negative impressions with their advertising, whereas the DP and the ARFY did not.[54] The accessibility and freedom of the media proved to be the most contested issue during and after the elections in Serbia. In March 1991, when street demonstrations erupted involving members and followers of the opposition (especially the SRM and its leader, Drašković), the catalyst was the question of media independence. Much of the distrust of the media shown by Serbs undoubtedly grew in the period 1990–91, when the populace grew disillusioned with Milošević. However, with the onset of war, the Serbian press closed ranks behind the war effort, becoming the only trusted source of information for Serbs. By 1992, *Politika* (and the publications of the Politika publishing house) and Radio-Television Belgrade were the most read and most trusted sources of information in Serbia.[55]

Serbian politics during the wars of Yugoslav succession

The aftermath of the elections and the outbreak of war

The elections and their aftermath coincided with the beginning of war in the former Yugoslavia. The period between the December elections and the outbreak of war in late June 1991 was loaded with conflicting signals, as it witnessed the election of ultranationalist Vojislav Šešelj (head of the new Serbian Radical party) in a by-election in Belgrade, a popular uprising in Belgrade against Milošević, violent unrest in Serbian districts of Croatia, and interrepublican negotiations on the fate of Yugoslavia. The war probably saved Milošević from a concerted effort to overthrow him. Unfortunately, with the outbreak of war, the general nationalist consensus that bound the opposition parties grew firmer, as they all moved to the extreme with the intriguing exception of Vuk Drašković, who turned pacifist as the tragedy unfolded.

The potential for a successful rebellion against the Milošević regime was shown by the demonstrations of March 1991 during which students and opposition leaders took to the streets of Belgrade. The movement focused on the undemocratic nature of the new regime and, especially, its monopoly of the media. The March demonstrations were a false prophecy of failure for Milošević. Although he was forced to reveal his undemocratic essence (his colleague on the Yugoslav presidency, Borislav Jović, had the Yugoslav People's Army (YPA) called in to patrol Belgrade's streets), and although the SRM gained immeasurable credibility as a result, in fact Milošević only had to substitute one supporter for another as general director at Radio-Television Serbia (RTS, formerly RT Belgrade).[56]

Any sense (or hope) that the formation of parties, the elections of 1990, and the street demonstrations of March, 1991 might have led to a true transition to democracy in Serbia was dashed with the outbreak of war in

June 1991. The war in Croatia brought mixed responses: it was clear to many in Serbia that the Milošević government had prepared the ground for the war with its media imagery of bloodthirsty Ustaša and cynical Slovenes, but it also was, quite simply, a real war after June, and as such demanded of the Serbian opposition a level of patriotism that it proved willing to provide. A year later the Bosnian war added to the internal confusion in Serbia, as the brutal nature of the war and the Serbian role in it clashed fundamentally with the general conviction of Serbs that their communities in Bosnia deserved protection and independence. With the imposition of sanctions on May 30, 1992 (they were made harsher on April 26, 1993, when they were increased to a total trade ban), the psychological dislocation of war was made complete, as conflicting senses of internal and international threats and a certain amount of shame resulting from the role of Serbs in Bosnia's tragedy produced a schizophrenic electorate. Nonetheless, that electorate quickly settled in to support the war. The politicians also adjusted. By 1993, Vojislav Koštunica, Zoran Djindjić (the new leader of the DP) and others were moving toward the nationalist consensus rather than disputing it. The only politician who has made the political mistake of repudiating the war (and only intermittently) has been Vuk Drašković, and he is openly reviled in Serbia today.

The outbreak of war signalled the arrival of Šešelj, the head of the Serbian Četnik Movement.[57] Šešelj was born in Bosnia and educated at the University of Sarajevo, where he received a doctorate in law. He spent much of the 1980s in jail as a critic of Titoism and the ruling LCY, but he only found his niche after the war in Croatia began in 1991. Until then, he was a caricature of the Četnik, the heroic Serbian nationalist of the Second World War. Although his open alliance with Milošević was not yet public, Šešelj's role as Milošević's surrogate radical nationalist was suspected by the opposition, as he had been treated leniently throughout 1990 in spite of violent public behavior. He competed with his former friend and political ally Drašković as Serbia's most atavistic nationalist. The Četnik movement was illegal, but Šešelj still came in fifth in the presidential election of 1990 and won a seat in the skupština in a by-election in the Belgrade suburb of Rakovica, in which he defeated Borislav Pekić, a novelist and one of the most well-known Democrats.

After his election, he officially formed the Serbian Radical party (SRP – Srpska radikalna stranka). At first glance, the success of this politician/warlord (his private paramilitary force was held accountable for atrocities in Croatia and Bosnia) was stunning: without much of an organization, Šešelj's Radicals won seventy-three seats in the December 1992 elections and have been an unavoidable element in coalition talks in Serbia since then. Many have pondered the appeal of Šešelj, as he appears on first glance to be a buffoon. However, research has demonstrated that the SRP and the SPS thrive among the same segments of the population and appeal to virtually the same voters. Both parties are popular among government employees, and the SRP appeals especially to former adherents of the SPS who have been disillusioned with the failure of Milošević to unify the Serbian communities of the former Yugoslavia.[58] The main difference in the appeal of the two parties is that those who support Šešelj are less likely to call themselves socialists and more likely to favor a more radical approach to the wars.

The failure of the opposition at the polls in 1990 and the outbreak of war also prompted the further fragmentation of the Democratic party. Following the election, Čavoški and Nikola Milošević left to form the Serbian Liberal party (SLP – Srpska liberalna stranka), and Koštunica took one faction out of the DP, first to join a new coalition with Drašković and then to form the Democratic Party of Serbia (DPS – Demokratska stranka Srbije, DPS). Remaining was the core of a now-moderate DP, still led by Mićunović. The issue that divided the Democrats was one that deserves our attention: the possibility of a radical transition to democracy in Serbia. The advocate of that type of transition was a new coalition known as the Democratic Movement of Serbia (DEPOS – Demokratski pokret Srbije), which was founded on May 23, 1992.[59]

DEPOS appeared in a period of international and internal crisis for Serbia. The war in Bosnia began in April, and sanctions would be put in place by the United Nations in late May. DEPOS brought together the SRM of Drašković (who became its president), the new DPS of Koštunica (who became its vice-president), the Serbian Liberal party, the People's Peasant party (PPP – Narodna seljačka stranka), and the New Democracy (ND – Nova demokratija) in a coalition that demanded a transition to democracy along the model of Poland, Hungary, and Czechoslovakia. This model, according to the coalition's leaders, demanded that the ruling party step down and a set of revolutionary bodies be established by democratic elements in Serbian society to completely recreate government.[60] DEPOS gained some authority when several members of the nationalist intelligentsia, including Matija Bećković, joined. Although it might have seemed that Bećković's inclusion signified a softening of the nationalism of some of the intellectuals, it probably illustrated more the essential similarity of the national goals of the various parties. In any case, DEPOS shared Panić's desire to end the war in Bosnia as quickly as possible, although there were tensions within the organization between Drašković, who was antiwar at this point, and Koštunica, who was not.

DEPOS announced its arrival with demonstrations lasting from Vidovdan (June 28, and a Serbian national holiday) 1992 through the first week of July. It seemed to be implementing its stated strategy of overthrowing the regime

Table 5.5 *Assembly and presidential elections in Serbia, 1992*

Party or candidate	Votes	%	Seats	%
Assembly				
SPS	1,359,086	28.77	101	40.4
SRP	1,066,765	22.58	73	29.2
DEPOS	797,831	16.89	50	20.0
DCVH	140,825	2.98	9	3.6
DP	196,347	4.16	6	2.4
Group of Citizens from				
Kosovo and Metohija	17,352	0.37	5	2.0
SPP	128,240	2.71	3	1.2
RDFV	71,865	1.52	2	0.8
DRPM	6,336	0.13	1	0.4
Total			250	

Presidency	Percentage of votes
Slobodan Milošević (SPS)	55.90
Milan Panić (Ind.)	34.30
Milan Paroski (People's Party)	3.31
Dragan Vasiljković (Ind.)	1.97
Jezdimir Vasiljević (Ind.)	1.38
Miroslav Jovanović (Ind.)	0.63
Blažo Perović (Ind.)	0.46
Others	2.05

Note: Voter turnout: 69 percent.
Source: Milan Andrejevich, "The Radicalization of Serbian Politics," *RFE/RL Research Report* 2, no. 13 (March 26, 1993), 15.

rather than negotiating a transition (as the DP wished). As the summer wore on, however, DEPOS became instead an actor in one of the surreal sideshows of Serbian politics since 1990: the attempt of the West and the opposition in Serbia to replace Milošević with Milan Panić, the Serbian-born American pharmaceutical magnate. Panić was chosen prime minister by the federal assembly in July 1992, one month after Dobrica Ćosić was made federal president. Initially, Milošević chose both Ćosić and Panić as a concession to the West, which had imposed the sanctions. But by August, Panić emerged as a serious alternative in Serbia, as he attempted to moderate aggressive Serbian policies in Bosnia. As a result, he and Milošević dueled through the fall as Western governments began to actively support Panić as a presidential candidate in opposition to Milošević.

Table 5.6 *Elections to Federal Assembly of Yugoslavia, 1992*

Party	Votes[a]	%[a]	Seats	%
SPS	1,478,918	31.4	47	34.1
SRP	1,056,539	22.4	34	24.6
DEPOS	809,731	17.2	20	14.5
DSP	130,431	2.8	17	12.3
DP	280,183	6.0	5	3.6
SPM	36,390	0.8	5	3.6
PP	34,436	0.7	4	2.8
DCVH	106,036	2.3	3	2.1
RFDV	101,234	2.2	2	1.4
DRPV	58,505	1.3	1	0.7
Total			138	

Note: [a]Other parties received votes but not seats.
Source: Andrejevich, "The Radicalization of Serbian Politics," p. 15.

The elections of 1992

Panić's presence only added insult to the injury of the sanctions: both reminded Serbs that they were international pariahs, outnumbered and surrounded by hostile forces. If the sanctions isolated Serbs, Panić himself represented the enemy in their midst. The Panić episode illustrates the extent to which the sanctions and other pressures from the West backfired: instead of affirming in the minds of Serbs the need to be rid of Milošević (as warmonger), they prompted Serbs to dig in their heels and resist the outsider. The fact that American policymakers openly labeled Panić the "candidate for peace" did not have the intended effect. Try as they might, DEPOS and other less popular civic opposition parties failed to overcome Milošević's media control, which played on Serbian paranoia. In the December 20, 1992, presidential election, 69 percent voted. In the event, after all of the threats and promises of the West, Milošević got 56 percent of the presidential vote to Panić's 34 percent. In the skupština elections, the SPS gained 29 percent of the vote and 101 seats, but the true victor in the voting was the SRP, with 23 percent and 73 seats, a massive gain at the expense of the SPS. DEPOS, the "vote for peace," gained only 17 percent of the vote and 50 seats, whereas the DP got 4 percent and 6 seats. Željko Ražnatović "Arkan," a paramilitary leader and war criminal, took advantage of extremely low turnout in Kosovo to win 5 seats. The DCVH, representing Vojvodina Hungarians, received 3 percent and 9 seats.[61]

Milošević's ability to turn the election into a referendum on the righteousness of the Serbian cause made it a loyalty test for voters. In the aftermath of the 1992 elections, the new Milošević majority was established with the open cooperation of the SRP and Šešelj. As it happened, Milošević's major goal was to use Šešelj to politically ruin both Panić and Ćosić. Šešelj's willingness to tar the two men with the brush of defeatism was enough to topple both by the summer of 1993. Thereafter, however, Milošević turned on Šešelj himself, allowing his press to attack the Čctnik leader relentlessly through the fall. Clearly, Milošević had exhausted the usefulness of the SRP, and he had no desire to make Šešelj into a more serious challenge to his own power. Instead, to satiate the radical nationalist element in Serbia, the SPS began to patronize the Serbian Unity party (Stranka srpskog jedinstva, SUP), Arkan's new party. With Arkan replacing Šešelj as Milošević's surrogate radical on the right, Milošević was able to be rid of his opponents in the moderate wing (Panić and Ćosić) as well as his most powerful potential opponent on the right (Šešelj).

The elections of 1993

By the December 1993 elections, Milošević had once again established his own equilibrium in Serbian politics. The 62 percent of the electorate who voted elected essentially the same constellation of parties. The SPS, with 37 percent of the vote, gained 123 seats in the skupština; DEPOS (composed in this election of the SRM, the People's Peasant party, the New Democracy, the Citizens' Alliance, and part of SLS) picked up some of the seats that the Radicals lost, receiving 45 seats; the SRP lost about half of its seats, getting 39; Djindjić's DP gained 29 seats (the remainder of the Radicals' loss); the DPS with 7, the DCVH with 5, and 2 Albanians (in spite of the continuing Kosovo Albanian boycott of the elections) completed the spectrum. The precipitous losses suffered by Šešelj's Radicals were no doubt due to negative media coverage, but Arkan's Serbian Unity party was also trounced. Still, the elections proved that the nationalization of politics had not changed much. In fact, in the aftermath of the elections, Djindjić, Koštunica, and Drašković would readily compete to best represent Serbian national interests in and out of Serbia proper (see table 5.7).

After the 1993 elections the SPS had difficulty forming a government. The only way for the opposition to stop Milošević was to form a coalition of its own – which was an impossibility. The SPS had merely to scrape up three more votes to control the skupština. They found them in the representative of the New Democracy party, which was led by Dušan Mihailović and had run as part of DEPOS. With the formation of an SPS/ND government in the spring of 1993, all that remained was for the entirely splintered opposition

Table 5.7 *Parliamentary elections in Serbia, 1993*

	Seats	%
SPS	123	49.2
DEPOS	45	18.0
SRP	39	15.6
DP	29	11.6
DPS	7	2.8
DCVH	5	2.0
PDA–DPA	2	0.8
Total	250	

Note: Voter turnout: 62 percent.
Source: Stan Markotich, "Postelection Serbia," *RFE/RL Research Report* 3, no. 3 (January 21, 1994), 8–12.

to once again discuss various combinations of alliances. The ominous point about this futile attempt was that the Radical Party was now free of obligations, leaving the road clear to negotiations between the democratic opposition and Šešelj. The catalyst to such a combination was Milošević's agreement, in the summer of 1994, to allow monitors along Serbia's Drina river border with Bosnia, to enable better policing of the Bosnian Serbs. Milošević agreed because it promised a lightening of the sanctions, and his acquiescence illustrated the fact that he was now beyond concern with the fate of the Serbs, instead opting to maintain power in ways he understood (coercive measures, control of the media and police). In the process, he left Koštunica, Djindjić, and Šešelj scrambling for allies, and they found each other. A further boon to the mutual interests of the opposition parties and their leaders came in May and August 1995, when Milošević allowed Croatia to retake Western Slavonia (the Daruvar region) and then the remainder of the Serb-held portions of Croatia without a fight.

The Milošević regime

One could not be faulted for hoping that a transition to democracy was in progress in the aftermath of the 1990 elections. Unfortunately, since then, it has been more than clear that there has been no transition and probably will be none until there are fundamental structural changes in Serbian institutions and especially in the political culture of the Serbian electorate. Simply put, there are neither the political alternatives available in Serbia nor the inclination to create such alternatives to challenge the regime. Slobodan Milošević and the SPS have retained predominance in all of the organs that assure power in an authoritarian state. Furthermore, no party or politician in Serbia has offered a powerful, antinationalist vision to compete with Milošević.

Milošević's ability to stay in power is founded on his control of two institutions: the media and the police. Regarding the media, little has changed since 1990. In July 1992, the government tried (and essentially succeeded) in returning *Politika* to the government fold after it tenuously opposed Serbian involvement in the Bosnian war, and in early 1993, RTS purged 1,000 employees deemed disloyal to Milošević.[62] The regime also assaulted the independence of the daily *Borba* in late 1994. *Borba*, which established its independent credentials (both journalistically and legally) in 1990 when Ante Marković's government allowed it to be privatized, remained a constant moderate voice in Serbia against the manipulations of the Milošević media. In November 1994, the regime challenged the private status of the paper. When the newspaper's staff resisted the crude attempt to reduce it to a government rag, the government simply began publishing its own *Borba*, side by side with the original one. But in January 1995, the newspaper's original staff began publishing *Naša Borba* (Our Borba).[63] The attack on *Borba* represented the latest and most aggressive of several attempts by the regime to reign in insubordinate media. Of the opposition media, today *Vreme*, *Naša Borba*, and *Republika* (an independent biweekly) continue to publish, and Radio B-92 still broadcasts. They have lost rather than gained support in Serbia, for which they can thank their limited range, their inability to get advertising and newsprint, and their allegedly treasonous approach to the news.

The Milošević regime has also retained firm control of internal security and the military. The status of the army has changed drastically in the past four years. Early in the wars in Croatia and Bosnia, besides its active role in the fighting, the YPA acted as a conduit to the paramilitary forces of Šešelj's Četniks, Mirko Jović's White Eagles, and Arkan's Tigers. In 1992, it was purged (for the first time) of virtually all non-Serbs and is now a Serbian, rather than Yugoslav, army. Today, the professional army (AY – Army of Yugoslavia) does not have the power or the privileges of the old YPA, although ironically it appears to have retained a high level of confidence among Serbs.[64] The army has been purged repeatedly, because it has proved to be quite factionalized, with supporters of various political leaders (namely, Milošević, Šešelj, and Radovan Karadžić) losing their positions as Milošević's policy has dictated.[65] Instead, the Ministry of Internal Affairs and its police occupy pride of place. They number up to 100,000, of which half are said to work for the secret police.[66] They have benefitted from the need to maintain tight security in Kosovo (where they, and not the military, provide that service) and the situation of the Serbian economy, which brought them, the government, and organized crime together in a conspiracy to evade the international sanctions. The Yugoslav judiciary is a partner to the Milošević regime rather than an external check to its abuses.[67]

One example of the interrelationship of the Milošević government, the state security services, and crime is the Jugoskandik bank affair of spring 1993. The head of that bank, Jezdimir Vasiljević, was a heavy contributor to the SPS (and apparently to other parties), a sanction-breaker, and is believed to have been part of an organized crime syndicate. When he disappeared in early 1993 with millions of dollars, and his bank was then looted with the complicity of the police, his relationship to the government became clear. The revelation had little negative effect on the regime (although a pair of ministers were arrested), but it did indicate that criminals had a special place in the state in Serbia.[68] In the summer of 1994, a series of revelations from within the ministry of internal affairs titillated the Belgrade public with details of the interrelationship of the police, organized crime, sanction-busting, and the government. The ministry appears to tolerate or even collaborate with the Serbian, Gypsy, and Albanian mafias in order to fund its own large payroll. [69]

Milošević's hold on the sources of power in Serbia is not threatened by any alternative civic organizations. The Serbian Orthodox Church has played an important role in the growth of the Serbian nationalist movement of the 1980s and in providing implicit support for the Serbian war effort in the former Yugoslavia, although it has not been an unconditional supporter of the Milošević regime. The importance of Kosovo and the Orthodox populations outside of Serbia has made it difficult for the church to place itself in open opposition to the regime or the nationalist opposition.[70] On the other hand, since the outbreak of the war in 1991, several organizations have been formed to provide an alternative to the ethnonationalist values which predominate in Serbian politics and society today. They emerged from the wreckage of the Alliance of Reform Forces, the all-Yugoslav party which suffered complete defeat at the polls in Serbia. The Civic Alliance (CA – Gradjanski savez) is the most important of these organizations, followed by (and linked to) the Center for Antiwar Actions, the Belgrade Circle, and others which are non-political groups proposing a civic, rather than nationalist, political culture in Serbia. The CA consists of four parties: the Reformist Party, Republican Club, People's Peasant party, and the League of Social Democrats of Vojvodina/Yugoslavia.[71] After the dust settled in the 1990 elections, the Civic Alliance had six representatives in the skupština; they have had none since then, however. Vesna Pešić, a Belgrade sociologist, is considered the leading figure of the organization, which can count on support from *Vreme* and Studio B, both of which share its political orientation, and the biweekly *Republika*, which is edited by one of its leaders, Nebojša Popov, a one-time member of the Praxis group. The Civic Alliance has little appeal within Serbia, where its antiwar stance, its antinationalist platform, and its vocal support of the rights of minorities in the new Yugoslavia have earned it the enmity of the mainstream opposition as well as of the SPS. Today, it is considered treasonous by the majority of Serbs. For its detractors, the fact that it finds financial support outside of Serbia only confirms this opinion.

Less sincere in its civic values is the Yugoslav United Left (YUL – Jugoslovenska udružena levica). YUL is a relatively new element in the Serbian political scene, formed in July 1994. Its leader is Mirjana Marković, the wife of Slobodan Milošević. YUL is a direct descendant of the League of Communists-Movement for Yugoslavia (LC-MY – Savez komunista-Pokret za Jugoslaviju, which first appeared in 1990 as a party of LC loyalists, especially from the military and the bureaucracy, who were Serbian but feared the breakup of Yugoslavia. It is most popular with young socialists who claim to reject Serbian nationalism, with Montenegrins, and with older member of the LC-MY. Powered by Marković's regular column in *Duga*, a Belgrade biweekly, YUL claims to be antibolshevik, antinationalist, and predicts the recreation of Yugoslavia: "I am convinced that the nations that lived together in the former Yugoslavia until two years ago cannot avoid living together again."[72] When queried, a YUL representative noted that the organization shares the Civic Alliance's "values of the independent citizenry, the values of a civil society, but we favor an autochthonous citizenry, an autochthonous civil society, not stimulated 'from outside.'"[73] It always helps to hint at foreign conspiracies in Serbian politics, even if YUL claims to be antinationalist. But, as one critic warned, "[i]f the YUL intends to be an important political factor, it must not support an unclear concept of the Yugoslav nation, or a certain European spirit, brotherhood with other people. The omission of the national component from the program can be negatively reflected in the public."[74]

The new Yugoslavia and its discontents

Within the new Yugoslavia, however, there is much diversity – ethnic diversity, diversity of state traditions, and debate on the future of the region. Serbia's ethnic complexity will be the greatest strain on any true transition to democracy that might occur in the future. The following section will survey four of the most vexing concerns for Serbian leaders: Kosovo, Sandžak, Vojvodina, and Montenegro.

The issue of Kosovo facilitated Milošević's ascent in Serbia. Its population today is at least 90 percent Albanian Muslim, but Serbian national ideology demands that Kosovo remain an integral part of the Serbian state. For the Albanians, Kosovo should be governed by its Albanian majority as a result of its Albanian majority. There is little dialogue in Serbia today regarding Kosovo. Martial law was declared in January 1990, when the YPA moved in to support police who had been subduing strikes and demonstrations in Kosovo since the summer of 1988. On July 5, 1990, the Serbian government suspended all vestiges of Kosovo's autonomy. The September 1990 constitution reincorporated Kosovo into Serbia, allowing the region to retain a territorial assembly, which existed only in theory, given the suspension of autonomy in July. In early 1991, the Serbian government made the Serbian language official in Kosovo, educational institutions began to teach only in Serbian, and a general purge of all Albanian employees in government service and industry began. Since 1991, Kosovo's political and social life has been stifled by repressive measures, but Serbia's ability and willingness to resort to open violence has been offset by international scrutiny and wars elsewhere.

The Sandžak is a region that straddles the Montenegrin/Serbian border along its length from Bosnia to Kosovo – to walk from Sarajevo to Priština would take one through its heart. The 1991 Yugoslav census, which both Serbs and Muslims have challenged where the Sandžak is concerned, tells us that the combined municipalities of the Sandžak had a population of 440,000, of which 52 percent were Muslim South Slavs. The Montenegrin portions were about 40 percent Muslim, whereas the Serbian ones were 61 percent Muslim.[75] The Sandžak rests in a critical geopolitical district linking Serbia, Montenegro, Kosovo, and southern and eastern Bosnian districts, leaving the Sandžak's Muslims as the only remaining Muslim South Slav population in the large Serbian state that is currently under construction. There is little agreement on the level of ethnic antagonism in the Sandžak. Many Muslims believe that it is rising, but others insist it is not. Many believe that coexistence in a large Serbia is the only hope for the Muslim South Slavs of the former Yugoslavia – Bosnia's fate being, for them, both a warning and a lament.

Vojvodina's ethnic composition is the most mixed all of the components of the new Yugoslavia. According to the 1991 census, 57 percent of Vojvodina's two million people are Serbs, 22 percent are Hungarians, and 7 percent are Croats. Vojvodina was one of two autonomous provinces within the Serbian Republic. It enjoyed (with Kosovo) almost complete freedom from Serbian control, which allowed the growth of a separate Vojvodinian bureaucracy which tended to empire building, as did that of Kosovo. The antibureaucratic revolution brought a leadership to Vojvodina that was loyal to Milošević. The 1990 constitution made the region an integral part of Serbia once again, retaining for it only its autonomous status, its provincial assembly (now quite circumscribed in its authority), and its member of the rotating presidencies of the party and the state. Since 1990, laws have been passed making Serbian the only official language in Vojvodina, the availability of schooling for ethnic minorities has been drastically reduced, and ethnic Hungarians have been removed from positions in government and business.[76] Unlike Kosovo, Vojvodina occupies no special place in the hearts of Serbs; in fact, historically Serbs from the region have been belittled as *prečani*, those from outside the Serbian heartland. But today Vojvodina is one of the most productive regions in Serbia, and the Serbian leadership has no intention of relinquishing it.

Montenegro is Serbia's partner-republic in the new Yugoslavia. Its relationship to Serbia is contentious today, just as it has been historically. The problem is simple to state: some Montenegrins believe they are part of the Serbian nation, others believe that they have their own unique national identity. Today Montenegro is governed by the heirs of the League of Communists of Montenegro (now known as the Democratic Party of Socialists [Demokratska partija socijalista, DPSo]), which is allied with Milošević's Socialist Party of Serbia. That relationship has been rocky, however. Montenegro's competing national identities, its underdevelopment, and its small size have all contributed to indecision about the role of the republic in the new Yugoslavia and in its relationship with Serbia.

Serbia's ethnic minorities have chosen to pursue widely varying political strategies since 1990. Their choice of strategies has depended on their circumstances. Some (Albanians in Kosovo, some Muslim South Slavs in the Sandžak) have chosen to boycott elections, calculating that their participation will do more to legitimate Serbian authority than it will to benefit themselves politically. Others (Hungarians in Vojvodina, some Muslim South Slavs in the Sandžak) have taken part in elections in the belief that only their participation will grant them the legitimacy necessary to ameliorate their position and perhaps change the dominant political culture of intolerant nationalism in Serbia today. There is no clear verdict on which strategy will succeed (if indeed either can succeed).

The single issue that divides Kosovo's Albanian leadership is that of the eventual fate of the region. After 1968, Albanian leaders demanded that Kosovo achieve the status of a republic within Yugoslavia. That goal was then moderate and attainable. Now, however, secession seems to be the only logical goal. Kosovo is no longer part of a multinational Yugoslavia with many constituent nations, it is part of a Serbian state that seems intent on creating a Greater Serbia. Ibrahim Rugova, the leader of the Democratic Alliance of Kosovo (DAK), has openly advocated Kosovo's independence, although not unity with Albania. Others, like Rexhep Qosija, an Albanian writer from Priština, openly favor union with Albania.[77] In spite of their subjugated status in Serbia, Kosovo's Albanian leaders have allegedly created an underground state of considerable authority. In summer 1990, after Serbia

Table 5.8 *Ethnic composition of regions of Yugoslavia, 1991 (in percent)*

	Kosovo[a]	Vojvodina	Montenegro	Serbia	Serbia (all)
Serbs	10	57.2	9.3	87.3	65.8
Albanians	90	-	6.6	-	17.2
Hungarians	-	16.9	-	-	3.5
Muslim Slavs	-	-	14.6	-	2.4
Montenegrins	-	2.2	61.8	-	1.4
Croats	-	4.8	-	-	1.1
Yugoslavs	0.2	8.4	4.0	2.5	3.2
Others	-	10.5	3.7	10.2	5.4
Total population	2,000,000	2,130,000	616,000	5,661,500	9,791,500

Note: [a]This table is drawn from census data except in the case of Kosovo, which is an estimate, since ethnic Albanians boycotted the census of 1991; *all* figures have been disputed by various groups, because the census was carried out by republican authorities.
Source: Susan L. Woodward, *Balkan Tragedy: Chaos and Dissolution after the Cold War* (Washington, DC: Brookings Institution, 1995), pp. 33-35.

suspended Kosovo's autonomy, ethnic Albanian legislators continued to meet secretly. They produced the Kačanik constitution, passed by the underground assembly on September 7, 1990. It claimed for Kosovo republican status within Yugoslavia. Kosovo's Albanians boycotted Serbia's elections of December 1990, but on September 26–30, 1991 an underground referendum that reportedly drew nearly all of Kosovo's Albanian voters endorsed the Kačanik constitution by a margin of nearly 100 percent. Soon thereafter, on October 19, 1991, the underground legislature declared Kosovo independent. Albania recognized Kosovo several days later; no other foreign state has done so.

The Muslims of the Sandžak suffer from a lack of unity, which is understandable, as they, unlike Kosovo's Albanians, have not been under the hammer of Serbian police for decades, and their population straddles the border of Serbia and Montenegro. In the Sandžak a variety of political options are available. The leaders of the kindred (Montenegrin and Serbian) Sandžak Parties of Democratic Action (Stranka demokratske akcije, PDA) as of 1991 were Sulejman Ugljanin in Serbia and Harun Hadžić in Montenegro. The stated goals of the party have been to attain autonomy for the Sandžak and its Muslim population. The Serbian and Montenegrin PDAs took part in the elections of 1990, achieving some success (three seats). In 1992, though, the PDA boycotted the elections, thus choosing the electoral strategy of choice for opposition parties in Serbia. Other initiatives include an October 1991 referendum on autonomy, which was sponsored by the PDA and other Muslim organizations under an umbrella organization, the Muslim National

Council.[78] Reportedly, 70 percent of the residents of the Serbian Sandžak districts voted, and an overwhelming majority (99 percent) of those who voted chose autonomy. The second major initiative of the PDA was its "Memorandum on the Establishment of a Special Status for the Sandžak," passed by the Muslim National Council on June 6, 1993.[79] The Memorandum seeks special administrative authority for the Sandžak as reflected by a local assembly and governor. Today the PDA is split, with Ugljanin and Rasim Ljajić leading rival factions.

None of the non-Serbian ethnic groups in the Vojvodina has demonstrated any intention to separate from Serbia. Rather, unlike Kosovo and the Sandžak, the most vocal minority in Vojvodina (the Hungarian) has taken part in the political process there, much to its apparent benefit.[80] The most popular representative of the interests of Vojvodina's Hungarian community of 400,000 is the DCVH, led by Andras Agoston. The approach of the DCVH is to assert the historical multiethnicity of Vojvodina and to try to maintain that special character in the face of nationalist extremism, war, and an influx of Serbian and Croatian refugees from Croatia. The Serbian government has not been receptive to the multicultural approach. The critical political event in the DCVH's history is its April 1992 "Vojvodina Hungarian Autonomy Memorandum," passed by the organization's general assembly.[81] The memorandum surrendered to the notion that in Yugoslavia, self-determination could only be achieved collectively. It proposed "tripartite autonomy" for Hungarians: personal autonomy, territorial autonomy, and local self-government. Since 1990, the DCVH has attempted to make its case by taking part in the political process in Serbia, as opposed to most other ethnic minorities and even many ethnically Serbian opposition parties, which have chosen to boycott elections. The DCVH has seen its representation in the Serbian skupština remain negligible (eight members elected in the 1990 elections, nine in 1992, five in 1993), but its successes on the local level have been more notable.

Montenegro, more than Serbia or its once-autonomous provinces, has celebrated the antibureaucratic revolution as its modern political rebirth: January 10 is the anniversary of the Montenegrin Uprising of 1989, and it is celebrated yearly.[82] This uprising, part of a series of massive demonstrations that plagued the party and state leaderships of Montenegro, Serbia, Kosovo, and Vojvodina, brought remarkably young new leaders to Montenegro. Momir Bulatović became the president of the party, and he is now the president of the Montenegrin state government. The political spectrum in Montenegro is similar to that of Serbia, with the exception of the fact that Muslim and Albanian parties have participated in elections. The DPSo has been joined by the People's Party (PP – Narodna stranka) of Novak Kilibarda and a changing constellation of oppositionists that include Montenegrin allies of Šešelj's Serbian Radicals and other Serbian parties. There has been considerable uncertainty in the Serbian-Montenegrin relationship since 1991. For its part, the ruling DPSo has proved opportunistic: it led Montenegro into the war in Croatia in late 1991, eagerly helping the Yugoslav army in its siege of Dubrovnik, which many Montenegrins consider to be part of Montenegro's Yugoslav inheritance. By late 1992, however, the intoxication of war had given way to dissatisfaction and, perhaps, even shame at the role Montenegrins had played in the war. As a result, the government and opposition sponsored a referendum on Montenegro's association with Serbia, in which 63 percent supported remaining with Serbia.[83] Today, the DPSo of Bulatović remains firmly in power, in control of the media and the police, occasionally voicing support for Montenegrin individuality.

Conclusion

Although the institutions have been in place since 1990 for a true democratic transition in Serbia, such a transition has yet to occur. The manipulations of the Milošević regime, the outbreak of war in Yugoslavia, and the inability of opposition to the regime to articulate anything but an ethnic nationalist alternative to Milošević have limited the potential effectiveness of Serbia's democratic institutions. The key reasons for this situation are: (1) at the time of the transition in 1990, Serbian society was obsessed with the fate of Kosovo, which led both the party and the nonparty opposition to frame the very notion of a democratic transition in ethnic nationalist terms; (2) by virtue of its financial means, its political experience, and its domination of the media in Serbia, the SPS was able to limit the ability of the opposition to function; (3) the war radicalized Serbian society to the point that Milošević has been able to present himself as the protector of Serbs outside Serbia; and (4) non-Serbs have been marginalized and treated as unwelcome participants in the Serbian political process.

In spite of that dispiriting summary of the state of the transition in Serbia, much has changed in recent months. In August 1995, Milošević allowed the Serbian region of Croatia to be overrun by the Croatian army without resistance. By November, those Croatian forces and their Bosnian allies had reduced Serbian holdings in northwest Bosnia considerably, again without vocal resistance from Belgrade. The Serbian opposition and refugees from the lost territories have blamed Milošević for betraying his promise to defend Serbs and even create a single state for all Serbs. Thus, Milošević has willingly relinquished one of the issues that contributed to his popularity: his ability to defend Serbs in a time of war. Unfortunately, all of the corollaries to that earlier promise remain: a nationalized electorate and opposition, a powerful state police apparatus, and marginalized ethnic groups, most importantly the Albanians in Kosovo. In spite of his abandonment of Bosnia, polling from 1995 indicates that Milošević retains much more support among Serbs than any of the mainstream opposition leaders. But extremists like Radovan Karadžić (head of the Bosnian Serb state) and Ratko Mladić (the head of the Bosnian Serb army) outpoll him.[84] Milošević now appears to be preparing for an open alliance with YUL and a move to appropriate some of the old Titoist language of brotherhood and unity. To these schizophrenic signs must be added the fact that fully a third of the population of Serbia is virtually disenfranchised because it is not ethnically Serbian. And a certain sign of turbulence ahead is the fact that Milošević's second term as president ends in 1997 and the constitution forbids him to run for a third. In other words, although there is potential for the peace in Bosnia to alleviate some of the tensions in Serbia, there are still many reasons for caution.

For the process of transition to democracy in Serbia to succeed, it would seem that two conditions must be met: first, Serbia's institutions must be reformed to create a less presidential and majoritarian system, and second, Serbia's ethnic minorities must be certain that their participation in the political process will not expose them to nationalist violence. Those are two utterly different types of changes: the first is purely institutional and could be accomplished (with the necessary will) by a series of votes in the Serbian assembly. The second would require the complete transformation of Serbian political culture, which is a much more daunting task and one which cannot be accomplished formulaically, according to a timetable. Ultimately, even those changes skirt the main issue, which is the fact that the current regime will not allow such institutional changes as are necessary. Until Slobodan Milošević endorses a change in the constitution of Serbia, supports the creation of a civic rather than ethnic definition of citizenship in Serbian political culture, and relinquishes his control of the security forces in Serbia, not much change can be expected.

Postscript: Serbia since January, 1996

Post-Dayton Serbia has passed through two distinct phases: one of disappointment and apathy provoked by the exhaustion of the war effort and the apparent defeat of the Serbian nationalist project, followed by an eruption of popular discontent with the Milošević regime following the Serbian supreme court's annulment of local election returns in November. The fact that the demonstrations provoked by that act continue as this postscript is being written makes any prognostications suspect. But a brief survey of the events of 1996 may help place the demonstrations in context.

Slobodan Milošević returned from Dayton with the material to create a new image: that of peacemaker. Most Serbs recognized the absurdity of such a pose, but believed that he had become the untouchable "American candidate" in Serbia as a result of the services he rendered at Dayton. The DS and the DSS continued their earlier tendency to build support as defenders of the Serbian communities of Bosnia and Croatia. In essence Djindjić and Koštunica, the leaders of the DS and DSS, switched roles with Milošević, he becoming the voice of moderation, they assuming ever more the role of defenders of the nation. The SRM continued to founder as the personal vehicle of Vuk Drašković, with no clear political message. The result was a palpable apathy in the Serbian capital through the first months of 1996. As an example, on March 9, the DS, SRM, and GS sponsored an anniversary demonstration to celebrate the movement of March 9, 1991, when demonstrators urged the overthrow of Milošević following a crackdown on the media. The few (perhaps 20,000) who attended the demonstration were entirely passive, in spite of weeks of preparation by the sponsors. Serbs, it appeared, had given up hope for change. Perhaps they were waiting for a fresh voice with a new message, but there was no one to fill that bill either.

Milošević, it appeared, needed only to solve the pressing political question of how to ensure his own continuity in power in Serbia. He is nearing the end of his second five-year term as president of Serbia, and is constitutionally prevented from seeking a third term. Given the obvious fact that he will not willingly step aside in Serbia, there are a few options available to him. One is a constitutional amendment allowing for more terms as president; another is for Milošević to seek the federal prime ministership, an office that he could occupy constitutionally so long as the SPS is the majority party in the federal parliament. The SPS has also floated the argument that Milošević's first term as president was not a full term (it was interrupted after two years by the creation of the new FRY), and thus does not count against the constitutional limit. In that case, Milošević could conceivably claim an entire new second term or the three unused years of his first term.[85]

The opposition to Milošević formed the coalition "Together" (Zajedno) in late July, although its final form was not clear until immediately before the federal elections which were held on November 3, 1996. The DS, the SRM, and the GS founded the coalition, while Šešel's SRS never considered joining. That left the DSS of Koštunica, which hesitated before finally agreeing to take part in the coalition in the federal elections.[86] In mid-August, news emerged that Dragoslav Avramović had agreed to head the Zajedno coalition. Avramović was the head of the National Bank of Yugoslavia who was most responsible for controlling Serbia's hyperinflation in early 1994 and would immediately make Zajedno a legitimate threat to Milošević.[87] At the end of September, he in fact was named the leader of the coalition.[88] Opinion polling showed that Zajedno, with Avramović as its leader, would run neck and neck with the SPS. Unfortunately, Avramović resigned from the coalition on October 9.[89] Conspiracy theorists proposed that he resigned under pressure from the West, which cynically supported Milošević, or that Milošević himself threatened to cut off Avramović's access to dialysis. Regardless, Zajedno lost any hope of defeating the SPS with the resignation of Avramović. In the November elections, 60 percent of the federal (Serbian and Montenegrin) electorate voted. Of 138 seats available, the coalition of the SPS, JUL, and ND received sixty-four; Zajedno attained twenty-two; the Montenegrin DPS got twenty, and the SRS received sixteen. Parties representing the Hungarian and Muslim Slav minorities received seats, as did smaller Montenegrin formations.[90] The results were thus dispiriting to the opposition coalition, which had now for the third time failed to unseat the SPS and in fact failed even to make inroads into that party's domination of Serbian politics.

All the more surprising, then, were the final results of local elections which took place on November 3 and 17. Zajedno (minus the DSS in these elections) won majorities in forty-four districts in Serbia, including twelve of the sixteen in Belgrade (where Djindjić thus became mayor), and those in Niš, Novi Sad, and Kragujevac. The SPS won majorities in 134 districts, while the SRS won in three (including Zemun, where Šešelj became mayor). The results were stunning, if limited to urban areas where the opposition had always polled well. But the understandable euphoria over the victory was rapidly transformed into anti-government demonstrations when the first district court in Belgrade rejected the victories of thirty-three Zajedno candidates in Belgrade and called for a third round of voting (Zajedno had won seventy seats, the SPS/JUL/ND coalition twenty-five in the city skupština). The government had already behaved heavy handedly in Niš, where a particularly loathed SPS mayor, Mile Ilić, had sponsored the falsification of ballots. Demonstrations beginning on November 19 in Niš found an echo in Belgrade, where a reported high of 150,000 demonstrators gathered. The demonstrations have been prompted by calls for peaceful opposition to the courts' actions, which were clearly the will of the SPS. The movement has remained resolutely peaceful, and at this time it is unclear how the demonstrations will conclude.

There are several theoretical possibilitics: the "Romanian" and "Czech" solutions have been suggested as plausible outcomes, but neither in fact are. Milošević has not had the time to create the sort of dictatorship that Ceauşescu built, and opposition to him is not nearly as powerful as it was in Romania in 1989. Therefore, Milošević need not fear a rebellion within his party, which was Ceauşescu's fate. Similarly, there is no chance for a Velvet Revolution in Serbia: there is no Vaclav Havel there, and if according to some unimaginable scenario Milošević were to fall from power, Serbia is far too divided to allow for a "velvet" conclusion to such an event. Instead, a more moderate outcome seems likely. The demonstrations are now finishing their third week, and signals have been mixed. The government shut down Radio B92 for a day (it responded to international pressure by reopening it) and has forced one independent newspaper (*Blic*) to end its enthusiastic coverage of the demonstrations. On the other hand, the government has not evidenced any willingness to use violence. The demonstrations do not appear to have become any larger, and workers have been notably absent. Coverage of events in Belgrade and Niš has apparently not reached much of the countryside. Members of the Serbian judiciary have publicly condemned the manipulation of the election returns, and Aleksandar Tijanić, the minister for information in the Serbian government, resigned in protest against the government's heavy handed treatment of B92. So while it is in fact a powerful movement that has taken over Belgrade's streets (and a great surprise given the apathy reigning in Serbia until it began), it does not appear that it will grow, nor does it appear that the government is in disarray. Milošević will probably take a page out of his own book from 1991 and sacrifice some of the more objectionable members of his ruling apparatus and then allow the original election results to stand. His control of the media and the security forces will not be challenged, and his dominance at the federal level will allow him to step into the post of federal prime minister next year. He will still have to face republican elections, which will be held in 1997.

Acronyms

ARFY	Alliance of Reform Forces of Yugoslavia (Savez reformskih snaga Jugoslavije)
AYDI	Association for a Yugoslav Democratic Initiative (Udruženje za jugoslovensku demokratsku inicijativu)
CA	Civic Alliance (Gradjanski savez)
DCVH	Democratic Community of Vojvodina Hungarians (Demokratska zajednica vojvodjanskih madjara)
DEPOS	Democratic Movement of Serbia (Demokratski pokret Srbije)
DP	Democratic Party (Demokratska stranka)
DPS	Democratic Party of Serbia (Demokratska stranka Srbije)
DPSo	Democratic Party of Socialists (Demokratska stranka socialista)
DUCV	Democratic Union of Croats in the Vojvodina (Demokratski savez Hrvata u Vojvodini)
LC–MY	League of Communists–Movement for Yugoslavia (Savez komunista–Pokret za Jugoslaviju)
LCS	League of Communists of Serbia (Savez komunista Srbije)
LCY	League of Communists of Yugoslavia (Savez komunista Jugoslavije)
ND	New Democracy (Nova demokratija)
ND–MS	New Democracy–Movement for Serbia (Nova demokratija–Pokret za Srbiju)

PDA	Party of Democratic Action (Stranka demokratska akcija)
PLPS	Party of the League of Peasants of Serbia (Stranka saveza eljaka Srbije)
PP	People's Party (Narodna stranka)
PPP	People's Peasant Party (Narodna seljačka stranka)
PRP	People's Radical Party (Narodna radikalna stranka)
RTB	Radio-Television Belgrade (Radio-Televizija Beograd)
RTS	Radio-Television Serbia (Radio-Televizija Srbija)
SANU	Serbian Academy of Arts and Sciences (Srpska akademija nauke i umetnosti)
SLP	Serbian Liberal Party (Srpska liberalna stranka)
SNR	Serbian National Renewal (Srpska narodna obnova)
SPM	Socialist Party of Montenegro (Socialistička stranka Crne Gore)
SPS	Socialist Party of Serbia (Socialistička partija Srbije)
SRM	Serbian Renewal Movement (Srpski pokret obnove)
SRP	Serbian Radical Party (Srpska radikalna stranka)
SUP	Serbian Unity Party (Stranka srpskog jedinstva)
YPA	Yugoslav People's Army (Jugoslovenska narodna armija)
YUL	Yugoslav United Left (Jugoslovenska udružena levica)

NOTES

The author would like to thank the East European Studies program of the Woodrow Wilson International Center for Scholars for a research scholarship that allowed him to begin work on this paper.

1 Robert M. Hayden, "Constitutional Nationalism in the Formerly Yugoslav Republics," *Slavic Review* 51, no. 4 (Winter 1992), 660.

2 Sabrina Ramet, *Nationalism and Federalism in Yugoslavia, 1962–1991*, 2d ed. (Bloomington, IN: Indiana University Press, 1992), pp. 20–1, 180, 206.

3 Susan Woodward, *Balkan Tragedy: Chaos and Dissolution after the Cold War* (Washington, DC: The Brookings Institution, 1995), pp. 42–3.

4 A good recent article on the 1974 constitution is Vojin Dimitrijević, "The 1974 Constitution and Constitutional Process as a Factor in the Collapse of Yugoslavia," in *Yugoslavia, The Former and Future: Reflections by Scholars from the Region*, ed. Payam Akhavan (Washington, DC: The Brookings Institution and The United Nations Research Institute for Social Development, Geneva, 1995), pp. 45–74.

5 Susan Woodward, *Socialist Unemployment: The Political Economy of Yugoslavia, 1945–1990* (Princeton: Princeton University Press, 1995), pp. 204, 209, 383–5.

6 Lenard Cohen, *Broken Bonds: Yugoslavia's Disintegration and Balkan Politics in Transition*, 2d ed. (Boulder, CO: Westview Press, 1995), p. 31.

7 Woodward, *Balkan Tragedy*, p. 59.

8 Woodward cites a figure of 25,661 Serbs and Montenegrins who emigrated from Kosovo between 1981 and 1988; Woodward, *Balkan Tragedy*, p. 485, n. 39.

9 Atanasije Jevtić, *Stradanje Srba na kosovu i metohiji od 1941. do 1990* (Priština: "Jedinstvo," 1990) is a statement of grievances by Serbs in Kosovo; Branka Magaš, *The Destruction of Yugoslavia: Tracking the Break-up, 1980–1992* (London: Verso, 1993) includes some of the petitions and commentary on them.

10 A crude indicator is that the percentage of members of the LCY's central committee with higher education was 69 percent between 1952 and 1958, 86 percent between 1964 and 1969, and 62 percent between 1972 and 1978; Miroslav Pečujlić, "U začaranom krugu politike: Političke institucije u Jugoslaviji (Srbiji) juče i danas," in *Radjanje javnog mnjenja i političkih stranaka: Analiza empiriskih istraživanja u Srbiji 1990–1991*, ed. Pečujlić et al. (Belgrade: Institut za političke studije, Centar za javno mnjenje i marketing "Medium," Pravni fakultet, 1992), p. 60.

11 For compelling English-language exposes of the intellectual uprising against Titoism, see Magaš, *The Destruction of Yugoslavia*, and Ivo Banac, "Historiography of the Countries of Eastern Europe: Yugoslavia," *American Historical Review* 97, no. 4 (October 1992), 1084-1104, on the revolt of Serbian historians against the party's version of history; see also Stevan K. Pavlowitch, *The Improbable Survivor: Yugoslavia and its Problems, 1918–1988* (Columbus, OH: Ohio State University Press, 1988), pp. 129–42.

12 Ćosić's speeches can be found in his *Stvarno i moguće: Članci i ogledi* (Ljublana: Cankarjeva založba, 1988), pp. 27–40, 121–33.

13 The memorandum has been reprinted in Bože Čović, ed., *Izvori velikosrpske agresije* (Zagreb: Školska knjiga, 1991), pp. 256–300.

14 Zagorka Golubović, "The Conditions Leading to the Breakdown of the Yugoslav State: What Has Generated the Civil War in Yugoslavia?" *Praxis International* 12, no. 2 (July 1992), 131.

15 Milošević's speech at the Eighth Session is published in Slobodan Milošević, *Godine raspleta* (Belgrade: Beogradski izdavačko-grafički zavod, 1989), pp. 170–9. On these events, see Slavoljub Djukić, *Izmedju slave i anateme: Politička biografija Slobodana Miloševića* (Belgrade: Filip Višnjić, 1994), pp. 59–102; Dragiša Pavlović, *Olako obećana brzina* (Zagreb: Globus, 1988); Magaš, *The Destruction of Yugoslavia*, pp. 109–10, 203–6.

16 Jasmina Vujović-Brdarević, "Pluralizam u predizbornom razdoblju," in *Od izbornih rituala do slobodnih izbora: Sondaža javnog mnjenja uoči prvih višestranačkih izbora u Srbiji*, ed. Srećko Mihailović et al. (Belgrade: Univerzitet u Beogradu, Institut društvenih nauka, Centar za politikološka istraživanja i javno mnjenje, 1991), p. 222; Dušan Radulović and Nebojša Spaić, *U potrazi za demokratijom* (Belgrade: Dosije, 1991), p. 34; Milan Andrejevich, "Milošević and the Serbian Opposition," *RFE/RL Research Reports*, 19 October 1990, p. 40.

17 Milan Andrejevich, "Milosević and the Socialist Party of Serbia," *RFE/RL Research Report*, 3 August 1990, pp. 41–5; Radulović and Spaić, *U potrazi*, pp. 30–3, 185–6; Vladimir Goati, "Višepartijski mozaik Srbije," in Pečujlić et al., ed., *Radjanje javnog mnjenja*, pp. 161–3.

18 Goati, "Višepartijski mozaik," p. 161.

19 The SRM emerged from an earlier party, the Serbian National Renewal, which was founded by Mirko Jović and Vuk Drašković in January 1990. The two leaders split in mid-1990 and Drašković founded the SRM. The SNR continued, but never became a mass party. See Mladen Arnautović, *Stranke u Jugoslaviji*

(Belgrade: Novinska agencija Tanjug, 1990), pp. 248–50; Radulović and Spaić, *U potrazi*, pp. 50–71, 187–8, 201–2; Goati, "Višepartijski mozaik," pp. 163–4.

20 Belgrade Domestic Service, in Foreign Broadcast Information Service, *Daily Report: Eastern Europe* (hereafter *FBIS-EEU*), 5 November 1990, p. 49.

21 Program of the SRM, in Arnautović, *Stranke u Jugoslaviji*, pp. 248–50.

22 Goati, "Višepartijski mozaik," p. 164; Radulović and Spaić, *U potrazi*, pp. 71–7, 190–91; "'We are Unstoppable': Interview with Djurdje Ninković," and "Serbian Democratic Party Founding Platform," *East European Reporter* 3, no. 4 (Spring/Summer 1990), 87–9.

23 Goati, "Višepartijski mozaik," p. 164.

24 "'We are Unstoppable,'" p. 88; *Borba*, 8 December 1990, in *FBIS-EEU*, 7 December 1990, pp. 62–3.

25 *Borba*, 5 December 1990, in *FBIS-EEU*, 7 December 1990, p. 62.

26 Radulović and Spaić, *U potrazi*, pp. 73–5.

27 Ibid., pp. 80–4, 192–3.

28 In Serbia, Marković found support among 81 percent of the population, according to polls taken in July 1990; Woodward, *Balkan Tragedy*, p. 129.

29 Andrejevich, "Milošević and the Serbian Opposition," p. 40.

30 "The fact that relations between the president, the government, and the assembly were not clearly delineated created fear of a new autocracy"; Radulović and Spaić, *U potrazi*, p. 45.

31 Hayden, "Constitutional Nationalism," pp. 660–1.

32 The law is printed in Arnautović, *Stranke u Jugoslaviji*, pp. 355–8; see also Andrejevich, "Milošević and the Serbian Opposition," p. 40; Vujović-Brdarević, "Pluralizam," p. 217.

33 *Politika*, 11 November 1990, in *FBIS-EEU*, 28 November 1990, p. 54.

34 *Vreme*, 23 March 1993, in *FBIS-EEU*, 21 April 1993, pp. 50–2.

35 *Belgrade Domestic Service*, 27 November 1990, in *FBIS-EEU*, 28 November 1990, p. 53.

36 Vladimir Goati, "Zaključno razmatranje," in Mihailović, *Od izbornih rituala do slobodnih izbora*, pp. 256–7. See also Radulović and Spaić, *U potrazi*, pp. 162–74; Dennison Rusinow, "To Be or Not to Be? Yugoslavia as Hamlet," *Field Staff Reports* (1990–91), no. 18; Sergije Pegan, "Pluralizacija parlamenta – socijalni sastav narodne skupštine Srbije," in Mihailović, ed., *Od izbornih rituala do slobodnih izbora*, pp. 231–49;

37 "Prilozi," in Mihailović, ed., *Od izbornih rituala do slobodnih izbora*, pp. 277, 280.

38 Radulović and Spaić, *U potrazi*, p. 39.

39 Ibid.

40 "Prilozi," p. 284.

41 Srdja Popović, "Political Opposition in Serbia," *New Politics*, Winter 1994, pp. 94–5; Srbobran Branković, "Determinante političkog javnog mnjenja u Srbiji," in Pečujlić et al., ed., *Radjanje javnog mnjenja*, pp. 210–211.

42 Pečujlić, "U začaranom krugu politike," p. 82.

43 Ibid., pp. 82–90.

44 The term "authoritarian" was used in the survey; ibid., p. 78.

45 Srbobran Branković, "How Bolshevik is Serbia?" *East European Reporter* 5, no. 1 (January-February 1992), 10–11.

46 Ibid., p. 9.

47 Pečujlić, "U začaranom krugu politike," p. 78.

48 Djukić, *Izmedju slave i anateme*, pp. 59–102; Mark Thompson, *Forging War: The Media in Serbia, Croatia, and Bosnia-Hercegovina* (London: Article 19, International Centre against Censorship, 1994), pp. 53–8; Milan Andrejevich and Gordon N. Bardos, "The Media in Regions of Conflict: Serbia and Montenegro," *RFE/RL Research Report*, 2 October 1992, pp. 86–91; Stan Markotich, "Government Control over Serbia's Media," ibid., 4 February 1994, pp. 35–9; Predrag Simić, "The Former Yugoslavia: The Media and Violence," ibid., 4 February 1994, pp. 40–7.

49 Andrejevich and Bardos, "Serbia and Montenegro," pp. 88–9.

50 *NIN*, 9 December 1994, in *FBIS-EEU*, 5 January 1995, p. 30.

51 Radulović and Spaić, *U potrazi*, p. 119; Djurdje Ninković, "How the Socialists Won in Serbia . . . and How They are Lost," *East European Reporter* 4, no. 4 (Spring/Summer 1991), 6.

52 *Borba*, 6 December 1990, in *FBIS-EEU*, 28 December 1990, pp. 40–1; Ljiljana Baćević, "Izmedju medijskog rata i rata za medij," in Mihailović, ed., *Od izbornih rituala do slobodnih izbora*, p. 165.

53 Baćević, "Izmedju medijskog rata i rata za medij," pp. 164–5.

54 Ibid., p. 167.

55 "Serbian Media Usage Reflects Political Landscape," *USIA Opinion Research Memorandum* (10 December 1992).

56 Thompson, *Forging War*, pp. 89–91.

57 Biographical information on Šešelj can be found in an article in the Belgrade weekly *Vreme*, 28 December 1992, in *FBIS-EEU*, 2 February 1993, pp. 66–8.

58 In that regard, it is worth noting that in June 1995, long after his split with the SPS in 1993, from his cell in Gnjilane prison, Šešelj's main reproach to Milošević was that he was "to blame that Dubrovnik, Zadar, Karlobag, Gospić, Ogulin, Karlovac, Pakrac, Virovitica, Osijek, Vinkovci, Sarajevo, and Tuzla are not in Serbian hands today"; *NIN*, 23 June 1995, in *FBIS-EEU*, 30 June 1995, p. 57.

59 Stan Markotich, "Opposition Parties Attempt Unity – Again," *Transition*, 9 June 1995, pp. 20–4.

60 "End Game: United for a Change: Interview with Vojislav Koštunica, Vice-President of DEPOS," *East European Reporter* 5, no. 4 (July-August, 1992), 58–60; Paul Shoup, "Serbia at the Edge of the Abyss," *RFE/RL Research Report*, 11 September 1992.

61 Milan Andrejevich, "The Radicalization of Serbian Politics," *RFE/RL Research Report*, 26 March 1993.

62 Stan Markotich, "Milošević's Renewed Attack on the Independent Media," *Transition*, 15 March 1995, pp. 27–8.

63 *Vreme*, 2 January 1995, in *FBIS-EEU*, 27 January 1995, pp. 77–80; *NIN*, 3 February 1995, in *FBIS-EEU*, 3 March 1995, pp. 55–7.

64 Of those polled, 67 percent of Serbs expressed confidence in the army in January 1995, while only 50 percent viewed the Serbian government favorably; "Serbian Confidence in Government Institutions Has Eroded over Past Year," *USIA Opinion Analysis*, 20 March 1995, p. 1.

65 James Gow, "Rump Yugoslavia: Perisic Replaces Panic as Chief of Staff," *RFE/RL Research Report*, 29 October 1993.

66 *Handelsblad*, 7 January 1995, in *FBIS-EEU*, 20 January 1995, p. 69.
67 Stan Markotich, "A Potent Weapon in Milošević's Arsenal," *Transition*, 28 April 1995.
68 *Vreme*, 22 March 1993, in *FBIS-EEU*, 21 April 1993, p. 57.
69 *Borba*, 16 August 1994, in *FBIS-EEU*, 17 August 1994, pp. 41-4; *NIN*, 5 August 1994, in *FBIS-EEU*, 25 August 1994, pp. 58-60.
70 Gordon Bardos, "The Serbian Church against Milošević," *RFE/RL Research Report*, 31 July 1992.
71 Popović, "Political Opposition in Serbia," pp. 97-8; "Hope Springs Eternal: Interview with Nebojša Popov," *East European Reporter* 5, no. 5 (September-October 1992), 56-7; and "The Belgrade Centre for Anti-War Actions," *East European Reporter* (January-February 1992), 17.
72 *Intervju*, 19 August 1994, in *FBIS-EEU*, 27 October 1994, p. 40.
73 *Duga*, 1-14 October 1994, in *FBIS-EEU*, 10 November 1994, pp. 57-8.
74 Živojin Djurić of the Institute for Political Studies of the University of Belgrade; *Politika*, 16 April 1995, in *FBIS-EEU*, 21 April 1995, p. 23.
75 Milan Andrejevich, "The Sandžak: The Next Balkan Theatre of War?" *RFE/RL Research Report*, 27 November 1992, p. 33.
76 Edith Oltay, "Hungarians under Political Pressure in Vojvodina," *RFE/RL Research Report*, 3 December 1993, pp. 44-5.
77 *Kosova Daily Report*, 10 March 1995, in *FBIS-EEU*, 13 March 1995, pp. 59-61; "Kosovo: For a Just and Permanent Solution; Interview with Redzep Cosja," *East European Reporter* 5, no. 4 (July-August 1992), 64-5.
78 Fabian Schmidt, "The Sandžak: Muslims between Serbia and Montenegro," *RFE/RL Research Report*, 11 February 1994, pp. 30-1, 34-5.
79 *Vreme*, 23 August 1993, in *FBIS-EEU*, 16 September 1993, p. 48.
80 On recent events in Vojvodina, see Hugh Poulton, "Rising Ethnic Tension in Vojvodina," *RFE/RL Research Report*, 18 December 1992; Stan Markotich, "Vojvodina: A Potential Powder Keg," ibid., 19 November 1993; Oltay, "Hungarians under Political Pressure."
81 *Dnevnik* (Novi Sad), 6 May 1993 in *FBIS-EEU*, 11 May 1993, pp. 44-5; *Borba*, 14-15 May 1994, in *FBIS-EEU*, 9 June 1994, pp. 60-1; Oltay, "Hungarians under Political Pressure," p. 46.
82 Srdjan Darmanović, "Montenegro: Destiny of a Satellite State," *East European Reporter* 5, no. 2 (March-April 1992), 27-9.
83 Darmanović, "Montenegro," p. 27.
84 The polling was done in January 1995; "Serbian Confidence in Government Institutions," p. 2.
85 Roksanda Ninčić, "Šta će Milošević biti posle 1997?" *Vreme*, 16 March 1996; V. Radivojević and I. Radovanović, "Novi vek sa starim šefom," *Naša Borba*, 10-11 March 1996, p. 6.
86 M. P. Brkić, "Pregovori sa svima sem sa SPO," *Naša Borba*, 1 August 1996; I. Kisić and M. Saponja-Hadžić, "Popravnog neće biti," ibid., 1 August 1996.
87 "'Morao bih da razmislim,'" ibid., 16 August 1996; "I dalje zavisimo od drugih," ibid., 26 August 1996.
88 J. Kosanić, "Posle pobede, biću premijer," ibid., 30 September 1996.
89 See "Povlaćenje pod pritiskom?" and "Zbog naglo pogoršanog zdravstvenog stanja," ibid., 10 October 1996.
90 *Beta* (Belgrade), 6 November 1996. There were reports that 63 percent of the electorate voted, but the subtraction of 242,808 invalid ballots reduced that total to 60 percent.

6   Democratization in Slovenia – the second stage

Sabrina Petra Ramet

The question of democracy is not so simple a matter as some writers suppose. Not only are there rival traditions of democracy, but even among those subscribing to the classical liberal tradition, there are differences between those advocating a maximal definition of democracy (and thereby imposing higher standards on the system) and those urging acceptance of a minimal definition (with the consequent lower standards thereby entailed).[1]

Nor do controversies end there. Should a political party be understood, in the first place, as an electoral organization that seeks to obtain sinecures for its members, or should the emphasis be shifted to the programmatic aspirations that unite the members in common action in the first place? Even equality may be thought to be a murky concept (though not by this author). After all, some say, if a constitution proclaims the equality of women, then should not women be satisfied that this, in and of itself, constitutes the full measure of equality? Others dispute the position implied in this rhetorical question, and urge that there is a distinction between formal equality and real equality.

In the ensuing chapter, I shall be concerned with the subject of democratization in Slovenia, and, in the course of examining the Slovenian case, shall endeavor to shed some light on the nature of democracy itself.

The legacy of the past

As is self-evident, the transition in Eastern Europe associated with the years 1989–90 was, among other things, a self-conscious attempt to escape the past. But as any cynic will remind one, it is never possible to escape the past entirely. There is always some legacy – and not merely from "the past" however defined, but also, as David Olson's chapter on the Czech Republic for this series[2] makes clear, from the "escape route" ("the transition"). But where, for example, in the Czech case, the rapidity of the transition assured

189

the primacy of parliament as the primary locus of interaction among political actors, resulting in the emergence of what Olson calls "Parliamentary-based parties,"[3] in Slovenia, by contrast, parliament played a much less important role in this regard in the early months of transition – or, more specifically, until the parliamentary elections of April 1990.

Where the communist legacy in Slovenia is concerned, as elsewhere, there are both direct and indirect legacies. In the former category one finds continued tendencies, in the short-term, for interest groups to look to the state, rather than to their own resources, to satisfy perceived needs, and temptations, on the part of the elected members of the political establishment, to hold onto communist–era tools of control, rather than dismantle them. One example of the latter has been in the matter of relinquishing the prerogative to name the directors and editors in radio and television, and of foregoing the opportunity to pass on unsolicited "advice" to newspaper editors.

In the latter category (indirect legacies) one finds the overload of work needing to be accomplished within a short time–frame with regard to the drafting of new laws, and – casting the net more broadly – the temptation for the Catholic Church to try to take advantage of the fluidity of the transition to impose its own agenda. Where new legislation is concerned, those laws that contribute to shaping the institutions and procedures of government have a most tangible force, with the potential for direct impact on the nature of the party system that emerges.

Before relinquishing the subject of legacies, there is one final aspect deserving of mention in the Slovenian case, namely, the legacy of communist understanding of liberalization and democratization. Specifically, Slovenia was in the vanguard of pressures for the liberalization and democratization of Yugoslav public life in the 1960s, as well as later, in the 1980s. While some features of this communist–era understanding of "liberalization" were consonant with Western concepts (for example, market economy, shift of priorities in investment from sectors favored for ideological or political reasons to sectors viewed as more profitable, emphasis on trade links with the West, reform of the banking system), other features advocated by Slovenian "liberals" in the 1960s and even later, such as the acceptance of the principle that Slovenia "should have a uniform system of education, health care, research, and scientific activities, and fiscal policy, directed from the center,"[4] reflected communist, rather than Western liberal, frameworks. Although Slovenian liberalism then, as now, was heterogeneous, it differed from its contemporary incarnation in that it subscribed to the more general Yugoslav tendency to view "liberalization" and "democratization" as processes to be unleashed, directed, inspired, controlled, and ultimately limited and circumscribed by the LCY.[5] As Božo Repe has noted, "The fundamental credo of Slovene 'liberalism' [in the 1960s] was that persistent internal criticism could change the structure of the system . . . Slovene liberals operated within the system, which was still Socialism, and they recognized the leading role of the LCY, but at the same time, expressed demands for pluralism in the existing socio-political organizations."[6]

The first stage

In June 1989, Dimitrij Rupel, a professor of sociology at the University of Ljubljana and a leading political activist, sounded a warning. In his view, Slovenia, like Yugoslavia itself, was "seriously late" in undertaking meaningful steps toward democratization and was being outstripped by several other countries in Central and Eastern Europe.[7] Rupel's anxiety notwithstanding, Slovenia was in fact one of the first republics of Eastern Europe to set out on the path toward democracy. Although neither the speed of transition nor the eventual scope could be divined at the time, the first stage in Slovenian democratization may be said to have begun in 1986, when the liberal wing of the League of Communists of Slovenia asserted its predominance over party conservatives, expelling the latter from the party leadership. Slovenian conservative France Popit was compelled to step aside,[8] and the new (and younger) leadership headed by Milan Kučan began to refashion the Slovenian political landscape. Among the first signs of change was a new boldness in the weekly magazine *Mladina* and in the Ljubljana daily newspaper *Delo*.

As late as November 1987, Ljubljana's Municipal Gallery offered the public an exhibition titled "Tito with us in Ljubljana." At the ceremony to open the exhibition, communist functionary Jože Smole told the small gathering, "I rejoice in the present day when we once again encounter our dearest friend, Josip Broz Tito, precisely here, in Ljubljana, which he first experienced as a jobless young metalworker back in 1911."[9] But such speeches were sounding ever more anomalous, as Slovenian culture and society experienced rapid change in several dimensions simultaneously.

One dimension of change was cultural, with the capital city of Ljubljana producing an impressive output in the visual arts, literature, drama, and music, especially popular music, in the course of the 1980s. Aleš Erjavec and Marina Gržinić credit this cultural efflorescence with contributing to ideological and political change. As they put it in a 1991 publication, "the 'authentic' art of the eighties in Ljubljana was alternative art and culture, or subculture, which demolished the established social schemes and patterns. Subculture penetrated even politics as 'art' and 'culture,' and under these guises, corroded and transformed the political status quo."[10] Any account of the players on the cultural scene in Ljubljana in the 1980s would have to include Radio Student (the independent radio station, set up in 1969),

Mladina (the youth magazine which became increasingly independent in the course of the 1980s), the Students' Cultural and Artistic Center (ŠKUC – which sponsored many cultural and artistic productions of the alternative movement), the punk scene, rock groups such as Laibach, Borghesia, and the Bastards,[11] the Anna Monro Theater (launched in 1981, combining a concept of "people's theater" with traditional stage action interspersed with critical commentary[12]), the Fiction Producer Company (another theater, featuring an all-women troupe),[13] the Helios Theater, the Glej Theater, the Ljubljana Dance Theater, and the Slovene Youth Theater, not to mention the fictional writings of Drago Jančar and others. The Slovene Youth Theater, like other sectors of Ljubljana's increasingly assertive cultural sector, marched straight into politics, offering, at one juncture, a program titled "Utopia instead of ideology."[14]

Of special interest, in the sphere of visual arts, was an exhibit staged by the Slovene Society for Aesthetics in Autumn 1989. Erjavec and Grižinić recall the exhibit:

The space was constructed out of flimsy, colorful relief ornaments or organic or geometric forms, produced out of pigments, sand, soil, glue, and wax. The exhibits consisted of shapeless masses of paint and molten lead. The objects were displayed on the walls and on the floor, with light installations helping to emphasize the colorfulness or the themes suggested by the scenography, as well as the illusive perspective of the gallery hall. The most interesting feature of the project was that it represented the salient trait of contemporary culture: the omnipresence of the visual and the promotion of the eye to the position of the foremost sense organ of our time.[15]

Changes in the cultural scene challenged Slovenes' perception of reality, challenged their cultural, social, and political values, and invited them to become active participants in a project of rethinking social existence. In all of these ways, the cultural sector proved to be a powerful force for social change in Slovenia.

A second dimension of change was associated with architecture and urban renewal. One does not ordinarily think of architecture as having political importance, even though utopian thinkers from Plato to Tommaso Campanella (1568–1639) have long understood the importance of architecture in affecting behavior and perceptions.[16] But Ljubljana's urban renewal in the 1980s showed the importance of architecture and urban planning for political behavior. In part, Ljubljana's renewal took on familiar forms – such as the rejuvenation of the Old Town, the opening of new shops, cafés, studios, and bars in the downtown area. The specific importance of Ljubljana's urban renewal lay in two aspects. On the one hand, what had been a quiet, run-down area became, in the course of the 1980s, revivified, with the restoration of both a lively day-time café life and an active night life. In this regard, too, the renewal of downtown Ljubljana was accompanied by a change in the local population structure, as young people moved into the center. That this change in population structure bore with it the capacity to affect political participation in Slovenia's most vulnerable point – downtown Ljubljana – is obvious. On the other hand, the renewal also involved the establishment of local institutions that became gathering places for people with common interests. Here one may mention the Škuc Gallery (established 1978), the Ars Gallery (established 1980), the Turist Discotheque (established 1980), the Society for Theoretical Psychoanalysis (established 1982), and the Slovene Society for Aesthetics (established 1983). The Roža Snack Bar and the Sax Pub, both established in the early 1980s, also proved to be important places for young people to gather. Nor should one omit the Cankar Center, completed in 1980, which hosted more than 7,000 events between 1980 and spring 1990.[17]

A third manifestation of social change in Slovenian society took place at the level of graffiti. In 1981, a local disco club called Disco FV began encouraging young people to write graffiti across the city. Given the hostility with which the authorities viewed this explosion of graffiti, the action was unavoidably political – both in the eyes of the graffiti artists and in the eyes of the authorities and public. Although short-lived, the outburst of graffiti art in 1981 provided a clue that Slovenian consciousness was changing.

A fourth level on which Slovenian consciousness changed was sexual, or one might say, sexual–political. The political coming-out of gays and lesbians in the mid–1980s "triggered off a whole sequence of socialization processes, of new patterns of social behavior and action."[18] The emergence of a Slovenian gay rights' movement – manifested in the launching of the Magnus section of the Škuc Forum, the creation of a gay disco at Club K4, and the organization of regular gay–lesbian cultural events – placed tolerance at the center of public dialogue. This newly explicit emphasis on tolerance as a social virtue satisfied an important cultural–ideological precondition for the creation of a liberal political system, insofar as classical liberalism has always held that "political choice is meaningless unless those to whom choice is granted are able to exercise their choice autonomously, and that autonomy, in turn, presumes toleration."[19]

And last, but by no means least, Slovenia experienced rapid change in the political sector, as outspoken opposition to the policies of Belgrade provoked the creation of embryonic parties. This incipient political pluralization (actually repluralization) had the character of pressure for democratization, and was foreshadowed already in late 1983 when France Klopčič, one of the oldest Slovenian communists, formally proposed a "Slovenian national program" oriented toward pluralization and the achievement of greater autonomy.[20] Four years later came the publication of a collection of articles on "the Slovenian national program," in the February 1987 issue of *Nova revija*, championing these same principles.[21] This intersection of "national" and "democratic" helped to frame the Slovenian public's response, in June 1988, to the arrest and trial of four young Slovenes (journalists Janez Janša, David Tasić, and Franci Zavrl, and army Sergeant Major Ivan Borštner) on charges of betrayal of a military secret. Their "crime" was to have appropriated a top secret military document with the intention of publishing it in *Mladina*.[22] Earlier, in May, *Mladina* had published in the pages of *Mladina* documented evidence of JNA preparations to arrest large numbers of Slovenian liberals and thereby put the lid on Slovenian democratization.[23] This article would be cited by the prosecution in the ensuing trial of the four.

The Slovenian public was outraged – not merely by the trial itself, which seemed to violate customary notions of protected speech, but also by the fact that the military conducted the trial in Serbo-Croatian (!), even though the trial was held in Ljubljana. Slovenes interpreted this fact as a violation of Slovenian sovereignty and constitutionalism, even though it was in accord with provisions of the federal constitution. Also troubling to some Slovenes was the fact that civilians were being tried by a military court in peacetime. On June 22, 1988, some 40,000 persons took part in a demonstration on Ljubljana's Liberation Square, to protest the trial. Although the four accused, among them journalist Janez Janša, were found guilty, the military failed to dampen the pressure for democratization. On the contrary, the trial only deepened and broadened Slovenian commitment to democratization, while convincing most Slovenes that the federal structure constituted an impediment to this process.

An independent Committee for the Protection of Janez Janša was formed in Ljubljana in response to this trial, enjoying the tacit approval of the communist government. Within a few days this committee renamed itself the Committee for the Protection of Human Rights. This committee issued periodical bulletins, and drew up protest petitions signed by more than 100,000 persons as well as several thousand organizations – a huge number for so small a society as Slovenia. In the course of the next few months following the trial, politically engaged intellectuals and labor activists set up a Social Democratic Alliance, a Slovenian Democratic Union, a Slovenian Christian Socialist Movement, and a Green Party. The Slovenian Peasant Union, which had been established just prior to the trial, experienced rapid growth in the wake of the trial and boasted some 25,000 members by September 1989.[24] At the same time, the League of Socialist Youth of Slovenia and the Socialist Alliance of Working People of Slovenia began to show a new independence, taking the first moves in the direction of transforming themselves into independent political parties.

The repluralization of Slovenian society, thus, was driven by energies released on several different levels, including the cultural, the sexual, and the political, as well as by freer religious life, and reinforced by conducive changes in the architecture and character of downtown Ljubljana. It was also charged with renewed nationalism, manifested in both grand and mundane settings. This nationalist charge seemed to provide evidence in support of Ghia Nodia's thesis that "nationalism is a component of the more complex entity that is called 'liberal democracy'" so that "democracy never exists without nationalism."[25] Although the dialectically conjoined forces, liberalism and nationalism, have always coexisted in tension, their combined force provided a more embracive challenge to communist hegemony than either liberalism or nationalism could have mounted in isolation from each other.[26]

In the face of this multifaceted change, the League of Communists of Slovenia was powerless to resist. The party wisely opted to embrace the inevitable and thereby to identify itself with the movement for repluralization. It therefore drafted a Program of Renewal and submitted it to public discussion. A mere dozen pages in length, this document called for the abandonment of one-party rule, the introduction of political pluralism, the recognition that legitimate differences of interests may be reflected in legitimate political conflicts, and the scuttling of the communist doctrine of a "single, eternal truth."[27] It is perhaps worth mentioning that this program was published in March 1989, at a time when Poland and Hungary were the only other republics to evince irreversible pluralizing tendencies. By endorsing repluralization ostensibly "voluntarily," Slovenia's communists, like Bulgaria's, gave the political transition the character of taking place within "the prescribed legal form, . . . rather than [involving] . . . the naked clash of powers."[28]

The Socialist Alliance of Working People of Slovenia, which had been established as a transmission belt of the communist party and which in some ways mimicked the activities of a political party, was by summer 1989 showing increasing independence of action and drew up a resolution on June 27. Among other things, this resolution called for "a democratic state of sovereign Slovene people and all the citizens of Slovenia, founded on human rights and civil freedoms . . . the rule of labor, and of the law, and independence of civil society."[29]

In late December 1989, the LC of Slovenia held a two-day congress in Ljubljana, agreeing to introduce a multi-party system within Slovenia.[30] Four days later, "after a lengthy and often polemical debate," the Assembly of the Republic of Slovenia adopted new laws on political association and on elections, at a stroke legalizing political pluralism in Slovenia. Multi-party elections were, thereupon, scheduled for April 1990.[31] The successful conclusion of these elections marked the end of the first stage of Slovenia's democratization and the inception of a second stage. The first stage had unfolded under the leadership of the communist party, within the framework of a moribund quasi-one-party system.[32] In this stage, Slovenia had laid the constitutional groundwork for eventual "disassociation" from the other Yugoslav republics, by passing a package of constitutional amendments in October 1989 that, *inter alia*, affirmed the sovereignty of the Republic of Slovenia.[33] In this phase, the Slovenes had also restored political pluralism and given birth to a new consciousness of Slovenian national identity, a consciousness played out and explored in diverse ways in Ljubljana's increasingly rich cultural life.[34]

It was left to Slovenia's postcommunist coalition governments to complete the process of separation from the Yugoslav federation, and to refashion the constitution and laws in such a way as to correspond to the functional requirements of a pluralist system.[35]

Rival concepts of democracy among Slovenia's new parties

The April 1990 elections were won by a coalition of seven non-communist parties under the umbrella-name "DEMOS" (a contraction of DEMokratična Opozicija Slovenije). Altogether the DEMOS parties won 127 out of the 240 seats in the Assembly. Left out of the coalition and thus in opposition were the Liberal Democratic Party (forty deputies) and the ex-communist Party of Democratic Renewal (thirty-five deputies) – ironically, the two parties which proved to be the biggest individual vote-getters (see tables 6.1 and 6.2).

Much has been made of the fact that the DEMOS government held a referendum on independence in late December 1990, a referendum in which a landslide of more than 88 percent of Slovenes voted for independence (with a 93.2 percent voter turn-out).[36] But what has not been sufficiently emphasized is the fact that some ten weeks before this referendum was held, the Slovenian Assembly had adopted a constitutional law annulling, in full or in part, some thirty federal laws in the spheres of the economy, politics, and defense.[37] In fact, some of the key figures in the DEMOS coalition had been thinking in terms of an independent Slovenia since at least summer 1989. In an interview in Ljubljana on September 6 of that year, for example, Dimitrij Rupel – then a professor of sociology but later to serve as Slovenia's first foreign minister – told me, "Sometime in the not so distant future, Slovenia will become an independent state . . . Slovenes should decide their own fate."[38] This was, as time would show, more than a hint; it was a programatic statement.

In the months between April 1990 and June 1991, the DEMOS government continued to prepare for independence – on the diplomatic level, the legislative level, and the military level. Independence was no longer in doubt

Table 6.1 *Legislative elections in Slovenia, 1990*

Political party	% of vote	No. of deputies in Assembly
DEMOS coalition:	55	
Slovenian People's Party		34
Slovenian Christian Democrats		26
Slovenian Democratic Union		25
Social Democratic Party of Slovenia		18
Green Party		17
Liberal Party		4
Unaffiliated		3
Liberal Democratic Party	16	40
Party of Democratic Renewal	17	35
Socialist Party of Slovenia	12	12

Notes: Absolute number of votes: 1,139,600; voter turnout: 77 percent; percentage of seats at stake: 100.
Sources: Miro Cerar, "Die verfassungsrechtlichen Grundlagen der Konstituierung des Staates Slowenien," in *Slowenien – Kroatien – Serbien: Die neuen Verfassungen*, ed. Joseph Marko and Tomislav Borić (Vienna: Böhlau Verlag, 1991), p. 105; Ali Žerdin, "Slovenia: Alone at Last," *East European Reporter* 5, no. 3 (May–June 1992), 54; and *The Economist* (London), 14 April 1990, p. 45.

Table 6.2 *Presidential elections in Slovenia, 1990*

Candidate	% of vote obtained
Milan Kučan	44.3
Joze Pučnik	26.3
Ivan Kramberger	18.9
Marko Demšar	10.5

Sources: *Chicago Tribune*, 9 April 1990, p. 5; and *The Times* (London), 10 April 1990, on *Nexis*.

in the minds of the leading figures in the Slovenian government and parliament. But DEMOS hoped to enjoy both the advantages of independence and the benefits of a security and customs association with the other Yugoslav republics. From the standpoint of Slovenia's new leadership, thus, the best option was to obtain a refashioning of the Yugoslav political system as a confederation. Comprehending that the Yugoslav federation was rapidly spinning out of control, the Slovenian government set a deadline of June 26,

1991 for the other republics to agree to a confederation. Consentaneity was not, however, the hallmark of relations among Yugoslavia's republics. Where Slovenia and Croatia insisted on a loosening of federal bonds, Serbia and Montenegro stood firm that the federation needed to be tightened. Bosnia and Macedonia tried, in vain, to produce a compromise. On June 25, 1991, the day before the deadline set by the DEMOS government, Slovenia declared its independence.

On the same day that Slovenia announced its secession, the Federal Assembly in Belgrade voted not to recognize Slovenia's independence. By June 26, 400 federal police and 270 federal customs officers, accompanied by 2,000 Yugoslav People's Army (JNA) troops, were sent to retake control of Slovenia's borders.[39] Only on June 27 were more consequential military operations launched by Belgrade ostensibly in an effort to thwart the wayward republic's quest for independence, but, in reality, to bring home to the Slovenes the costs of war and ensure their nonparticipation in subsequent operations against Croatia and Bosnia. Lt. Col. Lazar Drazić of the JNA passed along military information to the Slovenes and thereby undermined the JNA's half-hearted operations.[40] General Konrad Kolšek, a JNA general, would later claim to have contributed to the Slovenes' struggle by sabotaging general staff orders and preventing the use of special units and aerial strikes against Ljubljana and other towns.[41] After at least 100 persons had been killed or wounded, negotiations began between Belgrade and Ljubljana, culminating in an agreement that what was left of the federal government would order the withdrawal of the JNA from Slovenia. This withdrawal began on July 4.[42]

Like most of the other decommunizing governments of Eastern Europe, Slovenia's first postcommunist government set about the task of system change in a professional and scientific way. A commission headed by Miro Cerar was appointed (by the Assembly) and began studying the constitutions of sundry states. Among the constitutions they studied were those of Germany, France, Sweden, and – for certain rather specific ideas – Libya. The government soon found itself divided over four issues, and the nature of these issues tells us something about conflicts over values not just in Slovenia but in several countries of Eastern Europe. In brief, these conflicts related to:
- differences concerning the control of editorial appointments at Radio-Television Ljubljana and concerning the control of airwaves;
- differences over the most suitable scheme for privatization;
- a new drive by the Catholic Church, along with some Catholic parents, to rework the state school curriculum in such a way as to include Catholic religious instruction;

–   an effort, spearheaded by the Catholic Church and supported by the
    Christian Democratic Party, to obtain the criminalization of abortion
    and restrict women's access to abortion.

In combination, these controversies reveal fundamental differences not
only over how a democratic polity should arrange and regulate itself, but
concerning the very nature of democracy.

For those parties right of center – at that time: the Christian Democrats,
the Peasants, and the Liberals (not to be confused with the Liberal Democrats) – rapid privatization (giving priority to returning confiscated properties
to the Catholic Church), incorporating Catholic religion classes into school
curricula, and banning abortion became high priorities. On these counts, the
conservative parties were concerned, in the first place, to be of service to the
Catholic Church and to realize the programmatic ambitions of that organization.

For those parties left of center – at that time: the Party of Democratic
Renewal, the Socialists, the Liberal Democrats, the Greens, and the
Democrats – institutional transformation, including privatization, needed to
be more gradual. Spomenka Hribar, at that time a leading functionary in the
Democratic Party, told me in 1992, "I believe it would be catastrophic to
destroy the entire system set up by the communists at one blow. Privatization
[in particular] must be slow and gradual."[43] Parties on the left also opposed
the efforts to legislate Catholic values in school instruction and medical
services. The dispute over religious values revealed differences concerning
the meaning of democracy. And here, one may speak of three broad
approaches.

The first (traceable to Jean-Jacques Rousseau), dangerously simple in
concept, is that democracy is majority rule. Reducing democracy to majority
rule is dangerous both because it suggests that, at some basic level, "anything
goes," provided only that one can rally a majority of votes, at some
particular referendum, in favor (which is then equated with "the general
will"),[44] and because it glosses over the fact that issues are almost always
framed and spotlighted by specific actors and institutions already having
power. In other words, (as Alexis de Tocqueville realized) a purely
majoritarian concept of democracy inherently favors the rich and powerful,
and contains within itself the ever-present potential to manufacture reasons
to persecute "unpopular" (with whom?) minorities. In the Slovenian context,
this approach is most closely identified with Janez Janša, the darling of the
1988 trial but since then, increasingly the politician whose actions and
rhetoric have the most potential to subvert the liberal system in place.

A second approach (championed by James Madison and John Stuart Mill)
is more protective of both permanent and shifting minorities, construing
democracy in terms of choice balanced by toleration. In this scheme, the

emphasis on rule (as in majority rule) is misplaced, because it is not the outcome of the democratic process that should interest us above all, but the process itself, and the concept of equality requires that citizens be protected from abuse, even from "democratic" abuse. For this approach, toleration is inherent in the protection of free choice, because free choice presumes the autonomy of the individual, which in turn presumes toleration.[45] In the Slovenian context, this approach is identified with the centrist and left-of-center parties; among these one may include the Liberal Democratic Party and the United List of Social Democrats.

A third approach to democracy has, as its starting point, contempt – contempt for the very idea that fundamental principles of state might be subjected to popular approval and democratic debate. This is the line taken by the arch-conservative Joseph de Maistre (1753–1821) and by Josef Cardinal Ratzinger, who, in 1982, became the Prefect of the Sacred Congregation for the Doctrine of the Faith, as well as by conservatives within the Roman Catholic Church more generally (and in the Orthodox Church too, for that matter). De Maistre, whose hostility to republican forms of government was legendary, held that hereditary monarchy was "the most stable [form of government], the happiest, and most natural to man."[46] De Maistre refers the authority of laws to the authority of the lawgiver and criticizes British philosopher John Locke by name for having identified law with democratic consensus, which de Maistre calls "the characteristic which exactly excludes the idea of law."[47] Ratzinger, a close confidant of Pope John Paul II, has continued this tradition. For Ratzinger, one cannot vote about Truth, and hence, the doctrines of the Church have absolute priority over the preferences of any body of people.[48] Moreover, as Pope John Paul II has made clear on a number of occasions (including in his 1993 admonition to Bosnian Muslim women who had been raped not to have abortions, as well as in his insistence that the Polish Parliament make abortion illegal for all residents of Poland), Catholic conservatives are fully convinced that their moral strictures apply equally to Catholics and non-Catholics alike. In the Slovenian context, the Christian Democratic Party and the hierarchy and clergy of the Catholic Church stand out as the clearest exponents of this understanding of democracy. In one striking instance, despite the repeated rejection by the parliament of Church proposals to introduce Catholic religious instruction in state schools, the Catholic hierarchy has persisted in this demand, mobilizing its devout in support of this demand, despite the fact that parallel moves in Poland and Croatia have already shown that guarantees that such instruction be "voluntary" do nothing to relieve the inevitable pressure by "good Catholic children" on their peers (whether Protestants or Muslims or Jews or Orthodox or non-believers) to submit to Catholic religious classes.[49]

Paul Mojzes has suggested that the latter two approaches be termed, respectively, *secularism* and *reactive sacralism*. Mojzes' third model, *pluralism*, in which secular and sacralist tendencies coexist in harmonious and mutually tolerant balance, is, in fact, a null set, since the advocates of each approach must necessarily combat each other's ideas and program.[50] Thus, the *majoritarian* model listed above is not so much a species of pluralism *à la* Mojzes, as a populist manipulation of citizens which focuses more on *interests* than on values, except insofar as the manipulation of values may advance certain institution's vested interests. Majoritarian democracy is, in fact, the tradition which Talmon calls *totalitarian democracy*.[51]

In the Slovenian case, parties of the right championed the *reactive sacralist* model, while parties of the left advocated *secular* formulae that placed greater emphasis on toleration and choice. The tension between these two approaches grew until it overshadowed the initial unity that had been founded on opposition to the communist party and ripped the DEMOS coalition apart. In December 1991, DEMOS fell apart, and there was no doubt in anyone's mind that its collapse was permanent.[52]

By that time, the secular parties were increasingly fed up with Prime Minister Lojze Peterle, a Christian Democrat, whom they accused of having pursued a highly "ideological" program.[53] Critics charged, in particular, that Peterle "was spending too much time reopening churches and not enough mending the economy."[54] They swore that they would oust Peterle and make a new coalition in which the Christian Democrats would no longer hold the portfolio for education. Peterle's disgruntled coalition partners kept their word and in April 1992 were able to muster enough votes in the Assembly to topple him from the prime ministership. A new coalition government was eventually formed with Liberal Democrat Janez Drnovšek as prime minister. The Christian Democrats lost their control of the Ministry of Education, and were given, instead, the Foreign Ministry where, it was thought, they could do less damage. Peterle became foreign minister.[55] The United List was the third member of this coalition, but left the coalition in January 1996, complaining that its voice was being ignored in policy-making circles.[56]

Pluralism, liberalism, democracy

Political analysts often use the terms pluralism and democracy interchangeably, as if there were no distinction between them. This equation rests on two suppositions: (1) that there is no such thing as a democracy which is not pluralist in form; and (2) that the existence of choice and the staging of regular elections suffice not only for pluralism, but for democracy itself. I agree with the first supposition, but not with the latter. It is for this reason that I shall construe the project's definition of democracy – as "a political system in which the formal and actual leaders of the government are chosen within predictable intervals through a set of elections based on multiple candidacies, secret balloting, and other procedures that ensure real opportunities for electoral competition" – as more appropriate as a definition of pluralism. The definition makes no requirement that there be a written constitution, or a legal system of any kind, or any provisions for fair play or social justice, or a free press. A society which functioned in the absence of these factors would scarcely satisfy most observers as "democratic," even though it might have "pluralist" features. There is also a question as to whether *any* choice is sufficient. Is it the mere existence of clear choice that is at issue, or must there be the option of a moderate party? One can, for example, imagine a system in which three political parties competed for power – one racist-fascist, one Bakuninist and believing in the violent assault on churches and other institutions it deemed "reactionary," and one theocratic. Not everyone would find a satisfactory option within this system, but I would argue that such a system would meet the minimal standards for recognition as "pluralist." In the real world, El Salvador in the 1980s and Hungary in 1919–21 both serve as examples of systems with small and politically weak moderate parties, but with large and powerful right-wing and left-wing parties. In neither case was democracy served by the existence of extremes of choice, in the absence of a moderate middle. Indeed, the existence of a moderate center may be more important, in some ways, than the provision for choice of leaders.

I would like to suggest that pluralism may be viewed as the lowest niveau in the ascent to democracy, that liberalism – entailing a respect for the importance of tolerance – be interpreted as a high, more rarefied niveau, and that democracy – entailing not only a respect for the importance of tolerance but also an active promotion of social equality – be understood as representing yet a higher plane of political action. Under this scheme, all democracies are liberal systems, and all liberal systems are pluralist, but not all pluralist sytems are liberal, and not all liberal systems are democratic. In fact, as I shall argue below, there are very few systems that have actually approached what might be accepted as true "democracy" under this theory. And in this sense, democracy may be understood as a normative construct of an ideal to which societies may aspire. The normative component in the concept of civil society has already been noted by Nancy Bermeo.[57]

Elsewhere I have defined democracy *as a system based on the principles of political choice and social tolerance*,[58] thus signifying my subscription to the tradition embodied in the writings of James Madison and John Stuart Mill. But that definition might be usefully extended to add the following phrase: *and providing institutional protection of the legal, political, and social equality of all adult citizens*. Now it is true that there have been democracies which narrowed their scope by defining some of society's members as non-citizens: the ancient Greeks did this (thereby justifying both the exclusion of women and the enslavement of "barbarians"), and the United States did this in the eighteenth and nineteenth centuries, effectively disenfranchising the indigenous Indian population as well as blacks, women, and the propertyless. This expanded definition does not, however, address the issue of indigenous non-citizens. It is concerned, rather, with the concept of equality *of citizens themselves*, for it may be reasonably argued that if a system claims that all citizens are equal and then treats them unequally, then that system is not merely deficient where democracy is concerned, but profoundly hypocritical.

Most pluralist democracies are, quite self-evidently, hypocritical to one degree or another. This hypocrisy is manifest most pointedly where gender equality is concerned. This I shall take as my first criterion for success in the construction of democracy.

The case for gender equality is quite simple. If a system maintains that citizens are equal, then any distinction between broad groups of people on any basis other than merit or criminal record cannot be justified; (this qualification allows a state to disqualify convicted felons, for example, from holding public office). Moreover, if a system which minimizes the political participation of females and places males everywhere in positions of authority can be construed as somehow democratic, then, by the same virtue, a system which would minimize the participation of males and place females everywhere in positions of authority could, by the same virtue, be touted as equally democratic. Yet the latter picture will appear utterly absurd to most observers. *No more absurd than the reverse picture, which is the system under which most of the world lives!* As Rada Iveković put it in 1995, "Democracy without the [equal] participation of half of the population (women in this case) is no democracy."[59] It is no coincidence that J. S. Mill, who gave articulate expression to a liberal vision of social justice, was also a tireless advocate of gender equality.[60]

To Slovenia's credit, gender equality is enshrined in the very constitution (a guarantee pointedly absent, for example, from the US constitution). The US State Department's 1993 *Human Rights Report* for Slovenia expressly notes that "there is no official discrimination against women or minorities in housing, jobs, education, or other facets of the society."[61] The Slovene government set up an Office for Women's Policy in 1992, which has made some efforts to continue the communist-era policy of "positive discrimination for women." Moreover, among students in institutions of secondary and higher education, females outnumber males. But in other regards, Slovenia has no particular advantage over other European countries. Only 14 percent of deputies in the Slovenian Assembly are women, and among elected ministers, 15 percent are women. Of the sixty or so political parties in Slovenia (as of December 1994), not one is headed by a woman.[62]

Indeed, the US State Department's 1994 *Human Rights Report* for Slovenia noted that "women, even those employed outside the home, bear a disproportionate share of household work and family care" and that the average wage earned by Slovenian women is less than that earned by Slovenian men.[63]

Unfortunately for advocates of gender equality, many persons in Slovenia as in other countries of Eastern Europe, and most especially those of a conservative Christian cast, have been all too ready to associate gender equality with the communists, to condemn everything effected by the communists, and to assume that communism's support for gender equality constitutes some sort of "proof" that gender equality is a bad idea. The result has been the active promotion of "the cult of motherhood" by the Catholic Church in Slovenia,[64] the insertion into the constitution of a reference to the "sacredness of life" (as a non-commital palliative for conservative Catholics),[65] and a furious battle over Article 52 of the Constitution, which concerns women's right to an abortion. Ultimately, although the Catholic Church made the struggle against abortion its highest priority, Slovenian women of a more secular orientation organized pressure groups both within and outside the Assembly and successfully defended the Article.[66]

If Slovenia's success in satisfying the criterion of gender equality has been limited and rather mixed, on the second criterion – institution-building – Slovenia must be said to have been largely successful. This criterion embraces a cluster of closely related tasks, specifically: rewriting the laws to make them supportive of pluralism, reshaping Slovenian institutions toward the same end, decommunizing informal and formal networks and channels, and creating a stable party system dominated by a few strong parties, rather than by a swarm of small and weak parties.

I have written elsewhere of Slovenia's energetic efforts to reshape the legislative and institutional infrastructure bequeathed by "self-managing socialism,"[67] and will confine myself to observing that these efforts have been largely successful. Decommunizing the system has been more difficult because even though many of today's politicians are yesterday's dissidents, the political culture of self-management permeated the entire society and affected those out of power almost as much as those in power. Already in the first year of power, the DEMOS politicians found that, having protested for years against communist control of editorial appointments at Radio-Television Ljubljana, they no longer looked askance at this system once *they* had inherited control of the appointments. Needless to say, this gave rise to controversy.[68] As recently as February 1995, there were allegations of interference on the part of Slovenian politicians in the editorial policy of

Table 6.3 *Legislative elections in Slovenia, 1992 and party realignments as of March 1994*

Political party	% of vote	No. of deputies (Dec. 1992)	No. of deputies (March 1994)
Liberal Democrats (Janez Drnovšek)[a]	23.3	22 ⎫	30
Greens (Dušan Plut)[a]	3.7	5 ⎭	-
Christian Democrats (Lojze Peterle)	14.5	15	15
United List (Janez Kocijančič)	13.6	14	14
Slovene People's Party (Marjan Podobnik)	8.8	10	12
Social Democrats (Janez Janša)	3.3	4	4
Slovene National Party (Zmago Jelinčič)	9.9	12 ⎫	4
Slovenian National Right (Sašo Lap)[b]	-	- ⎭	3
Democrats (Tone Peršak)	4.5	6	4
Independents:			2
Italian minority: Roberto Battelli			
Hungarian minority: Marija Pozsonec			
Total		88	88

Notes: [a]Combined in 1994. [b]Split from Jelinčič's party in 1994. Voter turnout: 1,281,000, or 85 percent of those eligible to vote.
Sources: Milan Andrejevich, "Elections in Slovenia Maintain Status Quo," *RFE/RL Research Report*, December 18, 1992, p. 29; *Slovenia for Everyone*, 5th revised ed. (Ljubljana: Vitrum, 1995), p. 9; and Radio Slovenia (Ljubljana), December 9, 1992, trans. in BBC Summary of World Broadcasts (December 11, 1992).

Delo, the most respected Ljubljana daily.[69] There were also delays in depoliticizing the police force.[70] These and other considerations prompted a group of well-known Slovenian intellectuals to write an open letter (published in *Delo* in August 1993), warning about "cliques or informal groups from the former establishment" which constituted themselves as "secret power centers" and were allegedly "trying once again to deceive the Slovene public."[71]

But if decommunization seems to have encountered some obstacles, Slovenia's gravitation toward a stable party system has been nothing but robust. In a word, the highly fractured political landscape has been consolidated through the mergers of like-minded parties. First, the Peasant Party merged into the Christian Democratic Party. Then, in mid-1992, several left-oriented parties merged with the Party of Democratic Renewal to create the new United List of Social Democrats (sometimes called the Associated List). And finally, in March 1994, four moderate-left parties – among them, the Liberal Democratic Party – fused to form the Liberal Democracy of Slovenia.[72] Together these three parties controlled fifty-one of the eighty-eight seats in the State Assembly (as a result of elections of December 1992 which were conducted on the basis of a mixed proportional representation/single district system with a threshold of 3.4 percent).[73] (For a description of the constitutional/institutional structure of the government and brief account of electoral provisions, see the appendix to this chapter.)

If these three parties largely define right, left, and center in Slovenian politics today, there are, nonetheless, other political parties worth mentioning – above all, the Social Democratic Party of Slovenia chaired by Janez Janša (with 6,000 members as of April 1994) and the Slovenian National Party, an ultra-nationalist party chaired by Zmago Jelinčič (which claimed more than 4,000 members as of April 1994). By contrast, the Christian Democrats counted 35,000 members at that time, the United List 23,000, and the Liberal Democracy some 18,000, while the Slovene People's Party, which placed sixth in the December 1992 elections, claimed to have some 36,000 members organized in fifty-one county committees (see table 6.3).[74]

Political and economic criteria for pluralism

As Madison wrote in *The Federalist Papers*, it is first necessary to enable the government to control the governed (criterion No. 2, above). It is subsequently necessary to enable the government to control itself.[75] This is my third criterion for assessing the progress of Slovenian democratization.

Here, despite more than adequate constitutional and legislative safeguards, Slovenian authorities have repeatedly been accused of one infraction or another. Already in late 1991, there was the so-called "Slovingate" financial scandal, involving eighteen well-known Slovenian commercial enterprises and banking institutions in illegal transfers of money to Belgrade.[76] Later, there were charges that a local casino had bribed secret police agents,[77] and vague insinuations that Slovenian President Kučan had misappropriated state funds to fuel his reelection campaign in 1992. Then-Defense Minister Janša, who gave currency to these latter insinuations, also charged that former high-ranking communists were using illegal means to take control of Slovenia's major enterprises, banks, insurance companies, media outlets, and casinos.[78] The charge of embezzlement and misuse of state funds has more recently been leveled also against Jelko Kačin, Janša's successor as minister of defense.[79]

Beyond that, Helsinki Watch, the international non-governmental human rights organization, reported that it had received 270 reports of human rights violations in post-communist Slovenia by the beginning of 1995. Helsinki Watch rejected the Slovenian government's claim that "there are no systematic human rights violations" in the republic.[80] Dušan Jelušič, a Ljubljana lawyer and member of Helsinki Watch, called into question the independence of the Slovenian judiciary, claiming that the courts sometimes followed instructions from the Defense and Interior Ministries. Part of the problem is that Janša has a number of dossiers on individuals within the judiciary – dossiers containing compromising material – and has used his possession of these dossiers to blackmail certain judges into "cooperation" with him.[81] Noting other problems as well, Helsinki Watch issued a statement asserting its conviction "that with that kind of behavior, violating even the constitution and international legal principles, Slovenia is setting up for itself a very poor recommendation for admission to the European Union and to Europe in general."[82] I shall return to the theme of human rights violations in the penultimate section, within the context of a discussion of the "Janša affair."

The fourth and final criterion for the assessment of democratic construction is economic rehabilitation. The relationship between economic sufficiency and political moderation has been recognized since the time of Aristotle, and was a cardinal principle in the political philosophy of Thomas Hobbes. In the Yugoslav context, it was, after all, the growth of economic discontent in Serbia that provided the grist for Milošević's ethnic mobilization of Serbs, setting the stage for war. And in general terms, economic deterioration typically leads to an escalation of social tensions which, in turn, are apt to fuel political extremism, and most especially, right-wing extremism.[83]

In this regard, Slovenia's postcommunist economic managers have done well for their republic, as the figures in table 6.4 show. After two years of declining production and income 1991–92, Slovenia began to stage a recovery the following year, slowing the decline in industrial production from -13.2 percent to -2.8 percent, reducing inflation from a 1992 high of more than 200 percent to just over 30 percent annually, and recording the first, albeit modest, increase of 1.3 percent in the social product. But it was only in 1994 that the recovery gained momentum, as Slovenia recorded healthy growth rates of 5.5 percent in social product and 6.4 percent in industrial production, notching an increase in real income for the second year in a row, and stabilizing the rate of unemployment. The economic figures for 1995 showed continued positive trends, albeit at slower rates.

Slovenia has many economic advantages, including a well-developed industrial infrastructure, a well-educated population (see table 6.5), a successful tourist industry that attracts large numbers of visitors (especially from Austria and Germany), a strong tradition in printing and design, and some 100 highly professional advertising agencies.[84] Slovenia acceded to the General Agreement on Tariffs and Trade (GATT) in autumn 1994,[85] and in February 1995, reached an agreement for cooperation with the European Free Trade Association (EFTA).[86] Moreover, in September 1995, Slovenia was admitted to CEFTA, the Central European Free Trade Area,[87] and is

Table 6.4 *Indicators of economic trends in Slovenia since 1989*

	1989	1990	1991	1992	1993	1994	1995
GDP	-1.8	-4.7	-8.1	-5.4	1.3	5.5	3.5
Industrial output	-0.1	-10.5	-12.4	-13.2	-2.8	6.4	2.0
Rate of inflation	1,306	550	117.7	201.3	32.3	19.8	14.0
Rate of unemployment	2.9	4.7	8.2	11.6	14.4	14.4	14.5
GNP per capita	n.a.	n.a.	n.a.	n.a.	10,585	n.a.	n.a.
% Workforce in private activity	13.0	14.7	17.5	19.9	n.a.	n.a.	n.a.
% GDP from private sector	8.1	11.4	15.7	19.5	n.a.	n.a.	n.a.

Notes: GDP – % change from previous year; industrial output – % change from previous year; rate of inflation – % change in end-year retail/consumer prices, annual average; unemployment – % of labor force, annual average; GNP per capita in US dollars at PPP exchange rates.
Sources: European Bank for Reconstruction and Development, *Transition Report 1995: Economic Transition in Eastern Europe and the Former Soviet Union, 1995*; European Bank for Reconstruction and Development, *Transition Report Update, April 1996: Assessing Progress in Economies in Transition* (London, 1996); and Sabrina P. Ramet, *Whose Democracy? Nationalism, Religion and the Doctrine of Collective Rights in Post-1989 Eastern Europe* (Lanham, MD: Rowman & Littlefield, forthcoming 1997), tables 2.1 and 2.3.

expected to be among the first East-Central European countries to be admitted to the European Union.[88]

But Slovenia also has problems. Of the 640,000 families that make up the population of Slovenia, some 70,000 were reported to be near or below the poverty level.[89] In addition, Slovenia has had to cope with the presence of refugees from the war in Bosnia. In June 1992, after indigesting the first wave from the war, officials said there were more than 60,000 Bosnian refugees in Slovenia – an unmanageable number for the small Alpine republic.[90] About half of the refugees were later resettled outside the republic, but as of December 1994, there were still 24,156 Bosnian refugees registered in Slovenia.[91] Moreover, the general economic progress notwithstanding, the Slovenes have also made at least one serious mistake in the four years following the elections of April 1990. That mistake, according to Slovenian economist Jože Mencinger, was to allow salaries to grow at a rate faster than that of the social product. Mencinger warned, in May 1995, that "Large salary increases will hamper Slovenia's competitiveness on international markets in the future."[92]

The central element in the Slovenian program for economic recovery has been privatization. In practice, this has involved three facets: the return of

Table 6.5 *Demographic trends in Slovenia since the 1950s*

	1950s	1970s	1980s
Percentage of population	(1953)		
Rural	77.6		
Urban	22.4		
Average annual rates of	(1953–61)	(1971–81)	(1981–91)
population growth	0.6	0.8	0.3
Age distribution (%)	(1953)	(1971)	(1990)
15–24	18.4	17.4	14.8
25–49	21.7	34.9	37.1
50–59	10.3	8.6	11.7
Over 60	11.1	14.8	15.8
Levels of education[a] (%)	(1953)	(1981)	(1991)[b]
Without education or 1–3 years	15.2	3.6	0.7
Primary (4–8 years)	72.7	54.9	45.1
Secondary	11.2	34.5	42.4
Post-secondary	0.8	5.9	10.4

Notes: [a]Indicates attainment of completed education at each level among persons over 10 years of age. [b]Data are for persons over twenty-five years of age and include completed or partial education at each level.

Sources: Federal Institute for Statistics (Belgrade, Yugoslavia); US Department of Commerce, *Statistical Abstracts of the United States*; Paul S. Shoup, *The East European and Soviet Data Handbook*; UNESCO, *Statistical Yearbooks*; United Nations, *Demographic Yearbooks*; Eduard Bos et al., *World Population Projections, 1994–95 Edition*.

property confiscated by the communists to the original owners, or the payment of adequate compensation; the redesign of the legal system so as to encourage both the formation of private concerns and foreign investment; and the orchestration of the large-scale transfer of so-called socially owned enterprises to private ownership. All three have been controversial. The first issue has been particularly controversial where confiscated properties of the Catholic Church are concerned and as it relates to land confiscated from local Italians at the end of World War II. Ironically, the dispute with the Italians had been settled in the Osimo Accord (1975) and the Rome Accord (1983). But these accords were signed by Italy and Yugoslavia, and with the breakup of Yugoslavia, the Italian government (under pressure from the extreme right) has treated these accords as dead letters and has rekindled the dispute, using the dispute as a pretext to hold up approval of Slovenia's admission to the European Union. There are between 2,500 and 3,000 Italians living in Slovenia today.[93] Indeed, it was with an eye to appeasing Italy that, in May 1995, the Slovenian government agreed to change the constitution to allow foreigners to buy and own real estate in Slovenia.[94]

The second aforementioned issue (encouraging private enterprise and foreign investment) has been the least controversial of the three facets of the economic program. But, for all that, it has become bogged down, and a July 1995 report claimed that "Many foreign investors are frustrated at the slothful pace of Slovenian market capitalization."[95]

As for the third facet of the economic program (privatization), this proved extraordinarily difficult to work out, due to fundamental differences between those who wanted to use privatization to foster social justice (hence advocating the free distribution or discount sale of shares, under various percentage schemes, to enterprise workers and citizens at large), and those who wanted to use privatization to obtain capital and to promote profitability (hence advocating the sale of shares to investors, at the highest price obtainable, with the resulting capital being deposited in the national treasury). Between early 1991 and mid-June 1992, the Slovenian government entertained, and ultimately failed to adopt, four successive privatization schemes.[96] Finally, in November 1992, the Slovenian Assembly agreed on what must have seemed, by that point, the inevitable compromise: to let each enterprise decide on its own privatization scheme, within certain broad limits set by the government.[97]

In spite of this law, it was not until 1994 that privatization began in earnest, and by June 1995, only 200 of the 1,500 enterprises up for conversion had been successfully privatized. Even as late as October 1995, only 342 companies had completed the privatization process, while another 530 were said to be in the process of being privatized. Still, the government hoped to complete the transfer of the remaining enterprises to private hands by mid-1996.[98] By July/August 1995, Slovenian officials were taking up the partial privatization of the port of Koper and of Slovenia's national oil company, Petrol.[99] Meanwhile, Slovenia's slow pace of privatization had a direct impact on foreign investment, "Investors are waiting for the mass privatization process in Slovenia to finish because they want to deal with companies which have known owners," Matej Kovač, director of Slovenia's Office for Economic Promotion and Foreign Investments, told Reuters in October 1995.[100] At that time, foreign investments accounted for only 2.5 percent of all investments in Slovenia, with 20.4 percent of these coming from Austria and 19.6 percent from Germany.

The clerical challenge

A system's consolidation and stability may be gauged from its ability to withstand such tremors and challenges as it may face. As already noted, the chief challenges to liberal democracy in contemporary Slovenia are inspired respectively by clerical (sacralist) and populist (Rousseauian) premises.

The clerical challenge was scarcely a surprise to the Slovenian public. Although the Catholic Church in Slovenia had maintained a low profile in communist times, keeping its focus for the most part on narrowly defined ecclesiastical interests, it has become much more voluble since the communists were voted out of power in 1990. Some 72 percent of Slovenes are Catholic.[101] This preponderance of Catholics has encouraged the Church to demand that Catholic religious instruction be incorporated into the state elementary school system.

The Church had been severely restricted under communist legislation. But in May 1991, passage of an amendment to the Law on the Legal Status of Religious Communities abolished all formal obstacles to ecclesiastical involvement in public life. Taking advantage of the new liberalism, the Catholic Church immediately began organizing social services and established a small Catholic school system.[102] Even earlier, in October 1990, the Interdiocesan Catechetical Council had formulated a proposal that religious instruction be introduced in public schools, This demand was reiterated in a pastoral letter from the Slovenian episcopate circulated among Slovene Catholics in Lent 1991, and in a letter sent by Archbishop Šuštar to the government in August 1992.[103] Interestingly enough, Šuštar belongs to the "moderate" wing of the Slovenian Catholic Church. Anton Stres, an outspoken conservative theologian within the Slovenian Church, has joined other ecclesiastical conservatives in letting it be known that they will welcome Šuštar's eventual retirement, some of these conservatives even accusing Šuštar of being a "red archbishop."[104] An October 1995 poll revealed that 66 percent of Slovenes are opposed to the Church's demand that Catholic religious instruction be made part of the public school curriculum,[105] but widespread criticism has failed to deter the Church from its efforts to promote its agenda. Moreover, the Christian Democratic, People's, Liberal, and National-Democratic parties expressly supported the Church's demands on education and abortion, even pressing (unsuccessfully) to incorporate a ban on abortion into the constitution.

In the meantime, the Church, which had by 1995 already retrieved much of the land confiscated by the communists after World War II, continued to press for the return of forest lands to which it claimed title.

Whether one talks of the abortion debate or the dispute over religious instruction in the schools or the controversy over forest lands, the Catholic

Church has comported itself in the spirit of de Maistre and Ratzinger, identifying its own agenda with a superordinate "Truth" and refusing to submit its demands to majoritarian approval.

The populist challenge

Where the clerical challenge is explicit, even in its own way forthright, the populist challenge is both more insidious and more devious. Here it is the figure of Janez Janša who represents the most potent focus for populist authoritarianism. Janša has been described variously as social democrat and right-wing authoritarian. Central to his program is self-promotion, though nationalist appeals underpin his rhetoric. The populist challenge presented by Janša is identified, in the eyes of much of the Slovene public, with a series of scandals that may be subsumed under the rubric of the "Janša affair." It is, therefore, to a brief elucidation of the "Janša affair" that this penultimate section is devoted. I believe that it indicates, at a minimum, that there is some uncertainty in Slovenia as to whether the constitutional-legal foundations of the new state system are sufficiently stabilized as to withstand extra-legal attacks and informal political subversion.

Janša, the hero of the 1988 trial conducted by the JNA, had been known prior to 1990 for his pacifism and for his strong opposition to military budgets; in 1990, however, he became Slovenia's first postcommunist minister of defense. He joined the Social Democratic Party of France Tomšič, a slightly left-of-center political association, eventually becoming head of this party, after Jože Pučnik, Tomšič's immediate successor. Meanwhile, as defense minister, Janša enjoyed authority over the Ministry of Defense, Republic of Slovenia Brigade (the acronym formed from the Slovenian is MORiS Brigade). This brigade, consisting of several hundred elite troops trained as a rapid mobilization force, quickly displayed both political and criminal tendencies. For example, Anton Krkovič then head of the MORiS Brigade, not only modeled the brigade's uniforms – all black – on the Nazi-era SS, but even admitted in public that he viewed the SS as a model for MORiS to emulate.[106] Janša increasingly used the MORiS Brigade as his own personal force; when some MORiS Brigade members were indicted in 1994 on charges of bank robbery and other crimes, Janša intervened to obtain the dismissal of the charges.[107] By 1993, Janša was coming into conflict with Slovenian President Milan Kučan and, in an effort to embarrass Kučan, revealed (in July of that year) that weapons were being trans-shipped through Maribor Airport to the Bosnian Muslims. (The Slovenes, who had taken the side of Kosovo's Albanians in their quarrel with the Serbs and who had briefly fought against the Serb-controlled army in June–July 1991, were sympathetic to the Bosnian Muslims in their war with

Bosnian Serbs. Thus, the war itself did not rise to the level of constituting a major issue in Slovenian internal politics, but the illegal arms transfers, on the other hand, proved highly controversial, because they cast doubt on Slovenia's willingness to play by Western rules and on Slovenia's "good faith" in general.) Some 120 metric tons of weapons were "discovered" at the airport, at Janša's prompting, resulting in serious embarrassment to the Slovenian government in its relations with Western countries.[108] A few months later, however, Janša inflamed Kučan, by authorizing the arrest and beating of Milan Smolnikar, a former security agent of the Ministry of Defense. Kučan's allies were able to amplify the charges against Janša by claiming that he had tapped journalists' phones and engaged in subversive actions that "endangered civilian rule."[109] On March 29, 1994, on the recommendation of Prime Minister Drnovšek, the State Assembly voted forty-nine to thirty-nine to dismiss Janša from office; Jelko Kačin, erstwhile minister of information, was named to take over as minister of defense. Even as the Assembly was deliberating on this course of action, however, some 7,000–10,000 demonstrators rallied outside the Assembly building to express their support for Janša and to demand the resignation of Prime Minister Drnovšek (who had recommended Janša's dismissal).[110]

In the wake of Janša's dismissal, Kučan admitted that Slovenia had funneled arms to Croatia and to the Bosnian government but, in an effort to distance himself from the affair, demanded the appointment of a government committee to investigate the arms smuggling operation.[111]

Had Janša gone into quiet retirement, matters might have calmed down. But the thirty-six-year-old political activist was scarcely ready for retirement. As early as April 9, less than two weeks after his dismissal, Janša's party co-organized a rally with several other parties (including the increasingly alienated Christian Democrats). Some 5,000 persons attended the rally, demanding "a revision of procedures which led to the Slovenian public debt. . . more rigid sanctions for [the] illegal flow of capital abroad . . . [and] a rapid adoption of two laws on anti-corruption measures and money-laundering."[112] Meanwhile, Janša's supporters began a campaign of petty harassment and intimidation of the University of Ljubljana's internationally renowned professor of sociology, Rudolf M. Rizman, who had been quietly criticizing Janša among friends.[113] Undaunted, Rizman took his case to the public and charged that Janša had been "using his position as a defense minister to instrumentalize [the] military complex for the promotion of his authoritarian political ambitions."[114] Janša, in turn, claims that Slovenia remains under the control of scarcely-reformed communists (what he calls "the Udbomafia") and has demanded a "new Slovene spring."[115] The ruling coalition has fought back by dismissing large numbers of Janša's supporters within the Defense Ministry, purging the special MORiS Brigade, and replacing the head of the counterintelligence service.[116] Janša has remained popular, however, and his showdown with the government seems to have actually augmented his appeal. The upshot is that in the local elections of December 1994, Janša's party increased its strength by 300–400 percent.[117]

The swing of the pendulum

Slovenia's GDP and industrial production, which had grown at rates of 3.5 percent and 2.0 percent respectively in 1995, showed growth rates of 3.0 and -1.1 percent respectively in the first five months of 1996.[118] If these figures did not suggest robust performance, the figures relating to inflation and unemployment were more reassuring. Inflation, which had stood at 14.0 percent in 1995, was reduced to 10.5 percent as of June 1996, while unemployment, which had stood at 14.5 percent in 1995, was brought down to 13.7 percent as of June 1996.[119]

In other regards too, economic performance has been mixed. On the positive side, Slovenia was assigned the highest credit rating of any country in transition in 1996, by both Moody's and Standard and Poor.[120] Moreover, direct foreign investments in Slovenia in 1995 were nearly double the level of 1994.[121] Improvements in the export competitiveness of Slovenian industry during 1993 and 1994 created a momentum carrying well into 1996.[122] And in general, Slovenia was reported, as of May 1996, to have "developed a strong economy supported by a powerful export-led growth, a successful anti-inflation strategy, and sound public finances," reinforced by sturdy growth in the production of electrical machines, the manufacture of basic chemicals, non-ferrous metallurgy, wood products, rubber, machine industry, and transport equipment manufactures.[123]

On the negative side, there were some unfavorable changes in a number of sectors of the Slovenian economy in the second half of 1995, including an increase in stocks of finished industrial products, a halt in the growth of retail and wholesale trade sales, a drop in the number of overnight stays (especially of foreign tourists), higher than anticipated growth in wages, lower growth in savings by individuals, instability in the foreign exchange market, and high volatility in the tolar as of late 1995.[124] In these circumstances, the competitive position of Slovenian exports declined relative to several other countries in transition (Hungary, Poland, Czech Republic, and Slovakia) in 1995.[125] And finally, throughout 1995 and into 1996, Slovenia's foreign trade deficit was increasing. Indeed, Russia is one of the few countries, aside from the other Yugoslav successor states, with whom Slovenia has had a favorable balance of trade.[126]

It was against the backdrop of this somewhat mixed, if generally reassuring, economic picture that Slovenes went to the polls in November

1996, to elect a new government. On the eve of the elections, informed observers agreed that, regardless of the electoral outcome, Slovenia's next government would have to "cut welfare benefits, trim pensions, and reduce spending on education and health."[127]

The election results were not surprising, but the complexity of the situation created by those results seems not to have been entirely anticipated. The big winner in the 1996 elections was the Liberal Democratic Party, which increased its share of the vote from 23.7 percent in 1992 to 28 percent. The Social Democrats and People's Party (former Peasant Party) trailed at a distance, collecting only 19 and 18 percent respectively, while the fourth-place Christian Democrats won just under 9 percent of the vote. In fifth place stood the United List with 8 percent of the vote.[128] The difficulty was that the Social Democrats, People's Party, and Christian Democrats had entered into a pre-election coalition and that among them, they controlled forty-five of the ninety seats in the parliament. The Liberal Democrats, with fully twenty-five seats, thus found themselves negotiating from a weaker position, despite the increase in the number of seats they controlled.[129]

The right-wing coalition offered to include the Liberal Democrats in a coalition, but on the condition that Drnovšek step down as prime minister – a condition at once rejected by Drnovšek. In his place, the coalition proposed to install Marjan Podobnik, the thirty-five-year-old leader of the People's Party.[130] Although Drnovšek appeared to be at a disadvantage, his position was strengthened by the symbolically important unanimous endorsement of his continuance in the prime ministership on the part of the Democratic Party of Pensioners (who had elected five deputies to the legislature),[131] and by a survey conducted by the daily newspaper *Dnevnik* immediately after the elections, which showed that 53.6 percent of voters thought that Janez Drnovšek should remain prime minister.[132] Although there was still no solution at press time, informed observers speculated that the People's Party would break ranks and form a coalition with the Liberal Democrats, bringing in tow either the Christian Democrats or Janez Janša's Social Democrats. Under this formula, Drnovšek would retain the office of prime minister.

Conclusion

I have chosen, in the foregoing pages, to offer a somewhat controversial standard for assessing the progress of democracy, by placing gender equality at the center of discussion. I believe that this prioritization is justified and that those who advise that "women's issues can wait" cannot be said to be interested in human dignity, human equality, social justice, or democracy itself. But although gender equality is a necessary condition for authentic democratic life, it is not a sufficient condition. To that must be added further

Figure 6.1 *The ideological dispersion of Slovenia's political parties (January 1996)*

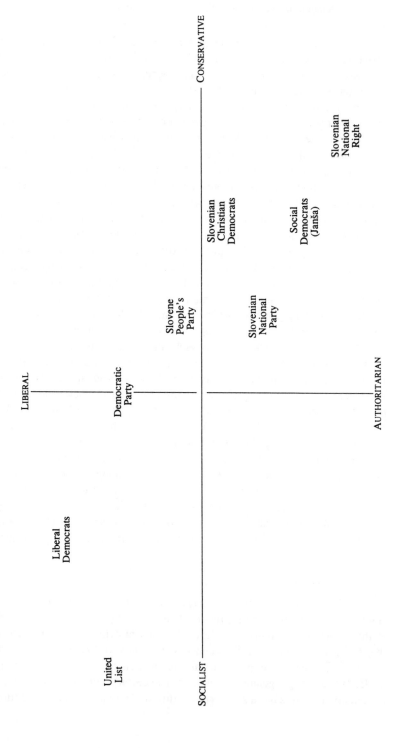

criteria – on my list: institution-building, the provision for adequate safeguards against abuses of power by the government, and economic rehabilitation. If I were to add a fifth criterion, it would be the creation or fostering of values conducive to democracy, tolerance occupying the place of honor among them.[133] Of these five criteria, three – institution-building, economic rehabilitation, and, up to a point, the provision of adequate safeguards against abuses of power by the government – may be seen as integral to the task of creating pluralism. The fostering of values conducive to democracy, most especially moderation and tolerance, is vital if a pluralist system is to rise to the higher level of liberalism. And the final criterion, namely, the fostering of social equality, including complete gender equality, is essential if a liberal system is to rise to the yet higher realm of democratic life, understood in normative terms. Thus, although equality is arguably no more essential than any of the other four criteria to the attainment of authentic democracy, it is the one key criterion that distinguishes authentic democracy from other forms of pluralism.

Emerging out of communism virtually overnight, the states of Central and Eastern Europe have had to confront all five tasks simultaneously. Conventional wisdom has held that this overloading of tasks contributes to making the transition in Eastern Europe difficult.[134] But Giuseppe Di Palma has reversed the argument and, in an interesting challenge, has suggested that the very opposite might be the case, that is, that the simultaneity of tasks, far from jeopardizing the process of democratization, might actually stimulate clarity of purpose and thereby reinforce the democratic transition.[135] Be that as it may, relative to other postcommunist states of Central and Eastern Europe, Slovenia can safely be said to enjoy especially favorable conditions and, despite the hesitant start with privatization, to be well on the way to establishing itself as a "First World" economy.

Appendix: Constitutional/institutional structure of the Government of Slovenia

After April 1990 a furious dispute developed between advocates of a bicameral legislature and supporters of a unicameral model. The eventual compromise, enshrined in the constitution adopted December 23, 1991, established a ninety-member State Assembly which exercises legislative competence, and a forty-member Council of State with purely advisory functions. The president of the republic is elected directly by popular vote, while the prime minister is chosen by whatever parties are able to put together a coalition embracing a majority of delegates in the Assembly. Members of the State Assembly serve for four years, members of the Council of State for five years, and the president for five years. The president may not be elected for more than two terms in a row. Article 111 of the constitution stipulates that "The prime minister is elected by the state assembly with a majority of votes of all delegates unless determined otherwise. . . If no candidate receives the required majority of votes . . . the president of the republic shall dismiss the state assembly and call [for] new elections." Under the constitution, judges are expected to be independent of political parties and political influence. The constitution of the Republic of Slovenia also makes provisions for local self-government, specifying that local communes shall finance their work through their own resources (Articles 139–142). The constitution may be changed by a two-thirds vote of the State Assembly, but must be submitted to the public for a referendum if at least 30 delegates demand it (Articles 169–170). The Slovenian constitution also makes provisions for all the usual guarantees and rights.

NOTES

I am grateful to Karen Dawisha, Bruce Parrott, Leopoldina Plut-Pregelj, Božo Repe, Rudi Rizman, and Vladimir Tismaneanu for helpful comments on the first draft of this chapter, and to Leopoldina Plut–Pregelj, Vladimir Pregelj, and Rudi Rizman for helpful comments on the second draft.

1 Huntington, even though advocating a minimal definition of democracy, acknowledges the dilemmas that such an approach entails (as per the apartheid-era South Africa and the Jim Crow-era United States, both of which Huntington considers to have been "democratic"). See Samuel P. Huntington, *The Third Wave: Democratization in the Late Twentieth Century* (Norman, OK: University of Oklahoma Press, 1991), pp. 5–13.
2 "Democratization and Political Participation: The Experience of the Czech Republic," in *The Consolidation of Democracy in East-Central Europe*, ed. Karen Dawisha and Bruce Parrott (Cambridge: Cambridge University Press, 1997), chapter 5.

3 Ibid.
4 Božo Repe, "Liberalization of Slovene Society in the Late Sixties," paper presented at the annual convention of the American Association for the Advancement of Slavic Studies, Washington, DC, October 26-29, 1995, p. 5. This paper is scheduled to be published in a forthcoming issue of *Slovene Studies*.
5 See Pedro Ramet, "Yugoslavia's Debate over Democratization," *Survey* 25, no. 3 (Summer 1980).
6 Božo Repe, *"Liberalizem" v Sloveniji* (Ljubljana: Narodna in univerzitetna knjižnica, 1992), p. 274.
7 Quoted in *Borba* (Belgrade), 16 June 1989, p. 7, trans. in Foreign Broadcast Information Service, *Daily Report: Eastern Europe* (hereafter *FBIS-EEU*), 26 June 1989, p. 82.
8 Popit resigned from the Slovenian party's Central Committee only three years later, however. See *Danas* (Zagreb), no. 396 (19 September 1989), pp. 16-17.
9 Quoted in Aleš Erjavec and Marina Gržinić, *Ljubljana, Ljubljana: The Eighties in Slovene Art and Culture* (Ljubljana: Založba Mladinska knjiga, 1991), p. 12.
10 Ibid., p. 18.
11 For details, see Sabrina Petra Ramet, *Balkan Babel: The Disintegration of Yugoslavia from the Death of Tito to Ethnic War*, 2d ed. (Boulder, CO: Westview Press, 1996), chapter 5; Sabrina Petra Ramet, "Shake, Rattle, and Self-Management: Making the Scene in Yugoslavia," in *Rocking the State: Rock Music and Politics in Eastern Europe and Russia*, ed. Sabrina Petra Ramet (Boulder, CO: Westview Press, 1994), especially pp. 117-23; and Marina Gržinić, "Neue Slowenische Kunst (NSK): The Art Groups Laibach, IRWIN, and Noordung Cosmokinetical Theater Cabinet – New Strategies in the Nineties," *Slovene Studies* 15, nos. 1-2 (1993), published July 1995.
12 Erjavec and Gržinić, *Ljubljana, Ljubljana*, pp. 44-5.
13 Ibid., pp. 47-8.
14 Ibid., p. 69.
15 Ibid., p. 137.
16 See Frank E. Manuel and Fritzie P. Manuel, *Utopian Thought in the Western World* (Cambridge, MA: The Belknap Press of Harvard University Press, 1979), pp. 271-9.
17 Erjavec and Grizinic, *Ljubljana, Ljubljana*, p. 27.
18 Ibid., p. 49.
19 I am quoting here from my own essay, "Democracy, Tolerance, and the Cycles of History," in *Politics and Society in Eastern Europe: From Socialism to Uncertain Pluralism*, ed. Sabrina P. Ramet (Bloomington, IN: Indiana University Press, forthcoming, 1998). For more in-depth discussion of this point, see Joseph Raz, "Autonomy, Toleration, and the Harm Principle," in *Justifying Toleration: Conceptual and Historical Perspectives*, ed. Susan Mendus (Cambridge: Cambridge University Press, 1988).
20 I am indebted to Božo Repe for pointing this out to me in a personal communication, November 7, 1995. For details, see Božo Repe, "Oris obravnave nacionalne problematike in nacionalnih programov v Sloveniji od konca druge svetovne vojne do začetka osemdesetih let," *Borec*, 3/475 (1992).
21 See Mirjana Kasapović, "O 'slovenskom nacionalnom programu,'" *Naše teme* (Zagreb) 32, no. 4 (1988), 771-86.

22 The document in question was never actually published in *Mladina*.
23 The article was written by Vlado Miheljak under the pseudonym Majda Vrhovnik. The article was based on a top secret recording of a secret meeting of the Central Committee of the LCY on 29 March 1988. Sergeant Major Ivan Borstner stole the tape and gave it to *Mladina* to publish. I am indebted to Božo Repe for these additional details.
24 This account is drawn from my *Balkan Babel*, chapter 2.
25 Ghia Nodia, "Nationalism and Democracy," in *Nationalism, Ethnic Conflict, and Democracy*, ed. Larry Diamond and Marc F. Plattner (Baltimore, MD: Johns Hopkins University Press, 1994), p. 4. For the Slovenian case, see Rudolf M. Rizman, "Die slowenische Nation im südslawischen Raum," in *Das Prinzip Nation in modernen Gesellschaften*, ed. Bernd Estel and Tilman Mayer (Opladen: Westdeutscher Verlag GmbH, 1994).
26 Elsewhere, I have portrayed chauvinistic nationalism as hostile to democracy. See Sabrina P. Ramet, *Whose Democracy? Nationalism, Religion, and the Doctrine of Collective Rights in Post-1989 Eastern Europe* (Lanham, MD: Rowman & Littlefield, forthcoming, 1997).
27 Belgrade Domestic Service, 11 March 1989, in *FBIS-EEU*, 16 March 1989, p. 60.
28 John D. Bell, "Democratization and Political Participation in 'Postcommunist' Bulgaria," chapter 9 of this volume.
29 *Delo* (Ljubljana), 28 June 1989, p. 3, in *FBIS-EEU*, 6 July 1989, p. 73.
30 *Tanjug* (Belgrade), 24 December 1989, in *FBIS-EEU*, 28 December 1989, p. 83.
31 Tanjug Domestic Service, 27 December 1989, in *FBIS-EEU*, 28 December 1989, p. 84.
32 I say "quasi-one-party system" because the *de facto* confederalization of the party itself had, by 1989 if not earlier, removed any higher arbiter in disputes between republic-based organizations of the League of Communists of Yugoslavia. For further discussion, see Sabrina P. Ramet, *Nationalism and Federalism in Yugoslavia, 1962–1991*, 2d ed. (Bloomington, IN: Indiana University Press, 1992), chapters 10 and 12.
33 Details in Robert M. Hayden, "The Beginning of the End of Federal Yugoslavia: The Slovenian Amendment Crisis of 1989," *The Carl Beck Papers* (University of Pittsburgh), no. 1001, December 1992.
34 See the magnificently illustrated volume, Erjavec and Gržinić, *Ljubljana, Ljubljana*.
35 For further discussion of the political transformations of 1988–90, see Sabrina Petra Ramet, "Slovenia's Road to Democracy," in *Beyond Yugoslavia: Politics, Economics, and Culture in a Shattered Community*, ed. Sabrina Petra Ramet and Ljubiša S. Adamovich (Boulder, CO: Westview Press, 1995).
36 *Frankfurter Allgemeine*, 27 December 1990, p. 2.
37 *Tanjug*, 4 October 1990, in *FBIS-EEU*, 5 October 1990, p. 48.
38 From the full text of the interview, published as "'Slovenia will Become an Independent State': An Interview with Dimitrij Rupel," *South Slav Journal* 12, nos. 1–2 (Spring-Summer 1989), 85.
39 Laura Silber and Allan Little, *The Death of Yugoslavia* (London: BBC & Penguin, 1995), pp. 169, 171.

40 For this, Drazić was sentenced in January 1995 to two years' imprisonment. See *Delo* (Ljubljana), 21 January 1995, p. 24, in *FBIS-EEU*, 24 February 1995, p. 39.

41 I am unable to confirm the truth of Kolšek's claims. See *Tanjug*, 3 August 1993, in *FBIS-EEU*, 4 August 1993, p. 51.

42 *New York Times*, 28 June 1991, p. 1; *Neue Zürcher Zeitung*, 5 July 1991, p. 1; and *Il Messaggero* (Rome), 5 July 1991, pp. 1, 7.

43 Spomenka Hribar, Democratic Party deputy in parliament, in an interview with the author, Ljubljana, March 24, 1992, as quoted in Ramet, "Slovenia's Road," p. 199.

44 See Jean-Jacques Rousseau, *The Social Contract*, trans. by Maurice Cranston (Harmondsworth: Penguin, 1968).

45 Raz, "Autonomy, Toleration, and the Harm Principle." For elaboration, see Sabrina Petra Ramet, *Social Currents in Eastern Europe: The Sources and Consequences of the Great Transformation*, 2d ed. (Durham, NC: Duke University Press, 1995), chapter 1.

46 Count Joseph de Maistre, *Essay on the Generative Principle of Political Constitutions*, reprint of trans. of 1847 (Delmar, NY: Scholars' Facsimiles & Reprints, 1977), p. viii.

47 Ibid., p. 27. See also Richard Allen Lebrun, *Throne and Altar: The Political and Religious Thought of Joseph de Maistre* (Ottawa: University of Ottawa Press, 1965), esp. pp. 49–70.

48 Ratzinger: "It is obvious that truth cannot be created through ballots. A statement is either true or false. Truth can only be found, not created." Joseph Cardinal Ratzinger with Vittorio Messori, *The Ratzinger Report: An Exclusive Interview on the State of the Church*, trans. from the German by Salvator Attanasio and Graham Harrison (San Francisco: Ignatius Press, 1985), p. 61.

49 For discussion of the Croatian case, see Sabrina P. Ramet, "The Croatian Catholic Church since 1990," *Religion, State and Society: The Keston Journal* (forthcoming).

50 Paul Mojzes, *Religious Liberty in Eastern Europe and the USSR: Before and After the Great Transformation* (Boulder, CO: East European Monographs, 1992), pp. 1–6.

51 J. L. Talmon, *The Origins of Totalitarian Democracy* (London: Secker & Warburg, 1952).

52 See *Delo* (Ljubljana), 3 January 1992, p. 2.

53 *Vjesnik* (Zagreb), 26 March 1992, p. 7.

54 *International Herald Tribune* (Paris), 15 July 1992, p. 4.

55 Two years later, Foreign Minister Peterle was charged with having taken an overly conciliatory stance in Slovenia's dispute with Italy. See *Agence France Presse* (Paris), 5 December 1994, on Nexis.

56 *Neue Zürcher Zeitung*, 27–28 January 1996, p. 1, and 31 January 1996, p. 2; and *Evropske novosti* (Belgrade/Frankfurt), February 1996, p. 6.

57 Nancy Bermeo, "Comments on the Research Agenda," paper prepared for the Workshop on Comparative Analysis of Post-Communist Democratization and Political Participation, SAIS and University of Maryland, Washington, DC, May 9–10, 1995.

58 Ramet, *Social Currents*, 2d ed., pp. 13–14.

59 Rada Iveković, "The New Democracy – With Women or Without Them?" in *Beyond Yugoslavia*, p. 396.

60 See Zillah R. Eisenstein, *The Radical Future of Liberal Feminism*, rev. ed. (Boston: Northeastern University Press, 1993).

61 US Department of State, "Human Rights Report: Slovenia Human Rights Practices, 1993," 31 January 1994, on Nexis.

62 Dragica Korade, "Struggling Against the Nationalist Right," in *Balkan War Report*, no. 30 (December 1994/January 1995), p. 36.

63 This is because of the disproportionate concentration of women in lower-paying jobs. See US Department of State, "Human Rights Report: Slovenia Human Rights Practices, 1994" (Washington, DC: US Government Printing Office, March 1995), on Nexis.

64 Korade, "Struggling," p. 36.

65 Iveković, "The New Democracy," pp. 404–5.

66 Silva Mežnarić and Mirjana Ule, "Women in Croatia and Slovenia: A Case of Delayed Modernization," in *Women in the Politics of Postcommunist Eastern Europe*, ed. Marilyn Rueschemeyer (Armonk, NY: M.E. Sharpe, 1994), p. 166.

67 Ramet, "Slovenia's Road," pp. 201–4.

68 See, for example, *Delo*, 7 October 1992, p. 2.

69 For details, see *Slovenec* (Ljubljana), 2 February 1995, p. 3, in *FBIS-EEU*, 6 February 1995, p. 49. My own interviews in Ljubljana in March 1992 convinced me that there was more than a bit of truth to these allegations. Still, these problems have to be viewed in perspective. The Slovenian media were, already in communist times, the most liberal media in Yugoslavia and enjoyed wide prerogatives tantamount, by the end of the 1980s, to virtual freedom of action. The scope of press freedom has expanded slightly since 1989. The controversy has centered not on on whether the Slovenian media have enjoyed some nebulously conceptualized "freedom," but whether Slovenian politicians have been using their positions to block stories on specific subjects or to influence the portrayal given to certain subjects in the press. These phenomena are not unknown in the United States, for example. For background on the communist era, see Pedro Ramet, "The Yugoslav Press in Flux," in *Yugoslavia in the 1980s*, ed. Pedro Ramet (Boulder, CO: Westview Press, 1985). For discussion of both the communist and postcommunist eras in Yugoslav media, see Ramet, *Balkan Babel*, 2d ed., chapter 4 ("The Press"). For a discussion of the media in postcommunist Slovenia, see Stan Markotich, "Slovenia's Early Reforms Laid the Foundation," *Transition*, 6 October 1995, pp. 36–8.

70 *Delo*, 28 February 1992, p. 10, in *FBIS-EEU*, 20 March 1992, p. 39.

71 *Delo*, 24 August 1993, p. 2, in *FBIS-EEU*, 17 September 1993, p. 58.

72 Radio Slovenia Network (Ljubljana), 12 March 1994, in *FBIS-EEU*, 14 March 1994, p. 55.

73 Milan Andrejevich, "Elections in Slovenia Maintain Status Quo," *RFE/RL Research Report*, 18 December 1992, p. 29.

74 *Dnevnik* (Ljubljana), 7 April 1994, summarized in *FBIS-EEU*, 22 April 1994, p. 53. Soon after the 1992 elections, the right wing of the Slovenian National Party split off and formed a new party organization, the ultranationalist Slovenian National Right, which some observers characterize as "neo-fascist" but which, in

any event, occupies a political position to the right of the Slovenian National Party.

75 Madison: "In framing a government which is to be administered by men over men, the great difficulty lies in this: you must first enable the government to control the governed; and in the next place oblige it to control itself." Alexander Hamilton, James Madison, and John Jay, *The Federalist Papers* (New York: New American Library, 1961), no. 51 (James Madison), p. 322.

76 *Delo*, 21 December 1991, p. 3, in *FBIS-EEU*, 17 January 1992, p. 31.

77 *Christian Science Monitor*, 25 October 1993, p. 1.

78 *Tanjug*, 13 September 1993, in *FBIS-EEU*, 15 September 1993, p. 48.

79 Details in Yugoslav Telegraph Service news agency (Tanjug), 19 January 1995, in BBC Summary of World Broadcasts, 21 January 1995.

80 *Večer* (Maribor), 7 January 1995, p. 2, in *FBIS-EEU*, 9 February 1995, p. 33.

81 Letter to the author from Rudolf M. Rizman, January 29, 1996.

82 *Večer* (Maribor), 7 January 1995, p. 2, in *FBIS-EEU*, 9 February 1995, p. 34.

83 I am paraphrasing here an argument I made previously in *Social Currents*, 2d ed., p. 373.

84 *The European-èlan* (London), 15–21 April 1994, p. 4.

85 See Radio Slovenia Network, 28 September 1994, in *FBIS-EEU*, 29 September 1994, p. 51.

86 *Balkan News International & East European Report* (Athens), 5–11 March 1995, p. 19.

87 *Neue Zürcher Zeitung*, 13 September 1995, p. 11.

88 *Balkan News & East European Report* (Athens), 19–25 March 1995, pp. 3, 18.

89 *Naša borba* (Belgrade), 21 March 1995, p. 6.

90 *Die Presse* (Vienna), 16 June 1992, p. 3.

91 *Slovenec*, 9 January 1995, p. 2, in *FBIS-EEU*, 17 February 1995, p. 53.

92 *Balkan News & East European Report*, 28 May–3 June 1995, p. 39.

93 *Neue Zürcher Zeitung*, 15 June 1994, p. 5; ibid., 26 November 1994 (Nexis); and ibid., 30 November 1994, p. 3.

94 Radio Slovenia (Ljubljana), 30 May 1995, in BBC Summary of World Broadcasts, 2 June 1995; and *Balkan News & East European Report*, 11–17 June 1995, p. 39. For more up-to-date reports on the Italo-Slovenian dispute, see *Der Standard* (Vienna), 23–24 September 1995, p. 2, in *FBIS-EEU*, 25 September 1995, p. 53; and *Slobodna Dalmacija* (Split), 12 October 1995, p. 11.

95 Euromoney Central European, 1 July 1995, on Nexis.

96 Details in Ramet, "Slovenia's Road," pp. 198–200.

97 Radio Slovenia Network, 12 November 1992, in *FBIS-EEU*, 12 November 1992, p. 36.

98 *Reuters European Business Report*, 7 June 1995, *Business Eastern Europe*, 12 June 1995, and ibid., 19 June 1995 – all on Nexis; and *New Europe*, 22–28 October 1995, p. 24.

99 Euromoney Central European, 1 July 1995, on *Nexis*; and *Financial Times*, 28 August 1995, p. 17.

100 *New Europe*, 15–21 October 1995, p. 24.

101 Reuter Textline, 9 February 1994, on Nexis.

102 Leopoldina Plut–Pregelj, "Changes in the Slovene Educational System, 1990–1992," *East/West Education* 14, no. 1 (Spring 1993), 59.
103 Ibid., pp. 60–2.
104 Oral communication from Leopoldina Plut–Pregelj, Washington, DC, 31 October 1995; and letter to the author from Leopoldina Plut–Pregelj, 15 January 1996.
105 Reuter Textline, 17 October 1995, on Nexis. In 1995, Krković became an innkeeper.
106 I am indebted to Rudi Rizman for this information from a personal communication on December 16, 1995.
107 Ibid.; partially confirmed in *Der Spiegel* (Hamburg), 6 June 1994, p. 130.
108 Radio Slovenia Network, 19 August 1993, in *FBIS-EEU*, 20 August 1993, p. 37; and *Vreme* (Belgrade), 18 July 1994, p. 32.
109 UPI, 28 March 1994, on Nexis.
110 10,000 on March 28, according to Yugoslav Telegraph Service news agency (Tanjug), 28 March 1994, in BBC Summary of World Broadcasts, 30 March 1994; 7,000 on 29 March, according to the *Frankfurter Allgemeine*, 30 March 1994, p. 2.
111 Yugoslav Telegraph Service news agency (Tanjug), 17 April 1994, in BBC Summary of World Broadcasts, 19 April 1994.
112 STA news agency (Ljubljana), 9 April 1994, in BBC Summary of World Broadcasts, 11 April 1994.
113 Details in Ramet, *Balkan Babel*, 2d ed., chapter 11. See also *Frankfurter Rundschau*, 17 October 1994, p. 20.
114 Rudolf M. Rizman, in a personal communication to the author on August 20, 1995.
115 *Frankfurter Rundschau*, 17 October 1994, p. 20; and *Slobodna Dalmacija*, 10 September 1994, p. 6.
116 *Delo*, 5 April 1994, p. 2, summarized in *FBIS-EEU*, 21 April 1994, p. 41; and *Delo*, 17 September 1994, p. 2, in *FBIS-EEU*, 28 September 1994, p. 55.
117 *Süddeutsche Zeitung* (Munich), 24 December 1994, on Nexis.
118 For 1996 figures, see *Neue Zürcher Zeitung*, 13–14 July 1996, p. 9, and 26 July 1996, p. 10.
119 Ibid., 26 July 1996, p. 19.
120 *New Europe*, 2–8 June 1996, p. 28.
121 Ibid., 26 May–1 June 1996, p. 25.
122 Ibid., 14–20 April 1996, p. 25.
123 Ibid., 19–25 May 1996, p. 25. Also ibid., 28 April–4 May 1996, p. 25.
124 Ibid., 31 March–6 April 1996, p. 25.
125 Ibid., 14–20 April 1996, p. 25.
126 Ibid., 19–25 May 1996, p. 25, and 24–30 March 1996, p. 25.
127 Ibid., 10–16 November 1996, p. 31.
128 *Neue Zürcher Zeitung*, 11 November 1996, p. 2.
129 Ibid., 12 November 1996, p. 1.
130 Reuter Financial Service, 25 November 1996, on Nexis; and Reuter Financial Service, 28 November 1996, on Nexis.
131 Radio Slovenia, Ljubljana, 13 November 1996, in BBC Monitoring Service: Eastern Europe, 15 November 1996.

132 Radio News Service, 14 November 1996, on Nexis.
133 For more on this fifth point, see Sabrina P. Ramet, "Democratic Values and the Construction of Democracy: The Case of Eastern Europe," in *Slavic Eurasia in Transition: Multiple Analyses*, ed. Tadayushi Hara (Sapporo, Japan: Slavic Research Center, Hokkaido University, 1994).
134 For the classic statement of this line of thinking, see Leonard Binder et al., *Crises and Sequences in Political Development* (Princeton, NJ: Princeton University Press, 1971).
135 Giuseppe Di Palma, "Why Democracy Can Work in Eastern Europe," in *The Global Resurgence of Democracy*, ed. Larry Diamond and Marc F. Plattner (Baltimore, MD: Johns Hopkins University Press, 1993), p. 265.

7   The Republic of Macedonia: finding its way

Duncan M. Perry

Macedonia declared independence from the rump Yugoslav Federation on November 21, 1991. In the transition from Yugoslav republic to the Balkan Peninsula's newest country, it carried with it the tradition of a strong leader and control by a political elite. Privatization and an ambitious effort to establish a market economy have brought significant social and economic hardships to the people of Macedonia. At the same time, tensions between ethnic Macedonians and Albanians, and problems with neighboring Greece – resulting in stunted economic growth – have made the transition even more arduous. This chapter is devoted to understanding the nature of Macedonia's democratization process and the difficulties it has faced and is facing in seeking to create a democratic state and civil society.

Some particulars

The Republic of Macedonia, with 25,713 square kilometers, is the smallest and newest Balkan country. Landlocked, it is the least developed of the former Yugoslav republics. Bordered in the north by Serbia, in the east by Bulgaria, in the south by Greece, and in the west by Albania, Macedonia is a multiethnic state, home to 2,075,196 people according to the 1994 census (see table 7.1 for some demographic trends). Ethnic Macedonians number 1,288,330 (66.5 percent), Albanians 442,914 (22.9 percent), Turks 77,252 (4 percent), Roma 43,732 (2.3 percent), Serbs 39,260 (2 percent), Muslims (Torbeši) 15,315 (.07 percent), and Vlachs 8,467 (0.004 percent). The remainder is made up of foreign nationals and small minorities, including Croatians, Bosnians, and Bulgarians.[1]

Although Albanians participated in this count, their political leaders claim that the census, like the preceding one held in 1991 which Albanians largely boycotted, was manipulated and that, as a result, the figure for Albanians is too low. Outside observers monitoring the census pronounced it accurate and

Table 7.1 *Demographic trends in Macedonia since the 1950s*

	1950s	1970s	1980s
Percentage of population	(1953)		(1990)
Rural	74.0	n.a.	41.9
Urban	26.0	n.a.	58.1
Average annual rate of	(1953–61)	(1971–81)	(1981–91)
population growth (%)	0.9	1.5	1.0
Age distribution (%)	(1953)	(1971)	(1990)
15–24	19.9	19.7	15.8
25–49	28.8	31.9	36.4
50–59	6.2	6.8	10.5
Over 60	8.2	8.9	11.7
Levels of education[a]	(1953)[b]	(1971)	
Primary	40.3	68.1	n.a.
Secondary	7.2	11.1	n.a.
Post-secondary	0.3	2.6	n.a.

Notes: [a]Indicates attainment of completed or partial education at each level for persons over fifteen years of age. [b]1953 data are for persons over ten years of age.
Sources: US Department of Commerce, *Statistical Abstracts of the United States*; Paul S. Shoup, *The East European and Soviet Data Handbook*; UNESCO, *Statistical Yearbooks*; United Nations, *Demographic Yearbooks*; Eduard Bos et al., *World Population Projections, 1994–95 Edition.*

fair, while noting that some irregularities occurred. Western governments consider the matter closed and most of Macedonia's Albanian political leaders accept the numbers (or at least recognize the reality that the results will not be changed). Since then Albanians have been demanding representation in the state infrastructure proportional to the number of Albanians making up the population in that count. To understand the complicated political and social picture that is Macedonia today, a brief expedition through Macedonian history is needed.

History

Ancient "Macedonia," or Macedon, once stretched from the Adriatic to India, from Egypt to the central Balkans, but that was in the days of Alexander the Great. What we know as geographical Macedonia, that region lying between the Šar and Osogov Mountains in the north, the Rila Mountains and Mesta River in the east, the Bistrica River, the Aegean Sea and the Pindus Mountains in the south, and the Albanian highlands in the west, has been a route for invaders and a thoroughfare for traders and merchants since before the days of Alexander.

The last empire to possess Macedonia was the Ottoman Empire, whose sultans ruled this territory from the late 1300s until 1913. A theocratic Muslim enterprise, the Ottoman Empire was, by the nineteenth century, well decayed. For the people living in those provinces making up geographical Macedonia, even for Muslim Albanians and Turks, the regime had become increasingly brutal and corrupt.

The year 1878 was a landmark in Macedonia's history. Defeated by the tsar's army in the Russo-Turkish War of 1877–78, the sultan concluded a bilateral peace with Russia at San Stefano, near Istanbul, in March 1878. The conditions of this accord established, among other things, a Great Bulgaria, which included most of geographical Macedonia. Threatened by and jealous of this large new state, Greece and Serbia protested and were championed by Austria-Hungary and Great Britain, whose leaders feared the expansion of Russian influence in the region. As a result, the accord made at San Stefano was superseded by the Treaty of Berlin, an agreement that created a rump Bulgarian principality, with Macedonia once again a part of the Ottoman holdings. Thereafter, Bulgaria, Greece, and Serbia, each born of revolution and warfare in the nineteenth century, and each motivated by nationalist considerations, competed for the allegiance of the Christian people living in Macedonia, most of whom were yet to develop a national consciousness.

In 1903 an uprising broke out on Ilinden, or St. Ilija's Day (August 2), the effort of a liberation/terrorist group best known as the Internal Macedonian Revolutionary Organization (IMRO). It failed to yield the desired goal of autonomy for Macedonia, but it subsequently proved to be an organization around which Macedonian (and Bulgarian) national myth-makers crafted a national history and from which they assembled a pantheon of national heroes. Nationalists argue that both IMRO and the revolt demonstrated the national will for the recognition of a Macedonian nation and the plea for a Macedonian homeland.[2] Neither was true as no widespread Macedonian national identity existed at the time and there was no discrete "homeland."[3]

Macedonia was pried out of the Ottoman Empire at the end of the Balkan Wars (1912–13) and was divided among neighboring states. Following World War I Greece retained the largest portion, more than 50 percent of geographic Macedonia; next came the newly created Kingdom of Serbs, Croats, and Slovenes (KSCS) with about 33 percent, followed by Bulgaria, which had briefly occupied much of Macedonia in both the Balkan Wars and World War I, with 10 percent. Albania received a sliver. This carve-up inflamed irredentist yearnings among Bulgarian nationalists, who ardently dreamed of recovering Macedonian territory granted by the Treaty of San Stefano, then lost with the Treaty of Berlin. Each country set about trying to assimilate the populations it inherited. KSCS Macedonia, which was to become in 1991 the Republic of Macedonia, was first dubbed "Southern Serbia" by Belgrade.

During the interwar period, the KSCS government, dominated as it was by Serbs, sought to make Serbs of Macedonia's inhabitants, no matter what their national consciousness might have been. No Macedonian nationality was registered in any KSCS census, political parties were prohibited, and Serbian was the official language of the region. Officials tolerated no one who spoke out for Macedonian autonomy, let alone independence. The same was true for the Albanians and Turks who lived there.

In 1929, King Aleksandar, in an effort to bring order to his increasingly fractious lands, declared martial law. He changed the name of the state to Yugoslavia and the name "Southern Serbia," to *Vardarska banovina* ("Vardar Province"). The name change was a deliberate effort to subvert any Macedonian consciousness and to foster a common identity within the Yugoslav state by avoiding reference to some national idea.

Following the assassination of the king in 1934, Yugoslav politics were chaotic. Macedonia, an extremely poor land, remained firmly under Serbian control. Although national consciousness seemed to be growing, particularly among intellectuals, and although there were scattered anti-Serbian conspiracies and terrorist activities, no sustained national movement developed. Paradoxically, Serbian leaders in Belgrade actually helped to strengthen the Macedonian identity by promoting a Serbianization policy that alienated, rather than assimilated, Macedonians. If people were unable to precisely identify what they were, they could clearly identify what they were not. They were not Serbs.

World War II

Skopje fell to the Axis in 1941 and Yugoslav Macedonia, along with a portion of Greek Macedonia, was turned over to Bulgarian occupation authorities, the third time in this century that Bulgaria occupied at least part of Macedonia. Bulgaria controlled all but a section north of Skopje and the predominantly Albanian Tetovo, Gostivar, and Kičevo regions, which were under Italian administration. Initially, Macedonians received the Bulgarians as liberators. However, instead of developing effective policies to assimilate the Macedonian Slavs, who were seen as "backward Bulgarians," they transformed their western cousins into adversaries by creating an oppressive regime that fed the development of Macedonian national consciousness. Macedonians thus realized that they were not Bulgarians.

The Macedonian national identity was first recognized by the Comintern in 1934 and was then promoted by Tito in 1942 at a congress held in Bihać, Bosnia. It was at that meeting that the Anti-Fascist Council for the Liberation of Yugoslavia (AVNOJ) was born. Partisans from all regions of Yugoslavia met in 1943 at Jajce, Bosnia, and further refined the blueprint for the future Yugoslav state, including the idea of a separate Macedonian nationality. After this, Macedonians, who had been wary of Tito's intentions given their previous experiences with Serbianization and Bulgarianization, joined the partisan war effort in significant numbers. As part of Tito's Macedonian nation-building program beginning in 1943, troops distributed literature written in Macedonian and encouraged the use of the Macedonian language, at that time still a collection of largely uncodified dialects. Schools were established in partisan-controlled territory in which the language of instruction was Macedonian.

Tito's inclusion of Macedonia (first called the Peoples' Republic of Macedonia and later the Socialist Federal Republic of Macedonia) as a constituent republic of Yugoslavia in 1946 and his recognition of the associated Macedonian nationality, served to differentiate the Slavs living in Macedonia from Bulgarians and Serbs. This was a fundamental element in Tito's Yugoslav nation-building activities, as it undermined Bulgarian territorial claims to Yugoslav Macedonia by denying that Macedonians were Bulgarians and blocked Serbs from arguing that Macedonians were part of the Serbian nation, while reducing the size of the "Great Serbia" that had dominated interwar Yugoslavia. Tito's strategy concerning Macedonian nationhood thus went a long distance toward clearing up the question for most Slavs from Macedonia about the nationality they belonged to; they were Macedonians.

Tito's experiment

Yugoslavia, in the aftermath of World War II, had much to do. Apart from physically rebuilding its devastated lands, Tito had to find ways to heal the wounds of deep-seated and deadly nationalism that had surfaced well before the war and that had, during the war, pitted Croatian fascists, Serbian Royalists, and Yugoslav communists against each other.[4] His tactic was to strike the chord of international communism in an effort to weld together Serbs, Croats, Bosnians, Slovenes, Macedonians, Albanians, Hungarians, and more in a common state which provided equal opportunity and full civil rights protection, while preserving individual ethnic identities. His ubiquitous motto was "bratsvo i jedinstvo" – Brotherhood and Unity. And in the early decades of the 1950s and 1960s, it appeared that the idea was working. Ethnic antagonisms diminished as economic conditions improved.

In the newly founded Macedonian republic, where there were no national institutions, and where there was no state infrastructure, no standard literary language, no official national history, and no national mythology, all had to be crafted. A literary language was developed based on four central Macedonian dialects, and it became the official language of the people.[5] Macedonian national identity was heavily promoted and Macedonian culture, especially literature and music, was nurtured. A Macedonian Church was established, over the loud protests of Serbia, giving Macedonia further legitimacy (see below).

In the immediate postwar years, Macedonia's communist party was fragmented between those who supported the Yugoslav federation and those who did not. Voices arguing for independent Macedonia were silenced, but not before a struggle between the new cadres and a collection of opposition groups, including a briefly resuscitated IMRO, occurred.[6] By 1948, following Tito's break with Stalin and two purges in Macedonia, a stable and, from Belgrade's point of view, reliable leadership made up of ethnic Macedonians was in place in Skopje.[7]

In the 1950s, the number of trained professionals capable of running a state infrastructure in Macedonia grew. A complement of them was mainstreamed in the federal system and representation at the federal level was roughly proportional to Macedonia's population. The same was generally true of the party. Kiro Gligorov, future president of the Republic of Macedonia, occupied one of the two vice-presidencies on the Council of the Federation.[8]

During the early years of Yugoslav nation-building, Belgrade poured money into Macedonia to build its economy. Plagued by underproduction, slow industrialization, and high unemployment initially, growth rates picked up in the late 1960s and in the 1970s, as a result of a policy of industrialization. By the 1970s Macedonia's economy was dominated by light industry, though overall, it remained underdeveloped.

Manifestations of reinvigorated nationalism in Yugoslavia occurred in 1968, when Kosovar Albanians, who then (as now) made up the vast majority of inhabitants in the Kosovo-Metohija region of Serbia, demanded that Kosovo, an area with great historic importance to Serbs, be granted republican status within Yugoslavia.[9] In Macedonia, sympathy demonstrations were held in which Albanian leaders called for the amalgamation of the Albanian-speaking sections of Macedonia with Kosovo as Yugoslavia's seventh republic. Macedonian authorities served up stiff jail terms for those involved in such activities and vocally denounced such ideas. They saw the Albanian moves as a step toward secession from Yugoslavia, union with Albania, and the creation of a Great Albania.

Signs of further troubles were clearly discernible during the 1970s in Yugoslavia. Ethnic fault lines crisscrossing the Federal Republic deriving from the war years and before, though papered over, were showing. In 1971, the greatest challenge to the Yugoslav idea, a bid by Croat nationalists for greater state decentralization, ended a period of liberalization and experimentation.[10] The fourth post-war constitution, promulgated in February 1974, signaled a "return to stricter control by a decentralized and redisciplined Party."[11] The aging Tito, evidently in an effort to provide for succession and build political cohesion among the republics, created a leadership collective in 1978 to replace him upon his death. Even before he died in 1980, resurgent nationalism and economic deterioration were feeding growing popular discontent.[12] The cumulative effect of these and other developments was to weaken the fiber of the state and strengthen national particularism.

In 1980, riots in Kosovo were especially violent. A period of repression directed at Albanian nationalists and orchestrated by Belgrade followed. Items in the press about increasingly virulent Albanian nationalism stimulated a general fright in Macedonia. Reports of soaring Albanian birthrates engendered fear that Muslim Albanians would eventually outnumber ethnic Macedonians, threatening the territorial integrity of the homeland.[13]

Such fears contributed to the failure of the government (both federal and state) to admit large numbers of Albanians to positions of importance in the infrastructure. Another factor was that Albanians received inferior education, limiting the ability of individuals to participate in government. If they had acquired university education at all, they did so at Kosovo University in Prishtina, not in Macedonia. As a response to press reports that Muslims were traveling to conservative Arab countries for religious instruction, the Macedonian government made it illegal for Muslim youth fifteen years old or under to receive religious education. It also attempted to block the building of mosques.[14]

With the advent of Slobodan Milošević in 1986, Serbs began to flex their muscles. Purging opponents, Milošević promoted the theme of Serbia first, a notion that readily found resonance in Serb enclaves outside of Serbia proper as well as among Serb nationalists who sought the elimination of Albanians in Kosovo and who went so far as to assert that most Macedonians were Serbs. In 1989, the last Yugoslav prime minister of note, Ante Marković, sought to hold the federation together. His efforts failed. With the ouster of Serbian Prime Minister Milan Panić, a Serb-American millionaire, in 1992, Milošević took full and uncontested control of the rump Yugoslav state. He supported the Serb faction in Bosnia until that proved no longer politic, then opposed it. In the process, he advocated that Greece and Serbia divide Macedonia, a suggestion the Greeks declined to accept.

Serb nationalists frustrated by, and angry at, Tito's having relegated Serbs to a non-dominant role in the federal enterprise, thronged to Milošević. Before them were visions of uniting all territories inhabited by Serbs into one Great Serbia. Serbian nationalism was of mounting concern to Bosnia-Herzegovina, Croatia, and Slovenia, as well as Macedonia, as the demise of Yugoslavia loomed.

Serbian nationalist politicians provocatively referred to Macedonians as members of an "artificial nation" whose state Serbia would seek to acquire if Yugoslavia broke up.[15] Skopje officials vainly sought accommodation with Belgrade over basic questions such as power-sharing, control of the national and state treasuries, control of the military, and nationality issues. In the end, Greater Serbian aspirations led to war elsewhere and drove a wedge of distrust between Macedonians and Serbs.

The first two Macedonian cabinets

While Slobodan Milošević was building an authoritarian state to the north, the Socialist leaders in Macedonia opened the door to political pluralism. Political parties multiplied rapidly as people coalesced around figures whom they felt represented their aims. Socialists faced off against non-Socialists. Nationalists formed ethnic parties.

In 1990, a year before Macedonia's declaration of independence, citizens voted for a new parliament in the first multiparty election ever. More than twenty parties were involved, although only eight won votes enough to secure more than single seats. These elections brought 80 percent of the electorate to the ballot boxes. The Internal Macedonian Revolutionary Organization-Democratic Party for Macedonian National Unity (IMRO-DPMNU)[16] won the most seats, thirty-eight (31.7 percent), making it the party with the largest representation in the parliament. The reform communists, now called the Social Democratic Union of Macedonia (SDUM), received thirty-one seats (25.8 percent of the vote), then came the Party for Democratic Prosperity/Peoples' Democratic Party Albanian coalition (PDP/NDP) with twenty-two seats (18.3 percent). The Markovićists, the Alliance of Reform Forces of Macedonia (ARFM), weighed in with eleven seats (9.2 percent). The remaining seats went to smaller parties and three independents. (See table 7.2.)

The first round election results indicated that ethnic Albanians were acting as a voting bloc. Fear that Albanians were seeking to either subvert the state or secede from it drove many ethnic Macedonians to select the nationalist ticket in the second round. For their part, Albanians voted against majoritarian rule and many saw the elections as an opportunity to register their demands for change. Some, too, were nationalists, seeking a separatist agenda. In the end, the election results reflected an ethnic divide between Macedonians and Albanians, with Turks voting a mixed ticket, the Roma opting for the Roma parties, Vlachs voting for Macedonian parties, and the Serbs generally choosing the Serbian party.[17]

The only truly supranational leader to emerge in the early days was Kiro Gligorov who became Macedonia's first president, elected by the parliament

Table 7.2 *Parliamentary elections in Macedonia, 1990*

Party[a]	Seats won	% of Seats
IMRO-DPMNU	38	31.7
LCM[b]	31	25.8
PDP/NDP	22	18.4
PDP - (17)		
NDP - (5)		
ARFM	11	9.2
ARFM/YDPP	6	5.0
SPM	4	3.3
PYM	2	1.7
NDP	1	0.8
SPM/ARFM/YDPP	1	0.8
SPM/PCER	1	0.8
Independent candidates	3	2.5
Total	120	

Notes: Voter turnout: 84.8% (1st round); 80.3% (2d round). [a]For a list of acronyms, see p. 274. [b]Reform communists are no longer called the League of Communists of Macedonia, but the Social Democratic Union of Macedonia (SDUM).
Source: Secretariat for Information, Republic of Macedonia.

on January 27, 1991. He favored a sovereign Macedonia that would "participate in the Yugoslav community."[18]

In a referendum on September 8, 1991, voters in Macedonia (minus most Albanians who did not cast ballots as a protest against their perceived inferior constitutional status) chose to separate from Yugoslavia. With the Wars of Yugoslav Succession in progress by then, Macedonia's parliament declared independence on November 21, 1991, following the path already trodden by Slovenia and Croatia. Macedonia had little choice, for otherwise it would have been drawn into the Serbian war machine.

European Community (EC) member states, unsure of what to do but seeking to take some action to halt the bloodshed in the former Yugoslavia and unwilling to commit forces to what could easily deteriorate into a protracted war, dithered. Croatia, Slovenia, and Bosnia were each recognized by the EC by April 1992, in spite of the EC's own Badinter Commission recommendations that argued only Slovenia and Macedonia met the minimum requirements for recognition as democratic states. Macedonia was kept out of the loop, a hostage of Greek policy (see below).

Nikola Kljusev's "government of experts," which contained but two politically affiliated ministers, was seated in 1991 and saw Macedonia through the initial phases of transition. Kljusev established a stable government, introduced a sound anti-inflation program which included the introduction of a new currency, the denar, which signaled monetary independence from rump Yugoslavia, and presided over the creation of a new military. He resigned in July 1992 after a no-confidence vote promoted by the Social Democrats, Liberals, and Socialists, who sought a political government.

IMRO-DPMNU, with the largest number of deputies in parliament, unsuccessfully tried to form a new government and called for elections in the fall of 1992. Instead, a new government, headed by thirty-year-old Branko Crvenkovski and made up of a four-party coalition including the PDP and its ally, the NDP, the Social Democratic Union of Macedonia (SDUM, formerly the League of Communists of Macedonia), and the Reformed Forces-Liberal Party (RF-LP), was brought in. It made stability and prosperity its chief goals.

Key to the Crvenkovski government's program was building interethnic tolerance between Albanians and Macedonians. Four Albanian ministers were appointed to the cabinet. Although there were several volatile issues and incidents that arose, the government, working closely with the state president and Albanian leaders, managed to resolve differences peacefully. The government ended its term in 1994, having presided over Macedonia's recognition by most states and by having been integral to finalizing an accord with Greece over the differences dividing the two countries. Finally, it was the Crvenkovski government that promulgated the 1993 privatization program, a plan that on paper, at least, promised much, though implementation was slow and at times ineffective.

The 1994 elections and their aftermath

One of the most consequential political developments in the Macedonian state's brief history was the fall 1994 election. Round one, held on October 16, 1994, saw a voter turn-out of 78 percent. It yielded a victory for the Alliance for Macedonia (AM), a three party coalition led by President Gligorov and made up of the SDUM, the LP, and the Socialist Party. The two main opposition parties, the Democratic Party (DP), headed by Petar Gošev, and IMRO-DPMNU, blasted the outcome as fraudulent. Both parties had done poorly in the vote and demanded new elections.[19] They accused the AM of manipulating registration rosters and gerrymandering voting districts.[20]

The DP and IMRO-DPMNU called upon all of their supporters to refrain from voting in the second round to be held on October 30, with the result that only 57.5 percent of the eligible constituency cast ballots. President

Table 7.3 *Parliamentary elections in Macedonia, 1994*

Party[a]	Seats won	% seats
SDUM[b]	58	48.3
LP	29	24.1
PDP	10	8.3
SPM	8	6.7
NDP	4	3.3
Democratic Party of Macedonia	1	0.8
Social Democratic Party of Macedonia	1	0.8
PCER	1	0.8
DPT	1	0.8
Independent candidates	7	5.8
Total	120	

Notes: Voter turnout: 78%. [a]For a list of acronyms, see p. 274. [b]Formerly League of Macedonian Communists-Party for Democratic Transformation (LCM).
Source: Secretariat for Information, Republic of Macedonia.

Gligorov was returned to office, though by a slim margin – 52.4 percent, defeating the IMRO-DPMNU candidate, Ljubiša Georgievski. Of the 120 parliamentary seats, 95 were captured by members of the Alliance for Macedonia – the SDUM gleaned 58 seats, the LP took 29, and the Socialist Party received 8. Of the remaining mandates, 10 went to the PDP, 4 to the NDP, and the remainder to an assortment of small parties and 7 independents.[21]

CSCE observers present during the 1994 elections spotted minor irregularities, but considered the elections valid. Nevertheless, allegations of ballot rigging, fraud and destruction of ballots lingered[22] and two election commissioners resigned their posts, apparently in protest to the manner in which the voting process was conducted.

The election outcome raised questions about the legitimacy of the new government, again headed by Branko Crvenkovski. With nominal opposition in the Sobranie (the legislative body), the cabinet and the parliament were unrepresentative; IMRO-DPMNU leaders called it illegal.[23] Recognizing its awkward position, the government sought to promote programs with broad popular appeal, in order to demonstrate that, despite the absence of a functioning opposition, it was providing broad leadership and promulgating the reform needed to move the state toward greater democracy, prosperity, and integration with Europe.

Four of the new government's ministers were PDP members, a figure proportionally greater than the number of the ten PDP deputies actually elected to the parliament. The LP, despite its twenty-nine seats, had the same numerical representation as the PDP in the cabinet, a fact which antagonized LP's leader, Stojan Andov. This arrangement, argued Crvenkovski supporters, reflected the coalition's strong commitment to integrate Albanians into the political mainstream. As further testimony to the government's effort, several places on the Constitutional Court and the Supreme Court were earmarked for Albanians. Further, in 1995, three Albanians were appointed to important diplomatic posts in Europe – in Belgium, Germany, and Switzerland. Finally, the first ethnic Albanian general had been appointed in the army in 1995. Not surprisingly, Albanian opposition members claimed such appointments were meant merely to pacify Albanian voters.[24]

While the DP and IMRO-DPMNU, the two strongest opposition parties, had relegated themselves to the political sidelines by refusing to participate in the 1994 elections, the LP gradually moved to a semi-opposition posture within the ruling coalition. Andov, who was also President of the Sobranie, nearly precipitated a crisis by trenchantly opposing Albanian demands that Albanian be an official language in the parliament. Further, he pressed for circumscribing Ministry of Internal Affairs (MIA) powers, and increasingly challenged the prime minister over privatization-related issues. Following the attempted assassination of President Gligorov (see below), Andov became acting president owing to Gligorov's precarious health. The struggle for power between Andov and Crvenkovski, simmering for some time, boiled over.

Meantime, public opinion indicated that the government was in need of an overhaul. In a poll taken in December 1995, 10 percent of the respondents said that the government was functioning well, 14 percent said it was too early to tell, and 7.33 percent did not respond. The rest, 68.67 percent, believed change was necessary. The same poll indicated that 35.67 percent of those consulted were satisfied with the government's performance, 26 percent were dissatisfied, 24.67 percent were uncertain, while 13.67 percent failed to respond.[25]

Mindful of the government's image as well as of the problems with the LP, on February 10, 1996, Crvenkovski announced the formation of a new government, which the parliament approved on February 21. It excluded LP members. Two Albanians were dismissed from their ministries, while the overall representation of Albanians in the government rose from four to six. The change was an inevitable one, given the failure of the SDUM and LP to find comity. The increase of Albanians in the government was both astute and necessary in order to give as broad a representation as possible in a country where a large, but undetermined number of voters supporting the DP and IMRO-DPMNU disenfranchised themselves in the last elections by opting not to vote. President Gligorov had opposed the government shuffle and had appealed on television that the old coalition members resolve their differences. In the end, Crvenkovski, too firmly committed to turn back, acted to disable Andov, his chief rival. Andov resigned as president of the parliament on February 23 and has moved his party into opposition to the government, calling for early elections.

In the early days of March the DP and IMRO-DPMNU raised their voices against the government and mounted a vigorous petition drive for early elections. The action, which yielded more than 600,000 signatures, was greeted by the Sobranic's rapid passing of a law governing petitions. It retroactively invalidated the March drive. Popular response was loud as people criticized heavily the parliamentary decision as self-serving and undemocratic.

The parties and the politicians

Across the political spectrum in Macedonia is an array of parties and most politically conscious people are sympathizers of one or another of them: a minority are party members. Lobbies and political action groups of the kind common in the United States are not in evidence in Macedonia, although in the Muslim communities, particularly among Albanians, benevolent societies from other countries are a presence (see below).

Many of the top leaders, are, like Gligorov and Andov, from the former ruling elite, people whose career paths often took them to Belgrade and/or through the halls of government in Skopje during the Socialist era. Most members of the government and of parliament are professionals including medical doctors, teachers, managers – in the main, intellectuals.[26] Dissident tradition in Macedonia is weak and dissidents played little role in the creation or development of the Macedonian state. Ideology does not drive state policy, rather, pragmatic issues such as creating a market economy and resolving ethnic tensions do. In 1995, the Sobranie enacted a law concerning the registration of political parties, stipulating that no party could be registered unless it obtained 500 valid signatures of members who possessed documentation of citizenship. At the beginning of 1995 there were some sixty parties, but this number will very likely decrease as a result of the law. Of the many parties, only a handful are of importance. Each is discussed below.

Social Democratic Union of Macedonia

The Social Democratic Union of Macedonia (SDUM), which adopted its present name in 1992, is the heir to the Yugoslav League of Communists (YLC). It supports democratic freedom for all, the rule of law, acceptance of the Universal Declaration of Human Rights, and democratic socialism. Founded in 1989 as the League of Macedonian Communists-Party for Democratic Transformation, it is the most influential party with a reported 150,000 registered members in branches in each county of the country,[27] a figure that is very likely inflated. It has dominated Macedonian politics since independence. The SDUM's economic program is centered on marketization and privatization and it favors joining the European system.

The party of the old guard as well as many technocrats, the SDUM has no ethnic emphasis, although it does not attract large numbers of ethnic minority members. The party chief and prime minister, Branko Crvenkovski, was born in 1962 in Sarajevo, the son of a military officer. He graduated from the Faculty of Electrical Engineering, Computer Science and Automation in Skopje in 1986 and worked in industry. He served as an MP in the parliament where he was president of the Commission for Foreign Political Affairs and Relations before becoming head of the SDUM in 1991 and premier in September of the next year. With significant support from Gligorov, Crvenkovski's rise has been nothing short of meteoric, in part a result of the need for a fresh face, but also attributable to his political astuteness.

Party for Democratic Prosperity

The Party for Democratic Prosperity (PDP) was formed in Poroj, near Tetovo in April 1990 by Nevzat Halili, an English teacher from Tetovo. He claimed his party was not an ethnic configuration. And indeed, the party program states that the organization is open to all citizens of Macedonia. In practice however, the PDP is an Albanian party.

The PDP, which recognizes the state borders and the legitimacy of the legally elected government, also recognizes the integrity of the ethnic Macedonian people and their history. The party was founded in part to win revision of the state's constitution to insure that Albanians are named a constituent people, with Albanian serving as an official language of the country. It demands that ethnic Albanians in Macedonia be considered equal to the ethnic Macedonians residing there and seeks equal opportunity in all spheres, including government, the police, education, and business.[28] As a measure of protest against the parliament's failure to accept this principal, PDP deputies in the Sobranie abstained from voting on the constitution's adoption in 1991.

Like many other parties in Macedonia and the Balkans, the PDP has been hierarchical with the leadership serving as the only official information channel.[29] In 1994 the party split over internal differences; Halili was ousted. Abdurahman Aliti emerged from the power struggle as head of the officially recognized faction. Arben Xhaferi became leader of the splinter group, PDP-Albanians (PDP-A). Both sides seek the same ends, though their means for achieving them differ.

The Aliti faction of the PDP, which has between 25,000 and 30,000 members, has been willing to work in coalition with the Crvenkovski governments, though the marriage has been at times tumultuous. PDP leaders, ever exposed to criticism from more radical groups, have been, despite the need to take tough positions, reasonable partners in the government. They have been willing to accept incremental change and prefer to work within the framework of state institutions. Aliti, who was born in 1945 in Zelin, Tetovo region, and who trained as a lawyer, says he supports integration but not assimilation. He protests that "Albanians are not separatists," and that they "want nothing more than what the Macedonians have."[30]

Party for Democratic Prosperity-Albanians

The Party for Democratic Prosperity–Albanians (PDP-A) leaders claim that Albanians have been marginalized in Macedonian society, demand that Albanian be made an official state language and that Macedonia be cantonized along ethnic lines. This group has not been willing to work with the government and opposes compromise. The number of members of this organization is not known, according to Xhaferi, the PDP-A's President.[31]

Xhaferi, who was born in 1948 and took a degree in Philosophy from Belgrade University, had worked for the state radio-television organization in Prishtina. He was elected to the Macedonian parliament in 1994. Xhaferi cautions that violence between the nationalities in Macedonia is a likely outcome if the government does not enact major reforms. He accuses Slavs (he means ethnic Macedonians) of wanting "to dominate non-Slavs."[32] The PDP-A's Vice President, Menduh Thaçi, a former dental student, is still more radical. He argues that if "Macedonians go on refusing Albanians' demands, there will be bloodshed here . . . Only Albania and Albanians hold the key to stability in this country."[33] Such talk frightens and alienates ethnic Macedonians and, evidently, many Albanians.

Socialist Party of Macedonia

The Socialist Party (SPM), whose leader, Kiro Popovski, a lawyer and vice-president of the Sobranie, died in 1995, is small but rather influential. The standard bearer of socialism in Macedonia now, it is a non-ethnically based party that claims 40,000 members,[34] a dubious figure at best. It formed a coalition with the Party for the Full Emancipation of Roma in the first state elections and together they won five seats in the parliament. Its platform calls for equal rights for all and designates Macedonia as a "common fatherland of the Macedonian people, the Albanians, the Turks, the Vlachs, the Gypsies, and the other nationalities living in the Republic of Macedonia."[35] The party platform notes that Macedonia's borders are inviolable and calls for good relations with all neighbors. Resembling the Socialists of yore, this incarnation supports conversion of at least some state properties into private industry. It calls for economic restructuring and economic reform.[36]

The Socialist Party, a member of the 1996 ruling coalition, will probably gain greater influence in the new government than previously held in the old cabinet. It has an excellent grass roots infrastructure, with activists in every part of Macedonia and can thus mobilize supporters around the country; it also has the know-how to get out the vote. In the previous government, leaders had felt that the party was neglected by its coalition partners.

People's Democratic Party

The People's Democratic Party (NDP) was founded in Tetovo in 1990 and is headed by Iljaz Halimi. An ethnic Albanian party, the NDP, like the PDP, is focused on assuring full rights for Albanians in Macedonia as a constituent people. The NDP asserts that the situation in Kosovo, where the majority of Albanians are under Serb domination in an authoritarian state, is the same as in Macedonia, where Albanians are a minority in a nascent democracy. It has encouraged international bodies not to recognize Macedonia until Albanians have equal status. The party also supports autonomy for the Albanian regions of Macedonia.[37] The number of NDP members is not known. The NDP is a small party, though it can influence PDP decisions.

Internal Macedonian Revolutionary Organization-Democratic Party of Macedonian National Unity

IMRO-DPMNU, founded in 1990, is an anti-Yugoslav, anti-socialist, nationalist party. It claims a membership of about 150,000,[38] a number that seems extremely high. It has branch offices in every region of Macedonia and abroad, notably in the United States, Canada, Germany, and Australia. By choosing to identify with the IMRO founded in 1893, the latter-day IMRO-DPMNU seeks to link one of Macedonia's most sacred historical icons with its own nationalist program. Unlike its namesake, IMRO-DPMNU has abjured violence.

IMRO-DPMNU, first and foremost, is an ethnic Macedonian party that seeks to unite Macedonians in a greater Macedonian state. Its constitution reads that it "seeks the spiritual, economic, and ethnic union of the divided Macedonian people and the creation of a Macedonian state in a future united Balkans and united Europe."[39] It advocates the return of property to dispossessed Macedonians in all three segments of geographical Macedonia and it refers to ethnic Macedonians as conquered peoples. IMRO-DPMNU stands for national "pride and dignity" and its constitution endorses democracy and respect for human rights for all people. Paradoxically, the party is anti-Albanian, fearing the creation of a Great Albania if too many rights are accorded Macedonia's largest minority.[40] In particular, it opposes allowing immigrant Albanians to obtain citizenship. Ethnic Macedonians living in regions populated by large numbers of Albanians tend to be ardent IMRO-DPMNU supporters.

In its foreign policy IMRO-DPMNU expresses concern for Macedonians in all neighboring lands. Its unabashedly irredentist approach in its earliest days did much to aggravate relations with Greece. IMRO-DPMNU's 1994 party platform, issued before it withdrew from the 1994 election, showed moderation with respect to irredentist claims. It called for a confederation of Balkan security and cooperation as the first step toward a Balkan union.[41]

The party president, thirty-one-year-old poet L'upčo Georgievski, maintains a tight control over who speaks for the party. He has been frequently accused of Bulgarophilism and stirred a massive controversy in 1995 when he wrote an article published in two installments, in the weekly news magazine, *Puls*. His claim was that Macedonians are Bulgarians.[42] In this piece, Georgievski shreds Macedonian history and calls revered figures of the incipient nineteenth century national awakening like the brothers Miladinov, Bulgarian.[43] Georgievski, sees the Tito era as a period of dictatorship and views Ivan Mihailov and Todor Aleksandrov, two IMRO leaders of post-World War I vintage, as national heroes who fought for an independent Macedonia.[44] In a biting response, journalist Mika Velinovska said Georgievski has an "ideological-political compass heading, whose magnetic needle is permanently fixed on the east."[45] This shrill debate is ample testimony that the question of national identity evokes passionate responses.[46]

Liberal Party

The Liberal Party (LP) began as the Reformist Forces of Macedonia-Liberal Party and was officially established in 1991. It was part of a coalition between the Alliance of Reformist Forces of Macedonia founded by Ante Marković, the last effective federal Yugoslav prime minister, and the Young Democratic Progressive Party. Renamed the Liberal Party in 1993, it had about 8,000 members in 1994 who were overwhelmingly ethnic Macedonians. The LP supports free market economy and full democracy.[47] A member of the Liberal International, this party controls much of the economy because its membership is made up of the captains of industry. The Liberals are accused, with some apparent justification, of maintaining the privatization process as the preserve for the few. Influential, but not popular, the LP sees itself as centrist, but actions in the Sobranie, such as its opposition to the use of Albanian in parliament, give it a nationalist tinge.

The president of the party, Stojan Andov, a former Yugoslav ambassador to Iraq in the 1980s, spent much of his career in Belgrade and abroad. Born in Kavadarci in 1935, he has a master's degree in economics and was a member of the LCY. Andov served as the vice president of the Yugoslav Republican Executive Council and was a deputy in the Yugoslav Federal Assembly. Elected to the Macedonian Assembly in 1990, he became its president in 1991 and retained this position until resigning in February 1996. In accordance with the constitution, he became acting president of the republic when Gligorov was incapacitated by the October 1995 assassination attempt. Andov, like Georgievski, runs his party using strict controls and the public knows little of its inner workings.

In February 1996, simmering, but arcane, differences between Andov and the prime minister boiled over with Crvenkovski forming a new government that excluded the Liberals. Thus, the gradual process of becoming a *de facto* opposition within the coalition government ultimately led to the creation of a full blown, if small, opposition outside the coalition. The long term effects of this could be very damaging to Andov, whose ability to dispense favors and maneuver policies ceased with the LP's role in government.

Democratic Party

The centrist Democratic Party (DP), founded in 1993, seeks to be an alternative to the SDUM and the LP. Petar Gošev, its head, had built his political career in Macedonia and was the only political personality whom the public knew at the outset of the new era. Gošev, who was president of the Central Committee of LCY in Macedonia, discarded communist ideology and set about reshaping the organization around social democratic principles. He failed to form a government in 1992 and in April 1993, resigned from the SDUM, accusing the government of dishonesty and a poor record.[48] Gošev went on to form the DP that stands for free market economy, democracy, and support of human rights. The party program proclaims the inviolability of Macedonia's borders, peaceful coexistence with neighbors, and a wish to join the EU. Not an ethnically based party, members, who number between a self-reported 12,000 and 15,000, are nevertheless mostly ethnic Macedonian.[49] Like IMRO-DPMNU, the DP's influence had been significantly diminished by its withdrawal from the political race in 1994. Whether the 1996 petition drive activities signal a comeback is unclear.

Democratic Party of Turks

The Democratic Party of Turks (DPT), first called the Democratic Alliance of Turks, was founded in 1990. Since 1992 it has been headed by Erdoğan Saraç, a businessman from Gostivar. It seeks to be the sole representative of ethnic Turkish interests in Macedonia. The DPT is neither strong, nor is its program coherent. Leaders advocate a free and sovereign Macedonia, but have also sought to arouse (unsuccessfully for the most part) Turkish nationalist sentiment. DPT leaders have approached the government to provide education in Turkish through the eighth grade and seek to integrate Turks more fully into the state's infrastructure. With ties to mainstream political parties in Turkey, including the Fatherland Party, it espouses the principles of Atatürk which include a secular state and equality for all.[50] The DPT supports the current government and wishes to resolve issues through dialogue.[51] Its influence is limited to supporters.

Democratic Party of Serbs in Macedonia

Another ethnic party active in Macedonia is the semi-militant Democratic Party of Serbs in Macedonia (DPSM), headed first by fire-brand Boro Ristić[52] and now by the equally strident Dragiša Miletić, a painter born in Serbia in 1956. The DPSM was officially registered in 1992 and has been involved in anti-Macedonian activity, notably riots in 1993. Claiming some 19,000 members (no doubt an inflated number given the size of the Serb and Montenegrin population in Macedonia), its leaders have significant ties to Serbian nationalist leaders like Zeljko Raznajtović-Arkan and Voijslav Šešelj.[53] The DPSM demands constituent status for the Serbian minority in Macedonia and claims that they are the most discriminated against group in the state. The party stands against their assimilation by the majority ethnic Macedonians.[54] It has close contacts with the Serbian Church, which seeks to discredit the Macedonian autochthonous church. An anti-American party, the DPSM stands against Macedonian involvement with NATO. DPSM influence does not reach beyond the Serbian/Montenegrin community and does not affect all members of this group. It does, however, represent a potential source of violence, especially if backed by nationalists in Serbia.

Agrarians and the role of labor

Unlike in neighboring Bulgaria, an agrarian party is absent altogether from the political scene, despite Macedonia's history as a peasant country with agriculture as a mainstay of the economy. The Democratic Alliance-Party of Farmers made a brief appearance in 1990, but soon fell apart. Labor unions have attained no political importance due both to a heritage of serving the communist state and a failure to understand how to mobilize membership. The Council of Trade Unions in Macedonia (SSM) inherited the old Socialist Labor Confederation's assets. It is the chief representative of labor to the government in Macedonia. It is independent of the government and operates without interference,[55] but is weak. People are free to organize and engage in collective bargaining, though there is no law governing collective bargaining and the concept is not part of the culture yet.[56]

Constitutional structures

Macedonia is a parliamentary democracy with a constitution modeled on those of established democracies. Legislative power is vested in the Sobranie, which is constitutionally "a representative body of the citizens."[57] Deputies are elected in "general, direct, and free elections and by secret ballot"[58] to single member districts. Each representative is elected for a four year term and the Assembly is considered to be in permanent session. It has a president and one or more vice presidents, each elected from among the membership. The constitution provides for as many as 140 mandates, although only 120 are filled at present and there appear to be no plans for increasing this number.

The government, where executive power constitutionally resides, is headed by a prime minister. The state president nominates the prime minister, who in turn recommends the government to the Assembly. The government is then elected by the parliament. It is the government's job to set policy for proposing laws and the budget, carrying out laws determining the work of ministries, and establishing diplomatic relations. A government may be removed by a no-confidence vote of the parliament.[59]

Members of the government cannot simultaneously serve as members of the parliament. The role of the Assembly includes setting taxes, adopting the state's budget, making and passing laws, ratifying international agreements, reckoning with border changes, deciding on war and peace, deciding issues of cooperation, association, dissociation, and union with other states, electing judges to the Constitutional Court, and appointing and dismissing public officials.[60]

Heading the state is the president, who is also elected by direct and secret balloting. The presidential term is five years and a president may not serve for more than two terms. The president must be at least forty years old and a citizen of the republic who has lived in Macedonia for at least ten of the previous fifteen years before the election.[61]

The president serves as commander-in-chief of the Armed Forces, appoints and dismisses ambassadors, proposes members to the Constitutional Court, performs many ceremonial duties, and heads the Security Council. The president cannot initiate legislation.

Although Macedonia has the constitution of a parliamentary democracy, the state has been run as a presidential democracy, owing to Gligorov's prominent role. He alone has been able to remain above allegations of corruption and has been the only unifying political force to transcend ethnic boundaries.

The Gligorov factor

President Kiro Gligorov is the best known of Macedonia's leaders and the most popular. His moderate approach, his conciliatory tone, and his facility for fairness between competing nationalities, have created for him the role of father of the state. In the central Balkans, only he and Zheliu Zhelev, president of Bulgaria, seem to be above corruption and exhibiting authoritarian behavior. But in the days of Tito, one hardly heard of Gligorov. He was a technocrat in Belgrade, not a personality on the Macedonian political landscape.

Gligorov was born in the eastern Macedonian town of Štip in 1917. He attended secondary school in Skopje and graduated from the Law Faculty in Belgrade in 1938. A Partisan sympathizer during World War II, he joined the League of Communists in 1944. He became the financial secretary of the Anti-Fascist Assembly of National Liberation of Macedonia (ASNOM) established in 1944 and which served as Macedonia's first executive body. He also became a member of AVNOJ (see above). From 1945 until the 1960s, he worked in the field of economics and finance, holding such posts as assistant to the secretary-general of the Federal Peoples' Republic of Yugoslavia, secretary to the Economic Affairs Commission of the Federal Executive Council, federal secretary of finance, and vice president of the Federal Executive Council. He was among the creators of an ill-fated 1965 marketization program that was never implemented. In the 1970s he was elected to the presidency of the Social Federal Republic of Yugoslavia. Later he was made president of the Yugoslav Federal Assembly and a member of the Central Committee of the LCY.

When he stepped down from the presidency of the Parliament in 1978, Gligorov's political career went into eclipse until reformist Yugoslav Prime Minister Ante Marković tapped him for help with a marketization program in the 1980s. As a strong supporter of multi-party elections and market economy, Gligorov's star was ascendant again by 1989, when Yugoslavia was spiraling out of control. He returned to Macedonia in 1990, by no means a well-known personality to his countrymen, but with a record of consistent support for economic reform and with broad experience. This CV catapulted him to the head of the list of people qualified to lead the fledgling state.

In office, Gligorov had to grapple with establishing a pluralistic democratic state while balancing the nationalist and exclusionary demands of IMRO-DPMNU and those of the PDP whose members sought inclusion. He quickly became the symbol of Macedonian reform and his activities overshadowed those of the government as he became a greater than life figure. For the majority of ethnic Macedonians, he symbolized the state and became the most powerful force within it. A 1995 poll gave him a 90 percent approval rating. Albanians were less taken with him and only 41 percent of those queried gave him high marks.[62]

The attempt on Gligorov's life on October 3, 1995, has had a significant impact on the popular psyche of this small country, which so far has been spared both civil war and significant criminal lawlessness. Two theories compete for explaining the assassination attempt. One has it that it was the work of ultra-nationalists, the other, that it was an act perpetrated by organized crime elements abroad or by malevolent foreign powers (read Russia), seeking to destabilize Macedonia. The authorities have released little information about the incident and speculation is rampant. Prime Minister Crvenkovski, speaking for most Macedonians, characterized it as a "plot against the state," an act intended to destabilize Macedonia.[63]

As soon as it was ascertained that Gligorov was unable to carry out his duties, Stojan Andov, president of the Sobranie stepped in, as is constitutionally mandated, to become acting president. While the transition was smooth and orderly, a process that displayed great political maturity in the young democracy, the threat of the loss of Gligorov from the scene, made the political situation instantly unstable. There is no leader among the potential candidates for president who possesses a stature or level of state-wide acceptability approaching that of Gligorov. All contenders have their constituencies and their enemies.

Gligorov returned to the job in January 1996, in part it seems, to give Macedonia a chance to find an appropriate successor. Unless a strong figure emerges who is above petty politics, the rationality that has allowed Macedonia to escape civil war could be abandoned in deference to scrappy politicians seeking economic and political advantage, and to organized crime.

The voters

Voters are little involved in daily politics, though they are attentive observers of the political scene. Lack of trust characterizes the public's view of politicians. In summer 1995, President Gligorov launched a campaign against corruption in state administration which resulted in the firing of a number of highly placed officials, including four deputy ministers. By the end of the year, however, the anti-crime initiative had stalled and rumors circulating in Skopje suggested that some people believed the attempt on the president's life was a consequence of his effort to root out the local mafia. Voters support the president's anti-crime efforts and call for an end to white collar crime which allows the wealthy to avoid its share of the tax burden.

Prime Minister Crvenkovski, in an interview in November 1995, acknowledged that there is indeed corruption but suggested that matters are improving. He noted that conditions in this regard are worse than in the days of Yugoslavia, but much better when compared to other states in transition.[64]

There are little data on which to draw in order to create an accurate picture of voter attitudes. Nevertheless, by evaluating voter turnout for both the 1990 and 1994 elections, some generalizations can be made. Firstly, voting patterns in Macedonia show a very pronounced tendency toward co-nationals and co-religionists. PDP and NDP candidates in 1990 won overwhelmingly in predominantly Albanian districts, notably Tetovo where they garnered 71,881 votes out of 97,946 cast.[65] While generalization is hazardous, it seems that of the seventy-six deputies who fell loosely within the governing coalition, twenty-four were from ethnic parties, while at least thirty-three of the forty-four opposition members represented nationalist perspectives. Thus ethnic issues played a major role in politics and national policy, not unlike in neighboring states such as Bulgaria, Rumania, Serbia, Croatia, and of course Bosnia. In the 1994 election, because IMRO-DPMNU dropped out, the nationalist Macedonian configuration is zero, while ethnic parties have fifteen seats, nine fewer than in the previous election. With the absence of IMRO-DPMNU and the DP from the elections, however, determining the true magnitude of ethnic voting preferences is not possible.[66]

The majority of ethnic Macedonians living in areas where Albanians are the dominant population voted a nationalist ticket in the first election. In the second, they chose either not to vote or to cast ballots for non-nationalist parties. Albanian voters, no matter where they lived, voted a straight Albanian ticket in both elections. Other minorities supported ethnic parties, and some crossed over to centrist, non-ethnic groups like the SDUM. Whether the motivation of most minorities was to vote against communism, or for nationalism, is unclear, though it seems the ethnic appeal was a strong factor. As to the non-ethnic parties, it appears they attracted better educated voters and non-Albanians involved in commerce.[67]

Secondly, a sizable number of voters in Macedonia voted for the party of the dominant national personality, Kiro Gligorov, the reformed socialists. In the first election, some thirty-one seats representing 20.4 percent of those voting chose this ticket; the only party to win more was IMRO-DPMNU with 22 percent.[68] In the 1994 balloting, the SDUM took fifty-eight parliamentary seats (48.33 percent of the ballots), a statement that there is no stigma to being either socialist or from the old party.

Macedonia's citizens are ethnically polarized, a common feature of the new postcommunist society everywhere. It will take time for the various sides to become involved in genuine multiethnic political activity, where membership in an ethnic group is not a prime requisite for party affiliation.[69] For now, it is impossible for mainstream political parties to be genuinely multiethnic. However, the sort of behavior evidenced by the Crvenkovski administrations, wherein Albanians are included in the government at ministerial levels is a major step toward a fully pluralistic society. For interethnic cooperation to prosper, positive examples must be set at the top. With these in place, interethnic compromise can incrementally develop.

Registering dissatisfaction with a government decision or action by withdrawing from politics or dropping out of a government coalition (as the PDP has done from time to time, or as the DP and IMRO-DPMNU have done prior to the second round of the 1994 elections), can have an adverse affect on consensus building and will inevitably polarize opposing groups. If the action is that of an ethnically-based party, it will also serve to alienate other ethnic groups.

Macedonia remains a male-dominated state. Only two women were in the last government, one is included in the new one. Four MPs are women. Women, who have the same constitutional rights as men, find themselves in a traditional, still patriarchal society, where prospects for professional development are limited. This is changing, but slowly, due to efforts of groups like the Union of Macedonian Women and the League of Albanian Women in Macedonia.

A matter of identity

In 1988, demonstrations by Albanians in Kumanovo and Gostivar demanding greater rights prompted arrests. In 1990, about 2,000 Albanians in Macedonia, taking a page from the book of activists in Kosovo, demonstrated in Tetovo for a Great Albania. No violence followed, but ethnic Macedonians nursed a fear of Albanian intentions.

Resolution of Macedonia's ethnic question will determine what form Macedonian democracy will ultimately take. For now, the course is unclear. Will the state become a fully civil society? That is, will Macedonia permanently become an ethnic state wherein national consciousness defines one's identity and where the dominant ethnos runs the state and equals the state? Or, will Europe's newest republic evolve into a pluralistic state where individual loyalty is to the state, not to an ethnos? To come to terms with these questions, an understanding of the problems between Macedonia's peoples is needed.

Macedonians

A Slavic-speaking people, today's ethnic Macedonians are descendants of Slavs who settled in the Balkans during the seventh century AD.[70] Five centuries of Ottoman domination generally precluded development of a national identity, creation of an intelligentsia, development of a national mythology, and the codification of a national language before the late nineteenth or early twentieth century. Into the twentieth century, Macedonia's Christian peasants, the majority of the population, tended to be inward looking and family/clan-centered. If they identified themselves as part of a group, it was seldom as part of a nation and most commonly as a member of a church – be it Bulgarian, Greek, or Serbian Orthodox – an inhabitant of a region, city, town, or village, or as a peasant, or as an Ottoman subject, or *reaya*. For its part, the state labeled people according to faith and vocation. Few people had a Macedonian national consciousness and those that did were chiefly members of the small intelligentsia. For the majority, Macedonian national consciousness, born in the nineteenth century, spread slowly in the twentieth century. Ethnic Macedonians were not considered to be members of an internationally recognized ethnos until following World War II.[71]

On a continent that exudes history, among neighbors like the Bulgarians, Greeks, Romanians, and Serbs who flaunt the achievements of glorious (if distant and often overlapping) pasts, it is little wonder that Macedonians have sought to hive off a slice of the Balkan heritage as their own. Nationalists, eager for a pedigree, have created a past linking today's ethnic Macedonians directly to Alexander the Great (an historical manipulation of which the Greeks are no less guilty insofar as their own lineage is concerned) and to great medieval Balkan empires. More rational lights reject this fabrication of history, but nevertheless seek to differentiate Macedonia's heritage from all neighboring histories, languages, and cultures to assure affirmation of the Macedonian nationality as unique. This task, by no means easy, involves at times staking a copyright to the likes of medieval folk hero Prince Marko, despite Bulgarian and Serbian claims on him, or determining that Tsar

Samuil, an eleventh-century regional potentate, was ethnically Macedonian, not Bulgarian, at a time when ethnic identity was a concept not yet conceived.

Efforts by the state, expressed through the media, in education, and in the arts assured ethnic Macedonians of their identities at every turn. Astutely, no attempt to construct an ancient history was made as there was no ancient lineage. The authorities turned instead to the recent past for validation, the past of IMRO between 1893 and 1903, an era wherein the actors were portrayed in greater than life proportions in the lore and the history books. The Ilinden Uprising was (and is) cast as a national revolt at a time when national consciousness was yet to be widespread and when those participants in the action, to the extent they had a "national" identity, tended to call themselves Bulgarians, largely a recognition of affiliation with the Bulgarian Exarchate Church. Still, it has become a national unifying symbol. Its "spirit" guides political parties and politicians, and it is interwoven deeply into ethnic Macedonian culture as evidenced by street names, music, folk culture, as well as textbooks and as measured by national pride and identity. Macedonians also looked to the future as a nation and a state as a unifying idea, while still within the Yugoslav federation.[72] The unifying theme remains the future, but it is a future of an independent state within a European context, a concept that is only partially understood by most, for limited experience and ethnic considerations cloud broader vision.

The defining characteristics of ethnic Macedonians are their religion, language, and most importantly, self-identity or national consciousness. To be an ethnic Macedonian, a *Makedonec*, one must be at least nominally Orthodox Christian and speak Macedonian.[73] Before the creation of the post-World War II Yugoslav Macedonian republic, how many people claimed to be members of a Macedonian nationality is moot. But now, nearly three generations after the recognition of this nationality in postwar Yugoslavia, one and a half million people know that they are Macedonian, are proud of this identity, and seek to foster and preserve it as a unique and cherished possession. This identity contributes greatly to the divide between the majority population and the next largest ethnic group, the Albanians.

Macedonians versus Albanians

Albanians claim to be the descendants of the now extinct Illyrians, who, along with Thracians, were resident in the Balkans well before the days of Alexander the Great.[74] In Ottoman times, primarily members of this group, along with Turks and some Greeks, made up the ruling elite.[75] Today, Albanians in Macedonia live in a crescent-shaped region that begins in Kumanovo in the northeast, stretches through Skopje to Tetovo in the northwest, then reaches south along the Albanian border to Debar, Gostivar, and Struga.

Albanians are not well integrated into the Macedonian state infrastructure politically, socially, or economically. Now, as in the past, Orthodox Christian ethnic Macedonians and predominantly Muslim ethnic Albanians live apart, though where historically religion separated them, now, ethnicity does. Ethnic Macedonians tend to be urbanized, while Muslims, chiefly Albanians, but also Turks and Macedonian Muslims or *Torbeši*, remain on the land.

Mutual suspicion and sometimes animosity characterize relations between the ethnic Albanians and ethnic Macedonians, although both groups practice religious tolerance, whether out of necessity or good sense.[76] But tolerance ebbs and flows with the magnitude of the threats each side perceives from the other. Both ethnic groups supported Macedonian independence, though perhaps for different reasons. That is, both clearly wanted to be out from under bellicose Serbia, but whereas ethnic Macedonians wanted independence and, along with many Albanians, security, some Albanians may have had their eye on creating a Great Albania and secession from Yugoslavia would facilitate that.

In the days following Macedonia's independence in 1991, Albanians claimed to have made up as much as 40 percent of the state's population, although a large number refused to verify this by participating in the census conducted that same year, arguing that the count was biased against them. To settle the matter, as mentioned earlier, the Council of Europe oversaw a European Union-sponsored census in 1994 that determined that Albanians make up 22.9 percent of the population.

While the percentage of Albanians residing in Macedonia may be a subject of dispute, no one contests the fact that Albanians are the second largest ethnic group in the republic. Far more numerous than any other minority, Albanians feel un-enfranchised and without significant influence in state structures. Their actual lot in the Yugoslav Federation was little better, but now, in a newly created country that aspires to be a pluralistic democracy, Albanians are staking out what they feel are minimally acceptable conditions for participation in this new land. Many, in fact, feel life is better now than under the Yugoslav regime.[77]

The preamble of the constitution states that the Republic of Macedonia "is established as a national state of the Macedonian people in which full equality as citizens and permanent co-existence with the Macedonian people is provided for Albanians, Turks, Vlachs, Roma, and other nationalities living in the Republic of Macedonia."[78] The last constitution of the Socialist Republic of Macedonia had read that Macedonia is "a state of the Macedonian people and the Albanian and Turkish minorities." Albanians and Turks were recognized as nationalities within Yugoslavia, but not as nations as their *heimat* was elsewhere.[79] Ethnic groups were not defined by that constitution. Nationalities were guaranteed the same rights as ethnic Macedonians, including the right to be proportionally represented in the legislature, fly their national flags, and have and use alphabets and languages considered to be of equal status with that of the majority Macedonians.[80]

Although the constitution provides "full equality as citizens" for all, it distinguishes between ethnic "Macedonians," that is, the majority, and all other peoples, called "nationalities," that is, minorities, a fact which most ethnic Macedonians regard as sufficient protection of civil rights for all.[81] Albanians, in particular, are angered by the wording of the new constitution and argue that it redefines the state as being of and for ethnic Macedonians rather than of and for the people of Macedonia. They demand that the constitution be amended to make them, like the Macedonians, a constituent people whose language and symbols have equal status. Interestingly, the Albanians make no plea on behalf of other nationalities or ethnic groups and neither ethnic Turks nor members of the smaller ethnic communities, except the Serbs, have actively pursued constitutional change.

Albanian nationalists, led by the PDP, sponsored a referendum in January 1992 in support of cantonization. The result showed that 74 percent of those voting (put at 92 percent of those eligible to vote) supported "territorial autonomy for Albanians in Macedonia."[82] The state, however, refused to recognize the vote and declared it illegal. The event was timed to precede the EC's June 27 meeting and seemed meant to cause the EC to force Macedonia into granting Albanian demands as a prerequisite for recognition.[83] It had no perceptible impact.

In the Republic of Macedonia's five year history several events stand out as having been dangerous to the stability of the state. Each was defused. In 1992, the Bit Pazar Affair, a confrontation between police and Albanian demonstrators polarized ethnic Macedonians and ethnic Albanians. Some Albanians feared that it signaled the beginning of police repression. Extremists were ready to fight, but the PDP leaders called for calm and no further incidents occurred.

The authorities announced in November 1993, discovery of a plot by a theretofore unknown group, the All Albanian Army (AAA), intent on overthrowing the government. This heightened fear of extremism in Macedonia. According to the MIA officials, the AAA had collected weapons and was seeking recruits. Part of the plan involved subverting the army. One of the key players was an Albanian deputy minister of defense. Another was a deputy minister of health. The Albanian community labeled the news a government hoax perpetrated as an excuse to move against Albanians and, if not to suspend rights, certainly to avoid having to enhance them. The PDP decried the government action and maintained that the allegations were trumped up. These events led to the PDP leadership shake-up of December 1994. Interethnic relations were tense.

Fear of a Great Albania continues to fuel nationalist sentiment among ethnic Macedonians. With western Macedonia, Kosovo, and Albania contiguous, it is easy enough to see how the populations there could unite. While Albania seems to understand that a Great Albania is not acceptable to Western powers, Albanian nationalists in Kosovo and Macedonia may not. For the moment, Albanian President, Sali Berisha, with prodding from the United States, has managed to keep the lid on such talk at home and seems to recognize that a whole Macedonia is critical to regional stability.[84]

As a mechanism for at least slowing the possibility of a Great Albania, the Sobranie passed a law in 1995 which provides that in order to be eligible for citizenship, one must reside in Macedonia for 15 years. This means that for the 150,000 or so Kosovars (and for that matter, some 30,000 Bosnian refugees) living in Macedonia entitlement to Macedonian citizenship is not automatic on the basis of having been a Yugoslav citizen. Should trouble erupt in Kosovo, the Macedonian government is prepared to close the border with Serbia to insure that refugees do not stream south. However, if waves of Kosovars seek to escape civil strife in Kosovo, both pressure from Macedonia's Albanians and the potential for a violent reaction against such a government decision, and possibly Western disapproval as a humanitarian concern, might force the government to rethink the issue.

Turks

Turks, who are Muslims, constitute the second largest minority, although their numbers represent only about 4 percent of the population. Historically, their fortunes have been mixed. Following the end of Ottoman rule, Turks left what was to become the Republic of Macedonia in large numbers. Those who remained coexisted with other peoples. Today, Turks are an integral part of Macedonian society and have cultural organizations, a newspaper, schools and even a theater. Politically, Turks are not influential or especially active. Many, perhaps most, Turks speak both Turkish and Albanian fluently (as well as Macedonian) and one can find members of the same family who identify themselves differently, some as Turks, others as Albanians.[85] Yet people who maintain a Turkish identity do not seem to have enlisted in the ranks of those pressing the Albanian cause. Unlike in neighboring Bulgaria, there is thus little friction between the Turkish minority and the ethnic Macedonian majority.

Roma

Roma, who constitute 2.3 percent of Macedonia's population, are, in general, regarded poorly across Eastern Europe. Characterized as thieves, ne'er-do-wells, and worse, they are especially unpopular in such places as the Czech Republic, Romania, and Bulgaria. Macedonia, curiously, is an island of comparative equanimity regarding its Roma population, which are even mentioned in the constitution as a legally recognized nationality. The Roma crime rate there is low and is not a concern to authorities,[86] unlike in neighboring Bulgaria or in Romania. Typically urban dwellers who live in ghettos, Roma males tend to be unskilled laborers, although there are entrepreneurs and skilled workers among them. Roma children are poorly educated and have no Romani schools to attend.[87] Plans have been laid to open a Roma faculty within the SS. Kiril i Metodij University in Skopje and the state has begun to respond to Roma pleas for establishing media in Romani.[88]

There are only two Roma political parties in Macedonia, the Party for the Total Emancipation of the Roma, headed by Faik Abdi, and the Progressive Democratic Party of the Roma led by Beki Arif.[89] The former is represented in parliament; leaders of both have had the ear of President Gligorov, but are poor at interparty cooperation.

Roma relations with ethnic Macedonians, as well as ethnic Turks and Albanians are generally good, in part a function of the fact that the politically complacent Roma rank-and-file threaten no one, and in fact have been the object of Albanian ballot and census courting.[90] Some leaders, however, deplore what they say has been a plot to coopt Roma by bribing and coercing them to identify themselves as Turks, thus reducing their potency as a force in politics and society.[91]

Vlachs, Serbs, and Montenegrins

Vlachs, traditionally a transhumant shepherd people related to Romanians, have nearly fully assimilated with ethnic Macedonians: today they are virtually indistinguishable. Vlach is not a language of school instruction. Historically, Vlachs were active in the revolutionary days of IMRO and were integral to that movement and perhaps in part owing to this, Vlachs are favorably regarded among Macedonians, who perceive little difference between the two peoples.[92] That Vlachs are not a political force in the state is also, no doubt, a factor.

Serbs and Montenegrins make up 2 percent of the population in Macedonia, although Serbian community leaders suggest that the population is actually many times greater. Serbs live in northeast Macedonia, in the

Kumanovo region. Many are politically active and support the DPSM. Some seek union with Serbia. While a small population, its substantial connections with Serbia could prove to be either a boon or deficit to the government, depending upon how relations with the former Yugoslavia unfold.

Macedonian Muslims

Macedonian Muslims, as they are officially designated, or *Torbeši*,[93] are a community in search of affirmation. Living in western Macedonia, these Macedonian-speaking, Slav Muslims are largely agricultural. During the Tito era, they were "encouraged" to adopt an ethnic Macedonian identity which ethnic Macedonian Christians were also prompted to accept.[94] Macedonian Muslim leaders fear assimilation by Albanians and in recent elections, Macedonian Muslims have tended to vote for Albanian candidates. In 1992 they attempted to form a political party, and some, in an effort to fight both Albanization and Macedonianization, demanded school instruction in Turkish from the state, in spite of no Turkish linguistic or cultural tradition. In May 1995, a controversy about forcing them to speak Albanian arose when the *Meshihat*, the Holy Synod of the Islamic Community in Macedonia, declared that Albanian was the language of Muslims. Leaders protested.[95] It seems that they at least do not want to be ethnic Macedonians, neither do they fancy being ethnic Albanians. The state sponsors the Association of Cultural and Scientific Manifestations of Macedonian Muslims that functions to promote preservation of their culture.

The religious factor

A major legacy of the 500-year-long Ottoman era is an Islamic/Christian divide, a direct result of the Ottoman theocracy's method of differentiating people according to faith. Christians and Jews occupied a place of inferior status to that of Muslims and all non-Muslim peoples were classified according to their faith into divisions called *millets*. There were Orthodox Christian, Armenian Christian, and Jewish millets. The leaders of each were responsible to the Porte on intracommunal legal matters, taxation, and education.[96] All functioned as religious communities and were not national entities although they were to contribute to national awakenings in the nineteenth and twentieth centuries.

In the quest for the affirmation of a Macedonian nation, the Orthodox Church has played an important role. Until the late nineteenth century, the Christian inhabitants of Macedonia worshipped predominantly in the Greek rite (and a few were Roman Catholic and Protestant). By the end of that century the Bulgarian and Serbian Orthodox churches were competing with that of the Greeks for the national and religious allegiances of the people.

The Macedonian Orthodox Church

For Balkan states the establishment of a national church was a key feature in nation building.[97] Macedonians claim various important figures in Orthodox Church history, including the ninth century missionary brothers, Kiril and Metodij, who hailed from what is now Thessaloniki and who are credited with developing the bases for the Slavonic alphabet. Their disciples founded an episcopate and the first Slavic university, both in Ohrid in the ninth century.[98] The episcopate came under Greek administration in the eleventh century and was closed in 1767 by the Ottomans.[99]

The Serbian Church was supreme during the interwar period in what was to become the Republic of Macedonia. Following World War II, Macedonians called for their own church and expelled Serbian bishops when the Serbian Orthodox Church refused to cooperate. The newly recognized nationality needed a separate church to further the affirmation process. In 1958, Skopje, with Belgrade's backing, and over the objections of the Serbian Church, seated an archbishopric in Ohrid. It was a semi-autonomous arrangement as the archbishop recognized the Serbian Patriarch. It was also the first step toward the Macedonian church becoming autocephalous.

The Macedonian Orthodox Church was created in 1967 over the howls of the Serbian Church's hierarchy. In time, this dispute subsided only to be reawakened with the formation of independent Macedonia. Since then, motivated by the Serbian national agenda of Slobodan Milošević and other nationalists, the Macedonian Church has come under renewed fire from clerics in Belgrade. Serbian Church officials have declared the autocephalous status of the Macedonian Church invalid and argue that the Macedonian Church is merely a wing of the Serbian Church. As such, Serbian Church fathers should have responsibility for Church governance. This problem, inextricably interwoven with Serbian-Macedonian relations, most likely will be resolved politically, now that Serbia and Macedonia have established diplomatic relations. Given the key role religion plays in the identity of ethnic Macedonians,[100] it is unlikely that the resolution will favor the Serbian Church.

Although the Macedonian Orthodox Church is the only religious institution recognized in Macedonia's constitution, it has no legal standing above other faiths. All faiths are allowed to run schools and philanthropic organizations. The Macedonian Church prelates have not interfered in the political scene, nor have they been in the vanguard of those seeking to resolve ethnic or social issues.

Islam in transition

If the Macedonian Church leadership is united as a force for national affirmation, the Islamic community leadership is divided. Since the end of Tito's Yugoslavia, Macedonian towns and villages where Muslims, who are overwhelmingly *Sunni*, are in the majority, have opened many mosques and religious institutions. The *Meshihat* coordinates affairs between institutions.[101] It adopted a new constitution in December 1995, though clerics disagree as to its legality and there are some who seek to splinter it.

The Meshihat opposes Muslim fundamentalism which has been spread allegedly by foreign-sponsored humanitarian groups such as the Saudi-sponsored Al Harameni and Islamic Vakuf. Both have been accused of interfering in domestic affairs by giving money to radicals and promoting Islamic fundamentalism. Such organizations are said to be pouring money into Macedonia.[102]

The unifying force of belief in Islam is not strong enough to enable Muslims to transcend ethnic boundaries fully. Religious leaders have no defined role in the political process, though they are influential. At the same time, religious leaders are not generally identified with the political factions within the Muslim community and are not in the vanguard of nationalist or separatist movements.

Education

As a measure of democracy-building, education is a double-edged sword in multiethnic states seeking to establish pluralistic societies. For ethnic Macedonians, it is and has been a primary vehicle for affirming Macedonian-ness among the majority population and a means by which minority peoples seek to maintain their cultural identities. It has also been a means for promoting the Macedonian language and culture among minorities. In Tito's Yugoslavia, it was one of the most effective mechanisms for building a Macedonian future.

Education is mandatory for children ages seven through fifteen. Where feasible, instruction is offered in Macedonian, Albanian, Turkish, or Serbian, depending on the first language of the students. Textbooks are printed in Macedonian, Albanian, and Turkish. Efforts to teach Romani have been made, but so far results have been frustrating because of wide dialectal variations. Although instruction may be in a pupil's native language, each child receives schooling in Macedonian as well.

About 80 percent of the children who complete elementary education go on to secondary schools. Approximately 25 percent attend high schools, the rest go to vocational or technical schools. Higher education is open to all qualified students and special quotas for affirmative action exist for Albanians. There is no constitutional obligation for the state to teach in minority languages at the secondary level, though the government seeks to do this when there are reasonable numbers of minority students of one language group. What textbooks there are, are printed both in Macedonian and Albanian.[103]

At the primary and secondary level, there is a shortage of qualified teachers able to offer instruction in minority languages. Recognizing this, then-minister of education, Emilija Simovska, in 1995 ordered the state teachers college, Kliment Ohridski Pedagogical Academy, to provide training for teachers in Albanian as well as in Macedonian. The staff protested and sued the ministry, which claims that all children are entitled to education in their own languages and thus trained teachers speaking the childrens' languages are necessary. The case was still pending in early 1996.[104] In those schools where Albanian is taught, the education is often inferior. Schools lack needed textbooks and other instructional materials. Albanian children regularly drop out after the eight years of compulsory education.[105]

The state universities, one in Bitola – St. Kliment Ohridski, and the much larger – SS Kiril i Metodij in Skopje, are granted autonomy by the Macedonian constitution. There are no private universities. Pedagogical academies, institutions where teacher education is taught, also have autonomy. Various laws for governing education are in draft form, none has yet been passed. Nevertheless, the intent is to guarantee equal opportunities in education to all qualified students.

According to the most recent available statistics, those for 1991–92, of the 27,000 students enrolled in higher education, only 1.5 percent were Albanian, while 88.7 percent were Macedonian, 0.6 percent were Turk, 4.2 percent were Serb, and 0.06 percent were Roma. What these statistics say is that almost no Albanians enroll in higher educational institutions. Although the number of Albanian dropouts from secondary school is apparently decreasing, very few attend university, despite special quotas available to encourage Albanian matriculation.[106]

Calls by ethnic minorities for instruction in their own languages threaten majority peoples, not just in Macedonia, but also in neighboring Romania and Bulgaria. Albanian community leaders claim that requiring Albanian students to study in Macedonian blocks Albanians from gaining a university education. Albanians are demanding higher education in the Albanian language and to that end created an Albanian language university in February 1995. The government forcibly closed this enterprise, causing a riot and the loss of one life. At issue was whether Albanians, without government sanction, could found such an institution. Although the university still functions in a much scaled back fashion, it failed to attract the world attention it was meant to win.[107] Instead, most who evaluate the events concur with the Organization for Security and Cooperation in Europe (OSCE) High Commissioner on National Minorities, Max van der Stoel, who noted that while people have the right to create educational institutions according to OSCE guidelines, this must occur within the framework of the country's constitution.[108]

Ethnic Macedonians saw the incident as a challenge to state authority which, if relinquished, would lead to certain federalization of the state, then secession by the Albanians. Albanians seemed to see it as an expression of frustration with the status quo and as a demand for greater educational opportunity and thus greater opportunity to participate in state administration. As a compromise, the Ministry of Education has made provisions for greater numbers of Albanians to attend the university in Skopje. State leaders seem to see the provision of full access to education, followed by opening professional careers in corporate and state enterprises for all, vital to the long term success of establishing a pluralistic society.

Media and the intelligentsia

A mark of an open society is a free press. In Macedonia journalism is a growth industry and a key to continued democratization. Two daily publications dominate the national print news market – *Nova Makedonija* and *Večer*. While both claim to have independent editorial policies, they support the government and receive financing from the government. *Flaka e Vlazerimit*, the Albanian language daily newspaper, and the thrice weekly Turkish language *Birlik*, are also under government subsidy. The contents of *Flaka* can be inflammatory and nationalistic, although this seems to escape the notice of ethnic Macedonian officials perhaps because few can read Albanian. In addition, *Puls*, a Macedonian language weekly news magazine, toes the government line. There are also various publications which present specific political perspectives such as *Delo* and *Makedonsko Sonce*, both of which reflect nationalist views; *Demokratija*, the paper of the opposition Liberal Party, *Glas*, IMRO-DPMNU's publication; and *Demokratski forum*, the gazette of the Democratic Party.

A third national daily, called *Dnevnik*, began publication in March 1996. It is a private enterprise supported by foundations and private business interests in Skopje. *Dnevnik* is meant to be a serious alternative to *Nova Makedonija*. *Fokus*, a weekly founded in 1995, is regarded by many as a scandal sheet, but it has a high readership. Although it is possible to start new publications within the state, newspapers from neighboring Albania, Bulgaria, Greece, and Serbia may be imported only if approved by the Ministry of Internal Affairs.

The electronic media in Macedonia are dominated by Macedonian Radio-Television, the state-owned and -operated radio and television network. Macedonian Television is the only state-wide television service, though there are 29 other local stations scattered throughout the country along with 91 combined radio/TV stations. A-1 is the chief privately owned television station. It broadcasts news and public affairs programming as well as entertainment and is a generally reliable source of information. Macedonian radio, with six channels, is aired twenty-four hours a day, with limited service in minority languages. Private stations also carry Albanian language broadcasts on local TV and radio.

The government controls one of the two printing plants in Macedonia and owns a majority of the newsstands in the country. Further, it sets customs duties on paper and other supplies. In effect, this gives the state control over pricing of printed materials and the power to put papers out of business. In the absence of a strong tradition of a free press, the media tend to follow the government lead rather than independently engaging in investigative journalism. The government does not appear to censor material printed or broadcast; however, it came under heavy criticism for seeking to close down approximately eighty radio stations in May 1995, allegedly for using pirated programming in contravention of international law.[109]

Journalists are among the core members of the Macedonian intelligentsia, along with school teachers and university faculty, artists, musicians, writers, poets, as well as movie and media personalities. They are revered in a country that prizes learning, and because Macedonia is a small country, they are generally well-known figures who have great influence on the direction of popular thought. Many are politically involved, as a glance at the parliamentary roster indicates.

Economy

Economically, Macedonia is seeking to pull itself out of the hole into which it fell because of the combination of the trade embargo imposed against it by Greece, enforcement of the commercial blockade against Serbia (see below), the substantial reduction of trade ties with other former republics, and the stresses of privatization and marketization. Thanks to a major in-dustrialization program during the Yugoslav era, Macedonia has a sizable industrial sector, although much of it is outmoded. Industries include oil refining, mining, textile production, and manufacturing. Macedonia's primary agricultural products are wheat, corn, tomatoes, rice, peppers, livestock, viticulture, and tobacco production.[110] Tourism, centered on the regions of Lake Ohrid and Prespa, is an important sector that fell into the doldrums in recent years – because Greek and Yugoslav tourists were only partly replaced

Table 7.4 *Indicators of economic trends in Macedonia since 1989*

	1989	1990	1991	1992	1993	1994	1995[a]
GDP	n.a.	-9.9	-12.1	-14.0	-21.1	-8.4	-4
Industrial output	n.a.	-10.6	-17.2	-16.0	-10.0	-9.0	-9
Rate of inflation	n.a.	n.a	n.a.	1,691	350	122	50
Rate of unemployment	n.a.	n.a.	18	19	19	19	n.a.

Notes: GDP - % change over previous year; Industrial output - % change over previous year; Rate of inflation - % change in end-year retail/consumer prices; Rate of unemployment - annual average. [a]Estimate.

Sources: European Bank for Reconstruction and Development, *Transition Report 1995: Economic Transition in Eastern Europe and the Former Soviet Union* (London: EBRD, 1995); European Bank for Reconstruction and Development, *Transition Report Update, April 1996: Assessing Progress in Economies in Transition* (London: EBRD, 1996).

by Bulgarian ones - but it should rebound strongly as economic relations with Greece improve.

Macedonian economic performance over the last four years or so has been characterized by several attempts at macroeconomic stabilization, the last of which began to show results in early 1994. Average monthly retail price inflation fell from 10.7 percent in 1993 to 3.9 percent in 1994, and about 0.7 percent in 1995, among the lowest in Central and Eastern Europe. This achievement is the result of the tight monetary policy promulgated by the National Bank of the Republic of Macedonia in cooperation with the International Monetary Fund (IMF). Fiscal policy has also been increasingly tight, and the budget deficit declined from about 4 percent of gross domestic product in 1994 to around 2 percent in 1995. The denar, after declining to an average of 47.52 to the dollar in February 1994, strengthened to finish 1994 at 40.60 and 1995 at 37.96. The differences between these official rates and black market prices have narrowed considerably, although there is still a divergence, with the latter at about 40 denars/dollar.

Such strict monetary and fiscal policy, combined with the various embargoes, has meant a sharp decline in production. The downward trend continued through 1995, long after it had stopped in virtually all other transforming economies, with social product declining in 1995 by 3 to 4 percent and industrial production by 9 to 10 percent. The fall in the latter was about 43 percent over 1991–95, while per capita GDP declined from $2,646 in 1988 to about $1,600[111] in 1995 (39.5 percent).

Unemployment, already among the highest in the region, continues to rise. In January 1995, unemployment stood at 197,678: by August 1995, it totaled 222,804, over 20 percent of the popultion. Statistics indicated that 119,711 people seeking employment were under 30 years of age. They also showed that 7,196 people with university education were waiting for jobs – 1,146 lawyers, 914 physicians, 882 economists, and 887 teachers. It is little wonder then that young people with education and training are seeking to emigrate.[112] Many of Macedonia's employed workers are not receiving regular pay and the pensions of the country's 200,000 retirees are declining steadily in purchasing power. In addition, fewer state funds are available for social services and health care delivery is deteriorating.

The monthly average wage expressed in dollars has remained high by Balkan standards. In September 1995, it was over $230, twice the corresponding figure in Bulgaria. The high cost of living and wage levels relative to the level of development have taken a toll on the trade and current accounts, both of which are in deficit. The small 1994 imbalances – a $441 million trade deficit and a $192 million current account imbalance – were expected to be replicated in 1995.

On March 31, 1995, the gross foreign debt was a moderate $844 million (or almost 28 percent of GDP), about evenly divided among the international financial institutions (especially the IMF and World Bank), the Paris Club of official creditors, and the London Club of commercial banks.[113] Macedonia signed an agreement in July 1995 with the Paris Club on rescheduling its $218 million share of the former Yugoslav debt to the group. Pursuant to that agreement, the country is signing bilateral deals with creditor countries, such as Switzerland (December 1995) and Austria in (February 1996). Official foreign currency and gold reserves remain negligible (about $21 million),[114] as does cumulative direct foreign investment (around $60 million).[115]

The country's relations with the IMF and the World Bank have developed well. The government has met the terms of the latter's $85 million interest-free Financial and Enterprise Structural Adjustment Credit. Macedonia was granted a $45 million stand-by facility by the IMF in early 1995. The European Bank for Reconstruction and Development has been particularly active, providing DM 40 million for support of small and medium-sized enterprises and DM 20 million for modernization of Skopje's airport. Is is also planning to buy shares in Komercijalna banka when that bank increased its capital in 1996.

In June 1993 the Sobranie enacted privatization legislation meant to stimulate the growth of entrepreneurship and private ownership. Some 1,217 enterprises – 113 large, 274 medium-sized, and 830 small – were to be privatized. These firms represent about half of the employment and half of the total assets in the economy.[116] The methods used emphasize leveraged buy-outs by firms' current employees and managers. Other sanctioned methods include direct sales via tender for all or part of enterprises, leasing arrangements, and privatization via bankruptcy proceedings. The key institutional actor is the Agency of the Republic of Macedonia for the Transformation of Enterprises with Social Capital (hereafter, the privatization agency).

The most recent figures, released in mid-February 1996, show that 604 enterprises have been privatized according to their chosen methods, while the process is ongoing at another 396. Some 216 failed to submit proposals by the deadline of December 31, 1995, meaning that they will be privatized according to a method decided by the privatization agency. The chosen methods, with their emphasis on leveraged buyouts, have not been very remunerative for the state budget, which has earned only DM 60.9 million (DM 19.2 million in cash) from the process. Moreover, one must be skeptical about the economic benefits – especially in the early years before a functioning stock market is in place – that will arise from these insider deals, which inject no new capital into the economy.

Although the government continues to extol the virtues of the privatization program, the scheme has been the target of corruption allegations. The government has been accused of handing companies over to managers, many associated with the SDUM and the LP, who, in return, promise to pay-off the purchase price from company profits over a five year period. The Democratic Party's Petar Gošev has been especially vocal in his accusations that the government is selling influence and political favors in return for financial support, real estate deals, and more.[117] To this can be added complaints that the parties in power are tied into tax evasion and protection rackets. There is a conspiracy of silence in the press regarding corruption, while the public is frightened and helpless.

A normal, if unattractive, aspect of democratization, corruption will be curbed only when popular revulsion demands action. Its origins, though, are easy to determine. Macedonia received negligible aid from Western institutions during its formative years, therefore, the new state faced a potentially ruinous economic situation that was exacerbated by being obliged to enforce the economic sanctions against Serbia and being the victim of Greece's blockades. Profiteers readily entered this vacuum and provided the goods needed to meet consumer needs. Stores were stocked: few items or food stuffs were scarce. In the Albanian sections, where recipients of large amounts of foreign capital resided, housing construction was widespread. Despite the lack of concrete evidence, it is clear that criminal groups carved up the marketplace to meet consumer demands. They delivered the needed goods and materials that could not have been obtainable through legal means. Paradoxically, these activities contributed to internal stability by keeping the population fed. The government, having little recourse, pragmatically turned a blind eye to such activities.

Increased trade with Albania, Bulgaria, and Turkey has been beneficial but insufficient to compensate for all of the losses sustained by Skopje since independence. Of course, the creation of the central Balkan trade route from the Albanian coast to Turkey will help, but what will really solve Macedonia's problems is the establishment of a Balkan peace and normalization of relations with all neighbors.

Judicial concerns

One measure of the success of democratization is how well the system of justice works. According to the Macedonian constitution, all courts are "autonomous and independent" and are expected to "judge on the basis of the constitution and laws and international agreements ratified in accordance with the constitution." The constitution expressly prohibits emergency courts (Star Chambers).[118]

There are municipal and district courts in a three tiered system headed by a supreme court. Court judges are elected to office and terms are open ended. The Supreme Court of Macedonia is established by constitution to provide "uniformity in implementation of the laws by the [lower] courts."[119] The state is represented by the Public Prosecutor's Office, the "single state body carrying out legal measures against persons who have committed criminal and other offenses determined by law."[120] A Republican Judicial Council, composed of seven distinguished jurists, is also provided in the constitution. Its role is to advise the parliament concerning appointments of judges and related matters. The Constitutional Court of Macedonia, composed of nine judges elected by the parliament, defends the constitution from encroachment.[121]

Local affairs

In the days of federal Yugoslavia, central control was lax and ineffective. In the new Macedonian republic, the central authorities have exercised strong control over the municipalities (units of local government) that make up the state, causing significant friction. In 1990, in Gostivar and Tetovo, Albanians won the elections, but the state would not allow them to take office, causing them to form a shadow administration.[122]

For four years the question of the relationship between municipality and state was a political football. Finally, in October 1995, the Sobranie passed the Law for Local Self-Government which provides municipalities with limited autonomy. The chief reason for the delay in writing and passing such a law was the question of what language may be used in official transactions.

The final version provides that in municipalities where national minorities are a significant part of the population, the language(s) of the minority will be used in addition to Macedonian in official deliberations. Signs may appear in both Macedonian and the other language(s).[123]

Each municipality is to have a directly elected mayor and council which are to deal with local issues. The compromise is significant and hard won. It is a building block in creating a multiethnic state, though there are those who see it and perhaps will try to use it as a means to segment the state.

Security in transition

Security forces

Macedonian security forces came under much scrutiny in the aftermath of the assassination attempt on President Gligorov. Then-minister of internal affairs, Ljubomir Frčkovski, whose staff were responsible for the president's security, submitted his resignation to the prime minister, though it was rejected.

Since the creation of the Macedonian republic, security forces, a symbol of the old regime, have been much criticized. The security services have been accused of abusing power and promoting corruption, and the LP in particular has been interested in circumscribing their authority. Evidence is scant and the accusations are partisan, still, after heated debates in parliament, several laws governing the intelligence service and security forces were passed in early 1995, part of a restructuring of the Ministry of Internal Affairs (MIA), making security services more accountable to elected officials. The MIA, with about 5,500 uniformed police and some 2,000 detectives or inspectors,[124] is the most formidable and best trained force in Macedonia. Approximately 4 percent of the police are Albanian though this number is increasing.[125]

The Intelligence Service, which deals only with external matters and whose director is appointed by and reports directly to the president of the Republic with a horizontal link to the government, is responsible for State Security. The Counter-intelligence Service deals with internal threats and has a staff of about six to seven hundred. Its director reports jointly to the minister for internal affairs and to the prime minister. The director is appointed by the government on the recommendation of the minister of internal affairs.

According to recent reports, there are no glaring human rights abuses in Macedonia; the police have been known to follow constitutional procedures concerning arraignments, detention, and rights to counsel for the accused when arrested.[126] The handling of the AAA defendants stands out as an exception. The accused were held incommunicado for a time and denied access to their attorneys. While the constitution prohibits torture and other cruel treatment, there have been isolated incidents of reported abuse. At the same time, the government has also prosecuted police officers on criminal charges for such actions.[127]

The Macedonian military

The military has not been a political force in post-Yugoslav Macedonia. Consisting of 10,000 lightly armed troops and 80,000 reservists, its leadership firmly backs the government. The arsenal is basically composed of light weapons inherited from the Yugoslav National Army. Macedonia has no air force, armored force, or heavy artillery; a few small boats constitute its modest navy. It has several traffic helicopters and little other hardware.[128]

The military, which relies on universal male conscription, has played only a supporting role in the democratization process. Its leaders have not become politicians, and Macedonia aspires to having a professional military force. Some 25 percent of the military is made up of Albanians, a percentage that coincides with the number of Albanians in the state's population.

Security policy

Macedonia's security policy is quite simple. It seeks to be a member of the European security structure, and indeed, must rely on it for protection. It has joined the United Nations, the Partnership for Peace, and the OSCE. NATO forces are stationed in Macedonia. The government seeks to join as many of these international bodies as possible, both to maximize protection and to insure the broadest affirmation of the state's existence against any future attempt by aggressors in the neighborhood who might question the existence of this state. At present, Serbia is the most worrisome in this regard. Belgrade is becoming a more repressive and authoritarian regime, one capable of turning Serbian nationalism into aggression against Macedonia.

Foreign policy

The Serbian threat

Serbia finally recognized Macedonia on April 8, 1996 thus stabilizing borders between the two countries. The Yugoslav National Army evacuated its bases in Macedonia in 1992, after very intense negotiations between Gligorov and Milošević. The departure of the troops was without incident, although all heavy weapons were withdrawn and installations were destroyed leaving Macedonia's army without an arsenal.

Fearing the spread of the Bosnian war southward, the United Nations sent an observation force of about 1,000 soldiers, including a contingent of 500 Americans to patrol the border between the two countries. From time to time, leaders in Serbia have issued aggressive sounding statements concerning forced union with the Republic of Macedonia. Serbia has made several threatening overtures, notably sending troops to occupy a narrow strip of Macedonian territory in 1994. Such actions have been evidently meant as a show of force and perhaps as a reminder that Macedonia is very vulnerable.

Serbia appears to have pulled out of Macedonia based on the calculus that opening a third, and non-contiguous front would have over-extended its army. Moreover, few in Belgrade seemed to expect an independent Macedonia to survive, as it appeared ill-equipped to withstand the economic and political pressures of the times. Because Macedonia was not the kind of emotional flash point that Croatia and Bosnia are and the intensity of animosities which characterized Serbian-Croatian, Serbian-Bosnian, and Serbian-Slovenian relations were not in evidence, Serbs seemed willing to depart – expecting a speedy return in any event. Belgrade no doubt also felt it imprudent to further antagonize world opinion over an invasion of Macedonia, especially since ethnic Macedonians are potential allies in the event of civil unrest in the neighboring, overwhelmingly Albanian, Kosovo region.

For their part, ethnic Macedonians have remained favorably disposed toward Serbia, which, during the Yugoslav years, was its chief trading partner, a relationship that is likely to revive now that the UN embargo against Serbia has been lifted. Macedonian political leaders, however, do not share their constituency's trust. The government remains wary of Serbia and has no wish to enroll Macedonia in a new Yugoslav federation led by Belgrade.

The southern neighbor

Macedonia, before declaring independence in 1991, had been a minor irritant to Greece because of the use of the word Macedonia in the then Yugoslav republic's name and the claims this implied. With independence, this simmering problem boiled over, scalding both sides.

The Greek-Macedonian dispute is rooted in World War II when Yugoslav partisans aided Greek communists in their struggle against the occupiers and subsequently against the royalists during the Greek Civil War of 1946–49. An uneasy marriage at best, it ended in divorce over Tito's aspirations to acquire Greek Macedonia. Slav inhabitants fled and today Greece denies the existence of a Macedonian minority within its borders, despite evidence that there is a small number, perhaps 50,000, whose linguistic and cultural aspirations are repressed.[129]

Greek-Yugoslav relations eventually became cordial, despite disagreement over the name of Yugoslavia's southern most republic. In 1982, however, amity gave way when then Prime Minister Andreas Papandreou inflamed Yugoslavs by denying the existence of the Macedonian nationality and thus also, the existence of a Macedonian minority in Greece. Yugoslavia argued that there were some 300,000 Macedonians in Greece.[130]

Accusations have been traded ever since between the sides with reverberations in both the Greek and Macedonian diasporas. Even before Macedonia's independence, public expressions of growing nationalist sentiment on the part of ethnic Macedonian nationalists, notably those belonging to IMRO-DPMNU, both in Macedonia and abroad, angered and threatened neighboring Greece. Such mantras as "Thessaloniki is ours!" and "On to the Aegean" caught the imaginations of many Macedonians and frightened many Greeks. Greece tossed back such claims as "Macedonia was is and always will be Greece!" and "No Macedonia for the Slavs." Both sides became irrational on the subject, while Athens vetoed Macedonia's membership in European and other international bodies as a means of pressing Skopje to drop the word "Macedonia" from its official name, change its constitution to unambiguously reject territorial aspirations, and to adopt a new flag.

Greece argued that the use of the name Macedonia was not only theft of a Greek birthright, to which Greece claims exclusive ownership, but also, in effect, amounted to staking a future claim to Greek Macedonia.[131] As further evidence of purported Macedonian expansionist intentions, Athens pointed to the use of the Star (or Sun) of Vergina (called Kutleš by Macedonians), a symbol of Philip of Macedon's empire uncovered at his ancient capital in Greece in 1978, as the centerpiece of the Macedonian republic's flag. Greeks also pointed to the Macedonian constitution which notes that the Republic of Macedonia "cares for" Macedonians, wherever they may be,[132] surely a subtle call for a Great Macedonia.[133]

Although interwoven with nationalist feelings, the subtext here from the Greek side has to do both with highly emotional feelings about Greekness and the Greek identity, as well as with Greek concerns that recognizing a Macedonian nation would both feed the national consciousness among its "Slavophone Greeks," and undermine the fundamental notion that Greece is a homogeneous state. It also claims to be threatened by some future Macedonian state that could, in collaboration with some other enemy, most likely Turkey, attack Greece. Recognition of Slavophones as Macedonians could very well lead Greece's more than 105,000 Turks, officially known as "Greek Muslims," to demand greater rights or autonomy; worse, they could seek to secede and thus threaten the stability of northern Greece on its border with Turkey.[134]

For Macedonia, the choice of its name was a natural outgrowth of the tradition begun in the Yugoslav federation where what was to become the new republic was first officially the Peoples Republic of Macedonia, then, later, the Socialist Federal Republic of Macedonia. A national consciousness had been intensively nurtured by the federal state and it matured quickly. From the Macedonian perspective then, there could not have been another choice.

The phrasing of the constitution to indicate that Macedonia "cares" for Macedonians outside the state was, it seems, bred out of the emotionally motivated concern for ethnic Macedonians in Greece, whose relatives and descendants carry great political weight in Skopje. That it was a provocation to Greece either mattered little or tickled nationalists who enjoyed getting the Greek goat. The flag too, seems to fall into this category and served as a second slap in the already smarting Greek face. With economic troubles at home, Greek politicians eagerly took up the call to fight the Macedonian menace, thus making political hay and deflecting popular attention from the internal issues plaguing Greece.

Greece imposed two economic embargoes on Macedonia, one briefly in 1992, the second in 1994 which lasted eighteen months. Richard C. Holbrooke, then US assistant secretary of state, managed to find the needed face saving formula required to end the dispute. The Greek government lifted the trade embargo on October 15, 1995, in exchange for two things: legislation that would change Macedonia's flag and Skopje's assurances that it harbors no claims to Greek territory. The Greek-Macedonian compromise, signed on September 13, 1995 by the foreign ministers of the two countries, signifies that the quest for Macedonia's full diplomatic recognition has ended. Macedonia then adopted a new centerpiece for its flag – an eight-ray sun or star, and has provided the pledges that it has no territorial aspirations. The question of altering the constitutional name, Republic of Macedonia, seems not negotiable from Skopje's point of view. Athens appears to recognize this, though it continues to argue that the matter is up for serious debate. Both sides will engage in diplomatic jousts over this issue to satisfy public opinion at home, but the question appears destined to eventually die,[135] the more so because of Athens' diplomatic recognition of rump Yugoslavia and "all the countries formed as a result of the dissolution of the former Yugoslavia" on April 25, 1996.[136] Without mentioning Macedonia, which it persists in calling the Former Yugoslav Republic of Macedonia (FYROM), Greece thus recognized the new state.

The world responds – sort of

On April 8, 1993, Macedonia gained UN recognition, albeit under the name Former Yugoslav Republic of Macedonia (FYROM). It was Germany, along with other EU countries, that brought charges against Greece in the EU Court of Justice in the hope of having the trade embargo lifted. Since the United Nations recognized the new state, many countries have established full diplomatic relations with Macedonia – notably absent from that list was the United States, which only recognized Macedonia in early 1996 (a testimony to the power of the US Greek lobby which seemed more influential than European leaders in this matter). Still, local politics notwithstanding, the United States has become a main supporter of Macedonia and has posted 500 troops to the new republic. Gradually, EU solidarity eroded to the point where various countries ignored Greek pleas to the contrary and recognized Macedonia by 1994. Some aid from the World Bank and other sources began to reach Macedonia as well.

Immediately after the signing of the September 1995 agreement between Greece and Macedonia, the new republic began to receive the international recognition for which it had been waiting. It formally joined the OSCE on October 14, 1995. It was admitted to the Council of Europe on November 9, 1995.

Turkey, Albania, and Bulgaria

Turkey, though not a contiguous neighbor, maintains an important place in Skopje's foreign policy. Macedonia has worked hard to forge close ties with Ankara, in part as a counter weight to Greece, but also because as a major trading partner, Turkey is a source of needed financial assistance. For Turkey, the Republic of Macedonia, with approximately 100,000 ethnic Turks within its borders, is of both symbolic and strategic importance. Turkey's Balkan strategy appears to be directed at insuring the welfare of ethnic Turks in the Republic of Macedonia, securing the new state as an ally as a possible counter force against Greece, and protecting itself against the possible influx of refugees from the region should war break out. Ankara has remained aloof from Macedonia's internal concerns, including matters having to do with Albanians, to both underscore that it is not a heavy-handed Muslim state and perhaps also because it is sensitive to criticism about its own internal crisis concerning the Kurds.

Whether Macedonian–Turkish relations will change now that the Greek embargo has been lifted and Macedonian–Greek relations are on the mend, is not clear. It is likely that Turkish influence will diminish if Turkish politicians turn away from secularism in politics. But even without such a shift, Macedonia will certainly look toward its southern neighbor for increased commerce, though with the full recognition that Skopje must remain guarded about Greece, a land that could again impose punishing economic penalties on it.

While Albania pursued a policy of support for and cooperation with Skopje, especially in the commercial sphere, it has meddled in Macedonia's internal affairs by openly supporting the Arben Xhaferi and Menduh Taçi and the PDP-A. In early 1995, Albanian President Sali Berisha loudly proclaimed his support for the creation of the Albanian university in Tetovo, unsettling the government which saw the institution as illegal and unconstitutional.[137] The Skopje government has repeatedly protested to Tirana about political interference.[138]

Bulgaria, the first country to recognize Macedonia diplomatically although it has failed to recognize the Macedonian nationality and language as distinct from Bulgarian, has proved to be a very helpful neighbor. Historically, the relationship between Sofia and Skopje has been torturous. Since the establishment of a modern Bulgarian state in 1878, Bulgarians believed that Macedonia was Bulgaria *irredenta*. They sought in vain to take what was theirs in the Balkan Wars, World War I, and World II. Only since the fall of communism in Bulgaria have Bulgaria's Macedonian aspirations dissipated, though whether they would regenerate if Macedonia were to collapse is not certain.

The diaspora

The Macedonian diaspora began in the nineteenth century and continued in waves throughout the present. Chiefly, emigration from Macedonia was a function of economic factors and often those who left, returned annually for visits. Many sent regular remittances to family remaining in Macedonia, a tradition that persists and that helps keep the economy afloat.

Centers of ethnic Macedonian emigration are Australia, Canada, North America, Sweden, and Germany. As is often the case, immigrants are more nationalistic than many nationalists in the homeland. Macedonian Albanians typically emigrate to North America, Germany, and Switzerland. They, too, send remittances, contributing to the apparent prosperity in Albanian villages.

Diasporas have, in effect, globalized nationalism as Danforth points out[139] and the influence of ethnic Macedonian immigrants on politics is clear. In federal Yugoslavia, *Matica na Iselenicite na Makedonija* (Queen Bee of the Macedonian Immigrants) was founded in the 1960s to promote national consciousness and to counter similar efforts abroad mounted by Bulgaria and Albania. There is no similar organization for Macedonia's Albanians, but then the state would be reluctant to promote Albanian national consciousness.

IMRO-DPMNU, which receives support from the immigrant communities, has called for a ministry to be added to the government purely for immigrant affairs.

The Macedonians abroad who are concerned with politics in Macedonia are those who were immigrants from Tito's Yugoslavia. They seek to affirm their nationality and do so by preserving Macedonian language, culture, and church abroad – often fiercely.[140]

The past as the future or the future as a new frontier?

The Republic of Macedonia was born, peacefully, bloodlessly. It came to democracy having no democratic tradition, yet it is a functioning constitutional democracy. Democratic pluralism in Macedonia, however, as in other democratizing countries, has given nationalism an unwelcome boost. As a result, interethnic issues are quite tense. The successive governments have had to both respond to the needs of the majority Macedonians in assuring them of a stabile and secure state and protection of their national identity, while according minorities, notably Albanians, greater rights and offering the promise of greater integration into the state. Macedonia has had more success than most emerging democracies regarding coping with ethnic issues, despite the international trend toward smaller but ethnically "pure" states (for example, Chechnia, Serbia, Croatia, and Bosnia). There is a recognition, and a *de facto* acceptance, that minorities, especially Albanians, will not countenance either assimilation or marginalization. Thus, the direction is clear: Macedonia, in an effort to preserve the state, must preserve its multi-ethnic character. In so doing it has little choice but to gradually let go of the nation state concept.

This goal is out of reach for now, though, and it would be political suicide for any leader to espouse it. Nevertheless, as the ethnic Albanian community continues to make headway in fulfilling its agenda, the government is incrementally changing the contours of interethnic affairs. Democracy has given Albanians and others a platform from which to speak and speak loudly. It has also integrated Albanians into more mainstream political activity. Minorities, who had little role in governance during the Tito era, now have more representation in government, and a growing role in society.

Although there has been a little interethnic violence, incidents have been few and contained quickly. They did not lead to further violence, in spite of the fact that the notion of ethnic unity outweighs allegiance to a supranational whole. The most eloquent testimony to a possible supranational future is the general interethnic peace that has been maintained throughout the six year existence of the state. As corroborating evidence, there is the popular response of pulling together both in the face of the attempted murder of Gligorov and the adversity of the Greek trade embargoes. Religion, while a contributing factor in the ethnic identity of citizens, and a potentially polarizing and destructive force in interethnic affairs, has not been excessively divisive. Whether clergy will contribute to the state building process, however, is as yet not clear.

Media play an important role in democratization; however, the free and open exchange of ideas in Macedonia currently has its limits. So, too, does the press's ability and willingness to offer news and analysis and to contribute to greater awareness of issues confronting ethnic groups. Both the people and the press have been self-censoring. At the same time, the people have not found the way to develop a sustainable and influential means of collective action in the interest of change. As a result, corruption bedevils society and the media have yet to fully mature as instruments of democracy.

Politically, while the newness of events makes any analysis seem more like star gazing, it appears that Macedonia may be entering a new phase of political activity. The attack on President Gligorov has altered the political situation – physically weakening him and thereby, the power he wields. Branko Crvenkovski was quick to see this, as was Stojan Andov. They collided in a contest of strength that is leading to a redefinition of roles and a realignment of relationships among parties and players. The role of prime minister will increase at the expense of that of president, for there is no one of the stature of Gligorov to succeed him. Andov has resigned the presidency of the Sobranie and has called for new elections along with IMRO-DPMNU and the DP.

Meantime, now that the Greek embargo and the UN sanctions against Serbia have been lifted, the promise of economic progress is real. An improved economic climate, to include further privatization, tax reform, and more marketization, would cool nationalist ardor in this state of entrepreneurs, shop keepers, and peasants. Attendant educational reform and greater access will further contribute to stabilization, as will greater integration with international organizations, and increased contact with the United States and other Western countries. Reckless behavior and irresponsible actions, which until now have not been frequent, are unlikely to grow. Macedonia's citizens seem instinctively to know that stability profits all and that it is in everyone's interest to allow the new Macedonian state to evolve, not explode.

Acronyms

AM	Alliance for Macedonia
ARFM	Alliance of Reformed Forces of Macedonia

ASNOM	Anti-Fascist Assembly of National Liberation of Macedonia (known by the Macedonian abbreviation, even in English)
AVNOJ	Anti-Fascist Council for the Liberation of Yugoslavia (known by the Serbo-Croatian abbreviation, even in English)
DP	Democratic Party (Demokratska Partija)
DPSM	Democratic Party of Serbs in Macedonia (Demokratska Partija na Srbite)
DPT	Democratic Party of Turks (Demokratski Sjuz na Turcite vo Makedonija)
IMRO-DPMNU	Internal Macedonian Revolutionary Organization-Democratic Party for Macedonian National Unity (Vnatrešna Makedonska Revolucionerna Organizacija-Demokratska Partija za Makedonsko Nacionalno Edinstvo - VMRO-DPMNE)
LCM	League of Communists of Macedonia (now SDUM)
LP	Liberal Party (Liberalnata Partija na Makedonija)
LYC	League of Yugoslav Communists
NDP	People's Democratic Party (Narodna Demokratska Partija) (known by the Albanian abbreviation, even in English)
PCER	Party for Complete Emancipation of the Roma (Partija za Celosna Emancipacija na Romite)
PDP	Party for Democratic Prosperity (Partia per Prosperitet Demokratik – PPD)
PDP-A	Party for Democratic Prosperity - Albanian (PDP splinter party)
RF-LP	Reformed Forces-Liberal Party
SDUM	Social Democratic Union of Macedonia (Socijaldemokratski Sojuz Makedonije – SDSM)
SPM	Socialist Party of Macedonia (Socijalistička Partija na Makedonija)
SSM	Council of Trade Unions in Macedonia
YDPP	Young Democratic Progressive Party

NOTES

I am indebted to Teuta Arifi, Branko Geroski, Jiri Pehe, Betty Perry, Trajko Slaveski, and Michael Wyzan for critically reading this chapter and to Ismije Beshiri for assistance in locating relevant materials.

1 Republic of Macedonia, Government Statistical Office, 1994 Census Data (Skopje). Demographic statistics in Macedonia are affected by cross-over between Albanians, Roma, and others. Sometimes it has been more advantageous to be considered a member of one group than another and in such cases, people have changed their national identities. Thus, the caveat "user beware" must be observed at all times when considering Macedonian demographic statistics.
2 See the works of such historians as Hristo Andonov-Poljanski, Krste Bitoski, and Manol Pandevski for examples.
3 See Duncan M. Perry, *The Politics of Terror: Macedonian Liberation Movements, 1893–1903* (Durham, NC: Duke University Press, 1988), pp. 17–24.
4 Sabrina Petra Ramet, *Social Currents in Eastern Europe,* 2d ed. (Durham, NC: Duke University Press, 1995), pp. 401–2.

5 Victor Friedman, "Macedonian Language and Nationalism during the Nineteenth and Twentieth Centuries," *Balcanistica* 2 (1975), 83–95.

6 See Stefan Troebst, "Yugoslav Macedonia, 1944–1953: Building the Party, the State and the Nation," unpublished paper presented at the ACLS/SSRC/Institut slavianovedeniia i balkanistiki Rossiiskoi akademii nauk, Moscow, 29–31 April 1994, pp. 42–5.

7 Stephen E. Palmer and Robert R. King, *Yugoslav Communism and the Macedonian Question* (Hamden, CT: Archon Books, 1971), p. 138.

8 Ibid., p. 139.

9 In 1389, the forces of medieval Serbia and its allies were defeated by the Ottomans. See *Kosovo: Legacy of a Medieval Battle*, ed. Wayne S. Vucinich and Thomas A. Emmert (Minneapolis, MN: MMEEM, 1991) and Alex N. Dragnich and Slavko Todorovich, *The Saga of Kosovo* (Boulder, CO: East European Monographs, 1984).

10 J.F. Brown, *Eastern Europe and Communist Rule* (Durham, NC: Duke University Press, 1988), pp. 352–6; Dennison Rusinow, *The Yugoslav Experiment, 1968–1974* (London: Royal Institute for International Affairs, 1977), pp. 248–307.

11 Rusinow, *Yugoslav Experiment*, p. 337.

12 See Lenard J. Cohen, *Broken Bonds: The Disintegration of Yugoslavia* (Boulder, CO: Westview, 1993), pp. 36ff.

13 Hugh Poulton, *Who Are the Macedonians?* (London: Hurst & Company, 1994), p. 128; Palmer and King, *Yugoslav Communism*, p. 178. Actual data concerning the birth rate increase of Albanians indicates that in the 1948 census, there were 179,389 Albanians in Macedonia, making up 17.1 percent of the population. When compared to the current count, which puts them at 22.9 percent of the population, it would seem that concerns have been exaggerated, given the international growth rate norms for this period.

14 Poulton, *Who are the Macedonians?* p. 132.

15 *Otechestven Vestnik*, 3 November 1990.

16 Trading on the IMRO name and associated mythology has become popular in Macedonia and Bulgaria. In both countries, nationalists claim political descendance from the ideals of IMRO, an organization that actually split after Ilinden, and became synonymous with terrorism in the 1920s and 1930s. See Elizabeth Barker, *Macedonia: Its Place in Balkan Power Politics* (Westport, CT: Greenwood Press, 1980 [1950]), for a succinct history.

17 Duncan M. Perry, "Macedonia: A Balkan Problem and a European Dilemma," *RFE/RL Research Report*, 19 June 1992, p. 37.

18 Quoted in Milan Andrejevich, "Macedonia's New Political Leadership," *Report on Eastern Europe*, 17 May 1991, p. 24.

19 See Robert Mickey, "Unstable in a Stable Way," *Transition*, 30 January 1995, p. 40.

20 Author's interviews with Petar Gošev in Skopje, 14 April 1995 and Dosta Dimovska, Skopje, 18 April 1995.

21 Hans-Joachim Hoppe, "Die politische Szene der Republik Makedonien," *Berichte des Bundesinstituts für ostwissenschaftliche und internationale Studien* 47 (1995), 34.

22 Interview with Gošev, Skopje, 14 April 1995.

23 Interview with Dimovska, Skopje, 18 April 1995.

24 See *Nova Makedonija,* 21 December 1994 for the government program.

25 This poll was taken between December 8 and 11, 1995 among 300 people of voting age (47 percent male, 53 percent female; 25 percent between the ages of 18 and 29; 24.33 percent between the ages of 30 and 39; 23.33 percent between the ages of 40 and 49; and 27.33 percent over 50, with a cross section of professions). *Puls,* 15 December 1995, pp. 16–17.

26 Hoppe, "Die politische Szene der Republik Makedonien," p. 35.

27 Ibid., p. 19.

28 *Nova Makedonija,* 26 January 1994.

29 See Robert W. Mickey and Adam Smith Albion, *Minorities: The New Europe's Old Issue,* ed. Ian M. Cuthbertson and Jane Leibowitz (New York: Institute for East West Studies, 1993), p. 67.

30 Author's interview with Abdurahman Aliti, Tetovo, 18 April 1995.

31 Author's interview with Arben Xhaferi, Tetovo, 18 April 1995.

32 Interview with Xhaferi. See *Flaka e Vellazerimit,* 14 and 22 April 1995 for more on the Aliti/Xhaferi differences.

33 Quoted in an interview with Thaci, *Observer,* 27 February 1994.

34 *Profile of Major Political Parties in Macedonia* (Skopje: MIC, 1994), p. 41.

35 Ibid., p. 42.

36 Ibid., pp. 42–3.

37 MAK-NEWS, 6 June 1995; *Nova Makedonija,* 14 July 1992.

38 *Profile,* p. 15.

39 Quoted in Janusz Bugajski, *Ethnic Politics in Eastern Europe* (Armonk, NY: M.E. Sharpe, 1995), p. 111.

40 "Izborna programa," *Glas,* October 1994, p. 30.

41 Ibid., p. 28.

42 Mika Velinovska, "Razgak'eniot L'u(b)pčo," *Puls,* 21 July 1995, p. 20.

43 L'upčo Georgievski, *Puls,* 14 July 1995, p. 22. In so doing, he has attempted to tear down national myths which, whether historically correct or not, are part of the nation building process that led to the affirmation of a Macedonian people. It happens that the figures he named as Bulgarian may have identified themselves as Bulgarian, a common choice for Slavs living in Macedonia who belonged to the Bulgarian Exarchate Church.

44 L'upčo Georgievski, "Za nacionalnoto pomiruvan'e po vtorpat," *Puls,* 7 July 1995, pp. 21–2. A review of Aleksandrov's and Mihailov's activities will convince most readers that they were gangsters rather than liberation fighters.

45 Velinovska, "Razgak'eniot L'u(b)pčo," p. 20.

46 See Kole Mangov, "Koj so kogo k'e se pomiruva," *Puls,* 29 September 1995, p. 26.

47 *Profile,* p. 34.

48 MILS, 2 April 1993.

49 Interview with Gošev; *Profile,* p. 48.

50 See Bernard Lewis, *The Emergence of Modern Turkey* (New York: Oxford University Press, 1976), pp. 239ff for elucidation of Atatürk's policies and programs.

51 MAK-NEWS, 6 June 1995.

52 Ristić in 1993 formed a new party, the Democratic Alliance of the Serbs in Macedonia. Its platform is like that of the DPSM and appears to be less influential.

53 *Profile*, p. 59; MAK-NEWS, 6 June 1995.

54 Bugajski, *Ethnic Politics in Eastern Europe*, p. 121; *Profile*, p. 62.

55 US Department of State, "1995 Human Rights Report Macedonia."

56 Ibid.

57 *Ustav na Republika na Makedonija* (Skopje: NIP, 1991), Article 61.

58 Ibid., Article 62.

59 See ibid., Articles 88–97.

60 See ibid., Articles 61–78.

61 Ibid., Article 80.

62 The survey was conducted by BriMa in late January-early February 1995 and included 1,083 adults over 18. Cited in USIA Briefing Paper, 15 August 1995.

63 Macedonian Information Service, 27 November 1995.

64 Interview with Branko Crvenkovski, *Nova Makedonija*, 25 November 1995.

65 *Profile*, p. 3.

66 See Hoppe, "Die politische Szene der Republik Makedonien," pp. 33–5, for a useful tabulation of election results.

67 These observations are drawn both from the results and discussions with journalists and other observers of the Macedonian scene.

68 Some of those originally elected on the IMRO-DPMNU ticket subsequently defected. One founded IMRO-DP, one went to a splinter, IMRO-Fatherland, two others joined the DP, and one went to the LP.

69 See Mickey and Albion, *Minorities*, p. 84.

70 There are Macedonian scholars who claim that Macedonians are among the earliest inhabitants of the Balkan peninsula. See Tasko D. Belčev, *Cetiri iljadi godini Makedonska istorija, civilizacija pismenost i kultura: ili etnogenezata na Makedonskiot narod* (Skopje: Strk, 1993), a book whose author argues that Macedonians predate the Slavs.

71 This, of course, is a highly sensitive subject, especially to ethnic Macedonians. There is evidence that a Macedonian consciousness existed among a small number of people in the nineteenth century. The idea of a Macedonian nationality spread during the twentieth, but did not find official expression or acceptance anywhere until the creation of the second Yugoslavia. See Loring M. Danforth, *The Macedonian Conflict* (Princeton: Princeton University Press, 1995), pp. 56–69. See also Krste P. Missirkov, *On Macedonian Matters* (Skopje: Macedonian Review Editions, 1974).

72 Troebst, "Yugoslav Macedonia, 1944–1953," p. 48.

73 Eran Fraenkel, "Turning a Donkey into a Horse: Paradox and Conflict in the Identity of *Makedonci Muslimani*," *Balkan Forum* 3, no. 4 (December 1995); Horace G. Lunt, "Some Sociolinguistic Aspects of Bulgarian and Macedonian," in *Language and Literary Theory*, ed. Benjamin Stolz et al. (Ann Arbor: Papers in Slavic Philology, 1984), pp. 87–9.

74 The origins of the Albanians are disputed. For pros and cons, see John V. A. Fine, Jr., *The Early Medieval Balkans* (Ann Arbor: University of Michigan Press, 1983), pp. 9–11.

75 See H. N. Brailsford, *Macedonia: Its Races and Their Future* (New York: Arno Press, 1971 [1906]), for a fascinating description of Ottoman Macedonia at the turn of the twentieth century.

76 A poll of 1,083 adults showed that 65 percent of ethnic Macedonians felt that interethnic relations were not good. Interestingly, only 48 percent of the Albanians consulted said the same. BriMa Poll, cited in USIA Briefing Paper, 15 August 1995.

77 BriMa Poll, cited in USIA Briefing Paper, 15 August 1995.

78 Preamble, *Ustav*, p. 3.

79 See Poulton, *Who Are the Macedonians?* pp. 125, 172–3.

80 Gjorgji J. Tsatsa, *The Constitutional Development of the S.R. of Macedonia* (Skopje: Macedonian Review, 1980), pp. 96–7.

81 Preamble, *Ustav*.

82 *Nova Makedonija*, 10 January 1992 and *Vjesnik*, 17 January 1992.

83 Mickey and Albion, *Minorities*, p. 65.

84 Macedonian Information Service, 17 May 1993.

85 See Fraenkel, "Turning a Donkey into a Horse," p. 158.

86 Zoltan Barany, "The Roma in Macedonia: Ethnic Politics and the Marginal Condition in a Balkan State," *Ethnic and Racial Studies* 18, no. 3 (July 1995), p. 520.

87 See Barany, "The Roma in Macedonia," pp. 519–20.

88 Ibid., p. 522.

89 See Ivan Ilchev and Duncan M. Perry, "Muslims in Bulgaria: Between East and West," in *Muslims in Europe*, ed. Gerd Nonneman (Leeds: Ithaca Press, 1996), pp. 115–37.

90 Barany, "The Roma in Macedonia," p. 526.

91 Fraenkel, "Turning a Donkey into a Horse," p. 161.

92 See T. J. Winnifrith, *The Vlachs: The History of a Balkan People* (New York: St. Martin's Press, 1987), for a comprehensive treatment of Vlachs.

93 To some, the term *Torbeši* is pejorative, hence the government's use of the more neutral but confusing term, Macedonian Muslims. Some leaders claim 100,000–200,000 Macedonian Muslims in the country. That figure seems quite high given the size of the population listed in the census.

94 Fraenkel, "Turning a Donkey into a Horse," pp. 154–5.

95 MILS, 29 May 1995.

96 Lewis, *The Emergence of Modern Turkey*, pp. 335–6; Norma Itzkowitz, *Ottoman Empire and Islamic Tradition* (Chicago: University of Chicago Press, 1972), p. 59.

97 Danforth, *The Macedonian Conflict,* p. 60.

98 The national identity of these monks and their followers is disputed by Bulgarians and Greeks. See Francis Dvornik, *Byzantine Missions among the Slavs* (New Brunswick: Rutgers University Press, 1970) for a dispassionate look at the issues.

99 For a contemporary discussion from the Macedonian perspective, see Miroslav Spiroski, *Borba za Avtokefalnost* (Skopje: Nova Makedonija, 1990).

100 See Fraenkel, "Turning a Donkey into a Horse," pp. 156–7.

101 RFE/RL Correspondent's Report, 31 October 1995.

103 "Review of the Macedonian Education System, Open Society Institute of Macedonia, Educational Programs, 1993-1995," unpublished report (Skopje, 1995).

104 Author's interview with Emilija Simovska, Minister of Education, Skopje, April 1995.

105 Aleksandr Soljakovski, "An Education in Complexity," *WarReport*, October 1992, p. 5, cited in Mickey and Albion, *Minorities*.

106 Author's interview with Emilija Simovska, Minister of Education, April 1995.

107 See Branko Geroski, "Tetovo Trials," *WarReport*, May 1995, p. 15.

108 Interview with Max van der Stoel, *Macedonian Times*, January 1995, p. 6. *Ustav*, Article 46 expressly governs the establishment of universities.

109 Branko Geroski, "Waiting for a Second Chance in Macedonia," *Transition*, 6 October 1995, pp. 42–5.

110 See *Doing Business in Macedonia: A Guide for Investors* (Skopje: Agency for the Republic of Macedonia for Transformation of Enterprises with Social Capital, 1995), p. 9.

111 *Business Central Europe: The Annual*, 1995, pp. 42–3.

112 *Nova Makedonija* and *Flaka*, 11–14 July 1995.

113 National Bank of the Republic of Macedonia, *Bulletin*, no. 1 (August 1995), 86.

114 The figure is from ibid., p. 20. Other sources, such as The Economist Intelligence Unit country report on the former Yugoslav republics for fourth quarter 1995 (p. 21), quote higher figures (e.g., $165 million at end-1994). The latter calculation seems to include claims on nonresident banks, which are usually not seen as part of the foreign reserves. In any case, even the larger numbers are low relative to imports.

115 *Business Central Europe: The Annual*, 1995, pp. 42–3.

116 *Doing Business in Macedonia: A Guide for Investors*, p. 17.

117 Speech by Petar Gošev, DP convention 1994.

118 *Ustav,* Article 98.

119 Ibid., Article 101.

120 Ibid., Article 106.

121 Ibid., Articles 105 and 109.

122 Mickey and Albion, *Minorities*, p. 77.

123 The law differentiates municipalities where the population is 50 percent minority (significant minority) and 20 percent (substantial minority). The distinctions are confusing, but such municipalities as Tetovo, Kumanovo, Gostivar, Debar and, of course, Skopje, qualify for using Albanian and/or Turkish in addition to Macedonian.

124 Author's interview with Ljubomir Frčkovski, Skopje, April 1995.

125 Ibid.

126 US Department of State, 1995 Human Rights Report, Macedonia.

127 Ibid.

128 Author's interview with Vlado Popovski, Minister of Defense, Skopje, 14 October 1992.

129 See the article by Anastasia Karakasidou, "Politicizing Culture: Negotiating Ethnic Identity in Greece," *Journal of Modern Greek Studies* 11 (1993), pp. 1–28.

130 *Mala Enciklopedija Prosveta* (Belgrade: Prosveta, 1969), II, p. 18.

131 Greece was willing to consider modifying the name by some designation such as "north," "Vardar," or "Slav." Macedonia refused to compromise.
132 *Ustav*, Article 49.
133 See Danforth, *The Macedonian Conflict*, pp. 30–7 for a very clear discussion of the problem.
134 See Yannis Valinakis, *Greece's Balkan Policy and the Macedonian Issue* (Ebenhausen: Stiftung Wissenschaft und Politik, 1992) for a lucid presentation of Greek concerns.
135 Interview, MIC, 27 November 1995, *Te Nea*, 24 September 1995.
136 *Dnevnik* and *Nova Makedonija*, 26 April 1996.
137 It is possible that Serbia had a role in this event, meant to destabilize Macedonia and set up the opportunity to intervene.
138 In Albania itself there is a small Macedonian minority, numbering perhaps as many as 20,000, to which limited linguistic and cultural rights have been granted. See Poulton, *Who Are the Macedonians?* pp. 144–7.
139 Danforth, *The Macedonian Conflict*, pp. 80–1.
140 "Izborna programa," *Glas*, October 1994, p. 28. See Danforth, *The Macedonian Conflict*, pp. 42–4. To look out for minority rights, the Sobranie has constituted several organizations, notably the Parliamentary Commission for Minorities, the Survey Commission, and the Council of the Nationalities. The first is a watch-dog for the Sobranie concerning legislation. The latter two are consultative groups. None has been especially active or effective, but all provide potential protection for ethnic minorities and indicate some thought about minority issues.

Albania, Bulgaria, and Romania

8 The process of democratization in Albania

Nicholas Pano

Introduction

Although Albania was the last of the East European Communist Party states to embark on the process of transition from political monism to democratic pluralism and from a centralized planned economy to a market economy, it has registered considerable progress in both areas since December 1990, when President Ramiz Alia acceded to the demands of student demonstrators at the University of Tirana for the establishment of a multiparty political system. Not surprisingly, the absence of a democratic political tradition; the fact that it is Europe's least developed state; the legacy of some four decades of domestic oppression coupled with the enforced isolation from much of the world during the unremittingly Stalinist regime of Enver Hoxha; and the vicissitudes in Tirana's relations with its neighbors in the context of the resurgent nationalism and political instability that have emerged in the Balkans during the postcommunist era have contributed to the tensions and periodic crises that have attended Albania's efforts to effect a democratic transition.

Albania's success between 1991 and 1996 in meeting the challenges arising from its precommunist and communist-era heritage owes much to the economic recovery the country has experienced since 1993; the generally strong and persistent popular sentiment for democratic reforms; the material and moral support of the United States, Western Europe, and a host of international agencies; and the charismatic leadership of the country's first non-communist president, Sali Berisha.

But while there has been discernible progress toward the establishment of a multiparty democratic political system in Albania during the initial six years of the postcommunist era, it is still uncertain whether the current momentum for political and economic reform can be sustained. It is apparent that, given Albania's economic heritage, the process of transforming the nation's economic system will be long and arduous. It is likely that any serious setbacks in this area could trigger internal unrest that in turn would endanger further progress toward democracy. The Albanian political culture, which has been characterized by a low level of popular participation in political activity, has produced a society in which the concept of democratic government, the rule of law, the accountability of public officials, and the expression and toleration of diverse opinions are not firmly rooted or fully understood by both the masses and the postcommunist ruling elite. This factor has contributed to the high level of corruption, abuses of power, and excessive partisanship which, if not checked, could lead to a disillusionment with democracy. Regional tensions in the Balkans also have profound implications for Albania. The problems arising from the presence of significant Albanian minorities in Serbia and Macedonia along with those posed by the small Greek minority in Albania have at times strained Tirana's relations with these states. So long as these issues persist, they have the potential to hinder Albania's economic recovery and to spark the growth of extreme nationalist fervor that could inhibit the transition to democracy – especially in the event that they would lead to hostilities directly involving Albania.

Although all of the former East European Communist Party states have faced similar problems in the transition to democracy and a market economy, they have each been required to confront the challenges posed by their respective historical heritages and by the legacies of their experiences under communism. Thus, my discussion of the Albanian transition process begins with a brief review of the country's historical heritage and continues with an analysis of the communist legacy; the abortive attempt of the ruling Albanian Party of Labor to initiate a controlled transition during the 1990–91 period; the multiparty transitional phase between June 1991 and March 1992; the postcommunist transition following the victory of the Democratic Party in the March 1992 parliamentary elections; an examination of the political, economic, social, and diplomatic aspects of the transition since 1992; and a consideration of the prospects for a successful democratic transition.

The historical legacy

Although the Albanians are the descendants of the ancient Illyrians, among the earliest of the inhabitants of the Balkan Peninsula, they were never able to establish a national state prior to the creation of an independent Albania in 1913, after nearly 450 years of Ottoman domination. Albania owed its existence to the efforts of those nineteenth- and twentieth-century patriotic intellectuals who had raised the national consciousness of their compatriots, the defeat of the Ottoman Empire in the First Balkan War (1912–13), and the decision of the European Powers to establish an independent Albanian state.

From its inception, Albania has confronted formidable obstacles in its struggle for survival.[1]

By sanctioning an independent Albania, the European Powers had frustrated the aspirations of Serbia, Montenegro, and Greece to partition Albania's territory among themselves. Greece was especially agitated at its failure to receive the southern region of Albania that it termed Northern Epirus. The Albanians in turn were disappointed that approximately 45 percent of their compatriots in Kosova and western Macedonia had been excluded from their homeland. These frustrations have contributed to the underlying tensions in relations with these neighboring states.

In respect to its population, Albania is one of the most ethnically homogenous countries in Europe, with Albanians accounting for over 95 percent of its inhabitants.[2] The Albanians themselves are divided into two subgroups: the Gegs, who live in northern and central Albania; and the Tosks, who reside in the south. Neither their differing physical characteristics, nor the distinctive but mutually intelligible dialects of Albanian they speak, had deterred them from cooperating during the era of the National Renaissance. But as Albania embarked on the process of state building in the 1920s, the Gegs, while patriotic, were somewhat resistant to the establishment of a strong central government that threatened their traditional freedoms.

There are also religious divisions among the Albanians. As a consequence of the Ottoman domination, nearly 70 percent of the Albanians had converted to Islam, while 20 percent – mainly among the Tosks – were Eastern Orthodox Christians, and another 10 percent – exclusively Geg – were Roman Catholic. Since Albanians, generally speaking, are not religious fanatics, religion was less a divisive factor than regional, tribal, or class differences. The claim of the Greek government during much of the twentieth century that all Albanian Orthodox Christians were ethnic Greeks coupled with the effort of the Orthodox Church of Greece to control its Albanian counterpart was an additional source of controversy in Greek–Albanian relations and spurred Albania to establish an autocephalous Albanian Orthodox Church.[3]

As is the case today, the Albanian economy in 1913 was the least developed in Europe. Industry was non-existent and both international and interregional trade limited. About 10 percent of the population lived in cities and some 90 percent were illiterate. The nation's infrastructure was primitive, and prospects for economic and social development were not promising owing to a lack of native capital and the limited interest of foreign investors in the country.

Finally, owing to the opposition of the Ottoman authorities and the hierarchy of the Greek Orthodox Church to Albanian-language instruction in the schools and the development of an Albanian-language press, Albanian national consciousness had not fully matured by 1913. The national identity of the Albanians of this era was based on their inhabiting what they viewed as a common domain; their spoken language; their common history, which they preserved and shared; and their pride in the exploits of their fifteenth-century national hero, Skanderbeg. The establishment of an Albanian-language school system and press coupled with the development of a uniform written language served to accelerate the process of national consciousness raising among the newly independent Albanians.

But before the Albanians could turn their attention to nation- and state-building initiatives under their ruler Prince William of Wied, who had been selected by the European powers, World War I erupted, and the country at various times between 1914 and 1920 was overrun and occupied by the armies of its Balkan neighbors as well as those of Austria–Hungary, France, and Italy. Albania's status remained uncertain until November 1921, when the European Powers reconfirmed its independence and boundaries.[4]

Following a period of instability between 1921 and 1924, Bishop Fan Noli (1882–1965), a Harvard-educated Orthodox clergyman, seized power in June 1924. He proclaimed a twenty-point reform program that pledged, among other things, to uproot feudalism, establish the rule of law, reform the judiciary and civil service, modernize the educational system, balance the budget, upgrade the infrastructure, encourage foreign investment, and improve relations with "neighboring countries." Since Noli was able to remain in office for only six months – owing mainly to his political ineptitude – his program was not implemented. But it remained an inspiration and model for future reformers and revolutionaries.

With the collapse of the Noli regime, Ahmet Zogu (1895–1966) emerged as the dominant political personality in Albania. The son of a Geg tribal chieftain, Zogu had studied in military schools in Monastir and Constantinople. He served ably at various times between 1922 and 1924 as minister of war, minister of the interior, and prime minister until forced into exile following the June 1924 Noli Revolution. After his return to Albania, Zogu served as president of the Albanian Republic from January 1925 until September 1928, when a constituent assembly proclaimed Albania "a parliamentary hereditary Kingdom" and bestowed the title "Zog I, King of the Albanians" on the president to underscore the unity of the Albanian nation.

Both as president and king (1925–39), Zog gave his highest priority to establishing a national police force and a central bureaucracy, disarming the northern tribesmen, and eliminating the practice of blood feuds. He supplanted Ottoman civil, commercial, and criminal codes with those based on West European models. But Zog continued his behind-the-scenes interference in the judicial process. Similarly, parliamentary elections were held regularly, but their manipulation by the king and his refusal to sanction a legitimate party system ensured a subservient legislature and fostered voter apathy and alienation.

During the Zog regime, the Muslim and Orthodox religious communities fell under the effective control of the state, and both recognized the primacy of secular law. By 1937, the Orthodox Church, with the strong backing of the monarch, obtained from the Patriarch of Constantinople the autocephalous status it had been seeking since 1922. While the Catholic Church enjoyed a greater degree of freedom owing to its ties with the Vatican and the support it received from Italy, its influence was confined mainly to northern Albania. Catholics, however, due mainly to their educational qualifications, were overrepresented within the central bureaucracy.

Although Zog sought to promote economic and social development, there was only limited progress in these areas, and by 1938 industrial production accounted for about 4 percent of the national income, 15 percent of the people resided in cities and towns, and 80 percent of the population were still illiterate. Zog's reliance on Italy for economic and military assistance resulted in a dependency that culminated in the Italian annexation of Albania in April 1939.

Zog's authoritarian leadership style paralleled that of the other Balkan "royal dictatorships" of the 1920s and 1930s. The Zog regime was characterized by a disregard for the legal and human rights of its citizens, the discouragement of popular participation in the political process, and pervasive corruption. There were anti-government uprisings in 1925, 1926, 1935, 1936, and 1937 which reflected the dissatisfaction of dissident intellectuals, civil servants, and officers regarding Zog's policies, but the Albanian ruler was able to quell these without undue effort. Zog's world outlook coupled with the conditions prevailing in the country ensured that even the rudiments of a civil society would not be found in pre-World War II Albania.

Prior to 1941 communism had been an insignificant factor in Albanian politics.[5] By the time of the Italian occupation, there were probably no more than 200 communists in Albania, and they lacked leadership, had minimal influence, and were divided into four major factions. Under these circumstances, the Comintern had refused to sanction the formation of an Albanian Communist Party. Thus, Albania was the only one of the future East European Communist Party states without an established Communist Party or formal affiliation with the Comintern prior to the outbreak of World War II.

The Albanian Communist Party was finally established in November 1941, following several initiatives from the Kosova–Metohija regional committee of the Communist Party of Yugoslavia (CPY). The

Yugoslav–Albanian cooperation was facilitated by the CPY's endorsement in 1928 and 1940 of Kosovar self-determination. An eleven-member Central Committee was elected with Enver Hoxha as provisional secretary. The majority of the party leadership and 130 original party members were students or young intellectuals, and the remainder were laborers or artisans. With very few exceptions, they had not been trained in the Soviet Union and did not have ties with the Comintern.

The immediate goals of the new Albanian Communist Party were to establish an organizational structure, expand its membership, enhance its influence with the masses, and play a leading role in the resistance movement.[6] By September 1942, the communists had succeeded in organizing the majority of the active anti-Fascist forces in the country into the National Liberation Movement (NLM) to coordinate the resistance effort and establish an administrative structure to govern the liberated regions of the country. As the only organized political party in the NLM, the communists were able to control it and its affiliated Albanian National Liberation Army by placing their growing number of members and supporters in key positions. Thus by the end of 1942, the communists were well positioned to play the leading role in the liberation of Albania.

After repudiating in August 1943 an agreement to join forces with the National Front (NF), the leading non-communist democratic resistance organization, the NLM found itself by year's end confronted by the combined forces of the German army (which had occupied Albania following the capitulation of Italy in September 1943), a pro-German Albanian puppet government, the NF, and the pro-Zog Legality Organization.

During 1944, the communists moved steadily to consolidate their power. At the May 1944 NLM Permet Congress, King Zog (whose exile government had not been recognized by the Allies) was formally deposed and forbidden to return to Albania. At the Congress of Berat in October, a provisional government headed by Hoxha and dominated by the communists was elected, and by December it was installed in Tirana following the German evacuation of Albania and the collapse of the organized non-communist resistance.

Thus, even before the end of World War II the transition to communist rule in Albania had been realized, and Albania had the distinction of being the only country in Eastern Europe where the communists had come to power without direct Soviet assistance and without the presence of Soviet troops on its soil. Albania's new communist leaders were generally young, patriotic, and ambitious, but they had only limited knowledge of and ties to the international communist movement.

The communist legacy

Enver Hoxha was the predominant political personality in Albania from the establishment of the communist regime in 1944 to his death in April 1985.[7] His imprint and influence on all aspects of Albanian life was so pervasive that it served as a restraint upon his successors in addressing the problems they had inherited. During the final years of his lifetime, he had come to view himself as the last of the true Marxist–Leninist leaders and resolutely opposed any change that would cause Albania to deviate from the course he had charted.

Hoxha's major objectives during his lengthy tenure remained constant. They were to maintain and strengthen the grip of the ruling Communist Party, under his leadership, on Albania and on all aspects of life in the country; to modernize Albania in accordance with the Stalinist Soviet model; and to preserve the independence and territorial integrity of Albania.

To achieve his objectives, Hoxha crafted a highly centralized political system in which the ruling Communist Party dominated every sphere of activity and discouraged individual initiative beyond the parameters of the party line. To ensure conformity to his policies, he employed the instruments of the Stalinist coercive compliance system such as the secret police (the *Sigurimi*), a prison camp network, forced labor, internal exile, and periodic party purges. In his efforts to preserve the Marxist–Leninist "purity" of the Albania he sought to fashion, Hoxha limited the country's external contacts, thereby relegating it to the status of the most isolated nation in Europe.

Although Hoxha could take satisfaction in the fact that his regime had succeeded in safeguarding Albania's independence and territorial integrity and in achieving progress in modernizing the economy as well as upgrading the quality of the country's social and cultural life, the price that the Albanian people were required to pay was high. Furthermore, the gains of the Hoxha era – especially in respect to the economy – have proven to be ephemeral, thus creating serious difficulties for his successors and the country.

Hoxha's rise to power was facilitated by the decision of the founders of the Albanian Communist Party (ACP) and their Yugoslav mentors to select a temporary party leader from outside the ranks of the existing communist groups. Hoxha was intelligent, articulate, personable, and apparently familiar with the fundamentals of Marxist–Leninist doctrine. Additionally, as has been observed, he possessed "a boundless and inalienable will to power."[8] These qualities and skills served him well as he consolidated his position in the party hierarchy.

The nature of Albanian communism during the Hoxha era was defined in a series of challenges to Hoxha's leadership that arose at various times from the late 1940s to the early 1980s. In responding to these threats to his authority, Hoxha skillfully capitalized on the divisions that arose within the world communist movement, resorted to repeated purges of party and state elites, and employed mass coercion to ensure that his line prevailed.

The first major test of Hoxha's leadership came between 1946 and 1948 from his major rival, Koci Xoxe, who advocated an accelerated implementation of measures to socialize the economy and the fostering of closer ties with Yugoslavia and the Soviet Union. Although Hoxha embraced the positions supported by Xoxe, the Yugoslavs persisted in their efforts to undermine Hoxha and replace him with the more pliant Xoxe. Hoxha seized upon the opportunity provided by the 1948 Soviet-Yugoslav split to purge Xoxe and his allies at the First Party Congress in November.[9] Following Xoxe's execution in June 1949, approximately 10 percent of the party membership were expelled, and the Ministry of the Interior, Xoxe's main power base, was restaffed with Hoxha loyalists. Hoxha now became an unswerving opponent of Tito and all manifestations of the Yugoslav dictator's "heretical ideology."

During the early 1950s a minority faction in the Albanian Politburo headed by Bedri Spahiu and Tak Jakova had urged a slowdown in the industrial development program launched in the late 1940s, a delay in the collectivization of agriculture, a softer line against religion, a "democratization" of the party, and, after 1953, the initiation of a program of de-Stalinization. Hoxha, who had enthusiastically embraced the Stalinist line in the late 1940s, strenuously opposed these positions as hindrances to the successful construction of socialism in Albania, and by June 1955 Jakova and Spahiu had been purged.

By the time of the Third APL Congress in May 1956, Hoxha had fully established his control over the party. The Politburo and Central Committee were now comprised of Hoxha stalwarts, and there would be no further significant challenges to his policies until the 1970s. Contrary to Soviet advice, Hoxha announced his intention to accelerate the pace of agricultural collectivization and industrial development. His resolve to stay the Stalinist course was reinforced by the turmoil that accompanied de-Stalinization in Poland and Hungary during 1956.

Hoxha's successful defiance of the USSR was made possible by the emergence of the Sino-Soviet rift during the early 1960s. Once Albania was assured of sufficient Chinese economic assistance to survive, Hoxha, beginning in 1964, prepared to implement the Albanian Ideological and Cultural Revolution. As outlined in a July 1964 speech by Ramiz Alia, the most pressing task confronting Albania at this point was to "cleanse the nation's superstructure" of remaining "bourgeois traces and influences" and to prevent the infiltration of "revisionist ideas" from abroad.[10] As the movement unfolded between 1966 and 1969, it was characterized by a series of initiatives to reduce the size of the bureaucracy, abolish military ranks and reintroduce political commissars into the armed forces, improve the status of women and expand their participation in the work force, narrow the salary differentials for all categories of workers, achieve the total collectivization of agriculture and reduce the size of collective farm private plots, and destroy the institutional church and the practice of religion. By 1969, when the Ideological and Cultural Revolution had run its course, it had – at least outwardly – achieved the majority of its objectives. Some 15,000 former bureaucrats were now "gainfully employed in productive labor"; the "military reforms" had been implemented; the Albanian version of the women's liberation movement had resulted in an increase of female representation in all sectors of the economy and all levels of education as well as in a national consciousness-raising campaign to eliminate discriminatory practices against women; and Albania had the distinction of being the only officially designated atheist state in the world.

The Ideological and Cultural Revolution represented a major initiative on the part of the Albanian leadership to mobilize the masses to accelerate the process of nation and state building within a "Marxist–Leninist" framework. Although in part inspired by the Chinese Great Proletarian Cultural Revolution, the Albanians seem to have regarded the contemporaneous Chinese initiative as a confirmation of the correctness of the course they were pursuing, and their common experiences strengthened the ties between Tirana and Beijing during the late 1960s. But unlike its Chinese counterpart, the Albanian Ideological and Cultural Revolution was well planned and controlled by the party, and it did not mask a power struggle between rival leadership factions.[11]

By 1969 most Albanians had tired of the seemingly endless activities associated with this initiative. Discontent was especially pronounced among the nation's youth, who resented the increasing regimentation to which they were subjected. Additionally, the insecurity that gripped Albania following the 1968 Soviet intervention in Czechoslovakia had caused the leadership to improve ties with Greece and Yugoslavia as well as Western Europe and led some of Hoxha's associates to question the wisdom of maintaining a radical domestic posture.

Thus, between 1970 and 1972 Albania enjoyed a period of somewhat relaxed party controls and opened its door a bit to foreign tourism and television. The restrictions and demands on the country's youth also eased, and writers, musicians, and artists with the encouragement of some party officials began to test the boundaries of their new freedom. The evolving realignment of Chinese foreign policy during 1970–72 had also triggered frank and uninhibited discussions in the defense and economic ministries concerning the implications of this development for Albania.[12]

By early 1973, however, Hoxha reversed course again amid reports of mounting school dropouts, high rates of unauthorized absences by young workers, the rise in juvenile delinquency, and the growing popularity of "Western" dress, hairstyles, and music among the nation's youth. Equally distressing to the Albanian dictator was the appearance of books, plays, and artworks that clearly violated the canons of "socialist realism."

The gravity with which Hoxha viewed these developments was reflected in the scope of the purge he initiated within the ranks of the nation's cultural elites and the ferocity of his denunciations of its leaders at the Fourth Plenum of the APL Central Committee in June 1973.[13] In addition to the dismissal and imprisonment of Central Committee members Fadil Pacrami, Todi Lubonja, and Agim Mero, who had promoted the "liberal" line toward youth and culture, there were extensive leadership changes in the Union of Albanian Writers and Artists and the Union of Albanian Labor Youth as well as administrative shifts at Tirana State University. The harshness of Hoxha's response to this perceived threat to the primacy of party authority from the nation's intellectuals and youth stifled creativity in Albania's cultural life for more than a decade and engendered resentment and alienation among the nation's youth.

After suffering a heart attack in October 1973, Hoxha turned his attention to the military establishment, which apparently advocated an easing of party controls over the armed forces and questioned the validity of Hoxha's concept of "people's war" – the mobilization of the masses to defend the homeland in the event of an invasion of Albania. In contrast, the military leadership urged that Albania develop a professional army with modern weaponry to combat aggression selectively from defensible strategic positions and by guerrilla warfare. Additionally, the military hierarchy seems to have questioned Albania's exclusive reliance on China and suggested a reorientation of the nation's foreign policy. Hoxha viewed these attitudes as a threat to party primacy in the military sphere and seems to have feared the possibility of a military putsch.[14] To reassert party control in this mainstay of the regime, Hoxha deposed the top echelons of the military establishment, including Politburo member and Defense Minister Beqir Balluku, reportedly the fourth-ranking member of the ruling hierarchy.

Alarmed by what he regarded as manifestations of "liberalism" in the management of the economy, Hoxha in 1975 unleashed a purge of the economic managerial elites. He was distressed by reports of "experiments" that provided workers with cash and consumer bonuses for exceeding production quotas, encouraged local initiatives in economic planning and management, and established semiautonomous marketing units within various economic enterprises. He was also irritated by suggestions that Albania reduce its dependence on China for economic assistance in light of the deteriorating relationship between the two countries and instead seek to partially finance the 1976–80 five-year plan by soliciting credits from capitalist countries. Hoxha saw these developments as a repudiation of "Marxism–Leninism" and a threat to his regime.[15] In response he proceeded to staff the ministries with carefully selected personnel who could be relied upon to hew closely to the party line. Hoxha thus precluded any possibility of a creative response to the systemic problems that plagued the Albanian economy, especially following the break with China in 1978.

Hoxha's purges during the 1970s had resulted in the dismissal of 41 percent of the Politburo, the expulsion or demotion of 49 percent of the Central Committee membership, and the firing or transfer of the majority of the district party first secretaries. Additionally, there were seventeen cabinet changes between 1972 and 1977.[16] Hoxha had succeeded in rebuffing what he had regarded as challenges to his primacy as a consequence of the tight control he exercised over the nation's internal security forces and the loyalty he commanded from such party stalwarts as Prime Minister Mehmet Shehu and Central Committee Secretaries Hysni Kapo and Ramiz Alia.

In the aftermath of the purges and concerns about his health, Hoxha sought to ensure the continuity of his line by promulgating in 1976 a new constitution. Although the document promised the Albanian people a vast array of human and civil rights, it declared the ruling Albanian Party of Labor as "the sole leading force in the state and society" and proclaimed Marxism–Leninism as the nation's official ideology (Article 3); limited property ownership to personal residences and household goods (Article 23); forbade the granting of concessions to, or the receipt of credit from, foreign companies or states (Article 28); forbade the practice of religion (Article 37); and subordinated the army to the party under the command of the APL first secretary. Additionally, the party statutes were revised to endorse such key Hoxha concepts as economic self-reliance and the struggle against "revisionism."

With the progressive decline in his health during the 1970s, Hoxha began to devote increasing thought to issues relating to the transfer of power following his death. It was apparent that he wanted the succession to be orderly so that party unity would not be undermined and its dominance in Albanian life be challenged; his policies would not be reversed; and his family's future and his place of honor in Albanian history would be secure.

In this connection Hoxha appears to have decided that his longtime ally, Prime Minister Mehmet Shehu (1913–86), should not be his successor owing to his age and health problems as well as personality conflicts with other leading communists. After apparently failing to convince Shehu to step aside in favor of Ramiz Alia, Hoxha's preferred heir-apparent, the Albanian dictator denounced Shehu at a December 1981 Politburo meeting, and subsequently the dispirited Shehu reportedly committed suicide.[17]

Shehu's death triggered, during 1982, the last of Hoxha's purges and was intended to ensure an orderly leadership transition. The victims at this time included such Shehu protégés as Defense Minister Kadri Hazbiu and Minister of the Interior Fecor Shehu. Mehmet Shehu's widow and other family members received prison terms of various lengths. Once the purges had run their course, Alia in November 1982 was appointed head of state (Chairperson of the Presidium of the People's Assembly). During the remaining years of the Hoxha epoch, Alia gradually assumed a greater share of his mentor's duties, and the two developed a close personal relationship. At Hoxha's death in April 1985, Alia succeeded to the party leadership without incident.

During his lifetime Hoxha appeared to have succeeded in achieving the objectives he set for himself and his party. The communists were firmly entrenched in power and Hoxha had managed to survive a series of external and internal threats to his leadership. Hoxha and his associates had imposed and maintained a rigid Stalinist variant of Marxism on Albania – long after this system had been repudiated in the Soviet Union and Eastern Europe. And they had protected the independence and territorial integrity of Albania.

Hoxha ruled through the Albanian Party of Labor, whose membership typically comprised no more than 3 to 4 percent of the population – the lowest ratio of party membership to population among European communist states. To transmit the party line and to mobilize the masses to achieve its objectives, however, Hoxha relied heavily on the mass organizations such as the Democratic Front, the umbrella political organization which all voting age Albanian citizens were expected to join; the United Trade Unions of Albania; Union of Albanian Women; and Union of Albanian Labor Youth. Under the highly centralized political structure that evolved in Albania, local and district party and state organs looked to Tirana for guidance. Similarly, the national legislature and judiciary were pawns of the party. Furthermore, with the abolition of the Ministry of Justice and the legal profession in 1966 even the pretense of the rule of law ceased to exist.

While there was orchestrated enthusiasm and better than 99 percent voter participation for the uncontested elections to rubber stamp the party choices for national and local legislative bodies, the masses had become thoroughly disenchanted with the political process by the end of the Hoxha era. The dreaded secret police, the *Sigurimi*, and its ubiquitous network of informers, coupled with the impact of the periodic purges unleashed by Hoxha, served to stifle public dissent, especially during the final decade of the dictator's life.

Under Hoxha, Albania had made the transition from a subsistence agricultural economy to a mixed economy, with industry and other non-agricultural sectors in 1985 accounting for 65.4 percent of the national income.[18] However, Hoxha's insistence upon implementing his policy of economic self-reliance ultimately put a brake on the pace of industrial expansion and additional exploitation of Albania's national resources. During the Seventh Five-Year Plan (1981–85) the average annual rate of industrial growth fell to 2.7 percent, substantially below the 6.2 percent of the preceding Five-Year Plan. Albania's efforts to underwrite the Plan by relying on its own resources made it difficult to acquire the modern technology necessary to enhance industrial output and to improve its quality. The inefficient highly centralized management structure; the discouragement of administrative innovation and experimentation; the regime's insistence on subsidizing inefficient and unproductive enterprises; the wastage of scarce resources on construction of the nationwide bunker defense system; and a poorly trained, disciplined, and motivated work force all contributed to the growing troubles of Albanian industry.

By the end of the Hoxha era, Albania had progressed further than the other East European party states in socializing agriculture, with about 80 percent of the land under cultivation organized into collective farms and the remaining 20 percent as state farms. Hoxha had sought to expand the amount of arable land by reclaiming marsh lands and terracing hillsides. But neither these measures nor the growth in farm mechanization, expanded use of chemical fertilizer and pesticides, and increase of trained agricultural specialists enabled Hoxha to succeed in realizing his goal to make Albania self-sufficient in food production by 1980. Rather, Hoxha's schemes to reduce the size of collective farm private plots and collectivize the personal livestock of collective farm families alienated the peasantry and contributed to the food shortages that led to rationing during the closing years of the Hoxha epoch. By the Seventh Five-Year Plan, the average annual increase in agricultural output had slipped to 2 percent – barely keeping pace with the 1.9 percent annual population growth for this period.

Although Albania had made economic progress under Hoxha, it nevertheless remained Europe's least developed state with an estimated per capita GNP in 1986 of $930.[19] At Hoxha's death, the deteriorating state of the economy was the most pressing problem confronting his successors. And it was apparent that the nation's problems in this sector had been aggravated by the economic rupture with China and Hoxha's subsequent decision to pursue his policy of self-reliance.

During the Hoxha era Albania experienced a social transformation. The size of the population nearly tripled, rising from 1,122,000 in 1945 to 2,962,000 in 1985. Throughout the period Albania's rate of population growth was the highest in Europe, with the result that by 1985 the average age of the population was 25.7 years, with about 34 percent under the age of

15. Approximately two-thirds of Albania's inhabitants in 1985 had been born during the communist era, and owing to Hoxha's isolationist policy, only a handful had traveled abroad or had direct contact with a foreigner. Indeed, the leadership restricted tourism in part out of fear that exposure to foreigners would have "negative influences" on their compatriots. The regime, however, could not insulate the nation's youth and others from the "harmful" influences of telecasts from such neighboring states as Italy, Greece, and Yugoslavia. With an estimated 200,000 television receivers in service in Albania by 1985, a sizable segment of the population was able to keep abreast of social and political developments in Europe and hope that these might one day encompass Albania.

Economic diversification had altered the profile of the social structure by 1985 with 51 percent of the labor force classified as farmers, 30 percent as factory laborers, and 19 percent as white-collar workers. However, Hoxha deliberately restricted rural-to-urban migration to ensure an adequate labor supply for the agricultural and mining sectors and to prevent urban overcrowding and unemployment. Consequently, 66 percent of the Albanians resided in the countryside, the highest percentage in Europe.

Hoxha's Ideological and Cultural Revolution had given a high priority to the "emancipation of Albanian women." With the establishment of communism, females, who generally comprised 49 percent of the population during this entire period, began to participate more fully in various aspects of national life and by 1985 comprised 47 percent of the labor force, 45 percent of the enrollments in secondary and higher education, and 15 percent of the membership in the APL Central Committee.

Similarly there was notable progress and success in the development of a comprehensive national education system, including the establishment of the State University of Tirana in 1957. The growth of an educated literate population gave impetus to the expansion of the nation's cultural and intellectual life. While it outwardly appeared that Albanian culture was flourishing under communism, the creativity of the nation's intellectuals was stifled by the controls exercised by party censors and the self-censorship practiced by individual writers and artists in the aftermath of the 1970s cultural purges. The conformity and mediocrity resulting from these cultural controls created resentment on the part of Albania's intelligentsia, students, and a growing segment of the public.

Ramiz Alia: the reluctant reformer

Alia was generally regarded as the logical successor to Hoxha and as the most competent member of the Albanian ruling elite.[20] Born in the northern Albanian city of Shkodër in 1925, Alia was one of the few Gegs in the inner circle of the Albanian leadership. He had joined the Communist Youth Organization in 1941 and was admitted to the Communist Party two years later. By 1948 he was a member of the party Central Committee and in 1949 he assumed the presidency of the Communist Youth Organization. After studying Marxist–Leninist theory in the Soviet Union during the early 1950s, Alia began his rapid ascent within the ranks of the communist leadership. In 1956 he became a candidate Politburo member and in 1960 was appointed the Central Committee Secretary for Ideology and Culture. At the Fourth Party Congress in February 1961, he was promoted to full Politburo membership.

Alia's rise to the inner circle of the Albanian party hierarchy was facilitated by his unswerving loyalty to Enver Hoxha and his friendship with Nexhmije Hoxha, wife of the Albanian dictator, with whom he had maintained close ties from their early association in the Communist Youth Organization and later in the Agitation and Propaganda Directorate of the Central Committee.

By the mid-1970s Alia was generally regarded as the fourth-ranking member of the party hierarchy after Enver Hoxha, Mehmet Shehu, and Hysni Kapo. Following the deaths of Kapo in 1979 and Shehu in 1981, Alia had emerged as Hoxha's closest and most trusted collaborator and the dictator's heir apparent. Although Alia had participated in and backed the purge of the opponents of the Hoxha line, he was nevertheless at the time of his succession regarded as one of the more enlightened members of the party leadership.

Alia recognized the gravity of the problems confronting Albania as the Hoxha era was drawing to a close. However, he was initially reluctant to embark upon a program of reform, owing to an unwillingness to call into question the legacy of his late mentor, the restraints of the 1976 constitution, and the conservatism of the majority of his Politburo colleagues and of Nexhmije Hoxha. And when Alia did move to introduce changes into Albania between 1986 and 1990, they were modest in nature and intended to maintain the integrity of the existing system, and especially the political monopoly of the Communist Party.[21]

Upon assuming power, Alia acknowledged that the targets established for virtually all sectors of the Seventh Five-Year Plan had not been fulfilled and that the prospects for the Eighth Five-Year Plan (1986–90) would be similarly bleak if the difficulties confronting the economy were not addressed. He also appears to have understood that the economic problems plaguing the nation along with continuing domestic repression lay at the root of the widespread alienation from and indifference to the regime.

Between 1986 and 1989, Alia sought to effect an economic turnaround by introducing wage incentives for those employed in the production sectors of the economy, granting factory and farm administrators some autonomy in the management of their enterprises, empowering agricultural cooperatives to sell their surplus production on the open market, and encouraging peasants to market the produce from their newly enlarged private plots. He also moved to increase the production and import of consumer goods and to upgrade the quality of consumer services. In this manner, the regime hoped to improve worker productivity and discipline. These measures, however, failed to have the positive effect on the economy that Alia had anticipated. A combination of worker apathy, bureaucratic resistance, unfavorable weather, and a lack of investment capital served to limit the implementation and impact of these reforms and to ensure the failure of the Eighth Five-Year Plan.

To combat the obvious disaffection of Albania's youth, a significant social element in a country where in 1989 the average age of the population was twenty-seven, Alia sought to increase recreational facilities and activities for this group and to ease regulations on clothing and hair styles. He also sanctioned special radio programming (including Western popular music), gave a high priority to creating positions for new entrants in the job market, and promised liberalizing curriculum reforms and the modernization of school buildings and equipment. These measures did not succeed in placating the majority of the country's youth, who remained dissatisfied with their lives and pessimistic about their future prospects in Albania.

Alia was also confronted with considerable discontent on the part of the Albanian intelligentsia and the growing ranks of secondary and university graduates regarding the burdensome strictures which inhibited creativity in literature and the fine arts, and which stifled open and meaningful discussion of issues confronting Albania. Alia and Foto Çami, his successor as Central Committee Secretary for Ideology and Culture, responded to this situation by signaling their willingness to relax somewhat party controls on the press and the arts. Thus, by the late 1980s, the Albanian press began to carry thoughtful articles dealing with social and economic questions confronting Albania. The most dramatic manifestation of this freer atmosphere of expression was the publication in August 1989 of Neshat Tozaj's novel, *Thikat* (Knives), in which the author – an employee of the Ministry of the Interior – presents a graphic account of the blatant violations of civil rights in Albania and other abuses of power by the Secret Police *(Sigurimi)*. Ismail Kadare, the nation's most distinguished writer, reviewed this work favorably in the October 15, 1989 issue of *Drita,* Albania's most prestigious literary newspaper. In this and a subsequent commentary, published in the November 19, 1989 issue of *Drita,* Kadare issued an eloquent plea for a more just Albanian society based on the rule of law, respect for individual rights, and freedom of expression for writers and artists.

Although Alia persisted in his predecessor's unwillingness to mend relations with the United States and the Soviet Union between 1985 and 1989, he did strengthen ties with Europe. By 1987 Greek–Albanian ties had been fully normalized and diplomatic relations with West Germany and Canada established.

In February 1988 Tirana ended its long-standing boycott of multilateral Balkan meetings and organizations by participating in the Belgrade Balkan Foreign Ministers Conference and agreeing to host in Tirana a second meeting of the group scheduled for October 1990. Thus, by the end of the decade of the 1980s, it appeared that in contrast to Hoxha, Alia was subordinating ideology to pragmatism in the conduct of Albanian foreign policy. The major motivations for Alia's diplomatic initiatives were economic – the need to develop markets for Albanian exports and to obtain technical and financial assistance to modernize the economy and improve Albania's competitive position. He also sought to change Albania's unfavorable external image as an isolated police state.

While it is significant that Alia had sought to encourage changes in key sectors of Albanian life prior to the demise of the East European communist regimes in 1989, he never developed a well-defined reform program or plan. It was also apparent that Alia's primary interest was in strengthening the existing socialist system and in ensuring that the leadership would control the process and extent of change in Albania. By 1989, there was still no organized opposition or dissident movement in Albania. Indeed, there was limited enthusiasm for reform within large segments of Albanian society. The party and state bureaucracies had exhibited little interest in implementing changes that would weaken their positions or might even threaten their jobs, and most workers and farmers were apprehensive at the prospect of having their wages based more heavily on the fulfillment of production quotas and quality standards.

Alia's reformist inclinations had elicited the greatest interest and support from intellectuals and students. But even within these groups, there was substantial dissatisfaction with the pace and scope of the changes Alia advocated. Many students, intellectuals, and young workers had developed doubts regarding Alia's commitment to reform following the publication in 1988 of the Albanian leader's sycophantic memoir of his relationship with Enver Hoxha titled *Our Enver*. And it was apparent that Alia himself continued to believe, even as the Romanian communist regime was being dislodged, that Albania could pursue a reform program without undermining socialism or the communist political monopoly. In a December 28, 1989 speech to the district party first secretaries, Alia observed:

The Eastern European crisis has nothing to do with us; it is not a crisis of socialism. For the past three decades our party has been denouncing revisionist treachery . . . but it had separated itself from the revisionists some time ago . . . Our party has not merely confined itself to criticizing revisionism, but has taken measures in our country to ensure that it is free of deviations of a revisionist character, and to be certain that its leadership role is not weakened . . . and that the position of socialism is continually strengthened.[22]

The demise of the Ceauşescus in Romania, however, which had a profound impact on Albanian public opinion, along with public manifestations of dissatisfaction with his policies and worsening economic problems, appear to have caused Alia to accelerate the tempo of reform. As unveiled by the Albanian leader between January and July 1990, changes he advocated focused on such areas as the economy, the political and legal systems, education and religion, and foreign relations. The economic reforms, especially, represented a reiteration and an extension of those initiated during the late 1980s. Alia also encouraged freer dialogue in the press to further the renewal process within the country.

In respect to the economy, the regime sanctioned a decentralization of economic planning and management; allowed the creation of a private sector in retail trade; removed price controls on "nonessential items"; permitted joint ventures and foreign investment in Albania; and guaranteed displaced workers 80 percent of their wages. These reforms, however, could not stem economic decline as work stoppages and political unrest spread and emboldened some critics of the regime to demand the repudiation of socialism and the establishment of a market economy.

There were more dramatic changes in the Albanian legal system and the regime's attitude toward the protection of civil rights. The Ministry of Justice, abolished during the Ideological and Cultural Revolution of the mid-1960s, was reinstated as was the private practice of law. The number of capital crimes was reduced from thirty-four to eleven and penalties for other crimes were ameliorated, the ban on religious worship was lifted, and laws governing the acquisition of passports and foreign travel were liberalized. By discarding some of the more undesirable aspects of the Albanian police state, Alia hoped to rally popular support for the regime and improve Albania's external image.

However, the Albanian leader's steadfast refusal during 1990 to surrender the communist monopoly on power and embrace genuine political pluralism gradually eroded his credibility with the nation's intellectuals, students, and young workers – the vanguard of the emerging opposition movement. Until December 1990, Alia's program for political reform consisted of such elements as contested elections and a ten-year service limit for most party and state offices as well as the transformation of the Communist Party–controlled mass organizations into quasi-political parties to nominate candidates for office. He also promised to convene a constitutional convention to replace the 1976 constitution with a new document that reflected the changing conditions within the country.

In July 1990, the regime had sought to enhance its popularity with the nation's youth by proclaiming a series of measures designed to address some issues of concern to students. These included the expansion of rural secondary schools; the depoliticization of university admission procedures; and the revision of curricula, textbooks, and instructional methodology in the schools to reflect the "new conditions" prevailing in the country.

In a significant departure from Hoxha's ideological legacy, Alia during the spring of 1990 communicated Albania's interest in normalizing relations with the Soviet Union and the United States. Responding to an equally dramatic request from Tirana for membership in the Conference on Security and Cooperation in Europe (CSCE), the organization was initially only willing to grant Albania observer status owing to its long-standing record of human rights violations and its failure to abandon its one-party system. In its quest for international respectability and acceptance, Albania signed the Nuclear Non-Proliferation Treaty, expanded its participation in the activities of the United Nations (UN) and UN agencies, and opened its doors to a host of foreign businessmen, journalists, and statesmen – including UN Secretary-General Pérez de Cuéllar.

A major impetus for change during 1990 had come from a small group of establishment intellectuals who had taken advantage of the relaxation of press censorship to urge a halt to civil rights violations, the expansion and implementation of democratic reforms, an end to Albania's isolation, and the transition to a market economy. The most prominent of these intellectuals was Ismail Kadare, who was joined by, among others, cardiologist Sali Berisha, physician Ylli Popa, economics professor Gramoz Pashko, and writer Besnik Mustafaj. Although the reformist intellectuals appear to have shared similar views regarding the problems confronting Albania, they largely worked independently of each other and continued to hold their Communist Party memberships until late 1990.

Lacking a well-organized opposition, Alia failed to appreciate the extent of the growing popular sentiment for more sweeping economic and political change. His support among the masses declined considerably following his denigration of the approximately 6,000 Albanians who fled the country in July 1990 after taking refuge in foreign embassies and the subsequent harassment of their families.

Alia's prestige further eroded when, during an August 1990 meeting with many of the country's leading intellectuals, he brushed aside the demands of Sali Berisha that Albania embrace genuine political pluralism by authorizing the creation of independent political parties.[23] Amid rumors of pending arrests and other reprisals against selected intellectuals, Ismail Kadare in October 1990 was granted political asylum in France after publicly expressing his disappointment with the unsatisfactory pace of change. The following month Alia announced a series of measures to "strengthen democracy" at meetings of the APL Central Committee and the People's Assembly.[24] They included the promised revision of the 1976 constitution; the passage of a new election law empowering the APL, the mass organizations, and "any other political or social organization or association recognized by law" to field their own candidates for the elections to the People's Assembly scheduled for February 1991; and the intent – at least outwardly – to lessen the role of the APL in government. Alia's initiative was intended to preclude the establishment of a genuine multiparty system and underscore the party's determination to safeguard its leading role in Albanian political life and to delineate the agenda for reform. It did, however, provide a mechanism for the recognition of political organizations outside the APL umbrella.

The postcommunist transition: the initial phase, December 1990–June 1991

As 1990 drew to a close, public disenchantment with Alia became more widespread as the economy headed toward collapse brought on by the breakdown of worker discipline, both in agriculture and industry, and bureaucratic snafus resulting from confusion in and resistance to implementing economic reform. With the government seemingly powerless to arrest the decline of the economy, there was an expectation on the part of at least some party intellectuals that, unless reversed, the situation could result in political and social unrest that could eventually topple the regime.[25] However, most Albanians as well as the inner circles of the leadership as late as the first week of December 1990 apparently did not believe that a confrontation between the regime and the masses was imminent.[26]

The event that triggered the first stage of the Albanian transition was a strike at Tirana University on December 8 by students protesting their miserable living conditions. During the next two days, after police efforts to end the strike had failed, the scope of the protest expanded to include such demands as the legalization of new political parties. Alerted to the growing support for the student demonstrators throughout the country, Alia on December 11 agreed to their demands, and by day's end the Presidium of the People's Assembly had issued a directive authorizing the registration of opposition parties.[27] Alia believed that by avoiding a confrontation that could have led to bloodshed, the APL would still be able to control the situation and follow through with its plans to hold elections in February 1991 and to implement the revised constitution prepared by his hand-picked committee. The first Albanian opposition party of the post-World War II era, the Democratic Party (DP), was thus established on December 12 and officially recognized on December 17.

In preparation for the February 10, 1991 parliamentary elections, the APL in late December 1990 held a national conference where it adopted a reformist party platform in which it affirmed its support for a multiparty political system, the protection of civil rights, and the implementation of a market economy. In his address to the conference, Alia, while defending the APL legacy to Albania, acknowledged that the party and the leadership had made mistakes in the past. He argued, however, that the responsibility for these shortcomings could not be assigned solely to Hoxha, but rather were attributable to the entire party.[28]

The press on December 30 published the text of a new Draft Constitution of the People's Socialist Republic of Albania.[29] The continued designation of Albania as a "people's socialist republic" and the inclusion of a paragraph in the preamble emphasizing the positive role of the ruling Party of Labor in the post-World War II history of Albania suggested that the communists envisioned an unhurried transition to a multiparty political system and market economy. Under the provisions of the draft constitution there were strong guarantees of civil rights for all citizens, including ethnic minorities (Articles 8, 33, 34, 35, 36, 37, 38), and political organizations were recognized as entities "separate from the state" (Article 10). The document recognized three categories of property ownership: state, cooperative, and private (Article 12); and permitted foreign investments and joint economic ventures in accordance with Albanian legislation (Article 19). The state, however, reserved the right to exercise control over the "creation and usage" of private property and "private [economic] initiative" (Article 18).

The draft constitution vested the president, who was to be elected for a five-year term by a two-thirds vote of the People's Assembly, with extensive powers (Article 89). It provided for a presidential veto of legislation, subject to a two-thirds majority legislative override; empowered the president to abrogate "unlawful or irregular acts" of the Council of Ministers, ministries, and local or district governmental bodies; and "when he deems it necessary, to preside over meetings of the Council of Ministers." Additionally, the president was designated as commander-in-chief of the Armed Forces in place of the APL first secretary, as chairperson of the Defense Council, and as chairperson of the Supreme Council of Justice. In this latter capacity the president was in a position to exert considerable influence in the appointment, transfer, disciplining, and discharge of judges and prosecutors.

Albania's initial steps toward political democracy were taken against a growing wave of unrest and violence in the country during December 1990. Noisy demonstrations and wanton acts of vandalism in such cities as Durrës, Elbasan, Kavajë, and Shkodër at this time served as an outlet for the pent-up hostility and rage that had built up among the masses during the 45 years of communist rule. The resulting destruction of machinery, vehicles, warehouses, greenhouses, and other property further disrupted the economy and swelled the ranks of the unemployed. This heightened political and social tension, along with the deepening economic crisis, inspired during late December 1990 and early 1991 a new exodus of some 10,000 refugees, including many ethnic Greek Albanians to Greece.

On December 22, the newly recognized DP inaugurated its first major public activity – a mass rally in Tirana – where its organizers such as Sali Berisha, Gramoz Pashko, Eduard Selami, Neritan Ceka, and Preç Zogaj pledged to persevere in their efforts to establish democracy in Albania until this objective had been achieved; announced that the party newspaper, *Rilindja Demokratike*, would soon begin publication; appealed for moderation and reasoned dialogue in the upcoming political campaign; and requested a forty-day postponement to prepare adequately for the elections.[30] The government initially rejected the latter request.

In the weeks following the legalization of the Democratic Party, the configuration of the new Albanian multiparty political system began to emerge. Following the lead of the United Trade Unions of Albania, the mass organizations proclaimed their independence from the APL. Only the Union of Albanian Labor Youth, however, appears to have made a clean break with the ruling party at this time. Although the mass organizations had slated their own candidates for the parliamentary elections, they had given individual endorsements to about 20 percent of the APL nominees.

The newspapers of the mass organizations such as the Democratic Front's organ *Bashkimi* and the Union of Albanian Labor Youth's *Zëri i Rinisë* began increasingly to take positions independent of those of the APL. Initially the newspaper of the United Trade Unions of Albania, *Puna,* advocated such reforms as higher wages, improved working conditions, and a shorter work week, while at the same time endorsing the government's vigorous measures to restore law and order in the wake of the December riots. Subsequently this newspaper changed its name and became more critical of the APL and the Alia regime. On the other hand, *Drita,* the organ of the Writers and Artists Union, strongly supported the democratic opposition from the onset of political pluralism.

The regime's domination of the press further eroded with the establishment of newspapers by the new political parties. The first of these was the Democratic Party's *Rilindja Demokratike,* which commenced publication on January 5, 1991. It was followed by *Republika,* the organ of the Republican Party, which first appeared on February 10, 1991. By March 1991, the two papers were published twice weekly and had a combined circulation of about 60,000 – with the DP newspaper accounting for about 80 percent – in contrast to the 103,000 of the APL's *Zëri i Popullit.* Owing to their limited distribution capabilities, the opposition newspapers circulated mainly in urban areas, where only 35 percent of the population resided and where the APL's grip on the masses was weaker than in the countryside. The opposition's ability to communicate its message to the electorate was also hindered by the regime's effective control of radio and television and its unwillingness to permit the opposition more than token access to these facilities.

As the initial phase of the electoral campaign unfolded,[31] the newly forming opposition parties joined the Democrats in requesting a postponement until May of the February elections to give them the requisite time to organize their campaigns. In the hope of calming the lingering labor and social unrest, Alia in mid-January 1991 agreed to delay the elections until March 31.

Between December 1990 and January 1991 a total of five opposition parties had registered to contest the APL. These were the Democratic Party, Republican Party, Ecology Party, Agrarian Party, and Democratic Union of the Greek Minority (Omonia). The challenges confronting the fledgling Albanian opposition parties were formidable, and their prospects for success were dimmed by their lack of organizational experience, limited financial resources, and minimal external political contacts.

By the time of the March 1991 elections, the Democratic Party was clearly the largest and most important of the opposition parties. On the eve of the elections, it claimed some 60,000 members, and its newspaper *Rilindja Demokratike* enjoyed the largest circulation of the opposition press. The Democrats favored the establishment of a pluralistic political system based on the rule of law, a full and sincere respect for human rights, and a rapid transition to a free market economy. In connection with the latter goal, the DP leadership advocated the encouragement of foreign investment and joint ventures to accelerate the pace of economic recovery. The Democrats favored scrapping the collective and state farms and returning the land to the peasants who worked it. They also favored Albania's close alignment with Western Europe and the United States to obtain the economic and technical assistance that would be required during the transition period. Additionally, the Democrats expressed their solidarity with the ethnic Albanians of Yugoslavia, rejected the permanent division of the Albanian nation, and pledged to work peacefully within the structure of "the integration process in Europe" to safeguard the civil and human rights of their compatriots and to achieve the long-sought national unity.

The major support for the Democrats came from students, intellectuals, and workers in Tirana and the larger and medium-sized Albanian cities. As noted above, the party in the relatively brief interval between its formation and the March 1991 election was unable to extend its power base to the countryside.

Initially the DP was led by a six-person steering committee whose most prominent members were Sali Berisha and Gramoz Pashko. By February 1991, Berisha, who had been entrusted with the responsibility of developing a nationwide party organization, had emerged as the dominant personality. Born in 1944 into a poor peasant family in the Tropojë district of northeastern Albania, Berisha received his medical degree from Tirana State University in 1967 and subsequently specialized in cardiology. After post-graduate study in France in 1979, Berisha joined the university medical faculty while continuing to practice and engage in research. He was an active member of the APL and served as secretary of the party organization at the hospital where he practiced. Berisha took his party responsibilities seriously and was regarded as an able and energetic administrator. Having mastered four foreign languages, Berisha was able to remain abreast of professional advances in his field and to develop a knowledge of European and American history and literature. Berisha had attracted considerable attention during 1990, when he became one of the most articulate advocates of reform in Albania. In December 1990, Berisha had served as the liaison between Ramiz Alia and the student strikers and had emerged as one of the founders and leaders of the Democratic Party. It soon became apparent that Berisha was the DP's most effective campaigner and organizer.[32]

The Republican Party, formed in January 1991, viewed itself as a moderate, right-of-center party that would offer voters an alternative between the left-wing APL and the centrist Democrats. It advocated a gradual transition to a market economy and the privatization of property to minimize economic and social disruption, favored strong ties with Western Europe and the United States, and paralleled the views of the Democrats on issues relating to civil and human rights.

Of the remaining parties chartered prior to the March 1991 elections, the Democratic Union of the Greek Minority (Omonia) was the most significant. It was originally a cultural association that later functioned as a political party when it obtained permission to nominate parliamentary candidates. Omonia's support was limited mainly to the ethnic Greek minority concentrated in the southern districts of Sarandë and Gjirokastër. The organization was dedicated to protecting the civil and human rights of the Greek minority, preserving its "ethnic and cultural identity," and maintaining economic and social stability in the regions affected by the ongoing exodus to Greece.

Neither the Ecology Party, which sought to raise the nation's awareness of environmental issues, nor the Agrarian Party, which aspired to serve as the advocate for the farmers, was able to attract popular support for their narrowly focused platforms, and the conviction that they were merely stalking horses for the APL further diminished their appeal. Following the new wave of political turmoil that gripped Albania during February, Skender Gjinushi, a former minister of education, and other APL dissidents established the Social Democratic Party (SDP) to promote a social democratic alternative based on West European models for Albania. The recognition of the SDP came too late for the party to compete in the 1991 elections, but it would later join with the Democrats and Republicans to form a loose coalition in opposition to the APL.

Originally, the strategy of the Democratic Party appears to have been to establish a parliamentary base to influence legislation and government policy to the extent possible and to begin to build viable party organizations at the district and local levels so that it could effectively participate in the elections scheduled at these levels in 1992. Once they had undercut the local base of the communists, the Democrats envisioned that their competitive position *vis-à-vis* the APL would be enhanced. In contrast to the gradualist approach of the party leadership, however, the most enthusiastic party supporters – students and young workers – became increasingly vocal in their demands for a total break with the communist past.

During February, student-led demonstrations in Tirana sought to have Hoxha's name removed from Tirana State University and called for the resignation of the government.[33] When these demands were rejected, some 700 students and faculty members went on a hunger strike. As the sympathy for the strikers and their demands extended to many parts of the country, the mobs which had gathered in the streets of Tirana to show solidarity with the strikers grew in size and became increasingly unruly. On February 20, more than 100,000 gathered in Tirana and toppled the larger-than-life statue of Hoxha that had become the focal point of the capital's central square. Apparently at Alia's behest, neither the army nor the security forces intervened to disperse the demonstrators or protect the monument.

Alia now reversed his position and accepted student demands to drop Hoxha's name from the university and replace the government. He requested the resignation of Prime Minister Adil Çarçani and his cabinet and appointed a new government headed by economist Fatos Nano (1952–), one of the APL's leading advocates of reform. Nano's cabinet, which included only four holdovers from its predecessor, was composed largely of communists who shared his views. Owing, however, to the rapidly escalating tension and sporadic clashes between diehard Hoxha loyalists and anti-communist students and workers, Alia declared a state of emergency and announced the formation of a nine-person presidential council to assist him in ruling the country for its duration. Except for Nano, this body was comprised of APL conservatives and hard-liners such as Nexhmije Hoxha, Xhelil Gjoni, and Çarçani. This latest wave of political unrest precipitated the flight of another 20,000 Albanians – this time to Italy.

It was against the background of this highly charged political environment that the election campaign entered its decisive phase in late March. The APL had sought to capitalize on this situation by portraying Alia as an indispensable national leader who alone possessed the experience and prestige to guide the country through the difficult transition it was experiencing. In mid-March Alia claimed that the release of the nation's remaining political prisoners had been completed, and the government made several revisions to the electoral law demanded by the opposition parties, including increasing their representation in the election commissions at all levels. The regime authorized further enlargement of the collective farmers' private plots and lifted the last of the restrictions on private ownership of livestock. It also profited from the March 15 announcement of the restoration of US–Albanian diplomatic relations. The APL may have further benefited from Republican Party leader Sabri Godo's endorsement of reformist APL candidates in districts not contested by his party.

Of greatest advantage to the APL were its well-entrenched national political organization, ample financial and logistical resources to conduct an active national campaign, control of the nation's radio and television facilities, and the conservatism of the rural electorate, who were apprehensive about uncertainties arising from a change of government. Capitalizing on these advantages, the APL conducted a well-coordinated campaign aimed primarily at undercutting the appeal of the Democratic Party by questioning the professional and personal qualifications of its leaders and sowing doubt about the potential negative impact of its reform program on the nation. Sensitive to its weakness in the larger cities, the APL focused its efforts in the countryside, where party leaders accused the opposition of harboring plans to restore farmland to its pre–World War II landowners and authorize foreign property ownership in Albania.

The government provided the opposition parties with office space and equipment, telephone service, motor vehicles, and funding to publish newspapers and finance their electoral campaigns. In the case of the Democratic Party, the cash subsidy amounted to about $150,000, but this along with the allotment of eight motor vehicles and a few fax machines and typewriters did not come close to matching the resources available to the APL. The government's rationing of newsprint to the opposition press and its limiting of the opposition parties' radio and television exposure – especially during the final stages of the campaign – could not be offset by a trickle of external funding to these parties and their utilization of international radio services such as the Voice of America to communicate with voters. Additionally, the relatively brief duration of the campaign did not afford the underfunded and outmanned opposition sufficient time to build the nationwide organization it required to compete effectively with the APL.

Table 8.1 *Parliamentary elections in Albania, 1991*

Party	No. votes	% vote	No. seats People's Assembly	% seats People's Assembly
Labor (APL)	1,046,120	56.17	169	67.6
Democratic	720,948	38.71	75	30.0
Republican	27,393	1.47	0	0.0
Omonia	13,538	0.73	5	2.0
Veterans' Committee	5,241	0.28	1	0.4
Agrarian	1,379	0.07	0	0.0
Ecology	65	0.00	0	0.0
Other	47,836	2.57	0	0.0

Source: *Zëri i Rinisë,* April 20, 1991.

The 1990 election law provided for the election by majority vote in single-member districts of the 250 representatives to the People's Assembly. Approximately 96 percent of the eligible voters participated in the March 31 elections, which resulted in a decisive victory for the APL. As noted in table 8.1, the APL won 169 of the 250 seats in the People's Assembly, giving it the two-thirds majority required to elect the nation's president and a comfortable legislative majority. As expected, the Democratic Party with 75 seats had emerged as the major opposition party, while Omonia with strong backing from the Greek minority concentrated in the Gjirokaster and Sarandë districts of southern Albania captured 5 seats. The Veterans' Committee, an organization sympathetic to the APL, won the final seat. Despite the APL electoral victory, the fact that the fledgling Democrats had garnered 39 percent of the popular vote did not bode well for the future of the ruling party. The poor showing of the Republican Party suggested it would not be a major factor in Albanian politics. And the parliamentary representation for Omonia ensured that issues of concern to the Greek minority would have a public forum.

The results of the election confirmed the rural–urban division of the Albanian electorate. APL candidates won handily in the rural districts in all regions of the country, including a sweep of the three parliamentary seats in Berisha's home district of Tropojë. In Tirana, on the other hand, the Democrats won seventeen of nineteen urban constituencies – even defeating Alia with a political unknown – while they were able to capture only one of the district's rural seats.

Although, as the Democrats correctly observed, there were some irregularities during the balloting and the election districts were drawn up in a manner that resulted in rural overrepresentation in the People's Assembly, the impact of these factors does not appear to have been sufficiently strong to have negated the APL victory. They did, however, contribute to the APL's attainment of its two-thirds parliamentary majority. Consequently, many rank-and-file DP adherents could not reconcile themselves to defeat, and their animosity toward and distrust of the APL was magnified by the shooting deaths on April 2 in Shkodër of four DP activists by police engaged in breaking up a protest demonstration outside the district APL headquarters.

The newly elected People's Assembly met on April 10, but opposition deputies announced a boycott of the session until responsibility for the April 2 Shkodër incident had been established. After eliciting a promise from the APL leadership to create a parliamentary commission to investigate this incident, the opposition members assumed their seats and participated in parliamentary deliberations. Within a week, the investigatory commission reported that the police were responsible for transforming an initially peaceful demonstration of Democratic Party members and sympathizers into a bloody confrontation between demonstrators and law enforcement officials that resulted in the four deaths and injuries to several dozen other marchers.

The People's Assembly gave its highest priority to the drafting of a new constitution for Albania. Although the APL had submitted a revised version of the December 1990 draft constitution to the People's Assembly on April 10 for approval, it did not seek to ram it through parliament when the Democrats objected. Instead the APL agreed to cooperate with the opposition to draft a new document. In contrast to the 129 articles of the December 1990 draft, the Law on Major Constitutional Provisions consisted of only 46 articles and was intended "to serve as the nation's fundamental law until a new constitution was adopted by the People's Assembly during the first quarter of 1992."[34]

The adoption of the provisional constitution, which was approved on April 29, 1991, represented a significant stage in the Albanian political transition by codifying substantive changes, including the endorsement of political pluralism (Article 6) and the renaming of the country. The country was now officially designated as the Republic of Albania and as a "parliamentary republic" (Article 1) based on the "rule of law" (Article 2). The document guaranteed the human and civil rights of all citizens, including the nation's minorities (Article 4); depoliticized the military, police, diplomatic corps, and judiciary (Article 6); endorsed the unfettered freedom and practice of religion (Article 7); recognized and provided equal protection for state, collective, and private property rights (Article 11); and sanctioned the acquisition and ownership of property by foreigners (Article 12). In contrast to the two draft constitutions prepared by the APL, the Law on Major Constitutional Provisions delegated extensive power to the legislative branch. In addition to electing the president, the People's Assembly was given substantial authority to define "the main directions of the internal and foreign policy of the state" and to control the activities of the judiciary and state-owned communications media (Article 16).

Reflecting DP reservations regarding the prerogatives of the president envisaged by the APL in the earlier proposed draft constitutions, the Law on Major Constitutional Provisions had designated Albania a parliamentary republic and enhanced the role of the legislature in the new political structure. Additionally, the April 29, 1991 document somewhat diminished the projected powers of the presidency by assigning responsibility for oversight of the judiciary to the legislative branch and depriving the president of the authority to set aside actions of district and local political units and of ministries that he considered incompatible with the laws of the land, or to preside over meetings of the Council of Ministers when he deemed it appropriate. The president did, however, retain the veto power, the position of commander-in-chief of the armed forces, and virtually all of the duties exercised by the head of state that had been included in the earlier draft constitutions.

Article 24 of the Law on Major Constitutional Provisions stipulated that "the president of the Republic of Albania is the Head of State and represents the whole unity of the people." This article was generally interpreted at the time of its adoption to mean that the office of the president should be nonpartisan in character, and that the incumbent should not hold office in a political party. Accordingly, upon his election as president on April 30 by the People's Assembly, Alia resigned his posts as APL first secretary and as a member of the party's politburo and central committee.

After APL feelers to form a coalition with the opposition had been rebuffed, Alia on May 4 reappointed Nano as prime minister. The new cabinet submitted a progressive legislative agenda intended to promote social reform and the transition to a market economy. However, with the expiration of a worker no-strike pledge in mid-May the newly organized Independent Trade Unions of Albania launched a general strike on May 15 to demand improved working conditions and pay increases ranging from 50 to 100 percent. Subsequently, there were demands for the arrest and trial of the police officers implicated in the April 2 Shkodër incident. Additionally, some opposition leaders hoped that the strike and the deepening national economic crisis could be exploited to demonstrate the inability of the Nano government to address the problems confronting the nation and the need to call for new elections.

As the strike continued into June, it became apparent to the APL leadership that even with their overwhelming legislative majority they could not govern without the support of the opposition, which commanded the loyalty of the factory workers and miners who had brought the economy to a standstill. After renewed appeals from Alia and Nano to form a coalition government, the country's political parties on June 4 agreed to participate in an interim multiparty government of national stability with a mandate limited to addressing the nation's immediate economic problems and to arranging for new elections to be held by May or June 1992.

The postcommunist transition: the second phase, June 1991–April 1992

Following the resignation of the Nano government on June 4, Ylli Bufi, who had served as minister of food since July 1990, was appointed as prime minister of the Government of National Stability. His cabinet consisted of 12 APL members and 7 Democrats with the other 5 posts shared by representatives of the Republican, Social Democratic, and Agrarian Parties. The DP appointees included Gramoz Pashko as deputy prime minister and minister of economics, Genc Ruli as minister of finance, and Perikli Teta as defense minister.

The establishment of the national stability government marked another stage in the postcommunist political evolution of Albania – the end of one-party communist rule. While the Democrats had assumed some serious risks, especially by virtue of their responsibility for the economics and finance ministries, they had decided to pursue this course out of a desire to assist in averting a total economic collapse and a potential descent into national anarchy as well as to preempt a possible effort by Alia to cope with the national crisis by assuming dictatorial powers with the backing of the military and security forces.[35]

As the June crisis reached its climax, the APL sought to come to terms with Albanian political realities in the postcommunist era at the Tenth APL Congress (June 10–13, 1991).[36] Following Alia's departure from the party leadership in April, hard-liner Xhelil Gjoni had emerged as his apparent successor, and his selection to present the keynote speech at the party congress seemed to confirm this speculation. Somewhat surprisingly, Gjoni in his address roundly condemned the main features of Hoxha's domestic and foreign policies, although he praised the late dictator for having preserved Albania's independence and serving as a source of national inspiration and unity. He also criticized politburo members for abusing their authority and even took Alia to task for his hesitancy in initiating reforms and his toleration of shortcomings in the party and government.

In an effort to change its image and better position itself in the political arena, the party changed its name to the Socialist Party (SP), elected former Prime Minister Fatos Nano as president, approved a new executive committee of fifteen members to replace the politburo and an eighty-one-person steering committee in place of the central committee, made numerous personnel changes in the party leadership, and expelled nine former politburo members from the party. The party program sought to emphasize that the SP would be a modern progressive party committed to the principles advocated by European social democratic parties and dedicated to an ongoing – but gradual – transition to a market economy and the continuation of Albania's efforts to strengthen its international ties.

The socialist members of the national stability government, however, took little interest in the restructuring of the former APL in order to avoid alienating their coalition partners. Indeed, the government during the summer of 1991 launched civil and criminal investigations into the activities of the deposed communist leaders following the publication of articles in both SP and opposition newspapers detailing the lavish lifestyles and privileges enjoyed by key members of the former ruling elite. It was apparent that there was growing popular sentiment to punish former rulers for their misdeeds.

Of more immediate concern to the new government, however, was the precarious state of the economy and the breakdown of law and order in many parts of the country.[37] By mid–1991 only about 25 percent of the nation's productive capacity was operational, and it was estimated that industrial and agricultural production for the first six months of 1991 was about half that for the same period in the previous year. Between December 1990 and July 1991, the foreign debt had risen from $254 million to $354 million. To provide the 80 percent wage guarantee for unemployed workers, the government increased the money supply, triggering a dramatic rise in inflation during 1991. The lack of well-defined property rights and the breakdown of law enforcement fueled squabbles over farmland and equipment and resulted in the theft and destruction of both state and private property.

In an effort to forestall economic collapse and to replenish the nation's dwindling food supply, the government appealed to Western Europe and the United States for economic and humanitarian assistance. In September 1991, Deputy Prime Minister Gramoz Pashko made a successful appeal to the G-24 membership for a $150 million emergency aid grant, and that same month Italy dispatched some 700 troops to Albania in what was termed "Operation Pelican" to assist in the distribution of the proffered humanitarian assistance. The Italian initiative was not entirely altruistic, since Rome hoped to stem the flow of illegal Albanian immigration to Italy. In October Albania joined the International Monetary Fund and the World Bank and became a participating member of the European Bank for Reconstruction and Development. With the technical and material assistance of these agencies, the Albanians looked forward to developing long-term strategies for economic recovery and the transition to a market economy.

To promote these processes, the national stability government had sponsored legislation privatizing collective farmlands and began to distribute these lands to the peasantry. It also established the National Privatization Agency to effect the privatization of retail shops and other small service enterprises. By year's end, the retail sector of the economy had largely been privatized. Legislation governing foreign trade was liberalized to permit greater private participation, and an agency was created to encourage foreign investment. While these measures initially had only a limited impact, they did underscore the new regime's commitment to economic reform and participation in the world economy.

The passage of legislation in July to abolish Hoxha's dreaded security force, the *Sigurimi*, at least outwardly, marked another step in repudiating the communist legacy. The *Sigurimi*, however, was replaced by the National Information Service (NIS), another national investigative agency with a nebulous mandate to enforce the provisions of the constitution and national legislation as well as to protect the rights of citizens. To assure an uneasy Albanian public that the new agency was more than a repackaged version of its predecessor, the NIS was prohibited from conducting unauthorized investigations and engaging in political activities. Nevertheless, many Albanians harbored reservations about the role of NIS, especially since it was impossible to purge the new agency of all *Sigurimi* personnel and influences.[38]

Although the government enjoyed greater success in restaffing the uniformed police force, the inexperienced and poorly equipped local public safety personnel were unable to cope with the wave of violent and petty crime that engulfed the nation as unemployment rose and the fear of the coercive power of the law enforcement agencies declined. In desperation, Albania turned to Italy and Interpol for assistance in training and equipping its beleaguered police.

Similarly the new Albanian government turned to the NATO countries as it sought to upgrade the outdated weapons systems, training programs, and command structure of the armed forces. During the last half of 1991, the regime also moved gradually to depoliticize the military by emphasizing its separation from party politics and its subordination to civilian authority. To enhance professionalism and symbolize a further break with the communist legacy, military insignia, which had been abolished in 1966, were restored in November 1991. At the same time, the government sought to reduce military appropriations, which accounted for approximately 15 percent of budgetary expenditures.

In addition to pursuing its domestic reform agenda, the national stability government persevered in its efforts to strengthen the nation's international ties. Albania's orientation toward Europe received a boost when the CSCE granted it full membership on June 19 and the European Community (EC) initiated diplomatic relations with Tirana on the following day. On June 22, an estimated 200,000 to 400,000 Albanians jammed the capital city to greet US Secretary of State James Baker to demonstrate their good will and affection for the United States and their desire for a close relationship between the two countries. Albania's relations with Italy and Greece were complicated by the desire of Rome and Athens to stanch the flow of Albanian refugees and to return those who had entered their borders illegally. Albanian–Yugoslav relations, which had been tense since the 1980s over the Kosova issue, were further stressed by the Kosovar declaration of independence in October 1991. Although the People's Assembly had urged recognition of the self-proclaimed state, the government hesitated to do so given the gravity of the challenges it faced at home.

As 1991 drew to a close, the economy continued to deteriorate, and despite the flow of relief shipments from abroad, there were periodic food shortages which heightened anxiety and undermined confidence in the government. The prestige of the Bufi administration was further diminished by reports of corruption in the distribution of relief supplies, the breakdown of law enforcement, and the appearance in major cities of shantytowns caused by a rural exodus. The widespread despair prevalent in Albania at this time intensified the desire, especially of young males, to emigrate.

By September 1991, it was apparent that differences had arisen within the Democratic Party regarding the domestic program of the national stability government. While Gramoz Pashko and DP Vice-President Neritan Ceka supported the efforts of the new regime, the party president, Sali Berisha, became increasingly skeptical of the government's ability to address the myriad problems it had inherited. At a November 26 party meeting, he threatened to end the DP's participation in the coalition government unless Hoxha's widow and other key members of the deposed communist ruling elite were arrested and tried, the directors of the Albanian radio and television services were replaced, and the date of the parliamentary elections was advanced to February 1992. Although the government response to these demands was generally positive, Berisha was not satisfied. On December 4 he called for DP members to resign from the cabinet and accused the Socialist members of the coalition government of obstructing land reform and of responsibility for the crime wave and refugee crises. He also intimated that the nation's economic crisis could not be resolved so long as the Socialists continued to exercise power. Although Ceka and Pashko did not hide their disappointment with Berisha's decision to force the resignation of the Bufi cabinet, they dutifully supported Berisha's action. Of the five participating parties in the coalition government (the Democratic, Socialist, Social

Democratic, Agrarian, and Republican parties), only the Democrats and Republicans favored its demise.

After consultation with the leaders of the five coalition parties, President Alia on December 14 appointed a new caretaker government comprised of independent technocrats, with outgoing Minister of Food Vilson Ahmeti as prime minister. The new government was charged with assuring that Albania had a sufficient supply of food and consumer necessities to survive the winter of 1991/92, restoring law and order throughout the country, and preparing for new elections.

After protracted discussion, the People's Assembly on February 4, 1992 adopted a new election law and scheduled the elections for March 22.[39] The legislation reduced the size of the People's Assembly to 140 and stipulated that 100 of the members would be elected by majority vote in single-member districts. The remaining forty seats would be apportioned among the parties that polled at least 4 percent of the total vote cast and fielded candidates in at least thirty-three electoral zones spread across at least nine administrative districts according to their percentage of the total vote. This formula was favored primarily by the Socialists and the smaller political parties. The Democrats, who sensed political victory, were willing to support this arrangement in order to avoid further delay in the balloting.

The 1992 Electoral Law specifically banned regionally, ethnically, or religiously based political parties. This provision, which was justified on the grounds that it was intended to discourage the fostering of regional, ethnic, and religious loyalties to the detriment of national unity and cohesion, resulted in the disqualification of the Greek organization Omonia from participation in the 1992 elections. Following protests from the Greek minority, the Greek government, and international civil rights organizations, the Human Rights Union Party (HRUP) was formed on February 24, 1992 to facilitate Greek minority participation in the political process.

Although some two dozen political parties had been registered by the beginning of 1992, only eleven participated in the March 1992 elections – the Agrarian, Communist, Democratic, Democratic Christian, Ecological, Popular Alliance, Republican, Social Democratic, Socialist, Human Rights Union, and Universal Parties. The eleven parties had nominated 521 candidates including but five women, but it was generally expected that the Democrats and Socialists would again be the leading contenders. The Republicans and Social Democrats cooperated with the Democrats in forming an opposition front to the Socialists.

Although it had been represented in the Bufi cabinet, the Social Democratic Party, which was not established until March 1991, was participating in its first national election. Led by Skender Gjinushi, a former minister of education, the party had attracted support from disaffected

Socialists and had been admitted to the Socialist International, thus enhancing its prestige within Albania. The Communist Party of Albania had been founded in January 1992 by hard-line members of the APL who opposed the reforms adopted at the party's final congress in June 1991.

In contrast to the 1991 elections, the Democrats were well organized and amply financed by donations from Albanian communities outside the country. They enjoyed better access to the nation's radio and television facilities and profited from the reconfiguration of the electoral districts, which now tended toward the overrepresentation of urban constituencies. As the campaign unfolded, the Democrats' charismatic leader, Sali Berisha, emerged as the country's most effective and popular political leader.

In the course of the campaign, the Democrats inspired confidence and raised expectations among the electorate by suggesting that their victory would result in a massive influx of foreign aid to Albania and that immigration quotas for Albanians would be established in EC countries. As the plight of the Albanians in Kosova worsened following the outbreak of hostilities in Bosnia in early 1992, Berisha pledged to his beleaguered compatriots that the Democratic Party would persevere in its efforts to ensure that the "great dream of uniting the Albanian nation is realized." In his election eve speech to a mass rally in Tirana's central square, Berisha exuded the optimism that had taken root among the Democrats as the campaign had progressed when he declared:

We are confident that 23 March will mark the end of the Communist night and the first day of the beginning of democracy . . . On 23 March Albania will begin to make its way toward Europe and its political and military integration with the venerable continent of Europe to which it will belong . . . We will be more united than ever under Skenderbeg's flag, around the ideals of democracy.[40]

Berisha's optimism was confirmed by the overwhelming victory of the Democrats in the March 1992 elections. With 90.5 percent of the eligible voters casting ballots, the Democrats garnered 62.1 percent of the popular votes and won 90 of the 100 seats chosen by direct elections. Although the Socialists polled 25.7 percent of the popular vote, they were able to capture seats in only six constituencies. Of the remaining four seats selected by the voters, the HRUP won two and the Social Democrats and the Republicans one each. The Socialists were the main beneficiaries of the allocation by proportional representation, receiving thirty-two of the forty parliamentary seats awarded through this process, with the Social Democrats gaining six and the Democrats two.

In contrast to the March 1991 elections the Democrats exhibited strength in all regions of the country and in both urban and rural constituencies. It was apparent that by the spring of 1992, the overwhelming majority of the Albanian electorate had lost confidence in the ability of the Socialists to

Table 8.2 *Parliamentary elections in Albania, 1992*

Party	No. votes	% votes	Seats direct	Seats proportional	Total seats	% seats
Democratic	1,046,193	62.09	90	2	92	65.71
Socialist	433,602	25.73	6	32	38	27.14
Social Democratic	73,820	4.38	1	6	7	5.00
Human Rights Union (HRUP)	48,923	2.90	2	0	2	1.43
Republican	52,477	3.11	1	0	1	0.71
Others	30,022	1.79	0	0	0	0.00

Source: *Rilindja Demokratike,* April 11, 1992.

address the plethora of problems confronting the nation and that they looked to the Democrats to accelerate the transition to democracy and the market economy as well as to attract the external technical and material support to realize these objectives. With the backing of its Social Democrat and Republican allies, the DP could potentially count on the support of 71 percent of the newly elected parliament to enact its legislative program and to provide the two-thirds majority required to approve a permanent constitution.

In contrast to the 1991 elections, there were few complaints regarding the conduct of the 1992 campaign or balloting. The Socialists accepted the voters' verdict without protest and initially assumed the stance of the loyal opposition. In his speeches to the jubilant Albanian masses in the aftermath of his party's victory, Sali Berisha sought to establish a positive tone by stressing that the Democrats did not intend to seek revenge for past wrongs, but rather would strive to unite the country and focus their efforts on revitalizing the economy, reducing crime, and strengthening Albania's external ties.

The transfer of power to the Democrats was facilitated by the resignation on April 4 of President Ramiz Alia, whose term of office would not have expired until 1996. This act marked the end of the public career of Alia, the sole remaining member of Hoxha's inner circle who was still active politically, and symbolized a new phase of the postcommunist transition.

With the election of Sali Berisha as president on April 9 by the Democratic-controlled parliament, Albania had its first non-communist head of state in nearly fifty years. Although Berisha resigned as leader of the ruling party and engineered the election of Eduard Selami (b. 1961) – the youngest member of the leadership – as his successor, he continued to play a prominent role in the party. His continued activity in the DP resulted from legislation approved on April 9 sanctioning presidential involvement in partisan politics. Other provisions of constitutional legislation approved on this date enabled the president to call, attend, and preside over cabinet meetings. Presidential authority subsequently was further enhanced by means of Law No. 7561, which defined the structure of the Albanian judiciary and established the High Council of Justice, headed by the president, to appoint, dismiss, and discipline all district and appeals court judges and prosecutors.[41]

The constitutional changes approved by the Albanian parliament during the first weeks of the Berisha administration represented a reversal of the 1991 position of the DP that the office of the president should be non-partisan and that the judiciary should be independent of the executive. These developments underscored Berisha's intent to enhance the powers of the president and his determination to continue to play a dominant role in the Democratic Party.

On April 13, the Albanian parliament ratified Berisha's selection of Aleksander Meksi (b. 1939) as prime minister. An engineer and archeologist, Meksi had been one of the founders of the Democratic Party in December 1990. As a Berisha loyalist, he was content to take his cues from the president in respect to both domestic and foreign policy initiatives. A multiparty cabinet in which the Democrats held fourteen seats, independents two, and Social Democrats and Republicans one each was formed to symbolize the unity of the pro-democratic coalition.

Following the installation of the Meksi cabinet on April 19, Berisha focused his efforts on obtaining moral and material backing from abroad. In an address to the European Parliament at Strasbourg on May 5, he made an eloquent plea for humanitarian, technical, and economic assistance; urged the European states to accept Albanian emigrants; and sought to mobilize support for the protection and enhancement of the civil rights of the Albanian ethnic minorities in Kosova and Macedonia. Berisha's post-election travels culminated in his June visit to Washington, where he received the unqualified endorsement of the Bush administration and a $60 million loan package to supplement the $35 million that had been promised in April.

In Albania, Meksi gave a high priority to accelerating the process of privatization, phasing out state subsidy of food prices and the 80 percent wage payments for unemployed workers, reestablishing law and order, combating corruption, and purging the civilian and military bureaucracies. Within the Democratic Party, the influence of the victims of communist persecution had grown as the party made a concerted effort to win their support during 1991 and 1992. The election of an anti-communist author, Pjeter Abnori, who had been interned for twenty-eight years during the Hoxha regime, as speaker of the DP-controlled Parliament and the subsequent selection of Tomor Dosti, another prominent persecuted anti-communist, as DP secretary general, suggested the growing influence of right-wing elements in the ruling party. This development, which had been encouraged by Berisha, was opposed by such DP founders as Gramoz Pashko, Arben Imani, and Preç Zogaj, who feared the party would take on a more decidedly rightist orientation, abandon its announced policy of national reconciliation, and weaken the role and influence of the students and young intellectuals who had established the DP.

Thus, there were tensions in the Democratic Party as the country prepared for local elections in July. Additionally, the Republicans and Social Democrats had decided against running in coalition with the Democrats. Prior to the election, Albania underwent an administrative restructuring which resulted in the division of the country into twelve prefectures, twenty-seven districts, forty-three municipalities, and 310 communes, and Parliament also approved constitutional legislation granting local and district governments greater autonomy from the central government, especially in the administration of public works and social services programs. And on the eve of the elections, the Communist Party, which occupied the extreme left of the political spectrum and which had polled some 8,000 votes in the March balloting, was outlawed.[42]

Despite the disqualification of the communists, the number of parties that competed in the July 26, 1992 local elections rose to thirteen from the eleven that had fielded candidates in March. As the campaign unfolded, it appeared that the Democrats would duplicate their performance in the parliamentary elections. Consequently, many Democratic Party supporters opted to spend election day at the beach rather than vote. The party was also hurt by the overconfidence of its leaders, discord within its ranks, and some popular disappointment with the pace of economic recovery and promised reforms.

According to the official election results, 70.5 percent of the eligible voters participated in the local elections, a 20 percent decline from the turnout in March. The Democrats polled 43.25 percent of the vote to the Socialists' 40.91 percent. An examination of election data suggests that the narrow Democratic victory in the overall popular vote resulted mainly from the failure of their past supporters to cast ballots rather than from the inroads the Socialists were able to make among voters following the parliamentary balloting. The election confirmed that the Democrats and Socialists were the dominant political organizations and that the minor parties, whose popular vote closely paralleled their earlier performance, enjoyed only limited popular support.

The Socialists constituted a plurality of the newly elected members of the municipal, district, and communal councils. They also won twenty-three of the forty-three mayoral contests. The strong showing of the Socialists in the

Table 8.3 *Local elections in Albania, 1992 (votes and seats in percent)*

Party	Votes	Municipal Councils	District Councils	Commune Councils
Democratic	43.25	41.24	38.95	35.76
Socialist	40.91	43.57	44.74	46.75
Social Democratic	4.36	4.81	4.51	5.14
Human Rights Union	4.30	4.96	5.69	4.19
Republican	3.42	3.88	3.43	5.15
Other	3.76	1.25	1.61	1.99

Note: Columns may not add to 100 percent due to rounding.
Source: *Koha Jone*, August 10, 1992.

local elections produced strains in the ill-defined relationship between the central government and the local political units administered by the Socialists. Additionally, it was now necessary to develop a local tax base to finance the activities of local government and to revamp the existing local bureaucracies to enable local governments to discharge their responsibilities more effectively. The challenges of divided government at the central and local levels have served to exacerbate the relations between the two major parties as the Democrats have sought to curb the prerogatives of local and regional government units.

Thus by the summer of 1992, Albania had outwardly made significant progress in its transition to democracy. However, as Albania's leaders sought to implement their program to ensure the definitive transition to political democracy, the market economy, and a more equitable and just society, they have been confronted with a series of challenges arising from the changes that have accompanied the postcommunist transition.

The challenges to democracy

The breakdown of the centrist democratic coalition

The unexpected Democratic setback in the July local elections intensified the strains which had been emerging within the party. There had been growing unease on the part of many of the young intellectuals who had played a leading role in party affairs during 1990 and 1991 regarding the growing authority exerted by Sali Berisha in the formulating of party policy as well as his emergence as its principal spokesperson and most popular personality.

These concerns had mounted as Berisha continued to exercise control of party activities after assuming the presidency.

The first significant break in the party leadership had occurred during the 1992 parliamentary elections, when Gramoz Pashko was elbowed out of the party inner circle and subsequently expelled from its ranks on the eve of the July local elections. Relations between Berisha and Pashko had soured during December 1991 when Pashko had only reluctantly agreed to the dissolution of the Government of National Stability in which he served as deputy prime minister, and they had further deteriorated as the influence of the victims of communist persecution increased within the ruling party.

Pashko's concerns were shared by other DP founders such as Preç Zogaj, Arben Imani, Perikli Teta, and others, who in August 1992 charged that the DP was evolving into a "right-wing party."[43] In this connection, they decried Berisha's initiatives to compensate victims of communist persecution with what they viewed as favored treatment in such areas as employment, university admissions, and housing. They also accused the president of seeking to divert attention from the nation's socioeconomic problems by his efforts to focus blame on the communists for Albania's sorry plight and by bringing former communist officials to trial for their economic crimes. The dissidents also took Berisha to task for parceling out party and state positions to friends and supporters in order to build a personal political power base. In addition, they were unhappy with Berisha's use of the state radio and television services both to combat the Socialists and to enhance his image as well as by the increasingly strident and narrowly partisan stance assumed by the DP's newspaper, *Rilindja Demokratike*. Finally, Berisha's detractors criticized the president and his supporters in the party leadership for having failed to mount an effective campaign in the 1992 local elections.

After the positions espoused by the dissidents had been condemned at a mid-August "extraordinary" party national convention, eight prominent DP founding members including Imani, Zogaj, and Teta either resigned or were expelled from the party.[44] Subsequently, seven of the twelve staff members of *Rilindja Demokratike* resigned to protest increasing DP control over the paper's content – especially the stifling of intraparty debate – and to express their sympathy for their purged colleagues.

Berisha, moreover, emphasized his determination to cement the DP alliance with the rightist forces by sanctioning the arrest in September of former president Ramiz Alia for corruption and initiating legal proceedings against other former APL Politburo members. In this connection, Hoxha's widow was convicted of misappropriation of state funds between 1985 and 1990 and sentenced in early February 1993 to eleven years imprisonment. The determination of the Berisha regime to muzzle what it viewed as irresponsible press criticism of its policies and its proposal to effect a massive removal of communist-era judges and state attorneys by establishing a six-month training program to prepare non-communist jurists and prosecutors provoked a confrontation between Berisha and Attorney General Maksim Haxhia, who had been appointed to his position in May 1992 by Berisha. Haxhia's expressed reservations concerning these initiatives resulted in his dismissal in September and created further tensions between the moderates and rightist factions within the DP.

Following their expulsion from the DP, the seven disaffected former Democratic members of Parliament formed the Democratic Alliance Party (DAP) under the leadership of Neritan Ceka. The DAP was harshly critical of the growing power of Berisha, the rightward drift of the Democrats, the seeming lack of respect for the rule of law and alleged toleration of corruption by the Berisha regime, and the insufficient efforts to address the economic and social problems confronting the nation. In turn, the Democrats argued that since the DAP parliamentarians had been elected under the banner of the ruling party, they should resign their seats and seek election under their new party designation. With the formation of the DAP, the Democrats were now dependent on their Social Democratic and Republican allies to provide the two-thirds parliamentary majority required to ratify a new constitution.

The Democratic Party experienced an additional defection after the forced resignation of Minister of Agriculture Petrit Kalakulla in October 1993 following his declaration during a parliamentary debate that he would have found it more honorable to have been branded a "fascist" than a "communist." Kalakulla, who had been appointed to the cabinet as a sop to the DP right-wing and to silence his criticism of corruption within the ruling party, announced in the spring of 1994 the formation of the Democratic Party of the Right (DPR). He was able to attract the support of only one other parliamentarian, Abdi Baleta – a political maverick who had drifted from the Democratic fold. The DPR favored the restoration of land and property to their pre-war owners, a harsher line against former communist officials and secret police agents, greater compensation and benefits for victims of communist persecution, and a more militant Albanian foreign policy in support of the rights and aspirations of the Albanians of Kosova, Macedonia, and Çamuria (northern Greece). Although Kalakulla and Baleta parted company in early 1995 – mainly for personal reasons – and became bitter rivals, the emergence of the PDR alternative and the formation in 1995 of the League of the Right – an umbrella organization of groups advocating the restoration of pre-World War II property rights – ensured that the Democrats would remain sensitive to the agendas of the League and other right-wing groups.

As the Democratic Party experienced minor defections on both the left and right, its ties with its Social Democratic allies also deteriorated. Relations between the two parties had taken a turn for the worse during the spring of 1993, when the Social Democrats had complained about the delay in presenting the draft of the proposed permanent constitution to Parliament for discussion. When the Democrats subsequently published the text of one of the versions of the document in *Rilindja Demokratike,* before its submission to Parliament, the SDs protested and led a three-month boycott of Parliament that enjoyed the support of the Socialists and HRUP members.

The decisive break between the Social Democrats and the DP occurred during the November 1994 constitutional referendum, when the Social Democrats opposed the draft constitution submitted by their former allies. The Democrats retaliated by fostering the establishment of a splinter party (the Social Democratic Union) comprised of SD supporters of the constitution.

Following the defeat of the draft constitution, the Republican Party, which had backed Berisha, acknowledged that the 1992 alliance of the anti-Socialist forces had collapsed. During 1995, the Republican Party strengthened its ties with the League of the Right, whose land reform program was antithetical to that advocated by the Democrats. The Social Democrats, in turn, entered into discussions with the Democratic Alliance Party with a view to forming a "center pole" that might prove attractive to moderates. The vehemence with which Berisha and other Democratic leaders attacked this initiative betrayed a fear that the "center pole" might have the potential to cut into the party's centrist electoral power base. But these apprehensions seemed groundless considering the results of political polls conducted in late 1995 and early 1996 that indicated the Democrats continued to enjoy the greatest popular support among the Albanian electorate and that the majority of the public endorsed the policies of the Berisha regime.[45]

The quest for a permanent constitution

Albania has since April 1991 been governed by an interim constitution, the Law on Major Constitutional Provisions. Although sporadic efforts had been made to draft a permanent constitution, this task was not pursued in earnest until after the March 1992 parliamentary elections. But the victorious Democrats apparently decided to proceed in two directions. They agreed to the formation of a drafting commission headed by Prime Minister Meksi and comprised of legal experts to prepare a new document, while adopting a series of amendments to "perfect" the interim constitution.

Thus, between April and November 1992, the Democratic-dominated Parliament approved a series of amendments which among other provisions enhanced the powers of the president; reorganized the structure of the justice system and established a Constitutional Court; effected an administrative reorganization; defined and strengthened the authority of the State Control Service; and designated the national flag, emblem, anthem, and holiday of the Republic of Albania. A subsequent amendment on March 31, 1993 outlined the fundamental freedoms and human rights of the Albanian people based on guidelines and advice provided by the Council of Europe.

By March 1993, however, there was growing impatience, particularly among the parliamentary opposition parties, with the delay in completing the draft of the new constitution. At this point the Social Democrats announced their intention to boycott Parliament if the draft constitution had not been submitted for ratification by June 16, 1993. The major remaining disagreement within the drafting commission centered on the powers of the president. Berisha's partisans favored an extensive delegation of power to the executive while the opposition wanted the preponderance of power vested in the legislature. It was the premature publication of an initial draft version of the constitution on June 15, 1993 by *Rilindja Demokratike* that precipitated the three-month parliamentary boycott by the Social Democrats, Socialists, and HRUP.

After the political furor accompanying this episode had subsided, the drafting commission resumed its effort to fashion an acceptable constitution. When the final draft had been completed and submitted to Parliament in late September 1994,[46] it was apparent that the document would not be able to command the two-thirds majority required for approval since it sanctioned the strong presidential powers favored by Berisha. The draft also aroused the opposition of the nation's Greek minority since it contained a clause stipulating that the heads of large religious communities must be native-born Albanians who had resided in the country for twenty years (Article 7). This provision would have called into question the status of the Greek-born Archbishop Anastasios Yanullatos, who had been appointed interim primate of the Autocephalous Albanian Orthodox Church in 1992.

Confident he enjoyed the backing of the majority of the Albanian people, Berisha over the protests of the opposition called for a national referendum to vote on the proposed constitution. Following parliamentary approval of this measure, the referendum was scheduled for November 6, 1994. Although the Socialists challenged the legality of the referendum, the Constitutional Court declined to hear the case, and three of the nine members of this body resigned in protest.

In a television address to the nation on October 3, President Berisha denied that the proposed constitution would establish a presidential republic. He reiterated his strong support for a parliamentary republic and observed that the presidential powers in the proposed draft were in essence similar to those in the amended interim constitution. The opposition in turn charged that Berisha had in fact transformed Albania into a presidential republic.

They focused much of their criticism on Article 109, which reconfirmed the composition and powers of the High Council of Justice, which was chaired by the president and comprised of the minister of justice, chief justice of the Supreme Court, attorney general, and nine lawyers selected by the Supreme Court and the attorney general's office. Since this body had the "sole authority" to appoint, promote, demote, discipline, and transfer judges and state attorneys at all levels, critics of this provision charged that it subordinated the justice system to the executive branch and deprived it of its necessary independence. There were also concerns regarding Article 84, which enabled the president to preside over cabinet meetings in "special situations" and delegated to the head of state responsibility for the implementation of measures submitted by the president for consideration by the cabinet. It was also noted that although under Article 81, the president was precluded from serving as chairperson of a political party, there were no further restrictions on presidential political activities, thus enabling Berisha to continue to exercise his *de facto* leadership role in the Democratic Party.

The proponents of the constitution emphasized the extensive guarantees of civil and human rights enumerated in the document, its specific reference to the separation of powers as an underlying principle of Albanian government (Article 4) as well as its protection of public and private property rights (Article 12), and its endorsement of the market economy. Berisha also pointed out that the document had been drafted with the assistance of foreign legal experts and that its adoption would pave the way for Albania's admission to the Council of Europe. President Berisha further sought to make the referendum a vote of confidence for democracy and the Democratic Party.

According to the report of the Central Referendum Commission on November 11,[47] 84.43 percent of the registered voters cast their ballots, underscoring the high degree of interest in this issue. Contrary to the expectations of the Democrats, the draft constitution attracted the support of only 41.70 percent of the voters while 53.89 percent opposed its ratification. An analysis of the voting patterns reveals that the draft constitution received the approval of the majority of voters in only nine of the thirty-seven administrative districts, mainly in northern Albania. The electorate in both rural and urban areas in central and southern Albania decisively rejected the proposed constitution. While the opposition of the Greek minority appears to have been overwhelming, it did not play a decisive role in the outcome.

The defeat of the constitution was a blow to the prestige and confidence of Berisha and the Democrats. Aside from the displeasure of the Greek minority with the constitutional provision regarding the leadership of major religious communities, the opposition to the constitution stemmed from a growing fear of a strong presidency, a general dissatisfaction with the pace of reform and the prevalence of corruption in Albania, and a negative reaction to the DP campaign strategy designed to make the vote a referendum on democracy.

Although Berisha was disappointed with the results of the referendum, he accepted the verdict and proceeded to initiate exploratory talks with delegates of the parties represented in Parliament to establish a new constitutional drafting committee. When the parties were unable to agree on the composition of the committee, Berisha proposed that Albania should adopt the constitution of one of the nations of Western Europe – an offer that was coldly received by the opposition parties and many intellectuals.

Thus by early 1995 Albania had failed to adopt a permanent constitution. As the country became more heavily embroiled in the political infighting associated with the 1996 parliamentary election campaign, this vital aspect of the political transition has been relegated to the political back burner. It remains to be seen whether the political climate in Albania following the 1996 balloting will be more conducive to the resolution of the constitutional question. But in the meanwhile Albania has taken on many of the characteristics of a presidential republic, a situation largely attributable to the DP's secure parliamentary majority and Berisha's dominance of the ruling party.

The restoration of religion

Hoxha's ban on the practice of religion and the destruction of the institutionalized church in 1967 created several problems for the re-establishment of organized religious activity following the lifting of restrictions on religion in May 1990.[48] Since all the country's churches and mosques had been closed and those not destroyed had been converted into museums or put to a variety of other uses, it was necessary to reconvert them so they again could be used for religious services. Given the fact that the country's clergy and other religious personnel had been forcibly laicized and most had been imprisoned, tortured, or executed, or had died of natural causes during the twenty-three-year period when Albania proclaimed itself the world's only atheist state, it was necessary to rebuild Albanian religious life virtually from scratch.

The various Albanian religious communities received support from their respective co-religionists abroad in rehabilitating their houses of worship and in training and retraining their clergy, obtaining the various liturgical supplies and other materials required to conduct services, and financing their activities. Of the nation's three major religious groups, the Muslims and

Roman Catholics have made the greatest progress in normalizing their situation. By 1996 mosques had been restored or constructed in almost all locations where they had existed prior to 1967. Muslim religious teachers and prayer leaders were retrained either in Albania or in various Islamic countries. The Albanian Islamic community continues to receive external financial and technical support as it seeks to reestablish its spiritual influence in Albania. The appeal of restored Islam in postcommunist Albania, however, appears to be confined largely to the older-generation faithful and to a smaller number of school-age youth, some of whom hope to qualify for study in one of the Islamic countries.

Although the Catholic Church had suffered the greatest degree of persecution during the communist regime, it has made remarkable progress in reassuming its position in Albanian life. The restoration of the administrative organization of the Albanian Catholic Church had been completed by April 1993, when Pope John Paul II visited the country to consecrate four ethnic Albanian bishops, three of whom were survivors of the communist persecution. There were at that time 65 priests, 38 monks, and 150 nuns to conduct the Church's spiritual and humanitarian activities. The Catholic seminary in Shkodër enrolled in 1995 about 100 candidates for the priesthood, with other young Catholic men and women in various stages of preparation for careers in the religious life. The ability of the Catholic Church to reconstitute a hierarchy comprised of ethnic Albanians – coupled with the fact that a substantial percentage of Catholics had remained loyal to the Church despite the pressures to which they were subjected – facilitated the restoration of Catholicism. The staunchly anti-communist Catholic population of northern Albania has constituted one of the major sources of support for the DP. And the historic close relationship between Albanian Catholics and Italy has contributed to the expansion of Italo-Albanian ties during the 1990s.

The restoration of the Albanian Orthodox Church, however, has proceeded less smoothly. This situation is attributable to the fact that all members of the church's hierarchy had died during the 1967–90 period, and there were no qualified Albanian candidates to fill the vacant bishoprics. After consulting with the Albanian government, the Patriarch of Constantinople in July 1992 appointed Archbishop Anastasios Yanullatos, a Greek citizen, to serve as head of the Albanian Orthodox Church until a native Albanian could assume this position. This appointment was welcomed by the country's Greek minority, but greeted with suspicion among large segments of the Albanian Orthodox community. They feared that Yanullatos would seek to "Hellenize" the Church and use its influence to support the demands of Greek ultra-nationalists for the annexation of the Greek-populated regions of southern Albania by Greece or the proposals by ethnic Greeks within Albania for autonomy in the region where they were heavily concentrated.[49]

The expulsion in June 1993 by Albanian authorities of a Greek Orthodox cleric for distributing separatist propaganda among the Greek population in southern Albania resulted in serious tensions between Athens and Tirana. Greco–Albanian ties further deteriorated following the arrest, conviction, and imprisonment during the spring and fall of 1994 of five ethnic Greek Albanians (the Omonia Five) for allegedly conducting an armed attack on a frontier military post that resulted in the deaths of two Albanian soldiers. These episodes strengthened the conviction of those Albanians who view the Orthodox Church of Greece as a driving force behind the nationalist activity of Albania's Greek minority. The 1993–94 tension in Greek–Albanian relations eased in early 1995, when the "Omonia Five" were released from custody by the Albanian Supreme Court.

Although Greek–Albanian relations have generally taken a more positive turn during 1995 and 1996, divisions within the ranks of the Orthodox community continue. The right-wing political forces in Albania, such as the Democratic Party of the Right, the Republican Party, and the right-wing of the Democratic Party, continue to view the Greek hierarchy of the Albanian Orthodox Church with suspicion and hostility. In November 1995, the Orthodox community in Elbasan split into pro- and anti-Yanullatos factions, and the archbishop has asked the courts to resolve this matter. The judiciary, however, has shown little interest in pursuing this delicate matter.

With the exception of banning the Church of Scientology for what it considered dubious and illegal activities, the state has been supportive of religious freedom. The government, however, is dedicated to maintaining the spirit of tolerance that has characterized the nation's religious heritage and has expressed the view that the preaching of fundamentalist religious doctrines is incompatible with this tradition.

Although the Albanian government made attempts to enact laws governing the practice of religion in 1992 and 1993, and in the draft constitution of 1994, these were not approved owing to both domestic and external objections. The present constitutional arrangement does guarantee the free practice of religion and the separation of church and state. Although the regime has sought to maintain cordial relationships with the major religious bodies, it has acted independently of their advice in matters of state policy such as in the approval of legislation in December 1995 legalizing abortion.

Freedom of information

The postcommunist transition to democracy has resulted in the breakdown in the monopoly of the communications media by the former ruling Party of

Labor.[50] Unlike the Soviet Union and several of the former Eastern European Communist Party states, there had been no *samizdat* or underground dissident press in Albania prior to the advent of political pluralism. But as new parties were established during the early 1990s, they published their own newspapers to propagate their views. Thus, the Albanian press that emerged in the postcommunist era has been highly partisan, more concerned with expounding the viewpoints of the respective parties than with factual news coverage. The most important of the party newspapers in mid–1996 were *Zëri i Popullit* and *Rilindja Demokratike*, the organs of the Socialist and Democratic Parties, respectively.

Additionally, "independent" newspapers, ostensibly unaffiliated with any of the political parties have appeared, beginning in 1991. Among the most significant of these are *Koha Jone* (1991), *Gazeta Shqiptare* (1993), and *Albania* (1995). Of the leading independent newspapers, *Koha Jone* and *Gazeta Shqiptare* have been viewed by the ruling Democratic Party as part of the opposition press while the opposition regards *Albania* as an ally of the DP.

The intensifying partisan and polemical character of postcommunist Albanian journalism had prompted seven staff members of *Rilindja Demokratike* to resign en masse in September 1992, explaining in a joint statement:

What really compels us to take this decision is the fact that we are experiencing more and more the burden of censorship. We note that the newspaper's bond with truthfulness which (as stressed in the first issue) was to have been its leitmotif has been shattered. This took place gradually, step by step; today we can say that the key criteria of professionalism and honesty have been replaced with militancy . . . We also observe with regret that the banalities plaguing almost the entire Albanian press are increasingly becoming the norm of *Rilindja Demokratike*. Insults, calumny and slander – now a part of this organ too – targeted against various individuals, are a flagrant breach of journalistic ethics and encroach upon respect for human rights . . . Thus, far from cultivating a new democratic culture, primitive instincts of vengeance-seeking and intolerance are being encouraged.[51]

This dramatic gesture, however, did little to promote professionalism or integrity in Albanian journalism. Additionally, by 1993, there were reports of Albanian and foreign journalists being subjected to police harassment for their writings and investigative activities. In July 1993, Idajet Beqiri, leader of the ultra-nationalistic Albanian National Unity Party and editor of its organ, *Kombi,* was sentenced to six months imprisonment for insulting and slandering President Berisha by characterizing him as "the assassin of the Albanian people" in an editorial in which he had taken the Democratic government to task for having failed to deliver its promised reforms as well as for its allegedly corrupt and anti-democratic practices. Beqiri was the first

Albanian journalist to be imprisoned since the overthrow of the communist regime.

In what was termed an effort to promote responsible journalism and define the legal rights and obligations of the press, a press law was adopted by parliament and approved by President Berisha in October 1993. Despite its being based on the relatively liberal press law of the North Rhine–Westphalia German state, the Albanian legislation has been criticized because, unlike its German counterpart, it is not backed by a constitution that defines the vaguely worded provisions of the law and is not administered by an independent judiciary. Although the DP has defended the law on the grounds that it was necessary to protect the press from arbitrary controls, most Albanian journalists viewed it negatively for restricting access to information and making reporters and editors subject to stringent punishments for violations of its provisions.

The enactment of the 1993 press law has provoked periodic confrontations between the opposition and independent press on the one hand and the government on the other. In one of the most notable of these cases, the editor of *Koha Jone* and one of his reporters were convicted in 1994 of publishing "state secrets" and jailed. Following domestic and external protests, President Berisha pardoned the defendants in this case as well as two other journalists who had run afoul of the press law. During 1995 and 1996, several other journalists were convicted and fined for various violations of the press law.

This legislation thus has not significantly curbed political polemics in the Albanian press nor succeeded in elevating its quality. The state has also apparently found it difficult to act as vigorously as it may have wished against those journalists who were most outspoken in their criticism of government leaders and policies owing to the growing interest of human rights organizations, the European Community, and the US Department of State in issues relating to civil liberties in Albania.

Reflecting the widespread popular distrust of the press and the reliance of younger-generation Albanians on radio and television for information, newspaper circulation has declined. By mid-1995 the Socialist Party organ, *Zëri i Popullit,* and the independent *Koha Jone,* with estimated daily circulations of 25,000 to 30,000, were the most widely read newspapers in the country. The independent daily *Gazeta Shqiptare* claimed a 1995 circulation of approximately 16,000, while the DP organ, *Rilindja Demokratike,* experienced a decline in its readership from 30,000 to 8,000 between 1991 and 1995, owing mainly to its heavily partisan content.

Since 1992, the independent and opposition press has complained about the high taxes and high cost of newsprint that they have been required to pay. During the winter of 1995–96, the government disrupted the distribution of the opposition and independent newspapers by impounding the vehicles used for this purpose for alleged safety violations. Additionally, the Albanian government and Democratic Party sought to undermine popular confidence in the opposition and independent press by alleging they are funded by Greek and Serbian interests and attempting to question the patriotism of their staffs. Despite these obstacles, a free press has managed to take root, if not yet flourish.

Unlike the press, the Albanian Radio and Television Service has remained under state control. Although Parliament has been granted responsibility for oversight of the broadcasting media, they are under the effective control of the executive branch. It is anticipated that legislation authorizing a private broadcasting sector will be passed following the 1996 parliamentary elections. Meanwhile the opposition has complained about the tight government control of radio and television and what it regards as their inadequate coverage of opposition party activities, especially during the 1996 campaign. Telecasts from Italy and Greece and foreign radio broadcasts, however, do enjoy large audiences in Albania and are important sources of information regarding developments both within and outside the country.

The Albanian press, television, and radio have the potential to play a significant role in the creation of a civil society by serving as a processor of public opinion, a government watch dog, and a source of factual information. It will be interesting to observe whether there is progress toward realizing these objectives following the 1996 elections.

Economic and social trends in the postcommunist era

Albania had initiated its privatization program during the period of the National Stability Government (June–December 1991). By the end of 1991, the retail trade sector had been fully privatized, and the transfer of state and collective farmland to private ownership was in progress and planning under way for the gradual privatization of medium- and large-scale enterprises. With the advent of the Berisha regime, the growth of the private sector accelerated, and by 1993 accounted for 20 percent of the employment in the nonagricultural sector.[52]

The privatization of farmland had been largely completed by 1993, and in 1995, 96 percent was independently owned and worked by some 400,000 farmers. The average size of the private farms created under this system was 1.5 hectares, thus rendering it difficult for farmers to support themselves and their families. Until the promulgation of the 1995 land law, farmers could neither purchase nor sell their lands. Under current legislation, peasants may acquire land or dispose of their holdings, but must first offer land they wish to sell to immediate family members or neighbors. In this manner the government hopes to encourage the consolidation of farms to facilitate commercial agricultural production. Although the privatization of agriculture stimulated a growth in farm output between 1992 and 1994 and contributed to Albania's economic turnaround, agricultural production by 1995 appeared to have reached a plateau, and Albania was obliged to increase its food imports to meet domestic demands. Agriculture, however, in 1995 accounted for about 40 percent of the Albanian GDP.

With the initiation of the privatization of housing in 1992, apartment dwellers and those occupying former private dwellings were able to acquire ownership at nominal costs. As in the case of farmland, there were complaints by prewar owners that they had not been compensated for the confiscation of their property. In both cases, the state has sought to satisfy the demands of claimants by compensating them in the form of "bonds" (vouchers) which can be used either to buy shares in enterprises that have been privatized or to purchase shares in state-owned coastal land parcels that will be commercially developed. Squabbles over privatized urban and rural properties have in some cases resulted in bitterly contested litigation and, in rural areas, led to violence.

Between 1991 and 1995, the privatization of some 2,715 small industrial establishments and mechanical enterprises that employed fifteen or fewer workers had been achieved. In 1993, a state agency had been established to restructure, phase out, or sell thirty-two large state enterprises (those employing more than 300 workers) and to dispose of over 300 medium-sized ones (15–300 workers). At year's end state subsidies for these plants were discontinued, and the search for buyers initiated. By 1995, the larger units had not attracted any purchasers and had been either shuttered or were operated as state enterprises. The Berisha regime has announced its intention to privatize the electrical power system, telecommunication services, water supply system, and the chrome and other mining enterprises, while it seeks joint ventures involving the state-owned Albpetrol firm and other foreign oil companies.

By 1995, in the manufacturing and service sectors, retail and wholesale trade and road transportation had been fully privatized; construction, 80 percent privatized; and food processing, 90 percent privatized. During that same year, 70 percent of total employment was estimated to be in the private sector, which accounted for about 60 percent of the country's GDP.

In addition to promoting privatization, the Berisha regime had during July 1992 adopted an IMF macroeconomic stabilization package that required Albania to end all quantitative restrictions on imports, abolish price controls, allow free movement of the exchange rate, reduce its government deficit, phase out its subsidies to unprofitable enterprises, and privatize farmlands. Although the "shock therapy" approach toward the establishment of a market economy succeeded in halting Albania's economic decline, it has created

Table 8.4 *Indicators of economic trends in Albania since 1989*

	1989	1990	1991	1992	1993	1994	1995[a]
GDP	9.8	-10.0	-27.7	-9.7	11	7.4	6
Industrial output	5	-7.6	-36.9	-44	-10	-2	2
Rate of inflation	0	0	36	226	85	22.6	8
Rate of unemployment	n.a.	7.6	11.7	30.3	22.4	19.5	13
GNP per capita	n.a.	n.a.	n.a.	n.a.	999	n.a.	n.a.
% GDP from private sector	n.a.	n.a.	n.a.	n.a.	n.a.	55.0	n.a.

Notes: GDP – % change over previous year; industrial output – % change over previous year; rate of inflation – % change in end-year retail-consumer prices; rate of unemployment, % change, domestic labor force, end of year; GNP per capita – in US dollars at PPP exchange rates. [a]Estimate.
Sources: European Bank for Reconstruction and Development, *Transition Report 1995: Economic Transition in Eastern Europe and the Former Soviet Union* (London: EBRD, 1995); European Bank for Reconstruction and Development, *Transition Report Update, April 1996: Assessing Progress in Economies in Transition* (London: EBRD, 1996).

significant unemployment and caused hardship for pensioners and other low-income recipients who had benefited from the subsidies and services they had received under the communist system.

The data in table 8.4 indicate the significant economic collapse that characterized the first years of the postcommunist transition. They also reflect the turnabout in the economy as a consequence of the policies pursued by the Berisha regime since 1992. The reduction and containment of inflation coupled with the revival of the industrial sector, if they can be sustained, will contribute to a successful transition to a market economy and should promote the internal stability required at this critical period in Albanian history.

Albania's economic recovery has also benefited from the remittances of Albanian emigrants employed abroad, most notably in Greece and Italy. In 1995, the approximately 400,000 Albanian overseas workers sent about $350,000,000 to their families in the homeland. These remittances equaled about 15 percent of the nation's GDP for the year. Additionally, Albania between 1992 and 1995 received $928.2 million in assistance from foreign governments and international agencies. Significantly, the pattern of aid flows to Albania during this time has switched from food and humanitarian relief to development and technical assistance.

Albania's economic survival between 1990 and 1995 was partially underwritten by the approximately $800 million foreign trade deficit the country had accumulated during these years. Owing to this situation, international commercial banks were reluctant to extend further loans to Albania, and this factor coupled with the unsettled conditions in the country discouraged private foreign investment. In June 1995, Albania reached an agreement with its commercial creditors that enabled Tirana to write off 80 percent of this debt and to woo foreign private investors.

As impressive as Albania's economic recovery and revival between 1992 and 1995 has been, it has followed a consumption-led rather than a manufacturing- or even agricultural-led strategy. It should also be noted that despite the impressive economic growth experienced by Albania between 1993 and 1995, the nation's 1995 GDP was still about 15 percent below that for 1989.

If the hundreds of thousands of concrete bunkers scattered throughout Albania symbolize the isolationism and xenophobia of the Hoxha era, then the ubiquitous television satellite dishes are reflective of the open society of the postcommunist transitional period. In contrast to the Hoxha epoch, when Albanians were actively discouraged from tuning in to foreign radio broadcasts or telecasts, by the mid-1990s over 80 percent of the time that Albanian youth spend watching TV is devoted to watching foreign programming.

The end of the Hoxha era resulted in the lifting of restrictions on internal and external migration. Within Albania, the newly acquired freedom has resulted in significant movement from the poverty-stricken rural areas of northern Albania to the cities. It is estimated that the percentage of urban dwellers has risen from 34 percent in 1989 to at least 40 and possibly 44 percent by 1995. The lack of sufficient housing and positions for the newcomers has resulted in the rise of shantytowns on the outskirts of Tirana and other cities.

The greater personal freedom that has characterized post-Hoxha society has also contributed to the rise in crime during the 1990s. Aside from the growth in robberies and burglaries, some Albanians have become active in the transportation of illegal immigrants and emigrants; drug trafficking; and smuggling cigarettes, oil, and stolen automobiles. Police have made an effort to combat crime, and profiting from professional training, they could claim in 1994 that they had solved 85 percent of cases assigned for investigation in contrast to 66 percent in 1991. The crimes that seem to cause the most general concern are kidnappings of children who are taken out of the country and sold for adoption or forced into prostitution. Although there were by the mid-1990s rumors of links between the Mafia and Albanian organized crime, it had not been established that the Mafia was operating in Albania, or whether there was mobster influence in Albanian political life.

During the democratic transition the political role of women has declined. Women comprised only 8 percent of the membership of the parliament elected in 1992, and no women served in the Berisha cabinet until the appointment of Suzana Panariti as Minister of Industry, Transportation, and Trade in 1995. During the 1996 parliamentary campaign, Sali Berisha promised to fill 25 percent of Civil Service positions with females and to provide state assistance to enable women to establish businesses. He appointed four women to the twenty-five-person cabinet that took office in July 1996.

Albanian women by the mid-1990s have succeeded in easing both divorce and abortion restrictions. Feminist activists were also strongly supportive of efforts to secure gay rights legislation and to end police harassment of gays and lesbians.

The passing of the communist era has also seen the establishment and proliferation of non-governmental organizations (NGOs) in Albania. There were an estimated 350 of these groups registered in 1995 and the majority appeared to be functioning. The NGOs include groups dealing with women's, youth, ecological, health, cultural, professional, and human rights issues. These organizations have focused on issues relating to the charters of their organizations and have served as a forum for dialogue in Albania's emerging democracy. Although the NGOs are still striving to establish a role for themselves in Albania, they do have the potential to play a significant role in laying the foundation for a civil society. The nature of the government reaction to the growing activism of the NGOs should serve as a barometer of its sentiments regarding the future role of these groups in Albania.

International trends

The overthrow of communism accelerated the realignment of Albanian foreign policy that had been evolving since the late 1980s.[53] Tirana's major diplomatic goals during the decade of the 1990s have been to strengthen its ties with Western Europe and to become a full-fledged member in good standing of the European community of nations. Albania has accorded an equally high priority to developing and maintaining a cordial relationship with the United States. Tirana has further sought to stabilize ties with its Balkan neighbors and Italy, which now all include significant Albanian minorities.

Albania has enjoyed considerable success in its quest for partnership with Europe. By 1996 it had been admitted to the Council of Europe, tapped for associate status in the European Union, invited to participate in the Central European Initiative, and accepted as a member of the Partnership for Peace. It was also expressing a strong interest in joining NATO. President Berisha traveled extensively through Europe to lobby for closer Albanian association with European nations and for increased infusions of government aid and private investment funds into Albania from these countries. Berisha had earned considerable respect and sympathy for Albania by virtue of the domestic reforms he had introduced as well as for his efforts to restrain further emigration from Albania and for his advocacy of a peaceful resolution to the Kosova question. The Albanian president had developed close ties with the European conservative right-of-center parties and sought to capitalize on this relationship to bolster his prestige and that of the ruling DP in Albania. There had been no major irritants in Tirana's ties with Western Europe until the crisis revolving around the 1996 elections.

US–Albanian relations had progressed satisfactorily following their restoration in March 1991. Prodded in part by the "Greek Lobby," Washington had at times between 1992 and 1996 expressed concern regarding the treatment of the ethnic Greek minority in southern Albania. In addition to providing economic assistance, the United States had taken an interest in the plight of the Albanian Armed Forces and had made available surplus equipment to them and initiated training programs for Albanian military personnel in both the United States and Albania. During the summer of 1995, Albania had provided the United States with a base from which to launch unmanned reconnaissance spy planes for service in Bosnia despite Washington's concerns about human and civil rights violations affecting the Greek minority, the press, and the judiciary. However, relations between the two countries remained cordial, and in September 1995 President Clinton had invited Berisha to Washington to bolster the DP parliamentary campaign. Moreover, during the final weeks of the campaign both Department of State and Department of Defense representatives appeared supportive of the Democrats in the course of visits to Albania.

In its relations with its Balkan neighbors, Greece, Macedonia, and Serbia, all states with sizable Albanian communities, Tirana has followed a consistent policy which holds that all issues relating to these nations must be peacefully resolved. While Albania's relations with Macedonia and Greece have on several occasions between 1992 and 1995 reached crisis proportions, the involved parties have managed to contain these crises before they escalated into a possible violent confrontation.

The most pressing of the regional issues confronting Albania concerns the status of Kosova. Under intensifying oppression from the Serbs during the mid-1990s, Kosovar spokespersons are becoming more insistent that this question be resolved within the context of the Bosnian settlement. While Berisha remains committed to a peaceful resolution of this matter, he has come under increasing pressure from compatriots in Kosova, nationalist elements in Albania, and Albanians of the diaspora to take a firmer stance in behalf of Kosovar independence.

The Kosova issue appears to be moving toward a critical phase at a time when Berisha's image has been tarnished by the irregularities associated with the 1996 parliamentary elections. It seems unlikely that Berisha would abandon his moderate position on this question at a time when Albania's standing with the majority of the European Community and the United States has declined. Berisha will most probably maintain his current responsible stance in order to try to restore Albania to the good graces of his European allies and Washington and preserve stability in the Balkans.

The 1996 parliamentary and local elections

The 1996 Albanian parliamentary election was both a triumph and a tragedy for President Berisha and the Democratic Party as well as for the transition to democracy in Albania.[54] It was a triumph in that the decisive Democratic electoral victory constituted a reaffirmation of the repudiation of communism and assured the DP of a commanding majority in the national legislature, but a tragedy in that the bitterly contested campaign had culminated in serious voting irregularities which had caused the defeated Albanian opposition as well as the European Union (EU), the Organization for Security and Cooperation in Europe (OSCE), the United States, and respected human rights organizations such as Helsinki Watch to question the integrity of the balloting and raise concerns regarding the prospects for democracy in the country.

The intensity with which the campaign was waged stemmed from the perceived decline in popular support for Berisha and the DP following the defeat of the draft constitution in the November 1994 referendum. A massive cabinet reshuffle and the government's announced anti-corruption drive in December coupled with Berisha's failure in February 1995 to muster sufficient parliamentary support to oust Supreme Court Chief Justice Zef Brozi (whose criticisms of political corruption and civil rights violations by law enforcement agencies had irked the president) reinforced the conviction of the Socialist, Democratic Alliance, and Social Democratic party leaders that the DP could be defeated in 1996. The opposition's confidence mounted following a confrontation between Berisha and his political protégé, DP chairperson Eduard Selami, arising from Selami's proposal that the party leader be designated prime minister. Berisha, who viewed this move as a threat to his political dominance, easily squelched this initiative and deposed Selami at a March 1995 party conference. The opposition, however, regarded this episode as further evidence of disarray within the DP and intensified its criticism of the corruption and authoritarianism of the Berisha regime.

Berisha and the DP, in turn, took the threat posed by the opposition seriously. The harsh tone of the DP campaign rhetoric and the no-holds-barred tactics it pursued reflected the extent of its determination to remain in power by discrediting the opposition and by capitalizing on its control of the executive and legislative branches to maximize the party's competitive advantage. Additionally, by September 1995, the party influence within the judiciary was strengthened when President Berisha finally prevailed in his ongoing effort to remove Supreme Court Chief Justice Brozi. Brozi's fate was sealed when he had approved a court review of the case of Fatos Nano, the Socialist Party leader who, following a controversial trial, had been convicted and imprisoned in April 1994 for misappropriation of state funds while serving as prime minister in 1991.

Both to placate DP right-wing elements, who clamored for a more stringent policy toward the nation's former ruling class, and to undermine the opposition, Parliament in September 1995 enacted the "Law on Genocide and Crimes against Humanity Committed during the Communist Regime in Albania." This legislation barred former top-ranking Communist Party and state officials as well as communist-era secret police informers from holding political office until January 1, 2002. A companion law approved in November established a seven-person government-appointed commission to verify the eligibility of candidates for office under the genocide law.[55] Of 139 parliamentary nominees disqualified by this legislation, only 3 were Democrats.

Interparty negotiations leading up to the development of election procedures exacerbated the tensions between the DP and the opposition parties. The opposition charged that the change in the electoral law raising the number of seats filled by direct election in the 140–member Parliament from 100 to 115 was designed to increase representation of the Democrats, who were expected to capture the majority of these constituencies. The remaining 25 seats would be apportioned among the parties that polled at least four percent of the vote on the basis of the percentage of the vote cast for their respective candidates. Opposition leaders also protested the composition of the 17–member Central Electoral Commission, where the Democrats were allotted nine seats, and two of the eight designated for the opposition were assigned to the right-wing Christian Democrat and National Front parties, neither of which was then represented in Parliament, while the Democratic Alliance Party, with seven seats in the legislature, was denied representation. Under another controversial feature of the electoral law President Berisha was empowered to approve the boundaries for the electoral districts. Finally, the president had the responsibility for setting the date of the elections. The president's delay in issuing the official call for the election until just forty-five days before its scheduled date created problems in the planning for and administration of the balloting, thus increasing the mistrust between the government and the opposition parties.

As the campaign unfolded, the DP appealed to the prevailing anti-communist sentiment in the country by branding the Socialists and the

Center Pole coalition of the Democratic Alliance and Social Democrats as a "Red Front" which intended to undo the economic and social reforms that had been instituted since 1992. The Democrats also alleged that the SP and several opposition newspapers such as *Koha Jone* were being subsidized by Serb, Russian, and Greek left-wing and nationalistic organizations. To underscore its unwavering anti-communist agenda, the government during early 1996 instituted legal proceedings against a number of top-ranking members of the former communist regime for "crimes against humanity."

In its quest for votes, the government announced plans for public works projects in various parts of the country and its intention to expand privatization initiatives to public utilities. Additionally, the DP sought to enhance its prestige by eliciting either direct or implied endorsements from the procession of West European and US officials and party leaders who visited Albania as the nation prepared to vote.

Although Berisha and the DP fully exploited the advantage of incumbency to ensure an electoral victory, these efforts were not sufficient to dispel the anxiety of some civil servants, zealous anti-communists, and other beneficiaries of the DP's largess concerning the potential consequences of an opposition victory. These elements, therefore, often with official connivance, sought to undercut the opposition campaign by disrupting their meetings, hindering distribution of their newspapers and campaign literature, and harassing their supporters. To counteract opposition protests concerning these activities, the DP accused the Socialists of having created a paramilitary force to terrorize voters and of having forged ballots to rig the elections in their favor.

It was in this highly charged atmosphere that the Albanians went to the polls on May 26. There were 1,180 candidates representing twenty-four political parties vying for the 140 parliamentary seats. About two hours before the polls closed, however, the Socialists and the Center Pole, subsequently joined by four other parties, announced that they were withdrawing from the elections owing to what they termed massive vote fraud and intimidation of their supporters, and ordered their local electoral commission representatives to leave their assigned polling stations. Two days later, riot police brutally suppressed a protest rally attended by some 800 opposition partisans in Tirana's main square. Although the government condemned the conduct of the police and fired seven high-ranking law enforcement officers for their role in this incident, it simultaneously announced a ban on further "illegal" opposition rallies.

Despite complaints of widespread "irregularities" and "flaws" in the electoral process by the opposition parties along with a majority of the official international monitors and foreign journalists who had observed the elections, President Berisha initially declared that the "shortcomings"

Table 8.5 *Parliamentary elections in Albania, 1996*

Party	No. votes	% vote	Seats direct election	Seats proportional representation	Total seats	% seats
Democratic	914,218	55.53	105	17	122	87.1
Socialist	335,402	20.37	5	5	10	7.1
Republican	94,567	5.74	2	1	3	2.1
National Front	81,822	4.97	1	1	2	1.4
HRUP	66,529	4.04	2	1	3	2.1
Others	153,943	9.36	0	0	0	0.0

Note: Columns may not add to 100 percent due to rounding.
Sources: Communiqué of Central Election Commission, June 17, 1996; ATA, June 21, 1996.

associated with the balloting, while "regrettable," were mainly attributable to the inexperience of election officials and to the disruptive tactics of the opposition, who had decided to abandon the contest when they sensed they had suffered a crushing defeat. Bowing to pressure from European governments and the United States, Berisha subsequently agreed to rerun the election in seventeen constituencies where the Albanian Central Election Commission had determined there had been "serious irregularities" in the voting procedures. This response satisfied neither the main Albanian opposition parties nor the United States, which urged a complete election rerun.

Based on reports of official monitors and journalists, it is apparent that in addition to problems arising from the inexperience of election officials and the inadequacies of the polling facilities, the Albanian parliamentary elections were marred by fraud and misconduct in the recording and tabulation of the vote. An OSCE report notes that the organization's observers had determined that thirty-two of the seventy-nine articles of the election law had been violated.[56] Among the most egregious of these violations were the casting of more ballots than voters assigned to a polling station, counting of opposition ballots for DP candidates, depositing of premarked ballots in ballot boxes, and early closing of some polling stations. Although the fact that these irregularities did occur has been well documented, the extent to which they occurred has not been definitively established.[57] It should also be noted that the opposition's decision to withdraw their representatives from the local electoral commissions facilitated vote fraud. And while these abuses do not appear to have been crucial to the DP victory, they – along with the SP decision to boycott the partial election rerun – seem to have contributed to the magnitude of the Democrat's parliamentary majority.[58] The DP's elation over its electoral triumph was tempered by the critical press and official reaction to the misconduct and shortcomings associated with the campaign and balloting, and the assignment of the lion's share of responsibility for these problems to President Berisha, the government, and the ruling party.

As the data in table 8.5 demonstrate, the DP's parliamentary majority – if it does not fragment – is more than sufficient to provide the two-thirds majority required for the ratification of a constitution and to ensure the re-election of President Berisha, whose term expires in 1997. Indeed, the excesses of the campaign waged by the Democrats aimed to achieve these objectives.

Although the Socialists retained their position as the major opposition party, their parliamentary representation declined by nearly 75 percent despite a drop of merely 5 percent in their share of the popular vote in comparison to 1992. This development, coupled with the SP's decision to boycott the newly elected Parliament, however, diminished the influence of the party. The Socialists had initially hoped to negate the results of the elections by refusing to recognize their validity, as the DP had done in 1991. Lacking the substantial strongly committed base of support their rivals had enjoyed, the SP was unable to achieve this objective.

The Center Pole parties, which between them had thirteen seats in the previous parliament, were also major casualties of the May elections. Neither party was able to win a single constituency or poll the 4 percent of the total vote required to qualify for the seats alloted by proportional representation. The electoral defeat of the Social Democratic and Democratic Alliance parties further weakened the left-of-center opposition to the Democrats and called into question their viability. The DP leadership took especial delight in the poor showing of the Democratic Alliance, which was comprised of defectors from the ruling party.

The remaining parliamentary parties – the Republicans, Human Rights Union, and National Front – are all right-of-center on the political spectrum. Each increased its share of the popular vote compared to its 1992 showing. Although these parties have their own political agendas, it nevertheless appears likely that they will more often be aligned with the DP than in opposition. Thus, if the Socialists decide to assume their seats in Parliament, they will find themselves a weak, isolated minority, even less able to exert their influence than in the previous legislature.

Although the Socialists during the summer of 1996 continued to protest the election results and boycott Parliament, the party at the behest of its imprisoned leader, Fatos Nano, engaged in intensive self-analysis to ascertain the causes of its poor electoral performance and to devise a strategy to enhance the party's image and appeal. At a late August party congress, the Socialists reelected Nano party leader and selected moderates for other leadership posts, agreed to delete all references to Marx and Marxist doctrine from all party documents, reaffirmed their commitment to the implementation of a market economy in Albania, and pledged to transform the SP into a social democratic party on the West European model.[59] Although the DP has sought to downplay the significance of this initiative, the Socialists' belated recognition of the need to unequivocally repudiate their Marxist and totalitarian past could make a positive contribution to effecting the revitalization the SP now requires to become a viable, competitive political party.

Throughout the summer of 1996, Berisha continued to brush aside all protests regarding the parliamentary election and reaffirmed his position that there would be no new elections until 2000. Accordingly, he convened the new Parliament on July 11 and reappointed Prime Minister Aleksander Meksi. Meksi's twenty-five–person cabinet included twenty-one Democrats, two Republicans, a Social Democratic Unionist, and a Christian Democrat. The presence of the non-DP members was intended to symbolize Berisha's willingness to govern with the cooperation of "genuinely democratic" forces. The majority of the cabinet, which included four women, consisted of newcomers – the most prominent of whom was Deputy Prime Minister and Foreign Minister Tritan Shehu, the DP chairperson.[60] It was not immediately apparent whether this appointment signaled Berisha's intention of playing a less visible role in the government or his intention to use Shehu as a counterpoise to Meksi.

Upon assuming office, Meksi indicated that his government would continue to pursue a program featuring balanced economic growth, modernization of the infrastructure, more effective law enforcement, enhanced state welfare programs, and expanded cooperation with Europe. During its first months in office, the new government was also preoccupied with planning for the October 1996 local elections. After initially refusing to participate in this contest as part of their ongoing protest of the May elections, the Socialists and Center Pole parties had by late September reversed their positions. The October elections would thus serve as an important test of the integrity of the Albanian electoral process and represent another important measure of the country's progress toward democracy.

In contrast to the close contest between the Democrats and the Socialists in the 1992 local elections, the DP won a decisive victory in the 1996 balloting for municipal and rural communal offices. Approximately 72 percent of the Albanian electorate participated in the two rounds of voting held on October 20 and 27, 1996.[61]

The DP polled 53 percent of the vote, just 2 percent below its performance in the parliamentary elections, while the Socialists garnered 31 percent – a 10 percent improvement over their showing in the parliamentary contest. The Democrats, however, won fifty-six of the sixty-two mayoralty seats with the Socialists capturing only four. One newly elected mayor was an independent and the other, from the DP stronghold of Shkodër, a coalition candidate running under the joint sponsorship of the National Front and the pro-monarchy Legality Organization. Although the defeat of the DP mayoral candidate in Shkodër appears attributable to local issues – especially official corruption – it remains to be seen whether the Democratic hold on northern Albania would be threatened by the emergence of a future NF–Legality alliance.

The DP also enjoyed considerable success in the countryside, electing 267 of 310 rural commune executives. The Socialists were able to win only fifteen of these posts and the HRUP nine (exclusively in constituencies with large ethnic Greek populations). And, the remaining nineteen positions went to candidates representing six other political groups.

According to the international monitors and journalists who observed the October election, the conduct of the electoral campaign and voting process represented a significant improvement over that of the parliamentary election. There were, nevertheless, some reported irregularities in the counting and recording of votes as well as documented cases of intimidation of DP and opposition voters and election officials. Both European and US observers agreed, however, that these incidences had not been of sufficient magnitude to affect the election results or compromise the voting. Both international and Albanian observers, however, urged the Berisha regime to continue its effort to improve the electoral process.

Prospects for democracy

The prospects for democracy in Albania remain clouded in the aftermath of the 1996 elections. The outbreak of widespread violence following the collapse in January 1997 of speculative pyramid investment schemes, to which some 65 to 75 percent of Albanian families had entrusted their savings, underscored the fragility of the democratic process. With the encouragement and support of a broad spectrum of the opposition parties, the protesters focused their ire on President Berisha and the Meksi government for the failure of the state to regulate or outlaw the speculative ventures whose demise had produced extensive economic misery. Following massive anti-regime demonstrations and armed conflict with the police and military units dispatched to quell the disturbances, the insurgents succeeded in gaining control of the major cities of southern Albania, securing in the process large quantities of military equipment. Confronted with the spread of rebel control in the south, the reluctance and inability of the army and police to undertake concerted action to subdue the uprising, and intense international pressure to resolve the crisis, Berisha agreed to request the resignation of the Meksi government and replaced it in March with a multiparty "government of national reconciliation" headed by the former Socialist mayor of Gjirokastër, Bashkim Fino. Despite rebel demands for his resignation as a precondition for the cessation of hostilities, Berisha on March 3 engineered his reelection for a second five-year term by a nearly unanimous vote of the DP-dominated Parliament. Although Berisha had played a significant role in the negotiations leading to the establishment of the new government, his political dominance in Albania appeared to have ended and his political future was in doubt.

Under the agreement hammered out by Berisha and opposition leaders with some prodding from the United States and the European Union, new parliamentary elections were scheduled to occur no later than June 1997. Additionally, an amnesty was proclaimed for all rebels who surrendered their weapons to the government. These measures, however, failed to placate the rebels, whose demands in mid-March included the resignation of President Berisha, the development of a plan to compensate the victims of the failed pyramid schemes, and the inclusion of representatives of the rebel forces in negotiations for a settlement of the crisis and other political issues. However, the disunity and lack of a stable and effective leadership within the rebel movement, required the development of an appropriate mechanism to facilitate their participation in the pacification and political processes. Meanwhile, conditions within Albania continued to deteriorate, and the country hovered on the brink of anarchy.

Albania's future progress toward democracy will depend heavily on the pace and degree of success in restoring law and order as well as in reasserting governmental authority throughout the country. A major factor in realizing these goals will be the ability of the state to reclaim the vast store of weapons acquired by the rebels and criminal elements from military and police armories as well as to restore the morale and professionalism of the military and police forces. It is apparent that Albania will require external humanitarian, economic, and technical assistance to ameliorate the economic and social consequences of the crisis. The international community must also be willing to provide the necessary encouragement, oversight, and expertise to assist Albania in strengthening its political and legal systems. Of special importance in this latter respect is the need to insist that the laws and procedures governing the forthcoming parliamentary elections ensure that they will be honestly conducted.

Assuming that Albania can transcend the immediate challenges it confronts, the longer term prognosis for democratic transition will be influenced by the nature of the permanent constitution it adopts. The results of the November 1994 constitutional referendum, the findings of a May 1996 poll conducted by the International Republican Institute, and the events that culminated in the 1997 political crisis demonstrate that the Albanians are wary of a strong presidential republic and prefer a parliamentary republic.[62] Albania's experience in the postcommunist era also demonstrates the pressing need to establish an independent judiciary and to delineate clearly the powers of the three branches of government as well as to define more precisely the rights of citizens and nongovernment entities in the constitution. The promulgation of a document embodying these provisions will mark a major stage in Albania's postcommunist evolution.

Prospects for Albania's successful democratic transition would be further enhanced by the establishment of a merit civil service system and improved compensation for government employees as components of a genuine effort to curb corruption. Also important in this respect will be the extent to which the Albanians are able to lower the heat of political rhetoric in the press and in partisan interchanges. The growth of Albanian NGOs in both numbers and influence in the democratization process since 1992, however, has been an encouraging development.

The reform and revitalization of the Albanian economy between 1992 and 1995, the pursuit of closer integration with Western Europe, and the commitment to seek peaceful resolution to issues threatening Balkan stability have undergirded the country's progress toward democracy, enjoyed broad popular support,[63] and enhanced Albania's international image. These efforts must continue to merit a high priority on Albania's agenda for democratization.

NOTES

1 For useful accounts of the Albanian national renaissance, see Stavro Skendi, *The Albanian National Awakening, 1878–1912* (Princeton, NJ: Princeton University Press, 1967); and Johannes Faensen, *Die albanische Nationalbewegung* (Wiesbaden: Otto Harrassowitz, 1980). For overviews of Albanian history, see Anton Logoreci, *The Albanians: Europe's Forgotten Survivors* (Boulder, CO: Westview, 1978); Ramadan Marmullaku, *Albania and the Albanians* (Hamden, CT: Archon, 1975); Nicholas C. Pano, "Albania," in *The Columbia History of Eastern Europe in the Twentieth Century,* ed. Joseph Held (New York: Columbia University Press, 1992), pp. 17–64; Stefanaq Pollo and Arben Puto, *The History of Albania,* trans. Carol Wiseman and Ginnie Hole (London: Routledge & Kegan Paul, 1981); and Miranda Vickers, *The Albanians: A Modern History* (London: I. B. Tauris, 1995).

2 Data from the most recent official Albanian census (April 1989) suggest that Albanians comprise 98 percent of the population. *Statisical Yearbook of the P.S.R. of Albania* (Tirana: Directory of Statistics of the State Planning Commission, 1990), p. 35. A recent analysis of the 1989 census data and 1992 election returns estimates the size of the Greek minority in Albania between 62,106 and 83,301, or 1.9 to 2.6 percent of the population. Arqile Berxholli et

al., "The Greek Minority in the Albanian Republic," *Nationalities Papers* 22, no. 2 (1994), 427–34. Greeks constitute the largest minority group in Albania.

3 See Kristaq Prifti, "The Albanian Autocephalous Church," in *70 Vjet të Kishës Ortodokse Autoqefale Shqiptare* (Tirana: Akademia e Shkencave e Republikës së Shqipërisë, 1993).

4 Two important complementary accounts of Albanian history between 1912 and 1939 are Brend Jurgen Fischer, *King Zog and the Struggle for Stability in Albania* (Boulder, CO, and New York: East European Monographs/Columbia University Press, 1984); and Michael Schmidt-Neke, *Entstehung und Ausbau der Königsdiktatur in Albanien, 1912–1939* (Munich: R. Oldenbourg, 1987).

5 For a discussion of the Albanian Communist movement between 1917 and 1941, see Nicholas C. Pano, *The People's Republic of Albania* (Baltimore, MD: Johns Hopkins University Press, 1968), pp. 26–43.

6 For the establishment of the Albanian Communist regime and its policies into the 1970s, see Pano, *People's Republic of Albania*; Peter R. Prifti, *Socialist Albania since 1944* (Cambridge, MA: MIT Press, 1978); and Luan Omari and Stefanaq Pollo, *The History of Socialist Construction in Albania* (Tirana: "8 Nëntori," 1988). For the World War II power struggle between the communists and non-communists, see Reginald Hibbert, *Albania's National Liberation Struggle* (London: Pinter, 1990).

7 For analyses of Hoxha's world outlook and his policies, consult *The Artful Albanian: The Memoirs of Enver Hoxha*, ed. Jon Halliday (London: Chatto and Windus, 1986); Bernhard Tönnes, *Sonderfall Albanien: Enver Hoxhas "eigener Weg" und die historichen Ursprünge seine Ideologie* (Munich: R. Oldenbourg, 1980); and Nicholas Pano, "Enver Hoxha's World," *The World & I* 2, no. 11 (November 1987), 410–16.

8 Milovan Djilas, *Rise and Fall* (London: Macmillan, 1985), p. 111.

9 At its First Congress the Albanian Communist Party was renamed the Albanian Party of Labor (APL) to better reflect "the social composition of the party and country." *History of the Party of Labor in Albania,* 2d ed. (Tirana: Institute of Marxist–Leninist Studies, 1982), p. 249.

10 *Zëri i Popullit,* 11 July 1964.

11 Nicholas C. Pano, "The Albanian Cultural Revolution," *Problems of Communism* 23, no. 3 (July/August 1974), 44–57.

12 Author's interview with Behar Shtylla, Tirana, September 1993.

13 See Instituti i Studimeve Marksiste–Leniniste, *Dokumente Kryesore të Partisë së Punës të Shqipërisë,* vol. 6 (Tirana: "Mihal Duri," 1978), pp. 347–99.

14 Enver Hoxha, *Vepra,* vol. 53 (Tirana: "8 Nëntori," 1987), pp. 395–516.

15 Ibid., vol. 54, pp. 408–98.

16 This analysis is based on data from the US Central Intelligence Agency's *Directory of Officials of the People's Republic of Albania* for 1970 and 1974, the *Directory of Officials of the People's Socialist Republic of Albania* for 1977, and Albanian press accounts.

17 The most detailed account of this episode is Bashkim Shehu, *Vjeshta e Ankthit* (Tirana: Albinform, 1994). The author, one of Shehu's sons, is unable to determine whether his father in fact committed suicide or was murdered on orders from Enver Hoxha.

18 Unless otherwise noted, the economic and social data reported have been derived from the *Statistical Yearbook of the People's Socialist Republic of Albania* for 1988, 1989, and 1990 published by the State Planning Commission.

19 World Resources Institute, *World Resources, 1990–91* (New York: Oxford University Press, 1990), p. 245.

20 My appraisal of Alia is based on numerous interviews and conversations with a broad spectrum of Albanian political leaders and citizens between December 1990 and August 1995.

21 For discussions of developments in Albania between 1985 and 1989, see Elez Biberaj, *Albania: A Socialist Maverick* (Boulder, CO: Westview, 1990); and *Albanien im Umbruch: Eine Bestandsaufnahme*, ed. Franz-Lothar Altman (Munich: R. Oldenbourg, 1990). For some interesting perspectives on Alia's policies through 1990, see Ismail Kadare, *Nga një dhjetor në tjetrin: Kronikë, kembim letrash, persiatje* (Paris: Fayard, 1991); Todi Lubonja, *Ankthi pa Fund i Lirisë: Shënime* (Tirana: Albinform, 1994); and *Unë, Ramiz Alia: Dëshmoj për historinë*, ed. Blerim Shala et al. (Prishtinë: "Zëri," 1992), pp. 115–205.

22 Ramiz Alia, *Fjalime e Biseda*, vol. 7 (Tirana: "8 Nëntori," 1990), p. 605.

23 For a partial transcript of this dialogue, see Shala, *Unë, Ramiz Alia*, pp. 159–72.

24 See Mehmet Elezi, *Shansi i tretë* (New York: Adam & Peck, 1993), pp. 13–20.

25 *Zëri i Popullit*, 12 December 1995.

26 The author was in Albania from December 1 to 15, 1990, and witnessed the transformation in Albanian public opinion and the growing militancy of students and young workers during this time. See *Chicago Sun-Times*, 17 December 1990.

27 Shala, *Unë, Ramiz Alia*, pp. 187–92.

28 Albanian Telegraphic Agency (hereafter ATA), 1 January 1991. Unless otherwise noted, all ATA citations are from its daily News Bulletin.

29 Ibid., 30 December 1990.

30 Ibid., 29 December 1990.

31 For useful discussions of the 1991 election, see National Democratic Committee for International Affairs (NDCIA), *Albania: 1991 Elections to the People's Assembly* (Washington, DC: NDCIA, 1991); and National Republican Institute for International Affairs (NRIIA), *The 1991 Elections in Albania: Report of the Observer Delegation* (Washington, DC: NRIIA, 1991).

32 Biographical information on Berisha derived from *Democratic Party of Albania* (Tirana: Democratic Party, 1992), p. 27; and *Aleanca*, 28 July 1995.

33 For varying perspectives on these developments, see Shala, *Unë, Ramiz Alia*, pp. 193–205; *Rilindja Demokratike*, 23 February and 19 June 1991.

34 For the text of this document, see Minnesota Lawyers International Human Rights Committee (MLIHRC), *Trimming the Cat's Claws: The Politics of Impunity in Albania* (Minneapolis, MN: MLIHRC, 1992), Appendix 2.

35 Author's interview with Gramoz Pashko, Tirana, 5 August 1995.

36 For a summary and analysis of these developments, see Elez Biberaj, "Albania at the Crossroads," *Problems of Communism* 40, no. 3 (September–October 1991), 9–12.

37 For a discussion of these economic trends and policies during 1991, see Mario I. Blejer et al., *Albania: From Isolation toward Reform* (Washington, DC: International Monetary Fund, 1992), pp. 53–7.

38 *Bashkimi,* 29 July 1991. One of the most comprehensive accounts of the domestic
    and foreign policies of the coalition governments of 1991 and 1992 is Ramiz Alia,
    Shpresa dhe zhgenjime (Tirana: "Dituria," 1993), pp. 75–215. Also useful is
    Petro Dhimitri, *Kundër Kommunizmit, "Jo" edhe Berishës!* (Tirana: "Monroe,"
    1995), pp. 61–71.
39 On the 1992 elections see Commission on Security and Cooperation in Europe
    (CSCE), *Albania's Second Multiparty Elections, March 22 and 29, 1992*
    (Washington, DC: CSCE, 1992).
40 ATA, 21 March 1992.
41 Ibid., 30 April 1992.
42 Louis Zanga, "Albania's Local Elections," *RFE/RL Research Report,* 18
    September 1992, 29–30.
43 *Rilindja Demokratike,* 7 August 1992.
44 For an overview of the breakdown of the unity of the Democratic Party, see
    Dhimitri, *Kundër Kommunizmit,* pp. 98–120. My perspectives on the dynamics
    of Albanian politics between 1992 and 1995 have benefited from interviews and
    conversations with Vangjush Gambeta (Tirana, September 1993, January 1994,
    and August 1995), Abdi Baleta (Tirana, September 1993), Sali Berisha and
    Eduard Selami (Tirana, January 1994), Maxim Haxhia (New York, January
    1995), Leka Toto and Tomor Dosti (Tirana, August 1995), Namik Dokle (Tirana,
    August 1995), and Gramoz Pashko (Tirana, August 1995, and Washington, DC,
    November 1995).
45 Polls conducted during November 1995 by Public Opinion Strategies, a US firm,
    and Eurobarometer, a European Union polling center, indicated that Berisha
    enjoyed a 60 percent approval rating and that among potential voters approxi-
    mately 40 percent supported the DP and 20 percent the Socialists. *Illyria,* 23
    January 1996; *Albanian Times,* 12 February 1996. An early 1996 poll conducted
    by the Tirana-based Society for Democratic Culture indicated that the Democrats
    held a lead of 38.4 percent to 20.5 percent over the Socialists and that Berisha
    was the most popular politician in the country. *Albanian Times,* 6 May 1996.
46 The text of the draft constitution was published in *Rilindja Demokratike,* 6
    October 1994.
47 ATA, 11 November 1994.
48 For a useful summary of trends in religion during the post-Communist transition
    in Albania, see Fabian Schmidt, "Albania's Tradition of Pragmatism," *Transition,*
    5 April 1996, pp. 33–5, 63.
49 For a discussion of issues relating to the Greek minority in Albania, see
    Minnesota Advocates for Human Rights (MAHR), *Trial Observation Report: The
    Albanian Trial of Five Ethnic Greeks for Espionage* (Minneapolis, MN: MAHR,
    1994); Human Rights Watch, *Albania: The Greek Minority* (New York: Human
    Rights Watch, 1995).
50 A comprehensive examination of issues pertaining to freedom of expression in the
    media appears in Human Rights Watch, *Human Rights in Post-Communist Albania*
    (New York: Human Rights Watch, 1996), pp. 64–92.
51 Quoted in *East European Reporter,* September–October 1992, pp. 64–5.
52 For a discussion of the economic and social policies of the Berisha/Meksi
    government, see *Kontrata e Partisë Demokratike më Shqipërine* (Tirana: "Rilindja
    Demokratike," 1995), pp. 28–108. For data and analysis on Albanian economic

and social changes from 1991 to 1995, cf. *Albania and the World Bank: Building the Future* (Washington, DC: The World Bank, 1994); *Human Development Report, Albania 1995* (Tirana: UNDP, 1995); *Financial Times,* 2 October 1995 (Supplement/Survey on Albania); and *Human Development Report: Albania, 1996* (Tirana: UNDP, 1996).

53 For perspectives on key aspects of Albania's foreign policy, see Fabian Schmidt, "Winning Wary Recognition for Democratic Reforms," *Transition*, 25 August 1995, pp. 3–7; Marianne Sullivan, "Seeking the Security of Military Might," ibid., pp. 8–10; Marianne Sullivan, "Mending Relations with Greece," ibid., pp. 11–16; and Fabian Schmidt, "Strategic Reconcilation in Kosovo," ibid., 17–19, 72.

54 For perspectives on the 1996 parliamentary elections, see Organization for Security and Cooperation in Europe (OSCE), "Report on the Parliamentary Elections in Albania: 26 May 1996" (Vienna, 1996); OSCE, Office for Democratic Institutions and Human Rights, "Observation of the Parliamentary Elections Held in the Republic of Albania: May 26 and June 2, 1996" (Warsaw, 1996); Republic of Albania, Central Electoral Commission, "Central Electoral Commission Response to the ODIHR Report 'On the Observation of May 26 and June 2, 1996 Parliamentary Elections in the Republic of Albania'" (Tirana: unpublished, 1996); Anthony Daniels, "Eye of the Beholder," *National Review* 48, no. 12 (1 July 1996), 43–5; and Human Rights Watch, *Democracy Derailed: Violations in the May 26, 1996 Albanian Elections* (New York: Human Rights Watch, 1996).

55 For translations of the texts of these laws, see *Human Rights in Post-Communist Albania,* pp. 140–9.

56 See OSCE, "Report on the Parliamentary Elections in Albania," pp. 12–13.

57 See Republic of Albania, Central Electoral Commission, "Press Release," 16 June 1996; Heritage Foundation, Executive Memorandum, "Setting the Record Straight on the Albanian Elections," 14 June 1996; *Albanian Times*, 16 July 1996.

58 Election-day exit polls conducted by the International Republican Institute and the Albanian Society for Democratic Culture projected the DP vote at 56 percent and the Socialist vote at 22 percent.

59 See *Zëri i Popullit*, 25–28 August 1996.

60 ATA, 21 July 1996.

61 For the official results of the October election, see ATA, 5 November 1996. For useful appraisals and analyses of the election, see *New York Times*, 21 October 1996; *Gazeta Shqiptare*, 23 October 1996; *Albania*, 29 October 1996; and *Zëri i Popullit*, 21 November 1996.

62 See "Opinion Poll Conducted in Albania by the Washington, DC based International Republican Institute on the Election Day (26 May 1996)" (Tirana, 1996), p. 3.

63 See "Opinion Poll Conducted in Albania . . . (26 May 1996)," pp. 1–2; USIA, "Albanian Public Broadly Positive on the Economy," *Opinion Analysis*, 2 April 1996; idem, "On Security Matters, Albanian Public Looks to the West," *Opinion Analysis*, 2 April 1996.

9 Democratization and political participation in "postcommunist" Bulgaria

John D. Bell

Introduction

Since the miraculous year 1989 Bulgaria has acquired a reputation as an island of stability in the Balkans. Bulgaria's progress toward the creation of a democratic order has been surprising since the country lacks a prosperous economy, a large middle class, and a developed civic culture – factors that scholars maintain provide the most fertile soil for democratic growth.

This chapter, taking a primarily chronological approach, begins with a brief description of the struggle for democracy that developed in the country following its emergence from five-hundred years of Ottoman rule in 1878, and it examines the social changes that took place under the communist regime. It then turns to the impact of Soviet perestroika and Gorbachevian "new thinking" that helped to undermine the regime of Todor Zhivkov.

The first stage of Bulgaria's transition lasted from the fall of Zhivkov to the adoption of a new constitution a year-and-a-half later. During this period, the influence of opposition leader Zheliu Zhelev was at its height and was reflected in the roundtable negotiations between the ruling Communists, who soon changed their name to Socialists, and the opposition. The critical June 1990 elections and the work of the Grand National Assembly laid the groundwork for the postcommunist era in politics.

The chapter then turns to the Union of Democratic Forces, which took power at the end of 1991, to explain the reasons for the failure of its government and its near marginalization as a political force. The capture of the organization by its far-right wing led to its loss of control of parliament and then to a seemingly endless round of recriminations among those leaders who remained.

The divisions in the Union of Democratic Forces contributed to the comeback of the Socialists. The final section of the chapter focuses on the Socialist Party to examine its efforts at internal reform and the emergence of a new leadership that led it to victory in parliamentary elections at the end of 1994. Within this basically chronological approach, the paper also presents material on the mostly abortive efforts at economic reform and on the more successful efforts to avoid serious conflicts over nationality issues.

Historical background

In facing the challenges of postcommunist democratization, Bulgaria is not without a usable past. Of course it is true that since 1878, when the country was liberated from five centuries of Ottoman domination, it has usually been governed by royal/military or Communist dictatorships that explicitly rejected democratic institutions as "anarchic" or "bourgeois." Yet the struggle for democracy is one of the central and recurring themes of Bulgaria's modern history. Democratic values motivated many of Bulgaria's political actors and were a cause to which the Bulgarian people contributed more than their share of martyrs. During the nineteenth century many of the Bulgarians who strove to awaken their people's sense of national identity hoped to create a state that was both independent and democratic. Vasil Levski, "The Apostle" of national rediscovery, wrote of his hope that Bulgaria would become "a sacred and pure republic," and the verse of Khristo Botev, the poet-laureate of the struggle for national independence, displayed a strong sympathy toward radical social and political ideals. When the modern Bulgarian state was created – at the convention held in Veliko Tûrnovo in 1879 – the delegates adopted a constitution with many liberal elements. Although the Great Powers insisted that the new government must be a monarchy, the Tûrnovo Constitution provided for a unicameral legislature elected on the basis of universal male suffrage, strict limitations on the monarchy, and a broad array of civil rights.[1]

This attempt to transplant a Western constitutional system into Balkan soil encountered many obstacles owing to a weak middle class and a low level of political consciousness among the rural majority. Nor did Bulgaria's imported monarchs have sympathy for democratic values, preferring to recreate the absolutist system in which they were raised. Nevertheless, the political institutions of a modern state were established.[2] The Democratic and Radical parties, drawing their support from the country's intelligentsia and professional classes, were usually loyal to the constitution; and the Social Democratic party (or "Broad Socialists") advocated gradual reforms within a democratic context and attracted the support of much of the country's civil service and part of the working class. The Bulgarian Agrarian National Union (BANU) became Bulgaria's party of mass democracy, aiming to bring the peasant majority into full participation in the country's political life. After World War I, the BANU government led by Alexander Stamboliski embodied popular, and populist, democracy. But Stamboliski was murdered in 1923 and his government overthrown by an alliance of the military, Macedonian terrorists and politicians who undid many of the Agrarian reforms.[3] When the People's Bloc, a coalition of the Democratic and Radical parties and the BANU, won a surprising election victory in 1931, it was followed by the military coup of 1934 that turned the country into a royal/military dictatorship.[4]

During World War II, some members of the democratic opposition joined the Communists in the Fatherland Front directed against Bulgaria's alliance with Germany. When the government collapsed and the Front took power, it became apparent that the Communists viewed the coalition as a stepping stone to their achievement of complete political hegemony. Resistance to communization was led by the BANU, which organized an Opposition Bloc under Nikola Petkov to compete with the Communist Party internally and to seek Western support. In the elections for a Grand National Assembly to write a new constitution, held on October 27, 1946, the Bloc polled nearly one-third of the votes in the face of a brutal campaign of intimidation. Western indifference to Bulgaria gave the Communists a free hand. Petkov was charged with treason, arrested and condemned to death, and the Opposition Bloc was suppressed. Petkov's execution by hanging, followed a week later by the extension of diplomatic recognition to the communist government by the United States, marked the end of the democratic resistance to communization.[5]

During the Communist era, Bulgaria developed a reputation for passivity. Alone among the states of Eastern Europe, it experienced no crisis in its relations with the Soviet Union, and the long tenure of Todor Zhivkov, who became party leader in 1954, suggested almost complete political immobility. Beneath the surface, however, the country experienced fundamental economic and social changes that provided the foundation for the developments of the late 1980s. At the end of World War II, three-fourths of Bulgaria's population lived in villages and the overwhelming majority of these villagers were engaged in small-scale, primitive farming. The Communist regime was committed to transforming Bulgaria by developing industry and educating the population for, in the phrase that appeared in countless Zhivkov speeches, "the scientific-technological revolution of the twentieth century." By the late 1980s about two-thirds of the population was urban, and only about one-fifth was still directly involved in farming.[6] Bulgaria ranked among the most advanced nations in terms of the proportion of its eligible population that received secondary and higher education.[7]

For the first time, Bulgaria possessed the equivalent of a Western middle class. It was not a bourgeoisie in the classical Marxist sense of owning the means of production. But in terms of psychology and outlook, skepticism

Table 9.1 *Demographic trends in Bulgaria since the 1950s*

	1950s	1970s	1990s
Percentage of population	(1956)	(1970)	(1990)
Rural	66.4	47.7	32.2
Urban	33.6	52.3	67.8
Average annual rates of	(1953-59)	(1970-74)	(1990-99)[a]
population growth (%)	1.0	0.6	-0.3
Age distribution (%)	(1956)	(1976)	(1990)
15–24	16.1	14.8	14.1
25–49	36.3	35.3	34.1
50–59	10.4	11.6	12.3
Over 60	10.7	16.0	19.1
Levels of education[b]	(1956)	(1965)	(1992)
Primary	89.1	81.9	49.1
Secondary	7.7	12.9	35.7
Post-secondary	3.2	5.2	15.0

Notes: [a]Estimate. [b]Indicates attainment of completed or partial education at each level among persons over 25 years of age.
Sources: US Department of Commerce, *Statistical Abstracts of the United States*; Paul S. Shoup, *The East European and Soviet Data Handbook*; UNESCO, *Statistical Yearbooks*; United Nations, *Demographic Yearbooks*.

toward inherited dogmas, desire for material success and personal autonomy, it resembled its Western contemporaries more than the generation of its parents and grandparents. Signs of the growing influence of this social group were mainly cultural: the development of Sofia's Vitosha Boulevard as a Bulgarian *via Veneto* of shops devoted to luxury goods; the opening of aerobic dance studios; the appearance of a teen-age counter-culture formed around the electric guitar; the growing popularity of tennis; the building of the country's first golf course; and the many pet dogs being walked in the country's parks. But there was also a political dimension, for this group proved receptive to the new currents set in motion in the communist world by Mikhail Gorbachev. And it is important to note in view of later developments that the largest element in this group was found within the Bulgarian Communist Party.[8]

In the 1980s Bulgaria was overtaken by the slow-motion crises developing throughout the Communist world. These included an economy becoming less competitive with the Western and rapidly advancing Southeast Asian countries, an environment ravaged by decades of pollution and neglect, and a demographic balance shifting steadily in favor of the country's ethnic, especially Moslem, minorities. Before the advent of Mikhail Gorbachev in the USSR, the Zhivkov regime had attempted to deal with these problems by fostering and identifying with nationalism. Zhivkov's daughter Liudmila, the virtual dictator of cultural affairs before her death in 1981, sponsored the construction of enormous museums and monuments and organized grandiose celebrations of Bulgarian achievements. At the 1,300th anniversary of the Bulgarian state in 1981, Zhivkov shared the dais with Patriarch Maxim in a ceremony designed to show that the party had inherited the Church's historic role as defender of Bulgarian culture. More ominously, the regime became increasingly intolerant of minorities. In the 1970s, the Pomaks were pressured to adopt a mainstream Bulgarian identity, and in 1984 authorities launched the so-called Revival Campaign that suppressed Turkish cultural activities, forced the country's ethnic Turks to adopt Bulgarian names and tried to promote the migration of Bulgarians into areas of heavy Turkish settlement.[9]

The impact of perestroika

Before the late 1980s there were dissidents in Bulgaria, but no organized dissident movement. In part this was due to Zhivkov's policy of heaping rewards and honors on compliant intellectuals and to the small size of the country and its intellectual communities. Secret clubs or an underground press were hardly necessary to facilitate discussion among people who saw each other regularly at work, in Sofia's cafe society, or during vacations together at the Black Sea. Conversation among trusted personal friends was the preferred Bulgarian method for advancing critical ideas, and it went on even in the antechambers of Zhivkov's office. For some, such as Georgi Markov or Vladimir Kostov, escape abroad provided greater opportunities.[10]

Because Zhivkov always stressed fidelity to the Soviet Union, going so far as to ask the USSR to admit Bulgaria as the sixteenth Soviet republic,[11] it was inevitable that he would have to adopt some version of Gorbachev's "new thinking" even though he had little appetite for it. In 1987, yielding to not-very-subtle Soviet pressure, he introduced the "July Concept," apparently embracing the cause of reform wholeheartedly.[12] Along with a wave of administrative and economic reorganization, the July Concept called for several steps toward political democratization, including an expansion of press freedom and experiments with multi-candidate elections. Both of the latter proved short-lived. Following the exposure of several cases of official corruption, the press was again muzzled, and uncompliant editors and reporters were fired.[13] In the elections for mayors and regional and municipal councilors (held on February 28, 1988), local electoral commissions disqualified all but the officially approved candidates in eighty percent of the electoral districts. Where "outsider" candidates managed to find places on the ballot, the authorities ensured their defeat by trucking in absentee voters from districts where there was no challenge to the official list and by changing the results on forms submitted by the election precincts.[14]

Despite government persecution, dissidence in Bulgaria continued to build in several quarters. Inspired by developments in the USSR and other East European countries and by Western support for human rights under the Helsinki Agreements, members of the Bulgarian intelligentsia dared to launch initiatives that would have been unthinkable a few years earlier. In print such writers as Blaga Dimitrova and the satirist Radoi Ralin managed to publish works exploring the stupidities and moral backwardness of the system. On television Kevork Kevorkian's "Every Sunday" continually tested the limits of permissible criticism. In the Sofia region, dissident philosopher Zheliu Zhelev, whose study of totalitarian institutions had created a sensation when it was published in 1981,[15] and other intellectuals created a Club for the Support of Glasnost and Perestroika, whose example soon spread to other parts of the country. In the city of Russe, which was being slowly poisoned by chlorine gas emissions from a Romanian chemical combine across the Danube River, celebrities from politics, the arts and sport formed an ecological movement, Ekoglasnost, that openly challenged the regime's indifference to the destruction of the Bulgarian environment. Poland's Solidarity inspired the physician Konstantin Trenchev to create Podkrepa (Support), an independent trade union, that began to challenge the monopoly of the party-controlled unions. In various parts of the country, groups were formed to promote human rights and religious freedom or to revive long-suppressed political parties. Among the latter were the Social Democrats of Dr. Petûr Dertliev and the Bulgarian Agrarian National Union–Nikola Petkov (BANU-NP) headed by Milan Drenchev.[16]

Zhivkov's response to this ferment was to revert to the methods of the past. Party members affiliated with dissident groups received sanctions or were expelled from the BCP. Many of them (along with nonparty members) were dismissed from their jobs and subjected to vicious slander in the press. In February 1989, Zhivkov met with "representatives of the intelligentsia," warning them that Bulgaria would not tolerate "national nihilism" or "negative attitudes toward our country or toward socialism."[17] But this time the opposition inside and outside the party did not retreat into passivity. Bulgarian dissidents carried on their activities in defiance of threats and actual persecution. During the year, most of the usually docile cultural unions turned out their old leaders in favor of critics of the regime.

During the spring, a new challenge to Zhivkov's regime emerged in the regions of heavy Turkish population. Since the brutal Revival Campaign of

1984–85, ethnic Turks had prepared an underground organization that now undertook a series of hunger strikes and demonstrations, soon escalating to violent clashes with the authorities and several deaths.[18] By the end of May there were demonstrations with thousands of participants, forcing Zhivkov to appear on national television to quell rumors of massive unrest. Denying that Bulgaria had a substantial Turkish minority, he repeated the fiction that most of the ethnic Turks were really Bulgarians who had been forcibly converted to Islam and a Turkish identity during the Ottoman period. He attributed disturbances among Bulgaria's Muslims to confusion over the terms of a new passport law and to an anti-Bulgarian campaign carried on by Turkey and he challenged the Turkish government to open its borders to Bulgarian Muslims, so that it would be clear how few were discontented with life in Bulgaria. When Turkey responded to Zhivkov's challenge by declaring that it would accept refugees from Bulgaria, the authorities launched a broad reign of terror against the ethnic Turks, forcing thousands to cross the border, where they found refuge in hastily organized camps. Before the Turkish government again closed the border, more than 300,000 ethnic Turks had abandoned or were driven from Bulgaria, an exodus that focused world-wide attention on Bulgaria's human rights record and disrupted an already shaky economy.[19]

The beginning of the postcommunist period

The events of November 10, 1989

The collapse of the "Old Regime" in Bulgaria differed in important ways from developments in neighboring Balkan countries. Outside Bulgaria the process began with a movement away from legality. In Yugoslavia escalating violations of the constitution by Serbia culminated in the outbreak of ethnic violence and war. Romania saw a managed revolution – perhaps better described as a coup – whose most dramatic event was the televised murder of the ex-dictator and his wife. In Bulgaria, on the other hand, whatever took place behind the scenes, the retirement/removal of Todor Zhivkov appeared to follow the prescribed legal forms, implying that further political and institutional change could take place within the framework of law, rather than through a naked clash of power.

Zhivkov's increasingly erratic performance, including an attempt to propel his wastrel son into the leadership, his poor relationship with Gorbachev, and the unravelling of communist regimes across Eastern Europe convinced the dictator's colleagues that a change had to be made. The details surrounding Zhivkov's actual removal are still not entirely clear, but its key figures were Petûr Mladenov, in charge of foreign affairs since 1971, and Dobri Dzhurov, the minister of defense. Mladenov may have stopped in Moscow for discussions with Soviet leaders on his return from a visit to China.[20]

On November 10, 1989, the day after East Germany opened the Berlin Wall, a meeting of the BCP's Politburo and Secretariat accepted Zhivkov's "resignation." The fiction that this resignation was voluntary lasted only days. Bulgaria's former "son of the people" was soon under attack by his former colleagues, accused of personal corruption and establishing a "totalitarian" regime. His relatives and closest supporters were quickly purged from their posts in the party and state. Many other "dinosaurs" of his generation went quietly into retirement; others found themselves the targets of popular demonstrations that began to play a growing role in putting pressure on the leadership to speed the pace of reform.

Mladenov and the rest of the new leadership pledged to welcome and promote the development of pluralism in the country and to respect the rule of law. To this end, they halted the persecution of the ethnic Turks and invited those who had fled to return to Bulgaria and to reclaim their abandoned property, allowed opposition groups to register as legal entities, and promised to eliminate the domestic role of the state security forces. Bowing to widespread demonstrations, the party also amended Article One of the constitution, which recognized the Communist Party as the guiding force in society.[21]

At an Extraordinary Congress that began at the end of January 1990, the BCP carried through a number of structural and personnel changes and took the first steps to separate the party from the state. Mladenov resigned the party leadership while remaining titular head of state. Andrei Lukanov, widely regarded at the time as the party's ablest statesman, became prime minister. And Alexander Lilov was elected chairman of a restructured Supreme Party Council.[22] Lilov had been purged from the leadership in 1983 by Zhivkov and was long known to favor liberalization.[23] The Congress adopted a "Manifesto on Democratic Socialism" that described the country as being in "an acute economic and political crisis," and it called for the BCP to transform itself into a "modern Marxist party of democratic socialism." To this end it specifically recognized the legitimacy of organized "ideological currents and associations" within the party and guaranteed their access to the party press. Concessions to factions in favor of faster or more radical reforms, however, did not mean that they had broad support among party officials; leading reform advocates, mostly Sofia intellectuals, were defeated in elections to the 131-member Supreme Party Council.[24]

Lilov and the new leadership continued to push for changes in personnel that favored younger and better educated leaders, denounced the "totalitarian" practices of the past and even conducted a party referendum to change the name from "Communist" to "Socialist." In the following months Lilov advocated making the party more open to a diversity of views and spoke of its development in a "Eurosocialist" direction, taking as a model the democratic socialist parties of Western Europe. Some former dissidents responded to these changes with enthusiasm. For example, Stefan Prodev, who had abandoned the party, returned to become editor of the party newspaper, making it as diverse and interesting as the opposition press. For others, the reforms did not go far enough, and a number of divisions began to appear. One was the Alternative Socialist Party, led by Nikolai Vasilev, which broke away to form its own organization. The sociologist, Petûr-Emil Mitev, formed a faction, "Road to Europe," within the party to promote more rapid democratization and to pursue a policy of reconciliation with the West. A conservative opposition to the party's new course also surfaced, objecting to the change in the party's name and all that it implied.[25]

In addition to the changes that took place within the party after Zhivkov's fall, most of the BCP's auxiliary organizations collapsed or undertook major internal reforms. The Central Council of Trade Unions declared its independence and elected a new leadership. Some unions dropped out altogether, while alternative unions, especially the independent Podkrepa, recruited thousands of new members. The Komsomol (Communist Youth League) disintegrated at its congress early in the year and was replaced by a new organization that declared itself independent of party control, and by a number of rival youth organizations, some of which were affiliated with the emerging political opposition. The official BANU purged its old leadership, declared its independence from the BCP, and elected Viktor Vûlkov as chairman of its governing council. Communist party cells in the workplace were dissolved or disbanded.[26]

The role of State Security, particularly its Sixth Department, whose activities focused on the domestic fight against anti-communism, was of great concern to both the political opposition and to Zhivkov's successors. On December 27, 1989 the minister of internal affairs, Georgi Tanev, who was closely linked to Zhivkov and who had been a major figure in the Revival Process, was dismissed from his post. He was replaced by Colonel General Atanas Semerdzhiev, a sixty-five-year-old career military officer, who was given a mandate to depoliticize and reduce the size of the security organs. According to official reports, the Sixth Department was disbanded altogether; the gathering of military intelligence was placed under the Defense Ministry, and the gathering of foreign intelligence was assigned to a "National Intelligence Service" under the head-of-state. While many in the opposition remained skeptical that State Security could actually be defanged so easily, it appears that in fact many of its personnel were rapidly making a transition to the private sector, taking advantage of their influence and contacts to initiate the "hidden privatization" of the state economy.[27]

In the precommunist era, the intervention of the army in political life was the greatest obstacle to democratic government, and steps to ensure the depoliticization of the military had broad support. Servicemen were forbidden to hold political affiliation, to attend political rallies in uniform, or to undertake political activities within barracks; officers who wished to remain politically active were required to resign. Between 1990 and 1994 approximately 6,000 officers left the service, although this large number is misleading because many officers, particularly younger ones, took advantage of it to cut short their military obligation.[28] During the period of the UDF government, Defense Minister Dimitûr Ludzhev described the depoliticization of the officer corps as "largely accomplished."[29]

Outside the BSP Bulgarian political life also began to quicken. The number of political parties and movements mushroomed – more than fifty sought official recognition. On December 7, 1989 ten parties and organizations came together to found the Union of Democratic Forces (UDF). They included the Federation of Clubs for the Support of Glasnost and Democracy (formerly the Clubs for the Support of Glasnost and Perestroika) led by Petko Semeonov, Dimitûr Ludzhev, and Zheliu Zhelev; the Podkrepa Independent Labor Confederation of Konstantin Trenchev; Milan Drenchev's BANU-NP; Dr. Petûr Dertliev's Social Democrats; Father Khristofor Sûbev's Committee for Religious Rights, Freedom of Conscience, and Spiritual Values; Ekoglasnost, led by the zoologist Petûr Beron; Rumen Vodenicharov's Independent Association for the Defense of Human Rights in Bulgaria, and three smaller groups. Before the June elections, six more members would be added, including the Green Party, the Radical Democratic Party and the Democratic Party. Owing to his prestige as Bulgaria's best known dissident, Zheliu Zhelev was the obvious choice to chair the UDF's coordinating council, and his understanding of the needs of the moment were fundamental in shaping the direction of change after November 10.

The influence of Zheliu Zhelev

Broadly speaking, in the immediate aftermath of the collapse of regimes across Eastern Europe, there were two approaches to the issue of "decommunization." One focused on *communists*, seeking to punish those held responsible for the deeds of the past. Because time had allowed most of the individual communists guilty of the worst excesses of the Stalinist era to escape justice in this world, the advocates of this approach sought to impose a collective guilt on all party members, holding the sons guilty for the sins of the fathers. Their goal was "to make them suffer as we have suffered," and they frequently favored using the same tactics that the communists had used against their opponents. Some would call for the banning of the

Bulgarian Socialist Party as a "criminal organization," and Alexander Karakachanov reported that when he was mayor of Sofia he was frequently asked why he did not solve the capital's housing problem by "throwing the communists into the street."[30]

The second approach saw *communism* as a system or set of institutions to be changed or eliminated. Its advocates considered the question of the punishment of individuals as either irrelevant or as an issue to be dealt with through law. During the critical period between the removal of Todor Zhivkov and the election of a Grand National Assembly in June 1990 it was the second approach, for which Zheliu Zhelev was the most consistent spokesman, that prevailed among the opposition and that guided it in its crucial negotiations with the government.

Born in 1935 in the mountain village of Veselinovo into a poor peasant family, Zhelev excelled in school and was allowed to enroll in Sofia University, where he studied philosophy under Dobrin Spasov. Spasov was at the center of a group of liberal minded faculty and students, but unlike them Zhelev refused to confine his critical views to a closed circle. In 1965, when he insisted on presenting a dissertation critical of Lenin's *Materialism and Empirio-criticism*, he was expelled from the party and exiled to a provincial town. Many of his friends stood by him, and in 1974 he was allowed to defend a new dissertation and was appointed a senior researcher in the Institute for Culture. He became a center of controversy again when his study *Fascism* was published at the end of 1981 and immediately suppressed when the authorities recognized that the author did not limit his concept of totalitarianism to fascist Germany, Italy, or Spain. He was a founder of Ekoglasnost and the Clubs for the Support of Glasnost and Perestroika and had publicly signed numerous petitions protesting the suppression of Bulgaria's ethnic Turks and defending the rights of various individuals persecuted for their beliefs.[31]

Zhelev's conception of what was necessary for the dismantling of the communist system can be seen in his study *Fascism*. Working from a limited resource base and without access to contemporary Western analyses, Zhelev arrived at a position similar to that reached by Hannah Arendt, Carl Friedrich, and others, that is that totalitarianism encompassed the experience of fascist *and* communist states. His description of the elements of fascism/totalitarianism were those found in most of the Western literature. They included a one-party political system, the fusion of party and state, an all-encompassing official ideology, a cult of party/state leaders, a monopoly on the means of communication and the dissemination of information, and the use of terror, including concentration camps, against real or potential opponents.[32] Clearly, for Zhelev totalitarianism was embodied in these institutions, not in the personality or the will of any individual or group, no matter how evil. Even Hitler, he wrote, could not have created the Nazi system by himself. "What allowed Hitler to turn the people into an amorphous, uncritical, unthinking mass – a mob – was not his oratorical skill, but totalitarian institutions. A people becomes a mob when it is deprived of political parties, political organizations, an opposition press, open politics, public opinion, free elections . . . ."[33] The importance of creating the political institutions characteristic of democracy was at the center of Zhelev's program and guided the UDF in its negotiations with the BCP/BSP on the future of the country, and it has been the consistent theme of his presidency.

The Roundtable

Beginning on January 4, 1990 the ruling Communist Party (which soon changed its name to "Socialist"), the UDF, and the official BANU[34] began roundtable negotiations that culminated in a series of agreements on political and institutional reform. During these negotiations, the UDF yielded on issues of personnel and tactics, for example, on retaining Mladenov as president and on the timing of the elections, but successfully held firm on a basic "bill or rights." The fruits of these negotiations were embodied in three agreements signed on March 12.[35] These provided for the election of a Grand National Assembly (GNA) to sit for a limited duration – eighteen months – to prepare a new constitution, during which time it would also exercise the functions of a regular parliament. The UDF accepted an early date – June 10 and 17 – for the election and agreed that Petûr Mladenov would hold the office of president until the completion of the GNA's term. Questions related to the election campaign would be resolved at the roundtable, and the current National Assembly would pass no law without the roundtable's approval. All parties agreed to abjure violence and to promote a transition to democratic government "in an unforced, bloodless, and civilized manner."[36] On April 3, the National Assembly altered the constitution to create the post of state president and then elected Petûr Mladenov to the office. On the same day it adopted laws on political parties and the electoral system based on agreements negotiated at the roundtable.

Key legislation

The law on political parties.[37] The law on political parties provided that every citizen had the right to join a political party without suffering any penalty or gaining any privilege. In a provision aimed at completing the removal of the BSP's party cells, the law prohibited political organizations and activities in the workplace. It gave to political parties the right to publish newspapers or other materials, required the state to provide the parties with free access to government controlled radio and television, and allowed them to accept contributions from foreign citizens. The last point was an important one for the UDF, which looked to such contributions to offset the BSP's huge advantage in resources.

Any group wishing to register as a political party was required to submit an application to the Sofia City Court that included a statement of the party's program and the signatures of fifty adult citizens. The court then had one week either to register the party or to reject the application with an explanation. Legitimate grounds for rejection included: a party's advocacy of compromising the sovereignty or territorial integrity of the country; its promotion of racial, ethnic, or religious hostility; or its advocacy of violence or other methods prohibited by law. The court was also directed to refuse to register any party "founded on an ethnic or religious basis." This language, which ultimately found its way into the constitution, reflected the fear of potential Turkish separatism on the part of both the BSP and the UDF as well as the desire of both to capture the Turkish voting bloc.[38]

In practice, the Sofia City Court rubber-stamped nearly all the applications presented to it. Approximately forty-five parties – including such examples as the "Organization of Cardiac Patients and Socially Vulnerable Citizens" – were registered by the time of the June 1990 elections. The most significant controversy focused on the MRF, whose initial attempt to register as a political party was rejected by the court on the grounds that it had an ethnic/religious foundation.

The Election Law.[39] The Grand National Assembly Election Act provided for the election to be conducted on the basis of "a universal, equal and direct suffrage by secret ballot." It gave the right to vote to all citizens aged eighteen or older, with the exception of persons convicted of "judicial disability" or serving prison sentences. Voters would elect a Grand National Assembly,[40] composed of 400 deputies, half to be elected from single-member electoral districts and half on the basis of proportional representation in twenty-eight multi-member districts. In single-member districts, if no candidate received a majority, or if the voter turnout was less than fifty percent, a runoff on June 17 between the two candidates with the highest number of votes would decide the election. The votes cast for party lists on June 10 determined the allocation of all 200 seats under the system of proportional representation; to gain any of these seats, a party had to receive a minimum of 4 percent of the national vote.

To administer the election, the law created 228 district electoral commissions (one for each of the 200 single-member and 28 multi-member districts) and approximately 13,000 precinct electoral commissions for each polling place. These commissions were established by local governments "in consultation with the leaderships of the political parties." In practice, this gave the major parties the right to nominate members of the commissions. A Central Electoral Commission (CEC) was charged with the law's overall implementation and the administration of the election. Naturally, the composition of this body was of great concern, particularly to the UDF. After negotiations among representatives of the BSP, UDF, and official BANU, the seventy-eight-year-old law professor Zhivko Stalev was selected to chair the body. Stalev belonged to no party and appeared to enjoy the confidence of all sides.[41] The BSP, UDF, and BANU (official) each nominated one of the CEC's other top officers (two vice-chairmen and secretary); of the other twenty members, by an agreement worked out at the roundtable, eight were named by the BSP, eight by the UDF, and four by other parties.

The CEC faced formidable problems. In an atmosphere of widespread apprehension that the ruling BSP would attempt to steal the election, it had to convince the population that the ballot would be truly secret, that votes would be honestly counted, and that all parties would receive fair play during the campaign. And it had to organize the mechanics of the election, in the face of shortages of even such basics as paper for the printing of ballots and voter registries, in less than two months. Moreover, it lacked the authority to investigate complaints of campaign or election abuses, and could only preserve them for future consideration by the GNA. Despite these formidable problems, the CEC developed and displayed a sense of professionalism that transcended partisan differences and ultimately earned a high degree of public confidence.[42]

In an extremely important decision early in the election campaign the CEC directed the district electoral commissions to register candidates nominated by the MRF, even though the Sofia Court had refused to register it as a political party. In the CEC's ruling, the MRF's earlier registration as an *organization* was sufficient to allow it to field a slate of candidates. Although the legal basis for this decision was shaky and it drew protests from both the BSP, which claimed that it was due to pressure from the American embassy, and the UDF, it undoubtedly was a fundamental contribution to the orderliness of the election and to the acceptance of its legitimacy by the country's ethnic Turks and Moslems.

In conformity with Bulgarian election practice before World War II, the law provided that instead of a single ballot listing the names of candidates and parties, colored ballots would be assigned to each party by the Central Electoral Commission.[43] The law also provided for "guests," understood to mean foreign observers, to be present in the polling stations or district commissions. This was an extremely important point for the UDF and other opposition parties, who counted on the presence of international observers to insure a fair vote. The BSP agreed, although it considered the term "observer" insulting and insisted on including "guests" from the USSR.

Agreements at the roundtable had also provided that national and local governments were to make available to the opposition office space, printing facilities, and other resources. These agreements were unevenly carried out. Many local authorities failed to act or delayed until the last minute, and Alexander Lilov argued that the influence of Radio Free Europe and other foreign broadcasters should be counted on the UDF side.[44] The UDF committee in the town of Gotse Delchev erected a tent in the central square as its "party headquarters" to dramatize the inequality of resources.[45] The BSP, of course, possessed its network of offices and clubs throughout the country, most government offices also flew the red banner rather than the Bulgarian state flag. Despite these obstacles, the UDF organized a vigorous campaign, culminating in the largest political rally ever held in Sofia. The entire campaign and the election itself were entirely peaceful.

Were the roundtable agreements, now translated into laws, a decisive defeat of the communist system? Zheliu Zhelev clearly thought so. As early as April he replied to a question on the state of totalitarianism in Bulgaria that "It's finished." And he explained that in a system with the free flow of information, the right to vote, and the right of political activity, totalitarianism cannot survive. He also predicted that the people, given a real electoral choice, would vote overwhelmingly to reject the communist system, and he predicted that the UDF would receive 70 percent of the votes.[46]

The June 1990 elections

Most of the political spectrum was represented in the June elections. On the far right, opposition to the restoration of full rights to the country's ethnic Turks had led to the formation of a Committee for the Defense of the National Interests (CDNI), led by a former state security officer, Mincho Minchev, that created a political party, the Fatherland Party of Labor, with a highly nationalistic program.[47] Opposition minority rights also inspired the formation of the Bulgarian National Radical Party (BNRP), led by the physicist Ivan Georgiev. Its program stressed "national pride" and opposition to "any concession to the claims of the ethnic Turks."[48]

The BANU (official) enjoyed the advantages of its former legal status, since it possessed a newspaper and network of clubs and was accorded more media time than the minor parties. Its leader, Viktor Vûlkov, was generally regarded the winner in the three-way television debate with Zheliu Zhelev and Alexander Lilov. He could not, however, stir real life into an organization that had had only a formal existence.[49] Moreover, as the campaign continued it appeared primarily to be a contest between the BSP and the UDF, and the BANU (official) became the odd-man-out.

The UDF entered the campaign with a high level of confidence. Assuming that if the populace were given the opportunity to vote freely it would automatically reject the BSP, the UDF sought to make the election a referendum on the past forty-five years of communist rule.[50] Consequently, much of the UDF campaign focused on the distant past, particularly on the atrocities committed by the BCP during the Stalinist era. By its very nature, the UDF coalition had difficulty speaking with a single voice or advancing specific measures to deal with Bulgaria's current problems. This was particularly evident with regard to the future of the Socialists. Some UDF leaders followed the example of Petûr Dertliev and spoke with sympathy of the BSP's efforts to reform itself, advocated an eventual reconciliation with its most liberal elements, and opposed the idea of reprisals against BSP officials. In this vein, Zheliu Zhelev and other UDF spokesmen advocated what they called a "Spanish policy," following the example of Spain's transition from fascism.

A growing number in the UDF, however, employed a far more strident tone, frequently referring to the BSP as "murderers" and a "mafia," giving the impression that the UDF would conduct a wholesale purge if it won. Both the BSP and some members of the UDF referred to this as a policy of "McCarthyism"[51] and some prominent figures who had left the BSP announced their return to it as "the lesser evil."[52] The UDF economic program called for shock therapy – an immediate and complete transition to a market economy – but did not make clear how this would be effected or how the most vulnerable elements in the population would be protected.[53]

Striving to distance itself from its past record, the BSP ran a campaign that was devoid of Marxist ideology. Indeed, BSP spokesmen rivaled the UDF in their denunciations of "totalitarianism" and stressed that they were the ones who had brought down Zhivkov's regime. The party's new symbols – a red rose and a cartoon boy who somewhat resembled Pinocchio – its thumbs-up gesture, and "Good Luck for Bulgaria" slogan replaced the heavy-handed mottoes and portraits of party leaders characteristic of past campaigns. The BSP presented itself as the party of "responsible, conservative change," stressing the experience of its leaders and minimizing its policy differences with the UDF. It denied seeking a monopoly of power and called for the formation of a coalition with the opposition either before or after the elections. The BSP also turned to "voodoo economics," pledging a gradual transition to a market economy in which no one would suffer. The party's claim that old-age pensions would be endangered by a UDF victory was particularly effective.

Table 9.2 *Elections to the Grand National Assembly of Bulgaria, 1990*

Party	Votes	% votes	Seats	% seats
BSP	2,887,766	47.15	211	52.75
UDF	2,317,798	36.20	144	36.00
BANU (official)	491,597	8.03	16	4.00
MRF	368,929	6.03	23	5.75
Others	158,279	2.59	6	1.50
Total	6,224,369	100.00	400	100.00

Seats distributed by the d'Hondt formula for proportional representation:		*Seats won in single-member districts:*	
BSP	97	BSP	114
UDF	75	UDF	69
BANU (official)	16		
MRF	12	MRF	11
		Fatherland Union	2
		Independents	2
		Fatherland Party of Labor	1
		Social Democratic Party (non-Marxist)	1
Total	200		200

Note: Voter turnout: 90.6 percent.
Source: BTA, June 19, 1990.

While cultivating a new image designed to appeal particularly to Bulgaria's middle class urban voters, the BSP apparently conducted a more traditional campaign in the countryside. There, local party and government officials put heavy pressure on the village population, whose habits of subordination, developed over the past forty-five years, were not easily broken. This pressure was admitted by BSP leaders, who attributed it to overzealousness on the part of local activists while denying that it was a tactic promoted by the national party leadership.[54]

The election results[55] (see table 9.2) came as a shocking disappointment to the opposition, whose expectations had been unrealistically high, but they were hardly the "overwhelming Socialist victory" that was reported in the Western press. The BSP failed to get a majority of the popular vote, and some of its leading figures, like Prime Minister Andrei Lukanov, were forced into embarrassing run-offs or, like Defense Minister Dobri Dzhurov, were actually defeated. The opposition dominated Bulgaria's cities, especially the capital, and enjoyed a commanding level of support from professionals and the young. And because decisions of the Grand National Assembly required a two-thirds majority, the opposition could exercise a veto on any Socialist proposals. The BANU (official) pledged to cooperate with the UDF and to seek unification with the BANU-NP.

Was the 1990 election fair? At the time, both foreign observers and the UDF leadership concluded that, however unbalanced the election campaign had been, the election itself was not manipulated. Over a year later, however, a statistician and UDF-supporter, charged that in fact the BSP had managed to add 500,000 votes to its total by some form of fraud, but offered no explanation of how it was done. Subsequently, several UDF politicians accepted this analysis and went on to argue that because the election was fraudulent, the GNA and the constitution it produced were also illegitimate.[56]

It seems highly unlikely, however, that significant election fraud actually occurred. The election was closely watched at every stage by foreign and domestic observers as well as representatives of the parties. Moreover, the Bulgarian Association for Fair Elections, whose members generally favored the UDF, and a West German polling organization, INFAS, independently carried out parallel vote counts that confirmed the official tallies.[57]

From red to blue

Political tension continued to run high after the elections because the UDF and other parties rejected all proposals to join the BSP in a coalition government. In the streets of major towns, protesters established "communist-free zones" occupied by tent cities and demanded full investigations of past communist crimes. A student strike at the University of Sofia spread to the provinces. Increasingly, protests focused on a statement made by President Mladenov the preceding December when, unable to gain a hearing from a hostile demonstration, he had told the defense minister that "the best thing is to let the tanks come." Although this statement was not acted on, it was captured on a videotape that was made available to the opposition and broadcast during the election campaign. Mladenov's immediate response was to charge that the tape had been fabricated by the opposition.[58] When its authenticity was upheld by a panel of experts, he maintained that his remark was "being taken out of context." Finally, he admitted having made the statement, but pleaded that it was due to the passion of the moment and that in fact he had never authorized the use of force against his opponents. Although this last argument was valid, the opposition focused on Mladenov's long effort to cover up the truth and called for his resignation. Even the BSP newspaper suggested that presidential dignity required Mladenov to leave office.[59] With support eroding even in his own party, Mladenov resigned on the evening of July 6, 1990, stating that he had no wish to be "a cause of tension."[60]

The question of Mladenov's successor led to a breakthrough in Bulgaria's political stalemate. After several votes in the GNA, no candidate gained the required two-thirds majority. At this point the various nominees withdrew in favor of the candidacy of UDF leader Zheliu Zhelev, who was elected with the support of a majority of the BSP's parliamentary group. Zhelev immediately nominated General Atanas Semerdzhiev of the BSP as vice president. Semerdzhiev, who as minister of the interior was responsible for depoliticizing the police and ending censorship, was elected with the support of the opposition.[61] Zhelev had never been enthusiastic about the UDF's decision not to participate in any coalition with the BSP, and his willingness to preside over the country while a BSP majority in the GNA prepared a new constitution alienated the UDF right wing. This segment actually became more influential because Zhelev had to resign as UDF leader when he assumed the presidency.

The erosion of the BSP's position continued as membership declined and factionalism increased. Days before the party's Thirty-Ninth Congress (September 22–25),[62] a street demonstration demanding a more rapid pace of decommunization attacked and partially burned the Party House.[63] When the congress convened, it showed sharp divisions between would-be reformers and conservatives, with the preponderance of strength lying with the latter. Although it voted explicitly to renounce the Leninist principle of "democratic centralism" and admit responsibility for past "distortions in every sphere of social life," the congress turned aside a proposal that it offer an apology to the people and it decisively rejected members of reform factions for positions in the party leadership. An open break also emerged between the party's two strongest figures, Alexander Lilov and Andrei Lukanov. This conflict came to a head in November, when Lukanov, supported by the pro-reform factions, attempted to remove Lilov from the chairmanship of the Supreme Party Council, accusing him of establishing an "authoritarian style" of leadership. Lilov prevailed, however, on a vote of 58 to 50.[64]

Lukanov was also hurt by his performance as prime minister. He had spent the last of Bulgaria's hard currency reserves to prevent a drop of salaries and pensions before the June elections, and when it became impossible to continue this policy, Bulgaria's economy and standard of living went into free fall. As the "hungry winter" of 1990–91 approached, Lukanov found himself both on the defensive against Lilov within the BSP and faced with a rapidly accelerating strike movement that demanded his resignation. He resigned as prime minister at the end of November.[65]

President Zhelev negotiated an agreement that turned the task of forming a new government over to Dimitûr Popov, a nonparty judge of the Sofia municipal Court who had won general approval for his work on the CEC during the June elections. On December 20 a cabinet of eighteen ministers was formed, consisting of eight Socialists, three members of the UDF, two Agrarians, and five independents. Three deputy prime ministers represented the major political forces – Alexander Tomov of the BSP, Dimitûr Ludzhev of the UDF, and Viktor Vûlkov of the BANU.[66] Although Zhelev and his supporters referred to this government as one of "cohabitation" rather than coalition out of deference to the UDF right, it clearly reflected the president's desire to proceed with the consolidation of a new political system while avoiding direct confrontation with the Socialists.

The resignations of Mladenov and Lukanov and the disarray in the Socialist camp contributed to a marked swing of public opinion in favor of the opposition. The UDF, however, experienced a setback when Dr. Petûr Beron, Zhelev's successor as chairman, suddenly resigned following allegations that he had once been an informant for State Security.[67] He was replaced by Filip Dimitrov, a lawyer and vice-chairman of the Green Party. The self-effacing Dimitrov won election essentially as a "broker" among the parties and factions of the UDF that were finding it increasingly difficult to maintain a united front.

The new constitution

During the following months the GNA undertook the contentious task of preparing a new constitution. Its basic principles are described below.[68]

Citizenship, national unity, and minority rights. The constitution provides for equal rights for all citizens without regard to "race, nationality, ethnicity, sex, place of birth, religion, education, beliefs, political affiliation, personal or social position, or property status," and it defines a citizen as "anyone who has at least one parent who is a Bulgarian citizen or who was born in the territory of Bulgaria." Orthodoxy is recognized as the traditional religion of the people, but is given no official status. Although it makes the government responsible for protecting Bulgarian citizens resident abroad, the Bulgarian constitution, in contrast with those of Hungary or Macedonia, makes no mention of any responsibility for ethnic Bulgarians outside the country's borders (see table 9.3).

The constitution reflected its drafters' obvious concern with national unity, a point driven home in its declaration of fundamental principles which states

Table 9.3 *Ethnic Bulgarians outside Bulgaria*

Country	Population
Ukraine	231,800
Moldova	88,419
Russia	32,785
Serbia	25,000[a]
Kazakstan	10,726
Uzbekistan	2,160
Macedonia	1,547[b]
Tajikistan	1,072

Notes: [a]A local organization in Serbia stated that the Bulgarian minority numbers 40,000 (*Demokratsiia*, May 30, 1992); the Agency for Bulgarians Abroad more recently gave an "unofficial" figure of 60,000 (*BTA*, June 12, 1995). [b]According to the 1994 Macedonian census (Macedonian Information and Liaison Service, January 5, 1995, distributed electronically).
Source: *Pismo ot Bûlgariia*, November-December 1993, p. 26.

that, while local self-government is recognized, Bulgaria is "an integral state," that its "territorial integrity is inviolable," and that no "autonomous territorial formations" may exist. These provisions reflected a fear of potential separatism among the country's ethnic Turks, and the example of Cyprus was frequently cited to emphasize the possible danger of autonomy or separation along ethnic lines. The constitution also carried over the agreement from the round table to ban (Article 11) political parties founded on an "ethnic, racial, or religious" base.

Republicanism. In September 1946 a referendum on the monarchy was held with 92 percent of the electorate voting in favor of its abolition. The heir to the Bulgarian throne, the then nine-year-old Simeon II was taken into exile, settling eventually in Spain as a guest of Juan Carlos. In the GNA there was a small, but vocal minority from the UDF that advocated the restoration of the monarchy either by restoring *in toto* the Tûrnovo Constitution or by creating a new monarchical constitution. During the debate on this question, supporters of republicanism, led by Petûr Dertliev, threatened to hold a popular referendum on the restoration of the monarchy. The monarchists, however, did not wish to risk a popular vote on the issue – little support for a monarchical restoration could be detected in public opinion polls, and openly monarchist parties received almost no support in the 1990 elections. The referendum was cancelled and Article 1 of the constitution was adopted, declaring Bulgaria to be a republic. Simeon was also in the minds of the Assembly majority when it drafted Article 93 (2), stating that to be elected president a candidate must have resided in Bulgaria for the previous five years. This measure was aimed at preventing Simeon, who has encouraged a monarchist movement, but has so far declined to return to Bulgaria, from offering himself for election as head-of-state.[69]

Separation of powers. Article 8 of the constitution provides that the state's power "shall be divided between a legislative, an executive, and a judicial branch." In defining the actual structure of government, the new constitution reflected the European tradition of parliamentary supremacy: the Council of Ministers, elected by the National Assembly, exercises the lion's share of authority; the presidency possesses only a suspensory veto on legislation passed by the Assembly. Moreover, the authority of the president as the representative of the country in relations with foreign governments and as commander-in-chief of the armed forces overlaps with that of the ministries of foreign affairs and of defense, a fact that has produced several subsequent conflicts among these institutions.[70] Independence of the judiciary was also provided in the constitution, and a Constitutional Court was created to pass on the constitutionality of legislation. Because of the mutual distrust of the main political factions, the high judicial institutions were to be filled in an unusual manner. One-third of the justices were appointed by the National Assembly, one-third by the president, and one-third by the judges of the Supreme Court of Cassation and the Supreme Administrative Court.

The breakup of the UDF

At the time of its formation, the UDF was dominated by center-left figures, usually intellectuals and former dissidents, many of whom had once been members of the BCP. But as the country made its first steps toward democratization, many new activists appeared who were much farther to the right. These elements, who came to be known as the "dark blues" had little patience with their more leftist colleagues, whom they suspected and often accused of being communist dupes or agents. Ianko Iankov, for example, was a dissident jailed during the 1980s for his political activities and was one of the UDF's founders. He wrote that as early as 1977, as part of an effort to recruit him as an agent for State Security, he was shown a secret plan code-named "Country X after Moment T" and was told that it was a blueprint formulated by the Soviet KGB for running Bulgaria after Todor Zhivkov. Part of this plan involved the creation of a "puppet opposition" that would be used to delude the population. As Iankov looked at the UDF, he observed that its leadership was filled with "former members of the *nomenklatura*, the sons of generals, and leftist fellow-travellers," and he concluded that the secret plan had been set in motion. Iankov, himself, temporarily abandoned the UDF for an association with the Movement for Rights and Freedoms

(MRF), representing primarily the ethnic Turkish minority, whose leader Akhmed Dogan, he had met in prison.[71]

As debate on the constitution progressed, a number of dark-blue UDF deputies began to argue that the process should be halted because no genuinely democratic constitution could be created by a body with a socialist\communist majority. They proposed that the GNA be disbanded and that new elections be held, elections that would presumably reflect a growth in UDF support. They were joined in this view by most of the deputies of the MRF, who concluded that the GNA would not accord sufficient protection to the rights of ethnic minorities. The majority of the UDF delegates, supported by President Zhelev, preferred to fulfill the commitment to the roundtable agreement and continued to participate in the drafting process.

When the commission presented its draft to the GNA, the UDF minority and nearly all the MRF deputies, walked out. As it became apparent that their number was insufficient to block approval of the constitution, they demanded that it first be submitted to a popular referendum. When the GNA voted down this proposal the UDF minority began a hunger strike in protest against what its members called the "communist document." Although relatively few in number – thirty-nine deputies at the beginning, later joined by another eleven – the UDF minority would form the core of the UDF-Movement. Outside the GNA, the position of the strikers was endorsed by the trade-union Podkrepa, and UDF Chairman Filip Dimitrov. Blaga Dimitrova, the wife of Iordan Vasilev who participated in the strike, and Bulgaria's most prominent writer, published a curse that called for the arms of all those signing the constitution to be cut off.

Despite the vehemence of the opposition, the constitution received 309 votes in the GNA and was adopted on July 12, 1991. The deputies who had walked out returned when the date for parliamentary elections was set. Although they continued to criticize the constitution, most admitted that their action had been directed less at the document itself, than at bringing about new elections.[72] After the October elections, none of the former strikers objected to taking an oath to uphold the constitution they had so recently denounced.

Before it adjourned, the Grand National Assembly adopted an electoral law to govern new parliamentary elections set for October 1991. The constitution set the size of the National Assembly at 240 deputies, and the electoral law provided that they be chosen on a basis of proportional representation. To qualify for the Assembly a party was required to poll a minimum of 4 percent of the total vote. All the major groups supported proportional over direct representation, presumably because it strengthened the power of party leaders who would determine the order of the party's electoral lists.[73]

Prior to these elections the UDF formally split. As most of its founders had originally conceived the organization, it was intended to be a vehicle temporarily uniting groups of widely disparate views whose sole common purpose was the end of the communist regime. Once this was accomplished, it was expected that the organization would dissolve into its component parties. Some of the organizations belonging to the UDF were, or at least claimed to be, parties with significantly large constituencies; others were smaller "movements" or special interest groups. Within the UDF governing council, each group possessed an equal voice, a fact that magnified the influence of the dark-blues. They wished to treat the UDF itself as a party so that their leaders would have a larger role in decision-making and, when elections were scheduled, in shaping the electoral lists. This provoked the largest coalition partners, the Social Democratic Party and smaller allies to withdraw to run as the UDF-Center. The BANU-NP also withdrew from the UDF to run independently.

The dark-blues moved to purge their remaining opponents, denying them positions on the UDF electoral lists and access to the UDF newspaper *Demokratsiia*. As a result another group, comprising many of the UDF's founders, withdrew to form the "light-blue" UDF-Liberals. Calling themselves the UDF-Movement, the hardline majority inherited the coalition's organization, newspaper, and blue ballot.

The breakup of the UDF was echoed in the splintering of some of its constituent organizations. Ekoglasnost, whose majority remained in the UDF, chose a new, stridently anticommunist leadership, while its previous chairman, the actor Petûr Slabakov, left the UDF to form the Ekoglasnost Political Club. The Democracy Clubs elected Iordan Vasilev chairman, while former chairman Petko Simeonov founded a new Club for Liberal Democracy, giving a home to light-blue intellectuals. Alexander Karakachanov, deposed as head of the Green Party, formed a new independent Green Party, while the old Greens changed their name to the Conservative-Ecological Party. Fractions of the Social Democratic Party and the BANU-NP chose to split off from the main body and to remain in the UDF.[74] The end result of these realignments was a significant rightward shift in the main UDF formation, the UDF-Movement, whose principal figures, in addition to Filip Dimitrov, were Stefan Savov, head of the Democratic Party, and Alexander Iordanov, leader of the Radical Democrats.

For its part, the BSP saw continual factional debate, although it managed to preserve formal unity at its pre-election national conference by leaving unresolved basic questions about the party's future direction. Its election campaign symbols, included both the red star of the communist past and the red rose of social democracy. Its election program emphasized "civil order,

Table 9.4 *Elections to the National Assembly of Bulgaria, 1991*

Party	Votes	% votes	Seats	% seats
UDF (Movement)	1,903,567	34.36	110	45.84
BSP	1,836,050	33.14	106	44.16
MRF	418,168	7.55	24	10.00
Left out of parliament:	(1,383,052)	(24.95)		
BANU (United)	214,052	3.86		
BANU-NP	190,454	3.54		
UDF (Center)	177,295	3.20		
UDF (Liberals)	155,902	2.81		
"Kingdom of Bulgaria"	100,883	1.82		
Business Bloc	73,379	1.32		
Bulgarian National Radical Party	62,462	1.13		
Others (none with more than 1%)	408,625	7.27		
Total	5,540,837	100.00	240	100.00

Note: Voter turnout: 79.2 percent.
Source: *Reporter 7*, October 20, 1991.

social justice, and democracy," without providing specific definitions for these terms.[75]

The elections, whose results are shown in table 9.4, were popularly perceived as a struggle between red and blue. The UDF-Movement[76] achieved a narrow plurality, the BSP declined but clearly remained a significant force, and the MRF continued to enjoy near total support among ethnic Turks and Bulgarian Moslems. No other party was able to meet the 4 percent minimum to qualify for representation in the new National Assembly. This meant that nearly a quarter of the electorate, representing primarily centrist political formations, failed to gain representation in the new Assembly, which was even more polarized than its predecessor. Because the UDF did not command a majority in the Assembly by itself, it formed a partnership with the MRF allowing a cabinet headed by Filip Dimitrov to take office in November 1991.

The UDF government

The Dimitrov government had several underlying weaknesses. Although the UDF was more unified than it had been before its split, it was still a coalition of separate parties and personalities with their own, often conflicting, agendas. After the fall of his government, Dimitrov compared himself to the prince of a Renaissance city presiding over an assembly of generals in command of their own private armies.[77] Particularly divisive within the UDF was the question of the restoration of the monarchy, for a significant number of deputies and ministers held monarchist views and expressed loyalty to the Coburg dynasty, while others remained in the republican camp. Several UDF leaders, including Stefan Savov, who became president of the National Assembly, visited "His Majesty" in Spain and urged his return to the Bulgarian throne.

The UDF, particularly its dark-blue core, did not interpret its narrow electoral victory as a mandate either to seek compromise with its opponents or to search for additional allies. Its reluctance to accommodate different views ultimately affected its critical relationship with President Zhelev and with the MRF, on whose votes in the Assembly its tenure in office depended.

The highest stated priority of the new government was to "complete the decommunization of the country," and one of the first acts passed by the Assembly provided for the confiscation of the property of the former Communist Party and its satellites: the Trade Union Confederation, Komsomol and official BANU. Even the BSP recognized the necessity, or at least inevitability, of this act and pledged to cooperate. It and the other successor organizations vacated hundreds of buildings, including the great Party House that dominates downtown Sofia, placing them at the disposal of the government.

The prosecution of former communist leaders was also broadly popular. Proceedings had already been launched against some figures, including Todor Zhivkov, under the government of Dimitûr Popov, but the UDF government appointed a more aggressive prosecutor who brought indictments against approximately fifty figures prominent in the Zhivkov and post-Zhivkov BSP governments. These included former Prime Minister Georgi Atanasov and former Economic Minister Stoyan Ovcharov. More controversial was the indictment of former BSP Prime Minister Andrei Lukanov, who was a sitting member of parliament. Lukanov's passport was taken and the Assembly voted to lift his parliamentary immunity. Zhivkov was ultimately convicted of embezzlement and given a term of house arrest that he is currently serving at the home of his granddaughter. Despite an extensive investigation, neither Zhivkov nor any other prominent official was charged with wrongdoing in connection with the Revival Process, a failing that also contributed to the rupture of the UDF-MRF alliance.

Some of the government's decommunization measures were more controversial. For example, the Assembly voted to deny pensions to retirees whose careers had been in BCP posts or the security organs, and it

introduced legislation that would have led to a broad purge of state administration by barring former members of the BCP or its satellites above a certain
rank from civil service posts or by denying the validity of any degrees earned
in Soviet educational institutions. The "Panev Law" also barred from any
position of leadership in an academic institution for five years anyone who
had ever held a post in the BCP or any of its satellites or the Security
Services. Such measures were widely regarded as unfair, and the Panev Law,
which brought about the purge of 1,637 individuals,[78] in particular was
criticized by international human rights organizations. President Zhelev
appealed it to the Constitutional Court, which upheld it in a surprise decision.

In February 1992 the "Group of Thirty-Nine," the former hunger-strikers
against the constitution, accused the BSP of preparing a coup and they
threatened the party with a ban. The BSP accused these opponents of "witch-
hunts and McCarthyism," and found support in President Zhelev, who
compared the dark-blue warnings to the rattling of an empty wagon when no
proof of an impending communist coup could be produced.[79]

The relationship between the President and the UDF government was poor
from the beginning, for in the October parliamentary elections, Zhelev had
made no secret of his sympathy toward the "light-blues," the groups that had
withdrawn from the UDF. When it was his turn to run for popular election
in January 1992, he received only lukewarm UDF support, and this only by
agreeing to accept the "dark-blue" Blaga Dimitrova as his running mate.
Zhelev received only 45 percent of the votes in the first round and was
forced into a run-off, winning with just 53 percent against the BSP-backed
candidate.[80] Following the election, the Assembly majority criticized his
tendency to appoint "pinks," such as Petko Simeonov, to positions in his
office, and its members sought to reduce the powers of the presidency below
even the limits of the constitution. In May, Defense Minister Dimitûr Ludzhev, who Zhelev once described as his "only friend in the Cabinet," was
fired by Prime Minister Dimitrov backed by a majority of the UDF members
in the Assembly.[81]

The economic policies of the Dimitrov government also alienated some
influential political forces. While a "small privatization" – placing shops,
restaurants, and other small businesses in private hands – was successfully
carried out, the government postponed decisions on the future of large state-
owned enterprises until the completion of a program of restoring the property
that had been confiscated by the communists. The policy of "restitution first"
both delayed more important economic reform and provoked a political
reaction, for it mainly benefited Bulgarians, including émigrés, who belonged
to or were descended from families wealthy in the era before World War II,
several of whom were UDF deputies.[82]

Table 9.5 *Presidential elections in Bulgaria, 1992*

President/Vice-President	Party	Votes	% votes
First round, January 12, 1992			
Zheliu Zhelev/	UDF	2,273,468	44.66
Blaga Dimitrova			
Velko Vûlkanov/	Independent[a]	1,549,754	30.44
Rumen Vodenicharov			
Georges Ganchev/	Bulgarian Business	854,020	16.77
Petûr Beron	Bloc		
Blagovest Sendov/	Independent	113,864	2.24
Ognian Saparev			
Slavomir Tsankov/	"Era 3"	50,307	0.99
Mikhail Milanov			
Others	(17 other tickets)	249,696	4.90
Total[b]		5,091,109	100.00
Second round, January 19, 1992			
Zheliu Zhelev/	UDF	2,738,420	52.85
Blaga Dimitrova			
Velko Vûlkanov/	Independent[a]	2,443,434	47.15
Rumen Vodenicharov			
Total[c]		5,181,854	100.00

Notes: [a]Endorsed by the Bulgarian Socialist Party (BSP). [b]Voter turnout: 75.41 percent. [c]Voter turnout: 76.02 percent.
Source: *NTsIOM Ekspres*, no. 1 (January 1992).

Bulgaria's trade unions were particularly disturbed by the sharp fall in living standards and slow pace of economic reform and by the government's decision to withdraw from the Trilateral Commission, a body including representatives of government, business, and labor that had in the past had a strong influence on economic policy. By the summer of 1992 both of Bulgaria's major trade-union organizations were calling for the resignation of the government. A shake-up of the economic ministries, including the firing of the minister of trade and industry, did not lead to a new approach to privatization.

One of the least edifying of the dark-blue efforts at decommunization was the assault on Bulgaria's religious institutions. To be sure, there was no doubt that during the communist era the hierarchy of the Bulgarian Orthodox Church had collaborated with the regime and was thoroughly penetrated by State Security agents.[83] Similarly Nedim Gendzhev, chairman of the Supreme

Table 9.6 *Religious affiliation in Bulgaria*

Religious institution	Membership
Bulgarian Orthodox Church	7,200,000
Supreme Muslim Theological Council	1,170,000
Roman Catholic Church (Latin Rite)	55,000
Roman Catholic Church (Bulgarian Rite)	15,000
Protestant Denominations	35,000
Armenian Orthodox Church	20,000
Central Jewish Theological Council	5,000

Notes: It should be stressed that these are the memberships claimed by the various institutions. Public opinion surveys have found that nearly six out of ten Bulgarians describe themselves as "non-believers," while only one of nine falls in the category of "deeply religious." NTsIOM, *Religiia i pûlnoletnoto naselenie, sotsiologichesko issledvane* (Sofia: NTsIOM, 1992), pp. 31–3. Among Bulgaria's prominent non-believers are President Zhelev, Prime Minister Videnov, and MRF leader Dogan.
Source: *Eastern Europe and the Commonwealth of Independent States 1992* (London: Europa Publications, 1992).

Muslim Theological Council, was an odious figure who openly admitted his ties to State Security and who had collaborated in the Revival Process.[84]

Shortly before Zhivkov's fall, the former physics student turned monk, Khristofor Sûbev, formed the Committee for the Defense of Religious Rights, Freedom of Conscience, and Spiritual Values that was one of the UDF's founding groups.[85] After the UDF election victory he became chairman of the National Assembly's Committee on Religious Affairs and with the assistance of a few dissident bishops and the approval of Prime Minister Dimitrov he moved to overturn the Orthodox hierarchy. When the aged Patriarch Maxim declined a request to resign, Metodi Spassov, a friend of Sûbev and newly appointed Director of the Office of Religious Affairs, declared that Maxim and the other members of the Holy Synod had been appointed illegally by the Communist Party and dismissed them in favor of a rival group led by Metropolitan Pimen of Nevrokop. Pimen promptly made Sûbev a bishop, and on the night of May 31, 1992 Bishop Sûbev and a group of clergy and police physically occupied the Headquarters of the Holy Synod. At the same time, the Board of Religious Affairs seized the Church's bank accounts, effectively halting the payment of salaries to the clergy.

Patriarch Maxim appealed to President Zhelev, who in turn submitted the question of the powers of the Board of Religious Affairs to the Constitutional Court, which ruled that the Board had exceeded its authority. This did not end the schism in the Church, although it ended state intervention. Maxim's supporters, armed with iron bars and bottles, attempted to retake the Synod building in July, but found a superior force waiting for them. The ensuing battle saw injuries to several priests and members of the laity. In the following months there were reports of commando-like attacks on isolated monasteries by one side or the other. After the fall of the Dimitrov government, President Zhelev invited Patriarch Bartholomeos of Constantinople to mediate the dispute, but his advice – "Let Pimen return to Maxim" – was not acceptable to the reformers, and the UDF accused "the atheist president" and the Ecumenical Patriarch of an "unwarranted intrusion into Bulgaria's religious affairs.[86] Most of the clergy, however, remained loyal to Maxim and public opinion turned sharply against the government's efforts to use "communist methods" to reshape the Church. Ultimately, the insurgency collapsed. Pimen returned to Maxim, and Sûbev faded into obscurity.[87] The Constitutional Court's ruling also blocked the Board's attempt to install a new Islamic leadership. The dispute between Gendzhev and an insurgent group of Imams led by Fikri Sali continues, with Gendzhev now enjoying the tacit support of the Socialist government.[88]

At the end of August President Zhelev convened a press conference at which he accused the government and Assembly majority of "having declared war on everyone." And he called on the "dark-blues" to end their policy of confrontation with the trade-unions, the Church, the presidency, and the democratic parties not in the Assembly. He directed his sharpest remarks toward Assembly president Savov, accusing him of exceeding his authority and adding that he considered it "immoral" for a deputy sworn to uphold the republican constitution, to work openly for the restoration of the monarchy. He warned that events in Yugoslavia illustrated the dangers of extremism and he stated: "We must turn from a policy of confrontation and the isolation of opponents toward a policy of national reconciliation and understanding, a policy of uniting all democratic forces . . . to lead the country from its present crisis."[89] A few in the government coalition, including MRF leader Akhmed Dogan, expressed support for Bulgaria's president, but most closed ranks against him. Prime Minister Dimitrov called his charges untrue, and the UDF's governing council accused Zhelev of "completely adopting the policies of the BSP Communists."[90] Stung by press criticism, the government issued an official declaration that the *168 chasa* publishing conglomerate was "biased" in its reporting on the government.[91]

The Dimitrov government could withstand criticism from the president, unions, and the press provided that its parliamentary group was united and its alliance with the MRF remained solid. By Fall 1992 it was apparent that both were coming apart. A group of BSP deputies charged that the MRF violated the constitution's prohibition of ethnically based parties and asked the Constitutional Court to invalidate the election of the MRF's deputies. The court ruled in favor of the MRF, but only by the narrowest of margins.[92] Although the challenge had come from a group of Socialist deputies, the MRF heard few expressions of support from the UDF. Moreover, during the year it failed to get UDF support for any measure to alleviate the economic plight of its constituents. Nor would the Dimitrov cabinet consult with its ally on policy issues. In July, when the BSP introduced a motion of no confidence in the Assembly, Dogan cast a single, symbolic vote in its favor, and in September the entire MRF parliamentary group voted with the Socialists to remove Stefan Savov from his post as president of the National Assembly. Hoping to force his critics into line, Dimitrov insisted on a parliamentary vote of confidence on October 28. This tactic backfired as the MRF deputies joined the Socialists to vote against the prime minister and bring down his government.[93]

From blue to colorless . . .

The defeat of the Dimitrov government was followed by two months of political uncertainty and maneuvering. In accordance with the constitution, President Zhelev asked the UDF, as the largest group in the Assembly, to propose a new government. It renominated Filip Dimitrov, who was again defeated by the combined votes of the BSP and MRF deputies. It was then the turn of the BSP to try to form a government, but the MRF refused absolutely to vote for any candidate nominated by the Socialists. When it appeared that the president would be forced to appoint a caretaker government and schedule new elections, the MRF put forward the name of Liuben Berov, a historian and economist who was also the president's chief advisor on economic affairs. Berov secured a majority in the Assembly with the votes of most of the BSP, the MRF, and at least twenty-three deputies from the UDF who broke ranks with their colleagues.

Berov, sixty-eight at the time of his election, belonged to no party, and he pledged to lead the country out of its "crisis of confrontation" by forming a "government of national responsibility."[94] Although his ministers were drawn primarily from high-level government administrators who were without party affiliation, the BSP was the principal force upholding the cabinet. Another member of the cabinet was Evgeni Matinchev of the MRF, who became a deputy prime minister and minister of labor and social affairs. Matinchev, who is of Bulgarian ethnicity, was the first representative of the MRF to serve at ministerial level. Two other deputy prime ministers belonged to the group of UDF deputies that voted for Berov. Once in office, Berov moved to revive the Trilateral Commission, limit the powers of the Board of Religious Affairs, and promised to speed the process of large-scale privatization.

Berov's coalition proved to be too fragile to allow for significant departures to deal with Bulgaria's problems. In retrospect, probably the most significant development that occurred while it was in power was the "hidden privatization" of much of the economy. Industrial conglomerates, such as Multigrup, Orion, and Tron, emerged in the shadowy world between the public, private, and illegal economic sectors. Many of the productive assets of the economy passed into private hands while the state was left with the inefficient and debt-ridden ones and often continued to subsidize the new private enterprises. International sanctions against the rump Yugoslavia and the Greek embargo against Macedonia provided opportunities for the rapid acquisition of substantial wealth through the smuggling of arms, fuel, and other commodities. As it actually developed, Bulgaria's "private sector" appeared to be dominated less by hardworking entrepreneurs than by "barons" operating at or beyond the fringes of legality. This new segment of Bulgarian society is difficult to analyze, for its activities for the most part are not publicized.[95] With the exception of the appearance of "businessmen" surrounded by an entourage of former athletes as bodyguards in the most expensive hotels, restaurants, and casinos and occasional outbreaks of gangland violence and assassinations, this institution operates in the shadows. Clearly, however, it was not threatened by Berov's government. His successor, Reneta Injova, in fact described the Berov administration as "The government of Multigrup," whose representatives were given access to the highest level of state power.

After nineteen months in office, Berov offered the resignation of his government on September 2, 1994, having come under increasing criticism from his parliamentary supporters. Because no proposed cabinet could muster majority support in the Assembly, President Zhelev appointed Reneta Indzhova, an economist and former head of the state's privatization agency, as caretaker prime minister.[96] Elections for a new National Assembly were scheduled for December 18.

. . . And back to red

The political parties

The UDF. Although there were obvious reasons for the fall of the Dimitrov government, the dark-blues interpreted it as the result of BSP machinations.[97] At its national conference it expelled the groups that had voted for the Berov Cabinet, adopted rules that prohibited not only former BCP members but also the children of BCP members from holding positions in UDF structures, and called for the resignations of the prime minister and president.[98] The National Council determined to pursue a policy of obstruction and confrontation in parliament.

The dark-blues increasingly turned their fire on President Zhelev, accusing him of acquiescing in the "recommunization" of the country. On June 7, 1993 *Demokratsiia* published an extended open letter to the president written by deputy Edvin Sugarev that was remarkable for its bathos and paranoia. Sugarev accused the president of having worked all along for the preservation of communism, restoring "lies and deceit" to public life, turning the economy over to "the launderers of red money," and destroying Bulgaria's chance to become a "normal country" with a "better and more dignified future." In the letter's conclusion, Sugarev announced that he would conduct a hunger strike to last as long as Zhelev remained in office.

I know very well that my decision will not trouble or disturb you. But this country will be doomed if civic vileness is left unpunished, if everyone accepts it as normal, if our sense of moral order is squandered. What will our children believe in and what will they live for?

You may peacefully continue to govern the country, but only if you pay the moral price. My life will be that price. Because Bulgarians must know that not everyone can be bought or intimidated. That there will always be found someone to pound the table and call things by their true names.

And so, Mr. President, I hope you live comfortably with your lies.

With no regard for you at all,

EDVIN SUGAREV[99]

Sugarev's broadside was followed by a walkout from parliament by the UDF's deputies, an escalating series of street demonstrations, and the erection of a "tent city" outside the president's office. At the end of the month Vice President Blaga Dimitrova demonstratively resigned, warning that Bulgaria stood "in the shadow of dictatorship."[100] Zhelev, who showed considerable calm through the crisis, delivered a radio address in which he attributed the downfall of the UDF government to the shortcomings of its own leaders and stated that such tactics as parliamentary boycotts and hunger strikes were neither necessary nor appropriate in a democratic society.[101] Sugarev abandoned his hunger strike after twenty days, stating that he had made his moral point and feared others might be inspired by his example to end their own lives. UDF parliamentarians followed his example, and returned to the Assembly bringing an end to the immediate crisis.

Although by this time, few but hard-core dark-blues remained in the UDF, they continued to be obsessed with the idea of subversion and intensified their struggle "to unmask the enemy with a party card." Alleged lists of State Security agents were produced, and some leaders accused others of being insufficiently firm in their anticommunism. Ianko Iankov, who had returned to the UDF when it swung to the right, warned that the organization

Table 9.7 *Ethnic groups in Bulgaria according to the 1992 census*

Ethnic group	Number	Percent
Bulgarian[a]	7,271,185	85.67
Turkish[a]	800,052	9.43
Gypsy	313,396	3.69
Armenian	13,677	0.16
Others	89,007	1.05
Total	8,487,317	100.00

Note: [a]Pomaks, Bulgarian-speaking Moslems, numbering about 270,000, are included in the Bulgarian and Turkish groups.
Sources: *Statisticheski godishnik 1993* (Sofia: Natsionalen statisticheski institut, 1993), p. 53; Ilona Tomova and Plamen Bogoev, "Minorities in Bulgaria," unpublished report of the President's Office on Minority Affairs, 1992.

was now being taken over by a leftist cabal, but he lost a showdown vote against the individuals he accused and was himself expelled.[102]

The Sixth National UDF Conference in May 1994 actually set up a "Clean Past Commission" to probe the backgrounds of UDF officials, but its chairman soon resigned when she realized that her investigations were being "implemented selectively."[103] A majority of the UDF's parliamentary group refused to obey the instructions of the National Council to walk out of the National Assembly, and this battle led to a further round of accusations, resignations and expulsions.[104] As one deputy argued, the UDF was turning into a sect of true believers divorced from political reality.[105] When the UDF celebrated its fifth anniversary in December 1994, not a single one of its founders was present. In his address, Filip Dimitrov stated that all those who had left the organization, "were now partners of the Communists."[106]

On the eve of the 1994 elections, Stefan Savov took his Democratic Party out of the UDF after a dispute with Dimitrov and formed a coalition, the Popular Union, with the BANU. The latter was itself the result of a merger of the BANU (official) and BANU-NP that had been effected by Anastasiia Dimitrova-Moser, the daughter of Dr. Georgi M. Dimitrov, who had returned to Bulgaria after many years in the United States.

The MRF. The restoration of full civil rights to the country's ethnic Turks and Moslems in December 1989 provoked a strong backlash among some Bulgarians, particularly in areas where they were in the minority. (The ethnic composition of the country as a whole is shown in table 9.7.) Although ultraright nationalist parties fared poorly in the 1990 election, the BSP made local electoral alliances with the Fatherland Party of Labor in October 1991 and attempted to present itself as the defender of ethnic Bulgarians against the "threat" represented both by domestic minorities and by the international power of "Islamic fundamentalism."[107] After the election, the Socialist press focused on the UDF's alliance with "the Turkish party" and in the 1992 presidential election made Zhelev's sympathy for the Turkish minority a central issue.[108] It was the BSP that carried the challenge to the MRF's legitimacy to the Constitutional Court, and a group of about twenty nationalist BSP deputies refused "on principle" to support the Berov government because it had been nominated by "the Turkish Party." Several developments, however, worked to lessen ethnic tensions. The Constitutional Court's decision that the MRF did not violate the constitution's ban on ethnic parties settled the nagging question of the MRF's legitimacy. Local elections, held in conjunction with the parliamentary elections in October 1991, saw ethnic Turks take over local councils and mayoralities where they were in the majority. Because they proved to be neither better nor worse than their predecessors, the fears of ethnic Bulgarians diminished.[109] And, finally, the growing estrangement between the MRF and UDF led to at least a limited *rapprochement* between the MRF and BSP and their informal collaboration in support of the Berov government.

During the period Berov was in power, Evgeni Matinchev of the MRF held the post of first deputy prime minister and actually ran the government for several months when Berov was hospitalized following a heart attack. But Matinchev was an ethnic Bulgarian (to this date no ethnic Turk has held ministerial rank in any Bulgarian government) and the MRF appeared to have little influence on Berov's policies. Its leadership appeared unwilling or unable to propose measures to halt the continuing decline of the standard of living of ethnic Turks, the majority of whom depended on tobacco production. Because they had generally not been owners of the land when it was collectivized, restitution did not benefit them. Moreover, the provisions of the land reform that provided for the distribution of some land to former collective farmers were not implemented. As a result, many of the ethnic Turks chose to emigrate to Turkey, diminishing the party's core electorate.

Some within the MRF were critical of the opulent style of life adopted by Akhmed Dogan and other members of the party elite; others objected to their relative indifference toward religion. In consequence, there emerged rivals and dissident factions. Mehmed Hodzha left the MRF to form the Party of Democratic Change and Nedim Gendzhev created the Democratic Party of Justice, both of which drew off some of the MRF's supporters.[110]

The BSP. Reformers in the BSP made their strongest bid to capture control of the party at its Fortieth Congress, held December 14–17, 1991, in the wake of the UDF's election victory. Alexander Lilov defended his concept of a "modern, leftist party" against an attack led by Chavdar

Kiuranov that advanced the alternative slogan "European Social Democracy."[111] The two formulations differed in three principal ways. Kiuranov's faction advocated a faster pace of reform in the party and society, full rejection of the idea of a planned, or state-directed economy, and the opening of the party to a broader range of opinion.[112] In balloting for the post of party chairman, 198 delegates voted for the Social Democratic faction's candidate, Georgi Pirinski, 243 for Lilov, and 203 for a surprise candidate, Zhan Videnov. Before the second round Lilov resigned from the leadership and threw his support to Videnov, who was promptly elected. In what appeared to be the result of a behind-the-scenes deal, Lilov was appointed head of a newly created Center for Strategic Analyses and Research, suggesting that he would continue to have a major influence on BSP policy.[113]

Videnov, only thirty-two at the time of his election, was generally regarded as Lilov's protégé, whose candidacy had been promoted to attract the votes of younger delegates and block the election of Pirinski. He was immediately labeled a "hardliner," and his victory was interpreted as a major setback for the reformist faction.[114] Indeed, the Congress failed to elect several reformers, including Pirinski himself, to the Supreme Party Council, and a few days later, thirty-eight delegates, including Pirinski, Andrei Lukanov, and Kiuranov, published a declaration critical of the congress and announced the formation of an "Alliance for Social Democracy" within the party.[115]

Until his election as BSP chairman, which came as a surprise even to himself, Zhan Videnov had little experience with political leadership. His career had been, until only a few months earlier, confined to the Komsomol, and in his initial public appearances he appeared hesitant and ill at ease. His election seemed one further step in his party's continuing decline. He had to weather a barrage of abuse from triumphalist UDF leaders in parliament, to supervise the transfer of BSP property to the state – symbolized by the BSP's move from the massive Party House to its present unimposing quarters at 20 Pozitano Street – and to deal with internal factions that threatened to bring about a formal split.

Videnov both symbolized and accelerated an ongoing generational change in the BSP leadership, transferring power to what one news-weekly described as "Daddy's gilded youth."[116] He was the model of a young, upwardly mobile beneficiary of the *nomenklatura* system. Born in Plovdiv in 1959, the son of a mining engineer and an agronomist, he attended the English-language high school favored by the party elite and graduated from the Institute for International Economic Relations in Moscow with a specialty in Arabic. He was then sent back to Plovdiv as Komsomol district secretary for seasoning in party work. In the late 1980s the Komsomol was the party institution most influenced by Gorbachevian "new thinking," and Videnov was not immune to it.[117] Moreover, during 1989 he was sent to Razgrad to "raise morale" at the time of the flight and deportation of ethnic Turks, an experience that demonstrated how far party propaganda was removed from reality.[118]

As party leader, Videnov favored people like himself, building a core of young, well-educated technocrats, usually from the former Komsomol and often from the Plovdiv apparatus. Representatives of the older generation, whether reformers or conservatives, were gradually relegated to the status of backbenchers. The most striking example was Lilov, who became one of Videnov's sharpest critics and who supported a challenge to Videnov's leadership at the 41st Party Congress in June 1994.[119] This congress also saw discussion of a draft program that was approved by a large majority in a party referendum during the fall. The result of prolonged negotiations among the party factions, the new program explicitly rejected the idea of class struggle and of the BSP as the representative of a class, permitted the formal organization of internal party factions, denied the idea that religious belief was a bar to party membership, and called for a continuing examination of all aspects of the party's past.[120] Chavdar Kiuranov considered the adoption of this program as the substantial victory of his Social Democratic faction.[121] Unlike the UDF, the BSP managed to contain its factions inside a "big tent" and was well positioned for the coming parliamentary election.

The December 1994 election

The election showed a clear shift of the electorate toward the BSP, which received a plurality of 43.5 percent of the vote and an absolute parliamentary majority. The UDF suffered a sharp decline as did the MRF. The remainder of the votes went to the Popular Union, which many perceived as the UDF shorn of its right-wing extremists, and the Bulgarian Business Bloc (BBB). Votes for the last group came from the personal appeal of Georges Ganchev, who sang his way into the hearts of a segment of the electorate, but who was expelled from the Assembly when it was revealed that he had declined to give up his American citizenship.[122] Approximately 15 percent of the votes were cast for parties that did not reach the 4 percent cutoff. The shift in the balance of forces was confirmed in elections for local governments held at the end of October. BSP candidates received 41 percent of the votes; the UDF 25 percent; the Popular Union 12 percent; the MRF 8 percent, and the BBB 5 percent.[123]

In the wake of defeat in the parliamentary elections, the leadership of the UDF resigned *en masse*. Ivan Kostov, who had been finance minister in the UDF government, was elected to replace Filip Dimitrov. His first priority

Table 9.8 *Elections to the National Assembly in Bulgaria, 1994*

Party	Votes	% votes	Seats	% seats
Coalition of the				
Democratic Left[a]	2,258,249	43.42	125	52.08
UDF	1,260,374	24.23	69	28.75
Popular Union	338,478	6.51	18	7.50
MRF	283,094	5.44	15	6.25
Bulgarian Business Bloc	244,695	4.70	13	5.42
Democratic Alternative				
for the Republic	196,807	3.78		
Bulgarian Communist Party	78,370	1.51		
"New Choice"	77,641	1.49		
Coalition - Patriotic Alliance	74,350	1.42		
Coalition "Kingdom of Bulgaria"	73,096	1.41		
Others	316,228	6.09		
Total	5,201,382	100.00	240	100.00

Notes: Voter turnout: 74 percent. [a]Coalition of the Democratic Left: the Bulgarian Socialist Party (BSP), the Bulgarian Agrarian National Union-Alexander Stamboliski, and the Political Club Ekoglasnost.
Source: Material supplied to the author by the Central Election Commission.

appeared to be to overcome the structural shortcomings of the coalition, particularly by moving to reduce the independence of its constituent parties and factions.[124] Over the following months, Kostov attempted to improve relations with the Popular Union and the MRF, but the goal of a united opposition remained elusive. For example, the UDF refused to support the candidacy of former prime minister Reneta Indzhova for mayor of Sofia, and when President Zhelev announced that he would seek re-election in 1997, the UDF declined to offer its support even though this would almost certainly guarantee the election of a BSP-backed candidate.[125]

The Videnov government

"There are always factions, even Zhivkov had them," Videnov stated while he was putting together his cabinet. A clear gesture toward the social democratic faction was the appointment of Georgi Pirinski as foreign minister. The forty-seven-year-old Pirinski, who was born in the United States,[126] had consistently joined or supported reform programs since Zhivkov's fall. The conservative/nationalist bloc in the party was rewarded with the appointment of Ilcho Dimitrov as minister of education. Dimitrov,

Table 9.9 *Indicators of economic trends in Bulgaria since 1989*

	1989	1990	1991	1992	1993	1994	1995[a]
GDP	0.5	-9.1	-11.7	-7.3	-2.4	1.4	2.5
Industrial output	-1.1	-16.0	-27.8	-15.0	-7.0	4.1	2.8
Rate of inflation	6.4	26.3	333.5	82.0	73.0	96.3	62
Rate of unemployment	n.a.	1.5	11.5	15.6	16.4	12.8	10.5
GNP per capita	n.a.	n.a.	n.a.	n.a.	n.a.	4,230	n.a.
% Workforce in private activity[b]	5.5	5.9	10.1	17.7	28.3	34.7	n.a.
% GDP from private sector[b]	n.a.	n.a.	16.6	25.3	35.9	40.2	n.a.

Notes: GDP – % change over previous year; industrial output – % change over previous year; rate of inflation – % change in end-year retail/consumer prices; rate of unemployment – % of labor force, end of year; GNP per capita – in US dollars at PPP exchange rates. [a]Estimate. [b]Not including cooperatives; data for 1994 are preliminary.

Sources: European Bank for Reconstruction and Development, *Transition Report 1995: Economic Transition in Eastern Europe and the Former Soviet Union* (London: EBRD, 1995); European Bank for Reconstruction and Development, *Transition Report Update, April 1996: Assessing Progress in Economies in Transition* (London: EBRD, 1996).

who had previously held this post under Zhivkov, had also been a prominent apologist for the Revival Campaign.[127] His appointment provoked a sharp protest from the MRF to which Videnov replied: "No-one cares about that anymore." Several ministers in the economic sector were close to Andrei Lukanov. During the summer, Lukanov himself upstaged Videnov by becoming the Bulgarian director of Topenergy, a Russian-Bulgarian firm that aimed to construct a pipeline across Bulgaria for the export of Russian natural gas to Western Europe. This positioned him at the head of the "red millionaires" close to Multigrup whose economic power rivaled that of the government.[128]

The data presented in table 9.9, showing the main economic trends since 1989, indicate that the BSP government inherited an economy that apparently had bottomed out in 1998 and was showing signs of recovery. It was widely expected that with its solid parliamentary majority, the government would proceed with long-delayed structural reforms. Indeed, it announced a plan for voucher privatization, modeled on the Czech reform. The implementation of this program, however, was repeatedly delayed, and the country was soon overtaken by a series of economic calamities.

The first came in agriculture, for the government's reluctance to carry through land restitution created a situation in which land ownership and the status of the remaining cooperative farms was unclear. Less and less land was put under cultivation, leading to steadily declining output. This was compounded by the government's issuing of export licenses to "certain groups" allowing them to purchase much of the 1995 harvest at low, state-regulated prices and to export it at the world market price. The result was a rapid rise in food prices, the introduction of bread rationing, and a humiliating plea to the European Union for emergency grain shipments.[129]

From the beginning of 1996 the *lev* began to lose its value, falling from seventy to the dollar to one-hundred-eighty to the dollar in July and nearly four-hundred to the dollar by November.[130] This was accompanied and in part caused by the collapse of the banking system and the revelation that several banks had served mainly to launder illegal money and to transfer it to foreign accounts. Rapid inflation and the banking crisis reverberated throughout the economy, causing a contraction of business activity and a sharp fall in GDP.[131] Because the government could not meet its foreign debts without loans from the International Monetary Fund, Videnov was forced to accept the demand of the IMF to establish a Currency Board under its observation. Although this promised to prevent hyperinflation, it also held out the prospect of further stringent austerity measures for an already hard-pressed population.[132] Tension rose further when, on October 2, Andrei Lukanov, the severest critic of Videnov's economic policies within the BSP, was assassinated.[133]

Bulgaria's economic setbacks, promoted the political revival of the UDF. President Zhelev had been the leading opponent of the Socialist government, appealing its legislation to the Constitutional Court, pointing out its "genetic links" to organized crime, and badgering it to make an unequivocal statement of Bulgaria's desire to join NATO and other European structures. The Popular Union and the MRF supported his re-election, but the UDF would not forgive him his criticism of Filip Dimitrov's government. The deadlock was broken by Zhelev's agreement to participate in a primary election against Petûr Stoianov, a forty-four-year-old lawyer, put forward by the UDF leadership. Stoianov won an easy victory, and went on to crush the BSP candidate, Ivan Marazov, by a 20 percent margin, a result that was widely interpreted as a popular vote of no confidence in the Socialist government.[134]

Following the Stoianov victory, demands for Videnov's resignation were widespread within the BSP itself. A plenary meeting of the party's Supreme Council gave him a narrow, eighty-seven to sixty-nine, vote of confidence, allowing him to remain in office, but did not silence his opponents. Foreign Minister Pirinski resigned to prepare to challenge Videnov at an extraordinary BSP congress scheduled for the December 21–22. He was joined by several other high-ranking party members, who indicated that they would prefer to split the party rather than allow Videnov to continue as prime minister.[135]

Conclusion

History provides few precedents by which we may gauge success or failure in the era that began with the collapse of communism. By the standard of the hopes that were raised in 1989, much of Bulgaria's subsequent experience engenders disappointment. Economic reforms have been glacially slow and have been stained by corruption and the rise of criminal activity. Disarray among the political opposition has so far kept the state in the hands of the heirs of the Communist Party. The West has shown no eagerness to welcome Bulgaria or to provide it with significant economic support.[136]

On the other hand, since 1989 the country has had three national elections for parliament, two for local governments, and two for the presidency, all conducted without violence or serious charges of fraud. The machinery of government created by the new constitution has functioned without crisis. The decisions of the Constitutional Court, despite complaints and disagreements, have been respected by the government and the public. Surveys of popular attitudes have consistently shown that however low the esteem in which some individuals or parties are held, there is broad acceptance of the basic ideas and institutions of political democracy.[137] Bulgaria has no serious dispute with any of its neighbors, and domestic ethnic tensions have significantly diminished. Measured against the standard of disasters avoided, never inappropriate in the Balkans, Bulgaria's performance allows a moderate degree of optimism about the future.

Acronyms

BANU	Bulgarian Agrarian National Union (Bûlgarski zemedelski naroden sûiuz)
BANU-NP	BANU-Nikola Petkov (BZNS-Nikola Petkov)
BCP	Bulgarian Communist Party (Bûlgarska komunisticheska partiia)
BSP	Bulgarian Socialist Party (Bûlgarska sotsialisticheska partiia)
CEC	Central Electoral Commission (Tsentralna izbiratelna komisiia)
CDNI	Committee for the Defense of the National Interests (Komitet za zashtita na natsionalnite interesi)
GNA	Grand National Assembly (Veliko narodno sûbranie)

MRF   Movement for Rights and Freedoms (Dvizhenie za prava i svobodi)
NA   National Assembly (Narodno sûbranie)
UDF   Union of Democratic Forces (Sûiuz na demokratichni sili)

NOTES

1 *Bûlgarski konstitutsii i konstitutsionni proekti*, ed. Veselin Metodiev and Lûchezar Stoianov (Sofia: Dûrzhavno izdatelstvo "D-r Petûr Beron," 1990), pp. 20–36.
2 Diana Mishkova, "Modernization and Political Elites in the Balkans before the First World War," *East European Politics and Societies* 9, no. 1 (Winter 1995), 63–89. A recent general history of modern Bulgaria is R. J. Crampton, *A Short History of Modern Bulgaria* (London: Cambridge University Press, 1987). The political ideas that inspired Bulgarians in the nineteenth century are examined in Cyril E. Black, *The Establishment of Constitutional Government in Bulgaria* (Princeton, NJ: Princeton University Press, 1943).
3 For Bulgarian politics from the end of the nineteenth century through 1923, with emphasis on the Agrarian movement, see John D. Bell, *Peasants in Power: Alexander Stamboliski and the Bulgarian Agrarian National Union, 1899–1923* (Princeton, NJ: Princeton University Press, 1977).
4 Nissan Oren, *Bulgarian Communism: The Road to Power* (New York: Columbia University Press, 1971), pp. 5–35. The politics of the interwar period from a monarchist point of view is presented in Stephane Groueff, *Crown of Thorns: The Reign of King Boris III of Bulgaria* (New York: Madison Books, 1987).
5 For a fuller description of the communist takeover and additional bibliography, see John D. Bell, *The Bulgarian Communist Party from Blagoev to Zhivkov* (Stanford, CA: Hoover Institution Press, 1986), pp. 55–101. Information about the reign of terror that accompanied the Fatherland Front's seizure of power has recently appeared in Polia Meshkova and Diniu Sharlanov, *Bûlgarskata gilotina* (Sofia: Agentsiia "Demokratsiia," 1994).
6 *Statisticheski godishnik* (Sofia: Natsionalen statisticheski institut, 1988), p. 47; Robert N. Taaffe, "Population Structure," in *Südosteuropa-Handbuch Band VI – Bulgarien*, ed. Klaus-Detlev Grothusen (Göttingen: Vandenhoeck & Ruprecht, 1990), pp. 445–9.
7 While it is dangerous to rely on a few selected indicators and on information drawn from official sources, it can be pointed out that Bulgaria consistently ranked in the top fifth on scales associated with modernity in George T. Kurian, *The Book of World Rankings* (New York: Facts on File, 1979). Kurian ranked Bulgaria 29th out of 190 nations surveyed. His rankings were generally consistent with those of Charles L. Taylor and David A. Jodice, *World Handbook of Political and Social Indicators*, 3d ed., vol. 1 (New Haven and London: Yale University Press, 1983).
8 Observations similar to those of the author were also made by the sociologist Chavdar Kiuranov, who became convinced that the social foundation of a movement for party liberalization had been established. Kiuranov currently leads the "social democratic fraction" within the Bulgarian Socialist Party. Interview with the author: Sofia, January 22, 1995. Information on the creation of a rock

subculture among Bulgarian youth was provided by Petûr Iovchev in a two-part article, "Bûlgarskiiat rok," published electronically in the internet newsgroup soc.culture.bulgaria, 18 June, 25 July, 1994. The archive of soc.culture.bulgaria may be accessed at: http://www.cs.columbia.edu/ ~ Radev/Bulgaria.

9 An official defense of the Revival Process is found in the collection of articles edited by Georgi Iankov, *Problemi na razvitieto na bûlgarskata narodnost i natsiia* (Sofia: Bûlgarskata akademiia na naukite, 1988). See also Kostadin Chakûrov, *Vtoriia etazh* (Sofia: K & M, 1990), pp. 186–91 and Orlin Zagorov, *Vûzroditelniiat protses* (Sofia: Pandora Ltd., 1993).

10 Markov and Kostov, whose broadcasts on the BBC and Radio Free Europe clearly disturbed the authorities, were targeted for assassination by "the Bulgarian umbrella." Markov died, but Kostov survived and is currently managing editor of the newspaper *Kontinent*. On dissent inside Bulgaria, see Bell, *The Bulgarian Communist Party*, pp. 137–42, and Chakûrov, *Vtoriia etazh*, pp. 51–144.

11 Zhivkov consistently denied this longstanding rumor, but the recent publication of the stenographic record of the BCP Central Committee Plenum of September 4, 1963, demonstrates that the offer was in fact made. *1963 – Otrichaneto ot Bûlgariia* (Sofia: Izdatelska kûshta Ogledalo, 1994).

12 *Rabotnichesko delo*, 29 July 1987. A glimpse of the pressure being placed on Zhivkov by Gorbachev and by Soviet ambassador Leonid Grekov was revealed in an interview with the latter published in the journal *Pogled*, no. 26 (1 July 1985). See also Chakûrov, *Vtoriia etazh*, pp. 111–44.

13 John D. Bell, "Bulgaria," in *Yearbook on International Communist Affairs – 1989*, ed. Richard F. Staar (Stanford, CA: Hoover Institution Press, 1989), pp. 300–1.

14 *Sofia News*, 2 March 1988. The description of the BCP's election tactics was given to the author by Vasil Gotsev, who was an official in the Ministry of Justice at the time of the election, in an interview in Sofia, April 19, 1990.

15 Ostensibly a study of fascist Germany, Italy, and Spain, Zhelev's *Fashizmût* drew obvious parallels with communist institutions. The book's suppression immediately after publication created a sensation in Bulgarian intellectual circles that is described in *Fashizmût sreshtu Fashizmût*, ed. Ivan Slavov (Sofia, 1991).

16 The appearance of organized dissident groups in the late 1980s was chronicled in Radio Free Europe's research reports. See also the surveys in *Yearbook on International Communist Affairs* for 1988–1990.

17 Todor Zhivkov, *Preustroistvoto na nasheto obshtestvo – prizvanie i otgovornost na intelligentsiiata* (Sofia: Partizdat, 1989).

18 Little is known publicly about the Turkish underground before the fall of the Zhivkov regime. Because some of those involved engaged in acts of terror (see the description in Georgi Sotirov, *Turskite teroristi i az, edin ot shesto* [Sofia: Mladezh, 1991]), there has been a tendency to avoid its discussion. When asked if his planned memoirs would cover the period from 1984 through 1989, Akhmed Dogan, leader of the Movement for Rights and Freedoms, only shook his head and laughed. Interview with the author: Sofia, February 22, 1992.

19 *Destroying Ethnic Identity: The Expulsion of the Bulgarian Turks* (New York: Helsinki Watch, 1989).

20 Mladenov denied stopping in Moscow, but his flight from Beijing was several hours longer than normal. The elevation of Mladenov, "a man well known to us," was reported as a victory for *perestroika* in the Soviet press (*Pravda* 13, 15, 18, 29 November, and 1 December 1989), and Mladenov paid a friendly visit to Moscow on December 4–5. The most detailed account of Zhivkov's removal appeared in the *Financial Times* (London), 16 November 1989. Further information appeared in *Sofia News*, 7 June 1990. Zhivkov's own account emphasized the desire of his colleagues to replace him "with someone enjoying the full confidence of Moscow." Todor Zhivkov, *Sreshtu niakoi lûzhi* (Sofia: Delfin pres, 1993), p. 49.

21 John D. Bell, "Bulgaria," in *Yearbook on International Communist Affairs – 1990* (Stanford, CA: Hoover Institution Press), pp. 313–16. It is an interesting comment on the role of the constitution during the communist period that this reform had suddenly to be delayed when it was pointed out by someone who had actually read the document that the constitution mandated a one-month period between the proposal of an amendment and a vote on its adoption.

22 *Bûlgarska telegrafna agentsiia* (BTA), 2 February 1990.

23 In a general way, Lilov's views were expressed in his book *Voubrazhenie i tvorchestvo* (Sofia: Nauka i izkustvo, 1986). This work, which discussed the ideas of Bulgarian and foreign Marxist philosophers, contained not a single reference to Todor Zhivkov; even the bibliography omitted the theoretical contributions of Bulgaria's "son of the people."

24 The leadership did persuade the congress to expand the Council to 153 members and to add several prominent reform proponents. Most of the latter, however, declined, stating that they did not want to be "beneficiaries of manipulation." *Rabotnichesko delo*, 6, 8 February 1990.

25 John D. Bell, "Bulgaria," in *Yearbook in International Communist Affairs – 1991*, ed. Richard F. Staar (Stanford, CA: Hoover Institution Press, 1991), pp. 260–2.

26 John D. Bell, "Bulgaria," in *Developments in East European Politics*, ed. Stephen White, Judy Batt, and Paul Lewis (London: Macmillan, 1993), p. 87.

27 Boncho Asenov, *Ot shesto za shesto* (Sofia: Poligraf, 1994), pp. 82–93. See also two articles by Kjell Engelbrekt from Radio Free Europe's *Report on Eastern Europe*: "Shakeup in the Ministry of Internal Affairs" (18 May 1990) and "The Lasting Influence of the Secret Services" (10 July 1991). According to a recent report in the newspaper *Trud* (15 October 1995), 80 percent of former State Security personnel are currently employed in the private sector.

28 Stefan Nikolov, "The Bulgarian Armed Forces in Transition," *DejaNews Service* (distributed electronically), 1 April 1995.

29 Interview with the author: Sofia, February 11, 1992.

30 "Kakvo stava v SDS?" *Demokratsiia-91*, 13 September 1991.

31 See Zhelev's own introduction to the American edition of *Fashizmût* (Boulder, CO: Social Science Monographs, 1990); Khristo Aleksiev, "Istinata za nego," *Demokratichna sedmitsa*, 7 June 1990; Dobrin Spasov, "A Friendly Letter to a Political Opponent," *Rabotnichesko delo*, 3 March 1990. On the controversies that surrounded the publication and withdrawal of *Fashizmût*, see Slavov, ed., *Fashizmût sreshtu "Fashizmût."*

32 While much of *Fashizmût* may seem familiar to Western readers who have had long familiarity with the totalitarian model, Zhelev's position as an insider led to a number of original observations. This includes his emphasis on the state's control of occupations and wage scales, the role of the professional unions, the system's "alliance" with mediocrity and, most notably, the system's weaknesses, which doomed it to ultimate collapse. Zhelev's analysis also benefited enormously from his interest in the case of Spain, which most prominent Western scholars were reluctant to classify as totalitarian.

33 Zheliu Zhelev, *Fashizmût* (Boulder, CO: Social Science Monographs, 1990), p. 158. This edition was a facsimile of the original 1981 Bulgarian edition.

34 The BANU (official) was the direct descendent of the BANU that had been a legal party under the communists. This designation reflects Bulgarian practice and was used to distinguish the organization from the BANU-NP. Ultimately there would be at least seven organizations that laid claim to the BANU title.

35 The background to the roundtable negotiations and a description of the basic agreements appear in Albert P. Melone, "Bulgaria's National Roundtable Talks and the Politics of Accommodation: Creating the Conditions for a Peaceful Transition to a Democratic Constitutional System," paper prepared for the 1993 Interim Meeting of the International Political Science Association Research Committee on Comparative Judicial Studies, St. John's College, Santa Fe, New Mexico, 1–4 August, 1993.

36 *Rabotnichesko delo*, 13 March 1990.

37 *Dûrzhaven vestnik*, 10 April 1990. A detailed study of the legislation affecting the elections appears in John D. Bell, Ronald A. Gould, and Richard G. Smolka, *The 1990 Bulgarian Elections: A Pre-Election Technical Assessment* (Washington, DC: International Foundation for Electoral Systems, 1990).

38 The BSP expected to gain credit for halting Zhivkov's "Revival Campaign" and restoring the rights of ethnic Turks. The UDF assumed that the ethnic Turks would hold the BSP, not just Zhivkov, responsible for their persecution.

39 *Dûrzhaven vestnik*, 6 April 1990.

40 The concept of a Grand National Assembly reflected precommunist tradition. The Tûrnovo Constitution stipulated that amendments could be made only by a Grand National Assembly, twice as large as the Ordinary National Assembly that dealt with normal parliamentary matters. The decision to hold the ceremonial opening of the GNA in Tûrnovo rather than Sofia was also an appeal to tradition.

41 One young lawyer and UDF activist argued that Stalev's selection owed much to his former students, "who never forgot his honesty." Interview with group of UDF activists: Sofia, April 18, 1990.

42 Dimitûr Popov's subsequent election to the post of prime minister in the "government of cohabitation" owed much to the reputation and visibility he acquired as secretary of the CEC and its main spokesman before the media. See also *The New Democratic Frontier: A Country by Country Report on Elections in Central and Eastern Europe,* ed. Larry Garber and Eric Bjornlund (Washington, DC, 1992), pp. 141–5.

43 This method was hardly appropriate in a country with near zero illiteracy, but it was generally believed that using the traditional ballot system would reduce apprehension. Because so many parties participated, single colors could not be assigned to all of them. The BSP ballot was red, the UDF blue, and the official

BANU had its traditional orange. The Independent Popular Democratic Party of Plovdiv, however, used a white ballot with blue, orange, and green stripes. The names of the candidates or parties were also printed on each ballot.

44 Interview with the author: Sofia, April 18, 1990.

45 Author's observation: Gotse Delchev, 9 June 1990.

46 Interview with the author: Sofia, April 23, 1990.

47 *Politicheski partii i dvizheniia v republika Bûlgariia* (Sofia: Confederation of Independent Trade Unions of Bulgaria, 1990), p. 68.

48 *Novi politicheski i obshtestveni sili* (Sofia: Pressluzhba "Kurier," 1990), pp. 15–16; *BTA,* 29 December 1989.

49 Viktor Vûlkov, interview with the author: Sofia, June 15, 1990.

50 Author's interviews with Zheliu Zhelev and with Petko Semeonov, director of the UDF's election campaign: Sofia, April 14–21, 1990.

51 Author's interviews with Zheliu Zhelev and Alexandûr Lilov in April and June 1990.

52 This attitude was illustrated by an open letter to Zheliu Zhelev from his old professor, Dobrin Spasov. It asked rhetorically how Zhelev could associate with the rabble in the UDF and argued that despite its past mistakes the BSP still included the bulk of the country's educated professionals and experienced administrators. *Rabotnichesko delo,* 3 March 1990.

53 See the discussion in the UDF's newspaper, *Demokratsiia,* 26 May 1990.

54 Author's interviews with Alexandûr Lilov and Alexandûr Strezov, deputy chairman of the BSP: Sofia, June 1990.

55 The figures given in table 9.2 are from the first round of voting on June 10 that decided the outcome in 119 single-member districts and the distribution of 200 seats in proportional representation. The remaining 81 seats were filled by runoff elections on June 17 in single-member districts where no candidate had secured more than 50 percent of the vote in the first round.

56 Veselin Georgiev, "40 'veliki' deputati sa vlezli nezakonno v parlamenta," *Bûlgarska korona,* 22 April 1994.

57 The Bulgarian Association for Fair Elections was founded by Kevork Kevorkian and received considerable support from the National Republican and Democratic Institutes for International Affairs. For a detailed report on the June election, see John D. Bell et al., *Bulgaria's Transition from Dictatorship to Democracy* (Washington, DC: International Foundation for Electoral Systems, 1990).

58 *Duma,* 14 June 1990.

59 Ibid., 6 July 1990.

60 Ibid., 7 July 1990.

61 *BTA,* 1 August 1990.

62 The party's previous congress was its Fourteenth. It was decided, however, to renumber party congresses to include those of the Social Democratic Party before the formation of the BCP in 1919. This gesture was intended to show that Social Democracy was part of the BSP's heritage.

63 The attack on the Party House, which is still a matter of some mystery and controversy, is the sole significant exception to the nonviolent character of Bulgarian politics since the fall of Zhivkov's regime.

64 Bell, "Bulgaria," *Yearbook . . . 1991,* pp. 264–6.

65 *New York Times,* 30 November 1990.

66 *BTA,* 21 December 1990.

67 *New York Times*, 4 December 1990. Beron, director of Bulgaria's Museum of Natural History, maintained that his "collaboration" with State Security consisted of filing routine reports on the activities of visiting foreign scientists. He resigned to avoid controversy and came bitterly to resent the distrust demonstrated by his colleagues. Interview with the author: Sofia, February 4, 1992.

68 This section relies extensively on the analysis of Professor A. E. Dick Howard, a specialist on constitutions at the University of Virginia Law School.

69 Simeon frequently comments on Bulgarian events, and members of the royal family have paid well publicized visits to the country. The publication of a Bulgarian edition of Stephane Groueff's *Crown of Thorns*, an adulatory biography of Simeon's father, Tsar Boris III, also helped to uplift the monarchist cause. But public opinion polls have never shown much more than a 15 percent approval rating for a restoration, and in the December 1994 elections the combined tally for all monarchist parties fell well short of the 4 percent barrier. Late in December 1995, Simeon announced that he would visit Bulgaria. No date for the visit was mentioned, but it was suggested that it might coincide with the fiftieth anniversary of the abolition of the monarchy. *BTA,* 13 December 1995.

70 Ambiguity in the constitution's clauses on the separation of powers along with Bulgaria's general lack of experience with the rule of law were described as the most serious problems to confront the Constitutional Court by two of its justices, Todor Chipev and Alexander Arabadzhiev. Interview with the author: Sofia, February 20, 1992.

71 Ianko Iankov, *Dokument za samolichnost* (Sofia: "Ianus," 1994), pp. 262–6.

72 This was confirmed by the UDF's Vice President of the National Assembly, Snezhana Botusharova, in an interview with the author: Sofia, February 19, 1992.

73 Interview with Petko Simeonov: Sofia, February 6, 1992. Tsentûr za liberalni strategii, *Izbiratelni sistemi i tiakhnata politicheska prilozhimost u nas* (Sofia: Center for Liberal Strategies, 1994), pp. 24–7.

74 Jozef Darski, "The Strange Case of Bulgaria," *Uncaptive Minds* 6, no. 2 (Summer 1993), 17.

75 *Duma,* 5 August 1991.

76 Hereafter, the UDF-Movement will be referred to simply as the UDF. This reflects Bulgarian practice and the fact that the UDF-Center and UDF-Liberal coalitions dissolved into independent parties and formations after the October elections.

77 Interview with the author: Washington, DC, April 28, 1993.

78 *Standart*, 6 February 1995.

79 *Trud,* 20 February 1992. Interview with the author: Sofia, February 25, 1992.

80 It was probably significant for future political developments that Zhelev's majority was made possible by the solid support of the MRF's constituency. In the first round 93 percent voted for him; 99 percent in the second. *Pismo ot Bûlgariia*, no. 6 (January 1992), 10–11.

81 Zhelev made this comment in a radio interview, cited in Radio Free Europe, *Report on Eastern Europe*, 22 June 1992.

82 According to BSP deputy Nora Ananieva, there were twenty-eight UDF deputies who benefitted directly and substantially from the law on restitution. Interview

with the author: Sofia, February 21, 1992. This information could not be independently verified.

83   Boncho Asenov, *Ot shesto za shesto* (Sofia: Poligraf, 1994), pp. 40–72.

84   *Duma*, 10 February 1992.

85   Sûbev was, in fact, one of the UDF's most colorful figures. He usually appeared at UDF rallies to bless the opposition and exorcise communist demons.

86   *Demokratsiia*, 13 September 1993.

87   Spas T. Raikin, "The Recent Schism in the Bulgarian Orthodox Church," unpublished paper presented at the Fifth Joint Meeting of the Bulgarian Studies Association (Pittsburgh, PA, 26 May 1994).

88   *BTA*, 28 February 1995.

89   "Preskonferentsiia na Prezidenta Zhelev," *Pismo ot Bûlgariia*, August 1992, 12–14.

90   *Pismo ot Bûlgariia*, September 1992, 12–14.

91   *168 chasa* publishes one of Bulgaria's most popular newspapers and weekly news journals. It was indeed highly critical of the Dimitrov government, and the former prime minister later stated that he was convinced it was a front for the old communist *nomenklatura* and the Bulgarian mafia. Interview with the author: Washington, DC, April 28, 1993.

92   There was a vacancy on the twelve-member court at the time of its ruling. Six justices actually voted to uphold the BSP petition and five voted against it. Court rules, however, required a petition to be upheld by at least seven votes. *Duma,* 22 April 1992. The decision appeared in *Dûrzhaven vestnik*, 22 April 1992. Transcripts of the minority and majority arguments were provided to the author by Justice Alexander Arabadzhiev.

93   Reuters, 29 October 1992. Kjell Engelbrekt, "The Fall of Bulgaria's First Noncommunist Government," *Report on Eastern Europe*, 3 November 1992.

94   *BTA*, 30 December 1992.

95   Zeljko Bogetic and Arrye L. Hillman, "Privatizing Profits of Bulgaria's State Enterprises," *Transition: The Newsletter about Reforming Economies* 6, no. 3 (March 1995), 4–6. Accusations that Multigrup was behind the attempt on the life of Macedonian president Kilo Gligorov, focused some light on that organization's background. See *Nova Makedonija*, 2 November 1995.

96   Zhelev apparently hoped that Indzhova could remain in office as head of a "presidential government." When the Assembly voted against this, he proposed a new government under Dimitûr Ludzhev, who was also unable to muster sufficient support in the Assembly.

97   *Demokratsiia*, 13 January 1993.

98   *BTA*, 17 March 1993.

99   Edvin Sugarev, "V kakvo shte viarvat detsata ni?" *Demokratsiia*, 7 June 1993.

100   *BTA*, 30 June 1993.

101   *BTA*, 13 June 1993.

102   *Standart*, 18 October 1993.

103   *Khorizont Radio Network*, 24 June 1994; distributed electronically by *East Europe Intelligence Report*, 27 June 1994.

104   *Demokratsiia*, 28 July 1994.

105   *Kontinent*, 14 August 1994.

106 *Demokratsiia*, 8 December 1994. The complete absence of UDF's founders from the anniversary was pointed out by the BSP newspaper, *Duma*, on the same date.

107 The leader of the FPL, Mincho Minchev, worked for State Security before Zhivkov's fall and had been an active participant in the Revival Process. *BTA*, 29 December 1989.

108 MRF support for Zhelev was in fact decisive, for a majority of ethnic Bulgarians voted for his opponent. *BTA*, 20 January 1992. In the campaign Zhelev was frequently depicted wearing a fez and accused of willingness to sell out "the Bulgarian nation." Interview with Zheliu Zhelev: Sofia, February 25, 1992.

109 This observation is based on the author's interviews with local officials and religious leaders in Kûrdzhali conducted in February 1992.

110 *168 chasa*, 30 August 1993; *Demokratsiia*, 4 August 1993; Venelin I. Ganev, "The Mysterious Politics of Bulgaria's 'Movement for Rights and Freedoms,'" *University of Chicago Law Center Review* 4, no. 1 (1995), distributed electronically.

111 *Duma*, 16 December 1991.

112 Chavdar Kiuranov, interview with the author: Sofia, January 25, 1995.

113 Kjell Engelbrekt and Rada Nikolaev, "Bulgaria: Socialist Party Elects New Leader," *Report on Eastern Europe*, 30 December 1991.

114 *BTA*, 17 December 1991.

115 *Duma*, 24 December 1991.

116 *168 chasa*, 9–15 January 1995.

117 Videnov had some input into a report on the state of Bulgarian youth that pointed to serious and worsening problems in the younger generation's health, productivity, and party discipline. A copy of this report was provided to the author by Alexander Mirchev, who was involved in its preparation and who was Videnov's immediate superior in the Komosomol.

118 Interview with the author: Sofia, February 7, 1992.

119 See Lilov's comments on Videnov's leadership in *24 chasa*, 12 January 1995. At the Forty-first Party Congress, Lilov supported the candidacy of Ianaki Stoilov. Stoilov, only a year older than Videnov, had been his first choice at the Fortieth Congress but declined to run at that time. Following the BSP election victory, the press reported that Stoilov would leave the country for studies at Harvard University (*Kontinent*, 10 January 1995).

120 *BSP informatsionen biuletin*, October 1994.

121 Interview with the author: Sofia, January 25, 1995.

122 *Demokratsiia*, 14 April 1995. Georges Ganchev is, perhaps, the most colorful of the political figures who emerged after 10 November. He was formerly coach of the Romanian fencing team and claimed to have made a fortune in Hollywood. He made a dramatic splash in Bulgarian politics with a surprise third place finish in the 1992 presidential elections. His principal appeal was as an "antipolitician," adept with songs and jokes. Although he has sometimes been called "the Bulgarian Zhirinovsky," such a characterization is not accurate, since he is neither an ultranationalist nor mentally disturbed. Interview with the author: Sofia, January 20, 1995.

123 *BTA*, 30 October 1995.

124 *Demokratsiia,* 1 March 1995.
125 *BTA,* 20, 22 November 1995. The Popular Union and MRF immediately announced their support for the president's re-election.
126 Pirinski's father, also named Georgi, was active in the CPUSA from the 1920s and was deported with his family in the early 1950s. His memoirs, *Izvikani ot spomena: Portreti na amerikanski i bûlgarski bortsi za mir i demokratsiia v SASht* (Sofia: Partizdat, 1986) provide a portrait of the American radical left in that period and of its efforts to organize Slavic and Balkan ethnic groups.
127 Dimitrov admitted having been head of a "Coordinating Committee" in the Bulgarian Academy of Sciences charged with implementing the Revival Process. *Standart,* 27 January 1995.
128 *BTA,* 25 May 1995.
129 *BTA,* 15 January 1996; Reuters, 28 July 1996.
130 *Demokratsiia,* 22 November 1996.
131 *Kontinent,* 21 November 1996.
132 *Duma,* 26 November 1996.
133 *BTA,* 3 October 1996.
134 *Demokratsiia,* 30 October 1996.
135 *Duma,* 14 November 1996.
136 The decision of the European Union to keep Bulgaria, along with Romania, on a "black-list," while extending the right to visa-free entry to citizens of the other East European states, was seen as a gesture of contempt and a repudiation of Bulgaria's reform efforts. *BTA,* 27 September 1995.
137 Jill Chin, "Political Attitudes in Bulgaria," *Radio Free Europe Report on Eastern Europe,* 11 April 1993; Deian Kiuranov et al., "Iz 'Politicheska stabilnost i obshtestvena modernizatsiia,'" in *Aspekti na etnokulturnata situatsiia v Bûlgariia* (Sofia: Asotsiatsiia AKSES, 1994), pp. 316-33; Richard Rose and Christian Haerpfer, *New Democracies Barometer III: Learning from What Is Happening* (Glasgow: Centre for the Study of Public Policy, University of Strathclyde, 1994).

10   Romanian exceptionalism? Democracy, ethnocracy, and uncertain pluralism in post-Ceauşescu Romania

Vladimir Tismaneanu

Introduction

Until the November 1996 presidential and parliamentary elections, postcommunist Romania presented scholars of the transition with a striking paradox: the most abrupt break with the old order seemed to have resulted in its least radical transformation. Many old faces remained in power while skillfully putting on new masks. Romania-watchers are thus divided between those who highlight the failure of the revolution, and those who think that former President Ion Iliescu did his utmost under the existing circumstances to turn his country into a functioning democracy. The major themes addressed in this paper are therefore linked to the widely perceived "exceptional" nature of Romania's transition from state socialism. In the concluding pages I will address the meaning of the 1996 elections which resulted in Iliescu's defeat and a major victory of his opponents, including Emil Constantinescu's election as Romania's president.

No other East European Leninist regime was overthrown by a violent popular uprising from below. In no other country of the region did the communist governments resort to ruthless forms of repression against peaceful demonstrators during the dramatic events of 1989. Yet the continuities with the old regime are in many respects more marked in Romania than in other East European countries (except perhaps the former Yugoslavia and Slovakia). I argue that some of these features are linked to the traditions of the country's political culture, but they do not make Romania a completely unique case. Indeed, populist authoritarianism and other illiberal features can be detected in other countries as well: Albania, Serbia, Croatia, Slovakia, Russia, and to some extent Poland. Furthermore, although changes have taken place slowly in Romania, they cannot be simply dismissed as a smokescreen for unreconstructed authoritarianism. During the years since the collapse of the Ceauşescu regime, Romania has established a proto-democratic institutional framework and reasonably fair electoral procedures. In addition, the country's civil society, although beleaguered, has continued to develop. What is missing is social trust, a civic commitment to the values and institutions of the emerging democracy, a "de-emotionalization" of the public discussion of fundamental issues regarding the country's future, and a truly liberal political center constituted primarily on the basis of shared ultimate values rather than immediate party affiliations.

Advances on the road to an open society have been accompanied, however, by disturbing attempts by the ruling elite to marginalize and de-legitimize the opposition, maintain tight controls over national electronic media, and perpetuate its economic and political domination by use of symbolic manipulation and democratic rhetoric. More than in any other East European country, the secret police continues to play a very significant role in orienting public opinion and influencing political debates and choices.[1] In other words, there is a deep contrast between the pluralist forms and the lingering authoritarian methods and mentalities that have beset the transition from state socialism. Whenever threatened in its control of political power, the government has resorted to populist, often chauvinist demagogy (that is, "the fatherland is in danger" – style rhetoric). But it would be absurd to deny that major progress toward democratization has been accomplished. The very victory of the opposition in the November 1996 presidential and parliamentary elections – indeed an "electoral revolution" – bears witness that the country has made significant advances toward pluralist procedures.

The centrally important moments in Romania's exit from authoritarianism are linked to a number of key events: the breakdown of Ceauşescu's dictatorship, the initial vacuum of power and the formation of the National Salvation Front (NSF) in December 1989; the growing polarization of the country's political life and the clashes between the newly formed democratic movements and parties and the NSF-controlled government (January and February 1990); the May 1990 elections and the conflict between the Ion Iliescu–Petre Roman group, on the one hand, and the democratic forces, on the other; the violent onslaught on the new parties and civic movements in June 1990; the break-up of the Iliescu–Roman alliance and the fall of the moderately reformist Roman government in September 1991; the February 1992 local elections and the opposition's success in major cities; the 1992 parliamentary and presidential elections and the attempts to interrupt the economic and political reforms; stagnation and further polarization of the political spectrum in 1992–95; and the victory of the opposition in the November 1996 elections.

A new generation has grown up in Romanian politics that cannot accept the return to the old status quo. This fact is valid not only for the former opposition, but also for members of the previously ruling party, Partidul

Democraţiei Sociale din România (PSDR – the Party of Social Democracy in Romania). Invisible to many, deep changes have taken place in the country, and even those often designated as hard-liners within the PSDR do not champion the revival of a monist, ideologically based system of command economy, cultural uniformity, and political repression. Even if a certain nostalgia for the Ceauşescu times surfaces occasionally, this is a marginal and politically weak sentiment. In reality, no major actor in contemporary Romanian politics unabashedly claims direct affinities with the deposed dictator and his legacy. For former President Ion Iliescu (who was involved in Ceauşescu's execution) such a position is quite logical. So is it for the pro-Western, democratic forces (former premier Petre Roman's Democratic Party included). But even the Socialist Party of Labor (PSL), a neo-communist formation, has not dared to publicly affirm its commitment to a full-fledged restoration of the old regime.[2]

This chapter addresses the main causes of communism's collapse in Romania and the stages of the country's democratic transition. It also identifies the main difficulties and the prospects for Romanian pluralism. First, I discuss the Leninist legacies by highlighting the institutional decline of the Romanian Communist Party (RCP) during the last decade of Ceauşescu's rule, the dismal state of the economy, and the psychological despair and social atomization. Second, the chapter explores the complexities of the transition, the ambiguities of the revolutionary breakthrough, the birthpangs of the opposition and the efforts to establish a presidential semi-authoritarian regime. The third part examines the causes of the enduring political polarization in the country's post-Leninist political culture, indicating that the responsibilities lie with both the power-holders and the opposition. Finally, I focus attention on the main threats to the emerging pluralism in Romania. I argue that these threats are not unique Romanian features, but they rather exacerbate trends that one can identify in other postcommunist societies as well. After all, the return of the "recovering communists" (a term proposed by Ken Jowitt) is not a Romanian peculiarity, as the November 1995 elections in Poland clearly demonstrated.[3]

Romania's future is not foreclosed. Even in the face of strong restorative trends such as the inordinately influential role of the secret police and the slowdown of privatization from 1992 through 1995, the old system of personal dictatorship exerted by a clique of corrupt sycophants serving the interests of one family has been dismantled. The new order, however, remains marked by hesitations, paternalist and collectivistic temptations, and resurgent forms of intolerance.

Romania's postcommunist dilemmas: an overview

The often convulsive and paradoxical regime transformation in post-1989 Romania cannot be thoroughly grasped and analyzed unless understood in the context of the communist political culture in that country. Although subsiding, the lingering climate of distrust, deception, and fear can be seen as a prolongation of the authoritarian patterns of leadership and domination exerted by the ruling elite in previous decades.[4] Indeed, the nature of Romania's post-1989 regime cannot be fully understood without reference to the cultural and political legacies of the past (both communist and precommunist). This is not to say that Romania is a case of complete restoration, but rather an emerging hybrid political culture that incorporates elements of the Leninist experience and nationalist trends, as well as embryonic forms of pluralism. To deny the existence of significant changes and consider the Romanian democratic process as irrelevant would be a gross exaggeration. On the other hand, the Romanian transition, especially after the 1992 elections, has been marred by lack of reformist will and imagination.

A "third way" approach is still dominant among the PSDR strategists.[5] Many of the opportunities created by the legal framework created between 1990 and 1992 have been missed. Confrontational, rather than consensual strategies remain the dominant note of Romanian politics: thus, until November 1996 the ruling party (the PSDR) governed in alliance with radical nationalist and leftist-populist formations.[6] The main oppositional force, Democratic Convention (DC), dominated by the National Peasant Christian and Democratic Party (NPCDP), regarded President Iliescu as a "crypto-communist." This diagnosis was endorsed by other oppositional formations, situated outside the Convention (Roman's Democratic Party, the Civic Alliance Party, the Hungarian Democratic Union). The accuracy of "neo" or "crypto" communist designations is doubtful, however. Ion Iliescu, like Slobodan Milosevič in Serbia, Algirdas Brazauskas in Lithuania, or Kiro Gligorov in Macedonia, is a populist leader whose ideological commitment to Leninism has long since disappeared.

Throughout his presidency, Iliescu exhibited residual forms of authoritarian behavior, resistance to full marketization, and attachment to the professed egalitarian values of state socialism.[7] Thomas Carothers gave an accurate description of the overall political situation in Romania five years after the May 1990 presidential and parliamentary elections (the first free, if not entirely fair, elections in forty-five years):

Romania is a greatly changed society, with many of the institutional features of democracy, a nascent capitalist economy and an identifiable path toward gradual integration with Europe. At the same time, however, it lags badly behind its neighbors in breaking clearly away from its communist past, has yet to face the most serious challenges of economic reform and seems unable to escape a turgid and often opaque political life. For most Romanians – who are struggling to stay afloat economically, fearful of rising unemployment and disgusted by the apparent corruption and inefficiency of "democratic politics" – the positive future they hoped for in December 1989 still appears quite distant.[8]

Compared with other cases of transition from state socialism, the Romanian one has a salient feature in the absence of a decisive break with the bureaucratic-centralistic and strongly statist traditions inherited from Leninism. The dismantlement of the old bureaucratic structures has been wavering and often inconclusive. One of Iliescu's former advisors describes the process as "spontaneous transition" and suggests that it responds to the political interests of the industrial managerial class.[9] No less symptomatic for the "Bucharest syndrome" of transition is the resurgence of "traditional," pre-World War II political parties, and the revival of a weak, but persistent monarchist trend.[10] It is thus significant that the most important oppositional party, the NPCDP, headed until his death in November 1995 by veteran politician Corneliu Coposu, remains unequivocally in favor of a return to the 1923 Constitution, including the re-establishment of constitutional monarchy (abolished by communist diktat in December 1947).[11] In other words, the strongest opposition party in Romania, which became the senior partner in the coalition government following the November 1996 elections, sees the fulfillment of the December 1989 revolution in the complete restoration of the precommunist political structures. To use Ralf Dahrendorf's concepts, the clash between the Romanian political forces bears upon constitutional as well as normal politics.[12]

Prior to the watershed November 1996 elections, Romania was a fragile democracy, with a strong presidential office, a divided opposition, and a real, but still weak civil society. The role of parliament had significantly decreased since 1993, and the country was governed primarily by government decrees (*ordonanţe guvernamentale*). Pressures on local officials to toe the government's policies intensified after 1993. By mid-1995, 10 percent of the mayors, councilors, and top local officials elected in February 1992 had been dismissed by the government. Out of these, some 80 percent represented opposition parties.[13] Iliescu appeared thus closer in political preferences, nostalgias and aspirations to Slovakia's Vladimir Meciar and Serbia's Slobodan Milosevič, than to the Czech Republic's Václav Havel or even Hungary's Gyula Horn. After having postured in December 1989-January 1990 as the symbol of the divorce from the old regime, Iliescu did very little to oppose the restorative trends in Romanian politics.[14]

The social base of the Iliescu regime was primarily the part of the population emotionally and professionally linked to the economic and social structures inherited from the old regime: primarily the large industrial and ministerial bureaucracy, the former apparatchiks converted into entrepreneurs, and a group of new barons of Romania's emerging private sector, often recruited among the former Communist Youth Union nomenklatura.[15] Given the ubiquitous presence of the Securitate in Ceauşescu's Romania, and its control over foreign trade companies, it is no surprise to see so many former secret police hacks now thriving as financial and industrial magnates.

The cleavage between the old order and the new one is less marked in Romania than in most other Central and East European countries. More than in any other country, the postcommunist secret services continue to directly influence the political process: they organize leaks of information about political personalities, publication of secret police files, and surveillance of journalists and other critics of the Iliescu regime.[16] Virgil Măgureanu, a former RCP Academy professor and one of Iliescu's closest associates has run the Romanian Service of Information since its establishment in March 1990. In fact, until 1996 Iliescu and Măgureanu were the only two personalities that have remained in office since 1990.[17]

For several years, the Iliescu regime appeared relatively stable.[18] While the president's achievement was "democracy by default,"[19] the opposition had excelled in hard-line anti-communist rhetoric, ceaseless calls for de-communization ("a trial of communism" – *procesul comunismului*), frequent espousals of nationalist themes (especially in its rejection of the Hungarian minority's demands), and lack of genuinely different economic solutions for the country's crisis. One could even say that President Iliescu's major asset was the anemic, fragmented and confused nature of the opposition. Secondly, and no less important, the president engaged in the fall of 1995 in a struggle against the România Mare Party leader, Corneliu Vadim Tudor, and other extremist forces. It may well be that this conflict was more important for the country's future than many among the centrist/moderate oppositional figures were ready to concede.[20] Indeed, the pact between PSDR and the România Mare Party came to an end in October 1995 and Vadim Tudor withdrew his representatives from the government.

In brief, at the end of Iliescu's second mandate the climate in contemporary Romania was dominated by disenchantment, frustration, malaise, anxiety, and insecurity.[21] Banking on these sentiments, radical nationalist movements have emerged, including attempts to reconstruct the Iron Guard, Romania's interwar fascist movement. There were official attempts to rehabilitate fascist Marshal Ion Antonescu. Members of the government participated in the consecration of monuments to this former pro-Nazi dictator executed in 1946 for crimes against humanity.[22] Leading PSDR politicians have often championed strong nationalist positions, especially regarding rights to native language education for the members of the Hungarian minority.

Support for the ruling coalition (PSDR-RNUP) also came from the neo-communist Socialist Party of Labor-SPL (headed by Ilie Verdeţ, a former

Ceauşescu premier and Adrian Păunescu, one of the most active sycophantic poets of the Ceauşescu era).[23] Most of the Ceauşescu era dissidents were marginalized, viciously besmirched in the pages of the pro-government parts of the media. Until November 1996, the official television was fully controlled by the president through the National Council of the Audiovisual. Although the separation of powers is still problematic, and the judges are still appointed by the government, one can identify the increased role of the Constitutional Court, which on several sensitive issues, turned down laws and decrees proposed by the president.

There is a growing and vocal civil society including human rights organizations, the nation-wide Pro-Democraţia movement, the Tîrgu Mureş Pro-Europa initiatives, and many organizations active in the areas of social services, public policy and children's issues. As of mid-1995, there were over 8,000 registered NGOs, out of which only about 200 were really functioning, with the vast majority relying heavily on funding from the United States and Western Europe.[24] So far, civil society, understood as the area of independent social initiatives from below, is still limited to pockets of urban intellectuals and its impact on national politics has been meager. Among students, once the most politically active group, one notices disaffection and profound demobilization. Portions of the media are outspoken and energetic, but the Iliescu regime used economic and political methods to intimidate and harass some of the more critical newspapers.[25] Minorities were expected to behave: in other words, their legitimate grievances were denounced by the ruling party and its allies as subversive actions meant to destroy Romania. What anthropologist Robert Hayden has aptly called *constitutional nationalism* best describes the ideological surrogate prevalent in Ion Iliescu's Romania.[26] It remains to be seen whether the new president and government who came to power after the November 1996 election will manage to break with this ethnocentric tradition.

The unmastered past, or facing the Leninist legacies

More than any other former Warsaw Pact country, the Romanian post-Ceauşescu regime had shunned the vital historical soul-searching needed for real national therapy. The archives are jealously guarded, the demons of an unmastered past are still there, and the Romanian political imagination continues to be haunted by the ambiguous narratives of unfulfilled desires and vengeful fantasies. Former President Ion Iliescu's unyielding refusal to allow for genuine elite circulation had a deep cause: it was related to the official orthodoxy which claimed that once Ceauşescu was ousted and liquidated, communism had ceased to exist and Romania became a democracy. In reality, only very little rigorous examination of the communist past has occurred after the December 1989 uprising: neither Iliescu, nor his supporters, were ready to engage in a soul-searching analysis of the Leninist experiment in that country. There were too many skeletons in their closets and they preferred to simply assign the guilt for past aberrations to the defunct dictator and his immediate subordinates.

No political formation has volunteered to assume responsibility for the Leninist heritage: even the Socialist Party of Labor prefers to distance itself from the dictatorial past and insists on its traditional socialist orientation.[27] Thus, the self-criticism professed by former communist parties in other East and Central European countries has been skillfully avoided in Romania. It is as if only a tiny Ceauşescu clique managed to impose a despotism now lamented and abhorred by the overwhelming majority of the population. The unanimousness of Ceauşescu's pageants has thus been replaced by a similar uncritical and unqualified monolith of perfunctory anti-Ceauşescuism.

Coming to terms with the past in contemporary Romania has been hindered by a combination of convenient silence on the part of the new leaders and amateurish, impressionistic, and often vindictive treatment of the communist period by exponents of the opposition. Few publications have engaged in releasing major archive documents and when they do, the critical-comparative analysis is conspicuously absent.[28] Little has been done to distinguish between individuals and institutions in the approach to the Stalinist terror and post-Stalinist repression: a systematically maintained oblivion often favors opportunistic alibis and self-serving legends of heroism and resistance.

At the end of his rule, Ceauşescu was universally seen as one of the world's last Stalinist dictators, totally obsessed with his grandiose industrial and architectural projects and viscerally hostile to Mikhail Gorbachev's reforms.[29] Romanians lived under immense hardships, the heat was cut down in apartments to freezing temperatures, and standing in endless lines was an everyday ordeal. Food was rationed as if the country was at war. A brazen propaganda was ceaselessly extolling the valiance of the fearless Great Leader and the scientific genius of his wife. Irritated by Gorbachev's reforms, Ceauşescu stuck to his Stalinist tenets and intensified repression. Romania appeared as a self-enclosed, nightmarish universe fully controlled by the dreaded secret police organization, the *Securitate*.

This picture, however justified in the light of the leader's terminal paranoid delusions, tended to obfuscate the existence of different stages in the evolution or devolution of the Ceauşescu regime: first, when he came to power in March 1965 as the youngest party leader within the Warsaw Pact, Nicolae Ceauşescu initiated a partial de-Stalinization by renouncing some of the most repressive features of his predecessor's (Gheorghe Gheorghiu-Dej) rule, by relaxing the party's ideological controls, exposing Dej's abuses, curtailing the secret police's influence through increased party surveillance of its operations, and opening Romania to the West. This period of "liberalization from above" lasted from 1965 to 1971.

The next stage, of regime radicalization, included a reassertion of ideological orthodoxy, cyclical anti-intellectual campaigns, dramatic elite transformation through the elimination of Dej's "barons" from all significant positions and the promotion of Ceauşescu's loyalists, and a growing fascination with gigantic economic investments (for example, the building of the Danube–Black Sea Canal). The leader's cult became all-pervasive and traditional Stalinist mobilization techniques were restored. After 1974, Ceauşescu engaged in a dynasticization of Romanian socialism through the advancement of close family members to high party and government positions. The most visible and influential was his wife Elena who, during the 1980s, became the second most important person in the party and state hierarchy.

Finally, the last stage, one of ineluctable regime decay, coincided with Gorbachev's reforms: an adamant, though primitive Leninist, Ceauşescu resented perestroika and did not make any secret of his condemnation of the Soviet attempts at systemic renewal. During this period (1985–89), Ceauşescu's policies became blatantly erratic and self-defeating. Relying more and more on his wife's advice, he antagonized the party bureaucracy deprived of authority and power. Although surrounded by cultic rituals of adoration, the general secretary was in fact ill-informed and prone to excesses of panic and hysteria. By the end of his life, Ceauşescu was a sick and isolated dictator, completely dependent on his secret police and manipulated by an inept and extremely corrupt camarilla.

The Romanian Communist Party, created in 1921, was ostensibly the ruling force in that country, but in fact Ceauşescu and his clan annihilated the party's collective leadership (the Political Executive Committee) as a decision-making body. During the 1970s and 80s, the Central Committee and the party congresses were mere sounding boards whose mission was to slavishly applaud Ceauşescu's initiatives. There was no trace of collegial behavior at the top of Romania's government. The political elite was demoralized and strictly subordinated to the Securitate, entirely dominated by Ceauşescu's appointees. This was indeed a peculiar Romanian phenomenon that explains many post-revolutionary tribulations: the almost complete emasculation of the party apparatus and the rise of the secret police as the crucial repository of political power, a real "state within the state." The explanation for this devolution of the party's traditional functions in a Leninist regime was linked to Ceauşescu's overblown suspiciousness as well as to the leader's awareness of mounting discontent even among his once loyal supporters within the nomenklatura. The case of Ion Iliescu was thus emblematic for this situation: a Ceauşescu protégé since the early 1960s, he became increasingly marginal as a result of his reservations about the post-1971 neo-Stalinist course.

Using the pretext of his opposition to Soviet hegemony, Ceauşescu constructed an original ideology of Romanian socialism, which mixed a Stalinist commitment to centrally planned economy and collective agriculture, with traditional themes of the extreme right (including the myth of the homogeneous nation, the exaltation of the feudal princes, the insistence on the Thracian-Dacian roots of the Romanian nation, the xenophobic fixation on the alleged conspiracies fomented by foreigners, and anti-intellectualism).[30] Gheorghe Gheorghiu-Dej (1901–65), succeeded in shunning de-Stalinization and in keeping Romania a fortress of Communist orthodoxy.[31] Whereas Dej ruled as the chief officer of an oligarchy and ingratiated himself with the party bureaucracy, power under Ceauşescu was exerted by a tiny coterie using the mechanisms of populist authoritarianism, symbolic manipulation, and, especially after 1980, psychological mass terror. Although Ceauşescu refrained from organizing show-trials and bloody purges, he allowed the Securitate to establish a huge network of informers and "collaborators" whose task was to prevent the rise of any critical current.

During the last years of Ceauşescu's rule, Romanians experienced not only the agony of terrible economic hardships, but also a state of moral despondency and universal fear. Since the leader imagined himself as the guarantor of the country's independence, all forms of opposition and dissent were treated as criminal offenses. To question Ceauşescu's infallibility was by definition an attempt to weaken the country's defense and sovereignty. In addition to the psychological obstacles linked to the anemic development of any intellectual resistance to tyranny, Romania's would-be dissidents encountered another obstacle related to Ceauşescu's image in the West as an opponent of Soviet hegemony. While in the case of post-1968 Czechoslovakia, Western chancelleries and media were almost instinctively favorable to any gesture of opposition to the Husak regime, it took them decades to abandon Ceauşescu's image as a genuine patriot.

Dissent in Romania was therefore reduced to individual protests against the most outrageous decisions made by the supreme leader or the *Conducător*, as the party propaganda referred to Ceauşescu. Those who dared to criticize the increasingly irrational policies of Nicolae and Elena Ceauşescu were automatically branded traitors to the national interest. Some were expelled, others were kept under house arrest, imprisoned or simply disappeared.[32]

The counterpart to political repression was Ceauşescu's domestic legitimation through nationalism combined with an autonomist course in foreign policy that ensured the regime a certain authority in international affairs. Unlike other Soviet-bloc leaders, Ceauşescu was not perceived as the

Kremlin's puppet, and his initiatives were often praised for their farsightedness. His notable policies in this regard included his refusal to break diplomatic relations with Israel in 1967 after the Six-Day War and his condemnation of the Soviet invasion of Czechoslovakia in August 1968. For many in the West, Ceauşescu was a maverick communist interested in defending his country's original course against Soviet interference.[33] Actually, the perception in the West was that in the event of war in Europe, Romania might not fight on the USSR's side.

As the West indulged in this friendly relationship with Ceauşescu, the Romanian critical intellectuals felt abandoned and powerless. According to Václav Havel, one of the premises for one's decision to engage in dissident activities is the sentiment that his or her acts would not pass unnoticed by democratic forces in the West.[34] Mental coercion, indoctrination and regimentation were the instruments for the perpetuation of the repressive system. No forms of organized working-class activism could emerge and the few attempts to establish independent unions were nipped in the bud.[35] The whole educational and cultural system was subordinated to Elena Ceauşescu's willful decisions.

If in the first stage of Ceauşescu's rule, he simulated tolerance for critical Marxism and permitted cultural experimentation, the situation changed dramatically after a visit to China and North Korea in 1971. Following that trip, Ceauşescu engaged in a mini-cultural revolution with disastrous consequences for Romania's spiritual life. Many of the country's brightest intellectuals emigrated or defected. Others withdrew in internal emigration, refusing to participate in the official pageants.

A vocal group of authors, however, endorsed the chauvinistic harangues of the official ideology and thrived as court writers for the *Conducător* and his wife. The most notorious were: Adrian Păunescu, Eugen Barbu, and Corneliu Vadim Tudor. These men did not simply vanish after the collapse of the Ceauşescu regime. Păunescu, Barbu, and Vadim have re-emerged as champions of a fundamentalist nationalism with racist overtones that simply jettisoned the perfunctory communist veneer of the previous times.[36] After 1989, they could publicly proclaim views they dared only to whisper before. They are now among the most active exponents of the radical ethnocentric alliance whose main targets are the democratic parties and all individuals who have a record of anti-Ceauşescu opposition.[37] During the September 1992 elections, they even managed to get parliamentary seats running on a platform imbued with xenophobic positions.

Romanian dissent reflected the peculiarities of the country's political culture under communism. Firstly, with the exception of Albania, no other East European country experienced such an uninterrupted exercise of Stalinist repression. Secondly, the destruction of the national intelligentsia in the 1950s went perhaps further in intensity and cruelty than in other countries: the explanation lies in the excruciating inferiority complex of the Romanian communists who tried to outdo Stalin himself in their endeavor to impose the new order. Thirdly, the national communist propaganda stirred responsive chords among many Romanian intellectuals who accepted or even volunteered to join the RCP in the 1960s and 70s.[38]

Certain groups and associations, however, did challenge the party's ideological monopoly. One example was the Writers' Union, an institution traditionally described as a Stalinist instrument devised in order to establish full control over literature. After 1971, the Union remained one of the very few institutions that allowed for meaningful debates on issues pertaining to ideology. The conflict within the Union between the nationalist Stalinists and the liberals was actually a political struggle.[39] The former faction enjoyed full party support. The latter had to pay lip service to the official dogmas, while repudiating their most grotesque and pernicious consequences. In the late 1970s, the nationalists asked Ceauşescu to allow them to form a truly communist Writers' Union, charging their liberal rivals with being "cosmopolites" manipulated by Radio Free Europe broadcasting. The last Writers' Union congress tolerated by Ceauşescu took place in 1981 and resulted in an inviable compromise between the two groups: the liberals realized their impotence and retreated into what they called "resistance through culture." Later, when conditions became unbearable, some of them engaged in open dissident activities.

Ceauşescu's December

The more personalist and authoritarian Ceauşescu's leadership methods, the less inclined he was to accept any form of collective leadership. During the 1970s, he completely dislodged the political faction that had helped him to establish himself as the absolute leader of the party. All significant personnel appointments were decided by Elena Ceauşescu and her most obedient servant, Central Committee Secretary Emil Bobu.[40] In the meantime, the couple's youngest son, Nicu, became a candidate member of the Political Executive Committee and head of the party organization in Sibiu County in Transylvania. Although notorious for his egregious life-style, Nicu was apparently groomed to succeed his father.

As the party became paralyzed, there was no support for the general secretary other than his seemingly faithful *Securitate*.[41] Headed by General Iulian Vlad, a professional policeman with no ideological convictions, this institution carried out Ceauşescu's draconian orders. At the same time, it appears now, the chiefs of the secret police were profoundly aware of the prospects for a popular explosion. The most clear indication that the proverbial patience of the Romanians had come to an end occurred in Braşov, the country's second largest city, in November 1987, when thousands of workers protested the plummeting living standards, ransacked the party headquarters and chanted anti-Ceauşescu and anti-communist slogans.[42]

In 1989 Ceauşescu realized that unless he intensified his repressive policy, the whole edifice of what he called the "multilaterally developed socialist society" would immediately and ingloriously crumble. Gorbachev's political reforms and their impact on the other bloc countries made the Romanian dictator and his clique increasingly nervous. On various occasions Ceauşescu proffered undisguised criticism of perestroika, which he called "a right-wing deviation" within world communism.[43] As a reformist trend was taking shape in Eastern Europe, Ceauşescu allied himself with stalwarts of Brezhnevism like Erich Honecker, Todor Zhivkov, and Milos Jakes. An anti-reformist alliance was formed between these diehard neo-Stalinists who understood that the winds of change that Gorbachev had unleashed would force them out of power.

Emboldened by Gorbachev's policy of glasnost, some Romanians took the risk of criticizing Ceauşescu publicly. In March 1989 six party veterans addressed Ceauşescu in an open letter, denouncing his excesses, his erratic economic policies, and the general deterioration of Romania's international image. The authors were not partisans of Western-style pluralism. One signatory, Silviu Brucan, was a seasoned party propagandist who had also served as the regime's ambassador to the United States and the United Nations in the late 1950s and the early 1960s. None of these figures enjoyed popular support, but they were well known within the party bureaucracy, and that was what mattered. Ceauşescu reacted furiously to the letter and placed the authors under house arrest. Their refusal to recant showed the limits of Ceauşescu's power.[44] Also in 1989, prominent intellectuals began to openly criticize the regime's obscurantist cultural policy. In November, dissident writer Dan Petrescu released a public appeal against Ceauşescu's reelection as general secretary at the Fourteenth RCP Congress.

Altogether, Ceauşescu's power – impregnable at first glance – was falling apart. Detested by the population, isolated internationally, living in his own world of delusions and fantasies, the aging leader could not understand what was happening to communism. He considered Gorbachev the arch-traitor to Leninist ideals and tried to mobilize an international neo-Stalinist coalition. In August 1989, he was so irritated with the formation of a Solidarity-run government in Poland that he proposed a Warsaw Pact intervention in that country. Every day the Romanian media highlighted the dangers of reformism and "de-ideologization." But breathtaking events were occurring in the other Warsaw Pact countries and Romanians were perfectly aware of them. Despite the regime's absolute control of the media, most Romanians were listening to Western broadcasts and watching Bulgarian, Hungarian, Yugoslav and Soviet TV. Videotapes were circulating underground with footage of the revolutionary changes in Poland, Hungary, East Germany, Czechoslovakia, and Bulgaria. Young Romanians knew that even the armed-to-the-teeth East German police did not dare to fire against peaceful demonstrators.[45]

An adamant Stalinist, Ceauşescu returned to his first ideological love, his master's theory of socialism within one country, and readied to turn Romania into a perfectly closed fortress, immune to the corrupting revisionist ideas that had destroyed the Bolshevik legacy. In November 1989, at the Fourteenth Congress of the RCP, Ceauşescu was enthusiastically, that is, mechanically, re-elected general secretary.

Conceived as a demonstration of force and a gesture of defiance to Gorbachev and his followers, the Congress only showed Ceauşescu's fatal alienation from the Romanian nation he claimed to represent. It became clear that far from accepting any limitation of his power, the leader was determined to fight with infinite obstinacy to carry out what he thought to be his mission in Romanian history.[46]

During his last month of life Ceauşescu's psychological features – an all-consuming sense of predestination, a failure to listen to other viewpoints, an immense vanity that made him blind to otherwise unmistakable signals of social unrest, but also an extreme perseverance, steadfastness and self-confidence – reached their climax. He desperately believed in his own star and refused to admit that a re-enactment of his most brilliant performance as a statesman – the August 1968 denunciation of the Warsaw Pact invasion of Czechoslovakia – had become impossible. No foreign power was interested in occupying Romania.[47] Deprived of either internationalist or nationalist demagogic alibis, Ceauşescu had no cards to play but violent repression against all protest.

The writing, however, was on the wall for Nicolae Ceauşescu and his regime. On December 16, 1989 a demonstration took place in Timişoara. The police tried to evict Laszlo Tőkés, a Hungarian Protestant pastor, from his parish house. When the protesters refused to disperse, the police and the army opened fire. The next day thousands took to the streets with anti-dictatorial slogans, and a carnage followed. Western radio stations were informed about the massacre in Timişoara, and all Romanians realized that Ceauşescu was ready to engage in total warfare against non-violent and unarmed demonstrators. At that moment there was no return for Ceauşescu: to accept the demands of the Timişoara protestors would have only shown how fragile his power was. Instead, he preferred to do what other Soviet-bloc leaders had avoided: he used force in an attempt to quell the unrest.

Ceaușescu underestimated the danger and left the country on December 18 for a state visit to Iran. On December 20, when he returned, he delivered an extremely provocative televised speech, and the next day he ordered a mass rally to endorse his intransigent opposition to reforms. On that occasion, however, Romanians refused to follow their leader's behest. Tens of thousands booed Ceaușescu in the Palace Square in front of the Central Committee building. For once, they abandoned their fear and interrupted the dictator's oratorical performance. Although Ceaușescu tried to accommodate the crowd, it was too late. Television had revealed his stupefaction and confusion. People saw that he was losing control. That same night, protesting students were massacred in the University Square, and the next morning a huge gathering took place in the Palace Square. The crowd stormed the Central Committee building, and Ceaușescu and his wife fled from its roof by helicopter.

The story of Ceaușescu's flight and his subsequent capture, secret trial, and execution on Christmas day remains to be clarified.[48] There are enough puzzling elements in it to make the official explanations provided by Ceaușescu's successors more than suspicious. For instance, who selected the judges and who wrote the indictment against Ceaușescu? Why was it necessary to have the leader and his wife executed when it was obvious that no serious threat coming from their loyalists was jeopardizing the new power?[49] One thing is now clear: once Ceaușescu left the Central Committee building, a vacuum of power was created that was swiftly filled by representatives of the disgruntled party apparatus, representatives of the army, and a few exponents of the rebellious masses.[50] As no organized underground opposition to Ceaușescu had been allowed to exist, this was not surprising. The postrevolutionary crisis, however, was determined by the growing chasm between the pluralist demands of the rapidly growing civil and political society, on the one hand, and the reluctance of the new leaders to accept them. For Iliescu and his associates, the creation of political parties fully committed to the establishment of a liberal democracy and the elimination of the former apparatchiks from key control positions, appeared as a personal threat. During the first year in power, they defended their hegemonic positions by resorting to manipulation, corruption, and coercion.

The resurgence of politics

After the revolutionary upheaval that swept away the Ceaușescu dictatorship in December 1989, Romanians rapidly discovered the flavor of politics. For the first time in forty-five years the people could enjoy unfettered freedom of expression, criticize the new leaders, and organize independent associations and parties. But the bureaucracy was not ready to capitulate and engineered an astute survivalist strategy. Thus, immediately after the revolution the National Salvation Front (NSF) was formed.

The Front's first statement announced its commitment to democratic principles, including the multiparty system and the need to organize free elections as soon as possible. The Front claimed to represent a decisive break with the detested Communist regime.[51] The RCP disappeared without a trace from the country's political life. Most of the 3.8 million party members lacked any emotional or ideological identification with the leadership. The NSF's announcement of the transition to a pluralist system was therefore welcomed and trusted. This was precisely one of the sources of the political tensions that followed: the contrast between the NSF's official pluralist pledges and its practical authoritarian actions. The Front's rhetoric and practice were seen by many Romanian intellectuals as shockingly divergent. Allegedly trans-ideological, the Front was in reality a movement of bureaucratic retrenchment whose initial main ideologue, Silviu Brucan, insisted on its integrative function. For Brucan, as long as the NSF allowed internal factionalism, there was no need for a competition of political parties.

The legitimacy crisis of the new regime was linked to the troubled circumstances of its birth. During their trial, the Ceauşescus challenged their judges and accused Romania's new leaders of treason and an anti-constitutional putsch. The NSF Council justified the summary execution by invoking reasons of revolutionary expediency. But many Romanians doubted this explanation and suspected that the purpose of this frame-up, with defense lawyers being more vituperative of their clients than the prosecutor, was to eliminate the dictator and his wife as potentially embarrassing witnesses in an inevitable trial of the RCP.

Pseudo-justice was summarily carried out in order to prevent true political justice.[52] Since such an occurrence would have involved an indictment of the very system that made possible the Ceauşescu phenomenon, the organizers of the secret trial preferred to transfer all the guilt to the two defendants and to silence them as soon as possible. In this sense, Romania's new leaders chose the worst of all alternatives: tyrannicide pretending to be law. By attempting to keep the revolution pure, they sullied it.[53] With the benefit of hindsight, one can say that the summary execution of Ceauşescu allowed the bureaucratic apparatus to maintain its position.

As for the composition of the new leadership, informed analysts were immediately struck by the emergence of Communist veterans and apparatchiks to prominent positions.[54] The NSF president himself, sixty-year-old Ion Iliescu, had served under Ceauşescu in the late 1960s as the first secretary of the Communist Youth Union and minister of youth.[55] Between 1970 and 1971 he was the RCP's Central Committee secretary in charge of ideology and an alternate Political Executive Committee member. In 1971

Iliescu opposed Ceauşescu's "minicultural revolution" and was criticized for "intellectualism and petty-bourgeois liberalism." Following this incident, Ceauşescu humiliated Iliescu for his unorthodox stances by assigning him to menial party and state jobs.

In 1984 Iliescu lost his Central Committee seat and was appointed director of the Technical Publishing House in Bucharest. Until the revolution he kept a low profile and did not engage in any daring anti-Ceauşescu activity. Although he was not among the signatories of the "Letter of the Six," Romanians knew about his political divergences with Ceauşescu. In the years that preceded the December explosion, he was widely perceived as a Gorbachevite whose arrival to power would permit Romania to embark on long-delayed reforms. But the violence of the revolution, the exponential rise in political expectations, and Iliescu's refusal to abjure his communist creed made him unsuited for the task of a radical tribune.

It was difficult to see Iliescu as the symbol of the anti-totalitarian revolutionary fervor of the youth. Somebody else had to be handpicked to play this role. Born in 1946, the new prime minister, Petre Roman, had no revolutionary credentials except that together with thousands of other Romanians he had participated in the December 22, 1989 seizure of the Central Committee building.[56] The young Roman could not invoke a single moment of his past when he had raised his voice in solidarity with the harassed dissidents. Fluent in French and Spanish, holding a doctoral degree from the Polytechnical School in Toulouse, Roman was supposed to provide the new leadership with a badly needed European veneer. Unlike Iliescu and Roman, Silviu Brucan (who was born in 1916) could invoke a dissident past. The same was true for Dumitru Mazilu, the fourth most visible member of the NSF leadership. A former international-law professor, he had criticized the abysmal human-rights record of Ceauşescu's government in a special report prepared in 1988 for the United Nations Human Rights Commission.[57]

To placate charges of a Communist plot to seize the still inchoate power, the NSF leaders decided to coopt in the larger Council a number of well-known oppositional figures. On January 12, 1990, a demonstration took place in Bucharest, where Iliescu, Roman, and Mazilu were accused of trying to preserve the communist system. Under the pressure of the crowd, the three announced the decision to ban the RCP. Mazilu engaged in a dialogue with the demonstrators that seemed to be an attempt to undermine Iliescu's authority. One day later, *România Liberă*, the country's most outspoken daily newspaper, published unknown data about Mazilu's political biography.[58] Upset by these revelations, Mazilu resigned and the NSF leadership remained in the hands of the Iliescu-Roman-Brucan troika.

Several other elements contributed to the political radicalization of the Romanians. One was the rapid constitution of political parties. During the first days after Ceauşescu's overthrow, the National Peasant and the National Liberal parties were formed. On January 5, 1990, Radu Câmpeanu, a Liberal politician who had spent nine years in Communist prisons, returned from Paris after fourteen years of exile. The National Peasants merged with a recently created Christian Democratic formation and became the National Peasant Christian and Democratic Party (NPCDP), headed by Corneliu Coposu, a survivor of Romania's Stalinist jails and one of the closest associates of Iuliu Maniu, the historical leader of the National Peasant Party who had died in the Sighet prison in the early 1950s.[59] Another important personality of the NPCDP was Ion Raţiu who returned to Romania after fifty years of exile in England and decided to run for president in the May 1990 elections (see table 10.1). The Social Democratic Party, the third of the traditional democratic parties in Romania, re-emerged under the leadership of engineer Sergiu Cunescu.

It seemed that in several weeks, Romania had experienced an extraordinary leap from the political numbness of Ceauşescu's years to the frenzy of a vivid and dramatic public life. Also in 1990, the nationalist forces formed their own movement, called *Vatra Românească* (Romanian Hearth), whose political arm, the RNUP, was created in 1991. Benefiting from Iliescu's and Roman's tolerance, Vadim Tudor started to publish his weekly *România mare* in 1990 and formed a namesake party in 1991. As for the opposition, in 1992, it formed its own bloc, the Democratic Convention, whose backbone was represented by the NPCDP. Endless strife among oppositional figures led to the fragmentation of the Liberal Party into several groups with little electoral support. In 1991, the Civic Alliance Party (CAP) was formed under the leadership of prominent intellectual Nicolae Manolescu. Its political platform was inspired by civic and liberal values. A part of the Democratic Convention during the 1992 elections, CAP broke with the oppositional bloc in 1994.

Problematic pluralism

The hallmark of the first stage of Romania's transition period was thus a blend of authoritarianism, paternalism, and embryonic political processes that kept the bureaucracy in positions of economic and institutional power and reduced the opposition to a powerless status. The chief instruments for the conservation of this state of affairs were: (a) the political apparatus grouped around Ion Iliescu within first the National Salvation Front (NSF) and then, after the split with Petre Roman's group, the Democratic National Salvation Front (DNSF), currently the PSDR; (b) the state economic bureaucracy and

Table 10.1 *Parliamentary and presidential elections in Romania, 1990*

Political party or candidate	Votes	% votes	Seats	% seats[a]
Assembly of Deputies				
National Salvation Front	9,089,659	66.31	263	68.0
Hungarian Democratic Union of Romania	991,601	7.23	29	7.5
National Liberal Party	879,290	6.41	29	7.5
Ecological Movement of Romania	358,864	2.62	12	3.1
National Peasant Christian Democratic Party	351,357	2.56	12	3.1
Romanian National Unity Party	290,875	2.12	9	2.3
Agrarian Democratic Party	250,403	1.80	9	2.3
Romanian Ecologist Party	232,212	1.69	8	2.1
Romanian Socialist Democratic Party	143,393	1.05	5	1.3
Romanian Social Democrat Party	73,014	0.53	2	0.5
Democratic Group of the Center	65,914	0.48	2	0.5
Others[b]	358,983	2.61	16	4.1
Parties failing to win seats	n.a.	4.59	–	–
Total			396	
Senate				
National Salvation Front	9,353,006	67.02	92	77.3
Hungarian Democratic Union of Romania	1,004,353	7.20	12	10.1
National Liberal Party	985,094	7.06	10	7.6
National Peasant Christian Democratic Party	384,687	2.50	1	0.8
Ecological Movement of Romania	341,478	2.45	1	0.8
Romanian National Unity Party	300,473	2.15	2	1.7
Romanian Ecologist Party	192,574	1.38	1	0.8
Parties failing to win seats	n.a.	11.24	–	–
Total			119	
Presidency				
Ion Iliescu	12,323,489	85.07		
Radu Câmpeanu	1,529,188	10.64		
Ion Rațiu	617,007	4.29		

Notes: Eligible voters: 17,200,722. Assembly of Deputies: voter turnout: 14,825,017 (86.2%). Senate: voter turnout: 14,875,764 (86.5%). Presidency: voter turnout: 14,826,611 (86.2%). [a]Column does not total 100% due to rounding. [b]Includes 16 additional parties, each receiving less than 0.4 percent of the vote and one seat in the Assembly of Deputies.
Sources: Domnița Stefănescu, *Cinci ani din istoria României* (Bucharest: Editura Mașina de scris, 1995), pp. 458–60, 468; and Kimmo Kuusela, "Emerging Party Systems and Institutions," in *Democratization in Eastern Europe: Domestic and International Perspectives*, ed. Geoffrey Pridham and Tatu Vanhanen (New York: Routledge, 1994), pp. 240–1.

parts of the new business elite; (c) the government-controlled national television; (d) the Romanian Service of Information (*Serviciul Român de Informaţii*), the Presidential Protection Service, and other secret police branches; and several fundamentalist-populist movements and parties, whose extremism has helped create the image of Iliescu's "centrist" position. Instead of a well-constituted and properly functioning system of political parties, Romania's public space was dominated by a self-styled version of majoritarianism favorable to the sweeping embourgeoisment of the nomenklatura (the formation of a financially omnipotent class of business mafiosi) and the predictable conversion of its political domination into economic supremacy.[60]

The peculiarities of Romania's exit from communism are thus caused by enduring authoritarianism, a profound moral crisis that affects negatively the development of civil society, reluctant privatization, and a beleaguered and factionalized status of the democratic forces.[61] Only by connecting these elements in a comprehensive analytic framework can sense be made of the results of the September–October 1992 parliamentary and presidential elections (see tables 10.2 and 10.3). Ion Iliescu was reaffirmed by over 60 percent of the Romanian voters as their president, and his political formation, the Democratic National Salvation Front (DNSF), with only 40,000 members, received 28 percent of the vote, constituting the parliament's largest faction.

The Election Law, under which the 1990 and 1992 elections were conducted, was adopted in 1990. Elections in May 1990 led to the formation of a bicameral parliament, comprised of an Assembly of Deputies and a Senate (see table 10.1). The parliament also functioned as Constituent Assembly until a new Constitution was adopted in 1991. In 1992 a new parliament was elected, with the Assembly of Deputies renamed the Chamber of Deputies. By that time, the NSF had split in two: one faction, directly associated with President Iliescu and advocating leftist values, called itself the Democratic National Salvation Front (DNSF). Later renamed the Party of Social Democracy in Romania, it won a plurality of votes and formed a coalition government with two nationalist parties, a neo-communist group and its own satellite called the Democratic Agrarian Party. Roman's National Salvation Front, later renamed the Democratic Party fared poorly, receiving only 10.39 percent of the vote. Most of the votes for the Democratic Convention went to the NPCDP and to the Hungarian Democratic Union.

According to the 1991 Constitution, the prime minister is nominated by the president, and ministers are nominated by the person selected to form the government. After 1992, Prime Minister Nicolae Văcăroiu, a former Planning Committee bureaucrat, managed to retain the necessary parliamentary support

Table 10.2 *Parliamentary elections in Romania, 1992*

Political party	Votes	% votes	Seats	% seats
Chamber of Deputies				
Democratic National Salvation Front	3,015,708	27.72	117	34.3
Democratic Convention	2,177,144	20.01	82	24.0
National Salvation Front	1,108,500	10.19	43	12.6
Romanian National Unity Party	839,586	7.72	30	8.8
Hungarian Democratic Union of Romania	811,290	7.46	27	7.9
Greater Romania Party	424,061	3.90	16	4.7
Socialist Party of Labor	330,378	3.00	13	3.8
Others[a]	155,773	1.40	13	3.8
Parties failing to win seats[b]	n.a.	18.60	–	–
Total			341	
Senate				
Democratic National Salvation Front	3,102,201	28.29	49	34.3
Democratic Convention	2,210,722	20.16	34	23.8
National Salvation Front	1,139,033	10.39	18	12.6
Romanian National Unity Part	890,410	8.12	14	9.8
Hungarian Democratic Union of Romania	831,469	7.59	12	8.4
Greater Romania Party	422,545	3.85	6	4.2
Democratic Agrarian Party	362,427	3.31	5	3.5
Socialist Party of Labor	349,470	3.19	5	3.5
Parties failing to win seats[c]	n.a.	15.10	–	–
Total			143	

Notes: Eligible voters: 16,380,663; voter turnout: 12,496,430 (76.3%). [a]Includes thirteen additional parties, each receiving less than 0.5 percent of the vote and one seat in the Chamber of Deputies. [b]Fifty-nine parties. [c]Fifty-seven parties.
Sources: Domniţa Stefănescu, *Cinci ani din istoria României* (Bucharest: Editura Maşina de scris, 1995), pp. 458, 475-6, and Kimmo Kuusela, "Emerging Party Systems and Institutions," *Democratization in Eastern Europe: Domestic and International Perspectives*, ed. Geoffrey Pridham and Tatu Vanhanen (New York: Routledge, 1994), p. 141.

for his coalition government. The opposition put forward several motions of no confidence and one impeachment motion; all failed. Although a law adopted in 1993 created a legislative council, this body did not come into being and most legislation was initiated by the government. There were limitations regarding the transparency of parliamentary procedures, and the parliament's control over the government is not seen by international observers as effective.[62]

Table 10.3   *Presidential elections in Romania, 1992*

Candidate	Votes	% votes
September 27, 1992 (1st round)		
Ion Iliescu	5,633,456	47.34
Emil Constantinescu	3,717,006	31.24
Gheorghe Funar	1,294,388	10.88
Caius Traian Dragomir	564,655	4.75
Ioan Mânzatu	362,485	3.05
Mircea Druc	326,866	2.75
October 11, 1992 (2d round)		
Ion Iliescu	7,393,429	61.43
Emil Constantinescu	4,641,207	38.57

Notes: 1st round: eligible voters: 16,380,663; voter turnout: 12,496,430 (76.3%).
2nd round: eligible voters: 16,597,508; voter turnout: 12,153,810 (73.2%).
Sources: Domniţa Stefănescu, *Cinci ani din istoria României* (Bucharest: Editura Maşina de scris, 1995), p. 458; "Results of the Presidential Election Reported," Bucharest Romania Network, 13 October 1992, *FBIS-EEU*, 16 October 1992, p. 19.

Together with the nationalist parties, the DNSF (now PSDR) represented almost half of Romania's voting population: in other words, almost half of the Romanians perceived sweeping reforms as more threatening than a continuation of the inefficient Iliescu regime. This hostility to radical privatization of the economy and flirtation with the chauvinistic parties was the main strategy pursued by Nicolae Văcăroiu prior to 1995. In 1995, the private sector share of the industrial production was only about 12 percent. At the end of that year, under pressure from international financial institutions the government rushed ahead with mass privatization. Vouchers exchangeable in almost 4,000 state companies were issued to the eligible population and the list of companies and the methodology for the exchange process were published. With a centrist coalition resulting from the November 1996 elections, one may hope that Romania will eventually engage in a full-fledged process of marketization of its economy.[63]

The key to overcoming the stalemate lay as much with Iliescu as with the opposition. During the 1992 election, an improvised, under-staffed and predominantly urban-oriented campaign failed to generate the long-expected electoral landslide on the latter's behalf. Disarticulated and plagued by inner factionalism, with personal interests and vanities often prevailing over the long-term goals and preventing a dynamic convergence of efforts, the oppositional Democratic Convention did not make the breakthrough meant to

Table 10.4 *Indicators of economic trends in Romania since 1989*

	1989	1990	1991	1992	1993	1994	1995[a]
GDP	-5.8	-5.6	-12.9	-8.8	-1.3	3.9	6.9
Industrial output	-5.3	-23.7	-22.8	-21.9	1.3	3.3	9.4
Rate of inflation	1.1	5.1	174.5	210.9	256.1	131.0	32.3
Rate of unemployment	n.a.	n.a.	3.0	8.4	10.2	11	8.9
GNP per capita	n.a.	n.a.	n.a.	n.a.	n.a.	2,920	n.a.
% Workforce in private activity[b]	5.9	9.2	33.6	41.0	43.8	51.4	n.a.
% GDP from private sector[b]	12.8	16.4	23.6	26.4	32.0	35.0	n.a.

Notes: GDP – % change over previous year; industrial output – % change over previous year; rate of inflation – % change in end-year retail/consumer prices; rate of unemployment, % of labor force, end of year; GNP per capita – in US dollars at PPP exchange rates. [a]Estimate. [b]Not including cooperatives.
Source: European Bank for Reconstruction and Development, *Transition Report 1995: Economic Transition in Eastern Europe and the Former Soviet Union* (London: EBRD, 1995); European Bank for Reconstruction and Development, *Transition Report Update, April 1996: Assessing Progress in Economies in Transition* (London: EBRD, 1996).

completely alter the existing "rules of the game." The economic situation, instead of improving or even bottoming out, continued to deteriorate during the 1990–92 period (see table 10.4). However, the opposition failed to convince the electorate that it had a viable or more attractive alternative to the ruling party's economic strategy (or lack thereof), thereby contributing to Iliescu's 1992 re-election. With about 20 percent support in the parliamentary elections, and with its presidential candidate, Emil Constantinescu, receiving less than 40 percent, the Convention did not succeed in articulating a forceful alternative strategy.

However, to indulge like many Romanian intellectuals in lamentations about electoral fraud is to miss the point of the 1992 elections: if fraud was present, it was symbolical. Iliescu and his party managed to obscure the real issues, advertised themselves as guarantors of social stability, and thus could better respond to the citizens' widespread grievances and fears.[64] In other words, a large segment among Romanians preferred continuity to discontinuity, stagnation to change, regime conservation to regime transformation, the quasi-revolution to the real electoral revolution. The main reason for the Convention's partial defeat was linked to the exaggerated emphasis on ideological themes (primarily anti-communism and the restoration of monarchy) in a country where all ideologies have lost their galvanizing power.[65]

The main source of Iliescu's 1992 victory is a phenomenon that transcends Romanian boundaries: the contrast between the anti-communist sentiment among the population at large and the existence of subliminal, but all the more real, interests of most social groups pointing to a vaguely socialist "third road." As Polish sociologist Edmund Mokrzycki put it:

> The idea of the "third road" (sometimes called that way, sometimes not) emerges from the grassroots rather than from the intellectual or political elites, it is clearly incoherent, if not outright naive . . . But this is precisely why it is so important and powerful. It gives clear answers to questions *people* ask. The answers correspond to people's knowledge, experience, needs, fears and expectations. The answers are simple and yet the idea is rich: there are plenty of alternatives from which to choose, depending on the circumstances. It is becoming the ideology of the masses – of this part of the masses anyway that actively oppose the liberal reform and see the political stage as a scene of war between "the people" and "them" – the corrupt and alien elites.[66]

Iliescu's strategy was to cater precisely to the fears, neuroses, and phobias among Romania's industrial workers, peasants in the less developed regions, and retired population. He has persuaded them that the transition would be less painful if effected gradually by "true patriots" like him, rather than the oppositional Westernizers, allegedly intent upon restoring big land estates and "selling the country out" to multinational corporations. During the 1996 campaign, all the populist stereotypes were used by the PSDR to instill among Romanians a sense of panic about the Democratic Convention's possible victory: anti-intellectualism, anti-Westernism, anti-capitalism, and flaming nationalism were used to ensure Iliescu's electoral triumph and preserve a structure of power still intimately linked to the authoritarian legacy of Ceauşescuism. With few exceptions, unions were brought under government control. Independent media were often critical of the power elite, and the effect of their revelations of corruption turned out to be pivotal for the opposition's victory.

By 1996, Romania had a semi-presidential regime with a weak parliament and a divided opposition. The real center of power was located in the presidential Cotroceni palace, rather than in the government or in the two parliamentary chambers. But the political struggle went on and the alliance between the Democratic Convention and Petre Roman's Democratic Party (supported by the Hungarian Democratic Union) ensured Emil Constantinescu's presidential victory with 54.4 percent of the vote on November 17, 1996.

The rise of civil society

No less important an element for the opening of the public space had been the swift reconstitution of the Romanian civil society.[67] For those accustomed to seeing Romania as a country without any opposition, this may have come as a surprise. But the truth of the matter was that even under the utterly unfavorable circumstances of the Ceauşescu regime, the germs of a civil society managed to survive. One of these, for instance, was the cultural circle surrounding Constantin Noica, a philosopher with Hegelian-existentialist propensities and a Socratic spirit whose disciples came into direct conflict with the official Marxist tenets.[68] Another center of dissent was the "Iasi group" of young writers and philosophers who had all been under continuous police surveillance.

In the same vein, it is interesting to note the existence of a group of young writers, art historians, sociologists, and philosophers in Bucharest who engaged in oppositional activities after 1988: Călin Anastasiu, Magda Cărneci, Dan Oprescu, Anca Oroveanu, Stelian Tănase, and Alin Teodorescu. Some of them signed in November 1989 an open letter of solidarity with other persecuted intellectuals. By the end of December 1989, these informal nuclei coalesced to form the "Group for Social Dialogue," an independent association dedicated to monitoring the government's observance of the democratic process and developing civil society in Romania. These young intellectuals came of age in a more urban and more educated, yet staunchly authoritarian Romania (see table 10.5). This more urbanized demographic structure helps to explain the results of the February 1992 local elections in which candidates of the Democratic Convention won mayoral office in many of Romania's cities (including Bucharest).

During the first months after the revolution, the "Group" – as it was usually referred to – became the center of a hectic search for alternatives to the official slide into a Romanian version of "neo-Bolshevism."[69] Its weekly publication, *22*, printed exciting reports of the Group's meetings with prominent NSF figures.[70] The major tension within the Group – a tension that would intensify in further months and would lead to its gradual loss of influence – was between those who saw its role as the backbone of an emerging political party (similar to the Network of Free Initiatives in Hungary that led to the forming of the Alliance of Free Democrats in 1989) and those who believed that such a community should situate itself *au dessus de la mêlée* (above the whirlwind) and preserve a supra-partisan, neutral status for itself. Initially, the Group played an important role in the crystallization of a critical discourse, the integration of Romania's opposition within the East European across-frontier dissident contacts and the restoration of communicative reason as a foundation for an open society. Later, however,

Table 10.5 *Demographic trends in Romania since the 1950s*

	1950s	1970s	1990s
Percentage of population	(1956)	(1970)	(1990)
Rural	68.7	59.2	45.9
Urban	31.3	40.8	54.1
Average annual rates of	(1970–74)	(1953–59)	(1990–99)[a]
population growth (%)	1.3	0.9	0.1
Age distribution (%)	(1956)	(1976)	(1990)
15–24	18.2	16.5	16.6
25–49	34.5	34.3	32.1
50–59	9.9	9.7	12.0
Over 60	9.9	14.2	15.7
Levels of education[b]	(1956)	(1966)	(1992)
Primary	93.7	81.8	29.8
Secondary	4.1	15.5	63.2
Post-secondary	2.1	2.7	6.9

Notes: [a]Estimate. [b]Indicates attainment of completed or partial education at each level among persons over 25 years of age.
Sources: US Department of Commerce, *Statistical Abstracts of the United States*; Paul S. Shoup, *The East European and Soviet Data Handbook*; UNESCO, *Statistical Yearbooks*; United Nations, *Demographic Yearbooks*.

the Group seemed to be increasingly self-enclosed, a sectarian community of self-appointed custodians of the country's spiritual values. This shift was linked to the demoralization of Romania's intelligentsia following the electoral success of the opposition and the widespread disgust with the restoration trends in Romanian politics.

At the same time, because of its outspokenness and moral authority, the Group became a favorite target for slanderous attacks waged by the Front-controlled media. Members of the Group were continuously smeared as "instigators to instability" or "crypto-Iron Guardists." Its inconsistencies notwithstanding, the Group was a significant catalyst in the awakening of the long dormant civil society. It established contacts with the Students' League, with independent unions, and with the military groups interested in the democratization of the army.

The difficulties encountered by Romania's emerging civil society during the first stage of the transition (1990–91) were linked to the NSF's hegemonic ambitions and its refusal to radically dismantle the Securitate. The much-decried "neo-Bolshevism" of the NSF's ruling team was less an ideological preference, but rather a matter of authoritarian political style and a continuous indulgence in self-serving half-truths and blatant non-verities. On the one hand, there was the Front, whose political options were often described as "neo-communist." On the other hand, there were the opposition parties and nascent civic initiatives from below. Among the latter, most active was the Students' League, the Romanian Helsinki Citizens' Initiative, several human rights groups, and the Timişoara Society.

The Hungarian minority formed its own political parties grouped within an alliance called the Hungarian Democratic Union of Romania (HDUR – *Uniunea Democrată Maghiară din România*) initially headed by writer and editor Geza Domokos and former dissident poet and human-rights activist Geza Szőcs. The honorary chairman of the HDUR has been, from the beginning, Bishop Laszlo Tőkés. In agreement with the other democratic forces, the HDUR advocated the rapid dismantling of the repressive structures and the establishment of a state of law that would guarantee and protect equal rights to all citizens. They also called for the restoration of Hungarian educational and cultural facilities suppressed by the Ceauşescu regime.[71]

The first stage of the transition was predominantly confrontational. The opposition could barely organize, because of logistical debility and general lack of experience. Its political discourse was not accessible to the population because of the obstacles created by the Front-run government to television appearances of Iliescu's critics. But discontent in Romania had deep social roots and could not be easily mitigated. The Front's aggressive warnings and monopolistic conduct could not but further irritate the revolutionary forces. It was perhaps Iliescu's major illusion that a Romanian version of perestroika would pacify even the most critical groups. To his dismay, instead of decreasing, the radical ferment was continuing to gather momentum. The students and the intelligentsia spearheaded this struggle for the fulfillment of the revolution.

The widespread sentiment that the NSF's hidden agenda consisted of the restoration of the old regime without the grotesque outgrowths of Ceauşescu's tyranny was not groundless. After all, Romanians knew that the abhorred Securitate had not been truly disbanded.[72] A few of Ceauşescu's henchmen were brought to trial only for their participation in the December 16–22 slaughter, not for the role they played in the functioning of one of Eastern Europe's most vicious despotic systems since Stalin's death. Instead of purging the administrative apparatus of the servants of the old regime, the NSF had appointed them to key positions. This situation was well known to the Romanians, and it accounted for the growing tensions that were soon to reach an explosive point in the spring of 1990.

Conceived by more or less reconstructed Leninists, the NSF's strategy failed to excite the youth and intelligentsia. It neglected the dynamism of society's self-organization, the force of the collective passions for justice, and the contagious effect of the democratic movements in the other Eastern European countries. The Front was living with the illusion that Romanians would accept a simple revamping of the Communist system. On March 11, 1990, the "Proclamation of Timişoara" articulated the political expectations and the values of those who had started the revolution. In effect the real charter of the Romanian revolution, the document emphasized the unequivocally anti-communist nature of the uprising in December 1989.

Article 7 of the "Proclamation" questioned the revolutionary bona fides of those who had emerged as the beneficiaries of the upheaval: "Timişoara started the revolution against the entire Communist regime and its entire nomenklatura, and certainly not in order to give an opportunity to a group of anti-Ceauşescu dissidents within the RCP to take over the reigns of political power. Their presence at the head of the country makes the death of our heroes senseless." This was political dynamite in a country still run by former luminaries of the communist nomenklatura.

To give this view even more poignancy, article 8 of the "Proclamation" proposed to set guidelines for the elimination of former communist officials and security police officers from public life for a certain period of time: "We want to propose that the electoral law, for the first three consecutive legislatures ban from every list all former Communist activists and Securitate officers. Their presence in the political life of the country is the major source of the tensions and suspicions that currently torment Romanian society. Until the situation has stabilized and national reconciliation has been achieved it is absolutely necessary that they remain absent from public life."[73]

Soon thereafter, the "Proclamation" became the rallying point of all democratic forces in Romania: the statement was endorsed by hundreds of independent groups and associations, including the "Group for Social Dialogue," the "Independent Group for Democracy," and the "December 21 Association." Even more emphatically, the document opposed the right of those who had served the communist regime to run as candidates for the presidential office. The "Proclamation" hit its target: the outraged nomenklatura reacted with its traditional weapons, including slander, innuendo, and intimidation. The pro-Front newspapers and the "free" Romanian Television tried to dismiss the relevance of the "Proclamation," calling it an unrealistic and potentially disruptive document.

By the end of April 1990, thousands of students, workers, and intellectuals seized the University Square in Bucharest, where they organized a sit-in to protest the government's refusal to consider the public demands formulated in the "Proclamation." The main organizers of the "Commune of

Bucharest" – which lasted several weeks – were the Students' League, "December 21" Association, and the Independent Group for Democracy. They were joined by hundreds of other informal initiatives. Although the government sent police troops to disband the demonstrators, who had camped in the Square, the around-the-clock demonstration continued until the May 1990 elections.

Another source of tension in the aftermath of Ceauşescu's downfall was the growing ethnic conflict in Transylvania regarding the grievances of the Hungarian minority. In March 1990 bloody clashes took place in Tîrgu-Mureş, and each side blamed the other one for these incidents. Romanian spokesmen deplored the radicalization of the Hungarian political demands, whereas Hungarian activists accused Vatra Românească, allegedly a Romanian cultural initiative, in fact a political movement with nationalist undertones, of having engineered the bloodshed. The government behaved in an erratic way, first playing neutral and then unqualifiedly embracing the Vatra approach. This in turn antagonized the Hungarians who spoke of the continuity of Ceauşescu's chauvinistic policy and accused the NSF of using nationalism for electoral purposes. Ominously, the Tîrgu-Mureş incident became the pretext for the reconstitution of a secret police under the name of Romanian Service of Information.[74]

Following the 1992 elections, Romania's civil society continued to grow, if in a less spectacular way than before. Ecological, women's rights, and gay groups were formed who opposed the intolerant views championed by the nationalist and other parties. Hundreds of NGOs have emerged in Romania's cities, advocating human rights, transparency of legal and government procedures, and ethnic tolerance. One of the most influential among these organizations is the Pro-Democraţia movement that has established a dynamic network of seminars and cooperative actions between its branches throughout the country. Members of these NGOs played a major role in monitoring the 1992 local, parliamentary, and presidential elections and they plan to do the same in 1996. Other groups have been engaged in watching and reporting persecution of the Roma population as well as police abuses. Contacts with similar groups in east-central Europe, participation in international initiatives and assistance from Western foundations have helped the new Romanian NGOs become part and parcel of the country's new civic culture.

Several of the civil society initiatives are part of the Democratic Convention: the Association of the Former Political Prisoners, the Civic Alliance, the pro-monarchist "România Viitoare" Movement, and the Ecological Party. As the archives remained strictly controlled by the government, civic initiatives were launched to preserve the memory of the victims of the communist regime. For instance, the Civic Alliance was instrumental in organizing the Sighet Memorial in the former penitentiary where many

Table 10.6 *The Romanian postcommunist political spectrum and associated prominent political figures*

The Left	The Center	The Right
Traditional Communists Socialist Party of Labor (SPL) Ilie Verdeţ, chairman Socialist Party (SP) Tudor Mohora, chairman *Nationalist Populist* Romanian National Unity Party (RNUP) Gheorghe Funar, chairman Agrarian Party (AP) Victor Surdu, chairman România Mare Party Corneliu Vadim Tudor, chairman Nationalist wing of the Hungarian Democratic Union of Romania (HDUR) Bishop Rudolf Tőkes, prominent figure *Socialist Populist* Party of Social Democracy in Romania (PSDR) Ion Iliescu, president Adrian Năstase, executive chairman Oliviu Gherman, honorary chairman	*Center Left* Democratic Party (DP) Petre Roman, chairman *Center Right* Civic Alliance Party (CAP) Nicolae Manolescu, chairman Liberal Party-93 (LP-93) Horia Rusu, chairman Liberal wing of the Hungarian Democratic Union of Romania György Frunda and György Tokay, prominent figures	*Christian Democracy* National Peasant Christian and Democratic Party (NPCDP) Ion Diaconescu, chairman Corneliu Coposu, former chairman (d. 1995) Civic Alliance Movement Ana Blandiana, prominent figure; various other groups belonging to the Democratic Convention (DC), including Former Political Prisoners and monarchists *Extreme Right (nationalists and religious fundamentalists)* Movement for Romania Marian Munteanu, chairman National Right Party and other chauvinistic groups and movements

Note: The author thanks Dorel Şandor, director of the Center for Political Studies and Comparative Analysis in Bucharest, for information regarding the ideological political spectrum in postcommunist Romania.

of Romania's precommunist elites perished in the 1950s. In 1995 a major international symposium took place in Sighet where survivors of the Romanian Gulag and researchers gathered to examine the legacy of communism in that country. In Romania, where the power-holders seem uninterested in confronting the past, the struggle for memory is an important task for those who believe that truth and politics are not incompatible.

But the real thrust of the political struggle takes place in the field of politics: parties, rather than civic movements, are the institutions that can articulate and aggregate social interests and expectations. This is not to deny the role of civil society in moderating the controlling appetite of the government, but simply to emphasize the nature of the current state of postcommunist politics. It is to political parties and the contemporary Romanian political spectrum that I now return.

Romanian Peronismo?

Left and right are elusive concepts in contemporary Romania. Can one simply depict someone like Vadim Tudor as a rightist politician, in spite of his nostalgia for the Ceauşescu regime? Is Iliescu a man of the left, in spite of his association with extreme xenophobic forces? The real spectrum should take into account the rapid changes and the versatility of political and ideological labels in times of transition (see table 10.6).

The left, in such a scheme, would include the following orientation: (a) traditional communism; (b) nationalist populism; and (c) socialist populism. Traditional communism emphasizes the "merits" of the Leninist order; the need to preserve the safety net for the economically challenged groups; and the hostility to "democratic chaos." The main proponents of this view are the Socialist Labor Party (Verdeţ, Păunescu), its splinter group headed by Tudor Mohora, and a former RCP and NSF leader, Alexandru Bârlădeanu. Nationalist populism characterizes the RNUP (especially Gheorghe Funar); the România Mare Party (Corneliu Vadim Tudor); and former Prime Minister Văcăroiu, whose open sympathies lie with the nationalist groups. Similar trends can be noticed among the HDUR, which is far from being a homogenous ethnic party, but rather an association of different, often contradictory ideological and political platforms going from nationalism to Christian Democracy. Socialist populism is predominant within the PSDR, with Ion Iliescu oscillating between his socialist preferences and a readiness to bend to the pressures of the electorate (populism). Among the main figures associated with this trend one can distinguish not only members of the ruling party (ex-President of Senate Oliviu Gherman, ex-Chairman of the Chamber Adrian Năstase), but also Mircea Ciumara, the main economist of the NPCDP, and former NSF grey eminence Silviu Brucan. One should notice that some groups here described as leftist share with the extreme right xenophobia, ethnocentrism, and an exaltation of a *völkisch* definition of the nation. In their case, anti-capitalism includes rejection of the West, hostility to market and financial mechanisms, and a glorification of a strong, centralized, ethnically homogeneous state.

Closer to the center, one sees the DP headed by Petre Roman, elected President of the Senate after the November 1996 elections. This orientation emphasizes the need to bring the secret police under genuine parliamentary control; to privatize the economy; integration within Euro-Atlantic structures; and observance of internationally required guarantees for minority rights.

The right includes: (a) proponents of civic-liberal values; (b) Christian Democracy, and (c) nationalist and religious fundamentalist groups and parties. Among the civic liberal formations, many would have serious problems in being seen as rightists. This is the orientation shared by CAP and its leader Nicolae Manolescu and a number of liberal formations (including groups within the HDUR) who favor a state of law, individual rights, a market economy, state support for free enterprise, a resolute break with the communist legacy, and who advocate the values of secularism and modernity. The spectrum of Christian Democracy goes from the Democratic Convention chairman and newly elected President of Romania, Emil Constantinescu to Civic Alliance leader and poet Ana Blandiana and the supporters of a return to the precommunist constitutional monarchy. The main exponent for this trend is the daily newspaper *România liberă*.

Further to the right one detects "mystical nationalists," fringe groups of neo-Iron Guardists, and some vocal exponents of the former political prisoners. For instance, a splinter group of the RNUP, headed by MP Cornel Brahaş, formed in 1995 a new party, called Dreapta Naţională [the National Right]. The logo of its namesake weekly is: *Noi facem ordine* [We make order].[75] What we notice from this inevitably cursory scheme is that the center is quite weak in postcommunist Romania: it includes DP, CAP, the liberal parties, especially PL-93, and several politically unaffiliated but very influential media and cultural personalities. The latter took the initiative to form in 1995 their own movement called Alternativa Pentru România which joined the Democratic Convention in 1996.[76] The fragility of the center is related to the nebulousness of the political platforms generated by different parties; the exaggerated preoccupation with the political backgrounds of different personalities; the lack of serious debate in the main media regarding the country's possible economic and political choices; and the confusions inherited from the previous regime regarding the distinctions between communism, socialism, nationalism, and fascism. The epitome of this epistemological mess is the RNUP. Its chairman, Gheorghe Funar, has made himself notorious with petty attacks on the Hungarian population of Cluj (20 percent of the city's inhabitants). At the same time, as the populist agenda requires, Funar (who was elected mayor of Cluj in February 1992), pledged a dramatic urban renewal and initiated, in 1994, programs to repair roads and finish off building projects.

From where do all these confusions come? What accounts for the ideological discombobulation in Romania? As the old saying goes, *ex nihilo nihil* (out of nothing, comes nothing). Post-Ceauşescuism includes many elements that had been part and parcel of the political style of the communist bureaucracy, including components of the symbolic structure of the old regime's legitimation: (1) a quasi-charismatic party/movement with a leader suspicious of and often hostile to impersonal democratic procedures and regulations; (2) an exaltation of the ethnically homogeneous community (*patrie, naţiune*) and an exploitation by some of the hegemonic forces of *völkisch* themes and mythologies; (3) an aversion to (or distrust of) market relations and the continuous appeal to "Third Way" formulas (as mentioned, this is a major trend within the PSDR); (4) an intense cultivation of collective identities, loyalties, and attachments combined with a suspicious attitude toward minority rights, aspirations, and grievances; and (5) regime anxiety demonstrated by a strong rhetoric of solidarity that insists on the need for Romanians to close ranks against all alleged foreign conspiracies meant to dismantle their unitary nation-state.

Under Iliescu, ethnic minorities (especially Hungarians and Gypsies) were described by government-connected media as disloyal, potentially treacherous, and inferior to the Romanians. That many of these themes and phobias pre-date communism and are indeed derived from the ideological-emotional constellation of the interwar extreme right makes the Romanian case even more puzzling and theoretically challenging in its political-cultural syncretism. One can even argue that by the end of the Ceauşescu regime, a strange ideological blending came into being as the belief system of the party bureaucracy and large segments of the intelligentsia: collectivism, ethnic purity, anti-Westernism, anti-liberalism, anti-capitalism, and a rejection of the Marxist vision of internationalism. This ideology has been an attempt to provide the postcommunist bureaucratic elite with a symbolic legitimacy and an alternative to the principles and methods of liberal constitutionalism.

Political polarization or national reconciliation?

So far, Romania has avoided major turmoil. Despite ethnic tensions in Transylvania, no mass clashes followed the 1990 Tîrgu Mureş incidents. Malaise, rather than anger seems to be the main sentiment. Many Romanians, including former presidential allies, have the feeling that because of Iliescu and his group, the country's fast transition to a market economy has been postponed.

A sober perspective on postcommunist Romania should avoid any apriorical conclusion: things are moving quickly, old alliances are falling apart, and there is hope that the 1996 elections will permit not only economic recovery (already suggested by recent economic figures), but also a regrouping of the pro-Western political forces and an end of the current stalemate. If Hungary's Kadarism was a model for Iliescu, one can assume that he may have understood that no political personality is forever bound to a certain choice. As Petre Roman is not the same person who ran Romania in tandem with Iliescu until September 1991, it is possible for the latter to have realized the perils of soft authoritarianism. This may explain Iliescu's readiness to concede defeat as well as his re-emergence as a PSDR chairman and member of the Senate. It is up to the opposition to persuade Iliescu and his allies that a centrist coalition would not engage in revenge and persecution of those long-decried as neo-communists.

Learning the democratic process is difficult in a country with few and long-repressed democratic traditions. On various occasions, Iliescu recognized the historical failure of the communist utopia, but warned against the dangers of a rapid transition to market economy.[77] At the same time, the past 5 years have shown that the old system has outlived itself and that economic development is hard to imagine in the absence of pluralism.

In 1990 and 1992, the opposition was fragmented and unprepared for decisive competition. Clinging to the memory of their bygone splendor, the "historical parties" failed to stir responsive chords among middle-aged Romanians who saw them as structurally different from what they had been accustomed to for decades. The Front's rhetoric sounded familiar, and many were ready to trust Iliescu because he appeared the closest to their understanding of politics. Thus, a paternalistic temptation motivated the decisions of the majority to support the NSF. This identification with the presidential father-like figure reached disturbing levels in such electoral slogans as "When Iliescu comes, the sun rises."

The NSF 1990 victory, however, did not mean an end to the democratic process in Romania. Neither did it imply a long-term victory for the Front, which, after all, was a heterogeneous formation whose initial leadership included former communist bureaucrats, technocrats, intellectuals, revolutionary romantics, and political adventurers.[78] The conflicts between different factions within the NSF intensified after the disastrous events in June 1990. The brutal evacuation of the University Square by police forces and the atrocities perpetuated by the miners invited by Ion Iliescu to defend him and Roman's government led to the country's international isolation. True, the opposition was for some time paralyzed, but that was a short-term effect.

Both the opposition parties and the independent civic groups realized that the struggle for Romania's democratization could not be continued on the streets. There was a clear awareness that new forms of oppositional activities had to be created in such a way that a true alternative to the NSF hegemony would become more than a mere desideratum.

In November 1990 the attempts to organize the extra-parliamentary opposition led to the formation of the Civic Alliance as a nation-wide movement from below committed to the development of democratic institutions and procedures. The first chairman of the Civic Alliance was student leader Marian Munteanu, who had been released from prison following mass demonstrations and international pressures.[79] The Alliance's convention in December called for a referendum on Romania's political system, to include consideration of a constitutional monarchy. In December 1990, the exiled King Michael (who had been forced to abdicate by the communists in 1947) tried to visit Romania but was forced out of the country.[80] The nationalist and populist media engaged in vicious denunciations of the King and his supporters. Later, the King was allowed to visit the country for the Easter celebrations in the spring of 1992. Enthusiastic crowds notwithstanding, only a minority of the Romanians were favorable to a Spanish-style monarchic solution and the King's visit remained a spectacular, but not sea-change event.

In July 1991, the CAP was formed under the chairmanship of Nicolae Manolescu, a prominent civic activist, political columnist and literary critic. For many, the creation of this party appeared as a new beginning for Romania's opposition. What made it attractive was its modernity, its refusal to embrace old-fashioned attitudes and choices, its rejection of any form of ethnic exclusiveness, and the moral authority of its leaders and primarily of Nicolae Manolescu himself.[81] Moreover, with the NSF leadership plagued with internal disputes and unable to propose a coherent program of reforms, CAP announced its commitment to a free market economy and the democratization of all institutions.

In August 1991, at the moment of the failed anti-Gorbachev coup in Moscow, CAP was the first Romanian force to protest the neo-Stalinist conspiracy. In September, the tensions reached their climax with the Jiu Valley miners coming again to Bucharest and asking for the resignation of both Prime Minister Petre Roman (also leader of the NSF) and President Iliescu. The latter managed to maneuver the miners and replaced Roman with the finance expert Theodor Stolojan, as head of a newly formed coalition government that included representatives of the Ecological Movement and the oppositional National Liberal Party. Offended by Iliescu's collusion with the miners' authoritarian leader, Miron Cosma, Roman and his supporters denounced a plot fomented by former communists and unreconstructed

Securitate members. The polemic between Roman and Iliescu turned especially bitter at the moment the former premier decried the presence of the nomenklatura at the country's highest levels and the president bitingly retorted by hinting at Roman's own nomenklatura background.[82] It was somewhat strange to watch Roman and his partisans using almost the same terms in their criticism of Iliescu as those in the "Timişoara Proclamation" they had so angrily rejected in March 1990.[83] The issue was in fact that Roman wanted to pursue a reformist program, whereas Iliescu expressed the interests of the most conservative forces in the country, including the former Securitate and administrative apparatus. In a way, even compared to postcommunist politicians in Poland or Hungary, Iliescu appeared as a political anachronism: he was formed in the Leninist tradition and could barely overcome it. His anti-capitalist views were deeply embedded and, although he may not be personally a staunch nationalist and an anti-Semite, he tended, until 1995, to rely on the most reactionary forces in Romania.

Endangered democracy?

So far, democracy in Romania has achieved a number of undeniable steps. We should therefore examine the half-full part of the proverbial glass. There are competing political parties that articulate their views and address relatively predictable political constituencies. The economy seems to be recovering and there are indications that the government may truly engage in mass-scale privatization.[84] Although the government monopoly on national television had been a major hindrance in the development of a true culture of dialogue, this situation improved after 1993 and Romania has now a number of non-governmental TV stations, including many local ones. In 1995 and 1996, several independent cable television channels began and expanded operation. Among these is Pro-TV which broadcasts news, talk shows and entertainment 24 hours per day. Pro-TV's dynamic and aggressive coverage of politics has served as an incentive for the national television station to adjust its news coverage and style and allow for more diversity of opinion. The independent printed media, among the most vivid in East-Central Europe, can barely reach the countryside or even remote urban areas, primarily because of the government control over distribution networks. Demagogic chauvinism and even nostalgia for Ceauşescu's times is rampant in the pages of the extremist media, but these publications represent a marginal portion of the press. *România Mare* has lost most of its initial appeal and it has become a simple vehicle for venting Vadim Tudor's hatred of both the opposition and more recently the president. The most circulated newspapers are not controlled by the government and often criticize its policies (*Evenimentul zilei*, *România liberă*, even the once pro-Iliescu

Adevărul). The weekly edited by the neo-Iron Guard "Movement for Romania" (*Mişcarea*) is printed for a small coterie of "true believers" and can barely be found in news kiosks.[85]

As, by the end of 1995, Iliescu moved quite decisively against Vadim Tudor, the chasm between the ethnocentric radicals (of rightist or leftist persuasion) and the proponents of democracy has further deepened, challenging much of the conventional wisdom regarding the viability of their alliance. This conflict has reached already spectacular dimensions as a result of the mutual accusations between Vadim Tudor and Virgil Măgureanu. The latter decided to preemptively publish his securitate file showing that between 1963–64 (at the age of twenty-two) he served as a collaborator of the secret police.[86] In so doing, Măgureanu deprived Tudor of a major blackmail instrument. Furthermore, appearing on national TV on January 15, 1996, Măgureanu publicly and unequivocally accused the România Mare Party leader of being the spokesman for a group of former Securitate hacks whose main goal was to prevent Romania's rapprochement with the West and its integration into the Euro-Atlantic structures. Măgureanu went so far as to describe this group as a "paramilitary formation that behaves like a state within the state" and appealed to all responsible institutions to strongly disassociate themselves from the "irresponsible behavior" of the PRM chairman.[87]

On the other hand, at the time of the November 1996 elections, there were several problems with Romanian-style democracy which one could see as the darker side of the story. Let us mention here: (1) a deeply ingrained authoritarian leadership style and a distrust of dialogue; excessive personalization of politics; (2) official attempts to curtail the independence of the media and to limit freedom of expression; (3) fragmentation of the opposition; (4) lack of a common vision of the public good; and (5) the rise of nationalist parties and their endorsement by the government. The main threats to Romania's democracy, disturbingly exemplified by the results of the September–October 1992 elections and which could seriously affect the long-term outcome of the 1996 elections, are therefore linked to the still low level of civic culture; the fragility of the democratic institutions; the inchoate and provisional nature of the political parties and their ideological preferences; the persistence of a mass psychology of nostalgia for collectivistic forms of social protection; the growing public dissatisfaction with the effects of half-hearted reforms; the endurance of the communist mentalities and methods in the functioning of important institutions, including the presidency, the Supreme Defense Council, the army, the Romanian Service of Information and the television; and the failure to launch a serious discussion of the country's precommunist and communist experiences. These elements can lead to a situation of profound despair and the rise of Peron-style social demagogues who claim to offer immediate and simple solutions to complex and intricate issues.[88]

The rhetoric of bellicose ethnic fundamentalism, including a religious Christian Orthodox dimension, could appeal to many dismayed, frustrated, and anguished individuals. To prevent the fulfillment of such an ethnocratic scenario, democratic forces have to close ranks, establish forms of cooperation and mutual support, overcome distrust and provide the citizens with a sense of their future. The "governance agreement" signed by Emil Constantinescu and Petre Roman in November 1996 is the basis for an overall program of major institutional and economic reforms.

The good news from Romania is that the age of monolithic authoritarian rule is over. Democratic political parties have emerged, although their identities are still quite elusive. Instead of being past-oriented, most of these formations try to articulate the political and social interests and aspirations of various categories of Romanian citizens. It is their task to familiarize Romanians with democracy and to make them understand the virtues of freedom.

Several scenarios can be envisioned regarding Romania's future. Likely, the PSDR itself will split between partisans of the status quo (who may eventually defect to the nationalist parties) and the proponents of reforms (who may break with Iliescu or force him to endorse their efforts). New coalitions are possible in the foreseeable future.

To put it briefly: by 1996, most of Romania's political actors were aware that the country could not afford to become the pariah of the international community. So, the most likely development was a continuous rapprochement between the two major forces (DC and PDSR), an overcoming of their mutual distrust, and the achievement of an anti-crisis pact. For this to happen, political forces in Romania needed to go beyond personal animosities and petty allergies, and discover the structures of interests and shared values that define genuine party politics.

The "national reconciliation" frequently proposed by Iliescu was not possible as long as reforms were postponed, the secret police organized provocations, and the Romanian political memory remained hostage to manipulation. The difficult, complicated, even daunting, and also the only solution is to replace a culture of fear, intimidation, and distrust with one of dialogue, procedures, and trust. The 1996 elections were indeed a major opportunity for the president and his supporters to go beyond their original illusions regarding the reformability of the Leninist system. Instead, Iliescu continued to resort to hackneyed propaganda cliches. Increasingly perceived as a man of the past, associated with rampant corruption and economic hardships, Iliescu lost the election. The vote was as much a protest against social and economic crises as an expression of the mass expectations for change. The alliance between the Convention, Roman's party, and the defection of the PUNR (which asked its supporters to vote against Iliescu) guaranteed Constantinescu's victory.

Taking into account the semi-presidential nature of the regime, and consequently the enormous powers invested in the presidential office, it is up to Constantinescu to direct the Convention, as well as the main state institutions, toward resolute reforms. Insisting on the need for public debate, implementing the rule of law and the separation of powers, and repudiating any form of ethnocentric self-glorification: these are the priorities that the new Romanian leader has to set for himself and for those who see him as the defender of their interests. The war of labels was extremely deleterious throughout Romania's first seven post-Ceauşescu years. In Romania, as in the other postcommunist countries, the outcome of the transition depends on the ability of the political elites to realize that trust, truth, and tolerance are indispensable ingredients of an open society. In this respect, Romania is not exceptional at all: it simply exacerbates political, moral, and psychological features one could notice in all the other societies long subjected to Leninist experiments in compulsory happiness.

Epilogue: a marriage of convenience ends the Iliescu era

On November 17, 1996, 54.6 percent of the Romanian voters elected Emil Constantinescu as their country's new president, completing the ex-communists' defeat, which began with the local elections in the summer and continued through the Fall parliamentary race. With Iliescu's departure from the helm, Romanians will once again try to reform the country, but this time with leadership which will hardly give a hand to Romania's communist and postcommunist predecessors.

The end of the Iliescu era was brought about because of the alliance between Roman and Constantinescu. Their alliance, however, is based on mutual concessions, and it is not exactly an easy one. The two leaders, and their parties, have different visions of the country's past, present, and future. Constantinescu, a member of the National Peasant Christian and Democratic Party, owes much of his career to the charismatic leader of this party, Corneliu Coposu (who died in 1995). The party's official line, codified by Coposu and the group of old leaders, calls for constitutional continuity; that is, it rejects the legitimacy of the commmunist-imposed abdication of King Michael in December 1947. Although during the campaign Constantinescu purged references to a referendum on the constitutional foundations of the state, it is hard to believe that this topic will simply vanish without a trace. From exile in Switzerland, King Michael congratulated the new president, admitting that this is not the time for questioning the constitutional order. At the same time, the problem of legitimacy will remain open as long as the Romanian republic does not procedurally confront the illegal coup d'etat that forced the king to abdicate and proclaimed the "Romanian People's Republic." The kind of continuity – whether it is the constitution of 1991 or pre-World War II – that remains following his presidency will define Constantinescu's place in Romanian history as either a pragmatist or a monarchist. For the short run, he is most certainly a pragmatist, and since in politics everything is short run, he can recall his monarchist leanings should he need them.

On the other hand, Petre Roman deems any such constitutional discussion inappropriate and dangerous. He was directly involved in the King's expulsion from Romania in December 1990 (when the ex-monarch came for a brief Christmas trip), and he has expressed uncompromising commitment to a republican form of government. Thus, the Democratic Party and its leader (who is the new chairman of the Senate, the upper chamber of the country's parliament and constitutionally the second highest position in the state) likely will obstruct any attempts to examine the many mysteries surrounding the December 1989 events and the miners' raid on Bucharest in June 1990 (which occurred during Roman's prime ministership under Iliescu).

If the tensions within the coalition deepen, the Democratic Party will leave the government and play the role of an independent oppositional force. Another factor which may lead to discord within the coalition is the personalities of the party leaders themselves. For example, the Democratic Party's leader, Roman, has presidential ambitions, and received 21 percent of the vote in the first round in the 1996 presidential race, which is an indication that a large segment of the electorate is ready to support him. In other words, the Democratic Convention and the Democratic Party alliance began as a marriage of convenience and is likely to remain one as long as there is a harmony of interests and incentives. Indeed, there are plenty of incentives, the act of governing itself perhaps being the strongest one, for these two formations to suppress their differences and keep the coalition stable for a relatively long period of time.

Meanwhile the once ruling party now in opposition, Iliescu's Party of Romanian Social Democracy, will likely adopt an obstructionist strategy which fans discontent with the costs of reforms, appeals to the losers of radical reforms, and mobilizes the unions against cuts in state subsidies for basic goods and services. As for Iliescu himself, it is hard to see a key political role for him in a modernized and Westernized Romania. Like Gorbachev, who was in many respects his model, he will be confined to a status of irrelevance. Among his party's elite there are too many "young

Turks" who are eagerly thinking about the next elections in four years and who regard Iliescu as a relic of the past.

Nationalism, an affliction that Adam Michnik aptly called the terminal disease of communism, already has been played *ad nauseam* in Romania. While it is true that national sentiment is strong, there is little reason to believe that it will take aggressive, violent forms. Romania's democratic engagement as 1996 closed was firm. The latent nature of this democracy remains mysterious: is it a civic-oriented community, based on liberal individualism, or is it rooted in nostalgia for archaic bonds of solidarity and group-defined loyalties? Will Romania accept the major trends of globalization, or will it try to oppose them in the name of vaguely conceived values of "one nation under God?" After seven years of missed opportunities, institutionalized squalor, and disgraceful plundering of national resources by those who were supposed to administer them, Romanians voted for renewal.

Political parties and movements in postcommunist Romania

Association of Former Political Prisoners
Civic Alliance Party (CAP – Partidul Alianţei Civice)
Civic Alliance Movement (Alianţa Civică)
Democratic Convention (DC – Convenţia Democratică [an umbrella movement])
Democratic National Salvation Front (DNSF – Frontul Democratic al Salvării Naţionale)
Democratic Party (DP – Partidul Democrat)
Future of Romania Movement (România Viitoare [pro-monarchists])
Greater Romania Party (România Mare)
Hungarian Democratic Union of Romania (HDUR – Uniunea Democrată Maghiară din România)
Liberal Party-93 (LP-93 – Partidul Liberal-93)
National Salvation Front (NSF – Frontul Salvării Naţionale)
National Peasant Christian and Democratic Party (NPCDP – Partidul Naţional Ţărănesc Creştin si Democrat)
National Liberal Party (Partidul Naţional Liberal)
Party of Social Democracy in Romania (PSDR – Partidul Democraţiei Sociale din România [formerly the DNSF])
Romanian National Unity Party (RNUP – Partidul Unităţii Naţionale a Românilor)
Romanian Ecology Party (Partidul Ecologic Român)
Romanian Communist Party (RCP – Partidul Comunist Român)
Socialist Party of Labor (SPL – Partidul Socialist al Muncii)

NOTES

The author wishes to acknowledge the research and editorial contributions made to this chapter by Stacy D. VanDeveer.

1 See, for instance, Petre Roman's frequent statements regarding the role of the Romanian Service of Information in the downfall of his government. Tape with the last meeting of the Roman government, September 1991, broadcast by independent TV station SOTI.

2 See Michael Turner, "The Political Inclusion of Romanian Illiberal Parties," paper presented at the AAASS Convention, Washington, DC, October 26–28, 1995. Excellent profiles of the Romanian political parties appeared during 1994–95 in *Sfera politicii*, a monthly journal of political analysis published in Bucharest.

3 See Ken Jowitt, "No More Normans in Europe," unpublished manuscript. Quoted with the author's permission.

4 For a thoughtful analysis of Romania's postcommunist political tremors, see Katherine Verdery and Gail Kligman, "Romania after Ceauşescu: Post-Communist Communism?" in *Eastern Europe in Revolution*, ed. Ivo Banac (Ithaca: Cornell University Press, 1992), pp. 117–47. For the climate of anguish and deception under the Iliescu regime, see William McPherson, "Intrigue, Illusion And Iliescu: Reaching for Reality in Romania," *Washington Post*, 13 September 1992. For a general assessment of political developments in Romania, especially during 1994–95, see my article "Democracy, Romanian-style," *Dissent*, Summer 1995, pp. 318–20.

5 The PDSR platform for the 1996 elections insists on the need to avoid both "capitalism" and "totalitarianism." Personal interview with Marţian Dan, vice-chairman of the PDSR, Washington, DC, December 1995.

6 In the September 1992 elections, the PDSR, then still called the Democratic National Salvation Front, got 27.72 percent of the votes for the Chamber of Deputies and 28.29 percent for the Senate. In the second round of the presidential elections in October 1992, the incumbent Ion Iliescu received 47.43 percent of the votes, while the candidate of the Democratic Convention, Emil Constantinescu, received 31.24 percent. For excellent data regarding Romania's postcommunist politics, see Domniţa Stefănescu, *Cinci ani din istoria României: O cronologie a evenimentelor. Decembrie 1989-Decembrie 1994* (Bucharest: Editura Maşina de scris, 1995).

7 For Iliescu's political views, see his book *Reformă şi revoluţie* (Bucharest: Editura Enciclopedică, 1994)

8 See Thomas Carothers, *Understanding Democracy Assistance: The Case of Romania* (Washington: Carnegie Endowment for International Peace, 1996).

9 See Vladimir Pasti, *România in tranziţie: Căderea in viitor* (Bucharest: Editura Nemira, 1995).

10 All polls indicate support for King Michael's return at about 12 to 15 percent of the population. Iliescu's popularity, although declining, remains quite high.

11 Personal interviews with Corneliu Coposu Bucharest, June 1994 and Washington, DC, February 1995. In the September 1992 elections, the Convention received 20.01 percent for the Chamber, and 20.16 percent for the Senate. The Convention

president and presidential candidate in both the 1992 and 1996 elections, Emil Constantinescu, announced in 1995 that he had joined the PNTCD.

12 See Ralf Dahrendorf, *Reflections on the Revolution in Europe* (New York: Random House, 1991).

13 See *Nations in Transit: Civil Society, Democracy and Markets in East Central Europe and the New Independent States* (New York: Freedom House, 1995), p. 112.

14 By the end of 1995, the split between Iliescu and Vadim Tudor became public and led to the elimination of România Mare Party representatives from the government. Vadim Tudor reacted angrily and accused Iliescu of having given in to pressures from Zionist and other anti-Romanian circles in the West. See "PRM Newspaper Accuses, Threatens Iliescu," in Foreign Broadcast Information Service, *Daily Report: Eastern Europe* (hereafter *FBIS-EEU*), 16 October 1995, pp. 63–5. This is not just a family quarrel, and other rearrangements of forces may occur that would distance the PDSR from its erstwhile political allies, including Gheorghe Funar's PUNR.

15 The business elite in Romania is deeply divided: on the one hand, there are those linked to Petre Roman's democratic party and his pro-Western strategy of opening the country to foreign investment; on the other, there are the exponents of secret police-linked new corporations and companies, enjoying government support for shabby financial operations. Romanian political analyst Andrei Cornea proposed the concept of "directocracy" to describe the ruling social group in Iliescu's Romania. See Andrei Cornea, *Maşina de fabricat fantasme* (Bucharest: Editura Clavis, 1995). An interesting phenomenon is the rise of this alliance between one portion of the business and financial elite, the ruling party and its acolytes, and the government bureaucracy. One should mention the success of Iliescu's party in attracting support from the unions, an indication of a corporatist trend in contemporary Romanian politics.

16 A massive exercise in this direction, *Cartea Albă a Securităţii* (five huge volumes) was published in 1995 by the SRI (Romanian Service of Information).

17 This situation makes the attacks against Măgureanu issued by România Mare even more significant.

18 I owe this distinction to Dorel Şandor, personal interview, Washington, DC, October 14, 1995. Şandor served as secretary of state in the Stolojan government (1991–92), and is currently running the Center for Political Studies and Comparative Analysis in Bucharest, an independent think tank.

19 A concept proposed by M. Steven Fish regarding Yeltsin's Russia. See his book *Democracy From Scratch: Opposition and Regime in the New Russian Revolution* (Princeton, NJ: Princeton University Press, 1995).

20 In 1995 Roman's party (PD) signed an alliance with the tiny Social Democratic Party headed by Sergiu Cunescu, and formed the Social Democratic Union. The objectives of the Union were common lists for the 1996 elections; coordination of actions within parliament and public debates; cooperation at local levels; and, most important for Roman, and irritating for Iliescu, mutual support for admission into the Socialist International. Cunescu's party has been accepted by the Socialist International, and this alliance will permit Roman to join it in the near future. This would deprive Iliescu's party (PDSR) of the same opportunity and would

seriously affect the efforts made by Iliescu, Adrian Năstase, and Oliviu Gherman to present their party (PDSR) as socialist in a Western and modern sense.

21 For instance, the extremely popular satirical weekly *Academia Caţavencu* published its 1996 Yearbook with the title *Cartea neagră a insecurităţii* (The Black Book of Insecurity) a pun on the title of the five volumes released by Măgureanu's service. (See note 16 above.)

22 See Andrei Codrescu, "Fascism on a Pedestal," *New York Times*, 7 December 1993.

23 PSM representatives hold important posiţions within the Ministry of Labor. Păunescu's political biography is worth a whole study: he started as an iconoclastic poet and journalist in the late 1960s, but moved toward increasingly nationalist stances in the 70s. He organized huge youth gatherings where folk music was accompanied by paeans to Ceauşescu's "genius."

24 See *Nations in Transit*, p. 109.

25 Iliescu himself has often engaged in polemics with "a certain part of the media," especially the dailies *România liberă* and *Ziua*. His language in criticizing opponents indicates a monolithic mentality: critics are perceived as apriorically malicious. One notices the rise of a sycophantic court around the president, and even a new "cult of personality." For an assessment of the proposed amendments to the Romanian Criminal Code, which will lead to the punishment of journalists who publish critical stories about officials even if the stories are true, see "The Not-So-Free Eastern European Press," *New York Times*, 2 October 1995.

26 See Robert Hayden, "Constitutional Nationalism and the Wars in Yugoslavia," paper prepared for the conference on "Post-Communism and Ethnic Mobilization," Cornell University, Ithaca, New York, April 21–23, 1995. Leaders of the Democratic Convention may disagree with the republican form of state, but they have not criticized the definition of Romania as a national unitary state as formulated by the 1990 Constitution. The same nervousness about the Hungarian demands for cultural autonomy can be noticed among other non-governmental forces (e.g., Roman's PD and PAC).

27 See the interview with Tudor Mohora, the PSM's secretary in charge of propaganda, *Flacăra*, no. 91, 1–7 September 1992. In the early 1980s, Mohora served as president of the Union of Communist Students' Associations.

28 This is the case with one of Romania's boldest weeklies, *Cuvîntul*, which has serialized a secret party report prepared in 1967–68 for the rehabilitation of former Politburo member and Justice Minister Lucreţiu Pătrăşcanu, executed after a pseudo-trial in April 1954. The lay reader is simply lost in the abundance of names and data, and the editors have not provided the needed background information to assess their meaning. The same can be said about the independent daily *România liberă*'s series of articles on "procesul comunismului" (the trial of communism), where testimonies of victims were published without any attempt to document the institutional and sociological foundations of political repression.

29 That Ceauşescu was personally an admirer of Stalin's model of socialism appeared clearly in his off-the-record statements to Ken Auchincloss of *Newsweek* in 1988. See Gail Kligman, "When Abortion is Banned: The Politics of Reproduction in Ceauşescu's Romania," a report for the National Council for Soviet and East European Research, 1992, p. 51.

30 An outstanding exploration of the cultural reverberations of Ceauşescuism is Katherine Verdery's *National Ideology Under State Socialism* (Berkeley: University of California Press, 1991). For analyses of Romania's political system under Ceauşescu, see Mary Ellen Fischer, *Nicolae Ceauşescu: A Study in Political Leadership* (Boulder, CO and London: Lynne Rienner, 1989); Michael Shafir, *Romania: Politics, Economics, and Society* (Boulder, CO: Lynne Rienner, 1985); and Vladimir Tismaneanu, "Personal Power and Political Crisis in Romania," *Government and Opposition* 24 (Spring 1989), 177–98.

31 For analyses of the Dej period, see Kenneth Jowitt, *Revolutionary Breakthroughs and National Development: The Case of Romania* (Berkeley: University of California Press, 1971) and Vladimir Tismaneanu, "The Tragicomedy of Romanian Communism," in *Crisis and Reform in Eastern Europe*, ed. Ferenc Fehér and Andrew Arato (New Brunswick: Transaction Publishers, 1991), pp. 121–74.

32 The case of writer Paul Goma, who in 1977 organized a human rights movement, is more than telling with regard to the fate of Romania's dissidents. After countless harassments and attempted bribes, Goma was forced into exile in France. Significantly, Goma still lives in French exile, although most of his books were published in Romania after December 1989.

33 See Harry G. Barnes, Jr., "Impressions on Romania," David Funderburk, "Relations Between the United States and Romania during the First Half of the 1980s," and Nastor Ratesh, "The Rise and Fall of a Special Relationship," in *The United States and Romania: American-Romanian Relations during the Twentieth Century*, ed. Paul D. Quinlan (Woodland Hills, CA: American-Romanian Academy of Arts and Sciences, 1988).

34 See Václav Havel, "The Power of the Powerless," in *The Power of the Powerless: Citizens against the State in Central-Eastern Europe*, ed. Václav Havel et al. (Armonk, NY: M. E. Sharpe, 1990), pp. 23–96.

35 The officially proclaimed ideals of equality and the myth of the leading role of the working class were contradicted by the egregious lifestyle of the presidential family. These values retained, however, a following among industrial workers such as coal miners, which explains both the 1977 working-class radicalism in the Jiu Valley and the manipulation of the miners' anger by the Iliescu regime in its attempts to topple the democratic opposition (June 1990) and the market-oriented reforms initiated by the Roman government (September 1991).

36 Eugen Barbu died in 1992.

37 The most active publications of the "green left" (or "red right" as this trend is often described), are the weeklies *România Mare* (run by Corneliu Vadim Tudor), *Europa*, and *Totuşi iubirea* (directed by Adrian Păunescu). For an examination of the extreme nationalist ideology of these publications, see Vladimir Tismaneanu and Mircea Mihăies, "Infamy Restored," *East European Reporter* 5, no. 1 (January-February 1992), 25–7.

38 For a remarkable collection of the Romanian dissident texts and testimonials, see the special issue of the monthly *Transilvania*, nos. 1–2 (1992).

39 The struggle was in many points similar to the conflict between the journals *Novy Mir* and *Oktiabr* – a point made clear by Verdery and implicitly denied by the "White Book of the Securitate."

40 After the 1989 revolution, Bobu was tried and received a life sentence for his "participation in the genocide of the Romanian nation."

41 I say "seemingly" because many documents released after December 1989 suggest that the Securitate was fully aware of the all-pervasive discontent and prepared itself for a post-Ceauşescu era. Thus, it is not insignificant that Virgil Măgureanu, whose anti-Ceauşescu views were known to the Securitate, was not arrested but simply assigned to a new job in the province, and could travel frequently to Bucharest, where he maintained relations with Iliescu.

42 See Vladimir Tismaneanu, "Tremors in Romania," *New York Times*, 30 December 1987; and Mark Almond, *Decline Without Fall: Romania under Ceauşescu* (London: Institute for European Defence and Strategic Studies, 1988).

43 See Michael Shafir, "Eastern Europe's 'Rejectionists,'" Radio Free Europe Research, RAD Background Report/121, 3 July 1989, pp. 1–6.

44 See Vladimir Tismaneanu, "The Rebellion of the Old Guard" and the full text of the "Letter of the Six" in *East European Reporter* 3, no. 4 (Spring/Summer 1989), 23–5.

45 Personal interviews with participants in the revolutionary uprising conducted by the author during his visits to Romania in February–March and June 1990.

46 See Nicolae Ceauşescu's report presented at the Fourteenth RCP Congress, *Scînteia*, 21 November 1989 (trans. in *FBIS-EEU*, 22 November 1989, pp. 59–84). For the anti-reformist direction of the Congress, see Alan Riding, "Romanian Leader Refuses Change," *New York Times*, 21 November 1989, and "In Romania, Fear Still Outweighs Hope," ibid., 24 November 1989.

47 Symptomatically, Ceauşescu's conspiratorial delusions about the Malta pact between the two superpowers to get rid of him have become the leitmotif of the nationalist revision of Romania's recent history. According to magazines like *România Mare* and *Europa*, the Timişoara uprising was the outcome of a well-prepared plan to destabilize Romania.

48 See Matei Calinescu and Vladimir Tismaneanu, "The 1989 Revolution and Romania's Future," *Problems of Communism*, January–April 1991, pp. 42–59. Theories abound about the various conspiracies that, in one way or another, prompted the end of Ceauşescu's dictatorship. So far, however, the only certain elements are that the Securitate and the army switched sides and abandoned Ceauşescu during the early hours of December 22, 1989.

49 On various occasions, Iliescu expressed regrets for the execution of the ex-dictator, but claimed that it was indispensable in order to avoid a civil war.

50 For a sober assessment of the events in December 1989 and their aftermath, see Nestor Ratesh, *Romania: The Entangled Revolution* (Washington: Center for Strategic and International Studies, 1991).

51 See Olivier Wéber, "La revolution confisquée," *Le Point* (Paris), 30 April 1990, pp. 46–7.

52 For the moral and philosophical aspects of political justice in post-totalitarian societies, see György Bence, *Political Justice in Post-communist Societies: The Case of Hungary* (Washington: Wilson Center, Occasional Paper no. 27, April 1991), with comments by Jeri Laber and Vladimir Tismaneanu.

53 See Alexandre Paléologue with M. Sémo and C. Tréan, *Souvenirs merveilleux d'un ambassadeur des golans* (Paris: Balland, 1990), especially pp. 219–28, and

Edward Behr, *Kiss the Hand You Cannot Bite: The Rise and Fall of the Ceauşescus* (New York: Willard Books, 1991).

54 See Jean-François Revel, "Roumanie: flagrant délit," *Le Point* (Paris), 12 March 1990, p. 87.

55 For Iliescu's biography and his role in the anti-student repression in the 1950s, see *22*, no. 40, 9–15 October 1992, p. 16.

56 See David Binder, "An Aristocrat Among the Revolutionaries," *New York Times*, 27 December 1989.

57 The principal author of the NSF first proclamation to the country, Mazilu broke with the NSF in January 1990 and wrote an interesting memoir serialized throughout 1991 in the Romanian emigre weekly *Lumea libera* (New York). According to him, it appeared very clear that Ion Iliescu and Petre Roman had a common agenda of stifling the spontaneous revolutionary ardor of the masses. Mazilu's criticism of the NSF resulted in a systematic besmirching campaign waged against him by the pro-government media. One element used by this campaign was Mazilu's past, including a short-lived tenure in the late 1960s as director of the Securitate school in Baneasa. It seems that Mazilu's former colleagues could not accept his genuine conversion to anti-communism and went out of their way to compromise him.

58 Later, *România liberă* would withdraw its charges against Mazilu.

59 For the destruction of the Romanian democratic parties during the years of unbound Stalinism, see Gheorghe Boldur-Lăţescu, *Genocidul comunist in România* (Bucharest: Editura Albatros, 1992).

60 The bureaucracy's status metamorphosis is characteristic of the postcommunist transition in other countries as well. See Lev Timofeyev, *Russia's Secret Rulers: How the Government and Criminal Mafia Exercise Their Power* (New York: Knopf, 1992).

61 For a brief, but convincing analysis of the post-1989 developments in Romania, see Richard Wagner, *Sonderweg Rumanien: Bericht aus einem Entwicklungsland* (Berlin: Rotbuch Verlag, 1991).

62 See "Romania," in *In the Public Eye: Parliamentary Transparency in Europe and North America*, ed. Edwin Rekosh (Washington: International Human Rights Law Group, 1995), pp. 191–206.

63 See "Romania-Country Survey," *East European Newsletter* (London), 15 December 1995, pp. 1–8.

64 For the "fraud claim" and the dissatisfaction of Romania's cultural elite with the election results, see *22*, no. 40, 9–15 October 1992.

65 See Andrei Cornea, "Mizeria ideologiilor," *ibid.*, no. 42, 22–28 October 1992, p. 4.

66 See Edmund Mokrzycki, "The Vicious Circle of Utopias in Eastern Europe," paper presented at the conference "Utopian Revisions: Nationalism and Civil Society in Eastern Europe," Institute for the Humanities, University of Michigan, Ann Arbor, 29–30 October 1992.

67 See Gail Kligman, "Reclaiming the Public: A Reflection on Creating Civil Society in Romania," *East European Politics and Societies* 4, no. 3 (1990), 393–439.

68 On Noica and his disciples, see Matei Calinescu's interventions in *Romania: A Case of Dynastic Communism* (New York: Freedom House, 1989); Verdery, *National Ideology under Socialism*; Alina Mungiu Pippidi, "Intellectuals as Political Actors in Eastern Europe: The Romanian Case," *East European Politics and Societies* 10, no. 2 (Spring 1996), 333-365.

69 Personal interviews with members of the Group.

70 *22* is still the most important tribune for Romania's independent thinking.

71 For the evolution of HDUR's views and its main political and social goals, see Aurelian Crăiuţu, "A Dilemma of Dual Identity: the Democratic Alliance of Hungarians in Romania," *East European Constitutional Review* 4, no. 2 (Spring 1995), 43-9.

72 As a matter of fact, a whole "revisionist" literature has emerged that presents the Securitate as a professional and truly patriotic organization. See William Totok, "Sindromul maltez: Falsificări istorice nationaliste in scrierile unor foşti securişti," German translation in *Halbjahreschrift für sudosteuropäische Geschichte, Literatur und Politik* (Fall 1995). One of the most egregious illustrations of this trend is Pavel Coruţ, *Fiul Geto-Daciei* (Bucharest: Editura Gemenii, 1995).

73 See "Proclamatia de la Timişoara," *România liberă*, 20 March 1990 (trans. in *FBIS-EEU*, 4 April 1990, pp. 60-3).

74 Virgil Măgureanu graduated from the University of Bucharest with a degree in philosophy in the late 1960s and received his PhD from the same institution in 1978 with a thesis on political power. See Virgil Măgureanu, *Puterea politică* (Bucharest: Editura politică, 1979).

75 See *Dreapta naţională*, 9-15 October 1995, p. 1.

76 I owe many suggestions regarding the ideological polarization of the Romanian political spectrum to Dorel Şandor, director of the Bucharest Center for Political Studies and Comparative Analysis.

77 See "Un entretien avec Ion Iliescu: Le large sourire du 'père de la nation,'" *Le Monde* (Paris), 17 May 1990.

78 One of these revolutionary adventurers seems to be former NSF senator Gelu Voican-Voiculescu, a former geologist and self-styled mystic, who participated in the storming of the Central Committee building on December 22, 1989 and was crucially involved in Ceauşescu's pseudo-trial and execution three days later. Between December 1989 and May 1990, Voican served as deputy prime minister in Petre Roman's government.

79 Soon thereafter, Munteanu resigned from the Civic Alliance and in 1991 he formed his own party, called "Mişcarea pentru România" (Movement for Romania). Formally a youth party, Munteanu's formation turned out to be close in both style and intellectual choices to Romania's interwar extreme right. The movement's weekly, named *Mişcarea* (The Movement), published its first issue in 1992 with a green frame on the front page, thereby indicating its sympathy for the Iron Guard Green Shirts. Munteanu's movement is a disturbing phenomenon of political despair and moral confusion among Eastern Europe's youth: a combination of religious mysticism and political radicalism, it may turn into one of those "movements of rage" mentioned by Ken Jowitt in his *New World Disorder: The Leninist Extinction* (Berkeley and Los Angeles: University of California Press, 1992).

80 For the issue of constitutional continuity in Romania, see the interview with King Michael, "Romania Past and Future," *East European Reporter* 4, no. 4 (Spring/Summer 1991), 81–3 and the King's article "Romania – Between Continuity and Change," *Common Knowledge* 4, no. 2 (Fall 1995), 158–83.

81 For Nicolae Manolescu's political views, see his article "How We Have to Destroy Communism," *East European Reporter*, pp. 78–81 and his book *Dreptul la normalitate: Discursul politic şi realitatea* (Bucharest: Editura Litera, 1991).

82 For details about this episode in the ongoing struggle among the initial allies within the NSF, see Michael Shafir, "'War of the Roses' in Romania's National Salvation Front," *RFE/RL Research Report* 1, no. 4 (24 January 1992), 15–22.

83 Ironically, Caius Dragomir, the NSF's presidential candidate for the presidential elections in the fall of 1992, tried to gain electoral capital by announcing that he had been a signatory of the "Timişoara Proclamation." After 1993, Dragomir served as Romania's ambassador to France.

84 See *Eastern Europe Newsletter*, 15 December 1995, pp. 2–6.

85 This is not the case with the books about the Guard or even pro-Guardist literature that are abundant, indicating a certain fascination with this element of Romania's past.

86 See the documents published in *Evenimentul Zilei* (Bucharest), 30 December 1995.

87 *Mediafax* (Bucharest), 15 January 1996. This press agency describes Măgureanu's statement as the staunchest ever to have come from an official personality against the PRM leader. Vadim responded by accusing Măgureanu of trying to sell Romanian territories to Hungary. In his response, Vadim called the SRI director a "madman" and an "adventurer" who represents a "public danger for Romania" (ibid.). As expected, President Iliescu (himself under Vadim's fire), endorsed Măgureanu. It is too early to draw any conclusions regarding this scandal, but one thing is clear: at this moment, Măgureanu's actions cannot but help the democratic forces get rid of one of the most obnoxious enemies of democracy in post-Ceauşescu Romania. Măgureanu's ouster would be indeed Vadim Tudor's triumph and a serious blow to Iliescu's increasingly pro-Western orientation (the România Mare Party is opposed to the country's integration into the NATO structures).

88 Gheorghe Funar is one example, but there are other demagogues, including nationalist generals, like the notorious Paul Cheler, the former commander of the Transylvanian Army, whom Iliescu forced to retire in 1995.

Appendix

Research guidelines for country-studies

Factors influencing the formation of political groups and parties

1. What are the key elements of the precommunist historical legacy of each country? Did the country have any precommunist experience of democracy, and have any elements of the postcommunist polity, such as particular government structures, intermediary associations, and political parties, been modeled on precommunist patterns?

2. What are the key elements of the legacy of the communist era? How has the political and social evolution of each country in the late communist era (e.g., the emergence or nonemergence of a significant dissent movement) affected the postcommunist formation of societal interest groups and parties?

3. How did the nature of the transition from communism (e.g., gradual versus abrupt; peaceful versus violent; internally – versus externally – precipitated) affect the formation of intermediary associations and parties in the early postcommunist period?

4. In the postcommunist selection of government leaders, what has been the importance of competitive elections and other forms of citizen political participation compared with threats of violence and the use of violence? Have military officers or the political police played a significant role in the selection process?

5. What political forces and calculations shaped the late-communist and especially the postcommunist electoral legislation and the timing of elections?

6. In brief, what are the main social and ethnic cleavages in postcommunist society?

7. In brief, what have been the pattern and pace of postcommunist economic change, and which social groups have been the winners and losers?

8. How has the presence or absence of violent conflict inside the country or with other states affected the inclination and ability of political parties or other organizations with political agendas to mobilize social groups in support of internal democratization?

The political evolution of society

9. Which types of political associations or actors have become most prominent in each country's political life? (For example, political parties, state sector managerial lobbies, trade unions, business organizations, professional associations, religious organizations, clans, paramilitary units, criminal groups, etc.) How has the public perception of political parties and what they claim to represent affected citizens' attitudes toward the political system? What is the relative importance of parties as vehicles for new elites intent on accumulating political power and wealth? What alternative vehicles have been used or preferred?

10. How have attempted marketization and privatization affected the political strength and behavior of business and managerial groups? Have labor groups formed or formally affiliated themselves with political parties, and what role have they assumed in the financing of elections and the control of the media?

11. How have attempted marketization and privatization affected the political strength and behavior of agricultural groups? Have these groups formed or formally affiliated themselves with political parties, and what role have they played in elections?

12. How have attempted marketization and privatization affected the political strength and behavior of organized industrial labor? Have labor unions sponsored or become affiliated with political parties? In their political programs and behavior (e.g., strikes), what is the relative importance of preserving democracy versus improving economic welfare?

13. What has been the political impact of organized criminal groups? Are associations or political parties linked with organized crime? How has the public perception of the role of organized crime affected citizens' attitudes toward the political system?

14. What do existing survey data show about the level of public support within the country for democratization? Do attitudes toward democratic governmental institutions, political compromise, participation in elections,

and membership in political parties and intermediary associations differ significantly between younger and older citizens? Do attitudes on these matters differ substantially between major ethnic groups? Similarly, are there significant attitudinal differences between men and women over democracy and the various forms of political participation? How has the performance of the postcommunist economy affected public attitudes toward democracy?

15. Have the media become a channel for the expression of a range of societal interests independent of the preferences of the government? How has control of the media affected the conduct of elections and other forms of political participation?

Political parties and the party system

16. How strong are the country's political parties and party system? Since the end of communism, has the country's party system been characterized only by the creation of ephemeral parties, or do patterns of leadership, electoral results, and survey data indicate that some stable parties have emerged?

17. How have the structure and durability of political parties been affected by the electoral law(s) and by laws – if any – on campaign finance? How have parties been affected by the timing of elections – including regional versus countrywide elections?

18. How have the cohesion and durability of political parties been affected by the structure of government – in particular, the existence of a parliamentary versus a presidential system, of a unitary versus a federal state, and the amount of discretionary power in the hands of a state bureaucracy independent of the top governmental authorities?

19. To what extent have the renamed communist parties actually changed (a) their attitudes toward liberal democracy (b) their political leadership, and (c) the interests that they represent? What role has been played by electoral competition in any changes that have occurred?

20. Apart from communist successor-parties, have anti-democratic parties or social movements based on clericalism, fascist traditions, or radical nationalism developed?

21. Among the major parties, what proportion consists of parties that are: a) disloyal or loyal to democratic procedures b) ethnically or religiously based c) based primarily in one geographic region d) willing to endorse political violence, and e) linked with paramilitary forces?

22. Has the party system facilitated or obstructed the creation of governments able to formulate and carry through reasonably coherent policies? How has the capacity of postcommunist regimes to formulate and implement policies affected citizen support of democratization and marketization processes?

Index